INSTRUCTOR'S RESOURCES

Richard O. Straub

to accompany

KATHLEEN STASSEN BERGER

The Developing Person Through Childhood and Adolescence

The Developing Person Through the Life Span

Invitation to the Life Span

ISBN-13: 978-1-4292-3450-4
ISBN-10: 1-4292-3450-4

WORTH PUBLISHERS

INSTRUCTOR'S RESOURCES

Richard O. Straub
University of Michigan, Dearborn

to accompany

KATHLEEN STASSEN BERGER

The Developing Person Through Childhood and Adolescence

The Developing Person Through the Life Span

Invitation to the Life Span

WORTH PUBLISHERS

Instructor's Resources
by Richard O. Straub
to accompany
Berger: **The Developing Person Through Childhood and Adolescence, The Developing Person Through the Life Span, Invitation to the Life Span**

Printed in the United States of America

ISBN 10: 1-4292-3460-1 (with binder)
ISBN 13: 978-1-4292-3460-3

ISBN 10: 1-4292-3450-4 (manual only)
ISBN 13: 978-1-4292-3450-4

First printing

Worth Publishers
41 Madison Avenue
New York, New York 10010
www.worthpublishers.com

CONTENTS

PREFACE

Teaching is always a challenge, and this is especially true in teaching development. It is not easy to find the right mix of theory and practice, research and application, that will help students to understand the major themes and concepts.

These **Instructor's Resources** are designed to to assist you in meeting this challenge when using any of Kathleen Berger's developmental psychology texts. A separate set of Lecture Guides is provided for each text. These Lecture Guides contain a Chapter Preview, the text "What Have You Learned?" questions, and a detailed outline of each chapter. Within each outline are listed all the relevant materials from these resources. The Preface to the Lecture Guides provides a chapter-by-chapter list of available audiovisual materials, as well as lists of the videos in the Tool Kits and DevelopmentPortal. Also listed are relevant videos from the introductory psychology series provided by Worth: *Digital Media Archive,* 1st edition; *Digital Media Archive,* 2nd edition, and the 2nd and 3rd editions of *Scientific American Frontiers.*

Part I of these resources contains suggestions for planning your course as well as ideas and guidelines for term projects such as case-study projects and portfolio assignments. It also includes instructions for the classroom debates, critical thinking activities, observational activities, and Internet activities found in Part II of these resources. The Internet activities are designed to foster student writing and critical thinking when using Internet resources. At the end of Part I are detailed descriptions of audiovisual materials, including directions for obtaining them, and descriptions of the Exploring Human Development tool kits and DevelopmentPortal.

Part II is a guide to teaching the text. Each unit begins with a concise listing of the relevant resources either described or provided in this manual—including films and videos, classroom activities, teaching tips, and easy-to-reproduce handouts.

Other teaching and learning aids that accompany each textbook are a Test Bank, a student Study Guide, and a companion Web site. Each Test Bank includes multiple-choice, fill-in, and true-false questions. In addition, several essay questions, with answer guidelines, are provided for each chapter. Each question is graded according to difficulty and keyed to the textbook topic. All the questions in the Test Bank are available for Windows and Macintosh on a dual-platform CD-ROM. This computerized test bank guides professors step by step through the process of creating and administering secure exams over a network. The Study Guide, which includes an abundance of practice test questions, helps students to improve their analytical, writing, and test-taking skills as it guides their active learning of the material presented in the text. Finally, the Web site, located at www.worthpublishers.com/berger, is a free, online educational setting for students and instructors. Resources on the site include detailed chapter outlines, learning objectives, annotated Web links, online quizzes with immediate feedback and instructor notification, Internet exercises, critical thinking questions, case study exercises, an English/Spanish glossary, interactive flashcards in both English and Spanish, frequently asked questions about developmental psychology, and a Quiz Gradebook for instructors.

Also available are two telecourses that were developed specifically to accompany the Berger texts. *Transitions Throughout the Life Span* is a telecourse produced by Coastline Community College. *Child Development: Stepping Stones* is the version available for those teaching the childhood and adolescence course. Information about these telecourses can be obtained by writing to Coast Learning Systems, 11460 Warner Avenue, Fountain Valley, CA 92708-2597, e-mailing CoastLearning@cccd.edu, or calling 1-800-547-4748.

Worth has also put together two collections of videos to accompany the Berger text. The first is taken from *Scientific American* "Frontiers," a series of programs dealing with topics related to both the social and biological sciences. The collection contains 17 video segments, ranging from approximately 6 to 14 minutes in length, that apply to topics traditionally covered in the developmental psychology course. These videos are available to users of the Berger text (see the Lecture Guides for a complete list). For more information, contact your sales representative or call 1-800-446-8923. The second collection, *The Journey Through the Life Span* (*The Journey Through Childhood* is available for instructors of the childhood and adolescence course), is a series of narrated segments that explore development in each of the three domains: biosocial, cognitive, and psychosocial. Each narrated segment is also accompanied by an unnarrated observation module that can be used to stimulate class discussion or test students' mastery of key developmental concepts.

I am grateful to the many instructors whose insights and advice have helped to improve this edition of these resources. I am especially grateful to Catherine Woods, who helped shape the final structure of these resources and continue to provide me with a stimulating publishing environment in which to write. Most important, I am profoundly grateful to Betty Shapiro Probert of The Special Projects Group, who has worked long and hard to make this the creative, comprehensive book it is. Betty shares equally in whatever credit I receive for the pedagogical success of this project. Thanks also to Don Probert for his skill and efficiency in word processing the final book, and to Sharon Prevost, Jenny Chiu, and Stacey Alexander for their skillful assistance in the preparation of these resources.

Any comments, criticisms, or suggestions that you may have about these resources or the textbook itself are welcome. I am especially interested in any classroom activities, new lecture topics, or testing and grading strategies that may be included in the next edition of these resources. I will, of course, credit you and your college for any material I use. Write to me in care of Worth Publishers, 41 Madison Avenue, New York, New York 10010.

Richard O. Straub

HOW TO USE THESE RESOURCES

Part I of these Instructor's Resources contains general resources that you might like to consult before the term begins; Part II consists of teaching resources for use throughout the term.

Part I includes the following:

1. *Suggestions for Planning the Course.* This section offers tips that should be especially helpful to instructors who are new to the course or who are more familiar with a topical approach to development. Suggestions for planning a syllabus are provided.
2. *Ideas for Term Projects.* This section lists a wide range of possible term projects, including topics for research papers, interviews, and institution reports. It also includes guidelines for preparing these, as well as for book reports, case studies, interviews, institution visits, and participant-observer logs. These lists and instructions for students may be photocopied and used as handouts.
3. *Instructions for Student Projects in Part II.* This section contains general instructions for some of the activities described in detail in the relevant teaching resources. These include the classroom debates, portfolio assignments, Internet activities, and observational activities.
4. *Audiovisual Materials.* This section first provides suggestions for importing videos into PowerPoint presentations. *Exploring Human Development: A Tool Kit for Understanding Development* (for students) and *Exploring Human Development: An Instructor's Media Tool Kit* (for instructors), *DevelopmentPortal* for instructors and for students, *The Journey Through the Life Span* video segments, and the Coast *Transitions Throughout the Life Span* telecourses are also broadly described. The Tool Kits are described in general on page G–24, and DevelopmentPortal is described in general on page G–24. Detailed descriptions of the activities and videos in the Tool Kits and DevelopmentPortal are provided in the Lecture Guides for your text.

    Note that the Lecture Guides for your text contain detailed descriptions of available films and videotapes relevant to each text chapter. Audiovisual materials are presented at the beginning of the Lecture Guides because they need to be planned for, ordered, and previewed weeks before the topic in question is to be discussed. Film distributors and their addresses are also listed.

Part II includes the following for each unit:

1. *Contents.* This is an outline of the materials in that unit of the Instructor's Resources. It is organized according to the text topic. Thus, all the pertinent audiovisual materials (abbreviated AV), classroom activities, "On Your Own" activities, critical thinking activities, observational activities, and Internet activities appear immediately below each topic heading. The Contents includes page numbers of the activities, along with the page numbers of the handouts.
2. *Suggested Activities.* The suggested videos and activities are designed to help you achieve each of the instructional objectives. They are as follows:

    The Journey Through the Life Span (or *The Journey Through Childhood* for the childhood and adolescence course). This is a description of the pertinent video program from the telecourse, as well as a description of the unnarrated observation module for the program. Because all three developmental domains are covered in a single segment, I describe the entire segment under biosocial development, then refer to it in subsequent units for that age group.

    Transitions Throughout the Life Span (or *Child Development: Stepping Stones* for the childhood and adolescence course). This is a description of the pertinent video segment.

    Teaching Tips. Some teaching tips are brief, focused suggestions for helping students make meaningful connections between course material and their own experiences. Other tips are more general and are designed to help you meet the challenges of teaching large sections of students, using technology, and so forth.

    Classroom Activities. Most activities are designed to inspire student interest and involvement in a topic, and some offer additional material for lectures. Also presented in this section are the classroom debates and problem-based learning activities (see the Introduction for a general description of how to use these).

"On Your Own" Activities. These optional assignments—ranging from simple observations, portfolio writing assignments, surveys, and interviews to guided library research—may be photocopied and distributed to students. For each activity there is a brief description of its purpose and an interpretation of likely student responses.

Critical Thinking Activities. Each unit contains a Critical Thinking Activity, asking the student to answer several questions that demand reflection, scientific reasoning, creativity, perspective taking, or persuasive argument. Sample answers are also included. An introduction to these activities can be found on G–21.

Internet Activities. Included where appropriate, these are assignments for researching developmental topics using the Internet. In some cases, a specific URL is provided; in other cases, the student is asked to locate resources for obtaining information about a topic.

Observational Activities. At least two fully planned observational activities are described for the major parts of the textbook. Each activity is designed to provide students with a "hands-on" research project highlighting the text coverage of biosocial, cognitive, or psychosocial development during a particular stage in childhood, adolescence, or adulthood. The handouts describe the assignment and then provide a series of questions to be answered by the student and returned to the instructor.

PART I

GENERAL RESOURCES

SUGGESTIONS FOR PLANNING THE COURSE

The particulars of classroom lectures, discussions, assignments, and tests will naturally depend on the needs and aspirations of your students, your own interests and goals, and the length and purpose of the course. The following guidelines and suggestions may help you tailor your course to maximize learning.

STUDENTS' INTERESTS AND GOALS

Students take this course for a variety of reasons, including several practical ones. Specifically, they want to understand their own developmental past, present, and future; they want to know how to raise their children or care for their aging parents; or they plan to have careers working with people of a specific age.

Since planning the course depends partly on the interests and goals of the students, you may ask them during the first class why they chose this course. Their responses will probably affect the kinds of projects you assign, the topics you emphasize, and the approach (research/theoretical or applied) you take. For example, if your students are of various ages or majors, you may allow more individual choice for project topics in order to meet their greater variety of experiences and interests. With younger students, you may want to emphasize the tasks of parenting. Older students, some already parents themselves, may be more interested in specific problems related to their children's development. Finally, human development is often a requisite for programs like nursing and education; your lecture and discussion emphasis may shift to applications of developmental principles in order to meet the goals of these students.

YOUR INTERESTS AND GOALS

It is impossible, and probably undesirable, to ignore your own personal interests and values in planning and teaching a course. Your theoretical biases, research experiences, and political or moral beliefs may all affect the text you choose, the topics you emphasize, and the approach you take. Indeed, students are usually very interested to learn about your own research and ideas. Therefore, it is best to acknowledge your approach to and beliefs about human development, but it is also important to balance your course with the presentation of other valid views.

Before you begin teaching the course, you may find it helpful to prepare a list of general objectives for yourself. (Specific goals for each class session are also desirable: the learning and instructional objectives provided for each chapter in the Lecture Guides will help with this.) Your general objectives may include any or all of the items on the following list, arranged in three broad categories.

Knowledge

1. To describe the developing person at different periods through emerging adulthood or over the life span.
2. To provide a perspective on the changes that take place during an individual's life.
3. To examine possible causes or sources of developmental change and reasons for disturbances in the developmental process.
4. To demonstrate how different theoretical perspectives affect or determine the research and applications that arise from them.
5. To describe objective techniques and skills for observing human behavior.

Skills

1. To sharpen students' observational skills, so that they can examine behavior more objectively.
2. To teach specific skills that will help students in various professions. For example, those who plan to continue in the social or behavioral sciences may need help understanding statistical charts and scientific analyses; those in education may need to strengthen their ability to interpret behavior so that they can respond appropriately; those in nursing need to understand the effects of the interaction of the family and professionals on the physical and emotional well-being of the individual.

3. To enhance students' cognitive-processing ability by focusing on careful reading, clear written expression, and concise oral communication.
4. To develop students' study skills, including listening, careful reading, time allocation, and note-taking.
5. To foster critical thinking, especially in the analysis of developmental controversies.

Values

1. To enhance students' awareness of the ways in which social, political, and cultural trends affect the individual.
2. To help students appreciate people of all ages, cultures, and backgrounds, and to gain insight into their similarities and differences.
3. To help students develop responsible personal behavior with regard to such important issues as drug use, sexual activity, and parenting.

Course Level

In setting your goals, you should bear in mind the level of the course you will be teaching. One of the hardest tasks in any college course is teaching at the level that is most appropriate to the students' level of preparation. While the Berger texts have been written for, and successfully used by, students ranging from poorly prepared first-year students to those enrolled in graduate courses, the specifics of course design and text use vary widely, depending on the student population. This is because the authors of the textbook and its ancillaries have taught at very different types of institutions—including Columbia University, Fordham University Graduate School, Bronx Community College, and the University of Michigan–Dearborn. Having myself taught the course at many different levels, I offer the following suggestions in the hope that they may prove useful, especially to new instructors.

In general, the less well prepared the students are, the more important it is to test their knowledge at frequent intervals. A quiz after each text assignment helps to verify that they have read the material, provides you with a measure of how well they have grasped the basic ideas, and tells you which concepts need to be emphasized in lecture. A test on each trio of chapters is also advisable. Classwork should focus on explaining text material; frequent written homework assignments help reinforce understanding. This manual contains a number of items that are suitable as homework assignments. The Study Guide, which encourages students to organize their thoughts in writing and tests their knowledge of the facts and concepts in each chapter, can be especially effective for students who need extra help.

If less well-prepared students are given assignments requiring long-range planning, many will need guidelines for the successful preparation and execution of the assignment. Providing students with specific steps to be followed and a schedule for completing each one can help students produce their best work. For example, for a term paper, you may require that a description of the topic be turned in by October 20, note cards by November 10, first draft by December 1, final paper by December 20. In this way, you can monitor progress, make suggestions, and help to ensure that adequate time and thought will have been devoted to the project.

As student background and preparation improve, testing need not be so frequent and more class time can be spent on formal lectures and enrichment material. If students can master text material on their own, you are free to devote class time to putting the text material into an interdisciplinary, cross-cultural, or ecological context to foster development of student written and oral communication skills and dialectical thinking processes. This manual includes much information that can be used for these purposes.

In addition, the manual contains many suggestions for student projects that can, when completed, be shared with the entire class. Ideally, students will work on their own and/or in small groups to prepare these projects. Students and instructors can learn a great deal from this process when it is done well, and classes are livelier than when the same old professional (you) talks day after day.

A word of warning: Many new teachers assume that their students are academically more mature and knowledgeable than they really are, because many students, in conversation and attitude, seem eager and bright. Even the best students, however, may need guidelines to help them accomplish what you assume they are quite capable of doing. When in doubt, give a test early in the term that demands conceptual as well as factual knowledge. Also, when assigning a class project or term paper, ask them how they would go about completing the project. On listening, you can decide whether specific guidelines are in order.

Course Organization

These resources have been designed for use with any of Kathleen Berger's texts: *The Developing Person Through Childhood and Adolescence, The Developing Person Through the Life Span,* and *Invitation to the Life Span.* Depending on which text you are using, you will want to refer only to the topics relevant to your course. For life-span development, simply follow the topic outline given here. If you are teaching either childhood and adolescence or a brief life-span course, the following table will help you to find the material you need.

Topics in this IR	Chapters in *The Developing Person Through Childhood and Adolescence*	Chapters in *Invitation to the Life Span*
Introduction	1	1
Theories of Development	2	1
Heredity and Environment	3	2
Prenatal Development and Birth	4	2
The First Two Years: Biosocial Development	5	3
The First Two Years: Cognitive Development	6	3
The First Two Years: Psychosocial Development	7	4
Early Childhood: Biosocial Development	8	5
Early Childhood: Cognitive Development	9	5
Early Childhood: Psychosocial Development	10	6
Middle Childhood: Biosocial Development	11	7
Middle Childhood: Cognitive Development	12	7
Middle Childhood: Psychosocial Development	13	8
Adolescence: Biosocial Development	14	9
Adolescence: Cognitive Development	15	9
Adolescence: Psychosocial Development	16	10
Emerging Adulthood: Biosocial Development	Epilogue	11
Emerging Adulthood: Cognitive Development	Epilogue	11
Emerging Adulthood: Psychosocial Development	Epilogue	11
Adulthood: Biosocial Development		12
Adulthood: Cognitive Development		12
Adulthood: Psychosocial Development		13
Late Adulthood: Biosocial Development		14
Late Adulthood: Cognitive Development		14
Late Adulthood: Psychosocial Development		15
Death and Dying		Epilogue

Chronological Versus Topical Approach

Another issue you will need to consider is the organization of course material. The *topical* approach allows the student to focus on specific aspects of the individual, such as personality, and to follow the development of these aspects from infancy through late adulthood. The *chronological* approach allows the student to comprehend the richness of development at any given period of the life span and to examine interactions among the different domains of development—biosocial, cognitive, and psychosocial.

Every developmental psychology course is both topical and chronological. However, unlike texts that cover chronological development within a topical framework, Berger's texts follow a topical organization within a broader chronological framework. Thus, if you are used to teaching a topical course, you will probably want to reorganize your lecture notes somewhat.

ADDITIONAL SUGGESTIONS

When planning special assignments, note the many projects described in the next two sections of these resources. For example, you may consider assigning one or more of the two Observational Activities provided for each of the five parts of the textbook. Formatted so that you can photocopy and distribute them to students, these activities are designed to help students make meaningful connections between the text material and their own life experiences. Most instructors find that requiring some form of objective observation reinforces text material and classwork very well.

You can anticipate an enjoyable class; the material is interesting and almost every student will have personal recollections and ideas to contribute to the topic under discussion. A word of caution, however: It is easy for the class discussion, along with general principles and overriding themes, to get lost in a sea of anecdotes ("When I had my baby . . .") or specific questions ("My little brother still sucks his thumb. Is that okay?") or uninformed opinions ("menopause causes depression"). You can turn these sidetracking comments into individual learning experiences. Anecdotes can be followed with questions from you, such as, "And how does that fit into Piagetian stages?" to reinforce the goals of your teaching. Questions not relevant to class issues can be answered after class, perhaps with a suggestion for a book or reading to help the student find his or her own answer.

If you emphasize the impact of social, economic, and cultural factors on development in your course, the following three general lecture suggestions may prove useful. These suggestions can be applied to any topic throughout the course.

Infusing Diversity Issues into the Teaching of Cognitive Development

Lisa Whitten of the State University of New York, College at Old Westbury, argues that psychology instructors need to place more emphasis in their courses on the impact of social, economic, and cultural factors on psychological development. In support of this contention, she notes that her student evaluations reveal that many students believe that racial and cultural factors are irrelevant to psychology because their textbooks give scant coverage to race, class, and other social forces that affect development. (Whitten surveyed 25 leading psychology textbooks to determine the extent of their treatment of several topics related to African American psychology: race, racism, culture, and prejudice. Although most of the texts included material on at least one of these topics, in many cases the coverage was limited to one page or less.)

Whitten suggests several ways of infusing diversity issues that pertain to African Americans, women, the disabled, and other disenfranchised groups into psychology courses. The simplest is to prepare one or two lectures that focus specifically on diversity. She offers the following sample outline for a lecture unit on black psychology.

- Introduction
  - Brief History of African Americans
  - The Origin of African Americans
  - The Triangle Slave Trade
  - The Civil Rights Movement
- The Black Psychology Model
  - Definition of Black Psychology
  - The Importance of Using African Americans as a Standard When Studying African Americans
  - Trends in the Study of African Americans
  - G. Stanley Hall
  - Cultural Deficit/Cultural Deprivation/ Cultural Difference
  - Blaming the Victim
- How Race/Culture Affect Development
  - Poverty
  - Social Policy
  - Prejudice
  - Institutional Racism
  - Stress/Illness
- Application
  - Scholarship on African American Families
  - Relation Between Family Style and History
  - Attempts to Correct Misperceptions
  - Impact on Policy Decisions
- Discussion
  - Large Group
    - Student Reactions
  - Small-Group Activities
    - Structured Activities

Conclusions
- Critique of Black Psychology Model
- Racial Attitudes
- What You Can Do to Make a Difference
- Future Trends in Black Psychology

Importance for All People to Understand the Relations Among Culture, Race, Politics, Economics, and Psychological Functioning

Other relevant lecture topics for developmental psychology classes include cultural/racial variations in child rearing, educational/intelligence testing, and child abuse; variations in family constellations and dynamics; the impact of the welfare system and migration on families; cultural and racial variations in learning style; and differences in infant mortality and morbidity.

Whitten notes that the most effective vehicle for immersing students into diversity issues is small-group interaction in multicultural contexts. "Strive to place students in cooperative and equal status relationships that require that they collectively share in the responsibility for the course of instruction." Among the topics Whitten suggests for small-group activities are the following:

1. Write intelligence test questions that tap knowledge about a specific cultural group and that people outside the group would fail.
2. Design a parent training program that takes into account the unique features of a particular cultural group.
3. Develop a program to improve the racial self-concept of African American (or immigrant or refugee) schoolchildren.
4. Develop a drug/AIDS prevention program that considers students' racial/cultural diversity.
5. Present debates between two opposing positions of a controversial topic regarding race (for example, the impact of single-parent homes, interracial marriage, and transracial adoption).

Whitten, L. A. (1993). Infusing black psychology into the introductory psychology course. *Teaching of Psychology, 20*(1), 13–21.

Using Literature to Teach Developmental Psychology

Chris Boyatzis of California State University–Fullerton assigns Maya Angelou's *I Know Why the Caged Bird Sings* in his classes to illustrate a broad range of child development topics.

Angelou's marvelous book recounts her own childhood from preschool through adolescence. The first part of the book, which spans early and middle childhood, provides vivid examples of many topics: the growth of logic and concrete operational thought; the development of self-concept and self-esteem; the impact of abuse, gender issues, child rearing styles, and sibling and friendship relations. The second half of the book, which could be assigned later in the course, illustrates the challenges of puberty and identity formation in adolescence, the impact of the peer group, the emergence of formal operational thought, the formation of sexual identity, and the beginnings of interest in parenthood and vocations.

Boyatzis instructs his students to write a term paper discussing "how Angelou's childhood experiences exemplify two or three aspects or topics of development. Use course materials (text, supplementary readings, class notes, films, handouts) to build a framework of theory and research to analyze Angelou's development. In short . . . make connections between the general and the particular: Use the course to explain Angelou's development and use Angelou's experiences to illustrate the course." An alternative approach is to assign sections of the book to be discussed in class.

Boyatzis notes that the project has been immensely successful with students. It "develops students' ability to integrate course materials and helps them understand the complex issues of race, gender, and social class in development. Angelou's childhood account is such a powerful psychological journey for the reader that I am confident students remember much about development because of this book. The potency of the assignment is captured in students' comments. One wrote 'I will remember the book and assignment for a very long time,' and another said the assignment was 'the most rewarding and beneficial I've had in college.'"

Boyatzis, C. J. (1992). Let the caged bird sing: Using literature to teach developmental psychology. *Teaching of Psychology, 19*(4), 221–222.

Incorporating a Semester-Long Scaffolded Assignment

For the major project in her neuropsychology course, Rebecca Achtman of Nazareth College requires each student to create a "Reader's Guide" for a neurological disorder of their choosing (e.g., amnesia, aphasia). Her model can easily be adapted to a developmental psychology course by having students choose from a list of disorders of physical, cognitive, or social development. Moreover, the project itself illustrates an important process in cognitive development: scaffolding.

Each Reader's Guide is divided into the following sections:

- Theorists and contributors
- Central concepts
- Controversial issue
- Major resources
- References

Achtman subdivides the assignment into five smaller ones that are distributed throughout the course to encourage continuous work and to allow for increased feedback and intervention when it is most useful. Each of the smaller assignments, except for Assignment 4 (the completed draft), receives a weighted grade toward the final, overall project grade. The five assignments are as follows:

Assignment 1: Topic identification (due week 4)

- What is your topic?
- Why are you choosing this topic?
- What resources will help in your research of this topic?

Assignment 2: Major contributors (due week 6)

Provide the following information on 4 or 5 people who have made significant contributions to your topic:

- Name, affiliation, important dates
- What questions did they ask?
- What technique did they use?
- References

Assignment 3: Oral presentation (due week 9)

- A 7-minute oral presentation that includes
  an introduction to the topic
  definitions of key terms (including relevant research techniques
  an explanation of why topic is controversial
  evidence supporting each side of the controversy?
  whether the controversy has been resolved

Assignment 4: Completed draft (due week 12, extensive feedback provided but no grade)

- Although students in Achtman's class had already received feedback on previous assignments, this was the first time they were required to write about the controversy regarding their topic. The students also received detailed guidelines on what should be included in this draft.

Assignment 5: Final product (due week 14)

- Students were permitted to submit the final product in a variety of formats (e.g., booklet, pamphlet, traditional essay).

Achtman notes that her students became increasingly knowledgeable and enthusiastic about their topics. This in turn increased motivation in the classroom as "they frequently made links between course readings and the disorder they were researching. They presented creative, high-quality, final projects that they were eager to share with one another."

Achtman, R. (2011). *Developing a semester-long scaffolded assignment*. Presented at meetings of the National Institute on the Teaching of Psychology. St. Petersburg Beach, FL.

READING RESOURCES

Keeping up to date is important because students invariably read reports of current research on human development in the media, and you will need to reply to their questions. In several areas, new research challenges what most developmentalists taught and believed as recently as five years ago. For example, genetic discoveries are reshaping the nature–nurture controversy; the information-processing model has increased our understanding of cognitive development; middle childhood may be just as "critical" as early childhood; and adolescents today face more serious potential threats to their development than at any other time in history.

If you wish to update or add material for your course, the extensive and current bibliography in the textbook is a good place to begin. I would like to call your attention to one especially comprehensive source. The four volumes of *The Handbook of Child Psychology* (6th ed.), edited by Paul Mussen and published by Wiley, cover most topics in child development, although there is greater emphasis on research than on applications.

In addition, three major professional journals deal with human development. These provide a good starting point if you would like more recent information on any topic.

Developmental Psychology, published by the American Psychological Association, 1200 17 St. NW, Washington, DC 20036 (www.apa.org).

Child Development, published by the Society for Research in Child Development, The University of Chicago Press, Journals Division, P. O. Box 37005, Chicago, IL 60637 (www.wiley.com/bw/journal.asp?ref=0009-3920)

Human Development, published by Karger, P. O. Box CH-4009, Basel, Switzerland (http://content.karger.com/ProdukteDB/produkte.asp?Aktion=JournalHome&ProduktNr=224249.

The Society for Research in Child Development (www.srcd.org) also publishes a very good index of recent research in their *Abstracts and Bibliography*.

IDEAS FOR TERM PROJECTS

This section provides suggestions and guidelines for term projects, including research papers, book reports, adult interviews, case studies, institution reports, and participant-observer logs.

No matter which type of project you assign, you may want to spend one class period preparing students for it. For instance, if you are asking students to do library research, you may arrange for them to be given a tour of the library resources. If you are asking them to conduct an interview, you may review the techniques that make for a good interview (such as ways of establishing rapport, how to be a good listener, what kinds of comments encourage an interviewee to offer more detail). If you are assigning a child-study project, for example, you may show one of the films in *The Child* series (see the audiovisual section and the relevant chapters in these resources), asking your students to write down what they observe and then to present their observations in the way suggested on page G–13. Having students compare their observations will demonstrate the many ways in which data can be classified and interpreted and will lead to the conclusion that some ways are better than others.

After students have completed their assignments, they may be required to share their findings with the rest of the class. This will help students understand points of view other than their own, as well as aid them in developing communication skills. For some students, giving an oral report requires them to spend more time and care on their project than they otherwise would.

GRADING TERM PROJECTS

Grading term projects is difficult. Some instructors find it useful to assign points for various elements of the paper and to explain this system to the students in advance. For example, John G. Hartung, of The University of Colorado, has developed the following guidelines for the research papers he assigns.

Criteria	Your Points/ Maximum
Technical Requirements	
1. Outline handed in, topic approved by ______ :	______ /10
2. Paper was handed in by ______ :	______ /10
3. Between 5 and 10 pages, double-spaced, typed:	______ /10
4. Minimum of 10 scientific references in bibliography:	______ /10
5. References are cited in the paper itself, according to a consistent format:	______ /10
Contents	
1. You report the scientific research accurately:	______ /10
2. Your writing is well organized: you followed the organizational guidelines that were provided; you used research to support your ideas; your writing is logical and sequential:	______ /10
3. Grammar, spelling, typing, syntax, and sentence construction are correct (a good proofreader can be helpful):	______ /10
Interest, Creativity	
1. Your paper is interesting and creative:	______ /10
2. You focus clearly on important points and are selective in choosing facts, ideas, and examples that are most significant to your topic:	______ /10
Total Points	______ /100

Note that these grading guidelines can be applied to any type of term project. Items 4 and 5 (under technical requirements), however, apply to research papers only, but they could be replaced by one or more of the following items, depending on the type of project.

Book Reports

The chosen book is a scholarly work relevant to child or adolescent development.

The chosen book was recently published and reflects current developmental thinking (unless it is a work of historical significance).

Adult Interviews

The topic and interviewees were carefully chosen to shed light on an important developmental issue.

Interview guidelines were followed accurately.

Case Studies

Methods chosen for conducting the case study were appropriate and well planned.

Guidelines for observation, interviewing, or testing were accurately followed.

Institution Reports

Choice of institution was appropriate for the topic.

Guidelines for conducting an institution visit or interview were accurately followed.

If you prefer giving more holistic grades, it is still helpful to establish for yourself the criteria you are using, so you will be fair in your grading. This also helps you if a student complains that his or her paper deserved a better grade.

RESEARCH PAPERS

Writing term papers helps students develop their research and writing skills, and encourages them to think about the issues in the study of human development. Unfortunately, many students find it extremely difficult (impossible?) to write a term paper without extensive help in finding resources, in organizing their ideas and time, and in actually writing the paper. Thus, before assigning research papers, consider your students' skills and how much time you want to spend helping them. If they are inexperienced in writing research papers, you may want to revise and then duplicate the following guidelines for writing research papers, along with the list of suggested topics, for distribution to your students. If your campus has an academic center that helps students develop sound writing skills, you may call this to your students' attention or have a representative from the center give a class presentation.

Guidelines for Research Papers

Instructions

Research papers are due by _______ . The topic must be related to human development.

Please return the top of this sheet to me by _______ to have your topic approved. Keep the remaining pages for reference in preparing your paper.

Your name ______________________________

Date _______________

Your topic ______________________________________

Briefly outline your topic:

Do you know how to use the reference library to find and read at least three scientific articles (journals, monographs, etc.) that you will use in preparing your paper?

Yes _______ No _______

Format

As you are working on your research paper, keep in mind that its primary function is to show your ability to read and understand scholarly research and to use it to support your own ideas and opinions.

1. *Due date.* Papers are due by 5 P.M. on _______ . Late papers will be accepted but graded more strictly. No late papers will be given an A.
2. *Length.* Your paper should be at least 5 and no more than 10 pages long.
3. *Form.* Your paper should be keyboarded, double-spaced. You must submit your original sheets. Photocopies of your paper are not acceptable.
4. *Textbook.* Read the relevant parts of the textbook before beginning your research to help you put your topic in its proper context. Consult the Subject Index to help you find the material you need.

5. *Organization.* Your paper should be organized as follows:

   (a) *Introduction.* A paragraph or two that clearly and concisely describes (1) the topic of your paper, (2) the question(s) you will investigate, and (3) the various points of view or differing explanations proposed in the scientific articles on which you are basing your paper.

   (b) *Research section.* The core of the paper—three to eight pages—must be a discussion of the scientific evidence. You should consult at least 10 sources (books, articles within books, monographs, or journal articles), at least half of which should have been published within the last five years. Try to find at least one relevant source published within the last year. While magazines written for a general audience sometimes pose provocative questions and contain interesting information, you should not rely on them for accuracy. Instead, you should find recent scholarly books and journals on your topic. If you have difficulty finding relevant material, ask the librarian.

   To effectively use the contents of journal or magazine articles to support your ideas, be sure to clearly describe (1) the topic of the research being reported, (2) the research methods used (and how these methods may have affected the results), (3) the researchers' conclusions, and (4) questions raised by the research.

   In the last paragraph or two of the research section of your paper, summarize the research findings and briefly state how the research relates to the topic of your paper. Good examples of how research can be used to support a discussion are given throughout your textbook.

   (c) *Your opinions.* A very important part of the paper is your own opinions and ideas, based on the research you have read. Indicate which sources you agree with and which you don't, and why. What conclusions can you draw from your reading? What important questions related to your topic remain unanswered?

   (d) *Bibliography.* All the books and journals used for your paper should be listed alphabetically in a bibliography at the end. You should follow a consistent format, such as the one in the text or in the style manual of the American Psychological Association.

6. *Plagiarism.* When you copy something word for word, or when you are merely rephrasing ideas from someone else's text, you must cite your source, including the last name of the author and the date of publication in parentheses (see examples in your textbook). If you use someone else's words and ideas without citing them, you are committing plagiarism and may receive an F.

7. *Topics.* A list of possible topics is available ____________________. For each topic, we have provided relevant questions to help you think of ways to organize your paper. You are not required to follow them, and you should not limit your paper to these questions. If you want to select your own topic, consult your instructor for approval and suggestions.

8. *Oral summary.* You will be required to give an oral summary of your findings to the class. Class members will have time to ask questions and to help in the evaluation of the research.

Possible Topics for Research Papers

This list represents only a very few of the almost endless possibilities for research topics. You may want to pursue a topic of particular interest to you, in which case you will need to set out the questions you intend to answer (your instructor can help you), as is done for each topic listed below.

Abuse

Cross-cultural analysis of child abuse Are some cultures more abusive than others? If so, why? What are the cultural variations in the modes of discipline? Is research based on the abuse and neglect of North American middle-class children valid for children from other groups?

Biosocial Development

Brain, eye, and hand specialization What is the usual developmental sequence of brain, eye, and hand specialization? What recent evidence is there concerning the relationship among these three body parts, especially with regard to left-right coordination? What conclusions can be drawn from studies of brain, eye, or hand injuries?

Dementia Identify the causes and symptoms of severe cognitive impairment in the elderly. How are different disorders distinguished? What is Alzheimer disease, and what does the latest research suggest about it? What methods are used to treat dementias?

Drug use What are the trends in adolescent drug use? To what extent do these patterns constitute a distinct subcultural pattern, and to what extent are they simply a reflection of the larger culture? What kinds of drug education programs should there be for adolescents?

Eating disorders What are some of the causes of or theories about anorexia and bulimia? the consequences of these disorders? Why are adolescent females particularly susceptible? What methods are being used to treat people with anorexia and those with bulimia, and how successful are they?

Health What are some common health problems for adults? What steps can be taken to prevent them? What do health clubs recommend for adults? Cite evidence for the effectiveness or ineffectiveness of their programs.

Perceptual development What are the interrelationships in the development of the various senses? How do they relate to motor-skill development? to cognitive skills? Does recent evidence allow you to reach a more complex conclusion than the generality that "maturation and learning interact"?

Puberty What psychological issues accompany puberty in adolescents? Are there sexual or cultural differences in the way puberty is viewed? What are the consequences of early or late maturation for the adolescent?

Cognition

Achievement in later life Find examples of individuals who produced great art or literature, or made a scientific discovery, late in life. Characterize their earlier productivity, and compare it to their later works. Is there evidence for a new wisdom or creativity in later life?

Children's art What are the theories that attempt to explain the sequence of children's art? Which aspects of children's art seem universal and developmental, and which seem bound by culture and personality? What function does art play in children's lives, as development of motor skills and development of emotional expression increase?

IQ Does intelligence decline during adulthood? Examine the arguments for and against this claim. Compare research on both sides of the controversy, including subjects and the research method used. Are standard IQ tests "age-biased"?

Language acquisition What are the universal similarities and individual differences in language acquisition? What light does research on Motherese shed on this question? How does language acquisition relate to later intellectual development?

Measuring intelligence What are the assumptions and theories underlying various tests of intelligence? Consider how tests change with the age of the individual and with the theories of the test makers. Can tests be culture-free? culture-fair?

Cultural and Socioeconomic Factors

Ageism What are some causes of ageism in our society? Which characterizations of the elderly are factual, and which are myths? How does ageism affect the elderly? How can ageist attitudes be changed?

Delinquency To what extent do the laws of your community treat juveniles differently from adults? Do these differences seem appropriate, given your knowledge of development? Would other differences be recommended? What is being done to prevent delinquency? What should be done? Be sure to consider research studies on this topic, especially large-group longitudinal research.

The generation gap Are there great differences between adolescents and their parents in values, ideals, political beliefs, or morals? What may cause the appearance of a gap? What do researchers think may help close the gap? Consider various theories and the evidence that supports them.

Minority-group children Pick one minority group—racial, religious, or cultural—and trace the development of children from that group. Which aspects of development are affected by minority status? What are the advantages and disadvantages of growing up as a member of that minority group? Are problems that occur caused by the majority culture, by the minority group itself, or simply by human nature?

Political attitudes How do political attitudes develop? What are the factors that influence the social values, voting patterns, and political protests of young people? What are the similarities and differences between the political attitudes of today's young people and those of earlier generations?

Senior housing What kinds of housing arrangements are available to the elderly today? Who seems to adjust to and like each type best? What are the advantages and disadvantages of age-segregated communities for the elderly? Evaluate your community's response to the housing needs of the elderly.

Death and Dying

Euthanasia and assisted suicide What laws govern these practices in your state? What ethical issues are raised by these practices? What rational arguments can you provide for and against euthanasia? Who should decide whether euthanasia and assisted suicides are legal?

Mourning rituals What funeral, burial, and bereavement customs are practiced by people living in your community? How do they compare with rituals practiced by their forebears a century ago? What accounts for these historical differences? What are the consequences of the changes?

Terminal illness How do people cope with a terminal illness? How do the reactions of dying children compare to those of dying adults? How can the responses of family members help or hurt the dying person? How can supportive care, such as that given in a hospice, help both the dying person and family members and friends?

Widowhood What factors make adjustment to widowhood relatively easy or difficult? How is the position of widows in your community today different from that of widows in other cultures? Other centuries?

Developmental Theory and Research

Behaviorism and current research What recent attempts have there been to apply behaviorist theory to human development? To what extent is behaviorism too narrow in focus to be able to take an ecological approach? What direction do you see behaviorism taking in the next decade?

Continuity and discontinuity According to recent thinking, is development more continuous or discontinuous? What are the strongest arguments for each side and the unresolved issues? Be sure to consider both longitudinal and cross-sectional research.

Eriksonian theory and current research What recent attempts have there been to validate Eriksonian ideas? How much of it is subjective and how much relatively objective? Evaluate both critical and laudatory approaches to Eriksonian theory.

Ethics and research What are the most recent formulations of ethical principles that should be upheld in psychological research? Is there widespread agreement on these? Is there any recent research that violates these standards? Do these ethical standards restrict scientific progress? Can they be bent to suit the experimenter?

Midlife crisis What evidence exists for a midlife crisis? Characterize the midlife crisis. What other factors could account for upheaval in an adult's life? Consider the various theories of adult development, both stage and continuity, in discussing the questions.

Moral development What evidence is there to support or refute the various theories of moral development? What is the relationship among moral attitude, gender, cognitive stage, and behavior? Consider cultural, familial, and personality factors in your answer.

Piaget's theory What do contemporary developmentalists say about Piaget's theory of cognitive development? Which aspects of the theory have withstood the test of time? Which have been modified, and how?

Play How does the play of children change as they develop? What are the various theories about the functions of play? What evidence is there to support each theory? What kinds of play patterns are ideal? Is play ever destructive to normal development?

Education

Bilingual education What are the various approaches to the education of children who speak a language different from that of the dominant culture? What are the advantages and disadvantages of each method for fostering the child's intellectual, linguistic, and emotional development? Consider the experiences of at least two different ethnic groups, such as French-Canadians, Mexican-Americans, Puerto Ricans living on the mainland, or Native Americans.

Education—Piaget Versus Skinner Compare books for educators written by followers of Piaget and by followers of Skinner. What are the similarities and differences in their assumptions and suggestions? What critical comments do you consider valid or invalid for these two approaches? Is there any research that helps resolve the controversy?

Employment

Career change What factors are involved in the decision to change careers? What programs are available to help with midlife career changes? How do the new careers differ from the original career choices? Are the new careers generally more or less satisfying than first careers?

Career selection What are the factors involved in career selection? What programs are available to help with career decisions? What effect do these programs have on career decisions? What factors affect an individual's satisfaction with a career? What factors are involved in the decision to change careers?

Families

Alternative lifestyles In terms of psychosocial development, what are the advantages and disadvantages for an adult who chooses to remain single? childless? who adopts a homosexual lifestyle? Be sure your paper reflects research findings as well as opinions.

Family patterns To what extent does the "traditional" family (father working, mother at home with the children) exist today? How are home-care responsibilities divided in families where the mother is employed? How do patterns in this country compare with patterns in other countries and/or earlier decades?

Siblings What effect do siblings have on development? Consider research on family size, birth order, and sex of siblings in connection with this topic. Is there an ideal family size and composition?

Learning Disabilities

Development of disabled children Pick one disability, such as blindness, deafness, mental retardation, or hyperactivity, and trace the development of children with that disability from birth to young adulthood. What periods of development, or aspects of development, are especially crucial? What can be done to minimize the impact of that disability?

Learning disabilities What recent evidence is there concerning the causes and treatment of learning disabilities? Which lines of research seem most promising? most popular? If children are diagnosed as having a learning disability during childhood, what predictions can be made about their later development?

Mainstreaming and special education What evidence is there that mainstreaming helps children? What evidence is there that it does not? What seem to be the crucial factors that should be considered in planning the education of a disabled child? Consider cognitive, emotional, and social development.

Marriage

Divorce What are the factors implicated in divorce and what are the factors that determine adjustment afterward? Consider the impact of divorce on children, adults, and grandparents.

Parenting and Caregiving

Alternatives to home care What evidence do we have concerning the differences and similarities between child care provided by the parents in the home and care provided by others outside the home? How do the advantages and disadvantages of alternative care change with the age of the child? with the type of family? with the type of alternative care? What can be learned from day-care experiences in other cultures?

Divorced and single parents How has the incidence of divorced and single-parent families changed over the last twenty years? How have these changes affected the experiences of children from these families? Which factors correlate with good adjustment and development in children from such families? Which factors correlate with poor adjustment? Are there periods of development when divorce is particularly difficult for children to cope with?

Fathers and mothers What are the differences between father–child and mother–child interactions? What are the similarities? Does this pattern change as the infant becomes a toddler? a preschooler? a school-age child? Does the sex of the child affect these differences? To what extent are these similarities and differences cultural? biological? psychological?

Peers and parents In what ways do peers have more influence with adolescents than parents do, and in what ways are parents more influential? Does the answer to this question depend on the subculture, the sex, and the familial pattern of the young person, or are there broad generalizations that can be made? Consider various theories, and the evidence that supports them.

Prenatal Development and Birth

Birth customs and traditions What are the variations in the birth process throughout the world? throughout North America? What are the reasons for the differences you find? Which traditions seem most beneficial for the baby? the mother? the father? other family members? the attending doctors, nurses, midwives? Consider psychological as well as biological advantages and disadvantages.

Medical procedures used during the birth process Fetal monitoring, cesarean deliveries, forceps deliveries, and especially drugs given to women during labor have both critics and champions. What recent evidence can you find that is relevant to the controversy over these procedures, and what are the possible interpretations of that evidence? Why do views diverge so widely on this issue?

Prevention of congenital problems Describe recent evidence concerning the cause and prevention of congenital problems. Consider topics such as genetic counseling, nutrition, education, drug use, and air and water pollution. What are the most recent developments in prenatal diagnosis and treatment?

Sex Differences

Female self-concept How has the women's movement affected the psychosocial development of adolescent girls? Compare research on this topic published within the last five years with research published a decade or more ago.

Gender roles What are the similarities and differences between male and female development in adulthood? Consider all three domains, but specialize in one area, such as sexuality, moral development, or employment.

Sex differences What are the sex differences in behavior, ability, and attitudes that emerge during childhood? Which theories explain these differences? What evidence supports the various theories? Since this is a broad subject, you may want to focus on a single aspect, such as the differences in motor skills, verbal ability, or rate of psychological disturbance.

Sexual-Reproductive System

Adult sexuality What does the most accurate and recent research say about sexual behavior after age 20? What are the difficulties in obtaining accurate information on this topic? What research do you think is most carefully done?

Family planning What predictions can you make about family planning in the year 2010? What cultural and socioeconomic variations will there be? Remember that predictions should be based on evaluation and interpretation of past data and history, and that family planning is a cognitive and psychosocial issue as well as a biosocial one.

BOOK REPORTS

If library research papers seem too time-consuming or complicated for your class, book reports may provide an alternative way to get students to read additional sources and think about the issues involved.

1. Make up a readings list of your own.
2. Permit students to select their own books, asking that they use books published in the last five years. In this case, ask them to bring the books to you for approval before beginning, and/or to lend you the book when they hand in the report, to help you evaluate their work.

You may find it helpful to photocopy and distribute the following book report guidelines.

Guidelines for Book Reports

One of the assignments for this course is that you read a book relevant to human development and write a report about what you read. In your report, answer the following questions:

1. What are the main ideas of this book?
2. What are the underlying assumptions of the author(s)?
3. To what extent is the book objective, and to what extent is it subjective?
4. Evaluate the main ideas and assumptions of the book. Criticize and praise, agree and disagree, point out omissions and overemphases, all with examples.
5. Why was this book written, and who is the intended audience? Would you recommend this book, and if so, to whom?
6. Your report should be at least 1,000 words. Type it if possible; if not, write neatly and legibly.

CASE-STUDY PROJECTS

There are many ways to structure reports on the development of an individual. The most elaborate includes longitudinal observation, informal interaction, testing, and interviews with other family members. The information presented should involve biosocial, cognitive, and psychosocial development, and include predictions about the person's future as well. (Although you may want to limit the scope of this assignment by omitting some of the research methods, you may profitably consider adding to it by requiring the students to study several people, perhaps in different age groups.) This assignment could be done in pairs or trios. Students can benefit from collectively performing these kinds of projects because they will learn how often subjective interpretations arise.

Structuring Case-Study Projects

Part of your work in this course is to study a child, adolescent, or adult closely, and report the results of your study.

Child-Study Project

1. When you have chosen a child for your study and are securing the parents' consent, explain that you are doing this research for a course in life-span development, that the child's name will not be used in the report, and that the main purpose of the report is to help you see the relationship between textbook knowledge of child development and real children. Also explain that you are not making a psychological evaluation of the child—you are not qualified to do so. (Indicate that you would be happy to talk with the parents informally about their child.)
2. *Before* you begin the study, read the trio of text chapters that apply to the age group to which your subject belongs.
3. Collect the information for your paper by using these research methods:

   (a) *Naturalistic observation* Ask the parents when the child is likely to be awake and active, and observe the child for an hour during this time. You should try to be as unobtrusive as possible: you are not there to play with, or care for, the child. If the child wants to play, explain that you must sit and write for now, and that you will play later.

   Write down, minute by minute, everything the child does and that others do with the child. Try to be objective, focusing on behavior rather than interpretation. Thus, instead of writing "Jennifer was delighted when her father came home, and he dotes on her," you should write "5:33: Her father opened the door, Jennifer looked up, smiled, said 'dada,' and ran to him. He bent down, stretched out his arms, picked her up, and said 'How's my little angel?' 5:34: He put her on his shoulders, and she said 'Getty up horsey.'"

   After your observation, summarize the data in two ways: (1) Note the percentage of time spent in various activities. For instance, "Playing alone, 15 percent; playing with brother, 20 percent; crying, 3 percent." (2)

Note the frequency of various behaviors: "Asked adult for something five times; adult granted request four times. Aggressive acts (punch, kick, etc.) directed at brother, 2; aggressive acts initiated by brother, 6." Making notations like these will help you evaluate and quantify your observations. Also, note any circumstances that may have made your observation atypical (e.g., "Jenny's mother said she hasn't been herself since she had the flu a week ago," or "Jenny kept trying to take my pen, so it was hard to write").

Note: Remember that a percentage can be found by dividing the total number of minutes spent on a specific activity by the total number of minutes you spent observing. For example, if, during your 45-minute observation, the child played by herself for periods of 2 minutes, 4 minutes, and 5 minutes, "playing alone" would total 11 minutes. Dividing 11 by 45 yields .244; thus the child spent 24 percent of the time playing alone. (If the figure in the third decimal place is 5 or more, round the second decimal place up to the next digit—for example, if your quotient were .246, you would round to .25, which is 25 percent.

(b) *Informal interaction* Interact with the child for at least half an hour. Your goal is to observe the child's personality and abilities in a relaxed setting. The particular activities you engage in will depend on the child's age and character. Most children enjoy playing games, reading books, drawing, and talking. Asking a younger child to show you his or her room and favorite toys is a good way to break the ice; asking an older child to show you the neighborhood can provide insights.

(c) *Interviewing parents and other adults responsible for the child's care* Keep these interviews loose and open-ended. Your goals are to learn (1) the child's history, especially any illnesses, stresses, or problems that may affect development; (2) the child's daily routine, including play patterns; (3) current problems that may affect the child; (4) a description of the child's character and personality, including special strengths and weaknesses.

You are just as interested in the parents' attitudes as in the facts, so it may make sense to concentrate on conversing during the interview, and then to write down all you have learned as soon as the interview has been completed.

(d) *Testing the child* Assess the child's perceptual, motor, language, and intellectual abilities by using specific test items you have planned in advance. The actual items you use will depend on the age of the child. For instance, you would test object permanence in an infant between 6 and 24 months old; you would test conservation in a child between 3 and 9 years old; and logical thinking in an adolescent. Likewise, testing language abilities may involve babbling with an infant, counting words per sentence with a preschooler, and asking a school-age child to tell a story.

4. When writing the report, do *not* simply transcribe your findings from the various techniques you used (although you can attach your raw data to your paper, if you want to).

   (a) Begin by reporting relevant background information, including the child's birth date and sex, age and sex of siblings, economic and ethnic background of the family, and the educational and marital status of the parents.

   (b) Describe the child's biosocial, cognitive, and psychosocial development, citing supporting data from your research to substantiate any conclusions you have reached.

   (c) Predict the child's development in the next year, the next five years, and the next ten years. List the strengths in the child, the family, and the community that you think will foster optimal development. Also note whatever potential problems you see (either in the child's current behavior or in the family and community support system) that may lead to future difficulties for the child. Include discussion of the reasons, either methodological or theoretical, that your predictions may not be completely accurate.

Adolescent- or Adult-Study Project

1. When you have chosen an adolescent or adult for your study, explain that you are doing this research for a course in life-span development psychology, that the person's name will not be used in the report, and that the main purpose of this study is to help you see how textbook knowledge applies to real life. Also explain that you are not making a psychological evaluation—you are not qualified to do so. (However, if your subject would like to know your ideas, you would be willing to share them.)

2. Before you begin the study, read the trio of chapters that apply to the age group to which the subject belongs.

   (a) *Naturalistic observation* Accompany the person to school, work, or to a social gathering. Try to be as unobtrusive as possible; maintain some distance from the person and those with whom the person interacts. Begin by describing the environment. For example, if you are observing the subject in his or her workplace, you may consider the following questions: Is it crowded? (How many people in how large an area?) Is it calm or busy? (How many phone calls, how many interruptions in how long a period of time?) On which skills, mental and physical, does the person's work depend?

Once you have collected some basic information about the surroundings, write down, minute by minute, everything the person does alone or with others. Try to be objective, focusing on behavior rather than interpretation. Thus, instead of writing, "Subject seems well-organized," you should note those factors that are the basis for the observation: "Subject keeps a calendar with notes for telephone calls and tasks to be performed each day." Or instead of noting, "Subject seems well-liked and respected by her co-workers," it is better to indicate, "At 3:05 P.M., a co-worker stopped by the subject's office to ask her opinion of how to solve a deadline problem. The subject came up with possible solutions; the co-worker thanked her and said that the ideas seemed good possibilities. At 4:15 the subject's manager asked her to interview a prospective employee."

After your observation, summarize the data in two ways: Note the percentage of time spent in various activities. For instance, "Talking on phone, 10 percent; typing, 20 percent; conferring with co-workers, 5 percent; attending meetings, 15 percent," and so on. (2) Note frequency of various behaviors (e.g., co-workers visited subject's office twice; subject visited co-worker's office once; subject made three phone calls and received two). Also note any circumstances that may have made your observation atypical (e.g., subject had just returned from a five-day, cross-country business trip and was tired and had a lot of catch-up work in the office).

(b) *Informal interaction* Interact with the person for at least half an hour. Some possible topics for discussion: What are the subject's favorite (and least favorite) activities? What experiences from the subject's past have been most influential to the subject's present life? What have been the influences of family, friends, and mentors in the subject's choice of employment and satisfaction with work? What other factors have been important (education, personal preference, financial needs, temperament, and so on)? How does the subject balance work responsibilities and family life? Questions about current events can elicit information about values and character.

Note the subject's attitudes and responses: Does the subject seem shy or open, easy-going or difficult to get along with, have a sense of humor about him- or herself? Does the subject accept responsibility for his or her life and actions, or blame others? Does the subject seem satisfied or dissatisfied with his or her personal life, family, choice of employment, etc.?

(c) *Interview* Conduct an interview with your subject and, if possible, with a relative or a friend of the subject. Keep these interviews loose and open-ended. Your goals are to learn (1) the person's history, especially any past illnesses, stresses, or problems that may affect development; (2) the person's daily routine, including patterns of school, work, and recreation; (3) current problems that may affect the person; (4) temperament, character, and personality, including special strengths and weaknesses.

Since you are just as interested in the person's attitudes as in the facts, it may be best not to take notes during the interview but simply to converse, and then to write down all you have learned as soon as the interview has been completed.

(d) *Testing the person* You can learn about your subject's thinking by planning in advance (with the help of your instructor) to obtain or design a test suitable for eliciting the type of information in which you are interested.

INTERVIEWING INDIVIDUALS

Asking your students to interview one or more adults is one way to help them understand the relevance of research in developmental psychology.

To help your students plan their interviews and gather information effectively, you may want to hand out the following guidelines.

Format for Adolescent and Adult Interviews

Students will better understand the issues important to adolescents and adults if you have them use the semi-structured interview technique. People are usually willing to talk about their lives if they feel that the researcher will treat their information confidentially and ethically. Their comments can be a rich source of information about human development.

To be sure they get the proper information during the interviews, students should develop a short list of questions in advance. (You may wish to review the students' questions before they go out on the interviews.) The interview subject should then be encouraged to talk freely about topics related to the original questions or to explore the questions in more detail. When the interviews are analyzed, both structured answers and related information should be considered.

To help your students plan their interviews and gather information effectively, you may want to hand out the suggestions and topics listed below.

Suggested Format for Interviews

Select a topic of interest, using the list that follows as a guide. Read the information about this topic in *The Developing Person Through the Life Span* or other sources. Draw up a list of about six questions that you want answered by all your interview subjects.

Select two people who fit the category described by the topic and ask them if they would agree to participate in a half-hour interview. Explain that you are working on a project for your class and that all information will be confidential.

Begin the interview by telling the subject that you will be asking some questions, but he or she should feel free to expand on the topic or talk about related ideas. Set a definite schedule for the interview (such as five minutes per question) and stay on that schedule. Either tape-record the session (with your subject's permission) or take thorough notes.

If a subject's answers are too brief or uninformative, follow up with questions like, "Why did you choose X?" or "Why do you think X happened?" If something the subject says seems important, follow up with additional probing questions, like "Tell me more about X."

Remember, you are interested in your subject's life and ideas. Do not involve yourself in a conversation, offer advice, or talk about your own experiences during the interview, except as a way of encouraging your interviewee to talk.

Prenatal development and birth (expectant parents) How many weeks along is your pregnancy? Do you have other children? What do they know about pregnancy and birth? Was the pregnancy planned? If so, what factors were involved in your decision to have this child? Are you aware of any possible genetic problems, and what are you doing about them? What steps for prenatal health are you taking (nutrition; exercise; avoiding drugs, alcohol)? What are your plans for the birth? Will the husband be involved in the birth? in child care?

Family planning options (childless couples) Did you choose not to have children, or are you childless for biological reasons? How difficult was your choice/recognition of a childless relationship? What are the advantages of being childless? the disadvantages? How has your child-free status affected your marriage? Is there a possibility that you will change your mind, or adopt, in the future?

Maternal employment (mothers employed outside the home) What are your reasons for working? Do you have any doubts about your decision to work? How old are your children? Are you having any problems with your children that may not exist if you were not working? What alternative child care have you used? What happens when your child gets sick? How much responsibility does your husband take for home and child care? How understanding is your employer? your family? How do you evaluate your children's development?

Schools and learning (high school students) What are your favorite courses in school? your best teachers? Why do you think they are better than other courses or teachers? Does your school encourage excellence in academic subjects? do your peers? How would you change your school if you could?

Independence (high school or college students) In what ways do you feel you have gained independence from your parents? What responsibilities go along with being independent? In what ways do your peers have more influence on your ideas, and in what ways do your parents have more influence? Do you feel that there is a generation gap between your parents and yourself? Have you thought of ways to reduce any differences while still developing your independence?

Moral reasoning (high school or college students) What are the moral issues in your life today? How are you resolving them? How would you approach a moral dilemma, such as finding out that a good friend cheated on an important exam? Do you have a trusted person with whom you discuss moral issues? Who is it? What are the important moral issues facing our country?

Sexuality (teenagers and young adults) When did puberty occur for you? Are you sexually active now? How long have you been active? If you are not sexually active, are you being pressured by your peers? How do you respond to that pressure? What is your current level of activity—frequency, number of partners, etc.? What birth control method do you use? What would you do if you/your partner became pregnant? What is the most important aspect of sex for you (love, pleasure, popularity)?

Drug use and health (teenagers and young adults) Do you smoke? drink alcohol? use other drugs? Why or why not? If so, how much? Would you like to quit? Why or why not? Do you think much about the health hazards? What drug habits do people you know engage in? What are the reasons? the results? What healthy activities do you engage in on a regular basis?

Decision making (young adults) What major decisions have you had to make in the past few years? How did you select your career goals? What resources did you consult in making your decisions? In retrospect, did you make the right decisions? What would you change? What decisions are you facing now? Has your approach to decision making changed in the past few years?

Life satisfaction (adults ages 45–65) How satisfied are you with your life today? Is it better or worse than you had expected when you were younger? What was (is) the happiest period of your life? the unhappiest? Why? Are you looking forward to the next decades? Why? Describe some of your plans for the future.

Cognitive development in adulthood (adults ages 45–65) What sorts of intellectual activities do you engage in (reading, games, taking courses, educational television, politics, debates and discussions)? What do you enjoy about these activities? Are you better or worse at them than you were as a young adult? in what ways? Would you take college courses now? Why? Would you choose different courses than you would have in your earlier school years? Explain.

Gender roles and society (adults ages 45–65) When you were young, how were males and females supposed to act? Did men do housework or women have careers? How have changes in the roles of men and women affected your own life? Do you think the changes are beneficial for men and women? for you?

Menopause (women ages 50–65) When did you begin (and complete) menopause? Did you experience symptoms such as hot flashes and discomfort? Do you think menopause caused a serious disruption of your life or your emotional stability? Are your attitudes about menopause different from those you held when you were younger? What do you think about the fact that you can no longer have children? Are you satisfied with your health in general?

Retirement (retired adults) What kind of job did you hold before you retired? When did you retire? Did you look forward to retiring? Did you plan for it financially and emotionally? Describe your adjustment to retirement. What factors made the adjustment easier or more difficult? How do you feel now about being retired?

Marital satisfaction (couples married more than 50 years) How have you kept your marriage interesting over the years? Has your relationship changed? When were your happiest years? your unhappiest years? Did you ever consider divorce? What kept you from divorcing? What do you think is the key to a successful marriage?

Bereavement (widows or widowers) How long have you been a widow(er)? What was your marriage like? What adjustments were the most difficult after your spouse's death? How did the advice or actions of friends and relatives help or hurt? How have you resolved your loss now? Would you consider remarriage? What would you look for in a new partner?

INSTITUTION VISITS

Visit an institution that is intended, at least in part, to serve developmental needs. It can be a formal organization (a school, a nursing home) or an informal institution (a park where preschoolers play, a health club). Use both naturalistic observation and information gathered from talking with various staff members and clients to understand the institution.

Begin your report by describing the institution, including the numbers of people it serves and their characteristics. Then evaluate the institution. In what ways does it foster and/or hinder development? What do the young people and the adults who are involved with the institution think about it? If you could change it, and had unlimited funds, what would you do and why? If you could change it, but had to stay within the present budget, what would you do and why?

Institution Interviews

People who work with an institution's clients can teach us a great deal about their unique needs, problems, and solutions. Using the semi-structured interview technique (described under "Format for Adolescent and Adult Interviews," page G–15), talk to a professional or lay worker concerned with human development in the institution you have selected.

Try to interview an experienced person who has been working directly with clients. Some sample questions are provided, although you would want to adapt your interview to your particular subject and institution.

Sample Questions

What are your goals and how are you meeting them?

What problems do you see in the group you work with, and what solutions have you developed?

What is your opinion of the clients you work with?

What measures does your organization take to encourage healthy development? How effective are these measures?

What changes would you like to see in the institution?

What gratifications and disappointments have you experienced in your work?

Suggested Subjects for Institution Interviews

genetic counselor

childbirth preparation class leader

neonatal care unit nurse

La Leché League coordinator

day-care worker

staff member at a children's park or camp

teacher (Montessori school, public school, private school)

school psychologist

social worker dealing with child abuse

lifeguard at local pool

Little League coach

juvenile court officials (police officers, probation officers, judges)

businesspersons working with children or adolescents

(record store, pizza parlor, toy store)
high school teacher, coach, or guidance counselor
college career counselor
Planned Parenthood counselor
health club exercise teacher
staff member of displaced homemaker center
member of Alcoholics Anonymous
minister, priest, rabbi, nun, or layperson concerned with religious values
retirement counselor
medical professional working with the elderly
activities director of a nursing home
coordinator of college courses or programs serving senior citizens

PARTICIPANT-OBSERVER LOGS

If you want your students to get more practical experience, and to be socially useful as well, you may assign them to spend at least two hours a week interacting with young people or senior citizens, and require them to write a log of their activities, observations, and impressions. This is a difficult assignment to grade, but if you can collect their logs weekly and comment on them quickly, you may create a dialogue that can be very educational.

Among the places where students may observe and participate are schools, hospitals, playgrounds, and senior-citizen centers. In addition, you may consider having the students care for one person on a steady basis. If you offer this option, consider whether it would be legitimate for the students to be paid babysitters, and whether the students can do this project with their own younger siblings, their own children, or their own elderly relatives.

PORTFOLIO ASSIGNMENTS

To help students make meaningful connections between course material and the "real world," you may want to create a Portfolio Assignment for a particular chapter or one for each chapter. The basic format for such assignments is provided on the next page; simply insert the chapter title and duplicate the form for distribution to students.

In Portfolio Assignments, students are asked to find a recent newspaper or magazine article or to think of a personal experience that illustrates a pertinent developmental phenomenon, concept, theory, issue, or research finding, and then write a brief description or explanation of how it relates to material covered in class or in the text. Students may choose from magazine articles, newspaper feature articles, editorials, commentaries, advice columns, medical columns, pictures, and even cartoons.

Elizabeth Rider of Elizabethtown College, who has used portfolio assignments extensively in her developmental psychology classes, suggests giving students a photocopy of a sample portfolio during the first class meeting to facilitate understanding of the project. The sample portfolio may contain 15 to 20 entries compiled from articles that the instructor has found in the media. (For subsequent terms or years, you may want to create a sample portfolio from previous student submissions.) Each entry should be annotated by the instructor to illustrate its relevance to the course. After discussing the entries, Rider distributes several additional media clippings to the class and has students spend about 15 minutes locating a pertinent section of the text chapter and drafting sample comments. Student comments are submitted to the instructor and returned with feedback at the next class.

Portfolio assignments can be graded chapter-by-chapter, or maintained in a folder by the student and submitted as a major project for a final grade. Portfolios can be graded on several dimensions, including relevance to course material, originality, and accuracy of student descriptions of psychological terms, concepts, and theories.

Rider has found that the overwhelming majority of her students report that the portfolio assignment was more valuable to them than other course projects, such as an oral presentation or a written term paper, were. The assignment, they felt, increased their ability to think about course material outside the context of the classroom. Furthermore, they enjoyed being able to write about a variety of topics rather than the usual single topic assigned as a term paper. Finally, this assignment encouraged students to distribute their writing across the course, which may have contributed to their feelings that this assignment improved their exam performance. An additional benefit of the assignment is that it stimulates critical thinking and nurtures students' writing skills.

Rider, E. A. (1992, October). Understanding and applying psychology through use of news clippings. *Teaching of Psychology*, *19*(3), 161–162.

PORTFOLIO ASSIGNMENT

Unit Title

Based on text and/or lecture material covered in this unit, prepare a brief (1–2 typed pages) essay or discussion that is divided into the following three parts.

1. Find and summarize a recent newspaper or magazine article or describe a personal experience or observation that illustrates, exemplifies, or pertains to one of the developmental phenomena, theories, processes, issues, or research findings discussed in class or the text. (Note: You may wish to check the original journal article on which the newspaper or magazine account is based to be sure that the author's findings are accurately reported in the media.)
2. Briefly explain the developmental phenomenon, theory, process, issue, or research finding described in item 1.
3. Explain why the phenomenon, theory, process, issue, or research finding applies to the article or to your personal experience or observation, and evaluate how well it "fits."

Instructions for Student Projects in Part II

Various chapters in Part II contain special activities that require general instructions for setup. This section provides the necessary instructions for these classroom debates, observational activities, and selected readings. The activities for your particular text are listed in the Lecture Guides that accompany the text.

CLASSROOM DEBATES

Thomas G. Moeller of Mary Washington College advocates the use of classroom debates in developmental psychology courses in order to teach students about controversial issues and to improve their thinking, oral communication, and research skills. If you wish to organize class debates, during the first or second class meeting give students a list of debate topics in a form such as the one provided in the Lecture Guides that accompany the text, asking them to rank topics in order of their preference. Note that you cannot assure them of being assigned their first choice. For each debate topic, set up two teams of four students each on the basis of topic preferences and, in order to balance the teams, your impressions of their academic and verbal abilities.

Several weeks prior to the actual debate meet with the two teams to clarify the debate procedures, provide some background information and suggested references (as presented in the relevant unit of these resources), identify important developmental issues, and answer any questions. To develop an effective rebuttal to their position, debaters should be required to prepare arguments and supporting evidence for both the affirmative and the negative positions on the issue in question. Approximately one week before the debate, have the two teams flip a coin to determine which side will argue each position.

For reference material, you may choose appropriate journals and textbooks and place them on reserve in the college library or you may want students to uncover them themselves. The latter approach has the benefit of giving students experience in conducting library research using the *Psychological Abstracts*, computer literature databases, and other available resources.

For a 50-minute class, you should divide the debate into eight 5-minute speeches. Beginning with the affirmative side, the sides alternate constructive (initial) speeches, with the order reversed during the second, rebuttal phase. Allow a 5-minute intermission/strategy review period between the constructive and rebuttal speeches. Have a nondebater keep time, signaling when a debater has 1 minute remaining and when time is up.

The overall grade for the debate should be a weighted average of the individual's oral presentation (60%) and the team grade (40%).

Moeller has found that students consider the debate to be a challenging and extremely positive learning experience. In addition, research has shown that innovative teaching techniques, such as a debate, foster critical thinking in students and a much deeper understanding of the complexity of child and adolescent development.

Moeller, T. G. (1985). Using classroom debates in teaching developmental psychology. *Teaching of Psychology*, *12*(4), 207–209.

Barnett, M. A., Knust, J., McMillan, T., Kaufman, J., & Sinisi, C. (1988). Research findings in developmental psychology: Common sense revisited. *Teaching of Psychology*, *12*(4), 195–197.

CRITICAL THINKING ACTIVITIES

Like most psychology courses, developmental psychology has two major goals: (1) to help students acquire a basic understanding of developmental psychology's knowledge base, and (2) to help students learn to think like a developmental psychologist. The second goal—learning to think like a developmental psychologist—involves critical thinking, those "thinking skills that promote conscious, purposeful, and active involvement of the thinker with new ideas" (Halonen, 2001). These skills include careful observation, asking questions, seeing connections among ideas, and analyzing arguments and the evidence on which they are based.

The critical thinking activities in these Instructors' Resources have been designed to help students develop their ability to think critically as they learn about developmental psychology.* Each exercise emphasizes one of six categories of critical thinking: pattern recognition, practical problem solving, creative problem solving, scientific problem solving, psychological reasoning, and perspective taking.

*The model for these exercises comes from J. S. Halonen (2001). *The critical thinking companion* (2nd ed.). New York: Worth.

As the foundation for all other forms of critical thinking, *pattern recognition* is the ability to use psychological concepts to describe behavior patterns and events, especially when a student's expectation of what is normal in a certain situation is different from what actually occurs.

When events or behaviors are unexpected, they may constitute a problem. *Practical problem solving* is the ability to use psychological concepts to develop a plan of action that will lead to the problem's solution.

Creative problem solving is the ability to make novel connections between previously unrelated ideas. This type of critical thinking often leads to new insights about behavior and developmental phenomena.

Developmentalists often employ the scientific method to develop comprehensive and systematic explanations of developmental phenomena. At the heart of this is *scientific problem solving*, which seeks to uncover relationships among the many factors, or variables involved in development.

Psychological information is transmitted through persuasive arguments that state a relationship between some aspect of behavior, such as intelligence, and another factor, such as age. *Psychological reasoning* is thinking critically about such arguments, especially the evidence on which they are based.

The final category of critical thinking is *perspective taking*, which refers to the ability to recognize the ways in which each person's thinking is shaped by his or her values and past experiences.

Before assigning any of these exercises, review these categories of critical thinking with the class. Each unit of these resources includes an activity focused on one of these categories. For some units, the exercise presents a hypothetical situation that students will need to think through. For others, students will be asked to evaluate arguments that are derived from actual psychological research. And for still other units, students' understanding of developmental concepts will be tested by asking them to apply them to a new situation.

Finally, encourage your students to polish their critical thinking skills by applying them to each of their college courses, and to other aspects of life as well, including advertising, political speeches, and the material presented in popular periodicals.

INTERNET ACTIVITIES

To help students broaden their "horizons" in finding developmental psychology resources, various chapters contain an Internet activity. Each activity asks students to search the Internet to find answers to questions regarding developmental issues, theorists, and recent research studies described in the text. In some cases, actual Web site URLs are provided. In other cases, students are simply given suggestions to guide their research.

OBSERVATIONAL ACTIVITIES

Two or three fully planned observational activities are presented for each major part of the textbook. Each activity is designed to highlight the text coverage of biosocial, cognitive, or psychosocial development during a particular stage of life.

These activities are described in the relevant units in Part II ("Teaching Resources") of this manual. Each activity begins with an overview ("orientation") of the project, then describes the assignment, and concludes with a series of questions to be completed by the student and returned to the instructor.

You may wish to assign a specific activity for each student to complete, or give students their choice of activities at the start of the semester. Another approach would be to divide the class into groups of three or four students and have each group complete one of the activities and then give an oral report to the class.

By assigning observational activities, rather than allowing students to select their own term projects, the instructor has greater control over the range of topics and developmental stages covered in "out-of-class" work.

Audiovisual Materials

Every class benefits from occasional deviations from the "talk and chalk" mode of instruction, especially since today's students are accustomed to receiving information through many media. Simple measures—such as posters or art on the walls or appropriate slides as each new chapter begins—are useful and welcome ways to supplement the more traditional modes of transmitting information. In some classrooms, use of an overhead projector or occasional use of filmstrips may be helpful, too. (Keep in mind that some students find filmstrips too evocative of elementary school.)

The most widely used audiovisual tool is the movie—either the 16 mm, the videotape, or the DVD. If you are unaccustomed to using these, read the tips on this and the following page. If you use them often, consult the Lecture Guides for your text, which lists all the clips suggested for each text chapter. Additional suggestions are welcome.

TIPS FOR IMPORTING VIDEOS INTO POWERPOINT PRESENTATIONS

The video clips that make up the Instructor's Media Tool Kit can be imported into PowerPoint to create a presentation for your classes (these instructions are also provided in the Faculty Guide that accompanies the tool kit). Please note that not all versions of PowerPoint are the same, and these instructions may not be compatible with your particular version or operating system. If you encounter any problems, see the Help menu in your program, contact BFW Tech Support at (800) 936-6899 or techsupport@bfwpub.com, or visit Microsoft's PowerPoint home page (http://office.microsoft.com/en-us/Fx010857971033.aspx).

Locating Video Files

Review the list of clips in the contents. Choose the proper CD for the clip you want to show and put it in your CD-ROM drive. If you are lecturing from the same computer every lecture, or if you have time and access to the hard drive in your lecture hall's computer, you can copy video files from the CD to the hard drive. Video files will run much better off of the computer hard drive than off the CD.

Be sure to check the drive space on the computer to which you are copying the files. Some of these video files are quite large. You should always do a test run with the videos you plan to show, whether off the CD or off the hard drive. Some machines will have difficulty running the largest files and the video clips may pause, jump, or stop.

Integrating Video Files into PowerPoint

When you insert a movie into a slide, PowerPoint actually creates a link to the original movie file and inserts a still frame image to represent the movie object. All inserted movies will be linked to your presentation. If you show your presentation on a different computer, remember to also copy the movie file when you copy the presentation. If you don't, you will just have a picture of the poster frame of the movie.

Importing videos into PowerPoint on a PC...

...in Windows 97/2000:

1. In slide view, display the slide to which you want to add the video.
2. On the Insert menu, select Movies and Sounds.
3. To insert a video from the Media Gallery, click Movie from Gallery, then double-click the video you want.
4. To insert a video from another location, click Movie from File, locate the folder that contains the video, then double-click the video you want.

Tip: By default, the video will start when you click it during a slide show. To change how you start a video—for example, by positioning the mouse over the icon instead of clicking it—click Action Settings on the Slide Show menu.

...in Windows XP:

1. Display the slide to which you want to add a movie or animated GIF.
2. On the Insert menu, point to Movies and Sounds, click Movie from File, locate the folder that contains the file you want, then double-click the file.

Note: A movie or .gif file that you've added to Clip Organizer is found in the Clip Organizer folder within the My Pictures folder on your hard disk. Or, go to the original location for these files.

3. When a message is displayed, do one of the following:
   a. To play the movie or GIF automatically when you go to the slide, click Yes.
   b. To play the movie or GIF only when you click it, click No.

Note: If you try to insert a movie and get a message that Microsoft PowerPoint can't insert the file, try inserting the movie to play in Windows Media Player, as follows:

1. In Windows, launch Windows Media Player (from the Start button on the Accessories submenu).
2. On the File menu in Windows Media Player, click Open, then type the path or browse for the file you want to insert and click OK.
3. If the movie opens and plays, complete the remaining steps in this task.
4. If the movie cannot play, then it won't play when you open the Windows Media Player in PowerPoint, so don't complete this task. You can consult Windows Media Player Help to try to troubleshoot the problem. Also, in PowerPoint, search on "Troubleshoot movies" in the Ask a Question box on the menu bar to get more suggestions.
5. Display the slide you want the movie on in PowerPoint; then on the Insert menu, click Object.
6. Under Object Type, click Media Clip and make sure Create New is selected. If you want the movie to display as an icon, select the Display as Icon check box.
7. Click OK.
8. On the Insert Clip menu in Windows Media Player, click Video for Windows.
9. In the Files of Type list, select All Files, select the file, then click Open.
10. To play it, click the Play button just below the menu bar, on the upper left; to insert it onto your slide, click outside the movie frame.

To add a motion clip from Microsoft Clip Organizer:

1. On the Insert menu, point to Movies and Sounds, and click Movie from Clip Organizer.
2. In the Insert Clip Art task pane, scroll to find the clip you want, and click it to add it to the slide.
3. If a message is displayed, do one of the following:
   a. To play the movie or GIF automatically when you go to the slide, click Yes.
   b. To play the movie or GIF only when you click it, click No.

Tip: To preview a clip, go to the Insert Clip Art task pane. In the Results box that displays the clips available, move your mouse pointer over the clip's thumbnail; click the arrow that appears; then click Preview/Properties.

Importing videos into PowerPoint on a MAC...
...in MAC OS/9:

1. In slide view, display the slide to which you want to add the video.
2. On the Insert menu, point to Movies and Sounds.
3. To insert a video from the Clip Gallery, click Movie from Gallery, then double-click the video you want. To insert a video from another location, click Movie from File, locate the folder that contains the video, then double-click the video you want.

Tip: By default, the video will start when you click it during a slide show. To change how you start a video—for example, by positioning the mouse over the icon instead of clicking it—click Action Settings on the Slide Show menu.

...in MAC OS/X:

1. Display the slide to which you want to add the video.
2. On the Insert menu, point to Movies and Sounds.
3. Do one of the following: To insert a video from the Clip Gallery, click Movie from Gallery, then locate and insert the video you want. To insert a video from another location, click Movie from File, locate the folder that contains the video, then double-click the video you want.
4. A message is displayed. If you want the movie to play automatically when you display the slide, click Yes; if you want the movie to play only when you click the movie during a slide show, click No.
5. To preview the movie in normal view, double-click the movie.

EXPLORING HUMAN DEVELOPMENT TOOL KITS

This series, available to instructors on CD-ROM, VHS, and DVD, was prepared by a talented team of instructors, including Victoria Cross, University of California, Davis; Sheridan Dewolf, Grossmont College; Pamela B.Hill, San Antonio College; Lisa Huffman, Ball State University; Thomas Ludwig, Hope College; Cathleen McGreal, Michigan State University; Amy Obegi, Grossmont College; Michelle L. Pilati, Rio Hondo College; Tanya Renner, Kapiolani Community College; Catherine Robertson, Grossmont College; Stavros Valenti, Hofstra University; and Pauline Zeece, University of Nebraska, Lincoln. Combining video, animations, self-tests, and interactive exercises, the student tool kit offers hands-on, interactive learning. The activities range from depictions of classic experiments (Piaget's conservation tasks, the Strange Situation, and the visual cliff) to case studies and investigations of topics such as malnutrition, bullying and Alzheimer's disease. In addition, the CD contains quizzes and flashcards tied to every chapter of the text. The instructor tool kit includes more than 500 video clips and animations. The descriptions of videos and activities in these tool kits are provided in the Lecture Guides that accompany the text.

DEVELOPMENTPORTAL

DevelopmentPortal is the complete online gateway to all the student and instructor resources available with Kathleen Berger's texts. DevelopmentPortal brings together all the resources of the media tool kits, integrated with an eBook and powerful assessment tools to complement your course. The ready-to-use course template is fully customizable and includes all of the teaching and learning resources that go along with the text, preloaded into a ready-to-use course; sophisticated quizzing, personalized study plans for students and powerful assessment analyses that provide timely and useful feedback on class and individual student performance; and seamless integration of student resources, eBook text, assessment tools, and lecture resources. The quizbank (featuring more than 80 questions per chapter) that powers the student assessment in both DevelopmentPortal and the Tool Kits was written by Pamela Hill, San Antonio College and Michelle L. Pilati, Rio Hondo College. These questions are not from the test bank!

Descriptions of the student activities within DevelopmentPortal are provided in the Lecture Guides that accompany the text. For the descriptions of the instructor's videos provided, please see the video descriptions for Exploring Human Development: An Instructor's Media Tool Kit.

THE JOURNEY THROUGH CHILDHOOD AND THE JOURNEY THROUGH THE LIFE SPAN

These two video series consist of 14 and 20 segments, respectively, that closely follow the organization of the Berger texts. The segments, which range in duration from 2 to 19 minutes, provide an engaging overview of physical, cognitive, and social development in each of the major periods covered in the text. S. Stavros Valenti, who edited the programs and wrote the accompanying student workbook, offers two alternative suggestions for using the programs. One is to show one or two segments at the start of each new developmental unit to give the class a sampling of the material that will be covered. The other is to play individual segments in the course of a lecture as a way to liven up the class.

Each video program is accompanied by one or more observation modules. These are unnarrated video segments that depict children, adolescents, and adults interacting in a variety of contexts. Valenti suggests presenting a module following a lecture or unit and asking students to identify key developmental concepts and behaviors

CHILD DEVELOPMENT: STEPPING STONES AND TRANSITIONS THROUGHOUT THE LIFE SPAN

These two video series are one-semester, college-level telecourses designed to cover the concepts, vocabulary, and subjects that are typical of an on-campus, development course. Closely following the chapters of Kathleen Berger's texts, the telecourses present the development process in three distinct domains: biosocial, cognitive, and psychosocial. The half-hour video programs feature an assortment of real-life examples, historical footage, and an array of subject matter experts. The programs emphasize how developmental principles can be used to improve the quality of students' everyday life.

The video and online components are produced by the award-winning Coast Learning Systems with funding support provided by the Coastline Community College District and Worth Publishers. Each video lesson includes real-life examples interwoven with commentary by subject matter experts. In addition to programs closely tied to each developmental domain at each age, there are video lessons on the whole child and special topics such as the role of the father, child maltreatment and abuse, school, and teen challenges.

TIPS ON USING FILMS AND VIDEOCASSETTES

Films and videocassettes should be ordered well before the term begins, since there is a limited supply and you want to be sure the best ones are available on the dates you need them. They are particularly apt to be unavailable if you wait until the last minute; most developmental courses are roughly chronological, which means everyone wants to show a film or video on the birth process in the first month, and so forth.

If you have not used films or videos before, you should probably acquaint yourself with the audiovisual department at your school as soon as possible. Most colleges not only have equipment and trained technicians but also own many films and videos. If this is the case at your institution, planning may involve nothing more than telling the audiovisual people what you want. Many audiovisual departments will also order for you. Audiovisual staff members might also be able to suggest films or videos for you to use, since they are likely to be aware of materials purchased by other departments, say, biology, that may be applicable to your course.

In some schools, however, good equipment and trained personnel are in short supply, so you may have to do most of the work yourself. (If you have never run a movie projector or VHS player, don't panic: neither is really very complicated, and chances are one of your students can help if you run into a problem.) Even if the "audiovisual department" is nothing more than a locked closet with a projector and VHS player in it, don't be put off. Whatever the effort required, it will be worthwhile: audiovisuals provide valuable education, as well as a break from usual classroom routines.

Many of the newer films and videos are available on DVD. This convenient format has many advantages over videotape, including virtual indestructibility, random access to specific video segments (for those who wish to show only parts of a film), and the ability to link video directly to computer PowerPoint presentations. If you have a notebook computer with a DVD drive, and an LCD projector with USB or serial port connections (or, even better, a multimedia classroom that allows you to simply bring your notebook computer), this makes for an excellent video display system.

I strongly recommend that you preview each title before showing it. Although the list of suggested materials was carefully prepared, some of the titles may not be appropriate for your class. If you can't preview a film or video (perhaps because it arrived late), tell the class that you haven't seen it and ask their opinion about it for future classes. Then, at least, you won't have to suffer the onus of having selected a bomb.

Even if you have previewed the movie or video and shown it to many classes, it is still a good idea to view each showing rather than turn to some other task while the class watches. Your students will be more attentive, you will catch nuances that you may have forgotten, and, probably most important, you will pick up valuable information from your students' reactions. Their laughter, comments, and restlessness during the showing reveal a great deal about the directions that subsequent discussion should take.

Many students view audiovisuals in class with the same mental set they adopt when watching television; that is, they see them as relaxing entertainment, nothing more. For this reason, it is useful (even essential) that you tell the class what you want them to learn from the film or video, then review its salient points as soon as it is over. One way to help your students focus their attention is to distribute a list of questions to be answered in writing at the end of class. Students' answers can be read aloud and used as a basis for class discussion. Or you might consider showing only part of a title or interrupting it to highlight the ideas presented up to that point.

Finally, although every class learns from seeing good films or videos, it is possible to show too many. Your class and your own evaluation are the best guide to the proper number, but as you are planning the course, keep in mind not to schedule too many audiovisuals back-to-back.

PART II

TEACHING RESOURCES

Introduction

Contents

Note: Worth Publishers provides online Instructor and Student Tool Kits, DVD Student Tool Kits, and Instructor and Student video resources in DevelopmentPortal for use with the text. See Part I: General Resources for information about these materials and the text Lecture Guides for a complete list by text chapter.

The Scientific Method

Cautions from Science

Suggested Activities

Introducing Development

"On Your Own" Activity: Developmental Fact or Myth?

Before students read the introduction to development, have them respond to the true–false statements in Handout 1.

The correct answers are shown below. Class discussion should focus on the origins of any developmental misconceptions that are demonstrated in the students' incorrect answers.

1. T 2. F 3. F 4. F 5. F 6. T 7. F 8. F 9. F 10. F

Teaching Tip: Semester-Long Scaffolded Assignment

The General Resources section of these resources includes a suggestion for assigning a project that can be carried out by students throughout the course (see p. G-4). Based on a project developed by Rebecca Achtman of Nazareth College, this assignment enables students to learn a topic in depth and to better understand the cognitive process of scaffolding.

Teaching Tip: First Day of Class: Developmental Milestones and Qualitative Versus Quantitative Change

What you do on the first day of class creates student expectations for the entire course. K. H. Grobman suggests building a framework for upcoming discussions of theories of development by asking the class to list milestones in their own lives. Start the discussion by noting that while theories of development are often very different, one thing many theories have in common is the identification of milestones over the life span. Then ask: "What are some of the important milestones in your life and the lives of others?"

Fill the board with your students' responses. Some, such as "taking the first step," will be obvious developmental milestones. Others, such as "getting my driver's license" and "voting for the first time" will be less obvious. Treat this part of the discussion as a brainstorming session and put everything on the board. Then ask: "Of everything on the board, which milestones would you say are important steps in development and which aren't?" Some clearly will be crossed out (e.g., driver's license, voting) and others clearly will be kept (e.g., first steps).

Other "milestones" will elicit differing viewpoints from students. For instance, is "mastering multiplication tables" development? Is any change development? From the responses, develop a set of class criteria for determining whether a change truly qualifies as an example of development.

Next, introduce the big question of whether developmental change is quantitative or qualitative, using a metaphor of a tree gradually growing larger (quantitative development) or a caterpillar turning into a butterfly (qualitative development). Now direct the class to think back to when they were 10 years old. Ask whether they see themselves now as simply more sophisticated and experienced versions of who they were at 10 (point to the tree metaphor), or if they look back and see an almost completely different person (point to the butterfly metaphor).

Grobman ends the first class with a brief discussion of why studying development matters. The reasons include practical ones such as parenting and teaching, understanding and shaping public policy (e.g., child labor laws imply a view of childhood as a special time), and fostering greater personal understanding of our own, personal development.

As students progress through the course, ask them to think about what they first identified as milestones, then consider whether they would add others or subtract some of those.

Grobman, K.H. First Day of Developmental Psychology Class. Retrieved on October 29, 2010 from www.devpsy.org/teaching/overview/first_day_of_class.

Teaching Tip: Asking Students What They Want to Know About Development

During the first meeting of my class, I ask students to think for a moment and then write down one or more questions they might have regarding human development, including their own. To preserve their anonymity and promote candor, I ask students to sign their questions with a pen name. After class, I sort the questions by category (prenatal development, hereditary influences, growth and motor development, research/ethics, working mothers, single parents, discipline, and so forth). The resulting list is almost always rich enough to provide one or more questions that I read aloud during each class as a means of introducing and organizing specific lecture topics.

The exercise has several benefits. First, student-generated questions help keep the course fresh by highlighting developmental topics you might have overlooked. Second, reading the questions and pen names tends to capture students' attention and lighten an occasionally heavy classroom atmosphere. Third, the questions promote a positive attitude toward the course, as students will usually perceive the class as more personalized and relevant when the instructor answers questions they themselves have generated.

Teaching Tip: Establishing Classroom Rapport

To establish rapport and spark interest, ask your students to introduce themselves, tell why they are taking this course, and relate a childhood memory. Encourage them to recall specific events rather than general behavior—for example, "I threw a brick at my brother, who was 6 years older than me, and made him cry," rather than "I fought with my brother." Shy students can be drawn out with such questions as "What do you remember about kindergarten?" "Name a game you played when you were about 8 years old." "What was your favorite toy when you were little?"

If the class is small and there is enough time, you can have each student tell a story. If the class is large and time is limited, you can divide the students into small groups and have them relate their memories to one another. Or you can ask them to write down their memories, and then you can read a few aloud. Choose cases that are interesting, funny, or universal, and make a few general comments. For instance, if someone reports stealing something, you might say, "Almost all children steal; the crucial thing is what happens when the theft is discovered."

To put students at ease, you might begin by sharing some personal information about yourself. This can be done by explaining who you are and why you are teaching the course or by relating one of your own memories before asking the students to do so.

Teaching Tip: Becoming a Master Teacher

Master teacher David G. Myers offers his 10 favorite teaching tips and secrets of success in the classroom:

- Be positive. Reinforcing students for doing something right is as important as correcting mistakes.
- Give frequent and fast feedback. It takes just as long to grade papers after a lengthy delay than it does soon after the assignment.
- Be enthusiastic. If you're a low-key person, don't worry about overdoing it and being considered a fake.

- Don't expect students to be as enthusiastic as you are. Although sleep-deprived and self-conscious undergraduates may not reciprocate your enthusiasm, it will likely still be welcomed.
- Give lots of practical examples. For every abstract point you make, strive to offer a concrete example.
- Make questions concrete. After showing a video, for example, ask a specific question such as "How do you feel about the argument that . . . ?" rather than a nonspecific "Comments anyone?"
- Have patience awaiting answers. Allow a few moments of silence . . . and don't answer your own question.
- Do say, "I don't know" and entertain ideas about how to answer a question. Doing so demonstrates your humility and can itself become a moment for teaching how scientists go about answering questions.
- Assume that your introductory students will never take another course in your field. Make sure they know the big lessons you hope they will never forget.
- Realize that in teaching, as in life, two things are certain: (1) you're going to make a fool of yourself at some point, and (2) you're going to have your heart broken. Recognize that it is virtually impossible to reach every student.

Myers, D. G. (2005). Teaching tips from experienced teachers. *Association for Psychological Science Observer, 18*(3). www.psychologicalscience.org/observer.

Teaching Tip: Exporting Developmental Psychology

Robert Baron describes his 1974 experience of receiving one of U.S. Senator William Proxmire's "Golden Fleece" awards for his National Science Foundation-funded research on the effects of heat on aggression. The Golden Fleece was awarded to faculty members who, in Proxmire's opinion, wasted taxpayers' money. Baron has spent the past 34 years striving to be "a true exporter of psychology, illustrating the intrinsic value of our field and the many ways it can be put to excellent use by non-psychologists."

Because developmental science can answer questions not easily answered elsewhere, exporting its principles and findings can help students lead richer, fuller, and more successful lives. For instance:

- Is using a cell phone to talk or send text messages when driving really dangerous? If so, how can we discourage this practice?
- Is punishment effective in disciplining children? When? How should it be used?
- Why do we find certain characteristics attractive in others? Is this the result of our inherited biological nature?
- How can people become truly happy?
- How can young people resist the many persuasive influences to which they are exposed every day?

Baron offers a good tip for exporting psychology: Invite guest lecturers from other fields to discuss how they use psychology in their work. In his invitation, Baron makes it clear that the goal is to illustrate how important knowledge of human behavior is in a wide range of fields. In one class, for instance, a stockbroker discussed how emotions often get in the way of investors' decisions about buying or selling stock.

Baron, R. A. (2007, June). "Exporting" psychology: Communicating the value of our field to students. *Observer of the Association for Psychological Science, 20*(6). www.psychologicalscience.org.

"On Your Own" Activity: "Dear Future Child"

When teaching courses in developmental psychology, instructors are typically frustrated by the many implicit, and often faulty, assumptions on which students base their beliefs about developmental issues. Ellen Junn of California State University, San Bernardino, identifies three illuminating examples. First, most college students have only vague knowledge regarding child development. Second, students typically have a false and idealistic sense of the degree to which parents control a child's development. Finally, students often rely solely on personal experiences and anecdotal evidence when evaluating research and arguing their viewpoints.

To help her students confront these hindrances to their own objectivity, Junn requires her students to write a letter to their future or actual child. The letters must address a number of developmental issues, including how they attempted to foster growth in their child's intellectual, social, and emotional development; the characteristics of "good" and "bad" parents; and why they decided to have this child. Students are encouraged to use their knowledge of relevant research and theory in composing their letters. Handout 2 provides guidelines for this exercise.

Junn reports that although some students find the exercise "difficult" or "stressful," virtually all feel that they profited from it and that it helped them "relate to the issues in class." Many even indicated that they intended to deliver the letter to their adult child. From a pedagogical standpoint, the exercise achieves at least two objectives. First, it is an effective way to make students more aware of "their implicit, often very unrealistic notions and attitudes regarding child development and parenting issues." Second, and perhaps more important, the exercise effectively "promote[s] students' ability to understand, apply, and integrate current research and theory with their own lives in a productive and potentially useful way."

An interesting variation on Junn's exercise is to return the students' letters at the end of the course and ask each student for a critique of the letter's factual content, based on the student's newly acquired (and empirically based) knowledge of development.

Junn, E. N. (1989). "Dear Mom and Dad": Using personal letters to enhance students' understanding of developmental issues. *Teaching of Psychology, 16*(3), 135–139.

AV: 21st-Century Sons and Mothers (48 min., Films for the Humanities and Sciences)

This Discovery Channel film presents scientific and anecdotal evidence for the changing dynamics of the mother/son relationship in a cultural and historical context in which single-mother households are on the rise and sons are taking longer to leave the nest. It provides a good vehicle for evaluating the quality of data as a means of answering questions about development and powerfully illustrates the influence of the social context on development and social constructions.

AV: Transitions Throughout the Life Span: Program 1: The Developing Person

The first program of the Coast Learning System's telecourse introduces the study of human development, first describing the three domains into which development is often divided, as well as the scope of the field, and then providing an overview of the major theories that have guided research over the past century. A philosopher once said that "nothing is more practical than a good theory," and such has proven to be the case in developmental psychology. Theories help psychologists organize large amounts of information and focus their research on specific, testable ideas about development.

Several major themes are introduced in Program 1 that will be woven throughout the telecourse, including the idea that development is influenced as much by external factors as by internal factors. This theme, framed initially by philosophers many years ago, continues to drive the field today as researchers weigh the relative contributions of biological factors (such as heredity) and environmental factors (such as learning) in development.

The impact of external factors on development is revealed in the many contexts in which development occurs, especially the context of social relationships. And therein lies a second theme: Each of us as individuals affects and is affected by other individuals (such as family members and friends), by groups of individuals (such as the neighborhood and community), and by larger systems in the environment (such as ethnicity and culture).

A third theme of the program and telecourse is that development is a lifelong process. Although some early theorists believed that our personalities and fates are fully shaped by the end of childhood, developmental psychologists today recognize that people continue to grow and change until the day they die.

AV: The Developing Child series: *History and Trends* (Magna Systems, Inc.)

Designed for educators, health care professionals, and parents, this series consists of 32 modules (averaging 30 minutes in length) that focus on specific developmental issues from childhood through adolescence.

AV: Child Development (60 min., Films for the Humanities and Sciences)

This videodisc program consists of one- to five-minute segments covering a wide range of topics that include genetic counseling, newborn behavior, child abuse and maltreatment, learning disabilities, and adolescent depression and suicide.

AV: Development (33 min., CRM/McGraw-Hill)

The growth of the child from birth to adolescence is shown through a series of illustrations of developmental research, including Kagan's research on infant cognitive development, Ainsworth's Strange Situation test of attachment, and Parke's "resistance to temptation" experiment. The film also includes some naturalistic observations of children at each major stage of development. This movie could be used in the first week of the course to illustrate various methodologies and ethical issues, as well as to raise some of the interesting issues within human development. As examples of the latter, Rhoda Kellogg makes a provocative statement in favor of nursery schools but against day care, and Elizabeth Douvan talks about our culture's failure to channel adolescent energy. The film is a good introduction to issues that will be explored in depth later in the course.

Teaching Tip: Developmental Psychology Scrapbook Albums

To help bring developmental psychology concepts to life for your students, consider having students assemble a scrapbook album consisting of items that for them are vivid illustrations of concepts or topics covered in the course. The assignment, which can be evaluated as a weighted portion of their final grade or for extra credit, could include clipped articles, photographs, and cartoons from magazines and newspapers; lyrics from popular songs; scenes from movies and television shows; and other media. Encourage variety by permitting no more than two examples from a given medium (e.g., newspaper articles) for each assigned text chapter. Encourage relevance and student understanding by requiring that each example be accompanied by a one-paragraph explanation of which developmental topic, issue, controversy, or concept the scrapbook entry pertains to and why. You may also allow students to describe personal experiences in their scrapbooks. The scrapbook albums could be submitted at the end of the course in a variety of formats, including traditional paper-based albums, PowerPoint presentations, Web pages, or even short videos.

Teaching Tip: Having Students Confront Their Biases and Assumptions

Objectivity is, of course, at the very heart of the scientific method. Scientists must constantly be on guard against allowing their own biases and assumptions to influence how they interpret research outcomes. This requires critical thinking, especially being aware of the existence of interpretations and perspectives other than your own.

An excellent way to develop students' critical thinking is to help them become aware of their own biases; without this awareness, they are not likely to realize how their reasoning and decision making suffer. If your students are typical, many will either deny having biases based on gender, ethnicity, socioeconomic status, religion, or age—or will be reluctant to admit them. (You may wish to discuss the candor of people participating in self-report studies as a separate issue in the scientific method.)

Jane Sheldon (1999, personal communication, 2007) suggests that an effective way of getting around students' tendency to deny their biases (which is, by itself, an example of self-serving bias) is to make confronting those biases a secondary agenda of another class activity. In doing so, students may unknowingly reveal their biases, which can later be discussed after finishing the primary activity. She offers two examples from her own classes:

- "One activity that lent itself to the secondary agenda technique had the students learning to apply psychological theories to a case study about a girl who is being aggressive and uncooperative with her science teacher. I purposely did not tell the gender of the teacher and found that the vast majority of students assumed that the teacher was male. Thus, subsequent class discussion involved analyzing what information students used to decide the teacher's gender. We also discussed sexism in psychological theory and research so students could see that researchers also may have gender biases."
- "In another activity, students were learning about parenting styles, and I had them discuss what they would hypothetically do if their 12-year-old was caught shoplifting. Over 90 percent of the time students assumed that the child was a boy, so this assumption initiated a discussion of gender bias, assumptions, and actual statistics concerning shoplifting by the two genders."

The discussion that ensues should be effective in conveying to students that biases are ever-present, and we must constantly guard against them.

Sheldon, J. (1999). A secondary agenda in classroom activities: Having students confront their biases and assumptions. *Teaching of Psychology, 26*(3), 209–211.

Classroom Activity: Introducing Problem-Based Learning

Problem-based learning (PBL) is a student-directed form of instruction that has proven to be highly effective in promoting deep mastery of a variety of types of academic material (Connor-Greene, 2008). Problem-based approaches generate enthusiasm among teachers who are frustrated with traditional lecture-focused instruction. While the distinction between PBL and other forms of cooperative or active learning are fuzzy, each of these approaches is fundamentally based on presenting students with an applied problem to be solved.

The model for problem-based learning comes from several innovative medical schools, where, more than 25 years ago, educators realized that traditional teaching methods seemed almost irrelevant to the practice of medicine, based as it is on problem solving and the need to be a lifelong learner. PBL was officially adopted in 1968 at McMaster University's medical school because faculty members were unhappy with students' inability to apply scientific knowledge to clinical situations.

Instructors who assign a PBL activity often begin with a brief discussion of concepts that are relevant to the specific task or situation. Afterward, the instructor presents a case example or engaging problem for students to solve either individually or working in small groups. Problems can come from real-life scenarios, videoclips, news stories, or journal articles. The University of Delaware hosts a Problem-Based Learning Clearinghouse, which includes a database of sample problems categorized by academic disciplines (https://primus.nss.udel.edu/Pbl).

Duch (2001) suggests the following steps for implementing a PBL exercise: (a) select a concept that is central to the course (e.g., continuity in development); (b) identify a real-world context for that concept (e.g., newspapers, magazines, and journals; (c) determine the structure and scope of the exercise (e.g., how much class time will be devoted to the activity); (d) prepare a schedule (e.g., mini-lectures, group and whole-class discussions); and (e) identify several good resources to get students started.

Because PBL is self-directed, the teacher may facilitate group discussion but the students alone must decide how to proceed and when they have solved the problem. A suggested model for the group work includes the following three stages.

1. The group must identify the FACTS in the problem.
2. A brainstorming period in which IDEAS are generated by group members without criticism.
3. The group attempts to create a synthesis of ideas that either solves the problem or identifies remaining things that they need to LEARN in order to test their hypotheses (ideas).

An example of a PBL classroom exercise to introduce developmental psychology could include one or both of the following activities: Design a model of relationships within a typical family using the dynamic-systems concept or explain how socioeconomic status affects biological, cognitive, or social development.

Connor-Greene, P. A. (2008). Problem-based learning. In W. Buskist & S. F. Davis (eds.). *Handbook of the Teaching of Psychology*. Oxford, UK: Blackwell Publishing.

Duch, B. J. (2001). Writing problems for deeper understanding. In B. J. Duch, S. E. Groh, & D. E. Allen (eds.), *The Power of Problem-Based Learning: A Practical "How to" for Teaching Undergraduate Courses in Any Discipline* (pp. 47–58). Sterling, Va.: Stylus.

Classroom Activity: The Blank Slate, the Noble Savage, and the Ghost in the Machine

Theories of Development includes an activity requiring students to discuss Steven Pinker's views on the relative influences of nature and nurture. You could use the activity in discussing evolutionary theory or you could use it here when discussing the nature–nurture debate.

Contexts of Development

"On Your Own" Activity: Your Cohort

To help students understand cohort effects, ask them to describe the cohort to which they belong, using Handout 3 as a guide. Students will appreciate the importance of cohort effects when they begin to understand the kinds of differences that exist among people born at different times. If your class includes both older and younger adults, this exercise may be especially interesting.

If there is enough diversity in the ages of your students, this activity will reveal cohort effects that might influence research. Compare the responses of those in different age groups. Use hypothetical cross-sectional and longitudinal studies to show how differences might be attributed to cohort effects.

Classroom Activity: Footnote from Past Cohorts: "How to Be a Good Wife"

The following is reputed to be an excerpt from a 1955 high school home economics textbook, defining a woman's "wifely duties." Although research has failed to find this in any 1950s text (see www.snopes.com), it is a vivid illustration of that period and the impact of cohort effects on all domains of development.

> Have dinner ready. Plan ahead, even the night before to have a delicious meal—on time. This is a way of letting him know that you have been thinking about him and are concerned about his needs. Most men are hungry when they come home and the prospect of a good meal is part of the warm welcome needed.
>
> Prepare yourself. Take 15 minutes to rest so you'll be refreshed when he arrives. Touch up your makeup, put a ribbon in your hair and be fresh looking. He has just been with a lot of work-weary people. Be a little gay and a little more interesting. His boring day may need a lift.
>
> Clear away the clutter. Make one last trip through the main part of the house just before your husband arrives, gathering up books, toys, papers, etc. Then run a dust cloth over the tables. Your husband will feel he has reached a haven of rest and order, and it will give you a lift, too.
>
> Prepare the children. Take a few minutes to wash the children's hands and faces (if they are small), comb their hair, and, if necessary, change their clothes. They are little treasures and he would like to see them play the part.
>
> Minimize all noise. At the time of his arrival, eliminate all noise of the washer, dryer, dishwashers or vacuum. Try to encourage the children to be quiet. Be happy to see him, greet him with a smile and be glad to see him.
>
> Some don'ts. Don't greet him with problems or complaints. Don't complain if he's late for dinner. Count this as minor when considering what he might have gone through that day. Make him comfortable. Have him lean back in a comfortable chair or suggest he lie down in the bedroom. Have a cool or warm drink ready for him. Arrange his pillow and offer to take off his shoes. Speak in a low, soft, soothing and pleasant voice. Allow him to relax and unwind.
>
> Listen to him. You may have a dozen things to tell him, but the moment of his arrival is not the time. Let him talk first.
>
> Make the evening his. Never complain if he does not take you out to dinner or other places of entertainment. Instead, try to understand his world of strain and pressure. It's good to be home and relax.

Classroom Activity: Similarities and Differences in the Experience of Growing Up

Ask your students to write down which period of their life they consider to have been the happiest, then which period they think most people in the class will report as the happiest. Tally the results on the board and have students discuss the differences among personal experiences, estimates, and general trends. (If the class follows the usual pattern, students will probably indicate middle childhood or late adolescence as their happiest years, but they will estimate that most class members will choose early childhood.)

The purpose of the exercise is to get students to think about their own childhood and that of their classmates, and about the differences between actual data and a hunch. However, it also provides an opportunity to introduce some statistics (e.g., measures of central tendency and rough estimates of the significance of the results).

As a follow-up to this exercise, you might report to your students the surprising finding that no particular cohort reports any greater happiness than any other cohort.

Koo, J., Rie, J., & Park, K. (2004). Age and gender differences in affect and subjective well-being. *Geriatrics and Gerontology International, 4,* S268–S270.

AV: Contexts of Development (30 min., RMI Media Productions)

Beginning with a description of the child's biological makeup, this film demonstrates how the interplay of the social, economic, and cultural contexts influences all aspects of development.

Classroom Activity: Context, Family Structure, and Divorce Rate

Each person belongs to at least three groups—a cohort, a culture, and a socioeconomic group—that tend to guide his or her life path by influencing the context in which development occurs.

To highlight the impact of context on development, you might discuss Census Bureau studies of poverty and family structure. Throughout the life span, poverty is a potent risk factor for many developmental outcomes. The percentage of Americans living below the poverty line in 2009 was the highest it has been in 15 years. In 2009, there were 44 million, or one in seven, people living in poverty in the United States.

Other findings of the 2010 report:

- About 14.3 percent (7.7 million) of the population were in poverty in 2006. Married-couple families had a poverty rate of 4.9 percent, compared with 28.3 percent for female-householder, no-husband present families and 13.2 percent for male-householder, no-wife present families.
- The poverty rate for children younger than 18 decreased slightly (17.4 percent). The poverty rates for people 18 to 64 (10.8 percent) and for those 65 and older (9.4 percent) also fell from rates in 2004.
- The official poverty levels in 2009, which are updated annually to reflect changes in the Consumer Price Index, were $22,050 for a family of four and $10,830 for an individual.
- In 2009, the poverty rate for non-Hispanic Whites was 9.4 percent. Among those who indicated African American as their only race, 25.8 percent lived in poverty. The corresponding rates of poverty among other racial and ethnic groups were as follows: Asian (12.5 percent) and Hispanic (25.3 percent).

Another example of the impact of context on development is the strong association between marital status and nearly any measure of health, including mortality rates. Married adults are the healthiest, and widowed adults are the least healthy. Single, divorced, separated, and cohabiting individuals fall somewhere in between in their general health scores. For instance, married adults are less likely to smoke cigarettes, engage in heavy alcohol use, struggle with obesity, suffer from severe psychological stress, or to have a physically inactive lifestyle (Schoenborn, 2004).

Eckholm, E. (2010, September 16). Recession raises poverty rate to a 15-year high. *New York Times*, A1.

Schoenborn, C. A. (2004). *Marital status and health: United States, 1999–2002* (Publication no. 351). Hyattsville, MD: National Center for Health Statistics.

"On Your Own" Activity: Community Service Projects

Many undergraduate students have difficulty comprehending developmental material because of a lack of personal experiences or interest in relevant issues. When this happens, they may become apathetic and minimize the material's importance. Even worse, students may engage in victim blaming and personal distancing when topics such as child abuse, adolescent pregnancy, and poverty are discussed. To counteract these states, some instructors give students an option of completing a significant community service project for extra credit, or as an alternative to a more traditional assignment such as a term paper. For students who select this option, you might require a minimum of one to two hours per week of service in settings relevant to the course. This amount of time is adequate to give students time to learn responsibility and to provide a significant benefit to the community served. To supplement their *practicum,* you might also assign relevant readings and require students to keep a daily journal, submitting a written summary of their work.

To implement this option, at the beginning of the course, provide students with a list of approved agencies that are willing to accept student volunteers. Representatives of the agencies may be invited to describe their agencies and answer questions for the class. Each student who chooses the community service option should sign a contract specifying his or her expected duties, copies of which are given to the student, the agency supervisor, and the instructor. Students should then summarize their experience, using the guidelines provided in Handout 4.

The Scientific Method

AV: Transitions Throughout the Life Span, Program 2: A Scientific Approach

Program 2 of the Coast Learning System's telecourse introduces the scientific study of human development as the science that seeks to understand how and why people change with increasing age, and how and why they remain the same. Central to this science is the set of principles and procedures scientists use to produce the most objective results possible. The program discusses these principles and procedures, beginning with the scientific method and including how researchers formulate, develop, and test hypotheses; how they draw conclusions; and how they make their findings available to other researchers. Naturalistic observation, correlational research, experiments, surveys, and case studies are also described, as are the special developmental tools of cross-sectional and longitudinal research. The program includes footage (and discussion) of Harry Harlow's classic studies of contact comfort in rhesus monkeys and Mary Ainsworth's Strange Situation measure of infant attachment.

Classroom Activity: Using "Telepathy" to Demonstrate Principles of the Scientific Method

My experience is that students' eyes often begin to glaze over as soon as I start lecturing about concepts such as independent and dependent variables, hypotheses, and so forth, so having them try to figure out how their instructor is seemingly able to perform a psychic phenomenon greatly improves students' motivation (and learning). Douglas Bernstein of the University of South Florida suggests a wonderful activity to bring research methods to life.

The "telepathy" trick is simple and needs no accomplice. You need only a clean wastebasket, a pad of paper, and a pencil. Stand at the front of the class with the pad and pencil and ask your students to name some European cities. Sooner or later, Paris will be mentioned. As each city is called out, you should appear to write the city name on a separate piece of notepaper, wad it up, and toss it into the wastebasket. The "trick," of course, is that you actually write "Paris" on every sheet, no matter what the students say. By the time Paris is actually called out, you will have a wastebasket full of wadded-up papers, all of which say "Paris," although your students will assume they are all different. (If Paris happens to be called out early in the demonstrations, simply keep going until you have a sizable collection of "different" city names in the wastebasket.)

The payoff comes when you ask a student to choose one of the wadded-up balls (holding the wastebasket high so the student cannot see into it), open the paper, and concentrate on the city name. After a minute or two of "reading" the student's mind, call out "Paris," and your students will surely be amazed.

The demonstration is even more effective if you know other tricks of this type and can demonstrate a few to the class. Once students are convinced that you have some telepathic ability, announce that what you did was actually a simple magic trick, which you would like them to figure out. As students suggest possible solutions, it is easy for you to introduce the proper terminology such as, "Your hypothesis, then, is that I prearranged this trick with the student who picked from the wastebasket." List these hypotheses on the board. In the process of asking the class how they might test their hypotheses, the concepts of independent variables, dependent variables, and other principles of the scientific method (especially those of experimentation) will arise, which you will then correctly label. For instance, "In scientific terms, whether or not I am blindfolded would be called an independent variable."

Bernstein notes that the most difficult part of the demonstration is that your students will eventually insist on knowing how you actually did the trick. If you ever want to use it again, don't tell them. One solution (which will undoubtedly elicit some student groans) is to tell them that a few of the hypotheses nearly hit the mark. Bernstein suggests the following: "Some of your hypotheses were very close to the truth. However, scientists never know for sure when they have found the truth; they can only eliminate plausible alternative hypotheses and reach a conclusion with a statistically significant, but not absolutely certain, likelihood of being correct. Like scientists, you will have to be satisfied with this situation." One piece of additional advice: Be sure to move toward an exit as you finish this statement!

Bernstein, D. (2002, January). *Sharing ideas on the teaching of psychology.* Paper presented at the meeting of the National Institute on the Teaching of Psychology (NITOP). St. Petersburg, FL.

AV: How Cultures Are Studied (30 min., Insight Media)

Researcher Napoleon Chagnon describes his seminal studies of the Yanomamo Indians of Venezuela, focusing on the importance of putting aside one's ethnocentric biases to become an active member of the society being studied. The film also touches on ethical issues in participant observation.

AV: How We Study Children (24 min., Insight Media)

This film explores observational and experimental methods for studying child behavior, focusing on the strengths and weaknesses of each method.

AV: Infancy Research Methods (18 min., Insight Media)

This brief video describes four methods for studying the sensory and perceptual capabilities of infants between 1 and 12 months of age: preferential looking, habituation, eye movements, and conditioning. The strengths and weaknesses of each method are thoroughly assessed.

Classroom Activity: Naturalism, the Scientific Method, and Classroom Debates

To prepare students for their debate assignment and to describe the use of the scientific method, choose a controversial issue and show how research is able to bring some resolution to the conflict. For instance, until relatively recently no one had been able to practically or definitively prove that children should not be whipped, that schools serve an important function, or that girls should be educated in the same manner as boys. Instead, people used rhetoric, religion, and emotional appeals to try to convince one another, and they often arrived at opposite conclusions. You might emphasize this point by citing one or more of these age-old controversies, asking students to argue for one side or the other. Following are two possible topics and opposing views:

Should boys and girls be raised in the same way?

> "The male is by nature superior, and the female inferior; the one rules and the other is ruled; this principle, of necessity, extends to all mankind." (Aristotle, *Politics*, Book 1, Chapter 5)
>
> "My law will apply in all respects to girls as much as to boys: the girls must be trained exactly like the boys. . . . [T]he present practice in our own part of the world is the merest folly; it is pure folly that men and women do not unite to follow the same pursuits with all their energies." (Plato, *Laws*, Book 7, Section 804)

Are people naturally good, bad, or indifferent?

> "In a state of nature, there would be no arts; no letters; no society; and, which is worst of all, continual fear and danger of violent death; and the life of men, solitary, poor, nasty, brutish, and short." (Thomas Hobbes, *Leviathan*)
>
> "Everything is good when it leaves the hands of the Creator; everything degenerates in the hands of man." (Jean-Jacques Rousseau, *Emile*)
>
> "I would imagine the minds of children as easily turned, this or that way, as water itself." (John Locke, *Some Thoughts Concerning Education*)

In expressing their opinions, students should be sure to explain their reasoning. Other members of the class should then comment on how convincing the arguments are. If the discussion goes well, students will see that mere personal testimony ("My neighbor's child . . ."; "My mother told me . . .") or hearsay ("I read somewhere . . .") is not as convincing as facts based on scientific evidence. This is an excellent time to point out that contemporary philosophy of science takes a naturalistic approach. Naturalism is the view that all statements are to be evaluated as they are in science—empirically. Developmental psychologists do not know all the answers, which is one reason they spend a great deal of time designing research, performing experiments, and reading each other's work.

This exercise will help students understand the importance of relying on scientific evidence, rather than personal experiences or anecdotal evidence, in the study of human development and in formulating their arguments for a debate.

AV: Research Methods (30 min., Insight Media)

This film is one of a series of programs created specifically for psychology classes. It discusses the impact of psychological research on society, explains the scientific method and its importance, and presents some archival film footage of research on autistic behavior.

Classroom Activity: Counting Fidgets: Bringing Naturalistic Observation to Life

If texts on research methods are any indication, psychology students spend much more time learning about experimentation than about scientific observation in a natural setting and other descriptive research techniques. As a result, students often do not appreciate the complexities of observation, which often involves the cataloging of many varied behaviors. Student disinterest is unfortunate, because this method is widely used in developmental research.

Barney Beins describes an activity to illustrate to students how they might approach naturalistic and systematic observations and the difficulties that must be overcome. Beins begins by asking for two volunteers who are wearing digital watches (or watches with sweep second hands). Beins suggests picking two students who are likely to respond differently to the task; for instance, one who seems very energetic and another who is calmer. This type of observer variation is likely to enhance the pedagogical effectiveness of the activity.

After the observers have been selected, Beins takes them outside the class to explain their roles. Beins gives the observers the following directions:

> I would like you to record the number of fidgets that the students in the class emit for a five-minute period. Break the five-minute period into separate one-minute segments and keep a count of the number of fidgets in each segment. Keep a written record of the number of fidgets in each segment. You will need to scan the entire class, so sit at the front of the class, facing them.
>
> When we go back into the classroom, take your observation seats and when I say "Begin," start recording the number of fidgets. For the first minute, I will be talking; for the second minute, I will explain that I want the students to sit with their eyes closed and imagine there are insects crawling on their skins. During the third minute, they will actually sit there with their eyes closed. During the fourth minute, they will begin a discussion of what they think is going on. It will continue into the fifth minute.

Make sure that you keep track of the time as accurately as you can.

Back in the class, and with the observers at their posts, use the following script over the five-minute period of observation.

Minute	Activity	Purpose
1	Talk about a topic unrelated to systematic observation	To generate a baseline period for the number of fidgets
2	Tell students that in one minute you will ask them to close their eyes and imagine insects are crawling on their skin	To prepare students for the period in which the number of fidgets is likely to increase
3	Students close their eyes and imagine the insects are there	After about half a minute, the number of fidgets typically begins to increase

Minute	Activity	Purpose
4	Begin a discussion in which students speculate on the reason for the activity and the role that the student-observers played	This creates a warm-down minute in which fidgets begin to decrease in number
5	The discussion continues	This provides another post-insect baseline

After the observation period, ask the class to speculate about the goal of the activity. Although sometimes the class is able to figure it out, Beins reports that in most instances the students generate inaccurate hypotheses. In many cases, students note that they changed their behaviors because they were being observed. The remaining time can be spent discussing how to make observations more reliable, for example, by generating behavior checklists, training observers, and so on. Students typically suggest using only one observer, thus preventing inconsistencies in recording. This suggestion makes for a good discussion of why this would be worse than using inconsistent observers (with only one observer, they have no idea about reliability; with inconsistent observers, at least they are aware if there is a problem).

Beins, B. (2002, January). *Counting fidgets: Teaching the complexity of naturalistic observation.* Paper presented at the meeting of the National Institute on the Teaching of Psychology (NITOP), St. Petersburg, FL.

AV: Observation (18 min., Insight Media)

Particularly relevant to developmental research, this short film describes techniques for observing children, including naturalistic and subjective observation. The film also contains a segment discussing the difficulties and responsibilities faced by researchers who study children.

Classroom Activity: Experimental Tests of Popular Advertising Claims

To help students understand the difficulties involved in conducting a valid experiment, you might tell them about a problem you personally have encountered, either in your current research or in your graduate work.

Alternatively, you might present a general observation, then ask students if they can find any flaws in the experimental procedures or in the conclusions drawn. For instance, if you use the memory-relating device for establishing rapport (see Teaching Tip on Exporting Developmental Psychology), you might ask someone to summarize the results. Because negative memories are usually cited more often than positive ones, such a summary might include observations such as these: "Most people hated school" or "Nobody had anything good to say about their brothers or sisters." Then ask the class if a valid conclusion would be that "Elementary school is a terrible experience" or "It's better to be an only child." The students should be able to see the bias in this kind of reasoning.

Another good way to increase understanding of the experimental method is to have students design a study to test a popular advertising claim, such as Gillette's claim that their M3Power razor raises facial hair up and away from the skin. You might pose this as a problem after discussing the basics of the experimental method with the class. Despite the difficulty of scientifically testing this claim, it was challenged by Schick-Wilkinson Sword—one of Gillette's main competitors. After evaluating the evidence, Judge Janet Hall of the United States District Court of Connecticut granted an injunction against Gillette on the basis that these claims were "unsubstantiated and inaccurate."

Your students are sure to think of other popular advertising claims that could be discussed and tested in class.

Associated Press. (2005, June 2). Judge rules Gillette M3Power ads are false. Retrieved from www.msnbc.msn.com/id/8074882.

AV: Experimental Design (2 segments, 30 min. each, Annenberg/CPB)

Divided into two segments, this film provides a broad overview of observational studies and experimental studies. Segment 1 focuses on basic principles of experimental design, including randomization, sampling, bias, and replication. Segment 2 focuses on the question of causation in research.

AV: Experiments in Human Behavior (35 min., Insight Media)

Describing landmark experiments concerned with obedience to authority, cult behavior, and addiction, this program explains research design and differentiates field research, observational studies, surveys, and experimentation.

AV: Research Methods for the Social Sciences (33 min., Insight Media)

Focusing on the experimental method, this program differentiates control and experimental groups, independent and dependent variables, and correlational research. It also discusses ethical issues in research.

"On Your Own" Activity: Wording Effects in Survey Questions

One potential problem of survey research involves the wording of questions. Improperly worded questions can result in biased responses. For this reason, surveys are used more often for political reasons than for legitimate research purposes. When people have "hidden agendas," the wording of survey questions can easily lead respondents toward particular answers. To illustrate wording bias at its worst, Barney Beins asks students to complete the questions that appear in Handout 5 before any discussion of survey methodology takes place. The questions came from a survey conducted by the American Policy Foundation (grammatical errors appeared in the original).

Afterward, Beins reads each question with the class to try to identify the specific components of the question that are likely to lead to the answer that the survey creators want. The problems include the following:

- Vaguely worded questions and unclear terminology
- The use of emotionally laden words
- Complex and lengthy sentences that may be difficult to understand
- Failing to include or allow for all possible responses
- Double-barreled questions: that is, multiple questions within a single question

Following the item-by-item discussion of the survey, students might be asked to reword some of the questions to be more neutral, that is, to create questions that a serious researcher would use. Only by asking neutral questions can responses be considered valid indicators of people's actual attitudes and opinions. Another activity is to have students reword the items so that the "correct" answer is opposite to the one that the creators of the survey intended.

Beins, B. (2002). *Identifying pitfalls in creating survey questions.* Paper presented at the meetings of the National Institute on the Teaching of Psychology (NITOP). St. Petersburg, FL.

Classroom Activity: Limitations of the Survey as a Research Method

The text notes notes that the survey is limited by the tendency of interviewees to present themselves as they would like to be perceived. Put another way, what people say they do is often very different from what they actually do. To prove this point, Martin Bolt suggested a simple classroom demonstration.

Purchase a tin of some exotic food (chocolate-covered ants work nicely) from the gourmet food section of a large grocery store. Bring the delicacy to class, concealed in your briefcase, and ask if anyone has ever eaten an exotic delicacy such as chocolate-covered ants. Pick a few students who did not raise their hands and ask, "Would you ever consider eating a chocolate-covered ant?" If you still get no "takers," offer an incentive ("Would you eat one for a dollar?").

If your class is typical, several students will publicly agree to eat the exotic food, which, unbeknownst to them, you actually have brought to class. At this point reach into your briefcase, reveal the delicacy, and invite your students to follow through on their boast. Most students will turn down your offer; even if they do not, the exercise can generate a good discussion of the "What would you do if . . .?" question on which many surveys and interviews are based.

Bolt, M. (2012). Instructor's resources to accompany David Myers' *Psychology in Everyday Life*, 2nd ed. New York: Worth.

AV: The Ethnic Flaw (30 min., Insight Media)

Focusing on the experiences of people who have emigrated from their country of birth to a foreign country, Thomas Sowell discusses the impact of culture on the individual. The affirmative action controversy is also explored, including how it has benefited middle-class African Americans while perhaps impeding progress among lower-income, unskilled African Americans.

AV: Race: The World's Most Dangerous Myth (60 min., Insight Media)

This program begins by differentiating various social, biological, and geographical categorizations of race. It next discusses genetic differences among races and how social institutions tend to perpetuate racial stereotyping.

AV: Social Constructionist Ideas About Research (30 min., Insight Media)

The central idea of this program is that how the choices researchers make—to observe certain people and disregard others, for instance—can dramatically affect their understanding of developmental phenomena. Attention-deficit/hyperactivity disorder is used as a model to illustrate the nature of social constructionist research.

AV: PsychNow: Interactive Experiences in Psychology (CD-ROM) (Insight Media)

This CD-ROM (Mac/Windows) uses animations, graphics, video clips, and interactive exercises to teach central concepts in psychology. Students can participate in memory exercises, view film clips of children in different stages of cognitive development, study cross-cultural issues in emotional expression, and investigate many other topics. There is a particularly good module on research methods and critical thinking.

Teaching Tip: Teaching Critical Thinking About Research Reports in the Media

Nearly every day, the Internet, television, radio, newspapers, magazines, and other media sources summarize the results of a research study—sometimes in ways that involve significant omissions or distortions of the original study. To teach students to think critically about research reports in the media, ask each student to find a recent news summary of a research study relevant to human development—and the original research article on which it is based. Make copies of the most interesting and relevant news summaries and divide the class into small groups of four or five students. After each group selects someone to record the discussion, give the students in each group a copy of one of the news reports and the five discussion questions below. After allowing the groups to read the article and formulate answers to the questions (which takes 30 to 40 minutes), reconvene the entire class to discuss students' responses.

At this point, you can use an overhead projector to provide excerpts from the original research article that is the subject of the news article. With your help, the class should attempt to identify omissions and distortions in the newspaper account.

As a follow-up to this classroom exercise, you might want to assign the Portfolio Assignment included in the General Resources of this manual.

Questions to consider:

1. What conclusion does this article imply? What statements in the article suggest this conclusion?
2. Is this conclusion warranted by the study described? Why or why not?
3. Is the title an accurate summary of the article described? Why or why not?
4. What questions do you have after reading this article?
5. If you had the power to create guidelines for the press's reporting of a research study, what would you recommend?

Teaching Tip: Motivating Students to Read Journal Articles

Exposing students to the primary research literature is a goal of many undergraduate courses in developmental psychology. By reading journal articles, students are able to see firsthand the practical application of methodological concepts that are covered in class. Reading such articles also stimulates critical reading and thinking skills that will help students develop a healthy skepticism for all information to which they are exposed.

David Carkenord of Longwood College offers a useful suggestion for increasing students' motivation for completing journal assignments. Each week of the semester, excluding weeks when exams are scheduled, Carkenord has students read an article to be discussed in class the following week. Students are told that exams will contain questions (both multiple-choice and short-answer/essay) about these articles.

In preparation for the class discussion and the exam, students are asked to briefly summarize, on an index card, the major points and conclusions of the article, along with his or her overall opinion of its merits. These cards may be turned in following the class discussion for students to receive 1 point extra credit (cumulatively worth 4 percent of total course points). More important, students who turn in cards are allowed to refer to them during the upcoming exam, which typically covers two or three journal articles in addition to material from the text and lectures. (To ensure that no other information is written on the note cards, they are returned to students just before the exams are handed out.)

Although some instructors "may take slight offense at the decidedly operant 'carrot-and-stick' approach of the technique," Carkenord notes that his students responded very favorably and turned in note cards for over 70 percent of the assigned readings. In addition to enjoying a bit of increased leverage on their exam and course grades, students reported that reading the articles "increased their knowledge of the subject matter" and was "a good learning experience." Another benefit is that more students came to class prepared to discuss the article. This made the discussions much livelier and more productive.

Carkenord's technique can be adapted to your own program of assigned readings.

Carkenord, D. M. (1994, October). Motivating students to read journal articles. *Teaching of Psychology, 21*(3), 162–164.

Classroom Activity: Cultural Influences on Research

Cultural diversity is an important topic in all of psychology's subfields, including developmental psychology. For this reason, developmentalists often compare people of different cultures. In a narrow sense, cross-cultural research simply compares people from different cultural backgrounds, testing for possible differences among them. In a broader sense, cross-cultural research is concerned with understanding developmental processes as either universal (that is, true for people of all cultures) or culture-specific (that is, true for people of some cultures).

The increased attention to culture paid by today's researchers certainly represents a huge stride forward from the days when psychology was a "science" of "White, undergraduate Americans." But we must be careful in conducting cross-cultural research and in interpreting the results from cross-cultural studies. This is because cross-cultural designs pose a number of unique challenges. For example, we have to consider the multicultural nature of society—a person can belong to many cultures—which makes comparisons particularly difficult. Discussing a few of these challenges with your students will increase their appreciation of cultural influences on development and encourage them to think critically about the scientific method.

- Culture refers to the shared values, attitudes, and behaviors of a group of people that are passed from one generation to the next. Unfortunately, however, psychologists have been unable to agree on how to measure these "shared" characteristics. Instead, they have relied on "easier" measurements that have equated culture with either race or nationality. This is not to say that these studies should be dismissed, but, rather, that there is a discrepancy between how culture is defined and how it is operationally defined for research purposes.

- Culture can influence the research process itself, including researchers' decisions regarding which variables are considered important for study. All researchers have their own cultural upbringing, which influences the hypotheses they choose to study. The problem is that a hypothesis that seems extremely important in one culture may be completely irrelevant to a person from a different cultural background. Too often, ethnocentric researchers develop hypotheses that are of interest to them in their particular cultural context, then impose those hypotheses on people from other cultures. Ask your students to think of examples of uniquely "American" research hypotheses that would make little sense in other cultures.
- Cross-cultural sampling is often problematic. When comparing U.S. or Canadian university students, for example, researchers typically take great pains to ensure their samples are representative of the population under study. Unless a cross-cultural researcher has a collaborator who is a native of the culture under investigation, researchers often simply assume that their samples are representative of the larger culture. When differences in the dependent measure are found, these differences are automatically deemed "cultural." Ask your students to come up with an example of how a random, and seemingly "representative," sample of their peers might in fact be biased. Pose the question from the standpoint of a researcher from another culture who selects a sample of American students for study.
- The data analysis from a research study may lend itself to more than one interpretation. For example, people in the United States are very familiar with questionnaires and generally feel free to answer them candidly in terms of how they truly think or feel about an issue. This is a reflection of the "individualistic" nature of Western cultural norms. People who grew up in a "collectivistic" culture, however, may react very differently to questionnaires. One possible manifestation of a collectivistic upbringing is that respondents may avoid choosing extreme values on bipolar response scales, following a norm that encourages group consensus. Although this type of response set is certainly a reflection of culture, it would be misleading for a researcher to draw a conclusion about a specific variable or measurement scale. In other words, it may be impossible to disentangle cultural differences in attitude from a cultural response set.
- To further stimulate student interest in this topic, have the class check your library's resources for materials related to cultural influences on research. One excellent resource is the journal *Culture and Psychology,* which can be accessed online at http://cap.sagepub.com. There, students can even view a recent sample issue.

Cornejo, C. (2007). The locus of subjectivity in cultural studies. *Culture and Psychology, 13*(2), 243–256.

"On Your Own" Activity: Teaching Students to Use PsycINFO Effectively

PsycINFO is an online abstract (not full-text) database of psychological literature from the 1800s to the present. An essential tool for students and researchers alike, PsycINFO covers more than 2,150 titles, 98 percent of which are peer-reviewed journals.

PsycINFO also covers chapters from books and publications from more than 50 countries and in 25 languages. Updated weekly and growing at a phenomenal pace, PsycINFO currently has more than 46 million cited references.

If you assign term papers or other projects that require students to conduct literature reviews, it is well worth taking class time to make sure your students fully understand how to use PsycINFO. Perhaps the best way to cover this material is to have an experienced librarian demonstrate for the class the use of PsycINFO, as well as other databases, with a "hands-on" approach. This can be done in the library where each student sits at an individual workstation, in a computer classroom using your campus network to access the library, or in a conventional, networked classroom using a desktop computer and some sort of monitor-projection system. After this overview, you might distribute Handout 6, which gives students the experience of locating primary source articles using PsycINFO. You might also point students directly to the APA Database site, which offers a great deal of information on using PsychINFO (www.apa.org/ psycinfo).

Cautions from Science

Classroom Activity: Limitations of Correlational Research

To help your students understand the limitations of correlational research, you might discuss one of the many developmental studies linking parental divorce or family conflict with the emotional and physical health of affected children (Hetherington, 2005; Gilstrap, 2003/2004). For example, one study reported that children in homes with absent fathers are more likely to suffer from antisocial personality disorder, child conduct disorder, and attention-deficit/hyperactivity disorder (Pfiffner, McBurnett, & Rathouz, 2001). Another study reported a higher incidence of adjustment problems among children of divorce compared with those in two-parent families (Simons, Lin, Gordon, Conger, & Lorenz, 1999). In their attempt to understand the relationship between these variables, the careful investigators examined several possible explanations, including loss of family income, parental conflict, the psychological adjustment and parenting practices of the custodial parent, and level of involvement of the noncustodial parent.

In contrast to this fine example of careful scientific reasoning, I am reminded of a radio talk show I was listening to some time ago concerning the impact of divorce on children. At one point the talk show host stated, "Scientists have proven that divorce stunts the growth of children." Although I recall no formal citation of the study and have been unable to locate it through online searching, the radio personality was apparently reading a news release of a journal article that reported a moderate negative correlation between family discord and the physical stature of young children. More specifically, parents who were divorced or separated tended to have smaller children. To conduct the study, the researchers apparently visited schools and measured the heights of a large group of children of the same age. These results were then statistically compared with their family circumstances.

Like many people, the journalist had fallen into the trap of inferring causality from a correlation between two variables (height and indicators of family conflict, one of which was divorce). In fairness, a speculative note from the research team that household stress might reduce growth hormone secretion in young children may have encouraged the journalist's conclusion.

In discussing this common form of faulty reasoning with your class, you might challenge your students with the following question: "Can we conclude that family conflict causes children to be smaller?" If their critical thinking skills are sharp, they should recognize that

- The journalist may have had a preexisting bias about the impact of family conflict on children and come to a conclusion that seemed reasonable without realizing that the converse was also a plausible explanation of the study's results. In stating this possibility, you might note that it is an example of *confirmation bias*, or the tendency of people (including careless scientists!) to interpret ambiguous outcomes as supporting their own beliefs rather than as neutral findings. In short, it would have been equally valid to conclude that having small children leads to divorce. (If you would like to expand on the important issue of belief bias in research, see the Classroom Activity "Experimental Tests of Popular Advertising Claims.")
- Another important point is that there may have been a third factor influencing the two variables identified in the study. For instance, children of poorer families may have poorer nutrition, resulting in slower growth. Furthermore, poverty might also lead to strained relationships among family members and higher divorce rates. Another plausible explanation is the presence of some genetic trait, which shows up in both the growth and temperament of family members.
- Finally, when scientists wish to establish a causal link between two factors, they conduct an experiment in which the independent variable can be controlled and other factors can be ruled out with certainty. For example, when a new drug is tested in a clinical trial, a large number of research participants is divided into two groups at random, with one group receiving the drug and the other a placebo pill. Neither the participants nor the person recording the data knows which group a given individual is in. Both groups are then monitored for possible effects (the dependent variable). The difference between this example and the correlational study is that the choice of who received the drug and who did not was *controlled*. In the correlational study that claimed to link divorce with stunted growth, there was no control over whose parents were divorced and whose were not. Thus, it was impossible to distinguish cause from effect or to rule out other intervening (confounding) factors.

Gilstrap, R. L. (2003/2004, Winter). Divorce, family structure, and the academic success of children. *Childhood Education, 80*(2), 97–111.

Hetherington, E. M. (2005). Divorce and adjustment of children. *Pediatrics in Review, 26,* 163–169.

Pfiffner, L., McBurnett, K., & Rathouz, P. (2001). Father absence and familial antisocial characteristics. *Journal of Abnormal Child Psychology, 29*(5), 357–367.

Simons, R. L., Lin, K., Gordon, L. C., Conger, R. D., & Lorenz, F. O. (1999). Explaining the higher incidence of adjustment problems among children of divorce compared with those in two-parent families. *Journal of Marriage and the Family, 61*(4), 1020–1033.

AV: The Way of Science (58 min., Films for the Humanities and Sciences)

"Humans are storytellers," notes this film's host Roger Bingham. "We tell stories to feel at home in the universe." This effort to "feel at home" has given rise to many ways of knowing, including science and mythology, both of which are explored here. The film provides a stimulating introduction to a lecture on the limits of the scientific method as a path to the truth.

Critical Thinking Activity: Breast-Feeding and Intelligence

Each unit of these resources contains a critical thinking exercise designed specifically to test students' critical thinking about a topic covered in the text. Handout 7 contains a brief scenario followed by a series of questions.

Answers to this unit's critical thinking exercise are as follows:

1. This study tested the hypothesis that breast milk offers a nutritional advantage over formula, resulting in increased intelligence in children, which the researchers defined as performance on an IQ test. The independent variable was the

duration of breast-feeding received by the infants in the study. The dependent variable was the child's IQ score, as measured by the Wechsler Adult Intelligence Scale (WAIS) at 27.2 years of age.

2. The evidence is based on empirical correlational research comparing IQ test scores of five groups of children who differed in how long they were breast-fed as infants. The research seems valid, especially because it attempts to rule out factors other than the independent variable that might have influenced the results, such as the mothers' social and educational status.
3. The researchers argue that the IQ advantage of infants fed breast milk is the result of nutritional factors that promote brain growth and thereby facilitate development of mental abilities. Based on the evidence presented, this explanation does make sense.
4. Because the evidence is correlational, not based on experimental data, we can't be sure that breast milk actually affects intelligence. Despite the researchers' efforts to rule out group differences in the mothers' social class and educational level, it is still possible that mothers who nurse their babies longer are more generally nurturing and produce better cared-for infants. To pinpoint breast milk as the causal factor, researchers could do an experiment using mothers who intend to bottle-feed rather than nurse. Half could be given formula and half breast milk from a donor.
5. We cannot yet be certain breast milk is better, but no evidence suggests that it is worse. Thus, mothers should be encouraged to breast-feed their babies, and mothers who will not or cannot breast-feed might explore alternative ways to provide breast milk. The nutritional advantage of breast milk, if reliable, should be particularly beneficial to premature babies, who are born at a stage of especially rapid brain growth.

AV: Ethics and Scientific Research (30 min., Insight Media)

This award-winning video explores ethical issues faced by scientists, focusing specifically on scientific misconduct. One intriguing segment discusses the case of a researcher who falsified findings on psychotropic drugs.

HANDOUT 1

Developmental Fact or Myth?

T F 1. The science of human development is the study of how and why people change as they grow older, as well as how and why they remain the same.

T F 2. Most developmental psychologists prefer not to use the scientific method in studying human development.

T F 3. Every difference between one developing person and the norm is a deficit.

T F 4. Children's development—both physical and mental—follows a straight, linear growth pattern.

T F 5. Culture, ethnicity, race, and SES are impossible for scientists to disentangle.

T F 6. Most of us are unaware of the culture we transmit.

T F 7. For the most accurate results, scientific observation should be performed in a laboratory.

T F 8. An experiment is always the best way to investigate a developmental issue.

T F 9. Developmental psychologists almost never base their research on the study of one group of people over a long period of time.

T F 10. When two variables are correlated, it means that one caused the other.

HANDOUT 2

"Dear Future Child"

Following the guidelines presented in class and below, compose a personal letter to a future or actual child (son, daughter, or both) on the occasion of the child's eighteenth birthday. Your letter will remain completely confidential. In your letter, be sure to cover the following:

1. When and why did you decide to have your child?
2. What qualities should a good parent possess, and why?
3. Which of your qualities do you believe will help make you a successful parent?
4. Which of your qualities may interfere with your ability to be a good parent?
5. What qualities do you want your child to possess, and why?
6. What can you do as a parent to promote your child's development in the following areas: cognitive development, social and emotional development, personality development, sex-role development, moral development, creativity?
7. What are your hopes for your child's future?
8. What bits of wisdom have you acquired that you wish to pass on to your child?

HANDOUT 3

Your Cohort

Describe the cohort into which you were born by answering the following questions.

1. In what year were you born?

2. Do you know of any important historical events that occurred at the time of your birth? If so, list a few of them.

3. What important events do you remember as having affected you and your classmates during your school years (for example, assassinations, space exploration, political upheavals or wars, natural disasters)? Describe, if you can, how these events influenced your development.

4. When you were in the fifth grade, what attitude did most of the people you knew have toward the following?
   a. mothers who worked outside the home

   b. fathers' roles in child rearing

   c. people of other ethnic groups

   d. senior citizens

HANDOUT 3 (*continued*)

e. couples without children

f. only children

g. handicapped children

h. birth control

HANDOUT 4

Community Service Projects

Following the guidelines presented in class, provide the information requested concerning your volunteer experience.

1. Describe the agency for which you volunteered.

2. Relate five things you observed while volunteering to material covered in the textbook or lectures.

3. In what ways do you think the agency benefited from your volunteer service?

HANDOUT 4 (*continued*)

4. In what ways did you benefit from your volunteer experience?

5. What is your opinion of allowing students to complete a community service project in order to fulfill course requirements?

HANDOUT 5

National Parents Survey on Public Education (sponsored by the American Policy Foundation)

1. In your opinion, which should be the primary goal of the public education system?

   A. teaching students basic skills such as mathematics, reading, history, and geography

   B. teaching students to "feel good"

   C. undecided

2. In your opinion, is it more important that students:

   A. be tested accurately on classroom work such as math, English grammar, geography, and history

   B. be graded on their ability to interact and get along with others

   C. undecided

3. In your opinion, who should have the stronger input in establishing student values, attitudes, and beliefs?

   A. the student's family

   B. teachers and government officials

4. In your opinion, what entity is better qualified to establish local school curriculum?

   A. community-elected school boards with input from PTAs and parents

   B. state and federal education agencies

   C. undecided

5. In your opinion, should basic reading, writing, and math skills be the major requirements for high school graduation?

   A. yes

   B. no

   C. undecided

6. In your opinion, should students be forced to perform free community service jobs such as working with suicide prevention hot lines and drug rehabilitation centers as a requirement for high school graduation?

   A. yes

   B. no

   C. undecided

HANDOUT 5 *(continued)*

7. In your opinion, are condom distribution and explicit sex education programs appropriate for students in kindergarten and elementary classes?

   A. yes

   B. no

   C. undecided

8. In your opinion, should schools have the right to administer some form of discipline on unruly students so that order and a learning environment is maintained in the school?

   A. yes

   B. no

   C. undecided

9. In your opinion, should schools have the right to expel students who have compiled long records of discipline problems, and who pose a threat to student and teacher safety, and show no interest in taking part in the educational process?

   A. yes

   B. no

   C. undecided

10. Which of the following best describes you?

   A. parent of student currently in public schools

   B. grandparent of student currently in public schools

   C. concerned taxpayer with no students currently in public schools

   D. other

Source: Beins, B. (2002, January). *Identifying pitfalls in creating survey questions.* Paper presented at the meetings of the National Institute on the Teaching of Psychology (NITOP), St. Petersburg, FL.

HANDOUT 6

Using PsycINFO

Following the guidelines presented in class and below, use your library's online search resources to conduct two searches for published research in primary sources *(peer-reviewed journal articles). In most cases, you will be able to access these resources by going to the college or university library Web page, where you will find a listing of PsycINFO and other databases to which your institution subscribes. If you have difficulty finding these databases, get help from any existing online resources. Even better, visit the library and arrange a consultation with a librarian.*

1. Conduct an author search

   Use PsycINFO to find a recent article in a peer-reviewed journal by someone who shares your last name. If you are unsuccessful, search for an article by someone cited in the first chapter of your textbook. To confirm that the journal is peer-reviewed, make sure that it is one to which your college or university library subscribes. Information on the journal's publication policies and review process can usually be found inside the front cover of the journal or in a separate section that you can locate from the index.

   In citing references to research, most psychology journals follow the style guide of the *Publication Manual* of the American Psychological Association. This style, which is referred to as "APA Format," will likely be the style your professors require as the format for references you cite in every term paper you write for your psychology courses.

   a. In the space below, provide complete reference information for this article following APA format: author's name, year of publication, title of article, journal name, volume number, page numbers.

   b. Briefly describe the publication policy of the journal in which your article was published.

HANDOUT 6 *(continued)*

c. Read the article's abstract and summarize the article in a few sentences.

2. Conduct a subject search

Use PsycINFO to locate an article on a developmental topic that interests you. If you can't think of a topic, skim through the textbook's index for ideas. Try to find an article that reports the results of a research study rather than one that is theoretical in nature or a review of other research. Locate this article online and then read it as carefully as you can. Depending on where the article was published, it may be difficult to understand, because most journals publish articles written by researchers for other researchers to read. Do your best to answer the following questions:

a. Using APA Format, what is the article's complete reference?

b. If the article reports the results of a research study, what type of study is it? Be as specific and complete as possible. For instance, is the research quantitative or qualitative? Is the study descriptive, correlational, or experimental?

HANDOUT 6 *(continued)*

c. Who were the participants in the study? How were they selected? Do they constitute a representative sample of a population?

d. What variables were investigated in the study? If age was a variable, how was it investigated (e.g., cross-sectional study, longitudinal study)?

e. If the study involves quantitative data, what types of statistics were used?

f. What was the study's major hypothesis, or research question? What were the major conclusions?

HANDOUT 7

Critical Thinking Activity: Breast-Feeding and Intelligence

Now that you have read and reviewed the introduction to development, take your learning a step further by testing your critical thinking skills on this scientific reasoning exercise.

Several studies suggest that breast-fed babies become more intelligent children than formula-fed babies. One such study (Mortensen, Michaelsen, Sanders, & Reinisch, 2002*) involved a sample of over 3,000 women and men born in Copenhagen, Denmark, between October 1959 and December 1961. The samples were divided into five categories based on duration of breast-feeding, as assessed by physician interview with mothers at a one-year examination. The child's intelligence was assessed using the Wechsler Adult Intelligence Scale (WAIS) at a mean age of 27.2 years.

The results showed that duration of breast-feeding was associated with significantly higher scores on the verbal, performance, and full scale WAIS IAs. This difference was observed even after the researchers adjusted for differences in the social class and maternal education of the two groups. (This adjustment allowed the researchers to rule out any preexisting differences in the groups that might have independently contributed to IQ differences in their children.)

The authors acknowledged that other differences between the groups, such as the children's genetic potential or their parents' caregiving skills or motivation to nurture, could explain the results. However, they believe that human milk contains various hormones and other factors that enhance brain growth and maturation.

1. State the research hypothesis in your own words. Identify the independent and dependent variables, and define all important concepts and terms as they are used in this study.
2. What evidence do the researchers offer as a test of their hypothesis? Is this evidence empirical (observable)? Is it valid?
3. What explanation do the researchers offer for their findings? Does this explanation make sense based on the evidence?
4. Given the results of this study, why can't the researchers draw a causal connection between type of food and later intelligence? What might be an alternative explanation for the results of this study? What could the researchers do in order to make a causal connection between the dependent and independent variables?
5. Are there any practical implications for this research?

*Mortensen, E. L., Michaelsen, K. F., Sanders, S. A., & Reinish, J. M. (2002). The relationship between duration of breastfeeding and adult intelligence. *Journal of the American Medical Association, 287,* 2365–2371.

Theories of Development

Contents

Note: Worth Publishers provides online Instructor and Student Tool Kits, DVD Student Tool Kits, and Instructor and Student video resources in DevelopmentPortal for use with the text. See Part I: General Resources for information about these materials and the text Lecture Guides for a complete list by text chapter.

Classroom Activities: Freud and Watson, p. 6
Using a Token Economy to Bring Behaviorism to Life (and Increase Class Participation), p. 7
Observational Learning, p. 8

Teaching Tips: Rehearsal, Reinforcement, and Learning Students' Names, p. 6
Basic Terminology of Behaviorism, p. 6

Cognitive Theory

Audiovisual Materials: Piaget's Developmental Theory, p. 9
How Young Children Learn to Think, p. 10
Jean Piaget: Memory and Intelligence, p. 10
Cognitive Development, p. 10

Teaching Tip: Developmental Stages of Family and Friends, p. 9

Classroom Activity: Classroom Debate: "Resolved: Cognitive Development Is Most Accurately Characterized as a Continuous Process Rather Than as Occurring in a Sequence of Stages," p. 9

"On Your Own" Activity: The Active Search for Knowledge, p. 9 (Handout 5, p. 24)

Newer Theories

Sociocultural Theory

Audiovisual Materials: I'm Normal, You're Weird: Understanding Other Cultures, p. 10
Culture, p. 10
Introduction to Culture and Diversity, p. 10
Social-Cultural Diversity, p. 10
Contexts of Development, p. 10
The Latino Family, p. 10
Street Children of Africa, p. 10
Vygotsky's Developmental Theory: An Introduction, p. 10
Play: A Vygotskian Approach, p. 11
Learning in Context: Probing the Theories of Piaget and Vygotsky, p. 11

Internet Activity: High-Quality Preschool Education: What Would Vygotsky Say?, p. 10 (Handout 6, p. 26)

The Universal Perspective: Humanism and Evolutionary Theory

Classroom Activities: Applying Humanism, Evolutionary Theory, and Other Theoretical Perspectives, p. 11 (Handut 7, p. 27)
The Nurture Assumption: Why Children Turn Out the Way They Do, p. 11
The Blank Slate, the Noble Savage, and the Ghost in the Machine, p. 12

Teaching Tip: Evolutionary Psychology: Raising the "Why of Behavior" Question, p. 13

"On Your Own" Activity: Introducing Evolutionary Psychology, p. 13 (Handout 8, p. 28)

What Theories Contribute

Audiovisual Materials: Theories, p. 14

Classroom Activities: A Test of Three Theories of the Work–Family Interface, p. 14
Designing a Developmental Brochure for Targeted Audiences, p. 15
Positive Psychology, p. 16

Teaching Tip: The Role of Theories in Developmental Study, p. 14

"On Your Own" Activities: Applying Principles of Positive Psychology: Well-Being, p. 17 (Handout 9, p. 29)
Applying Principles of Positive Psychology: A Beautiful Day, p. 17 (Handout 10, p. 30)

Critical Thinking Activity: Theories, p. 17 (Handout 11, p. 31)

Suggested Activities

What Theories Do

On Your Own Activity: Developmental Fact or Myth?

Before students read about the theories of development, have them respond to the true–false statements in Handout 1.

The correct answers are shown below. Class discussion should focus on the origins of any developmental misconceptions that are demonstrated in the students' incorrect answers.

1. T	6. T
2. F	7. F
3. T	8. F
4. T	9. F
5. T	10. T

AV: Transitions Throughout the Life Span, Program 1: The Developing Person

Program 1, The Developing Person, is described in detail in the Introduction of these resources. It applies also to Theories of Development in its discussion of theories and different theoretical perspectives.

Teaching Tip: Differentiating Facts, Laws, Hypotheses, and Theories

Because many students find the distinctions among facts, laws, hypotheses, and theories to be extremely confusing, it is a good idea to spend a few minutes making sure everyone in your class is "on the same page" on this issue. As noted by one researcher:

> Many believe that scientific ideas pass through the hypothesis and theory stages and finally mature as laws. A former president [Reagan] demonstrated his misunderstanding of science by saying that he was not troubled by the idea of evolution because it was . . . "just a theory." The president's statement is the essence of this myth; an idea is not worthy of consideration until "lawness" has been bestowed upon it. The problem created by the false hierarchical nature inherent in this myth is that theories and laws are very different kinds of knowledge. Laws are generalizations, principles, or patterns in nature, while theories are the explanations of those generalizations. Thus, the "law of gravity" expresses the relationship of mass and distance to gravitational attraction as described by Sir Isaac Newton. The more thorny, and many would say more interesting, issue with respect to gravity is the explanation for why the law operates as it does. At this point, there is no well-accepted theory of gravity. Some suggest that gravity waves are the correct explanation; with clear confirmation and consensus lacking, most feel that a theory of gravity still eludes science.

As the crowning achievement of science, then, theories are used to organize and explain existing facts. Facts (also referred to as observations) are objective statements based on direct, empirical measurement. In psychology, facts are usually particular behaviors or reliable patterns of behavior. For example, the unvarying sequence in which children acquire the various rules of grammar in mastering their native language is a "fact." Noam Chomsky's model of an innate language acquisition device is a theory that was formulated from (and designed to explain) this fact. Thus, in the grand scheme of science, facts are observations, laws are regularities, and theories are explanations. To follow up on Newton's example: I release a ball at a certain time and place and it falls to the ground (fact). Balls and other objects descend according to a certain mathematical relationship between distance and time (law). The law is explained by the theory of gravity.

The word *hypothesis* is especially problematic for students, many of whom confuse it with "theory" (especially those who have taken a science course in which the two terms are, in fact, sometimes used interchangeably.) The word *hypothesis* is used in at least three different ways. It has come to mean (1) an immature theory, (2) a tentative prediction, and (3) a tentative law. In psychology, it means a testable prediction. As valuable as it is, hypothesis testing has several limitations. Failure to confirm a hypothesis, for example, may be due to apparatus failure or some other factor apart from a deficiency in the hypothesis.

In the cycle of science, facts lead to theories, which lead to hypotheses, which are tested with experiments or other research designs, which lead to new facts, which may lead to a reformulation of existing theories, and so on.

Proctor, R. W., & Capaldi, E. J. (2007). Teaching scientific methodology. *Association for Psychological Science Observer.* www.psychologicalscience.org/teaching/tips.

"On Your Own" Activity: The "Lifeline"

To help your students become more aware of the implicit stages in the life cycle, have them construct a personal "lifeline" by following the directions in Handout 2. Then discuss with them the kinds of events they recorded and when these events occurred or would occur.

Students should discover that they have already formed a relatively clear picture of the life cycle as being divided into distinct stages that correspond to childhood, adolescence, early adulthood, middle age, and old age. Some students may focus more on categories of events, dividing their lifelines into separate stages devoted to education, career, family, retirement, and so on. This activity can also serve as the basis for a good class discussion of why people tend to organize their lives in these ways. As an alternative, discussion can proceed with students comparing their lifelines in small groups.

"On Your Own" Activity: Major Developmental Theories: Discover Your Bias

Before discussing the psychoanalytic, behaviorist, cognitive, sociocultural, and universal theories at length, you might use the quiz in Handout 3 to encourage your students to explore their biases or predispositions.

As will be obvious to most of your students, *a* responses suggest a bias toward psychoanalytic thinking; *b* responses, toward behaviorism; *c* responses, toward cognitive theory; *d* responses, toward sociocultural theory; and *e* responses, toward evolutionary theory. While many students will answer consistently, some may choose more than one answer to a question or answer reflecting different biases for different questions, thus revealing an eclectic orientation. The items on the handout should stimulate students' thinking about themselves and the theories they will encounter. (NOTE: The test should *not* be used to categorize students or their orientations.)

Grand Theories

Classroom Activity: "Development" as a Social Construction

As noted in the text, economic, social, and cultural events and trends shape the thinking of individuals living in a particular time period. Even the most fundamental ideas about development are sensitive to the historical context. For example, the concept of childhood as a separate and extended life stage is a recent social construction.

Many students today too quickly dismiss the grand theories of Freud, Piaget, Skinner, and other pioneers of psychology as being overly simplistic, mechanistic, or even bizarre. To appreciate the genius of these and other early theorists, students should consider their unique historical contexts.

Both Freud and Piaget built on a classic notion of social development that can be traced from Greek philosophy to early Christianity, to political theorizing during the age of the Enlightenment, to nineteenth-century evolutionary biology. According to this view, developmental change is inborn, directional, and continuous.

Some thinkers have criticized the classic concept of development, declaring it to be vague and empirically inadequate. Beginning with pioneering behaviorists Edward Thorndike, John Watson, and Clark Hull, American psychologists in the first half of the twentieth century replaced the early concept of development with principles of learning and information processing. Whereas Watson attempted to explain developmental change in terms of conditioned Pavlovian associations, Hull argued vigorously for the removal of any general concept of development, along with "all other vestiges of vitalistic biology." By the late 1960s, the classic concept of development had come under so much fire that Sidney Bijou, in his 1968 presidential address to the American Psychological Association, declared that "the field does not any longer need the grand theoretical designs proposed by Piaget, Freud, [Erik] Erikson, [Arnold] Gesell, and Emmy Werner."

John Dollard, Neal Miller, John Flavell, and other contemporaries of Bijou continued that trend of transforming developmental principles into concepts that were compatible with learning theory and the then-emerging information-processing model of cognitive development. Thus, for example, Freud's theory of sexual identification as the culmination of the Oedipus complex was recast as an example of modeling, reinforcement, and other principles of observational learning. Similarly, a child who had demonstrated mastery of Piaget's conservation experiment had merely learned to filter out irrelevant situational cues while attending to those relevant to mastery of the principle.

The goal, of course, was parsimony—the replacement of vague, mentalistic concepts with "more precise," measurable ones. Piagetian and Freudian processes were either discarded or simply viewed as examples of information processing and learning.

James Youniss maintains, however, that these apparent gains in empirical precision occurred at the expense of an accurate understanding of what Piaget and Freud were attempting to explain. "For Freud," notes Youniss, "identification entails more than coming under the influence of a powerful model. It is a crucial step in a longer process of constructing a personality that is socially adaptive, yet autonomous."

Youniss also urges that contemporary developmental psychologists should not lose sight of the historical and cultural contexts in which Freud and Piaget developed their ideas. According to this viewpoint, many psychoanalytic and Piagetian concepts are social constructions that can give us important insights into the ways in which context influences contemporary thinking concerning developmental issues. As Youniss notes,

> Freud reached intellectual maturity when Viennese scholars were fixated on the failed promise of the Enlightenment that freedom from autocratic rule would release the natural human capacity for rationality and moral virtue. But to late nineteenth-century Viennese scholars, a review of the century's political events could not validate this idealistic position. Within the beneficent Austrian monarchy, Vienna was run as a model democracy with the city revamped according to technical planning and a social welfare policy. However, by the century's end, Vienna had become not a utopia but a hotbed of anti-Semitic and antislavic forces, fervid nationalism, and deep class divisions. It was clear to Freud, and to his artist, dramatist, and philosopher

> peers, that rationality was not natural and morality was not inborn. Freud's solution was to ground human behavior in unconscious irrationality that had to be penetrated and developmentally overcome. The capacity for reason had to be struggled for; it was not a natural grant. Hence, the need for an extended Oedipal process with the eventual transcending of childhood authority and the subsequent possibility for the individual to form a conscious relationship with society.

Although Youniss certainly does not advocate that developmental psychologists reembrace Freudian and Piagetian theories wholesale, he reminds us that many of the processes about which they wrote were constructed to address the unique social and cultural problems of their cohorts.

Youniss, J. (1995). The still useful classic concept of development. *Human Development, 38*, 373–379.

Youniss, J. (2006). G. Stanley Hall and his times: Too much so, yet not enough. *History of Psychology, 9*(3), 224–235.

Psychoanalytic Theory

AV: Young Dr. Freud (99 min., Films for the Humanities and Sciences)

This film portrays the early scientific life and discoveries of Freud and shows the excitement and frustrations he experienced as a scientist and theorist. It also places Freud's work in its historical context, making many of his ideas easier to understand. The movie was originally produced by Austrian and German television and is in German with English subtitles.

AV: Freud: The Hidden Nature of Man (27 min., Learning Corporation of America)

Freud's most significant discoveries about human sexuality and its role in neurotic disorders are dramatically reenacted. The film includes a staged session of analysis in which a woman remembers an incestuous relationship with her father, and Freud gradually realizes that this "memory" is actually part of an unconscious fantasy that is common to many women. The id, ego, and superego are also acted out in two vignettes, as is one of Freud's childhood dreams and his analysis of it. The movie provides a vivid though somewhat simplistic grasp of basic Freudian ideas.

"On Your Own" Activity: Freud's Influence on Psychology and American Culture

Freud's influence continues to permeate American culture 100 years after his concepts, theories, and terms were introduced. Freudian concepts can be found almost everywhere, from literature and motion pictures to philosophy and religion. In a computer search of the PsycINFO database, which indexes publications from 1967 to the present, the keyword "psychoanalytic" appeared in amost 72,000 references!

To help students appreciate the extent of Freud's influence, Marianne Miserandino of Beaver College offers a simple exercise that can be used in class or as an outside assignment. Using a five-point scale, students indicate the extent of their agreement or disagreement with the statements in Handout 4.

Miserandino suggests administering the scale before psychoanalytic theory is discussed in class or assigned in course readings. Students' responses can then form the basis of a good class discussion focusing on why students believe as they do and how their attitudes were formed. Would it be possible to use the scientific method to evaluate the statements? Which ones? What role does an individual's social and cultural background play in the formation of his or her responses to these statements? Would a person with a different sociocultural background respond differently? Do cohort differences play a role in a person's responses?

Each student should score his or her own responses as follows: For items 1, 2, 7, 9, 13, and 15, strongly disagree = 5, disagree = 4, neutral = 3, agree = 2, and strongly agree = 1. For the remaining items, strongly disagree = 1, disagree = 2, neutral = 3, agree = 4, and strongly agree = 5. The total of the student's scores indicates the extent of his or her agreement with a Freudian perspective. The higher the score (minimum = 15, maximum = 75) the greater the student's concurrence with a psychoanalytic perspective.

Miserandino, M. (1994). Freudian principles in everyday life. *Teaching of Psychology, 21*(2), 93–95.

AV: Sigmund Freud (17 min., Insight Media)

Using documentary footage, this film takes viewers into Freud's home in Vienna and offers a rare view of Freud's personal world. Narrated by Eli Wallach, it shows Freud's collection of antiquities and points out the parallels between his interests in archaeology and in exploring a person's past to gain insight into his or her personality.

AV: Erik Erikson: A Life's Work (38 min., Insight Media)

Working from the perspective of the biopsychosocial model, this film combines biographical information and interviews with Erik Erikson with a thorough description of the theorist's eight psychosocial crises.

Behaviorism

AV: Learning (30 min., Insight Media)

This video (1990) reviews the basic principles of Pavlovian and operant conditioning. Highlights include an interview with B. F. Skinner and a segment in which operant conditioning principles are used to help hyperactive children.

Teaching Tip: Rehearsal, Reinforcement, and Learning Students' Names

Mastering the names of your students early in the course is a powerful way to make them feel important, and to demonstrate that you are genuinely interested in them. Doing so in a large lecture class, however, can be a real challenge. Although some teachers rely on seating charts, composite photos, and other devices, a simple and fun in-class activity is to ask the first student in row 1 to say his or her first and last name, the second student to repeat that name and to add his or her own, the third student to repeat the names of the first two and add his or her own, and so forth, concluding with YOUR repeating all the names, followed by your own. This works very well for classes up to about 30–35 students, and offers a number of added bonuses. First, it is a great icebreaker for the class as memory lapses, mispronunciations, and the like create some comic relief from the tension of being "up next." Second, the activity can later be used to illustrate a number of psychological principles, including the benefits of repetition, rehearsal, and reinforcement.

Teaching Tip: Basic Terminology of Behaviorism

To help students master the complex terminology of behaviorism, ask for volunteers who want to change some aspect of their behavior—for instance, studying more and watching television less, controlling their temper, or speaking up when they have something to say. When you have a volunteer, put these terms on the board*: stimulus, response, classical conditioning, operant conditioning, reinforcement, reinforcer,* and *modeling.* Then ask your volunteer to identify the current link between the stimulus (the environmental conditions that trigger the behavior) and the response (the behavior in question), and the desired link. Have the class offer examples of classical and operant conditioning that might be useful in effecting a change. In the course of the discussion, note which suggestions are classical and which are operant, and so forth. In addition, be sure to emphasize the degree to which reinforcers are specific (and intrinsic) to the individual (ideally, one of your students will point out that the volunteer has to be asked what he or she enjoys before the class can decide on the best reinforcers).

AV: Pavlov: The Conditioned Reflex (25 min., black and white, Films for the Humanities and Sciences)

This documentary makes a good introduction to behaviorism. Originally produced for Russian television, the film reviews the life and career of Nobel Prize–winning scientist Ivan Pavlov and includes rare footage of Pavlov at work.m

Classroom Activity: Freud and Watson

Sigmund Freud and John Watson are two of the most influential theorists in psychology, yet they are rarely considered as having an influence on each other's work. However, in a careful review of the history of both men's writing, Mark Rilling (2000) argues that the early connections between psychoanalysis and behaviorism were extensive. In fact, he argues that Watson played a major role in the process by which Freud's ideas were assimilated into American culture.

Watson contributed to the "Americanization of psychoanalysis" in two important ways. First, Watson was influential in urging psychologists to adapt their methodology to conduct a scientific appraisal of Freud's theories. Second, as one of America's first great "pop psychologists," Watson used the language of behaviorism to "explain" psychoanalytic concepts in numerous popular articles and books.

Freud's ideas were becoming increasingly influential in the United States between 1909 and the mid-1920s, at about the same time that Watson was developing behaviorism. Although Watson was initially ambivalent about Freud, his autobiography reveals that an anxiety attack "in a way prepared me to accept a large part of Freud when I first began to get really acquainted with him around 1910."

In 1909, Freud made his only visit to America to deliver a series of lectures on psychoanalysis at Clark University. Although Watson did not attend the conference, he apparently recognized the challenges it placed on his own theory of behavior. Watson's solution was to explain Freud in terms of Pavlov's classical conditioning theory, with the ultimate goal of assimilating psychoanalysis into behaviorism.

Rilling notes that the impetus for Watson's infamous Little Albert study was his desire to adapt Pavlov's methods to study the emotions of infants. Why study emotions? Because Freud considered emotional disturbance a cornerstone of psychopathology, and Watson sought to empirically test this aspect of psychoanalytic theory by studying it in the laboratory. The ensuing program of research on children's learning of fears led to Watson's most original contribution to learning theory: the discovery of a new category of conditioning called *conditioned emotional responses (CER).*

The idea of the CER is that a strong, learned emotion, or *conditioned response*, can be established when a neutral (nonemotional) stimulus becomes associated with an unconditioned stimulus that automatically triggers a strong, involuntary emotional state, or *unconditioned response.* Rilling's thesis is that this important idea emerged from two sources: Watson's interest in classical conditioning and his effort to explain psychoanalytic concepts behavioristically, using concepts from classical conditioning.

Watson coined the term *conditioned emotional response* to compete with two psychoanalytic concepts that were part of Freud's theory of affect: transference and displacement. But Freud's influence on Watson was lost to history, because use of Pavlovian vocabulary masked the psychoanalytic influence on his work.

Watson described how he differed from Freud when he first introduced the concept of the CER in the following way.

> As I view the matter we have here just the situation for arousing *conditioned emotional reflexes*. Any stimulus (nonemotional) which immediately (or shortly) follows an emotionally exciting stimulus produces its motor reaction before the emotional effects of the original stimulus have died down. A transfer (conditioned reflex) takes place (after many such occurrences) so that in the end the second stimulus produces in its train now not only its proper group of motor integrations, but an emotional set which *belonged originally to another stimulus*. Surely it is better to use even this crude formulation than to describe the phenomenon as is done in the current psychoanalytic treatises. (Watson, 1916, cited in Rilling, 2000)

With the CER, Watson finally had a concept that could explain the transfer of emotion without an appeal to Freud's unconscious. Fears could be transferred from one stimulus to another in the laboratory by means of classical conditioning. Although Watson understood that Freud's patients entered psychoanalysis with their transferences already in place, this simplified analogue of transference in the laboratory satisfied the behaviorist, who "must have a uniform procedure which will allow at least approximate reproducibility of his results. He must have his phenomena under such control that he can watch their inception, course, and end" (Watson & Morgan, 1917, cited in Rilling, 2000).

Following publication of the successful conditioning of 11-month-old Albert's fear of a laboratory rat, which *generalized* to a variety of other furry objects, Watson went on the offensive with this direct attack on psychoanalysis.

> The Freudians twenty years from now, unless their hypotheses change, when they come to analyze Albert's fear of a seal skin coat—assuming that he comes to analysis at that age—will probably tease from him the recital of a dream which upon their analysis will show that Albert at three years of age attempted to play with the pubic hair of the mother and was scolded violently for it. (Watson & Rayner, 1924, cited in Rilling, 2000)

As Rilling notes, this parody was probably intended to indicate the unparsimonious nature of an Oedipal interpretation of adult psychopathology. More important, it thus appears that Freud deserves credit for the origins of Watson's thinking about transference, and Watson emerges from the Little Albert study as a pioneer in the scientific appraisal of Freud.

In describing the shift in Watson's thinking regarding psychoanalysis, Rilling notes that between 1910 and 1916, Watson was quite enthusiastic about Freudian concepts as a fertile source of ideas for research. Between 1916 and 1920, Watson absorbed Freud's work on emotions along with Pavlov's work on classical conditioning. In the end, of course, Watson became an arch anti-Freudian. This phase began after 1920 when Watson left academic life for a career in advertising. His treatise *Behaviorism* was liberally sprinkled with attacks on psychoanalysis, which was referred to as "Voodooism" (Watson, 1924, cited in Rilling, 2000). Watson went on "to predict that 20 years from now an analyst using Freudian concepts and Freudian terminology will be placed in the same category as a phrenologist" (Watson, 1924, cited in Rilling, 2000).

Rilling, M. (2000). John Watson's paradoxical struggle to explain Freud. *American Psychologist, 55*(3), 301–312.

AV: B. F. Skinner on Behaviorism (28 min., RMI Media Productions)

The late eminent behaviorist discusses behavior modification, behavioral technology, the role of reinforcement in shaping human behavior, and the application of principles of learning to larger social concerns.

AV: B. F. Skinner and Behavior Change: Research, Practice, and Promise (45 min., Research Press)

This film takes behaviorist principles out of the laboratory and shows that they have many practical applications. It features six actual situations, including one in which parents work with an autistic child and another in which future dentists learn how to reduce children's fear of dentistry. Particularly interesting to the more sophisticated student is a discussion of ethical and philosophical questions and the future of behaviorism. The discussion is between Skinner and a dozen well-known behaviorist researchers, including Sidney Bijou, C. B. Ferster, Fred Keller, Joseph Cautela, and Gerald Patterson.

AV: Childhood Aggression (30 min., Research Press)

In this case study, the parents and teacher of a hostile, difficult child learn to use time-outs, tracking techniques, and positive reinforcement for desirable behavior. Specific changes for the better, as well as a general improvement in the milieu, occur. This approach is explained in the film by Gerald Patterson of the Oregon Research Institute.

AV: The Power of Positive Reinforcement (28 min., CRM/McGraw-Hill)

This film provides a good introduction to the application of principles of operant conditioning to business and industry. Its message is that all workers—from factory workers to executives—are searching for feedback (reinforcement) for their job performance. The effectiveness of positive reinforcement is examined at a 3M plant in California, an amusement park in Minnesota, on members of the Minnesota Vikings football team, and with sanitation department workers in the city of Detroit.

Classroom Activity: Using a Token Economy to Bring Behaviorism to Life (and Increase Class Participation)

Extensive research attests to the importance of active learning, which occurs when students engage and process information rather than passively receive it. Instructors facilitate active learning by frequently challenging the class with questions related to the material and by encouraging students to offer their own questions and comments. However, many of these instructors panic when they experience the "dreaded silence"—the uncomfortable time following the question when no one responds. This is a particular problem in large classes in which students feel anonymous and are reluctant to participate.

Kurt Boniecki and Stacy Moore of the University of Central Arkansas propose a procedure for increasing student participation that has the added benefit of bringing behaviorism to life for students. The procedure involves establishing a token economy in which students earn tokens for participation and then exchange those tokens for extra credit. This can be accomplished in several ways; the most effective technique involves tossing an actual poker chip, wooden checker piece (available at most hobby shops), or some such token to the student immediately after a correct answer. (This itself can be discussed as underscoring the greater effectiveness of immediate reinforcement as compared with delayed reinforcement.) At the end of each class meeting, students turn in any tokens they collect and the instructor immediately records the amount of extra credit earned. Instructors who do not like to use extra credit in their courses might consider making the tokens worth credit toward "purchasing" desirable options, such as dropping a quiz. Another possibility is not to use tokens but to toss a piece of candy or some other easily delivered reward.

Boniecki and Moore field-tested their token economy over 11 class meetings near the end of the term of a relatively large ($N = 63$) undergraduate psychology course. Each class meeting, the instructor periodically posed a question to the class (averaging 4.18 questions per class meeting). The instructor called on students in the order they raised their hands until the question was correctly answered. If no one raised a hand within one minute, the instructor announced the answer and continued with the lecture.

During each class, a research assistant, posing as a student, sat in the last row of the classroom where he or she had an unobstructed view of all students. The assistant recorded the amount of direct participation (the number of students raising their hands in response to the instructor's question), latency of participation (the amount of time following a question until the first hand was raised), and the amount of general, nondirected participation (the number of times any student spontaneously asked the instructor a question or engaged the instructor in discussion). To determine the effectiveness of the token economy, these data were collected during the first 4 of the 11 class meetings, constituting a baseline period during which no tokens were delivered.

Over the next four classes, the token economy was put in place. At the end of each class, students could exchange each token for one point added to their next exam grade. Each exam point was worth 0.25 percent of the final grade. Tokens had to be turned in immediately after the class in order to be exchanged for credit, thus ensuring that the instructor needed only enough tokens for one class. During the final three classes, the token economy was removed. The instructor told the class that tokens would no longer be offered for correct answers. Students who had not earned extra credit during the token economy were allowed to complete alternative extra credit assignments during the removal period.

The amount of directed and nondirected participation dramatically increased during the token economy. Students were more than twice as likely to raise their hands to answer a question during the token economy than during the baseline or removal periods. Similarly, students were more than twice as likely to spontaneously ask questions and make comments during the token economy than during the baseline or removal periods. All these differences were statistically significant. Equally significant was the fact that students enjoyed the procedure, with many commenting that it made the class more exciting and interactive. The researchers did notice an increase in student attendance, enthusiasm, and preparation during token economy classes.

Another benefit of this exercise is to bring to life a discussion of the pros and cons of active learning in the high school or middle school classroom—a topic that is covered later in the text as part of a discussion on changing educational curricula. You may wish to discuss it here as well; at the beginning of the course, this type of "applied psychology" may have an impact on how students study the material in your course, as well as others.

Boniecki, K. A., & Moore, S. (2002, January). *Breaking the silence: Using a token economy to reinforce participation in a college classroom.* Paper presented at the meeting of the National Institute on the Teaching of Psychology (NITOP), St. Petersburg, FL.

AV: Observational Learning (23 min., HarperCollins)

Written and narrated by Robert Liebert, who is responsible for some of the best research on the effects of television on children, this film provides a good general introduction to the social learning approach to developmental psychology, as Liebert explains how parents, peers, and the media affect a child's behavior.

Classroom Activity: Observational Learning

To extend the text coverage of social learning theory and modeling, you might discuss social psychologist Robert Cialdini's suggestion that our tendency to model the behavior of other people is often exploited. For example, when advertisers tell us their product is the "biggest seller" or the "fastest growing" product of its type, they hope we will be encouraged to buy it because so many others have already done so. For the same reason, contributors' names are often listed during charity telethons to encourage imitation from viewers who have not yet phoned in their pledges.

Your students are sure to come up with other everyday examples of the ways in which the human tendency to imitate the behavior of others is often exploited.

Cialdini, R. (2007). *Influence: The psychology of persuasion.* New York: Collins Business Essentials Series.

AV: Learning: Observational and Cognitive Approaches (30 min., Insight Media)

Profiling pioneering researcher Albert Bandura, this video explores observational learning, focusing on the cognitive components of modeling. Also discussed are latent learning, cognitive maps, learned helplessness, and instinctive drift. A final segment describes the role of vicarious conditioning in teaching new skills and the use of behavior modification.

Cognitive Theory

Teaching Tip: Developmental Stages of Family and Friends

To enhance student understanding of the developmental stage theories of Piaget and Erikson, help them make connections between the course material and their own lives. After your students have read the text discussions, spend a few minutes of class time reviewing Piaget's periods of cognitive development and Erikson's psychosocial stages. Next, ask your students to list each period on a piece of paper. Then, have them think of a friend or relative whom they would place in each stage. Have students briefly explain why they put that individual in a particular stage, including actual examples of behavior whenever possible.

Classroom Activity: Classroom Debate: *"Resolved: Cognitive Development Is Most Accurately Characterized as a Continuous Process Rather Than as Occurring in a Sequence of Stages"*

As early as the seventeenth century, philosophers such as John Locke and Jean-Jacques Rousseau noted the importance of early life experiences on later development and the uniqueness of childhood as a separate stage of life. Developmentalists since then have generally agreed that development from childhood to adulthood involves an orderly sequence of behavioral changes. They have not agreed, however, on whether development occurs gradually and continuously or in a series of discrete, and qualitatively distinct, stages.

Stage theorists such as G. Stanley Hall, Jean Piaget, Sigmund Freud, and Erik Erikson assume a biological, cognitive, or psychoanalytic perspective on development, respectively. Those who endorse a nonstage view, such as B. F. Skinner and Albert Bandura, assume a learning perspective on development and perceive development as a gradual and continuous process, without stages that differ qualitatively from one another.

On no other issue has the debate between stage and nonstage theorists been more heatedly waged than on that of how best to describe cognitive development in children. After years of careful observation of children, Swiss psychologist Jean Piaget developed his enormously influential (and widely accepted) stage theory of cognitive development, which is outlined in the text. Newer procedures for testing the cognitive functioning of children suggest, however, that Piaget, who used the method of scientific observation, underestimated the intellectual abilities of children. For example, if test conditions are arranged so that children's responses depend less on their language ability than is the case in standard Piagetian tasks, the quality of their thinking does not change significantly from one stage to another. Similarly, the fact that young children do not perform as well as older children on tests of memory may be due to differences in memory capacity rather than to stages of cognitive development, as was once believed.

To help your students understand differences between stage and nonstage theories, as well as how theory and methodology sometimes bias experimental results, follow the guidelines in the General Resources section of this manual for scheduling a classroom debate on the preceding resolution. Reference material from journals and textbooks may be chosen by the instructor and placed on reserve in the college library or left for students to uncover. Alternatively, you may wish to schedule this debate later in the course, after your students have studied the material on Piaget's theory provided later in the text.

"On Your Own" Activity: The Active Search for Knowledge

Intelligence involves the continual adaptation of organizational structures to make sense of new ideas and experiences. To help your students understand that this cognitive processing operates throughout the life span, ask each student to interview an older adult who has returned to school. (If older adults are in your class, you might simply have them answer the questions in Handout 5 during a discussion period.)

Students should discover that older adults remain active searchers for knowledge and that they continually adapt to new ideas and experiences. Older adults may report changes in their memory, motivation, or ability to master abstract material. They may say that they do not learn as quickly as younger adults or that they need more careful preparation. They will probably cite stronger motivation and a firmer base of life experience within which to organize new material. Although responses will vary, most answers will reflect some changes in the way older adults think and learn. You may want to take this opportunity to link adult learning with the stage theory of cognition.

AV: Piaget's Developmental Theory (Set of three films: *Classification,* 17 min.; *Conservation,* 28 min.; *Formal Thought,* 32 min., Davidson Films)

Piaget's theory, methods of classification, and stages in

the development of intelligence are described. This film incorporates many demonstrations of children's thinking at different stages of development and explains how educational programs based on Piagetian principles can help children make transitions from one stage to the next.

AV: How Young Children Learn to Think (19 min., Insight Media)

This brief video conversation with Constance Kamii presents an especially clear and concise explanation of Piaget's theory of childhood cognition.

AV: Jean Piaget: Memory and Intelligence (44 min., Davidson Films)

Piaget is filmed giving a lecture to a Japanese conference on preschool education. In the first half of the film, Piaget effectively contrasts his views of education with traditional approaches. The second half deals specifically with Piaget's experiments on reconstructive memory. The film, which is in French with carefully written English subtitles, avoids being boring (as many filmed lectures are) because of Piaget's enthusiasm and charisma.

AV: Cognitive Development (20 min., CRM/McGraw-Hill)

This film, which is best shown after the students have read the text discussion of cognitive theory, begins with a brief review of Piaget's stages and some of his terminology. It then shows two contrasting kindergartens, one based on "discovery" learning and the other on a strict application of behaviorist principles, as interpreted by Bereiter and Englemann. In class, the instructor and the students can identify comparable types of education for older children and for adolescents (and college students?), and then discuss the merits of carefully preprogrammed instruction versus more spontaneous learning. Showing this movie is a good way to help students see that various theoretical ideas can lead to contrasting and controversial applications.

Newer Theories

Sociocultural Theory

AV: I'm Normal, You're Weird: Understanding Other Cultures (23 min., Insight Media)

In this entertaining film, a group of aliens prepares to take human form. As they rehearse their new roles, they discover that human behavior has an extensive cultural basis.

AV: Culture (30 min., Insight Media)

Taking the viewer to different regions of the United States, this video vividly displays the ways in which different subcultures address individual needs. The societies explored include Chinese settlements in the South, Cajun settlements in Louisiana, and Native American.

AV: Introduction to Culture and Diversity (60 min., Insight Media)

Beginning by differentiating culture, macroculture, and microculture, this film considers various subcultures and religious groups in the United States. A student discussion focuses on the dangers of viewing groups from ethnocentric perspectives.

AV: Social-Cultural Diversity (30 min., Insight Media)

Developed for classroom teachers, this program explores the role that a student's cultural background plays in his or her learning style and behavior. The effects on students of stereotypes based on culture, socioeconomic status, and gender are also discussed.

AV: Contexts of Development (30 min., RMI Media Productions)

(See description in the Introduction.)

AV: The Latino Family (28 min., Films for the Humanities and Sciences)

In following three generations of one Mexican American family, this film illustrates both the changes and the endurance of traditional Latino family member roles. In doing so, it provides a good introduction to sociocultural theory.

AV: Street Children of Africa (52 min., Films for the Humanities and Sciences)

This captivating film explores a tragic worldwide phenomenon: homeless children. Focusing on children in West Africa with no means of support other than what they scrounge from the street, the program invites comparisons with American children and poignantly highlights sociocultural influences on development.

Internet Activity: High-Quality Preschool Education: What Would Vygotsky Say?

The Internet is an excellent resource for learning about prominent developmental theorists. For example, a Web site devoted to Lev Vygotsky contains a wealth of biographical and professional information. Have students search the Web to find answers to the questions in Handout 6.

AV: Vygotsky's Developmental Theory: An Introduction (30 min., Davidson Films)

Hosted by psychologist Elena Bodrova, this film introduces the life and theory of the seminal Russian theorist who increasingly is being cited in developmental research today. The program focuses on four integral concepts: children construct knowledge; learning leads development; development cannot be isolated from its social context; and language plays a key role in development.

AV: Play: A Vygotskian Approach (26 min., Davidson Films)

Using enchanting sequences of young children at play, this video reviews the various methods of studying play. These include the Freudian–Eriksonian emphasis on emotional content, the Piagetian emphasis on symbolic representation, the social psychological approach, and, especially, Lev Vygotsky's view of play as a zone of proximal development.

AV: Learning in Context: Probing the Theories of Piaget and Vygotsky (31 min., Films for the Humanities and Sciences)

This program examines three sets of experiments that demonstrate the influence of contextual factors in learning: (1) tasks involving gender-biased instructions; (2) tasks that require cooperation with others; and (3) tasks involving the training of students by peers and adults. The film provides a segue for a discussion of the impact of stereotyping on performance, the effects of self-perception on competence, and how different methods of teaching influence student performance.

The Universal Perspective: Humanism and Evolutionary Theory

Classroom Activity: Applying Humanism, Evolutionary Theory, and Other Theoretical Perspectives

To stimulate students' understanding of humanism, evolutionary theory, and developmental psychology's other theoretical perspectives, give them some practice in applying these perspectives to several behaviors not discussed in the text. Divide the class into small groups of four and five students each and have them identify a behavior they find interesting. Randy Larsen and David Buss suggest using personality characteristics such as narcissism, perfectionism, and procrastination, but almost any behavior pattern or developmental trait will work. Ask each group to prepare six sentences about the characteristic, one to represent each of developmental psychology's major theoretical perspectives: psychoanalytic, behavioral, cognitive, evolutionary, humanist, and sociocultural. Each sentence should make a statement or pose a question about the specific behavior or trait from a given perspective. Allot 15 or 20 minutes for the task and then have each group report to the full class.

As an alternative, or in addition to the above class exercise, Martin Bolt suggested distributing Handout 7 to each student or each small group. The handout provides six sentences regarding prosocial or helping behavior. Each statement represents one of the major theoretical perspectives. Give students 5 or 10 minutes to connect each statement to its appropriate perspective. The correct answers are as follows: 1. Evolutionary, 2. Psychoanalytic, 3. Cognitive, 4. Sociocultural, 5. Behaviorism, 6. Humanism.

Bolt, M. (2011). Instructor's resources to accompany Myers *Exploring Psychology* (8th ed.). New York: Worth.

Larsen, R. J., & Buss, D. M. (2008). *Personality psychology: Domains of knowledge about human nature* (3rd. ed.). Boston: McGraw-Hill.

Classroom Activity: The Nurture Assumption: Why Children Turn Out the Way They Do

Even before Judith Rich Harris's book *The Nurture Assumption: Why Children Turn Out the Way They Do* appeared in bookstores, the popular media was ballyhooing its seemingly novel insight. Before this book, Harris had written several developmental textbooks that mostly maintained that children were shaped by their parents' child-rearing style. On January 20, 1994, she reportedly experienced a moment of revelation regarding why children often turn out in unexpected ways: "Genes matter and peers matter, but parents don't matter" (as stated in the book's foreword).

Critics were surprised at the magnitude of the public response to Harris's book. After all, the fact that offspring raised side by side often develop very different personalities has been well known to parents since antiquity. And although some developmentalists before Harris emphasized parental style over peer groups in determining how children turn out, parents have always been concerned about peer-group influence and have tried to turn their kids away from negative peer influences toward more positive ones.

People may have accepted Harris's views in large part because several generalizations from developmental psychology permeate her writing: (1) development is discontinuous; (2) children who flounder developmentally compared with their peers tend to be propelled downward, while those who achieve success are pushed upward; and (3) there is no unified organization of personality, such as a self-concept, that remains constant in all or most situations.

Harris's newest book, *No Two Alike: Human Nature and Human Individuality,* has breathed life into the nature–nurture controversy and has spawned a national debate on its political implications. For example, her analysis of how young people naturally form peer groups that define themselves by excluding others helps us understand why multicultural and bilingual education, college-admission quotas, and coed military training unintentionally worsen race and sex relations.

Critics have noted that Harris's assertion that parents don't matter is plausible only within a very narrow, arbitrary boundary. For example, to show that peers outweigh parents in importance, Harris cites studies of how young immigrant children take on the accents of their playmates, not their parents. "True," argues businessman and writer (and blogger) Steven Sailer, "but there's more to life than language." Immigrant parents do pass down numerous aspects of their culture, especially those that are more often home-based, such as food preferences, attitudes and values, and so forth. "To fully explain human behavior," he maintains, "everything matters. Anything conceivable (whether genes, peers, parents, cousins, teachers, TV, incest, martial-arts training, breast-feeding, prenatal environment, etc.) can influence something (whether personality, IQ, sexual orientation, culture, morals, job skills, etc.)."

Sailer also finds fault with Harris's distinction between "direct" and "indirect" parental influence. (For example, parents who work overtime and make financial sacrifices to get their kids into neighborhoods and schools offering better peer groups are said to be exerting an "indirect" influence.) Sailer suggests that the failure of developmentalists to find reliable relationships between "direct" influences (e.g., different child-rearing styles) and how children turn out may reflect a methodological shortcoming rather than the absence of an actual relationship.

As a case in point, Sailer attacks Harris's assertion that studies prove it doesn't matter whether mothers work or not. "But the same methodology," he notes, "would report that it doesn't matter whether you buy a minivan or a Miata, since purchasers of different classes of vehicles report roughly similar satisfaction. In reality, women don't randomly choose home or work; they agonize over balancing career and family. They tailor their family size to fit their career ambitions, and vice versa. Mothers will then readjust as necessary, looking for the compromise that best meets their particular family's conflicting needs for money and mothering. For instance, a working mother might quit when her second baby proves unexpectedly colicky, then return when the children enter school, then shift to part-time work after her husband gets a big raise. This nonrandom behavior of moms is bad for these studies, but good for their kids."

To stimulate a good class discussion on this subject, you might assign a portion of each of Harris's books for the entire class to read. Alternatively, you may have different groups of students read and report on separate chapters of the book. However you choose to bring the subject up, students are sure to have strong feelings about it.

Harris, J. R. (1998). *The nurture assumption: Why children turn out the way they do.* New York: The Free Press.

Harris, J. R. (2007). *No two alike: Human nature and human individuality.* New York: Norton.

Sailer, S. (1998, October 12). The nature of nurture. *National Review, 50*(19), 57–58.

Classroom Activity: The Blank Slate, the Noble Savage, and the Ghost in the Machine

The application of evolutionary theory to human development brings the nature–nurture debate back to the forefront. In his book, *The Blank Slate,* MIT Professor Steven Pinker argues that many contemporary intellectuals deny the existence of human nature by embracing three dogmas: the blank slate (the mind has no innate traits that will come to identify the person), the noble savage (people are born good and corrupted by their environments), and the ghost in the machine (each person has a soul and free will apart from his or her biology).

The "slate" of Pinker's title refers to the popular *tabula rasa* concept introduced by philosopher John Locke and carried down through the centuries. According to this doctrine, personality, behavior, and intelligence cannot be inherited and so are shaped completely by parenting, culture, and society. This argument is, of course, simply a variation of the nurture side of the nature–nurture debate, which Pinker concludes is over, with nurture failing to win—by a long shot. Pinker's conclusion is based on the body of empirical results that have been replicated time and again over the past 40 years. Pinker maintains that the three fundamental laws of behavioral genetics that derive from this body of evidence are the most important discoveries in the history of psychology. These laws are that

- All human behavioral traits are heritable.
- The effect of being raised in the same family is smaller than the effect of genes.
- A substantial portion of the variation in complex human behavioral traits is not accounted for by either genes or families.

Stated another way, Pinker breaks down the influences that shape development in the following way: "genes, 50 percent; shared environment, 0 percent; unique environment, 50 percent." Shared environment consists of experiences that impinge on the child and his or her siblings alike, including parental behaviors, home life, and neighborhood. Nonshared (unique) environment is everything else. This includes anything experienced by one sibling but not by another, such as parental favoritism, and unique experiences such as a childhood accident.

If shared influences do not shape children significantly, as Pinker contends, what is the missing environmental factor? Pinker's answer is to agree with Judith Rich Harris (see earlier Classroom Activity), that this factor is the child's peer group. "One way that peers could explain personality," Pinker states, "is that children in the same family may join different peer groups—the jocks, the brains, the preppies, the punks, the Goths—and assimilate their values. But then, how do children get sorted into peer groups? If it is by their inborn traits—smart kids join the brains, aggressive kids join the punks, and so on—then effects of the peer group would show up as indirect effects of the genes, not as effects of the unique environment. If it is their parents' choice of neighborhoods, it would turn up as effects of the shared environment, because siblings growing up together share a neighborhood as well as a set of parents." Like Harris, Pinker concludes that which child fills which niche in any specific peer group is largely a matter of chance.

In addition to discussing Pinker's take on the nature–nurture debate in your class, you may wish to assign different groups of students to read the award-winning book and report back to the class on each of the three dogmas.

Pinker, S. (2003). *The blank slate: The modern denial of human nature.* New York: Viking Penguin.

Teaching Tip: Evolutionary Psychology: Raising the "Why of Behavior" Question

Fundamentally, a "genetic predisposition," or developmental force, is presumed to exist because (1) genetic diversity promotes the survival of a species; and (2) through the process of natural selection, those predispositions and developmental forces that promote reproductive success (fitness) are passed on to the next generation.

If your students are typical, many are likely to have misconceptions about evolution. Peter Gray notes that one common misconception is that "lower" species are slowly evolving into humans. Another is that evolution is a mystical force working toward some planned end or future purpose.

For example, some students are likely to think of humans as the "most evolved" creatures, followed by chimps and other apes, mammals, and so forth. Following this line of reasoning, the "lowly amoeba" is viewed as an early step toward becoming a human being. But, as Gray notes, the amoeba has been evolving just as long as humans have and "is as complete and adapted to its environment as we are to ours. The amoeba has no more chance of evolving to become like us than we have of evolving to become like it."

To help students overcome such misconceptions, you may need to do more than simply remind them that only genetic changes that are immediately beneficial to the organism (that is, those that increase survival and reproduction) will survive through natural selection. Gray suggests giving examples of current evolution. For example, you might cite the small-scale rapid evolution of wing color that occurred in peppered moths living in and around London over the past 150 years. Before the mid-nineteenth century, the wings of peppered moths were a very light, mottled color that matched the lichen growing on the trees on which they spent much of their time. This coloration provided an effective camouflage against the trees that kept them from being seen and eaten by birds. But with the Industrial Revolution, the air of cities became so polluted that the lichen could not survive and the tree bark became much darker. In this new environment, the few mutant moths that occurred in each generation with darker wing color (which in earlier generations almost never survived) now were more effectively hidden and therefore were more likely to survive and reproduce. By the mid-twentieth century, over 90 percent of London's moths had dark wings.

Another way to get students to focus on the evolutionary perspective is to ask them to consider the possible evolutionary advantage of specific behaviors and traits that are universally human. Gray suggests using the example of children's resistance to going to sleep at bedtime. Ask the class, "What advantage to our species could possibly be served by young children resisting going to bed?" A sharp student is sure to realize that some children resist bedtime because they are afraid of being alone in the dark—a healthy fear during prehistoric times, when the hazards to survival were quite real. Children who managed to keep the attention of adults on them probably were more likely to survive the night than their uncomplaining counterparts.

If students protest that this type of after-the-fact reasoning proves nothing, play your "ace" by noting that cross-cultural studies provide a converging line of evidence. Among present-day hunter-gatherer societies, putting a child to bed alone is frequently considered a form of child maltreatment. Moreover, in cultures where young children generally sleep with an adult, bedtime protests are much less common. Finally, you might note that light-colored wings are once again becoming prevalent on peppered moths, as antipollution laws have cleaned up London's air over the past few decades.

As a preface to this discussion, you might wish to assign the "On Your Own" Activity that follows, which introduces the evolutionary perspective in a provocative way that is sure to stimulate students' interest.

Gray, P. (1996). Incorporating evolutionary theory into the teaching of psychology. *Teaching of Psychology, 23,* 207–214.

"On Your Own" Activity: Introducing Evolutionary Psychology

To introduce several basic principles of evolutionary psychology (see also the relevant Classroom Activities), Martin Bolt suggested distributing copies of Bernard Weiner's (1992) handout (8) during class (it takes about 5 minutes to complete).

The basic premise of evolutionary psychology is that the human body (and human behavior) is just the vehicle and mechanism by which our genes reproduce. According to this viewpoint, the fundamental motive for all behavior is to act in ways that enhance the likelihood of sending our genes into the future.

Reflecting this motive, students are more likely to choose the 5- and 20-year-olds in response to questions 1 and 2. According to Weiner, this is because children are more likely to die before age 5 (and so the 5-year-old is more likely to reproduce), just as 20-year-olds are more likely to have additional children than are their older counterparts.

According to the evolutionary perspective, males and females are selected for somewhat different traits of attraction to the opposite gender. Due to the essentially infinite supply of sperm, males presumably are more likely to be attracted to young, fertile-appearing women. Because the reproductive potential of females is much more limited, however, females are believed to be selected for attraction to males who have more resources to assist in child care. Thus, in response to question 3, females should choose older males, while males should choose younger females. Following the same logic, females should choose items *a, c,* and *e* in question 4, while males should choose *b, d,* and *f.*

For question 5, females have the advantage of knowing that any child they bear is genetically "theirs," so maternal grandparents—assured that the grandchildren are genetically related—should be pleased with the birth.

Finally, the greater the parental investment in a child and the greater each child's reproductive potential, the greater the expected grief upon the death of a child. Thus, for question 6, mothers, parents of the mother, and older parents (who are less likely to reproduce again themselves) should experience greater grief. For question 7, grief should be greatest for parents of a healthy child.

Bolt, M. (2012). Instructor's resources to accompany Myers *Psychology in Everyday Life* (2nd ed.). New York: Worth.

Weiner, B. (1992). *Human motivation: Metaphors, theories, and research*. Newbury Park, CA: Sage.

What Theories Contribute

AV: Theories (27 min., Magna Systems, Inc.)

One of the modules from the Developing Child Series, this film reviews the major developmental theories: cognitive, behaviorist (including social learning), sociocultural, and psychoanalytic. Specific theorists discussed include Piaget, Vygotsky, Skinner, Erikson, Freud, and Gesell.

Teaching Tip: The Role of Theories in Developmental Study

Most students tend to wonder, "Why can't we just concentrate on the facts and dispense with hypothetical or theoretical statements?" To help explain the role of theories in developmental study, you might offer everyday examples of the ways in which theories clarify, interpret, and suggest new hypotheses—for example, "Eating breakfast before a test helps me do better" and "If I take an umbrella, it's certain not to rain today." Have students come up with others. You might also point out that even simple items that we take for granted—an eggbeater, a pencil sharpener, a light switch, rollerblades—would not exist without the theories behind their design and manufacture. In addition, you might explain that seemingly practical approaches to problems are based on theory. For example, the idea of providing alternative behaviors through rehabilitation reflects the prison system's realization that positive reinforcement is more effective than punishment.

To approach the broader issue of the role of theories, find a topic of current interest—one on which students are sure to have differing views due to conflicting interpretations of the facts. Examples include drug use and whether it should be legalized, how we should respond to acts of terrorism, whether handguns should be outlawed, whether capital punishment is a deterrent for potential criminals, and how society should treat victims of AIDS. Local news events, sports, or campus controversies might also be discussed.

Classroom Activity: A Test of Three Theories of the Work–Family Interface

To help your students understand how developmentalists use the scientific method to carefully formulate hypotheses that, when empirically tested, shed light on the strengths and weaknesses of various theories, you might discuss a study on the work–family interface.

Three different theoretical models have been advanced to explain the interaction between work and family life. According to the *role strain theory*, the responsibilities from different, separate domains compete for limited amounts of time, physical energy, and psychological resources. According to the *role enhancement theory*, participation in multiple roles provides a greater number of opportunities and resources to the individual that can be used to promote growth and better functioning in other life domains.

In contrast to these models, Bronfenbrenner's ecological-systems model suggests that the work–family experience is a joint function of process, person, context, and time characteristics. Ecological-systems theory suggests that each type of characteristic exerts an additive, interactive, and potentially positive or negative effect on an individual's work–family experience.

As a test of these theories, Joseph Grzywacz and Nadine Marks (2000) formulated two major hypotheses:

- The work and family contexts overlap via four dimensions of *spillover*: negative spillover from work to family, negative spillover from family to work, positive spillover from work to family, and positive spillover from family to work.
- A higher level of negative spillover between work and family, both work to family and family to work, will be associated with fewer ecological resources (for example, less support from coworkers and supervisors, and a lower level of family support).

To test these hypotheses the researchers used data from the National Survey of Midlife Development in the United States (MIDUS) collected in 1995 by the John D. and Catherine T. MacArthur Foundation Research Network on Successful Midlife Development. The sample consisted of employed respondents aged 25 to 62 years (N = 1,986; 948 women and 1,038 men).

Dependent Variables

Factor analyses of survey responses were used to assess each dimension of spillover. Response categories for each of the items were 1 (*never*), 2 (*rarely*), 3 (*sometimes*), 4 (*most of the time*), and 5 (*all of the time*). Each item began with the question, "How often have you experienced each of the following in the past year?" This was followed by outcomes such as those listed below.

Negative spillover from work to family: (1) Your job reduces the effort you can give to activities at home. (2) Stress at work makes you irritable at home.

Positive spillover from work to family: (1) The things you do at work help you deal with personal and practical issues at home. (2) The things you do at work make you a more interesting person at home.

Negative spillover from family to work: (1) Responsibilities at home reduce the effort you can devote to your job. (2) Personal or family worries and problems distract you when you are at work.

Positive spillover from family to work: (1) Talking with someone at home helps you deal with problems at work. (2) Providing for what is needed at home makes you work harder at your job.

Independent Variables

The family microsystem was assessed by adding up the research participants' responses to items such as "How much does your spouse or partner really care about you?" and "How often do members of your family make too many demands on you?" Spousal disagreement was measured by adding responses to items measuring the level of disagreement between the respondent and her or his spouse regarding money matters, household tasks, and leisure activities.

For the work microsystem, researchers assessed the amount of perceived control each respondent had over his or her work environment with items such as "How often do you have a choice in deciding how you do your tasks at work?" and "How often do you have a choice in deciding what tasks you do at work?" In addition, psychological strain associated with work was measured by adding responses to questions such as "How often do you have to work very intensively—that is, are you very busy trying to get things done?" and "How often do different people or groups at work demand things from you that you think are hard to combine?"

Individual Characteristics

Measures for age, race/ethnicity, gender, level of educational attainment, household earnings, and two aspects of personality (i.e., neuroticism and extroversion) were also included.

Results

The results strongly supported ecological theory's broader conceptualization of work–family spillover, while indicating the incompleteness of both the role strain and role enhancement theories. Simply stated, the work and family contexts were found to be overlapping and interdependent, with both positive and negative potential effects. Among the specific findings were the following:

- A lower level of spousal disagreement was associated with less work-to-family conflict for both men and women.
- A low level of spousal support was associated with more negative spillover (and less positive spillover) from family to work.
- A lower level of decision latitude was associated with less positive spillover from work to family and from family to work among both women and men.
- A lower level of support at work from co-workers and supervisors was strongly associated with less positive spillover from work to family.
- Younger men reported more negative spillover between work and family (both work to family and family to work) and less positive spillover from family to work than older men.
- Younger women reported more positive spillover from work to family and more negative spillover from family to work than did older women.
- A low level of spousal and other family criticism/burden was strongly associated with less negative spillover from family to work.
- Education and household earnings were significantly associated with positive spillover from work to family, although these associations differed significantly by gender. Specifically, lower levels of education and income were strongly associated with a lower level of positive spillover from work to family among women but were not associated with this outcome among men.
- Having a child of any age (in contrast to having no children) is associated with more negative spillover from family to work for both women and men.
- Although previous research had found that family factors were the primary source of family-to-work conflict, these researchers found that pressure at work was also associated with negative spillover from family to work, supporting the interrelationship between work stress and family stress.
- In terms of personality characteristics, a higher level of neuroticism was associated with more negative spillover between work and family (in both directions) for both women and men, and less positive spillover between work and family among women only.
- A higher level of extroversion, on the other hand, was associated with less negative spillover and more positive spillover for both women and men.

Grzywacz, J. G., & Marks, N. F. (2000). Reconceptualizing the work–family interface: An ecological perspective on the correlates of positive and negative spillover between work and family. *Journal of Occupational Health Psychology*, *5*(1), 111–126.

Classroom Activity: Designing a Developmental Brochure for Targeted Audiences

Dani' Raap of the University of Alaska, Fairbanks, suggests a lively project to bring developmental theories to life. Raap divides the class into groups of three to six students, with each group choosing one domain of development (biological, cognitive, or social). Their task is to summarize development in that domain throughout the life span to a targeted audience—a group of nurses wanting to better understand their patients. They are permitted to choose from one of the areas of development (or come up with their own, instructor-approved topic): physical, motor, neuronal, intellectual (includes cognition, learning, and memory), emotional, sensation/perception, moral, social, personality, meaning of life, identity, health, toys, or gender. The groups are told they will set up a table at a mock nurses' convention, for which they are to design and produce a brochure to inform the nurses of what they can expect individuals to be experiencing at any time in their life span (pertaining to the area the students have chosen). The brochure should also include major developmental milestones, what stays the same and what changes throughout life, descriptions of major influences on this aspect of development, lists of myths versus facts, and recent scientific findings. At the end of the semester, Raap schedules a "developmental symposium," in which each group briefly summarizes its project and distributes copies of its developmental brochure.

The idea of a group-designed brochure can be adapted to many different aspects of development. For instance, different groups could be assigned the task of producing a brochure that describes development in one domain according to the various major theories. Another variation would be to have different groups produce brochures for different targeted audiences, especially those identified by Kathleen Berger in her marginal questions (teachers, social workers, first-time parents, grandparents, and so on).

Raap, D. (2002, January). *Course projects for targeted audiences.* Paper presented at the meeting of the National Institute on the Teaching of Psychology (NITOP), St. Petersburg, FL.

Classroom Activity: Positive Psychology

The field of positive psychology is a rich resource of ideas for college and university teachers. Insights from the field complement many educational and developmental findings on topics such as active learning, autonomy, and dignity at work. If you wish to devote a portion of a lecture to outlining this relatively new perspective, the following information should be helpful.

At its inception, psychology's focus was threefold: curing mental illness, making the lives of all people more fulfilling, and identifying and nurturing high talent. After two world wars and an economic depression, however, the focus shifted to curing mental illness. This was, perhaps, an understandable reaction to the political, economic, and social climate of the day. When civilizations face warfare, poverty, and other ills, it is only natural that science focus on trying to alleviate suffering. To this end, psychology has largely been successful. For instance, some 14 different psychological disorders have been identified and can be successfully treated. But this success has come at the expense of the other two original goals. Psychologists have scant knowledge of what makes life worth living. Since World War II, psychology has become a science largely about healing, a field that concentrates on repairing damage within a disease model of human functioning.

Proponents of the positive psychology movement believe that the time is ripe for refocusing the science of psychology toward the second and third of the field's initial goals. During times of relative peace and prosperity (at least in developed countries), the arts and sciences have historically flourished—as was the case in Athens in the fifth century B.C.E., when democracy flourished; and fifteenth-century Florence, when the arts flourished.

Positive psychology has been defined as the scientific study of optimal human functioning. It aims to discover and promote factors that allow individuals and communities to thrive. More specifically, the goal of positive psychology is to consider optimal human functioning at several levels, including biological, experiential, personal, relational, institutional, cultural, and global. Simply stated, positive psychology seeks to understand and encourage factors that allow individuals, communities, and societies to flourish.

These goals are, of course, reminiscent of Bronfenbrenner's ecological-systems model (discussed earlier in the text) and the three domains of development. For instance, the first of these goals—individual well-being—is influenced by several factors:

- *Temperament*—the inborn qualities that determine how well people interact with the environment.
- *Learned positive outlook on life*—People learn optimism and hope through experience. In addition, people achieve greater life satisfaction when they work for things they value rather than merely for things that bring immediate pleasure.
- *Strongly held values and goals related to these values*—People who have clear goals and who make progress toward achieving them report higher levels of subjective well-being.
- *Sociocultural differences*—Within limits, socioeconomic and cultural differences predict increased well-being. For example, Latin cultures report higher levels of subjective well-being than one might expect from their socioeconomic status. In addition, psychological measures such as self-esteem more accurately predict positive subjective experiences in individualistic cultures (the United States and Western Europe) than in collectivistic cultures (Japan and communist cultures).
- *Age*—People's age brings perspective and experience that affects how they view life situations. For instance, older people are more likely than younger people to view illness as part of the normal aging process. Moreover, they may have greater confidence in their ability to deal with illness and prefer a greater quality of life to mere survival.

Understanding the sources of positive subjective experiences can lead to better individuals and societies. People who report higher subjective well-being tend to contribute more to their communities; have better relationships with others; are more creative; excel in sports and academics; provide leadership; are more likely to help others; and are less of a drain on psychological and medical health systems.

To help bring the new positive psychology perspective to life, you might have students complete the following two "On Your Own" Activities on positive psychology.

Bolt, M. (2005). *Pursuing human strengths: A positive psychology guide.* New York: Worth.

"On Your Own" Activity: Applying Principles of Positive Psychology: Well-Being

To assess the content of a person's emotional life, researchers sometimes ask volunteers to keep a record of their daily experiences for weeks or even months. They can then use this information to determine how much positive and negative affect people experience. To help your students become more aware of the positive psychology movement, have them make copies of the Daily Mood Form in Handout 9 and instruct them to record their levels of affect at approximately the same time each day for a few days.

Have students calculate their affect scores as explained in the handout. If the global daily mood score is greater than zero, the student reported more positive than negative affect. If it is less than zero, the student reported more negative than positive affect.

Positive affect scores are associated with a number of traits reflecting psychological well-being and adjustment, including high self-esteem, self-confidence, satisfaction with one's life, and cheerfulness. Positive affect is strongly related to the personality trait of extroversion. In contrast, negative affect is related to neuroticism, defined as the tendency to worry and easily become upset. Interestingly, these relationships were found even when the mood measures were taken a decade after the participants' personalities were measured.

As a follow-up to this activity, consider assigning the following "On Your Own" Activity, which asks students to design a beautiful day.

Fineburg, A. C. (2002, January). *Positive psychology: A seven-day unit plan for high school psychology.* Paper presented at the meeting of the National Institute on the Teaching of Psychology (NITOP), St. Petersburg, FL.

"On Your Own" Activity: Applying Principles of Positive Psychology: A Beautiful Day

After discussing the positive psychology perspective (see the Classroom Activity "Positive Psychology") and the qualities of positive experiences, have students design a beautiful day that is within the realm of possibility and explain why they chose each element of the day (have them use Handout 10).

Have students share their "beautiful days" with the class. Once the sharing is complete, pose the following questions: How difficult would it be for you to actually live your beautiful day? Are there any actions you might take to move toward achieving a beautiful day on a more regular basis? How does your conception of a beautiful day fit in with your life's goals?

Critical Thinking Activity: Theories

Each unit of these resources contains a critical thinking exercise designed specifically to test students' critical thinking about a topic covered in the chapter. Handout 11 contains a brief statement regarding the major theories followed by a series of questions.

Answers to this unit's critical thinking exercise are as follows:

1. Freud's psychoanalytic theory, Erikson's psychosocial theory, and Piaget's cognitive theory each view development as a succession of stages of growth, with each stage characterized by its own unique challenges and achievements. Instead of developing a stage theory, behaviorists have formulated laws of behavior that are believed to operate at every age. Similarly, sociocultural theory views development as a much more gradual and continuous process, in which the factors that govern development remain more consistent throughout life. Although humanism does not postulate stages, a developmental application of this theory is that the satisfaction of childhood needs is crucial for later self-acceptance. Evolutionary theory does not regard development as a series of stages.
2. Cognitive and sociocultural theories and humanism emphasize the individual's conscious thought processes, individual knowledge, competencies, and the way these affect the person's understanding of the world; psychoanalytic theories emphasize unconscious urges; learning theories emphasize observable behavior; evolutionary theory emphasizes the interaction between genes and the environment.
3. Psychoanalytic and evolutionary theories and behaviorism suggest that early experiences, such as nurturing relationships, have long-term effects on development. Cognitive and sociocultural theories recognize early experiences but concentrate on current development, thought processes, and the dynamic interaction between developing persons and their surrounding culture. Humanism focuses on current experiences.
4. Each theory views the child differently: psychoanalytic theories regard the child as a collection of hidden impulses; behaviorism, as a passive individual to be molded by the environment; cognitive theories, as a thinking, rational being; and sociocultural theory as an apprentice who will grow in response to the social interactions that are shared with more mature members of the society.
5. The theories reflect different opinions on adult development. Cognitive theories generally do not consider cognitive advances that occur after ado-

lescence to be very important. Behaviorism recognizes the existence of a constant learning process throughout the life span, with adults obeying the same laws of behavior as children. Psychoanalytic theories are divided on this issue: Freud's psychosexual theory "stopped" personality development at age 6, whereas Erikson's psychosocial theory stressed the continuation of personality development throughout the life span. Although sociocultural theories place less emphasis on developmental changes that occur after adolescence, they do emphasize the changing nature of the sociocultural context and, therefore, that development continues throughout the life span.

6. Each theory applies a different methodology: behaviorism and information-processing theory, the experiment; cognitive theories such as Piaget's, the clinical interview method; psychoanalytic theories, the case study. Sociocultural theory applies a variety of methodologies, but most often relies on observation, including cross-cultural field work. All the theories emphasize careful observation in combination with theoretical principles; however, only behaviorists and cognitive theorists have made extensive efforts to test their theories through the use of the scientific method.
7. Psychoanalytic theory has been faulted for being too subjective; behaviorism, for being too mechanistic; cognitive theory, for undervaluing emotions; sociocultural theory for neglecting individuals; and universal theory, for slighting cultural, gender, and economic variations.

HANDOUT 1

Developmental Fact or Myth?

T F 1. Psychoanalytic theory, behaviorism, and cognitive theory are considered "grand" because they are comprehensive, enduring, and widely applied.

T F 2. Proponents of behaviorism believe that all behavior arises directly from operant or classical conditioning.

T F 3. Piaget believed that how people think and how they understand the world depends on their age.

T F 4. Developmental psychologists are increasingly aware that culture shapes our responses.

T F 5. According to sociocultural theory, learning is active.

T F 6. The newest theory of development stresses that all humans, at the basic level, are alike.

T F 7. According to evolutionary theory, some traits result from genetic inheritance alone.

T F 8. All developmental theories attempt to explain the broad spectrum of human development.

T F 9. Cognitive theory has been faulted for overvaluing emotions.

T F 10. Most developmentalists incorporate ideas from several theories into their thinking.

HANDOUT 2

The "Lifeline"

Most people naturally divide the life cycle into separate periods of time, or stages, during which they expect certain events to occur (starting a family, establishing a career, retirement, etc.). To clarify your own view of the life cycle, fill in the details of your life up to this point and as you project them to be for the future, along the "life line" that follows. At the top of the line, list your date of birth. At the bottom, list a projected date of death. At an appropriate spot midway along the line (depending on your age), list today's date. Now, summarize your life to the present by listing any especially significant events at the appropriate points along the line above today's date (starting school, moving to a new neighborhood, puberty, etc.). Next, project your future as you see it today by filling in the bottom part of your lifeline. List who you hope to be (your profession or family plans, for example), what you hope to accomplish, and any expected pressures and responsibilities (dealing with adult children and elderly parents, for example) 5 years from now, 10 years from now, and so forth until your death.

Moment in Time **Event, Goal, or Expected Role**

Date of Birth

Expected Date of Death

HANDOUT 3

Major Developmental Theories: Discover Your Bias

Most students come to class with a bias or predisposition toward one or more of the five basic theoretical frameworks. Answer the following questions to see whether you can discern a pattern in your responses that might indicate a bias toward one theory or another. You may check more than one answer if both reflect your opinion.

1. The father of a 2-year-old finds that he becomes very impatient with his daughter when, night after night, she claims she cannot fall asleep because of a "monster that comes out in the dark." Although each night the father tries to reassure and comfort his daughter, the next morning she does not remember his attempts to reason with her regarding her fear. He should probably

    ______ a. try to understand the hidden causes and meaning of his daughter's dreams.

    ______ b. give his daughter a reward the following morning if she stayed in bed until falling asleep the night before.

    ______ c. realize that, because of her limited intellectual abilities at age 2, she cannot be rationally reasoned with.

    ______ d. consider how he can structure his interactions with his daughter to "mentor" her through her fear.

    ______ e. recognize that fears of the dark are partly genetic, because they undoubtedly helped our species survive.

2. Most adults become physiologically aroused when they hear the sound of a baby's cry. This is because

    ______ a. the baby's cry evokes unconscious memories of their own painful childhood.

    ______ b. at some time during their past, the sound of a baby crying became associated with another stimulus that naturally elicited physiological arousal.

    ______ c. they consciously become irritated by the distracting sound.

    ______ d. nurturing young babies is a developmental challenge that all humans face and address in culture-specific ways.

    ______ e. humans are biologically predisposed to respond favorably to an infant crying.

HANDOUT 3 *(continued)*

3. A preteenage boy is not interested in having sexual experiences. The most reasonable explanation is that

_____ a. he feels threatened; he is denying his true feelings, possibly without realizing what they are.

_____ b. he has probably had anxiety-producing experiences with sex and wants to avoid any repetition of these experiences.

_____ c. his ideas and values make sexual experiences seem wrong or inappropriate for him right now.

_____ d. his social, or cultural, background has not yet fostered such interests.

_____ e. his biological immaturity means he has not yet experienced the hormonal surge of puberty.

4. Nine-year-old David is more aggressive in the classroom than Maria is. His teacher should probably

_____ a. refer David to a therapist who can get him to talk about his repressed urges.

_____ b. give him stars and privileges whenever he behaves appropriately.

_____ c. find out why he is not concentrating on the material; to begin with, have his vision, hearing, and other perceptual abilities tested.

_____ d. realize that David's past social interactions have not challenged him to develop certain social competencies.

_____ e. consider that boys are naturally somewhat more aggressive than girls are.

5. Advertisers often incorporate "babyishness" in their promotional symbols because

_____ a. most adults have hidden consummatory urges stemming from their childhoods.

_____ b. people are conditioned to act impulsively (and, perhaps, spend money) around children.

_____ c. they are afraid of making their sales pitches too intellectually complex for the average consumer.

_____ d. people in most cultures are socialized to respond favorably to babies.

_____ e. adults are genetically predisposed to respond favorably to images of infancy.

HANDOUT 4

Views on Development

The following questions relate to your views about human development and behavior. Please indicate your degree of agreement by answering ***strongly agree, agree, neutral, disagree,*** *or* ***strongly disagree****. There are no right or wrong answers.*

__________ 1. Events that occurred during childhood have no effect on one's personality in adulthood.

__________ 2. Sexual adjustment is easy for most people.

__________ 3. Culture and society have evolved as ways to curb human beings' natural aggressiveness.

__________ 4. Little boys should not become too attached to their mothers.

__________ 5. It is possible to deliberately "forget" something too painful to remember.

__________ 6. People who chronically smoke, eat, or chew gum have some deep psychological problems.

__________ 7. Competitive people are no more aggressive than noncompetitive people.

__________ 8. Fathers should remain somewhat aloof from their daughters.

__________ 9. Toilet training is natural and not traumatic for most children.

__________ 10. The phallus is a symbol of power.

__________ 11. A man who dates a woman old enough to be his mother has problems.

__________ 12. Some women are best described as being "castrating bitches."

__________ 13. Dreams merely replay events that occurred during the day and have no deep meaning.

__________ 14. There is something wrong with a woman who dates a man who is old enough to be her father.

__________ 15. A student who wants to postpone an exam by saying, "My grandmother lied . . . er, I mean died," should probably be allowed the postponement.

HANDOUT 5

The Active Search for Knowledge

Piaget has said that intellectual growth continues throughout life. Interview an older adult who has returned to school—for example, a middle-aged person who is preparing for a new career or a senior citizen who is seeking intellectual enrichment. Record answers to the following questions. (If you are an older adult who has returned to school, answer the questions yourself.)

1. At what age did you return to school, and why?

2. Do you think that you learn new information now in the same way you did earlier in your life? If not, how has the process of learning changed for you?

3. What kinds of things seem more difficult to learn now? What seems easier?

4. How have your study methods changed over the years, and why?

HANDOUT 5 *(continued)*

5. How have your life experiences influenced your learning abilities?

6. Compare yourself with younger students in your classes. In which ways, if any, are you intellectually stronger? In which ways are you weaker?

HANDOUT 6

Internet Activity: High-Quality Preschool Education: What Would Vygotsky Say?

Over the past 20 years, interest in applying Lev Vygotsky's ideas to early-childhood education has increased dramatically. Imaginative play, for example, is the leading educational activity of preschool children, according to sociocultural theory. Another idea is the importance of amplification or enrichment of learning via each child's zone of proximal development. To learn more about practical applications of Vygotsky's theory, search the Web to research answers to the following questions.

1. What is the Tools of the Mind project? How and why did it begin? What specific problems or issues was the project designed to address?

2. What are "play plans"? How do preschool programs derived from sociocultural theory incorporate play plans into daily activities?

3. What is scaffolded writing? How is it used in preschool education?

4. How are teachers trained in Vygotskian-based preschool programs?

5. What evidence is there that Vygotskian-based preschool programs are working?

HANDOUT 7

Link each of the statements regarding prosocial, or helping, behavior to the appropriate developmental perspective.

1. By helping each other, we are more likely to survive and reproduce.
   Perspective ______________________________

2. Unconscious sexual motivation prompts our willingness to help others.
   Perspective ______________________________

3. We are most likely to help those we perceive as similar to ourselves and whom we believe deserve our assistance.
   Perspective ______________________________

4. The willingness of people to help varies greatly across the world's societies.
   Perspective ______________________________

5. Children who have been rewarded for helpful behavior are more likely to be helpful in future interpersonal interactions.
   Perspective ______________________________

6. The desire to help others is a basic human need shared by all people.
   Perspective ______________________________

Source: Adapted from Bolt, M. (2011). Instructor's resources to accompany David G. Myers *Exploring Psychology* (8th ed.). New York: Worth.

HANDOUT 8

Introducing Evolutionary Psychology

1. You are on a boat that overturns. It contains your 5-year-old and 1-year-old children (of the same sex). The boat sinks and you can save only one. Whom do you choose to save? Circle one:

   5-year-old   1-year-old

2. That same boat (you are slow to learn lessons) contains your 40-year-old and 20-year-old children (of the same sex). Neither can swim. As the boat sinks, whom do you choose to save? Circle one:

   40-year-old   20-year-old

3. Have you (or would you) rather marry someone older or younger than yourself?

   older   younger

4. Of the following six factors, which are most important in the selection of your mate? Circle the answers:

   a. good financial prospects
   b. good looks
   c. a caring and responsible personality
   d. physical attractiveness
   e. ambition and industriousness
   f. an exciting personality

5. You and your spouse are proud new parents. The grandparents are ecstatic. Who do you think will be kinder to the child? Circle one:

   the mother of the mother   the mother of the father

6. Who will mourn more at the death of a child? Circle the answer in each pair:

   a. father   mother
   b. parents of the father   parents of the mother
   c. younger parents   older parents

7. Which will elicit more grief?

   a. death of a son   death of a daughter
   b. death of an unhealthy child   death of a healthy child

HANDOUT 9

Daily Mood Form

Make seven copies of the Daily Mood Form below and use one sheet each day to record your emotional state at approximately the same time each day (before you go to bed, when you wake up in the morning, at lunch, and so on). After the one-week period, calculate your affect scores and frequency of affect in the following way:

Compute a positive affect score by finding the average ratings for "happy," "joyful," "pleased," and "enjoyment." Compute a negative affect score by finding the average of the ratings for "depressed," "unhappy," "frustrated," "angry," and "worried." Subtract the negative score from the positive one to obtain a global daily mood score. To compute frequency of positive affect, divide the number of days in which you had a positive score by the total number of days on which you reported your mood.

DAILY MOOD FORM

Name ________________________________ Day # __________ Date: __________

Please indicate how much of each emotion you felt today.

1	2	3	4	5	6	7
Not at all	**very slight**	**somewhat**	**moderate amount**	**much**	**very much**	**extremely much**

_____ Happy
_____ Depressed/Blue
_____ Joyful
_____ Frustrated
_____ Pleased
_____ Angry/Hostile
_____ Enjoyment/Fun
_____ Worried/Anxious
_____ Unhappy

Positive affect score _____

Negative affect score _____

Global daily mood score _____

Source: Larsen, R. J., & Diener, E. (1987). Affect intensity as an individual difference characteristic: A review. *Journal of Research in Personality, 21,* 1–39.

HANDOUT 10

A Beautiful Day

Design a beautiful day (a 24-hour day) that is within the realm of possibility for you to live currently. Next, try to live your beautiful day and then answer the following questions:

1. List the elements and activities that make up your day, and briefly explain why you chose each element.

2. Were you successful in living that day? Why or why not?

3. Were all of the qualities of your beautiful day truly beautiful? Why or why not?

4. What would you now change about your perception of a beautiful day?

5. Is there any action you might take to move toward achieving a "beautiful day" on a more regular basis?

6. How does your conception of a "beautiful day" fit in with your life's goals?

Source: Seligman, M. E. P. (1998). *Learned optimism: How to change your mind and your life* (2nd ed.). New York: Pocket Books.

HANDOUT 11

Critical Thinking Activity: Theories

Now that you have read and reviewed theories of development, take your learning a step further by testing your critical thinking skills on this scientific reasoning exercise.

Five major theories of human development are described, compared, and evaluated in this section. These are the psychoanalytic theories of Freud and Erikson; the behaviorism of Pavlov and Skinner and the social learning theory of Bandura; humanism and evolutionary theory; Piaget's cognitive theory; and Vygotsky's sociocultural theory. Although each theory is too restricted to account solely for the tremendous diversity in human development, each has made an important contribution to developmental psychology.

To help clarify your understanding of the major developmental theories, this exercise asks you to focus on the similar, contradictory, and complementary aspects of the five theories.

1. Which of the major developmental theories are stage theories? Which are not?

2. Which theories emphasize individual conscious organization of experience? unconscious urges? observable behavior? the interaction of nature and nurture?

3. Which theories emphasize the impact of early experience on development?

4. How does each theory view the child?

5. How do the theories view adult development?

6. Do the theories use the same methodology? How does each make use of the scientific method?

7. Which theories have been criticized for being too subjective? too mechanistic? too deterministic? for neglecting the role of biological maturation in guiding development?

Heredity and Environment

Contents

Note: Worth Publishers provides online Instructor and Student Tool Kits, DVD Student Tool Kits, and Instructor and Student video resources in DevelopmentPortal for use with the text. See Part I: General Resources for information about these materials and the text Lecture Guides for a complete list by text chapter.

Genotype and Phenotype

Chromosomal and Genetic Problems

Suggested Activities

Introducing Heredity and Environment

"On Your Own" Activity: Developmental Fact or Myth?

Before students read the text discussion of heredity and environment, have them respond to the true-false statements in Handout 1.

The correct answers are shown below. Class discussion can focus on the origins of any developmental misconceptions that are demonstrated in the students' incorrect answers.

1. T	6. T
2. F	7. F
3. F	8. F
4. F	9. T
5. F	10. F

Teaching Tip: Teaching a Large Class

If your campus is typical, the number of students in your developmental psychology classes has probably been increasing every year . . . perhaps to the point where you are teaching a very large, 100-plus student course. As Todd Zakrajsek (2007) has noted, "Faculty responses to increased class sizes often resemble Kubler-Ross's stages of grief and loss: denial ("There is no way to increase the size of this class and maintain academic integrity!"); anger ("I can't believe they did this; administrators don't care about students or faculty!"); bargaining ("If I teach 20 percent more students without additional compensation, what do I get in return?"); depression ("How am I ever going to teach this class in a meaningful way again?"); and finally acceptance ("OK, my class is larger. How do I deal with the hordes?")."

Here are some tips to improve your experience, and that of your students, when class size grows.

- Encourage faculty–student contact. Learning students' names and something about them works wonders. A good way to get to know students in a large class is to arrive at class early enough to spend a few minutes talking to students before class begins. You might also try the name-learning exercise in the Theories of Development unit. Another useful technique is to periodically ask students to provide written feedback about how the class is going.
- Promote cooperation among students. Even the largest class can be divided into groups of four or five on the first day. After 10 minutes or so of discussion, call on one individual from each group and have him or her introduce the others in the group. Reinforce the value of group membership by encouraging students to e-mail one another for missed course material, announcements, and the like.

- Encourage active learning. The biggest mistake you can make when a class gets larger is to resort to lecturing only. Even the largest class can benefit from "concept test lectures," in which you present a mini-lecture of 15 minutes or so and then project a multiple-choice question or two, asking the class "How many think *a* is the correct answer, how many *b,* and so on." If most students "get it," move on to the next material. Some instructors incorporate "live" survey technologies to facilitate this—for example, iClickers (see www.worthpublishers.com/bergerca8e for more information on this new technology). Another strategy is to break lectures up with case studies and other problem-based assignments to which small groups of students must respond.
- Give prompt feedback. This may be the toughest challenge with large classes, causing some teachers to abandon student writing assignments altogether. "Grading rubrics" are scoring templates that identify the three to five most important aspects of a written assignment. For a research article review, these might include accurate description of methodology, major results from the researchers, and the student's overall response. Each area is allocated a specific number of points. Giving the rubric to the students at the time of the assignment also leads to better papers. A suggested grading rubric for major term papers is provided in the General Resources section of this instructor's manual.

Zakrajsek, T. (2007, May). Effective teaching when class size grows. *Association for Psychological Science Observer, 20*(5). Retrieved from www.psychologicalscience.org/ observer.

AV: Transitions Throughout the Life Span, Program 3: Nature and Nurture: The Dance of Life

Program 3 discusses the biological and genetic mechanisms by which normal, and sometimes abnormal, chromosomes and genes are transmitted to the developing person. The program emphasizes that although the direction a person's life takes is strongly influenced by heredity, its ultimate course depends on the interaction of many biological and environmental factors—that is, on both nature and nurture.

Through the story of identical twins Mohammad and Ali, the program also discusses how developmentalists use twin studies to tease apart the contributions of genes and environmental factors to development. Genotype and phenotype are distinguished, and the benefits of genetic counseling for prospective parents who are at risk of giving birth to children with genetic disorders are discussed. Advances in prenatal diagnostic techniques allow prospective parents to make more informed decisions about the risks of childbearing.

Classroom Activity: What Do Kids Cost?

No one, of course, should decide whether to have children solely on the basis of cold, economic facts. But not only don't kids come free; their cost is skyrocketing. According to one estimate, the cost of raising a child from birth to puberty has increased dramatically since 1960, after adjustments are made for inflation and changes in the average family size. As your students embark on their study of human development, it might be a good time to cite a few sobering statistics. After all, we want them to take this business seriously, don't we?

In 2010, the U.S. Department of Agriculture released a government report that a middle-income family with a child born in 2009 will spend about $286,050 for food, shelter, and other necessities to raise that child to 18 years of age. The projected figures for low-income and upper-income families are $205,960 and $475,680, respectively. To put this into perspective, in 1960, a middle-income family could expect to spend $25,230 ($182,857 in 2009 dollars) to raise a child to age 18.

The pie charts on the next page illustrate how child-rearing costs have changed over the past 5 decades. Most dramatic are the increases in child care, education, and health care costs.

1960 Child-Rearing Expenses

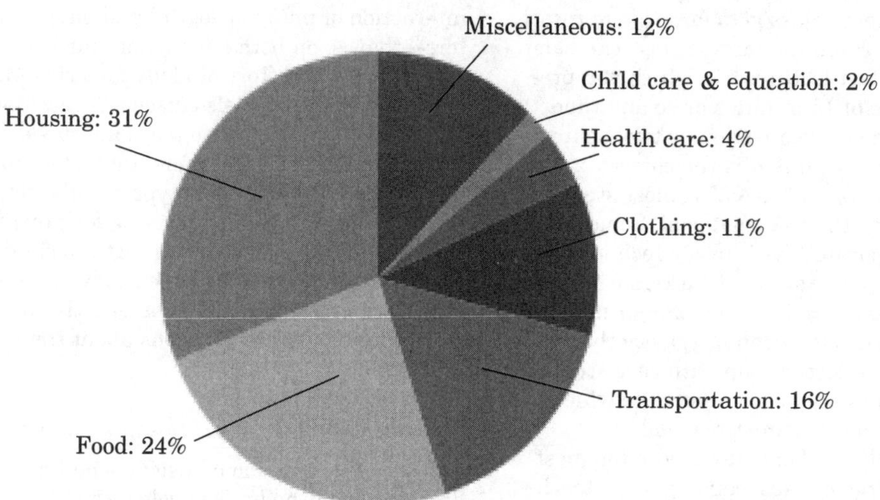

2009 Child-Rearing Expenses

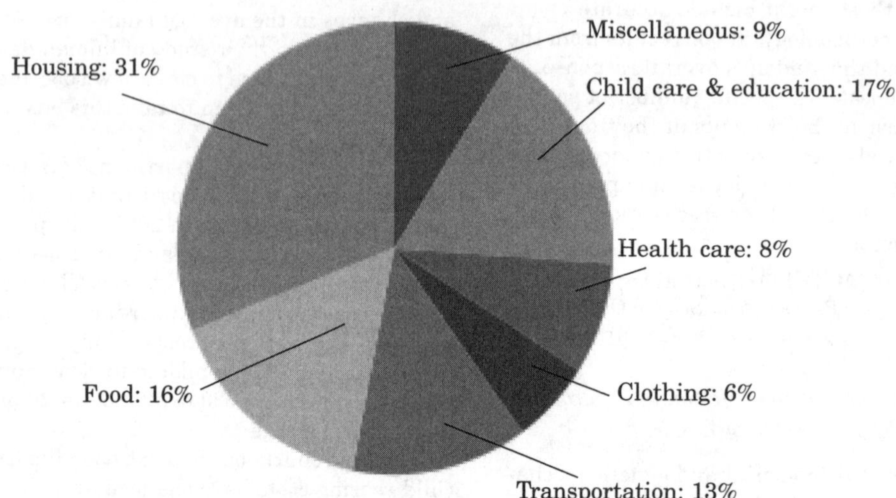

Lino, Mark. (2010). *Expenditures on Children by Families, 2009.* U.S. Department of Agriculture, Center for Nutrition Policy and Promotion. Miscellaneous Publication No. 1528-2009.

The Genetic Code

AV: Blueprint for Life (30 min., RMI Media Productions)

This program discusses the mysteries of genes and charts the evolution of the zygote into the fully formed infant. Graphic footage illustrates how teratogens endanger the developing individual.

AV: The Developing Child: Conception and Heredity (15 min., Magna Systems)

This brief video module provides a concise overview of the beginning of life. Topics explored include cellular duplication, genetic abnormalities and diseases, the determination of sex, mechanisms of heredity, and genetic counseling.

AV: How Life Begins (46 min., University of Southern California Film Library)

This film provides an extraordinary look at the beginning of life, from conception to birth, throughout the animal kingdom. One theme is the miraculous nature of prenatal development; another is the common ground humans share with other animals. Originally an ABC news special, the film won critical acclaim for both its photography (magnificent) and its narrative.

AV: Life's Greatest Miracle (57 min., Time Life Video, NOVA)

This biological view of conception—including male and female anatomy and the actual moment of fertilization inside the woman—and prenatal development was filmed by justly famous Swedish photographer Lennart Nilsson. The film might provide good background information if you want to emphasize the importance of preventing unwanted pregnancy before it occurs.

Classroom Activity: Sociobiology, Culture, and Sex Selection

To reinforce the idea that the 23rd chromosome on the sperm is the crucial factor in sex determination (although many other factors may be involved in a particular couple's chances of having a boy or a girl), as well as to provide an interesting discussion of science and fantasy, you might elaborate on the idea of sex selection. The following background material can be used as the basis for a lecture.

Historically, and almost universally, male offspring have been preferred, and women have generally been blamed for "failing" to produce male children. For instance, in some cultures a woman who bore only daughters was thought to be poisoning the sperm. Perhaps not surprisingly, then, various prescriptions for assuring male children have been advanced. Interestingly, some of these have been associated with the ancient notion of superiority of the right side of the body. Following the advice of Hippocrates, for example, Greek husbands eager to have a son tied up their left testicle during intercourse so that only sperm from the right testicle would fertilize an ovum. In addition, wives were required to lie on their right side during intercourse so that the right ovary would be the repository of sperm. One theory that achieved some scientific respectability in the early twentieth century was also based on the idea that the right ovary ovulated boys and the left, girls. This theory further suggested that these "boy" and "girl" ova were ovulated alternately; thus a couple could, subsequent to the birth of their first child, calculate which ovary would be ovulating when, and so produce a boy or girl at will. Other theories have focused on such things as the relative strength of character, activity, or passion of the man and woman in question. Weather was also supposed to be a factor, with the full moon and the north wind both favoring boys.

One widely advertised modern method of sex selection involves the use of in vitro fertilization in which the sperm have been separated into sperm cells containing X chromosomes and those containing Y chromosomes. Separation is achieved by measuring the amount of DNA each cell contains. Artificial insemination is then used to produce embryos of the chosen sex, supposedly with 93 percent accuracy.

The procedure, known as *preimplantation genetic diagnosis,* or "MicroSort," is based on the fact that sperm carrying the Y chromosome have 2.8 percent less DNA than sperm with the X chromosome. To measure the DNA of a sperm cell, the researcher stains the cells with fluorescent dye using a laser. The labor-intensive sorting procedure is not cheap. In 2006, Sharla and Shane Miller paid $18,400, plus travel, to guarantee the sex of their baby.

It is interesting, however, to speculate about parents' choices if sex selection were 100 percent accurate and practical. You might ask your students to describe their ideal family, in terms of sex as well as size. Most Americans prefer to have a boy first, then a girl—although, of course, there is some variation—and most would rather have two boys and a girl than two girls and a boy. This preference for males is even stronger in developing countries.

Over the past 15 years, Chinese demographers have been tracking birth sex ratios with great accuracy. One concern is family size—specifically the connection between overpopulation and poverty. To stimulate economic development, the Chinese government recently began requiring couples to postpone marriage and limit family size. Consequently, average family size in China has decreased dramatically, down from 6 children per couple in 1950 to fewer than 2 today. Although family size is certainly not the only factor in China's economic success story, the Chinese economy increased by a factor of 10 during the same time.

Another concern is that in China the reported number of male births exceeds female births by amounts much greater than would be expected naturally: the ratio is 114 males to 100 females on average, and 130 or 140 males to 100 females in rural areas. Although female infanticide is illegal in China, some families apparently resort to this practice to guarantee a son. The problem is compounded by government policy that limits most families to having only one child. As noted in the text, the law prohibits prenatal testing to determine sex, but the law is not well enforced.

Researchers speculate that these skewed birth rates will have far-reaching social and possibly even evolutionary effects. For one thing, demographers project that there will be a severe shortage of marriageable women. In a country where 96 percent of the population marries, such a shortage could translate into millions of unmarried men emigrating to countries where they can find a partner. For another, cultural practices that increase the number of adult males eventually will biologically favor parents of daughters, who are more likely to reproduce and pass on their parents' genes.

Using a sophisticated mathematical model, Marcus Feldman and colleagues at Stanford University have predicted that within 200 generations, China's cultural bias favoring sons could shift evolutionary pressures to favor female-based birth ratios. The gene–culture evolutionary model "is our response to simple sociobiological arguments about human evolution," says Feldman. "It is a structured methodology for exploring how two direct transmission systems, genetic and cultural, can interact to influence biological evolution and cultural change."

Other researchers speculate that if we had even more males in our population, there would be more crimes, more children with problems in school, and more handicapped infants, because each is more common among males than females. Would the social cost become too much for society to bear? Would families quickly realize that the natural population balance is probably better and therefore try to keep the sex ratio constant? Or would they try to switch to a higher proportion of females? Finally, would it be easier to achieve zero population growth if sex selection were possible? How many families with all boys or all girls would keep trying to have more babies in the hope that the next child would be of the opposite sex? Such questions should help your students focus on the interrelationship of individual childbearing and social forces.

Kalb, C. (2006). Brave new babies. *Newsweek Health.* www.msnbc.msn.com/id/3990309/site/newsweek.

Stern, H., Karabinus, D., Wiley, S., et al. (2003, October). MicroSort babies: 1994–2003 preliminary postnatal follow-up results. *Fertility and Sterility, 76*(3S), 54.

World youth report 2007: Young people's transition to adulthood. (2008). New York, United Nations Publications.

"On Your Own" Activity: Similarities Among Twins: Coincidence or Evidence of Genetic Influence?

If your students are typical, they will be fascinated by research studies on identical twins. Many of them have probably heard accounts of twins who have been reunited after years of separation, only to find striking similarities in their personalities, attitudes, and virtually every imaginable aspect of their lives. Do similarities such as these indicate the importance of genes in personality and behavior? Or will any two people find some surprising similarities just by chance? As is often the case, the truth probably lies somewhere in between. However, to help ensure that students maintain a healthy dose of skepticism in their thinking about such similarities, David Myers suggests a provocative activity that will keep students talking long after the class ends.

Distribute copies of Handout 2, then ask each student to pair off with another student (preferably someone the other student does not know) and give them 5 to 10 minutes to see how many similarities they can uncover. Be sure to tell them that although they are sure to find many differences between them, they shouldn't worry and should continue searching for similarities. If you have an odd number of students, pair off with a student yourself or put a group of three together.

The first time Myers did this with a student, within 5 minutes they discovered that they "both like basketball, hate Brussels sprouts, sleep seven hours, chew Wrigley's spearmint, use Crest, read *Time*, prefer nonfiction books, view the nightly news and not much else, and are right-handed, outgoing persons." Most likely, you will obtain similar results.

AV: Body Doubles: The Twin Experience (50 min., Films for the Humanities and Sciences)

This visually stunning HBO documentary discusses the vital contribution of the study of twins in developmental psychology. Tracing the history of twin research from Josef Mengele to the University of Minnesota Twin Research Center, the film presents a balanced treatment of both sides of the nature–nurture controversy.

Classroom Activity: Classroom Debate: *"Resolved: Embryonic Stem Cell Research Should Be Outlawed"*

The text does not discuss cloning or stem cell research, but the topics work well as a natural extension of the discussion of identical twins. The debate is certain to be a lively one.

As we move closer to the day when the possibility of cloning a human being becomes a reality, many scientists are raising concerns about the ethical implications of this biological revolution. Currently, 13 U.S. states ban any type of human cloning, 2 prohibit use of public funds for reproductive cloning, and 6 states have laws preventing embryonic stem cell research. To encourage students to think about some of these issues, and to increase their understanding of the complexity of the issues, follow the guidelines in the General Resources section of this manual for scheduling a classroom debate on this resolution. You might prefer to select the reference material yourself and place the relevant journals and textbooks on reserve in the college library, or you might want students to find their own by surfing the Internet.

Advocates of cloning and stem cell technology believe that this approach could one day be used to provide tissue transplants to treat juvenile diabetes and Parkinson's disease and to repair severed spinal cords. Unlike adult stem cells, embryonic stem cells have the potential to develop into any cell or tissue in the body. "The hope the research offers is enormous," notes neurosurgeon Dr. Anil Nanda. "In a spinal cord patient, it can bring back function. In a stroke patient, you could put them in the stroke area and there is some evidence that it would help."

The process of using stem cells to treat a diseased person begins with the creation of embryonic stem cells in a process called *somatic cell nuclear transfer.* First, scientists remove the nucleus from an unfertilized human egg cell. The scientists then remove the nucleus of a skin cell from the patient needing treatment. The skin cell nucleus is implanted in the egg cell, replacing the egg's original nucleus. The nuclear transferred egg cell is then stimulated electrically or chemically, which causes it to begin to divide in a Petri dish. In the final step, the dividing cells are implanted in the patient. Because the cells contain the patient's own DNA (from the donor skin cell), the chances of tissue rejection are dramatically reduced.

Although The National Institutes of Health has ruled that embryonic stem cells are not a form of human embryo, opponents equate embryonic stem cell research with cloning that leads to the creation of a human being. "Everything discussed comes down to life," notes Louisiana State Representative Gary Beard, who is opposing legislation to lift the ban on stem cell research in his home state. "We have always placed life in the highest pinnacle of life. This bill is the antithesis of life. It allows for a darkness that you cannot possibly imagine." Central to the issue from Beard's point of view is the question of whether cloning a cell for research is equal to the creation of life. Equally disturbing to anti-abortion activists who oppose the legislation is the fact that because the research requires the destruction of cloned human embryos, it is actually a form of abortion.

Internet Activity: Cloning

To help students learn about cloning, and the many ethical, moral, and philosophical issues raised by the growing possibility of human cloning, have them surf the Internet to find brief answers to the questions in Handout 3. The handout also lists several Internet sources to get them started.

AV: Adoption and Assisted Reproduction: A Look at the Children (26 min., Films for the Humanities and Sciences)

Shifting social norms and increasing medical options have redefined traditional concepts about reproduction and parenting. This program focuses on several case studies: a couple who underwent in vitro fertilization, surrogate motherhood, a single woman who chose to be artificially inseminated, and a bachelor who adopted a child. The program emphasizes the impact of various types of parenthood on children.

AV: The Baby Makers (43 min., CRM/McGraw-Hill)

This film, produced by CBS, explains many of the new methods of fertilization (including surrogate motherhood and test-tube babies). It also explores the ethical questions raised by these methods. At times, the treatment seems to skirt the deeper questions in favor of newsworthy footage, but that allows you to probe more deeply during class discussion.

Polygenic and Multifactorial Interaction

Classroom Activity: Genes for Obesity

To expand on the discussion of dominant–recessive gene interaction and the multifactorial nature of most human characteristics, you might discuss research regarding a genetic component to obesity. The role of genes in obesity has long been debated, no more heatedly than today, when 65 percent of Americans are overweight. Following is some background information.

Evidence for a genetic contribution to obesity comes from a large number of twin, adoption, and family studies. Identical twins have similar body weights, even when reared apart, and the body weights of adopted children most closely resemble those of their biological parents, despite sharing meals with their adoptive parents.In fact, having one obese biological parent makes a young girl six times more likely to be obese than her counterparts with non-obese parents.

Using animal genetic models, researchers have found evidence of an obese gene (OB, for short) that triggers abnormalities in a number of physiological systems involved in obesity. For example, this gene may cause thermoregulation (which lowers the body temperature) and the abnormal functioning of the adrenal and thyroid glands (which affect the regulation of metabolism and energy).

Research studies have demonstrated that, in mice, daily injections of the hormone leptin can lead to weight loss in a matter of weeks. Increasingly, researchers are referring to leptin as "the satiety hormone," because blood levels of leptin are directly correlated to fat stores in obese and lean people. Leptin, which is also found in humans, may regulate weight by controlling how much fat is stored in the body. When injected into mice, leptin quickly decreases appetite and increases metabolic rate.

The production of leptin apparently is governed by the OB gene. When the OB gene is defective, not enough leptin is produced to regulate normal fat storage. Animals with mutated OB genes may grow to three times normal weight! Believing that injections of leptin can help obese humans, researchers have managed to manufacture leptin by cloning the OB gene into bacterial "factories" that then produce the hormone.

Although human trials with leptin are under way, other researchers are skeptical about its efficacy. Endocrinologists Robert Considine and José Caro were unable to detect OB gene defects inside the fat cells of a sample of obese men and women. Caro also has measured leptin levels in 140 obese people and so far has been unable to find a single person with below-normal amounts of the protein. In fact, most of the people had an overabundance of leptin. "The majority of humans with obesity are insensitive to their own leptin," says Caro. "Their bodies simply aren't getting the blaring message to slim down." To determine why these people don't get the message, researchers are trying to locate leptin's target, thought to be a receptor in the brain. Learning why this hypothetical receptor becomes insensitive to leptin could lead to the design of a drug to enhance the receptor's sensitivity.

Other studies point to a gene called GAD2, which sits on chromosome 10. GAD2 acts by enhancing production of gamma-amino butyric acid (GABA), a neurotransmitter in the brain. When GABA interacts with proteins in the paraventricular nucleus of the hypothalamus, hunger results. Researchers believe that people who carry a more active form of the GAD2 gene build up unusually high levels of GABA in the hypothalamus, which may be one reason that obese people overeat.

Researchers doubt that obesity is determined solely by genes. Rather, the predisposition to obesity is influenced by a variety of social, behavioral, and biological factors. From the research currently available, a good number of genes seem to have the capacity to cause obesity or increase the likelihood of a person becoming obese. But because a larger percentage of the population than predicted by genetic factors is obese, environment obviously is important. As the text emphasizes, most human characteristics are multifactorial; that is, they result from the interaction of many genetic and environmental factors. Therefore, people who are genetically prone to obesity can minimize the risk of obesity by altering equally important environmental risk factors, such as high-fat, excessive calorie diets and lack of exercise. Conversely, people who inherit a predisposition to slimness may still become obese if they consume more calories than they expend in their daily activity levels.

In the final analysis, researchers caution against taking an overly simplistic view of obesity. "The genetics of obesity are not so simple," says biologist Juergen Naggert. "Even in mice, there are at least five genes involved in different aspects of obesity." The list of human obesity genes also continues to grow with the recent discoveries that an energy-regulating gene called BDNF is linked to obesity in children with *WAGR syndrome,* a rare genetic disorder that also causes kidney and urinary problems (Han, et al., 2008). Leptin is likely to be just one of many biological cues, as well as social and psychological influences that tell us when to eat. "We don't always eat because we have a signal that we're hungry," says James Hill of the University of Colorado. "We see a wonderful cake in the window and it looks good and we're not hungry, but we eat it."

One promising benefit of identifying an obesity gene is that a diagnostic test can be developed to identify risk of obesity when children are very young. Early identification and intervention through diet and exercise programs may help reduce the risk of obesity, as well as health conditions that are more common in the obese, such as coronary heart disease.

Gene linked to adult-onset obesity. (2008, June 11). *Science Daily.* Retrieved from www.sciencedaily.com.

Han, J. C., Liu, Q. R., Jones, M., Levinn, R. L., Menzie, C. M., Jefferson-George, K. S., et al. (2008). Brain-derived Neurotrophic factor and obesity in the WAGR syndrome. *New England Journal of Medicine, 359,* 918–927.

Rankinen, T., Zuberi, A., Chagnon, Y.C., Weisnagel, S. J., Argyropoulos, G., Walts, B., et al. (2006). The human obesity gene map: The 2005 update. *Obesity, 14,* 529–644.

Classroom Activity: Genetic Influences on Taste

Martin Bolt suggested a simple demonstration of genetic influences on behavior: the ability to taste the bitter substance phenylthiocarbamide, or PTC. If your class is typical, approximately two-thirds of your students will be "tasters" and one-third will be "nontasters." Begin by explaining to the class that certain taste preferences are genetically determined. Most people, for example, have an innate preference for sweet tastes, find sour and bitter tastes unpleasant, and prefer salt in low concentrations. These preferences have even been demonstrated in newborns, who purse their lips and wrinkle their noses when stimulated with a sour taste and stick out their tongues when stimulated with a bitter solution.

Bring some PTC-containing salt substitute (potassium chloride) to class and pass it around. Have students sprinkle a small amount in their palms and, by a show of hands, determine which students are "tasters" and which are "nontasters." To a taster, the salt substitute will seem equally salty and bitter. To a nontaster, it will only seem salty. As a follow-up, have students test their parents and other family members. Because the ability to taste is determined by a dominant–recessive interaction, two nontasting parents should produce only nontasting children.

Bolt, M. (2012). Instructor's resources to accompany David G. Myers' *Psychology in Everyday Life,* 2nd ed. New York: Worth.

Genotype and Phenotype

AV: The Ecology of Development (30 min., Insight Media)

Profiling children in 12 families in 5 countries, this program explores how genetic and environmental factors influence development in every domain. Working from an ecological, or systems theory, perspective, the video considers the influence of family and peer relationships, schooling, history, and culture on development.

Classroom Activity: Shopping for Genes

To introduce students to the ways in which the probabilities of certain traits are calculated, try this fun activity suggested by the National Corn Growers Association. In the activity, pipe cleaners of various colors are used to represent genes controlling eye color, the ability to curl or roll one's tongue, whether one's earlobe is attached, gender, and number of fingers. The traits were chosen because each is coded as a single gene in humans (traits such as height and weight are coded by multiple genes).

Bring to class 10 small bags, into which you will place various combinations of colored pipe cleaners. The bags represent the genes contributed by hypothetical parents in this exercise: five for "Mom" and five for "Dad." Fill the bags with pipe cleaners as follows:

- Bag 1 (Mom's eye color): Mom has blue eyes (recessive). Fill the bag with 100 percent short brown pipe cleaners.
- Bag 2 (Dad's eye color): Dad has brown eyes because he received a dominant "brown gene" from his mother and a recessive "blue" gene from his father. Fill the bag with 50 percent short brown pipe cleaners and 50 percent long brown pipe cleaners.
- Bag 3 (Mom's tongue-rolling ability): Mom can roll her tongue because she received a dominant tongue-rolling gene from her mother and a recessive non-tongue-rolling gene from her father. Fill the bag with 50 percent long red and 50 percent short red pipe cleaners.
- Bag 4 (Dad's tongue-rolling ability): Dad can also roll his tongue. He received a dominant tongue-rolling gene from his mother and a recessive non-tongue-rolling gene from his father. Fill the bag with 50 percent long red and 50 percent short red pipe cleaners.
- Bag 5 (Mom's earlobe attachment): Mom has attached earlobes. She received dominant (attached) genes from both her parents. Fill the bag with 100 percent long white pipe cleaners.
- Bag 6 (Dad's earlobe attachment): Dad also has attached earlobes and received dominant genes from both his parents. Fill the bag with 100 percent long white pipe cleaners.
- Bag 7 (Mom's gender): Females have two X chromosomes. Fill the bag with 100 percent short yellow pipe cleaners.
- Bag 8 (Dad's gender): Males have one X and one Y chromosomes. Fill the bag with 50 percent short and 50 percent long yellow pipe cleaners.
- Bag 9 (Mom's finger genes): Mom has five fingers and no mutant finger genes. Fill the bag with 100 percent long green pipe cleaners.
- Bag 10 (Dad's finger genes): Dad has six fingers due to his possession of mutant finger genes inherited from both his parents. Fill the bag with 100 percent short green pipe cleaners.

Write the following on the board:

Pipe Cleaner	Trait
Brown	Eye color (long = dominant = brown) (short = recessive = blue)
Red	Tongue rolling (long = dominant = can roll; short = recessive = can't roll)
White	Earlobe structure (long = dominant = attached; short = recessive = not attached)
Yellow	Gender (two longs = girl; one long and one short = boy)
Green	Number of fingers (long = dominant = five fingers; short = mutant recessive = six fingers)

Line the bags up at the front of the class, labeled "Mom's eye genes," "Dad's eye genes," etc. Divide the class into several teams (the number of which must equal the number of pipe cleaners in each bag), then have each team pick one pipe cleaner from each bag. After all the teams have picked, ask each team to decide what their person would look like (male or female, blue eyes or brown, tongue-rolling ability, attached or unattached earlobes), and then describe the person for the class.

The results, which you can post on the board after the activity, will be as follows:

- Eyes: Offspring should be 50 percent blue-eyed and 50 percent brown-eyed.
- Tongue rolling: Offspring should be 75 percent tongue rollers and 25 percent non-tongue rollers.
- Earlobes: 100 percent of the offspring should have attached earlobes.
- Gender: Half of the offspring will be females and half will be males.
- Fingers: All offspring will have five fingers. Point out how dominant normal genes can cover up a "defect" caused by recessive genes. The offspring, while having five fingers in their phenotype, are carriers of the recessive mutant gene in their genotypes.

National Corn Grower's Association. (1999). NCGA Corn Curriculum (Genetics & Biotech; Lesson 2, Worksheet 1). www.ncga.com.

"On Your Own" Activity: Calculating Phenotypes and Genotypes

To introduce students to the ways in which the probabilities of certain traits are calculated, have them work through the Punnett square exercises on Handout 4.

In the first example, because both parents have two brown-eye genes, the children's phenotypes and genotypes will be the same: All brown-eye genes and brown eyes will be expressed. The same is true of the second example, except that all the children will have blue-eye phenotypes and genotypes. In the first example on page 19 of this resource unit, all the children will have brown eyes; their phenotype will be for brown eyes, but in their genotype, they will be carriers for blue eyes. In the second example, the children have two chances in four of inheriting the phenotype for brown eyes; the possible genotypes are Bb and bb. In the last example on page 21, the probability of a blue-eyed child being produced by these two parents is one in four.

AV: Heredity and Environment: Blueprints for a Baby (29 min., Magna Systems, Inc.)

One of the modules from the Developing Child Series, this film describes conception, the function of genes and chromosomes, and the earliest days in the life of the developing person. Graphics and animation are also used to explain the determination of sex, how traits are inherited, the interaction of genes and environment, and the impact of genetic and chromosomal abnormalities on the developing fetus. An overview of the field of genetic counseling is also provided.

"On Your Own" Activity: Temperament and Heredity

Nothing brings a discussion of heredity to life like having students evaluate themselves for the presence of a trait that is largely inherited. Martin Bolt suggested a good one for the class to consider: temperament, generally described by developmental psychologists as a broad personality disposition rather than a specific trait. A specific temperament is more a matter of style (how responses to the environment are made) than of content (which responses are made).

Handout 5 presents Buss and Plomin's EAS Temperament Survey, which measures three temperaments: activity, sociability, and emotionality. Activity represents a person's general level of energy output. People who score high on this dimension prefer an active lifestyle and tend to stay busy most of the time. Sociability refers to a person's tendency to affiliate with others. Adults who score high on this dimension seek out others and generally prefer company to being alone. Emotionality refers to how intensely emotions tend to be expressed. Adults who score high on this dimension have "short fuses" and easily become upset.

To score the survey, students should reverse their responses to items 6, 18, and 19 (1 = 5, 2 = 4, 3 = 3, 4 = 2, 5 = 1). The sum of their responses to items 2, 7, 10, and 17 yields their activity score. Adding their responses to items 1, 6, 15, and 20 yields their sociability score. The emotionality dimension has three parts: the sum of items 4, 9, 11, and 16 yields a distress score; adding items 3, 12, 14, and 19 produces a fearfulness score; and 5, 8, 13, and 18 produce an anger score. Average (mean) scores for men and women are as follows:

	Women	**Men**
Activity	13.40	12.80
Sociability	15.24	14.60
Emotionality		
Distress	10.08	9.72
Fearfulness	10.60	8.92
Anger	10.28	10.80

Identical twins have significantly more similar temperaments than do fraternal twins. The average correlations for emotionality, activity, and sociability are .63., .62, and .53 for identical twins, and only .12, –.13, and –.03 for fraternal twins. Still, it is important to note that while heredity may predispose a certain disposition, the expression of that trait is also influenced by the environment. Thus, while a highly emotional child may be predisposed toward fearfulness or anger, parents who nurture problem-solving skills over overt expressions of these emotions may help shape the child into a less fearful or angry adult. Stated another way, "nurture works on what nature endows."

Burger, J.M. (2008). *Personality* (7th ed.). Belmont, CA: Thomson Wadsworth.

Buss, A.H., & Plomin, R. (1984). *Temperament: Early developing personality traits.* Hillsdale, NJ: Erlbaum.

Bolt, M. (2010). Instructor's Resources to accompany David G. Myers *Psychology* (9th ed.) New York: Worth.

Chromosomal and Genetic Problems

AV: Pregnancy After 35 (22 min., Polymorph Films)

This film considers the physical and emotional aspects of pregnancy during the later childbearing years. It shows that although pregnancy after 35 should be planned carefully—including amniocentesis and good medical care—it is a joyful experience. Misconceptions about pregnancy after 35 abound, and this film will help clear them up.

Internet Activity: Cystic Fibrosis

To help students learn more about genetic disorders, and the Internet resources available to individuals affected by them, have them surf the net to find brief answers to the questions in Handout 6. The handout also lists several Web sources to get them started.

"On Your Own" Activity: Becoming Aware of Serious Genetic Problems

To give your students a clearer sense of the incidence of serious genetic problems, ask them to respond to the questions in Handout 7.

Although the 1-in-30 estimate seems high to many students, a little thought will usually lead to greater awareness of genetic disabilities among people the student has encountered in his or her life. Be sure to remind your students to take into account children who died in infancy. You should also point out that not every genetic problem is visible or observable and that we tend to omit people who have adjusted successfully to a disability or handicap.

The estimates students make on the basis of their experiences are therefore likely to be on the low side. The tendency to isolate or institutionalize people with certain kinds of defects or disabilities may also reduce our awareness of the incidence of genetic problems.

AV: Sickle-Cell Anemia (22 min., Filmakers Library)

Sickle-cell anemia is carefully explained, from its origins as a defense against malaria in Africa to its tragic outcome in the lives of many African Americans. Included is the story of a close-knit African American family with six children, three of whom have sickle-cell anemia. The mother explains that neither she nor her husband knew that they were carriers until their children were born.

"On Your Own" Activity: Raising a Child with a Serious Genetic Disorder

To help bring to life for your students the difficulties of nurturing a child with a serious genetic or chromosomal problem, assign the exercise on Handout 8. You might facilitate this exercise by identifying beforehand several parents who are willing to discuss their experiences with your students.

The point of this exercise is to demonstrate that genetic and chromosomal problems influence pychological and social development as well as biological development. As your students discuss their interview experiences in class, ask them whether they learned anything from these special parents that perhaps could not be learned from the parents of children who are not genetically challenged.

Teaching Tip: Genetic Counseling

To help your students understand the process and importance of genetic counseling, you might invite to class a speaker from an organization that provides genetic counseling. Two very helpful resources are the National Society of Genetic Counselors (NSGC), 401 N. Michigan Avenue, Chicago, IL 60611 (312-321-6834); and Genetic Alliance, 4301 Connecticut Avenue NW, Suite 404, Washington, DC 20008-2369 (202-966-5557). These organizations can give you the addresses of counseling centers near you. The Web sites of the NSGC (www.nsgc.org) and Genetic Alliance (www.geneticalliance.org) contain a wealth of information about genetic counseling for consumers, students, and professionals.

In addition, national organizations for the most common genetic diseases can provide more information; they may also have local groups in your area. Among these are the Cystic Fibrosis Foundation (www.cff.org/home/), the National Foundation for Jewish Genetic Diseases (www.healthfinder.gov/orgs/HR0556.htm), the American Sickle Cell Association (www.ascaa.org), the Cooley's Anemia Foundation (www.thalassemia.org), and the National Hemophilia Foundation (www.hemophilia.org).

Critical Thinking Activity: The Genetic Counselor

Each unit of these resources contains a critical thinking exercise designed specifically to test students' critical thinking about a topic covered in the text. Handout 9 contains a brief scenario about a genetic counselor and is followed by a series of questions. In this exercise, students are asked to play the role of genetic counselors advising healthy young couples who are at the beginning stages of their pregnancies. Based on their own phenotypes, as well as those of their parents and grandparents, they seek help in predicting those of their offspring.

Answers to Handout 9's critical thinking exercise are as follows:

1. The genes that affect skin color usually interact in an additive fashion. In this example, the offspring of a dark-skinned woman (whose parents and grandparents were also dark-skinned) and a light-skinned man (whose parents and grandparents were light-skinned) would likely be of middling skin tone.
2. This example is a bit trickier. First, you must realize that the woman must have one recessive red-hair gene (inherited from her red-haired mother), while the man has two recessive red-hair genes. The chances that their first child will have red hair are two in four. The odds are the same that their first child will have black hair.
3. In this example, you must realize not only that both parents have a recessive gene for blue eyes (How else could their children be blue eyed?) but also that heredity "has no memory": The odds of blue eyes for each child born to that couple are one in four, no matter how many previous children already have blue eyes.
4. There is one chance in two that the boy's sister is a carrier, and no chance that she will develop the disability herself. In this example, you must remember that each woman who is a carrier of an X-linked learning disability must have a healthy gene on one of her two X chromosomes. Therefore, all her offspring have a 50/50 chance of receiving the normal X chromosome. The normal X chromosome from their fathers will protect daughters who receive the defective X chromosome; sons will not receive an X chromosome from their fathers and therefore will manifest the learning disability.

Classroom Activity: Should Minors Be Tested for Incurable Genetic Conditions?

On a fall day in 1993 at the University of Michigan Medical Center, 16-year-old Melissa Drake, her father, an aunt, and a cousin gathered to hear whether Melissa carried the gene that triggered the deaths from breast cancer of her mother, grandmother, and numerous other women on her mother's side of the family. "I'm going to get it," she lamented to her boyfriend, at the same time mentally steeling herself for the day when she would be forced to take the only step that might prevent the disease: double mastectomy.

To initiate a class discussion of genetic testing and bioethics, ask your students the following question: If your 16-year-old daughter was fated to develop breast cancer, would you want her to know? Given recent developments in genetic testing, families will increasingly be confronted with such questions.

In fall 1994, researchers at the University of Utah pinpointed the actual gene, called BRCA1, responsible for about 5 percent of inherited cases of breast cancer. Women who carry the mutated BRCA1 gene and who have a strong family history of breast cancer have up to a 90 percent lifetime risk of developing the disease. It is estimated that half a million American women are BRCA1 carriers, making it one of the world's most common disease-triggering genes.

Barring unforeseen difficulties, researchers predict that routine tests for BRCA1 and hundreds of other disease genes will soon be available. Medical writer Terence Monmaney maintains that "it's not far-fetched to think DNA testing labs will someday be as common as fortune-telling parlors or at least the cholesterol-screening vans that visit malls."

One problem with this development, according to a survey conducted by the National Institutes of Health of over 1,000 commercial and nonprofit laboratories, is that some of the laboratories do not follow the admittedly vague and inadequate regulatory controls that help ensure the validity of genetic tests. And some laboratories are marketing genetic tests to physicians, obstetricians, and primary care providers who lack expertise in medical genetics.

Another problem has to do with genetic testing of untreatable diseases. For treatable conditions, genetic testing is rarely controversial. After researchers found the gene for retinoblastoma, an inherited childhood cancer of the eye, new procedures for preventing the formerly inevitable blindness were developed. But untreatable diseases are another story. "We need an extra layer of caution when dealing with young people," says Katherine Schnedier, a genetics counselor in Boston. "There are questions about their ability to give informed consent to these tests or to understand the tests' implications. Until we get more experienced in telling people about their genes, we'd rather work with adults."

Other counselors are even more adamant. The International Huntington Association has issued strong guidelines against having minors take DNA tests for incurable Huntington's disease. "You endanger a young person's ability to dream about an unlimited future by telling them at an early age what's in store," says Indiana University psychologist Kimberly Quaid. Quaid is also concerned that children identified as carriers of serious genetic disorders will be discriminated against. In one case, a New York school board pondered whether special education students should be tested for fragile X syndrome, which causes mental retardation. The issue was brought to the board by an advocate who argued that the school district could save money by "weeding out the kids" with the syndrome.

A related concern is the real possibility that insurance companies will deny coverage to individuals who have a predisposition toward developing a particular disease. To date, no federal laws prevent insurers from doing so.

Should parents have the final word in deciding whether their minor children should be tested? In one recent case, a father with a family history of Huntington's disease asked that his two young children be tested for the gene because he was concerned about saving enough money to meet their college expenses! "It may sound paternalistic," says genetic counselor Barbara Biesecker, "but sometimes we have to protect children from their parents." And in an article in the *Journal of the American Medical Association* (Stephenson, 1995), geneticist Dorothy Wertz argued that parental requests should be turned down if the child won't derive any medical benefit from knowing whether he or she carries a damaging gene.

Proponents of limited genetic testing of children, such as geneticist and lawyer Mary Pelias, feel differently. "Who are geneticists to be guardians of the world?" she asks. "We need to make sure the family understands that this kind of information has an upside and a significant downside. That's all we can do. We shouldn't step between parent and child."

And in some cases, such as Melissa Drake's, the results of testing can be liberating. When researchers told Melissa she did not have the breast cancer gene, she was initially stunned. But she gradually lost the fatalistic attitude that had caused her to dread her developing sexuality. Even so, breast cancer researchers at many medical centers (including the one that tested Melissa) now refuse to perform genetic analysis on minors.

You might expand on this classroom discussion by scheduling the Classroom Debate described on the next page, which calls for mandatory genetic testing of prospective parents.

Geller, G. (2005). The ethics of predictive genetic testing in prevention trials involving adolescents. In E. Kodish (Ed.), *Ethics and research with children: A case-based approach* (pp. 194–220). New York: New York University Press.

Monmaney, T. (1995). Genetic testing: Kids' latest rite of passage. *Health*, 46–48.

Stephenson, J. (1995, December 6). Questions on genetic testing services. *Journal of the American Medical Association, 274*(21), 1661–1662.

"On Your Own" Activity: Reaching Out

To demonstrate for students that they can easily obtain information for making informed decisions about genetic problems, you might assign the exercise in Handout 10 for homework. Begin by filling out the top of the handout, which identifies the genetic defect the student will be investigating.

Students may consult a variety of resources—including the telephone book, their physicians, the student health clinic or local hospital, or popular books at the bookstore or library. Many genetic disease foundations, support groups, and professional health organizations also maintain home pages on the Internet (see the Internet Activity on Cystic Fibrosis in this resource unit). The point of the exercise is to provide them with experience in taking action to acquire information. Students' resourcefulness will probably be enhanced by hearing about the different ways in which class members completed this exercise. Actions that might be taken in the absence of a local chapter of a particular organization include writing to the national organization for the address of the nearest chapter, or even organizing a local chapter.

Classroom Activity: Classroom Debate: *"Resolved: All Prospective Parents at Risk as Carriers of Abnormal Genes Should Be Subjected to Mandatory Genetic Testing"*

With the completion of the government's Human Genome Project, many people are expressing concern that genetic testing may pose serious threats of discrimination and violation of privacy rights. To encourage students to think about some of these issues, and to increase their understanding of the issues' complexities, follow the guidelines in the General Resources section of this manual for scheduling a classroom debate on this resolution. You might prefer to select the reference material yourself and place the relevant journals and textbooks on reserve in the college library, or you might want students to find their own.

One concern has to do with what could happen when the genes for diseases such as Alzheimer disease or alcoholism have been pinpointed.

On the other side of the issue are those scientists, counselors, and concerned citizens who believe that mandatory genetic testing will help reduce the emotional and financial burdens that the most serious genetic disorders create for the individual, the family, and society.

You might encourage your debaters to prepare arguments that address some of the following questions: Should genetic screening be required of every couple? For some couples? Who should decide who must be screened? To what extent, if any, should the government be involved in genetic screening? How far should such technology be permitted to advance? What are some of the negative effects of genetic technology on the individual? On the family? On society?

HANDOUT 1

Developmental Fact or Myth?

T F 1. No two cells of the human body contain exactly the same genetic instructions.

T F 2. The genetic contribution of the father's sperm determines whether a fertilized egg develops into a male or female.

T F 3. Not all individuals are born genetically unique.

T F 4. Humans have more than 100,000 genes.

T F 5. All the genes a person has show up as observable characteristics.

T F 6. The genomes of humans and chimpanzees are 99 percent identical.

T F 7. Alcoholism is inherited.

T F 8. Middle-aged couples are less likely than younger couples to produce a child with a chromosomal abnormality.

T F 9. Everyone carries several genes that could produce serious diseases or handicaps in their offspring.

T F 10. Most of the known genetic disorders are transmitted through recessive genes.

HANDOUT 2

Similarities Questionnaire

	ALIKE	DIFFERENT
Politics		
Music		
Religion		
Clothes		
Jobs held		
Job goals		
Sports		
Hobbies		
Favorite school subjects		
Subjects you dislike		
Favorite foods		
Foods you dislike		
Favorite colors		
Regional (climate) preferences		
Automobile preferences		
Sleeping habits		
Reading tastes		
Talents		
Aversions (What bugs you?)		
Chewing gum brand		

	ALIKE	DIFFERENT
Cigarette brand		
Toothpaste brand		
Coffee brand		
Newspapers read		
Favorite magazines		
Any special or unusual talents or abilities		
Pets owned		
Family members (names, ages, interests)		
Educational interests (major)		
TV programs		
Habits		
Personality traits		
Vacation—activities, preferences		
Social preferences (gregarious/reclusive)		
Marital status		
Handedness		
Grade point average		
Major illnesses (age of occurrence)		
Sensitivity to drugs		

Source: Adapted from a questionnaire by W. Joseph Wyatt. Used by permission. Used in Bolt, M. (2008). Instructor's resources to accompany David Myers, *Exploring Psychology* (7th ed.). New York: Worth.

HANDOUT 3

Internet Activity: Cloning

To learn more about cloning, and the many ethical, moral, and philosophical issues raised by the growing possibility of human cloning, surf the net to find brief answers to the following questions. (Hint: To get started, you might consult the Web sites listed below. From each home page, search on the keyword "cloning.")

www.ornl.gov/sci/techresources/Human_Genome/elsi/cloning.shtml
Human Genome Project information with a variety of authoritative links to Web sites describing the latest cloning research

www.newscientist.com/specials.ns
Search on "cloning" for the latest research summaries compiled by *New Scientist* magazine.

http://ethics.sandiego.edu/applied/bioethics/index.asp
Web site examining the ethics of artificial reproductive technologies

1. What is cloning?

2. When was cloning first demonstrated? What was the first species to be cloned?

3. What are some practical uses of animal cloning?

4. For what technical reasons was human cloning considered essentially impossible until recently? What new developments have changed the reasoning of some scientists regarding this possibility?

HANDOUT 3 *(continued)*

5. What are several common misconceptions about cloning?

6. State at least three arguments in support of research into human cloning.

7. State several ethical, legal, and moral issues raised by the possibility of human cloning.

8. Which of the issues identified above do you find the most troubling?

HANDOUT 4

Calculating Phenotypes and Genotypes

One way to calculate the odds that parents with a particular gene in their genotype will pass it on to their children is to draw a table with the father's two genes for that genotype on the top and the mother's two genes on the left.

Father's two genes

Mother's two genes	F_1	F_2
M_1		
M_2		

The box is filled in very simply. The letters at the top of each column are written into the boxes reading down and the letters at the side are written into the boxes reading across.

Father's two genes

Mother's two genes	F_1	F_2
M_1	F_1M_1	F_2M_1
M_2	F_1M_2	F_2M_2

As you can see from examining the boxes, a child could inherit any one of four possible combinations from the parents' two pairs of genes. The chances of each child inheriting one of these combinations is one in four, or 25 percent.

HANDOUT 4 *(continued)*

Consider how this works in practice. When both parents have two brown-eye genes, all the children will have brown eyes as well as two brown-eye genes.

Parents' phenotype: brown eyes. Father: BB; Mother: BB.

Parents' genotype: sperm and ova each carry the brown-eye gene. Father: B; Mother: B.

Using B to represent the gene for brown eyes, fill in the table to show the possible genotypes of the children.

Father's two genes

Mother's two genes	B	B
B		
B		

What is the children's phenotype? ____________

What genes will the children carry in their sperm or ova? (What is their genotype?) ____________________

The same pattern holds true if both parents have two blue-eye genes. Here we use b to represent the blue-eye gene.

Parents' phenotype: blue eyes. Father: bb; Mother: bb.

Parents' genotype: sperm and ova each have the blue-eye gene. Father: b; Mother: b.

Using b to represent the gene for blue eyes, fill in the table to show the children's genotype.

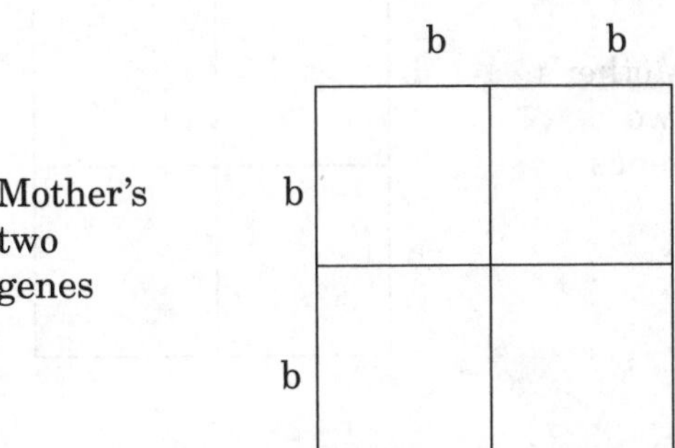

It gets more complicated if one parent—for example, the father—has two brown-eye genes (BB) and the other, the mother, has two blue-eye genes (bb). All of the children will inherit one brown-eye gene and one blue-eye gene. This means that they will all have brown eyes, because the brown-eye gene is dominant over the blue-eye gene. The sperm or ova of each child will have a

HANDOUT 4 *(continued)*

50 percent chance of having the dominant brown-eye gene and a 50 percent chance of carrying the recessive blue-eye gene. The latter are called carriers of the recessive gene, even though the gene does not affect their appearance (or phenotype). Complete the table for this pair (one combination has already been filled in for you).

Father's two genes

	B	B
Mother's two genes b	Bb	
b		

What is the children's phenotype?_______________
What possible genes will the children carry in their sperm or ova? (What is their genotype?) __________________

Now, what if one parent—let's say the father—has one brown-eye gene and one blue-eye gene (Bb), while the mother has two blue-eye genes (bb)? Each child will have a 50 percent chance of having blue eyes and a 50 percent chance of having brown eyes; in the latter case, they will carry the recessive blue-eye gene. Complete the table for this pair.

Father's two genes

	B	b
Mother's two genes b		
b		

All the possible genotypes of the children are___________________.
The chance(s) that one of the children will inherit the phenotype for brown eyes is (are)_____ chance(s) in four.

HANDOUT 4 *(continued)*

If, in the preceding case, the mother's eyes were brown and she had two brown-eye genes, all of the children would have brown eyes. However, each would have a 50 percent chance of carrying the blue-eye gene, just like their father, as you can tell by filling in the table.

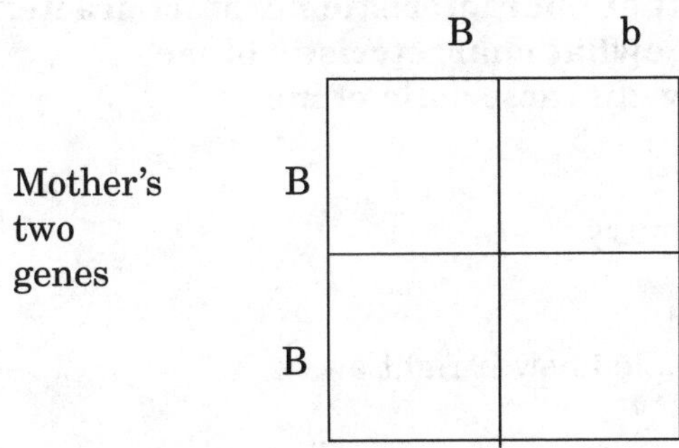

The following possibility is the most surprising: Two brown-eyed parents can produce blue-eyed children if each parent has one brown-eye gene and one blue-eye gene.

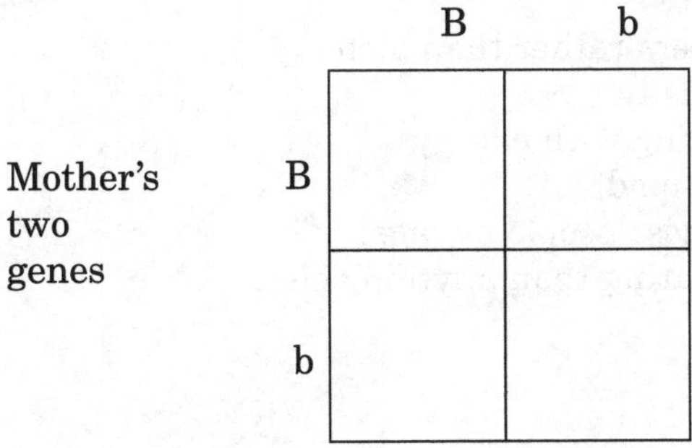

After filling in the table, you can predict that the probability of a blue-eyed child being produced by these two parents is ________________ .

HANDOUT 5

EAS Temperament Survey

To assess your own temperament, rate each of the items using the following scale.

1 = Not at all characteristic of me
2 = Somewhat uncharacteristic of me
3 = Neither characteristic nor uncharacteristic of me
4 = Somewhat characteristic of me
5 = Very characteristic of me

______ 1. I like to be with people.
______ 2. I usually seem to be in a hurry.
______ 3. I am easily frightened.
______ 4. I frequently get distressed.
______ 5. When displeased, I let people know it right away.
______ 6. I am something of a loner.
______ 7. I like to keep busy all the time.
______ 8. I am known as hot-blooded and quick-tempered.
______ 9. I often feel frustrated.
______ 10. My life is fast-paced.
______ 11. Everyday events make me troubled and fretful.
______ 12. I often feel insecure.
______ 13. There are many things that annoy me.
______ 14. When I get scared, I panic.
______ 15. I prefer working with others rather than alone.
______ 16. I get emotionally upset easily.
______ 17. I often feel as if I'm bursting with energy.
______ 18. It takes a lot to make me mad.
______ 19. I have fewer fears than most people my age.
______ 20. I find people more stimulating than anything else.

Source: Reprinted by permission of Lawrence Erlbaum Associates, Inc., and the authors from Buss, A. H., & Plomin, R. (1984). *Temperament: Early developing personality traits.*

HANDOUT 6

Internet Activity: Cystic Fibrosis (CF)

To learn more about genetic disorders, and the Internet resources available to individuals affected by them, surf the net to find brief answers to the following questions. (Hint: One URL you might consult is the Family Guide to Cystic Fibrosis Genetic Testing, at www.phd.msu.edu/DNA/cf_fam.pdf.)

1. What is cystic fibrosis (CF)?

2. What are the major symptoms of CF?

3. How is CF usually diagnosed? What is direct testing?

4. What causes CF?

HANDOUT 6 *(continued)*

5. One in _____ (how many?) people in the general population in the United States is born with CF.
6. Based on your ethnic background and family history, how likely are you to be a CF carrier? Explain your answer.
7. If two parents who carry the CF gene have a child, what is the likelihood that that child will carry the CF gene?
8. Assume that you have a brother or sister with CF and that you and a White partner who has no family history of CF have a child. What is the likelihood of your child being affected?
9. Is prenatal diagnosis of CF possible?
10. State the URL (Internet address) of at least one relevant Web page other than the one identified in the introduction to this activity.

HANDOUT 7

Becoming Aware of Serious Genetic Problems

About 1 baby in 30 is born with a serious genetic problem. Because this is so, you will have encountered many people who have such problems. Indeed, in any population of 30 people you might expect to encounter one person who has a serious genetic problem. Remember that "serious" does not mean "disabling." Review your experiences with the help of the questions below.

1. Think back to your fifth- or sixth-grade class. About how many children were in the class? ____________

   Were you aware that any of these children had a serious genetic problem (for example, cleft palate, diabetes, sickle-cell anemia, hemophilia)? If so, describe the problem.

   Did any of your classmates have a sibling who had a serious genetic problem? If so, describe it.

2. Consider the children of your parents' closest friends. About how many children are in this population? ________________

   How many of these children have a serious genetic problem? ________________

   Describe the problem(s).

HANDOUT 7 *(continued)*

3. Think of the group of children in your building or on your street now or at some specified time in the past. In this population of neighborhood children, how many had serious genetic problems? ________________

   Describe the problems.

4. Finally, think of your extended family: your first and second cousins and other close relatives who are your age or younger. How many people are in this population? ________________

   How many of the people in this population have serious genetic problems?

   Describe these problems.

5. Does your experience substantiate the estimate that about 1 child in 30 is born with a serious genetic problem?

HANDOUT 8

Raising a Child with a Serious Genetic Disorder

When development does not proceed normally, life becomes more difficult for everyone involved. Parents find that it takes more time and effort to raise a child with a serious genetic problem and that other people are often hurtful in their comments and behavior toward the child. To help bring some of these developmental issues into focus, set up an informal interview with one or both parents of a child with a serious chromosomal or genetic problem (for example, Down syndrome, cystic fibrosis, muscular dystrophy, or sickle-cell anemia). If you do not know such a family, you can probably get a referral from someone at the local chapter of the national organization that provides information about one of these diseases. Alternatively, ask if you can interview a representative from the organization itself. Use the following questions to organize your interview; afterward, write out answers to the questions and return these to your instructor.

1. Whom did you interview, why did you choose them, and how were they contacted?

2. What experience do your participants have with serious genetic or chromosomal problems? Which one(s)?

3. What (if any) was the impact of this problem on the development of the parent's child in each of the three domains? Give specific examples. (If your participants are not the parents, discuss the developmental impact of the genetic or chromosomal problem in general terms.)

   Biosocial Domain:

HANDOUT 8 *(continued)*

Cognitive Domain:

Psychosocial Domain:

4. In what ways has your *participant's* own development been influenced by raising a child with this genetic or chromosomal problem?

5. What advice would your participants offer to prospective parents who may have a child with this condition?

HANDOUT 9

Critical Thinking Activity: The Genetic Counselor

Now that you have read and reviewed the material on heredity and environment, take your learning a step further by testing your critical thinking skills on this practical problem-solving exercise.

Conception brings together genetic instructions from both parents for every human characteristic. Genotype refers to an individual's entire genetic makeup, including those genes that are not expressed outwardly. When a trait is apparent, it means that the genes have expressed themselves in the developing individual's phenotype. We all have many genes in our genotypes that are not actually expressed. In genetic terms, we are carriers of these unexpressed genes.

How genetic instructions work to influence the specific characteristics an offspring will inherit is usually quite complex, because most traits are both polygenic and multifactorial. To further complicate things, the phenotype of any given characteristic is often influenced by additive or nonadditive patterns of gene–gene interaction.

In this exercise, you are asked to play the role of a genetic counselor advising healthy young couples who are at the beginning stages of their pregnancies. Based on their own phenotypes, as well as those of their parents and grandparents, they seek your help in predicting those of their offspring. (Hint: You might find it helpful to diagram each situation, using uppercase letters to indicate dominant genes and lowercase letters to indicate recessive genes.)

1. A dark-skinned woman, whose parents and grandparents all had very dark skin, marries a light-skinned man, whose parents and grandparents were all very light-skinned. What is the probable skin tone of their offspring?
2. A man with red hair (recessive) marries a woman with black hair whose mother had red hair. What are the chances that their first child will have red hair? Black hair?
3. A woman and a man both have brown eyes, but their first child has blue eyes. What are the chances that their second child will have blue eyes?
4. An apparently healthy couple has one normal daughter and then a son who develops a learning disability, an X-linked recessive disease. What are the chances that the boy's sister is a carrier of the learning disability? What chance is there that she will develop the learning disability herself?

HANDOUT 10

Reaching Out

Prospective parents and other family members work closely with physicians and genetic counselors to predict genetic problems and treat them. National organizations have been established to provide information on most genetic diseases and to help families cope with their medical and biological effects.

Assume that your special need is to find out more about the genetic disease called ______________________.

1. Use your resources to find the address(es) of the national organization(s) that provide(s) information about this disease. Write the address(es) below:

   ____

   ____

   ____

2. Many national organizations also have local chapters. If you can find a local chapter or a group that meets in your immediate area, write the address and/or telephone number.

   ____

   ____

   ____

3. If there is no local chapter in your area, what further steps might you take to meet others who are either interested in or affected by this genetic problem?

Prenatal Development and Birth

Contents

Note: Worth Publishers provides online Instructor and Student Tool Kits, DVD Student Tool Kits, and Instructor and Student video resources in DevelopmentPortal for use with the text. See Part I: General Resources for information about these materials and the text Lecture Guides for a complete list by text chapter.

Problems and Solutions

The New Family

Suggested Activities

Introducing Prenatal Development and Birth

"On Your Own" Activity: Developmental Fact or Myth?

Before students read about prenatal development and birth, have them respond to the true–false statements in Handout 1.

The correct answers are provided below. Class discussion can focus on the origins of any developmental misconceptions that are demonstrated in the students' incorrect answers.

1. T	6. T
2. T	7. F
3. F	8. F
4. T	9. T
5. F	10. F

Teaching Tip: Covering Sensitive Topics

Sensitive ("touchy") subjects come up often when teaching developmental psychology. As a teacher, you face the dilemma of not wanting to offend students while wanting your students to benefit from how psychological research can inform their understanding. You may want to challenge some of your students' beliefs, but you don't want to insult them by telling them they are wrong.

Retta Poe notes three related challenges that can occur in the classroom when a sensitive area is being covered. First, students and instructors can lose their composure, even bursting into tears or speaking in anger. Second, some students seem to engage in too frequent or inappropriate self-disclosure, as when recounting their own use of drugs or engaging in other risky behaviors. Finally, students sometimes state as "fact" something that is objectively wrong or confuse anecdotal or personal experience with fact.

Whether you choose to deliberately raise a touchy subject or it comes up during class discussion, you should definitely have a plan for handling scenarios that might provoke emotional responses in both students and yourself. Poe offers a number of strategies for preventing problems and resolving conflicts during such moments.

1. Develop class ground rules for discussion. Examples of good rules to go over with the class are
   - Treat others' opinions with courtesy and respect.
   - Maintain confidentiality of experiences shared by class members.
   - Don't monopolize discussion.
   - Attack ideas rather than persons.
   - Don't tell things that are too personal.
   - Exercise your right not to share your thoughts and ideas if you are uncomfortable talking about something.
2. Respect students' feelings. Be careful, for instance, when using role-playing to teach certain topics, and never force students to disclose personal experiences about certain topics. You may need to give some students permission to skip a class meeting if they believe the topic will be too upsetting. If a student completely loses his or her composure in class, your best option may be to dismiss the class, take the student aside, and, if necessary, refer the student to the appropriate counselor.
3. Take advantage of teachable moments. Having controversies come up in class can be good opportunities for teaching and stimulating growth in your students. Always try to turn a heated difference of opinion into a learning experience, even if you have to resort to discussing research findings about group dynamics, persuasion, and the like.
4. Model tolerance. As an instructor, it is vital that you deal with sensitive issues in an open, honest way that conveys acceptance of divergent beliefs and values. This is especially important in a class where students differ in age, ethnicity, culture, and religion.
5. Have a planned activity. When you anticipate difficulty in getting students to discuss a sensitive topic, come to class with a short assignment to get the ball rolling. Before opening the floor for discussion of racism, for instance, Poe assigns a short "writing to learn" exercise in which students are asked to jot down a few of their own ideas and questions. She then asks students to share what they have written.

Poe, R. E. (2000). Hitting a nerve: When touchy subjects come up in class. *Association for Psychological Science Observer, 13*(9). Retrieved July 10, 2007 from www.psychologicalscience.org/teachingtips.

AV: Transitions Throughout the Life Span, Program 4: The Wondrous Journey

As Program 4 opens, we meet Sandra and Darrin Nealy in the anxious moments just before Sandra gives birth. The personal experiences of this young family throughout Sandra's pregnancy and delivery form the backdrop for the program's exploration of prenatal development and birth.

The period of prenatal development is a time of incredibly rapid growth during which the emerging person develops from a single cell into a fully functioning individual. This development is outlined through the germinal, embryonic, and fetal periods of development, vividly illustrated with in vitro footage.

The second segment discusses some of the problems that can occur—among them prenatal exposure to disease, drugs, and other hazards—and the factors that moderate the risks of exposure to such factors. Next, the program examines the process of birth, its possible variations and problems, including anoxia and low birthweight. The program concludes with a discussion of the significance of the parent–newborn bond, including factors that affect its development. Kathleen Berger provides expert commentary.

Classroom Activity: The Evolutionary Perspective on Prenatal Development

The following discussion of some aspects of pregnancy, childbirth, and infant development from an evolutionary perspective is sure to spark interest in your students.

By mammalian standards, the nine-month gestation period in humans is relatively long. But according to evolutionary biologists, based on other aspects of life, a nine-month gestation period is actually a relatively short period. They further note that the period probably ought to be 15 or 16 months! But, of course, that's impossible. (Your students are sure to see that it is indeed impossible. If not, ask them if they really would want to give birth to a 15- to 20-pound baby.)

As a result of our slow rate of physical maturation and "abbreviated" gestation period, the human infant is exceedingly helpless and relatively less well developed when compared with most other animals. Anthropologists believe that the relatively short gestation period may be a response to the evolution of our species' large brain, which, while providing humans with a high level of intelligence and cognitive flexibility, resulted in a large skull that makes birth difficult.

Why did the forces of evolution produce a relatively short pregnancy in humans, rather than widening the birth canal in order to allow babies to develop more fully in the womb? Anthropologist Barry Bogin believes the answer lies in the unique way that humans move. "Unlike other animals," says Bogin (personal communication, 2007), "we walk upright on two legs. We don't have tails to balance us, like kangaroos do, or birds. We don't have other bodily projections to support us or to counterbalance our weight. We just have our legs." Thus, the duration of prenatal development represents somewhat of a compromise between brain maturation and bipedalism (the upright posture of humans): Babies are born at a point when the brain is as big as it can be without requiring a wider birth canal, which would impair a female's ability to walk.

According to this line of reasoning, then, there are two competing evolutionary pressures on the shape of the human female's hips. The first is bipedalism. The second is the advantage of giving birth to babies with large brains, ready for learning. There came a moment in the evolution of our species when we couldn't have it both ways. We couldn't keep the advantages of getting around on two feet and still have that large complex brain of ours.

Another interesting example of the evolutionary perspective on human development concerns the newborn's body fat composition. Compared with other primates, human infants are remarkably fat when they are born. Fat ensures that the developing brain—which has attained only one-quarter of its mature size at birth—is adequately nourished. In the precarious world in which humans evolved as a species—a world of constant walking, hunting, and gathering—fat evolved as an efficient way of storing resources, a sort of nutritional backpack to tide the individual over periods of short food supply.

Even before infants are born, their mothers store fat for them. The mother's fat ensures a rich supply of breast milk for nursing. Storing maternal fat, which is used up later in lactation, is so important that if a mother-to-be has not stored enough fat by the last trimester, she will continue to store fat even if her baby turns out to be low birthweight.

Further, each species' milk has a special profile of nutrients that exactly matches the species' specific developmental needs. Cow's milk, for example, has twice as much protein as human milk. Rabbit milk has six or seven times as much protein as that of humans. Cow and rabbit milk are designed to grow muscle mass. In contrast, human milk, which is relatively low in protein but very high in sugar, is designed to provide energy for the baby's rapidly developing brain—not to grow a large body. And indeed, the newborn's development reflects this nutritional profile. During the first year of life, the infant's body weight will at most double or triple; compared with other mammals, this is a very slow rate of growth of muscle and bone. By contrast, the infant's brain grows at an extraordinarily rapid pace.

Bogin, B. A. (2001). *Growth of humanity.* New York: Wiley.

"On Your Own" Activity: Folk Wisdom and Pregnancy

To help students appreciate the continuing strength of fallacious folk wisdom about pregnancy and to help them apply knowledge gained in the text discussion, have them answer the questions in Handout 2, drawing on the folk tales of family and friends.

This exercise should reveal a range of beliefs, depending on the ages and backgrounds of your students. Relevant to the discussion may be such factors as age (Do the older and younger members of the class have different varieties of folk wisdom to relate?), culture, and gender (some of the men may be less familiar with "accepted wisdom" than the women). If students have difficulty with these questions, you might ask them to interpret the following examples.

"Don't stretch your arms above your head or the umbilical cord will get tangled around the fetus's neck." (Not true; the umbilicus stays taut like a high-pressure hose.)

"Intercourse during pregnancy will cause miscarriage." (Not true, although during the last months of pregnancy vigorous intercourse can sometimes trigger premature labor. This myth may have arisen because the normal rate of miscarriage is high during the early months of pregnancy. In addition, the need to lay blame made it convenient for people to point the finger at the husband's sexual appetite, especially when the double standard made the male the usual initiator of intercourse.)

"You can tell whether a woman is carrying a boy because her face glows more, because the fetus is more active, or because she is carrying 'low'." (All myths.)

"Every baby costs a tooth." (When calcium in the woman's diet was in short supply and dental care was poor, pregnancy may have weakened the tooth and gum structure, causing loss of teeth in women who bore many children.)

"Eat for two." (If this is interpreted as eating twice as much, it's not only false but potentially harmful. If it means that the mother must be better nourished in order to carry and deliver a healthy baby, it's true.)

Observational Activity: Pregnancy's Impact on Expectant Parents

As described in the General Resources section of this manual, panel interviews are an excellent (and sometimes the only) practical means of giving students real-life experience with certain developmental stages and issues. One example is the impact of pregnancy on expectant parents. Departing from the traditional lecture/textbook format by allowing students to interview couples in various stages of expectancy is an especially useful technique for increasing student awareness of the impact of this significant developmental transition—that from adult offspring to parent.

This observational activity involves inviting several expectant couples to the class. Ideally, the couples selected will represent the diversity of the group under study (expectant couples at early, middle, and late stages of pregnancy) and will be comfortable with student questioning. Students are directed to use the "before and after" approach to the interview, as explained in the General Resources section, to integrate text information, lecture material, and personal life experiences in order to pull together all they know about the impact of pregnancy on couples. Then they are directed to construct a set of expected behaviors, developmental tasks, issues, and stresses that they will use to assess the panelists.

Handout 3 provides information on setting up the interviews; Handout 4 contains the developmental assessment form and the follow-up questionnaire.

Prenatal Growth

AV: Life's Greatest Miracle (57 min., Time Life Video, NOVA)

(See description in Heredity and Environment.)

AV: Developmental Phases Before and After Birth (28 min., Films for the Humanities and Sciences)

Stunning photography is used to probe physical development from the fetal period through the first year of life.

AV: Prenatal Development (30 min., Insight Media)

Focusing on physical development from conception to birth, this film dramatically illustrates the effects of drug use on a developing fetus. Ultrasound "photography" shows a fetus responding to a variety of sensory stimuli, including music. The film closes with the baby's birth.

AV: Prenatal Development: A Life in the Making (26 min., Magna Systems, Inc.)

This film traces the story of life, from a one-celled zygote into a fully functioning human being 266 days later. Each of the three stages of prenatal development is fully described, along with the impact of environmental factors on the developing person.

AV: Psychological Development Before Birth (22 min., Films for the Humanities and Sciences)

This film discusses high-tech methods of determining the well-being of the fetus and the beginnings of sensory-motor responsiveness to environmental stimuli. It also explores how mothers-to-be prepare themselves for having a baby.

AV: Nature's Child: Biological Growth (60 min., RMI Media Productions)

This film explores the many influences of biological processes on behavior and prenatal development. It also describes the three stages of labor, the birth process, and possible complications of birth, including prematurity and anoxia.

AV: Pediatric Brain Development: The Importance of a Head Start (13 min., Films for the Humanities and Sciences)

Hosted by ABC newsperson Diane Sawyer, this short film reports on neural development in the brain during fetal development and early childhood. PET scans (explained by UCLA's Michael Phelps, inventor of the technology) are used to illustrate the long-term effects of sensory stimulation and deprivation, early language development, and the possible connections between premature birth and attention-deficit disorder.

Classroom Activity: Birth and Prenatal Development Resources on the Internet

The Internet is full of empirically and medically sound information and advice for prospective parents. If your classroom has direct access to the Internet, you might devote one class session to checking out a couple of these large sites. There, you and your students will find extensive information on every imaginable issue related to childbirth. Several of the sites also provide good photographs, graphs, tables, and charts that are helpful teaching aids. Following are several such sites.

www.ivf.com
The Web site of Georgia Reproductive Specialists is an extensive Internet resource that includes information on twins, a discussion of various types of birthing, and a pregnancy primer.

http://parenting.ivillage.com/pregnancyh/calendar
The Interactive Pregnancy Calendar will build a day-by-day customized calendar detailing the development of a baby from conception to birth. The pregnancy calendar should be seen as a general guide: Every pregnancy is unique, and some babies are faster or slower developers than others.

www.efn.org/~djz/birth/birthnew.html
The Online Birth Center is an expansive site that discusses a host of topics related to pregnancy with an emphasis on natural childbirth. It features sections on pregnancy, birth stories, fetal monitoring, and midwifery, for example, in addition to book reviews and a resource area. This site also provides a link for downloading The Baby Calculator, which is designed to help parents-to-be keep track of special dates such as each trimester, their conception date, and the due date. Pictures show the different stages of the baby's development with a written description of what is taking place during each period.

Classroom Activity: Fetal Ultrasound: "The Best Physical You'll Ever Have"

Sophisticated new developments in ultrasound imaging provide parents-to-be and researchers with a wealth of information on the progress of the developing person in utero. "It's the best physical you'll ever have, because the quantity and quality of information ultrasound reveals is astonishing," says George Leopold of the University of California San Diego's Department of Radiology. "We can measure the fetus's size and estimate age extremely accurately just four to six weeks after conception. We can monitor fetal movements to see if the central nervous system is developing normally. We can see if the heart has four chambers and if the spinal cord is closed."

Here are just a few of the things that modern ultrasound has helped us to understand about normal prenatal development.

- Fetal movements change predictably. "At seven to eight weeks," notes Leopold, "the embryo's entire body jerks and twitches. At 13 to 14 weeks we see movements in the limbs, not the entire body. By 20 weeks, we should see purposeful movements, like a hand opening and closing or sucking a thumb. If these movements are not happening according to this schedule, we look for a problem in the central nervous system or metabolism."
- Ultrasound is often used to resolve questions of fetal size and age when a mother-to-be's size doesn't correspond with her due date. Notes Leopold, "We can measure the head diameter and circumference and the length of the femur, the large bone in the leg, and very accurately determine the age." This helps establish the appropriate delivery date. "Before ultrasound helped us estimate age women could be induced into labor too soon, before the baby was ready to be born, or allowed to carry a child past the time when the uterus could nourish it."
- With an incidence of 1 in every 600 births, Down syndrome (trisomy-21) is the most common cause of severe cognitive handicap. With advancing prenatal ultrasound technology, screening for this condition has moved from the second to the first trimester.
- Ultrasound is routinely used to detect growth disorders (which occur in 10 percent of all fetuses), and to help diagnose the cause of abnormally large maternal weight gain during pregnancy. "The mother," Leopold explains, "may be too big because she is carrying an overly large fetus; she may have developed diabetes during pregnancy, or there is simply an excess of amniotic fluid and the baby is really the right size. Depending on the answer, the obstetrician can make a better decision whether to intervene."
- Uneven growth is fairly common in multiple births, with one twin being much larger than the other, for example. Because ultrasound illuminates blood flow, it can indicate whether the smaller twin's blood supply is normal or is being unduly influenced by the larger twin. In the latter case, treatment involving removal of some amniotic fluid around one of the twins can actually improve the chances that both will thrive.
- Leopold even believes that ultrasound can actually give mothers a headstart on bonding. "Ultrasound pictures are so good that even the patient can identify the baby's profile, arms, legs, and so on. At that point, the pregnancy becomes 'real' for most mothers. The result is that they take better care of themselves and their babies."

The Nemours organization maintains an excellent Web site (http://kidshealth.org/parent/system/medical/prenatal_tests.html) that describes a variety of prenatal diagnostic tests, including fetal ultrasound. There, prospective parents can read more about how the test works, what to expect during the test, how to prepare for the test, and any possible risks.

Vankayalapati, P., & Hollis, B. (2004, April). Role of ultrasound in obstetrics. *Current Obstetrics and Gynecology, 14*(2), 92–98.

Birth

Classroom Activity: Preparing for Birth

To give your students an idea of what it is like to prepare for the birth of a baby, you might acquire (or ask a few interested students to acquire) examples of the information packets obstetricians and family planning clinics hand out to their pregnant patients. In addition to providing information on prenatal health, these packets describe the birth process and tell couples what to expect at the hospital or in case of emergency. Information may also be included on how (and when) to check in at the hospital, the advantages of taking a tour of the delivery or birthing room, and related matters. For the most part, the material is written in simple and appealing language and includes helpful illustrations. And, of course, the tone is usually reassuring and positive.

AV: The Journey Through the Life Span, Program 1: Birth

Program 1 (9:20) introduces the developing person as embarking on a journey of biosocial growth. The program begins by depicting and explaining the physiology and process of birth. Annette Perez-Delboy of Columbia-Presbyterian Medical Center explains the use of the Apgar scale to rate the newborn twice: immediately after birth and five minutes later. Richard Polin, also of Columbia-Presbyterian Medical Center, describes the special needs and potential problems of preterm babies and infants.

In addition to the narrated video segment, the program includes an unnarrated observation module. This observation module (4:15) explores the problems of Taylor, who along with his twin Alec was born prematurely and of low birthweight (the combined weight of the twins at birth was 3 pounds). It focuses on the care Taylor received at 28 weeks' gestational age.

AV: Newborn (28 min., Filmakers Library)

Three of the most highly respected neonatal researchers—T. Berry Brazelton, Lewis Lipsitt, and Louis Sander—are shown testing newborns. The impressive array of newborn reflexes, sensory abilities, and learning potential is demonstrated. Probably even more important, these neonatal abilities are put into context, showing the infants able and willing to respond to their parents. Thus, the film goes beyond the clinical test procedures and captures some of the warmth that is possible in the parent–newborn relationship.

"On Your Own" Activity: Reading About Birth

The last 15 or so years have seen a growing media interest in pregnancy and birth. First-person accounts of births, as well as news features on all aspects of the birth process, regularly appear in newspapers, in magazines, and on television. In 1998, for the first time the birth of a baby was "broadcast" on the Internet. Since then, a number of mothers have shared their birth experiences on the Internet. As a class project, ask students to bring in examples of recent articles on these subjects. For those students who do not bring in an article, distribute a few of the most interesting articles you have seen.

When each student has an article, use Handout 5 to help your students relate lecture and text material to their outside reading.

The articles supplied will probably touch upon a wide variety of topics, including the father's role in birth; the role of midwives and birth attendants; the presence of siblings at birth; home birthing; the patient's role in decision making about obstetrical procedures; the use or abuse of cesarean section; nontraditional birth methods (birthing chairs, etc.); malpractice suits in obstetrics; and medical responses to preterm birth. There may also be first-person accounts of birth and its psychological impact on the parents. The main role of the instructor will be to show students how their learning experience in the text can help them interpret and understand information from all kinds of sources. Focusing on articles that have an obvious relationship to material in the text and lectures will be especially valuable.

"On Your Own" Activity: Birth in Fiction and Film

Your students may have noticed that many biographies and novels begin at the beginning—with birth. A remarkable example is *David Copperfield*, by Charles Dickens, in which the first chapter is titled simply "In Which I Am Born." This chapter sets the stage for much of what happens in the novel. The reader learns about the time of birth, the physical and emotional health of the mother, and the expectations of an important relative (especially regarding sex—David was supposed to be a girl). Also mentioned are a minor birth abnormality (the presence of a caul, or membrane, partially covering the head) and the absence of the father (who was dead). Virtually all the facts and events of "In Which I Am Born" influence the shape of the narrative that follows.

To help your students think about the ways in which the birth experience can "set the stage" for the life that follows, you might ask them to look at the ways in which birth is treated in fiction and other literary forms (examples include Somerset Maugham's *Of Human Bondage*, Günter Grass's *The Tin Drum*, Laurence Sterne's *Tristram Shandy*, and William Shakespeare's *Richard III*). Then, have them try the exercise in Handout 6.

Students should come to see that each of us uses facts and fictions about our births to set the stage for or "explain" developments that come later, much as an effective novelist does.

AV: The Process of Birth (23 min., Films for the Humanities and Sciences)

This excellent video explores how different cultures and individuals view the process of birth, including where it should occur, who should be in attendance, and how long infants should be breast-fed.

AV: Pregnancy and Birth: Caring and Preparing for the Life Within (26 min., Magna Systems, Inc.)

Part of the *Developing Child* series, this module takes a contemporary look at pregnancy and birthing, focusing on how technological advances have affected both.

AV: Understanding Pregnancy (30 min., Magna Systems)

Focusing on relatively recent developments in pregnancy and birth, this program explores the stages of labor, medical monitoring and intervention, and various birthing situations.

AV: Birth Without Violence (21 min., black and white, New Yorker Films)

The film shows a Leboyer birth, with Frederick Leboyer himself as the obstetrician. As soon as the baby emerges, he is placed on the mother's abdomen and caressed, first by Leboyer and then by the mother. After several minutes, the umbilicus is cut and the infant is placed in the warm bath. This is an awe-inspiring, even eerie film: the black-and-white footage in dim light (one of Leboyer's prescriptions) with no narration creates a strong visual message.

As a teaching tool, this movie is best shown after the students know what a standard delivery involves for the infant (measuring, weighing, suctioning, identification, Apgar rating, etc.) and the reasons for each procedure. Certainly, the standard birth takes less time for the hospital staff and may allow medical problems to be spotted more quickly. Because there is no commentary with the film, you might want to add your own, pointing out things students might otherwise miss—for instance, the birth cry is spontaneous and short (no need for a slap), the reflexes are already functioning (this newborn sucks his finger moments after birth), the head is somewhat misshapen (a natural consequence of the birth process), and the newborn's breasts are somewhat enlarged (again normal, the temporary result of hormones produced as part of the birth process).

Classroom Activity: Are Vaginal Births Best?

Based on the best judgments of a large group of health experts, the government report *Healthy People 2010* (www.healthypeople.gov) set a number of specific health objectives to be achieved by the year 2010. One of these was to reduce the rate of c-sections, the most common major operation performed in the United States.

This objective seemed appropriate because vaginal deliveries generally are associated with lower maternal and neonatal illness, and therefore cost substantially less than cesarean deliveries. However, there is mounting concern that the objective of reducing the rate of cesarean delivery may be backfiring, leading to more complications for mothers and their babies, as well as higher medical costs.

To bring this issue to life, assign groups of students to research the question, "Are vaginal births best?" and report back to class. Ask different students to tackle specific aspects of the question, much the way a team of investigative journalists would. One student, for instance, could examine the question from the perspective of public health policy, focusing on cost and other large social issues. Another student could tackle the question of how the government set the 2010 target that no more than 15 percent of all deliveries in this country should be by c-section. It is now 2011. Ask students if the objective has been achieved. If so, has it made a difference in the health of mothers and newborns?

Classroom Activity: Classroom Debate: *"Resolved: The Increasing Medicalization of Birth Is Harmful to Both Mothers and Their Babies"*

To help your students develop informed opinions about the medical procedures used during the birth process, follow the guidelines in the General Resources section of this manual for scheduling a debate on the advantages and disadvantages of these procedures. You may wish to introduce the debate topic by preparing a brief lecture that summarizes both sides of the argument. The following information should be helpful.

Critics of the medical establishment argue that most procedures are for the convenience and wealth of doctors and hospitals. The administration of drugs to start and speed up contractions, which in turn necessitate anesthesia to lessen pain, is a prime example. Other examples include the practice of having the woman lie on the delivery room table with her legs in stirrups (making it easier for the doctor to see but harder for her to push); predelivery "prepping" (shaving the pubic hair and administering an enema), which is done, say the critics, so things will be neat for the hospital rather than convenient for the woman; and the general atmosphere, which makes the woman feel that birth is a dangerous rather than a natural event. After the birth the newborn is wheeled away, and the mother can usually see her infant and other members of her family only at scheduled times—again for the convenience of the hospital rather than the health and happiness of the baby. Advocates of home births cite the many birth complications that are brought on by overuse of drugs, by surgery, and by staphylococcal and other infections that are more common in hospitals than in homes. The (over)use of cesareans has come under attack as the rate of surgical deliveries has risen beyond what many believe to be a safe or necessary level. As many as 32 percent of all births in some teaching hospitals are now cesarean.

On the other hand, the fact that the number of perinatal deaths has steadily decreased in recent years is directly tied to new medical procedures. Many women with diabetes or sickle-cell anemia, for instance, are much more likely to give birth to a viable infant today than they were even 10 years ago, because fetal monitoring and other techniques are saving infant lives. The incidence of cerebral palsy is down, partly because the incidence of cesareans is up. Doctors believe that they are being attacked for the overuse of drugs that occurred a generation ago, when not as much was known about the effects of medication on the fetus. Many obstetricians say they are much more cautious today.

An interesting related issue is the increase in malpractice suits, which some say is making doctors more reluctant to intervene unnecessarily; others claim that the increase in suits actually forces doctors to undertake needless procedures "just in case."

Although about 90 percent of all births could occur just as safely at home as at a hospital without any medical intervention at all, about 10 percent of all births require medical assistance to avoid or treat complications. The problem, doctors argue, is that one cannot be sure which births will be part of that 10 percent. While one can prepare for complications due to some risk factors—such as the age and the health of the mother—sometimes a healthy woman in her prime childbearing years suddenly develops complications during the last moments of birth, complications that necessitate immediate medical help. Without the ready availability of that help, the baby or the woman could suffer permanent injury or even death.

Critical Thinking Activity: Medical Attention

Each unit of these resources contains a critical thinking exercise designed specifically to test students' critical thinking about a topic covered in the text. Handout 7 briefly outlines the opposing positions on medical intervention followed by a series of questions. If you have not used the Classroom Debate regarding the medicalization of birth, you might want to make this critical thinking exercise an outside assignment.

Pro-Protective Custody Laws Position:
Assume that you are an attorney arguing a hypothetical test case involving an ailing fetus, for whom surgery within the uterus can be performed. Although there is a 50/50 chance that the surgery will save the fetus, it may also endanger the mother's life. What arguments could you use to support your position that the surgery should be performed?

Anti-Protective Custody Laws Position:
Now assume that you are an attorney arguing against the increasing medicalization of prenatal treatment and birthing. What key points would you propose in arguing that the surgery should not be performed?

Answers to this unit's critical thinking exercise are as follows:

Pro-Protective Custody Laws Position:
Those who believe that "protective custody" laws should be extended to allow doctors to protect endangered fetuses assume that a developing fetus has some (or all) of the rights and needs previously reserved for a fully formed, independently breathing newborn.

Anti-Protective Custody Laws Position:
Critics of protective custody laws caution that it is easy to imagine the frightening scenario in which pregnant women lose their personal freedom in the face of overzealous doctors, courts, or societal values regarding childbearing.

AV: Birth at Home (14 min., Filmakers Library)

This film is unusual in many ways. It shows a home birth in Australia, assisted by a midwife who uses massage and herbal medicine. The actual birth occurs as the woman is on her hands and knees. The baby is born with the umbilicus around the neck and initially appears to be in danger of anoxia. The midwife resuscitates him and all seems well by the end of the film. This is a fascinating and provocative film, even for those who are familiar with the usual birth process.

Classroom Activity: Midwifery and Doulas

As noted in the text, many expectant mothers are considering options other than medicated hospital births, especially the use of trained assistants (*doulas*) and midwives. Following is some basic information about these alternatives, which might be of interest to your students. The dictionary defines *doula* as a Greek word meaning "a woman experienced in childbirth who provides continuous physical, emotional, and informational support to the mother before, during, and just after childbirth." There is some evidence that the presence of a labor doula

- decreases labor length.
- decreases the use of labor-inducing drugs.
- decreases the mother's request for pain medication.
- reduces the rate of cesarean birth.
- lessens postpartum depression.
- reduces the need for epidural anesthesia.
- increases the father's participation level.

A *Certified Nurse Midwife (CNM)* is a board-certified nurse with advanced training and education to deliver babies and care for pregnant women. Many CNMs also provide well-woman care such as Pap tests. These midwives are certified and registered by the ACNM (American College of Nurse Midwives), which now owns the additional titles of DEM (Direct Entry Midwife) and CM (Certified Midwife). However, this is an area of confusion because many traditional midwives refer to themselves as DEM or CM. Because CNMs must work under the direction, license, and/or supervision of a board-certified and licensed physician they do not deliver babies at home in southern Nevada, for example. Many CNMs in other areas of the United States are also *Certified Professional Midwives* (CPMs).

A CPM is a board-certified independent care provider with advanced training and education to deliver babies and care for pregnant women. CPMs may also provide well-woman care, well-baby care, counseling, and other services throughout life. They have additional training and certification in nutrition, naturopathy, and emergency care. These midwives are certified and registered by NARM (North America Registry of Midwives). Because CPMs are not required to work under the direction, license, and/or supervision of a physician, they do not ordinarily deliver babies in the hospital in southern Nevada, for example. Many CPMs in other areas of the United States are also CNMs. Of the total 4,138,349 births in the United States in 2005, 7.4 percent (306,377) were attended by CNMs. Considering vaginal births only, the percentage of CNM-attended births is even higher (10.6 percent).

In comparison to the cost of a physician-assisted birth in a hospital, a midwife birth can be considerably less expensive. For instance, a CNM-assisted birth at a hospital birthing center may cost $1,800 to $3,000, while a CPM-assisted birth at home may be only $1,200 to $1,800.

In September 2000, the governor of California approved State Bill 1479, which declared that

- Every woman has a right to choose her birth setting from the full range of safe options available in her community.
- The midwifery model of care emphasizes a commitment to informed choice, continuity of individualized care, and sensitivity to the emotional and spiritual aspects of childbearing. It includes monitoring the physical, psychological, and social well-being of the mother throughout the childbearing cycle; providing the mother with individualized education, counseling, prenatal care, continuous hands-on assistance during labor and delivery, and postpartum support; minimizing technological interventions; and identifying and referring women who require obstetrical attention.
- Numerous studies have associated professional midwifery care with safety, good outcomes, and cost-effectiveness in the United States and in other countries. California studies suggest that low-risk women who choose a natural childbirth approach in an out-of-hospital setting will experience as low a perinatal mortality as low-risk women who choose a hospital birth under management of an obstetrician, including unfavorable results for transfer from the home to the hospital.
- The midwifery model of care is an important option within comprehensive health care for women and their families and should be a choice made available to all women who are appropriate for and interested in home birth.

For more information on doulas and midwives, direct students to one of the following organizations, which are happy to provide a wealth of information on these birth options. *The Journal of Midwifery and Women's Health* (www.jmwh.com) is another excellent source of information.

American College of Nurse Midwives
1522 K Street NW
Suite 1120
Washington, D.C. 20005
(202) 347-5445
www.acnm.org

Midwives Alliance of North America
P.O. Box 1121
Bristol, VA 24203
(615) 764-5561
www.mana.org

Another excellent resource is www.mymidwife.org. Sponsored by the American College of Nurse-Midwives, this consumer-oriented Web site provides parents-to-be with a wealth of information regarding pregnancy, planning, and women's health.

AV: The Newborn (30 min., Insight Media)

This film examines physical and social development in the newborn. The newborn's physical appearance, physiological functioning, and reflexes are discussed, and the Apgar scale and Gestational Age Test are explained. On-camera demonstrations show newborns imitating adult movements.

AV: The Story of Eric (34 min., Centre Films)

A birth story that gives proper recognition to the father's role during pregnancy and birth, this film shows the parents-to-be learning the Lamaze method and then using that knowledge to have an exhilarating birth experience. The movie can be considered propaganda for the advantages of prepared childbirth with minimal medical assistance. However, unless students already understand that birth can be a joyful family event, this movie is well worth showing. The only drawback is that students might believe that every birth can be like this one; as a result, those who have cesareans and/or need more medical assistance when they give birth may feel that they have failed. You can point out that the basic principles (involvement of the father, preparation for birth) hold true, no matter what the actual balance between nature and hospital.

AV: Some Babies Die (54 min., University of California Extension Media)

This documentary follows a family coping with the death of their newborn and the counseling process that encourages them to acknowledge their baby's life and death, to grieve, and then to proceed with their lives. Narrated by Dr. Elisabeth Kübler-Ross, the film contrasts this family's experiences with those of a woman who was not permitted to see any of her three stillborn children and who, after many years, has not yet gotten over her grief and depression.

Problems and Solutions

Classroom Activity: The Role of Nutrition in Prenatal Development

To help students better understand the role of nutrition in the short- and long-term psychological health of the developing fetus, you might begin by pointing out how the popular and scientific consensus on this subject has zigzagged over the past 60 years. Medical textbooks published in the 1950s warned future obstetricians about the dangers of overeating in pregnant women. For one thing, they assumed that overeating (rather than retention of water in the body) caused the sudden weight gain that was one of the first symptoms of eclampsia, a disorder of late pregnancy characterized by convulsions, high blood pressure, and an abnormal accumulation of fluid in the body cells.

Then, as cross-cultural research showed a correlation between malnourished mothers and intellectually and physiologically retarded offspring, and animal research found that severe malnutrition led to the destruction of brain cells, the scientific and medical communities began to appreciate the value of proper nutrition during pregnancy. The idea that future learning problems could be prevented by better nutrition was the most important argument in favor of a federal program to allow impoverished pregnant women and mothers of newborns to obtain free high-protein foods. Congress passed legislation creating this program in the belief that a well-nourished newborn would become an intellectually capable adult, and that a poorly nourished one would be intellectually impaired.

However, later evidence suggested that this, too, was an oversimplification. Nutrition is probably not as crucial a determinant as most researchers two decades ago believed it to be. Yet it may still be one of a series of crucial factors in later intellectual development.

A major reason that the mother's nutrition before and during her pregnancy is so critical is that it determines whether she will be able to grow a healthy placenta. The consensus of many researchers on prenatal nutrition is that although temporary malnutrition probably does not cause permanent damage, if an infant is adequately stimulated, chronic malnutrition—especially if it begins during the fetal period and continues into toddlerhood—may cause deficits. The most damaging effect of malnutrition on development may not be in the destruction of brain cells but in the malnourished newborn's relative inattentiveness and lack of responsiveness to the environment, which in turn retards the formation of the parent–infant bond. This reduces the frequency of parent–infant interaction, thus affecting the child's future intellectual and social development. In this sense, the effect of prenatal malnourishment is quite similar to that of prenatal exposure to certain drugs, such as cocaine.

In the latest edition of their popular nutrition textbook, Frances Sizer and Ellie Whitney (2008) list the most severe risk factors for malnutrition in pregnancy: a mother who is 15 or under; an unwanted pregnancy; many pregnancies at intervals of less than a year (this depletes nutrient stores); a history of poor outcome (premature births, small-for-date newborns); poverty and lack of family support; food faddism; heavy smoking; drug addiction; alcohol abuse; chronic disease requiring special diet; and a mother who is more than 15 percent over- or underweight. These factors at the start of a woman's pregnancy indicate that poor nutrition is likely to be present and to have adverse effects on the developing organism.

Sizer, F., & Whitney, E. N. (2008). *Nutrition: Concepts and controversies* (11th ed.). New York: Cengage Learning.

AV: Pregnancy: Caring for Your Unborn Baby
(20 min., AIMS)

The importance of good nutrition and avoiding drugs during pregnancy is emphasized, especially through footage of a 2-pound malnourished premature infant. This film is not appropriate for all classes; the points made are so obvious that the film may come across as "preachy" to more sophisticated groups. For them, however, you might ask what can or should be done to ensure fetal well-being in all pregnant women, or you might ask whether the film overstresses the role of the individual woman and understresses the role of society. The need for an ecological approach to development will probably become obvious.

"On Your Own" Activity: Avoiding Teratogens in Your Life

To emphasize the variety of specific teratogens to which students may be exposed every day and to help them understand how a person could continue to be exposed to them despite being aware of their dangers, have students complete the exercise in Handout 8, a checklist of possible teratogens to which they have been exposed during the last month. (Let students know that their answers are for discussion only and will not be handed in.)

From students' scores, construct means, medians, and ranges for the class on the measures in question. A comparison of the scores should form the basis of an interesting discussion, because our society makes it difficult to avoid both exposure to pollutants and the use of social drugs (especially alcohol). NOTE: You may notice a gender-based difference: Men in the class may say that avoiding teratogens is not so important for expectant fathers. Such an opinion could well trigger heated debate and discussion.

Internet Activity: Clinical Teratology

To help students learn more about the effects of teratogens on the developing person and the Internet resources available to prospective parents, pick a teratogen from among those mentioned in the text and surf the net to find brief answers to the questions in Handout 9. For example: What are the potential short- and long-term effects of this teratogen on the developing person? Has this teratogen become more of a problem in recent years as a result of technological advances? Explain. What steps can prospective parents take to minimize the effects of this teratogen?

AV: Teenage Pregnancy (26 min., Films for the Humanities and Sciences)

By following several teenagers through the births of their children, this film offers a sobering look at the realities of this worldwide problem.

AV: Pregnancy After 35 (22 min., Polymorph Films)

(See description in Heredity and Environment.)

AV: 39, Single, and Pregnant (18 min., Filmakers Library)

In contrast to the optimistic view presented in *Pregnancy After 35*, this film is the story of a 39-year-old woman who encounters difficulties. She is single, wants to become a mother, and is delighted to be pregnant. As the film follows her pregnancy and the first years of motherhood, the serious implications of parenthood are revealed. While this woman loves her baby, the social and financial problems that she encounters prove more worrisome in reality than she anticipated. This film helps students see that "having a baby" means a lot more than the biology of conception and birth.

AV: DES: The Timebomb Drug (27 min., Filmakers Library)

The DES story is told by the drug manufacturers, doctors, consumer advocates, and mothers and their children (both sons and daughters) who were affected by it. Among the points that can be highlighted in class is the difficulty of conducting research on teratogens and the consequent need for caution in using any drug during pregnancy. Class discussion can be supplemented by information on Accutane, a drug taken by many young women to treat acne. According to some estimates, hundreds of babies were born with birth defects because women took this drug while pregnant.

AV: Pregnancy and Substance Abuse (28 min., Films for the Humanities and Sciences)

This program follows several couples through pregnancy and early prenatal development of children exposed to various addictive drugs. Former U.S. Surgeon General C. Everett Koop discusses the impact of cigarette smoke on the developing child. Michael Dorris, author of *The Broken Cord*, discusses his experiences raising a son with fetal alcohol syndrome.

Classroom Activity: Frequent Drinking Among Pregnant Women

No one took him seriously when, 40 years ago, French pediatrician Paul Lemoine first reported facial deformities in babies of mothers with alcoholism. At the time, many suspected Lemoine's findings were denied because France is Europe's biggest consumer of alcohol. Soon enough, however, the link between alcohol and birth defects was confirmed by others and named "fetal alcohol syndrome." By 1989, alcoholic beverage labels began carrying warnings to pregnant women. According to the American College of Obstetricians and Gynecologists, women who are heavy drinkers before, during, or after pregnancy, face a slew of serious health problems:

- Vitamin and mineral deficiency
- Damage to their internal organs, including the brain, liver, and digestive system
- Depression
- Increased risk of certain types of cancer

For their babies, the effects of heavy alcohol use during pregnancy include

- Miscarriage
- Fetal alcohol syndrome, the most common cause of mental retardation in children
- Physical defects
- Low birthweight
- Hyperactivity
- Decreased attention span

Even so, approximately 10 percent of pregnant women use alcohol, and approximately 2 percent engage in binge drinking (defined for women in 2006 as four or more drinks on any one occasion) or frequent use of alcohol.

To help students gain insight into this complex issue, and their own behavior, project the following Web page, which lists state-by-state alcohol consumption rates among women of childbearing age: www.cdc.gov/ncbddd/fasd/data/html.

Then ask the class the following: Knowing the dangers alcohol poses for the developing organism, why do so many pregnant women continue to drink? Although no one knows for sure, some researchers speculate that reports of health benefits of moderate wine drinking could be one factor. Another is that because most women don't know they are pregnant until eight weeks or so after conception, many have had a few drinks. Other possible reasons tap into the issue of why adolescents and young adults engage in any risk-taking behaviors, including illusions of invulnerability, gradients of reinforcement, and so forth.

AV: Fetal Alcohol Syndrome and Other Drug Use During Pregnancy (19 min., Films for the Humanities and Sciences)

This brief film profiles an 8-year-old boy born with fetal alcohol syndrome. Beginning with a clear description of how alcohol passes through the placenta into the bloodstream of the fetus, the program describes the common characteristics of children born with this disorder, including learning disabilities, cognitive handicaps, and behavioral problems. The program also takes a brief look at babies who are born addicted to crack cocaine.

AV: David with Fetal Alcohol Syndrome (45 min., Films for the Humanities and Sciences)

This film provides a unique, personal look at David Vandenbrink, a seemingly bright and articulate 21-year-old man, who suffers from fetal alcohol syndrome. The teratogenic cause of David's condition went undiagnosed for the first 18 years of his life, causing confusion and pain for both him and his adoptive family.

AV: Fetal Alcohol Syndrome: Life Sentence (24 min., Films for the Humanities & Sciences)

This brief film explores the symptoms of FAS, including learning disabilities, poor judgment, and antisocial behavior. It also discusses a controversial study, which suggests that maternal drinking may explain why 1 out of every 4 prison inmates is a victim of FAS.

AV: One for My Baby (Fetal Alcohol Syndrome) (28 min., AIMS)

This film portrays the tragedy of fetal alcohol syndrome by interviewing doctors and parents of FAS children. The film dramatically emphasizes the importance of avoiding risk factors in pregnancy, even though most fetuses born to drinking mothers are unaffected in any obvious way. In addition to convincing future mothers to avoid alcohol, this film can be used in the same way as the one titled *Pregnancy: Caring for Your Unborn Baby.*

AV: Having a Mentally Handicapped Baby (50 min., Films for the Humanities and Sciences)

This poignant program explores the joys and sorrows faced by families with a handicapped baby. It also addresses some of the numerous difficult decisions parents face, including whether to terminate a pregnancy, day-to-day problems coping with a special-needs child, and whether to give up a handicapped child to foster parents or an institution.

AV: Prenatal Diagnosis: To Be or Not to Be (45 min., Filmakers Library)

This film demonstrates the use of amniocentesis, fetoscopy, and ultrasound in prenatal diagnosis. A couple who lost one child to Tay-Sachs disease is shown rejoicing when amniocentesis reveals that their second child is a healthy, normal girl. Other, more difficult examples of prenatal decision making are shown—for instance, in Down syndrome and spina bifida the outcome of the disease is less clear than in Tay-Sachs disease, making the parents' and doctor's jobs more difficult. The ethical dilemmas inherent in genetic testing are made clear.

Classroom Activity: Classroom Debate: *"Resolved: A Fetus Has the Same Moral and Legal Rights as Its Mother"*

South Carolina is the only state in which, by law, a fetus able to live outside its mother's body is considered a person with legal rights. Abortion advocates see it as a particularly egregious attempt by anti-abortionists to establish fetal rights in any area of law they can. Their purpose, says the pro-abortion camp, is ultimately to overturn *Roe v. Wade,* the 1973 Supreme Court ruling that made abortion legal in America.

The legal system continues to struggle with the issue of fetal rights. In Racine, Wisconsin, Deborah Zimmerman was charged with trying to kill her 6-month-old daughter, Megan, *before her birth.* The night of the birth, her blood alcohol level was 0.30, three times the legal level in Wisconsin. When she was delivered, Megan had a blood alcohol level of 0.199, nearly twice the level considered to make an adult legally drunk. Like many victims of fetal alcohol syndrome, Megan was born with facial abnormalities and, in all likelihood, severe cognitive impairment.

And this was not the first time Megan's mother had run afoul of the law due to her problems with alcohol. She had been convicted of the 1983 drunken driving death of a Milwaukee man, for which she served one year in prison.

Perhaps the most significant factor in the case was that the night Zimmerman gave birth to Megan, hospital workers overheard her threatening to kill her unborn child by drinking. It was their testimony, showing Zimmerman's intent to do harm, that led prosecutors to file charges of both attempted homicide and reckless injury.

The implications of the developing fetus's emerging identity as a person pose a number of legal, medical, and ethical questions. For example, the medical community's ever-increasing technology and understanding of prenatal hazards raise important questions regarding the balance between the mother's rights as an individual and those of the developing fetus she is carrying. Increasingly, doctors are able to treat the fetus itself as a patient with distinct medical needs. As technology advances, should women be expected, and even legally required, to submit to medical intervention—including surgery—that might save a fetus but risk their own lives? Similarly, what about mothers-to-be who knowingly endanger their unborn offspring by continuing to use addictive drugs or by engaging in other potentially harmful behaviors?

Some experts believe that "protective custody" laws should be extended to allow doctors to protect endangered fetuses when deemed necessary. On the other hand, it is easy to imagine the frightening scenario in which pregnant women lose their personal freedom in the face of overzealous doctors, courts, or societal values regarding childbearing. The recent successes that researchers have had in cloning embryonic stem cells has added fuel to the fire (Serour, 2006). The process begins when scientists remove the nucleus from an unfertilized human egg cell. The scientists then remove the nucleus of a skin cell from a patient needing treatment. The skin cell nucleus is implanted in the egg cell, replacing the egg's original nucleus. The transferred egg cell is then stimulated electrically or chemically, which causes it to begin to divide in a Petri dish. Although The National Institutes of Health has ruled that embryonic stem cells are not a form of human embryo, opponents equate embryonic stem cell research with cloning that leads to creation of a human being, begging the question of whether every embryo has the right to be implanted and to develop into a fetus.

To encourage your students to think about some of these issues and their complexity, follow the guidelines in the General Resources section of this manual for scheduling a classroom debate on this resolution. You might prefer to select the reference material yourself and place the relevant journals and textbooks on reserve in the college library, or you might want students to find their own.

Serour, G. I. (2006). Human reproductive cloning and embryonic stem cell research and use. *International Journal of Gynecology and Obstetrics, 93,* 282–283.

Classroom Activity: Low-Birthweight Risk Factors

You may wish to reinforce the text discussion of the risk factors associated with low birthweight with the following additional data and analysis.

According to the most recent UNICEF estimates, more than 96 percent of low-birthweight babies are born in developing countries. South Asia has the highest incidence of low birthweight (31 percent), more than four times higher than the incidence found in industrialized countries (7 percent). In the United States, the percentage of births born preterm declined in 2008, the most recent year for which there are data, to 12.3 percent. The 2008 rate of low birthweight was 8.2 percent, unchanged from 2007. In developing countries, the rate of low birthweight is much higher—16 percent according to the UNICEF estimates.

The National Academy of Sciences has published a report suggesting that much can be done to remedy the problem. It has compiled a table of risk factors and is beginning to examine how some of these factors might work. Following are some examples:

(a) Twenty-four percent of all low-birthweight babies are born to teenagers. However, except for very young teens (under age 15), simply being a teen does not increase the risk. In all probability, the teenager's nutrition and prenatal care are more important than her chronological age. The teen birth rate in the United States decreased in 2008, reversing two years of consecutive increases.

(b) Low birthweight is four times as common among women who gain less than 15 pounds during pregnancy than those who gain 30 to 35 pounds. Nutrition before conception is probably also an important variable.

(c) Unmarried women are twice as likely to have low-birthweight babies as married women, perhaps because husbands can provide help, reassurance, and stability, as well as financial assistance in paying for prenatal care.

(d) Prenatal care is a crucial variable. Health insurance coverage for pregnancy is often unavailable to those who need it most—women who are young, unmarried, and employed in marginal work or unemployed. Medicaid has fairly strict eligibility requirements, and even if a woman is eligible, she may have trouble finding a doctor sufficiently public-spirited to accept Medicaid payment for prenatal care.

The difficulty of paying for prenatal care, and consequently the numbers of women who get inadequate care or no care at all, may be the major reason the low-birthweight incidence in the United States is higher than in other industrialized countries. Other studies have suggested that unemployment, excessive stress, and other social factors are often associated with low birthweight.

To help students appreciate the limited choices of a low-income woman in their area, have them gather information on the following topics. In addition to searching printed resources, encourage your students to surf the net to find the most up-to-date resources.

- How much do a standard delivery and prenatal care cost at a local hospital? At a birthing center? With a private obstetrician?
- What birth-related procedures does Medicaid cover in your state?
- If students or faculty have recently given birth, what were their options and how much did each birth cost?
- What do articles in consumer magazines directed at pregnant women assume about their ability to pay for births and the options available?

Hamilton, B. E., Martin, J. A., Ventura, S. J. (2010, April 6). *Births: Preliminary data for 2008. National vital statistics reports, 58*(16). Hyattsville, MD: National Center for Health Statistics.

UNICEF. (2007). *Low birthweight.* Retrieved July 10, 2007 from www.unicef.org/nutrition.

The New Family

AV: After the Baby Comes Home (19 min., Films for the Humanities and Sciences)

This brief film explores steps new parents can take to prepare for the various potential stresses associated with bringing a baby home, including postpartum depression, marital stress, physical exhaustion, and sibling reactions.

AV: Right from the Start (55 min., Prime Time School Television)

This videocassette focuses on the importance of early contact between mother, father, and newborn. The research of various experts—Harlow, Spitz, and Bowlby, for example—is cited to prove the importance of bonding, and Klaus and Kennell's research is described in detail. The opposite position is not fairly represented, so bonding is probably overstressed here. However, film clips of parents and newborns and Brazelton's wise words on parent–newborn interaction make this film worth showing.

Classroom Activity: "Dancing Baby Down" and Cultural Differences in How Newborns Are Welcomed

Throughout the world, newborns are greeted with a variety of wonderful traditions. In Israel, for example, proud Jewish parents plant a tree—cedar for a boy, pine for a girl. The branches are later used for the wedding canopy. Here are some other examples to share with the class. See if the members of the class can add to the list.

- Flying a kite (JAPAN)
- Giving the parents an odd (never even) number of fresh flowers (RUSSIA)
- Tossing colored confetti (MEXICO)
- Placing nutritious foods around the infant (ISRAEL: ARABIC COUNTRIES)
- Playing drums (BRAZIL)
- Planting a tree: apple for a girl, nut for a boy (SWITZERLAND)
- Opening a bottle of rum (JAMAICA)
- Serving red-dyed eggs (CHINA)
- Sprinkling the infant with water to protect him or her from future danger (NIGERIA)
- Dressing the newborn in the clothing of the opposite sex (GREAT BRITAIN)
- Passing the baby around to family and friends, who whisper prayers in his or her ear (IRAN)

You might extend this activity by assigning individual students (or small groups of students) to report on cultural variations in the birth experience. For instance, kangaroo care, which is described in the text, was first initiated by two South American neonatologists to involve parents in the care of their preterm children and to decrease some of the stress associated with an infant needing neonatal intensive care. Parents who have experienced kangaroo care have expressed excitement and joy with the practice, and many feel like parents for the first time since their infant's birth. In Guatemala, traditional midwives provide the majority of maternity care and are responsible for 60 to 75 percent of all births. Government-run midwifery training programs are grounded in a holistic model, which views childbirth as a normal process having powerful emotional, physical, cultural, and spiritual dimensions. As a third example, many cultures have dances that have roots in childbirth preparation. These dances often center around pelvic movements and exercises that help women's bodies to relax, stretch, and open naturally during birth. These include cultures in Hawaii, Seneca (Native American), Tunisia, and several other areas throughout the Middle East, North Africa, and parts of Asia. In certain parts of the Orient, for instance, the practice of "dancing baby down" includes the techniques of "belly roll" and "flutter." These movements are virtually identical to two of the exercises commonly taught in Lamaze classes to help prepare women for the stresses of labor: "pelvic rocking" and "deep breathing."

Spencer, P. (2000, March). How newborns are welcomed around the globe. *Parenting, 14*(2), 30.

Classroom Activity: Maternal Bonding Reconsidered

As the text notes, some developmental psychologists now believe that the importance of early contact between mother and child has been overly popularized and that the events right after birth are just one episode in a long-term process of bonding between parent and child. This comes as good news to adoptive parents, as well as to those who have quietly resented the "campaigns of blame" that perpetuate the myth that every poor outcome of child development is due to a failure to form a positive parent–newborn bond.

In a provocative article, Alice Adams of Miami University notes that psychology, sociology, medicine, and literature have traditionally regarded mothering from the perspective of the developing child. "These fields," Adams writes, "present middle-class White mothers as the norm and consider them as functions (or, more frequently, dysfunctions) of a child's developing psyche. Mothers who are women of color, or who live in poverty, or who work outside the home, or who are single, lesbian, younger than average, or otherwise beyond the narrow limits that define the normal mother are generally represented by writers in these disciplines as dangerous, psychologically and socially."

Adams reviews several books on maternal bonding that avoid the tendency to diagnose dysfunctional families and blame mothers. A common theme of these works is criticism of bonding theory in psychology and medicine for promoting the idea that a mother's success or failure in bonding with her newborn is directly responsible for the presence or absence of child abuse and neglect, failure-to-thrive, juvenile delinquency, and childhood depression.

Criticizing the "faulty science that produced and continues to promote bonding theory," Adams objects to the tendency of this and other theories "to reduce the complex practices of mothering to a simple functional process. It is not the mother's intentions but the mere fact of immediate postbirth physical contact, and in some theories the hormonal effects of that contact, that supposedly effects the bond."

Several of the works Adams reviews focus on mother–daughter relationships, noting the prevalent perception of mothers as sources of anger and emotional pain for their daughters. "The choice that daughters seemed to face," summarizes Adams, "was either to reject mom or to replicate her limited identity as homemaker, her economic dependence on men, her annoying and fruitless attempts to live through her children, her years of thankless, stultifying service as wife and mother, and especially her lack of a sense of self-worth."

Adams is critical of social histories that imagine a "golden age" of mother–daughter relationships prior to the development of "the new woman in the late nineteenth century." Often viewed as the cultural and historical "epicenter of fundamental mother–daughter hostility," the creation of the new woman led to the disturbing view of mothers who "let go" of their daughters as "healthier" than mothers who strive to remain connected, a view perpetuated by an overly psychoanalytic postwar climate in the United States in which motherhood was steeped in biological and psychological pathologies. In *Motherhood and Sexuality* (2000), for example, Marie Langer proposed that "fear of separation is the most profound anxiety of pre-birth labor. According to Langer's psychodynamic viewpoint, each mother-to-be presumably fears not only the pending separation from her own child, but also the reexperiencing of her own traumatic separation from her mother.

Several of the works reviewed analyze social and historical changes in the depiction of motherhood in film, television, and other popular media. The mostly male-written films of the World War II era, for example, depicted sacrificial working-class mothers giving everything for their children so that they presumably could then enjoy a better life. Adams notes that as Freudian constructions of familial relationships gained popularity, American films increasingly portrayed pathological mother–daughter relationships.

The television shows of the 1950s changed this portrait of motherhood. "No longer sacrificial victims or maternal vampires feeding on the emotional lives of their children," writes Adams, "television mothers are passive. The father-who-knows-best becomes the key to his daughter's successful development to femininity (defined as a marital commitment to a man like Dad)."

Beginning in the 1970s, the popular media depicted more complex mother–daughter relationships. Novels by Alice Walker, Paula Marshall, Amy Tan, Toni Morrison, and others—even sitcoms such as *Maude*—portray a more powerful and complex relationship. More recently, researchers found that the infants of psychotic mothers showed more eye contact avoidance toward their mothers. The key point, of course, is that dysfunctional cognitive styles in mothers may adversely influence their interaction with their babies and disrupt the emotional bond.

To stimulate deeper thinking about the roles of ideology and cohort effects in research on bonding and the depiction of motherhood, you might assign different groups of students to read the books listed below and then report back to the class. You might also invite to class several women who became mothers at different times in recent cultural history. Their reflections in the context of the literature discussion are sure to provoke a good classroom experience.

Adams, A. (1995). Maternity and motherhood. *Signs: Journal of Women in Culture and Society, 20*(2), 414–427.

Eyer, D. E. (1994). *Mother–infant bonding: A scientific fiction*. New Haven, CT: Yale University Press.

Friday, N. (1997). *My mother, myself: The daughter's search for identity.* New York: Dell Publishing.

Hornstein, C., Trautmann-Villalba, P., Hohm, E., Rave, E., Wortmann-Fleischer, S., & Schwarz, M. (2006). Maternal bond and mother-child interaction in severe postpartum psychiatric disorders: Is there a link? *Archives of Women's Mental Health, 9*(5), 279–284.

Mazzon, C. (2002). *Maternal impressions: Pregnancy and childbirth in literature and theory.* Ithaca, NY: Cornell University Press.

Rich, A. (1977). *Of women born.* New York: Bantam.

Walters, S. D. (1994). *Lives together/worlds apart: Mothers and daughters in popular culture*. Berkeley: University of California Press.

Warner, J. (2005). *Perfect madness: Motherhood in the age of anxiety.* New York: Riverhead Hardcovers

Teaching Tip: The Impact of Birth on the Family

To help your students understand the psychological significance of birth for family members, you might ask the members of your class (or other students who are parents) to describe their firsthand experiences of the birth process. If possible, select as discussants some who had their babies recently and others whose babies were born some time ago. This will give the class the opportunity to compare childbirth methods over the years. (This activity can be combined with the panel interview of expectant parents detailed in the Observational Activity.) Ask the participants to be sure to discuss the following:

- whether any medication was used, and if so, what kind and why (more than 90 percent of hospital births involve medication)
- whether any other medical intervention was used and why (the increase in cesareans nationwide may be evident from the number of cesareans among your students)
- whether the birth process happened in the way they had anticipated it would
- their reactions to first seeing their baby

To prevent this exercise from becoming simply an exchange of stories, ask all class members to try to think of a general statement that will summarize the experiences described. For instance, the father's role or early mother–newborn contact may show interesting trends.

If the student body at your college contains very few parents, here are several alternatives.

(a) Invite an articulate new parent (for instance, a faculty colleague) to talk to the class about his or her experience of the birth process. In this case, it would be interesting to find out what choices the person made (for example, home versus hospital, childbirth classes, natural childbirth) and why.

(b) Contact a local organization concerned with birth and arrange for a speaker. For instance, a Lamaze-method teacher or a nurse-midwife might be invited to speak to the class about new trends in delivery procedures or a similar topic.

(c) Ask your students to recount what they know about their own birth and/or the births of their siblings. Misunderstandings and ignorance on these topics should be just as interesting as accurate accounts.

(d) Ask your students to discuss their own birth with their parents. If they are firstborns, they will probably find that their mothers were medicated, didn't know what to expect, and were frightened by the experience. Their fathers may not have been present at the delivery and may have had only a glimpse of them as newborns. Have students compare their parents' experiences with those they hope to have as future parents or have had as recent parents.

"On Your Own" Activity: What Are Your Attitudes Toward Birth?

As the text notes, prospective first-time parents may approach birth with a host of fears and negative feelings. At least this was the case in the past. However, attitudes toward birth are changing. It is not unusual to read first-person accounts celebrating the birth experience. Today, pregnant women (and their husbands) are increasingly well informed and highly positive as they prepare for the birth of their babies.

To help your students uncover their own attitudes toward the subject of birth, have them complete Handout 10, which asks them to respond to such questions as: What was your reaction to the photos of the birth process in the text? Did these photos interest you? engross you? or put you off? Compare your response to the birth photos with your response to the photos of the newborns in the text. How do your responses differ, and what, if anything, does this suggest about your attitudes toward birth and newborns?

Students will quickly see that the first response choices to questions 3–6 reflect a positive attitude toward the subject of birth; subsequent responses reflect less positive feelings. Some responses ("maybe" or "interested *and* uneasy") reflect ambivalent attitudes. Many students can be expected to choose these responses.

"On Your Own" Activity: Saying When

Throughout, the text emphasizes the interaction of the biological, social, and psychological domains. For each domain there is a developmental clock that suggests the "proper timing" of each event. In several lessons, students are asked to consider the settings of these clocks in their own lives. In Handout 11, students are asked to do so regarding the timing of births by responding to such questions as: If you (or your subject) are (is) not a parent but contemplate(s) having a child or children, at what developmental "time" do you foresee your birth(s)—according to your own biological clock? Your social clock? Your psychological clock? How does this compare with the settings of your parents' developmental clocks when you were born? With the settings of your grandparents' developmental clocks when your parents were born?

Because there are no correct or incorrect answers for this exercise, the most appropriate feedback might be a summary of the class's answers. The summary need not be exhaustive but should note any age cohort effects in the timing of births. Regarding the actual (or anticipated) timing of their children's births, are there generational differences in the settings of the students' developmental clocks?

HANDOUT 1

Developmental Fact or Myth?

T F 1. At the end of the third month, the fetus has all its body parts.

T F 2. Fetuses jump in response to sudden noises.

T F 3. When drugs such as marijuana and alcohol are taken together, a higher dosage of each is required before either becomes harmful.

T F 4. (A View from Science) Even moderate drinking by a pregnant woman may be harmful to the developing organism.

T F 5. If the mother carries the virus that causes AIDS, nothing can be done to prevent the fetus from becoming infected.

T F 6. Officially, a baby's "due date" is established as 38 weeks after conception.

T F 7. Cesarean sections account for less than 10 percent of all births in the United States.

T F 8. Today, most U.S. births occur at home.

T F 9. Malnutrition is the primary reason teenage girls often have small babies.

T F 10. In both humans and other animals, there is a critical period for the formation of the parent–newborn bond.

HANDOUT 2

Folk Wisdom and Pregnancy

Perhaps no other period in the life of the developing person generates as much fascination and misinformation as the gestation and delivery of a new baby. Folk wisdom, or old wives' tales, concerning pregnancy and birth is still passed on today. Some is based on fact and observation; other bits of wisdom are derived from fears or are no longer true for a healthy mother who receives good prenatal care.

1. If you are a parent, think of a piece of advice that you were given during your pregnancy on the subject of your health or the health or possible gender of your baby, and write it in the space below.

2. If you aren't a parent (if you are, you'll find this interesting, too), ask a friend of your own age who is a parent to think of a piece of advice he or she was given during the pregnancy, and write it in the space below.

HANDOUT 2 *(continued)*

3. Ask a parent or other adult relative or friend who is older than you whether he or she remembers any old folk tales about pregnancy, and write down one example.

4. On the basis of what you have learned from the text discussion of prenatal development and birth, which of the folk tales you have documented are accurate/helpful/true? Which are not? Why or why not?

HANDOUT 3

Observational Activity: Pregnancy's Impact on Expectant Parents

Following discussion of the text material on this topic, invite several expectant couples to the class. If couples cannot easily be found from among friends, relatives, students, or colleagues, try contacting local hospitals that conduct childbirth classes. Ideally, the couples selected will represent the diversity of the group under study (expectant couples at early, middle, and late stages of pregnancy) and will be comfortable with student questioning.

Developmental Assessment

Have students use the "before-and-after" approach to the interview, as explained in the General Resources section. The assessment requires students to integrate text information, lecture material, and personal life experiences in order to pull together all they know about the impact of pregnancy on couples and then construct a set of expected behaviors, developmental tasks, issues, and stresses with which they will attempt to assess the panelists.

Before the Panel Interview

Distribute copies of the Developmental Assessment Form to students about one week before the panel interview is scheduled. Have students complete the "expected responses" column and bring the handout to the class meeting prior to the panel interview. At this time the class should plan the interview and generate a list of questions for the panelists.

To get things started, encourage your students to consider some of the following questions: "How has your pregnancy changed your everyday life?" "How has pregnancy changed your marital relationship?" "What new emotions, if any, have you felt during your pregnancy?" "How has the prospect of being a parent changed your own sense of identity?" "What fears/joys have you experienced during your pregnancy?" "What new responsibilities do you have as an expectant parent?" "How do you feel about these responsibilities?" "How active a role is the father taking in the pregnancy, and why?" "What are some of the stresses of being an expectant parent?" "Where have you been able to turn to find help and support in coping with these stresses?" "What advice do you have for those considering childbearing?"

During and After the Panel Interview

Your role during the panel interview is to rephrase student questions when necessary, ask questions, and ensure the comfort of all involved. Both students and panelists need a great deal of support, especially when sensitive issues and questions arise. Be sure students understand that they are to complete the "observed responses" column of the Developmental Assessment Form during the interview.

Use the class meeting following the panel interview to discuss the panelists' comments and the students' interviewing techniques. Students will probably be surprised at how very differently other students reacted to the panelists' comments. An added benefit of this activity is that students will learn a great deal about the strengths and weaknesses of the interview method.

As an extension of this activity, distribute copies of the Follow-Up Questionnaire and have students turn it in at the next class meeting.

Source: Dodendorf, D. M. (1981). A "real-life" developmental psychology course. *Teaching of Psychology*, *8*(3), 172–173.

HANDOUT 4

Observational Activity: Pregnancy's Impact on Expectant Parents: Developmental Assessment Form

Based on lecture material, textbook content, and your own personal experiences, think about the ways in which pregnancy affects expectant parents.

Category	Expected Responses	Observed Responses
Developmental Tasks of Pregnancy:		
for Mom		
for Dad		
Changes in Interpersonal Relations:		
with friends		
and relatives		
with partner		
Stresses of Pregnancy:		
for Mom		
for Dad		
Responses to Stress:		
by Mom		
by Dad		

HANDOUT 4 *(continued)*

Category	**Expected Responses**	**Observed Responses**
Physical Changes During Pregnancy		
Psychological Changes During Pregnancy		
Emotional Changes During Pregnancy		
Developmental "Gains" from Pregnancy:		
for Mom		
for Dad		
Developmental "Losses" from Pregnancy:		
for Mom		
for Dad		

HANDOUT 4 *(continued)*

Follow-Up Questionnaire

1. Describe the panelists who participated in the expectant couple interview.

2. Did your class encounter any difficulties in conducting the panel interview? What were they?

3. Briefly summarize your reactions to the interview. Was it enjoyable? informative?

4. What personal experiences and expectations (for example, friends or relatives who have gone through pregnancy) did you bring to the panel interview?

5. In what areas (for example, psychological changes, developmental tasks, stresses) did the panelists' responses confirm your expectations?

HANDOUT 4 *(continued)*

6. In what areas did the panelists' responses conflict with your expectations?

7. Has your assessment of pregnancy's impact on expectant couples changed following the panel interview? If so, how?

8. In a paragraph, summarize your assessment of the ways in which pregnancy affects an expectant couple.

HANDOUT 5

Reading About Birth

1. In the space below, write the title, author (if given), and source (magazine, newspaper, or journal) of an article on birth that interests you.

2. Who is the article written *for* (for example, women in general, pregnant women, husbands, the public at large)?

3. What can you tell about the author of the article? For example, what are his or her credentials? his or her biases?

4. What experts, authorities, or studies are quoted or referenced in the article?

5. In what ways, if any, does the article seek to increase understanding of birth/the birth process?

6. Is the reader urged to take any specific actions? If so, what are they?

7. Does the article discuss matters that seem to be controversial? What are they?

HANDOUT 6

Birth in Fiction and Film

Novels or films that portray the life of a single individual sometimes begin with birth; the circumstances of birth (time, place, weather, the significance of the birth to family members or community) are recounted, and the reader or viewer knows that the details presented will have a bearing on the story that follows.

1. Can you think of a novel or film in which the birth of the hero was portrayed as being highly significant to the story that followed? If so, name the novel or film, and briefly explain why the birth scene was significant.

2. At some point in your school career, you may have been asked to write an autobiographical composition. If so, what kind of attention (if any) did you give to the circumstances of your own birth? For example, did you describe the time and place of birth? your parents' hopes and expectations? Did you emphasize any special joys or problems associated with your birth? In the space below, describe how you began (or would begin) an autobiographical or fictionalized account of your life.

HANDOUT 7

Critical Thinking Activity: Medical Attention

Now that you have read and reviewed the material on prenatal development and birth, take your learning a step further by testing your critical thinking skills on this perspective-taking exercise.

The implications of the developing fetus's emerging identity as a person pose many legal, medical, and ethical questions. For example, the medical community's ever-increasing technology and understanding of prenatal hazards raises important questions regarding the balance between the mother's rights as an individual and those of the developing fetus she is carrying.

Increasingly, doctors are able to treat the fetus itself as a patient with distinct medical needs. As technology advances, should women be expected, and even legally required, to submit to medical intervention—including surgery—that might save a fetus but risk their own lives? Similarly, what about mothers-to-be who knowingly endanger their unborn offspring by continuing to use addictive drugs, or by engaging in other potentially harmful behaviors?

Your task in this exercise is to develop arguments for and against "prenatal protective custody laws" and to identify the values that might underlie each of these positions.

Arguments:

Pro-Protective Custody Laws Position
Assume that you are an attorney arguing a hypothetical test case involving an ailing fetus, for whom surgery within the uterus can be performed. Although there is a 50/50 chance that the surgery will save the fetus, it may also endanger the mother's life. What arguments could you use to support your position that the surgery should be performed?

Anti-Protective Custody Laws Position
Now assume that you are an attorney arguing against the increasing medicalization of prenatal treatment and birthing. What key points would you propose in arguing that the surgery should not be performed?

HANDOUT 8

Avoiding Teratogens in Your Life

Understanding the danger of potential teratogens isn't the same as automatically avoiding the use of or exposure to such agents. Imagine that you have decided to become a parent. To ensure that your body is teratogen-free for the year during which fertilization and gestation occur, consider the following potentially hazardous behaviors. For each behavior or exposure you have experienced over the past month, assign a score of 1 (totals are for discussion only and will not be handed in). Then estimate how difficult it would be for you to avoid the proposed teratogen in the following year, by assigning a score of 0 for each you could change easily, 1 for each you could change without too much difficulty, 2 for each that would be difficult to change, and 3 for each you would consider virtually impossible to change or avoid.

	Violation This Month	Difficulty Score
Use alcohol		
Use marijuana		
Use tobacco		
Take prescription drugs		
Use over-the-counter drugs (aspirin, cough medicine, allergy tablets)		
Use hard drugs (heroin, cocaine)		
Drink too much caffeine (coffee, tea, and sodas)		
Use artificial sweeteners		
Use or be exposed to pesticides		
Breathe polluted air		
Avoid contact with viral diseases (rubella, influenza, chicken pox)		
TOTAL SCORES		

HANDOUT 9

Internet Activity: Clinical Teratology

To learn more about the effects of teratogens on the developing person and the Internet resources available to prospective parents, pick a teratogen from among those mentioned in the text and check the Internet to find brief answers to the following questions.

1. Which teratogen did you choose? Why?

2. What are the potential short- and long-term effects of this teratogen on the developing person?

3. Are other risk factors associated with damage from this teratogen? That is, who is most (and least) likely to suffer teratogenic damage?

HANDOUT 9 *(continued)*

4. Has this teratogen become more of a problem in recent years as a result of technological advances? Explain.

5. What steps can prospective parents take to minimize the effects of this teratogen?

6. State the Internet address (the URL) of at least one relevant Web page.

HANDOUT 10

What Are Your Attitudes Toward Birth?

1. What was your reaction to the photos of the birth process in the text? Did these photos interest you? engross you? or put you off? Did you look at them for a relatively long time, short time, or not at all?

2. Compare your response to the birth photos to your response to the photos of the newborns in the text. How do your responses differ, and what, if anything, does this suggest about your attitudes toward birth and newborns?

To learn more about your attitudes toward the subject of birth, examine your responses in the following situations.

3. You buy a magazine and discover that it contains a mother's personal account of giving birth. Do you:

   ______ read it right away?

   ______ read it later?

   ______ maybe read it later, maybe not?

   ______ avoid reading it?

4. You learn that your class is scheduled to see a film of a birth. Are you:

   ______ very interested in seeing the film?

   ______ somewhat interested in seeing the film?

   ______ somewhat uneasy about seeing the film?

   ______ very uneasy about seeing the film?

   ______ both interested *and* uneasy?

5. A close friend or relative asks you to be present during her labor and at the birth of her child. You feel like saying:

   ______ Yes, I want to be there!

   ______ Yes, if you need me.

   ______ Maybe; let me think about it.

   ______ It's something I don't think I can do.

   ______ (Don't know; it's hard to imagine.)

HANDOUT 10 *(continued)*

6. You learn that someone took a photograph of the moment of your birth. Are you:

    ______ very eager to see the photograph?
    ______ interested in seeing the photograph at some time?
    ______ turned off by the thought of the photograph?
    ______ both interested *and* turned off by the idea of the photograph?
    ______ (Don't know.)

HANDOUT 11

Saying When

The three developmental domains come into play in every major transition of life. No transition is greater than the change from being pregnant to being a parent. The setting of the developmental clocks can affect the timing of births and the adjustment of first-time parents to their new roles, and can have long-term life-span consequences for both parents and their children. Unlike the biological clock, which changes little from generation to generation, the social and psychological clocks can be reset. The settings of these clocks reflect each individual's culture, historical context, and life experiences.

1. If you (or your subject) are (is) a parent, please discuss the timing of your child(ren)'s birth(s) by answering the following questions. If you (or your subject) are (is) not a parent, skip to question 2.
   a. If you have recently had a child or children, according to the settings of your social, biological, and psychological clocks, was the timing of your child(ren)'s birth(s) "on time" or "off time"? That is, were your children born when you felt biologically, socially, and psychologically ready to have children?

   b. If your child(ren)'s birth(s) was (were) not recent, would its (their) timing mesh with the present settings of the developmental clocks and the trend toward "early" and "late" births?

   c. What factors (career, education, health concerns, etc.) influenced the timing of your child(ren)'s birth(s)?

HANDOUT 11 *(continued)*

2. If you (or your subject) are (is) not a parent, but contemplate(s) having a child or children, at what developmental "time" do you foresee your birth(s) according to your own biological clock? Your social clock? Your psychological clock? How does this compare with the settings of your parents' developmental clocks when you were born? with the settings of your grandparents' developmental clocks when your parents were born?

3. In your opinion, from the standpoint of the three developmental clocks, what is the ideal timing for the birth of a child? You may conclude that the ideal time is never. Whatever the case, please explain your reasoning.

4. What is your current age (or the age of your subject)?

The First Two Years: Biosocial Development

Contents

Note: Worth Publishers provides online Instructor and Student Tool Kits, DVD Student Tool Kits, and Instructor and Student video resources in DevelopmentPortal for use with the text. See Part I: General Resources for general information about these materials and the text Lecture Guides for a complete list by text chapter.

Brain Development

Audiovisual Materials: Birth of a Brain, p. 8
The Development of the Human Brain, p. 8
The Brain, p. 8
Pediatric Brain Development: The Importance of a Head Start, p. 8
Pediatric Neuroscience: Rage of Innocents, p. 8

"On Your Own" Activity: BYOB: Bring Your Own Brain, p. 8 (Handout 3, p. 18)

Sensation and Movement

Audiovisual Materials: The Discovery Year, p. 8
Discovering the Outside World, p. 9
The Newborn: Development and Discovery, p. 9

The Five Senses

Audiovisual Materials: Seeing Infants with New Eyes, p. 9
Helping Babies Learn, p. 9
Simple Beginnings?, p. 11

Classroom Activities: Incorporating a Comparative Perspective into Developmental Psychology, p. 9
The Development of Visual Perception, p. 10
Facial Expression Processing: Neurobehavioral Maturation or Cognitive Scaffolding?, p. 11

Observational Activity: Time Sampling of Newborn Behavior, p. 9 (Handout 4, p. 19, and Handout 5, p. 20)

"On Your Own" Activity: Infants' Shape Preferences, p. 11 (Handout 6, p. 24)

Motor Skills

Audiovisual Materials: A Child Grows: The First Year, p. 12
Infancy: Landmarks of Development, p. 12
See How They Move, p. 13

Classroom Activities: Normal Development of Motor Skills, p. 12
Nature and Nurture in Motor-Skill Development, p. 13

"On Your Own" Activity: Basic Motor Skills: Learning Like an Infant, p. 13 (Handout 7, p. 26)

Observational Activity: Gross Motor Skill Development in the Infant, p. 13 (Handout 8, p. 27, and Handout 9, p. 29)

Critical Thinking Activity: The Effects of Biosocial Experiences on Cognitive and Psychosocial Development, p. 14 (Handout 10, p. 31) (This activity is in effect a summary of the major biosocial changes during infancy.)

Surviving in Good Health

Audiovisual Materials: Keeping Babies Healthy and Safe, p. 14
Bottle Babies, p. 15
Nutrition, p. 15

Classroom Activity: Nutrition for Children, p. 15

Internet Activity: Childhood Infections, p. 15 (Handout 11, p. 32)

Suggested Activities

Introducing The First Two Years: Biosocial Development

"On Your Own" Activity: Developmental Fact or Myth?

Before students read about biosocial development during the first two years, have them respond to the true-false statements in Handout 1.

The correct answers follow. Class discussion can focus on the origins of any developmental misconceptions that are demonstrated in the students' incorrect answers.

1. T
2. T
3. F
4. F
5. F
6. T
7. T
8. T
9. T
10. T

Teaching Tip: Using Presentation Software Effectively

PowerPoint and other presentation software programs have become almost as common as chalk in the classroom. Advocates maintain that the visual dynamism afforded by presentation software captures and focuses student attention. In addition, they maintain, the variety of available formats—including video, extreme close-up images, sound, and three-dimensional representations—can elevate students' understanding more than less technologically rich lectures.

Critics of presentation software contend that succinct, bullet-pointed information stifles critical thought. They are fond of pointing out that one NASA official blamed presentation software for some aspects of a mission failure, claiming that engineers were more likely to fail to grasp the seriousness of data that were presented via PowerPoint slides. Students, too, often complain of being overloaded with onscreen information. In my early days of using PowerPoint, students frequently asked me to slow down my lectures as they scrambled to copy the content of slides verbatim. Although many instructors have solved this problem by providing students with the slides before class or on a Web site, students have another gripe. They complain that so much time is spent viewing slides in a darkened classroom that discussion is stifled, along with their alertness!

Cathy Sargent Mester offers several useful tips for preparing presentation software slides and effectively showing them in class.

Slide Preparation

- Avoid presenting too much information in a single slide. Too many instructors use slides as speaker notes, or as excerpts from the text. The best slides are "highlights" that clarify and emphasize rather than provide complete explanations. To this end, the "6 × 6" rule should be followed whenever possible. Derived from visual perception research, this rule states that six words or numbers across the field and six down is the maximum that viewers can process in a single look.
- Choose uncomplicated images that are large enough for every student in the class to see. Images should have high contrast and clear labels that are readable from the back of the classroom. The simplicity rule also applies to slide backgrounds, fonts, and the many sounds that presentation software companies have made available.
- Keep the room lights on. Before using a slide deck in class, preview it in the classroom while experimenting with different light settings. Choose a setting that affords the greatest visibility of the slides without triggering dark adaptation in your students' eyes. Lecturing in the dark puts a barrier between you and your students. It also makes it hard for students to take notes as a way of actively engaging in the learning process.

Presenting Slides in Class

- Synchronize slide information with your narration. Slides can be manually advanced as you lecture or triggered automatically on a timer. In addition, information on each slide can either be gradually revealed or shown all at once. Pedagogically, the most effective combination is to manually advance the slides and gradually reveal the content of each slide so that at any moment you are showing only the specific information you want to address. By using a wireless mouse, you can stand anywhere in class, spending as much or as little time on each slide as you need.
- Speak to the class, not the screen. Inexperienced and underprepared lecturers often make the mistake of looking at the slides instead of at the class, sometimes even reading the information. Doing so raises doubt in students' minds about your familiarity with the material and cuts off eye contact with the class. Whenever the human connection is lost, students' attention will wander.
- Be prepared for snafus. Like all forms of teaching technology, computers and projectors malfunction. Be prepared by arriving early to the class. Doing so will help ensure that your presentation is indeed on the flash drive and that there is time to call a technician to get the projector to communicate with your laptop and to deal with the host of other problems that can arise. Ideally, you will also have a contingency plan, either by having backup visual aids such as handouts or by switching to another classroom activity.

Mester, C.S. (2006, September). Technology is not a toy! *Association for Psychological Science Observer.* Retrieved July 11, 2007 from www.psychologicalscience.org/observer.

AV: The Journey Through the Life Span, Program 2: Early Infancy

Program 2 (12:10) examines biosocial development during the first weeks of life. Four-week-old Lily and 7-week-old Julia demonstrate the reflexes we are all born with and the developmental trajectory of those reflexes. The regulation of sleeping and other physiological states is also discussed, along with the underlying neurological development that enables this regulation. A highlight of this segment is a discussion of cultural differences in sleep patterns led by Charles Super and Sara Harkness of the University of Connecticut. The final segment of the program is a delightful exploration of the first exogenous smiles during infancy, the first true social smiles that occur at about 2 months of age, and the pain and hunger cries that infants use to convey their needs.

The unnarrated observation module for Program 2 is divided into two segments. In the first (3:15), the Moro, rooting, sucking, and Babinski reflexes are vividly demonstrated in a 4-week-old infant. The second segment (5:35) depicts a 7-week-old infant in various states of arousal.

AV: Transitions Throughout the Life Span, Program 5: Grow, Baby, Grow

Program 5 begins with observations on the overall growth and health of infants, including their size and shape during the first two years. Next is a discussion of brain growth and development, noting the importance of experience in these processes. At birth, the brain contains over 100 billion nerve cells, or neurons, but the networks of dendrites that interconnect them are rudimentary. Over the course of the first few years, extensive growth occurs in these neural pathways, enabling the emergence of new capabilities in each domain of development.

The program then turns to a discussion of motor abilities, including infant reflexes, walking, and gross and fine motor skills, and the ages at which the average infant acquires them. The final segment discusses the importance of nutrition during the first two years and the consequences of severe malnutrition and undernutrition. During the program, pediatricians Beverly Hendrickson, Alberto Gedissman, and W. Donald Shields, along with developmental psychologist Claire B. Kopp, provide expert commentary.

AV: The Journey Through the Life Span, Program 3: Infants and Toddlers

Program 3 introduces the developing person during infancy and toddlerhood as embarking on a journey of sensorimotor and social change that will affect every domain of his or her development. The first segment of the program, physical development (7:00), begins by pointing out the changes in size, weight, and shape that occur during infancy. Charles Nelson of the University of Minnesota outlines the stages of brain growth, focusing on the myelination of the central nervous system. A highlight of the segment is the depiction of the universal developmental pattern by which infants around the world develop postural control, the ability to sit up, crawl, stand, and take the first tentative steps.

The second segment of the program describes cognitive development (18:30) and so might be held for your discussion of cognitive development during the first two years. It begins by describing infants' emerging perceptual abilities. The development of reaching and grasping is depicted, as is the ability to differentiate mother's voice from other people's. Charles Nelson discusses infant face perception and recognition of emotional expressions in other people and the developing awareness of the affordances that objects provide. Karen Adolph of New York University explains how infants perceive surfaces and how they learn more and more about affordances as they refine their locomotion skills. At each developmental milestone (cruising, crawling, sitting, etc.), babies must essentially relearn to perceive the world around them. The segment then describes the development of perceptual constancy and how researchers use the habituation procedure to test infants' abilities. The final portion of the segment centers on Jean Piaget's stage of sensorimotor development. The development of object permanence, memory, and imitation are discussed, and the six substages of the sensorimotor period are delineated and described in detail. In the closing minutes of the segment, Steven Pinker of MIT describes the language explosion that occurs during the first three months of life, focusing on Noam Chomsky's notion of universal grammar. In their need to communicate, infants first make sounds that develop into cries and then babbling, which forms the building blocks of speech. These lead to the first words and holophrases and then, telegraphic speech. More than any other skill, the emergence of language signals the end of infancy and the beginning of childhood.

The final segment of the program, social development (10:20), begins by exploring synchrony between infants and caregivers throughout the world. Separation anxiety and stranger anxiety are described and the biological advantages conveyed by the infant–caregiver bond are discussed. The strange situation test is depicted and the nature of secure attachment and avoidant attachment is explored. In a fascinating segment, Gilda Morelli of Boston College describes her research studies of attachment among the Efe people of the Congo region in Africa. The program concludes with an exploration of toddlers' emerging self-awareness and temperament. The temperamental types of "easy," "difficult," and "slow-to-warm-up" are differentiated and depicted.

The observation module for this unit is divided into three segments. In the first segment (0:50),

5-month-old Skye and 6-month-old Boris illustrate the development of coordinated arm and leg movements. In the second segment (5:00), 1-year-old Rylen and Maya and 11-month-old Lilith demonstrate a variety of locomotor and manual skills. In the third segment (4:20), 18-month-old Emma demonstrates her remarkable skills of speech and coordinated hand–eye movements. Because her arms are short, she can reach only to the top of her head, which provides a good illustration of infant body proportions.

Teaching Tip: How Biology and Culture Shape Parenting

A good way to begin discussion of this material is to pose the following problem to your students:

> It's 3 A.M. and little Davy is wailing in the nursery. Shaking her husband, Mom says: "Get up. It's your turn to feed our son. Don't you hear him crying?" Dad rolls over and says: "Davy has to learn to sleep through the night sooner or later. Let him cry." Who's right? Mom or Dad?

According to the sociocultural perspective on development, there are as many different views on how to raise children as there are parents, relatives, and pediatricians eager to offer opinions. If your class is like most, your students' reactions to this example will reveal that even the most basic questions can be quite polarizing. Some will argue that if you let a baby cry, the child will become an emotional cripple. Others will argue with equal passion that the opposite will occur and the child will eventually adjust by becoming a self-possessed, independent adult. If you want to push this exercise a bit further, here are some other good questions to pose: If a child sleeps in his or her parents' bed, will he or she become overly dependent or more affectionate and secure? Does breast-feeding on demand lead to an overweight, demanding child or a lean and healthy, loving one?

These examples also are a good way to introduce the scientific study of ethnic and cultural variations in parenting. Consider the Gusii, an agricultural people of southwestern Kenya, who would never allow an infant to remain alone and crying. Gusii infants are carried around by their mother or a nurse all day long, and they are never left alone to play by themselves. In addition, they are breast-fed whenever they cry, even if it means that the mother must leave her work in the fields. Yet, these mothers rarely talk to their babies, believing that doing so fosters a child who is self-absorbed and too individualistic for the communalistic society in which they live. Contrast this lack of concern for early linguistic stimulation with the views of parents who miss no opportunity to provide cognitive stimulation to their offspring, beginning almost from the moment of conception.

But parenting is shaped by natural as well as cultural evolution. This means that child-rearing practices that may seem beneficial from a societal standpoint are sometimes not optimal to the well-being of the infant. Regarding the issues of nursing on demand and sleeping with parents, all primates evolved to be held, fed, and slept with until they were ready to fend for themselves. Thus, it may make sense to allow children to sleep with parents and to be breast-fed on demand until they wean themselves.

Epigenetic inheritance can account for the transmission of parental behaviors (and other phenotypic responses) from one generation to the next. Although psychologists have long maintained that behavior can influence evolution, until fairly recently, plausible mechanisms have not been identified. One example of epigenetic inheritance is relatively common; in this case, typical responses made by a parent to environmental threats or challenges are displayed by offspring, even when the offspring have not themselves encountered the same threats or challenges. Likening the phenomenon to "phenotypic inertia," Lawrence Harper of the University of California, Los Angeles, suggests that gene expression is altered in subsequent generations, resulting in a type of "intergenerational continuity" of response.

Harper, L. V. (2005). Epigenetic inheritance and the intergenerational transfer of experience. *Psychological Bulletin, 131*(3), 340–360.

Body Changes

Body Size

Teaching Tip: The Evolutionary Perspective on Infant Growth

To stimulate thinking about the evolutionary perspective on human development, you might remind your students that any specific pattern—such as a growth spurt—must have evolved because it added some benefits to the life of the species. Then ask them to speculate as to what these benefits might be.

All placental mammals, including humans, share some fundamental physical skeletal and neurological adaptations. Among these are those related to rapid and flexible locomotion, brain capacity suited for high levels of learning by offspring, and intense attachment to parents.

In contrast to these universals of mammalian development, humans differ from most other mammalian species in our postnatal growth patterns. For example, whereas mice reach their maximum rate of growth after birth (during the infancy stage), humans achieve their maximum rate of growth in length and weight during prenatal development, with growth rates slowing during infancy. This difference is probably due to the fact that humans typically have only one fetus per pregnancy, while competition among multiple fetuses in mice and other mammals in which litters are the norm limits prenatal growth rates. Another difference is that the human placenta is much more efficient in providing nutrition than that of other mammals. Cows, for example, grow much more rapidly after birth than before because lactation provides much better nutrition than that received via the placenta.

Another major difference is that among most nonhuman mammals, puberty begins when growth rates are decelerating but still near the maximal rate of infancy. In contrast, human puberty takes place when the rate of growth in weight and height are at their lowest points since birth. A fourth difference is that while human adolescence is marked by a cascade of endocrine changes that trigger the pubertal growth spurt, growth rates in other mammals continue to decline following puberty. A final difference is that while humans generally delay the adult reproductive stage for some years after puberty, other mammals generally begin to reproduce soon after they are fertile.

Thus, while most mammals develop "seamlessly" from infancy to adulthood, humans show patterns of growth that are much more stagelike and include a long interval between weaning and puberty that is almost completely absent among other nonprimate mammals. One hypothesis to explain the juvenile stage is that this period enabled an extended time for brain growth and the social learning necessary to ensure reproductive success (*learning hypothesis*). To survive, social animals such as primates must learn how to live within the group's social hierarchy. They must also develop the skills necessary for locating food, hunting, competing for mates, and caring for offspring. An extended period for learning also permits a species to adapt to unpredictable changes in climate, food availability, and so forth.

Another hypothesis for the existence of a juvenile stage is that individuals with delayed reproductive maturity may have survived to adulthood more often (and achieved greater reproductive success) than individuals who matured at a younger age. Support for this *dominance hypothesis* comes from evidence that among wolves, lions, and other social carnivores, high-ranking individuals in the dominance hierarchy seem to be able to inhibit the reproductive maturation of younger, low-ranking individuals. This may occur as a result of stress-related hormonal changes triggered by social intimidation, or as a result of inadequate nutrition because of competition for food.

As a final quiz for your students, ask them to speculate as to why humans and most primates delay body growth and sexual maturity, but do not delay brain growth. As noted in the text, the human brain reaches 75 percent of its adult weight by age 2, while body growth obviously continues until age 18 and beyond.

According to the evolutionary perspective, this pattern of growth gives primates their incomparable ability to learn (note that for most children, formal schooling is delayed until approximately the age of brain maturity). It may also be the case that rapid brain growth and delayed body growth and sexual maturation also contribute to the overall reproductive success of the species. Older, "prereproductive juveniles" can help their parents care for new infants (and develop their own caregiving skills at the same time).

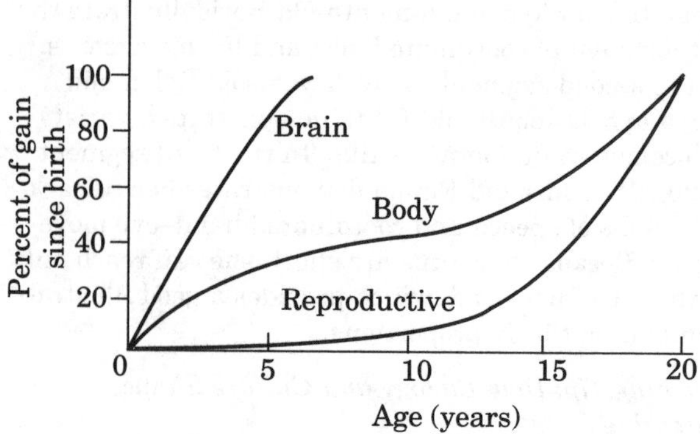

Mascie-Taylor, C. G., & Bogin, B. (2005). *Human variability and plasticity.* Cambridge: Cambridge University Press.

AV: Developmental Phases Before and After Birth (30 min., Films for the Humanities and Sciences)

This film describes milestones of physiological and psychological development during the fetal period and the first year of life. A major theme is that these milestones are identical for children throughout the world. It also examines the impact of the mother–child relationship on child development.

AV: The First 365 Days in the Life of a Child (13 programs, 28 min. each, Films for the Humanities and Sciences)

This 13-part series describes normal development of an average healthy child during the first year of life. The series focuses on the research of a group of pediatricians at the University of Munich who systematically observed and filmed five babies for a year. From these observations, the researchers developed a system of developmental tests that measures a baby's most important developmental functions monthly. The first program shows the reactions of the newborn 10 days after birth. Programs 2–13 show the baby at 1 month, 2 months, and so on until the first birthday.

AV: A Baby's World (3 volumes, 60 min. each, Insight Media)

This three-part series provides a detailed depiction of the remarkable process by which helpless infants develop biologically, cognitively, and socially into walking, thinking, and talking human beings.

AV: In the Beginning: The Process of Infant Development (15 min., Davidson Films)
Nurturing (17 min., Davidson Films)

These two movies can be shown together. Both feature Dr. Bettye Caldwell describing infant development. *In the Beginning* shows stages of development in several children, illustrating normal variation in growth rates. *Nurturing* examines the role of the caregiver as an active contributor to optimal growth. Caldwell offers several suggestions for fostering curiosity, exploration, and stimulation.

Classroom Activity: Evolutionary Theory and Head-Sparing

Head-sparing is the process by which the nutrition stored as body fat is used to protect a baby's brain during times of inadequate nutrition. Even if the body stops growing as a result of dietary deficiency, the brain's development is protected, or "spared." This fascinating developmental phenomenon is an excellent starting point for a class discussion of whether evolutionary pressures and definitions of "fitness" have shifted over the millennia. Get the ball rolling by pointing out that head-sparing was viewed as an adaptive response to the immediate environmental challenge of a less-than-optimal pregnancy. Students will readily understand that, from the standpoint of species survival, during such times the brain's needs must take precedence over those of the body.

However, the long-term developmental consequences of head-sparing are potentially quite negative, including increased risk of obesity, impaired cognitive development, and a greater risk of metabolic diseases later in life. More recently, some developmental psychologists have suggested that the adaptive process of head-sparing evolved (and was appropriate) in the challenging environments of prehistory, when a steady supply of food was difficult to come by. Today, however, head-sparing is mismatched with the modern environment of the developed world. Ask the class whether this argument makes sense, and if so, whether new approaches to intervention and prevention might be appropriate.

Gluckman, P. D., & Hanson, M. A. (2006). The consequences of being born small: An adaptive perspective. *Hormone Research, 65*(3), 5–14.

"On Your Own" Activity: Growth Rates During the First Two Years—On an Adult Scale

Using their own weights and heights, students can answer the questions in Handout 2 to see how dramatically the developing person grows in the first two years of life. The first statement is, "If you were gaining weight at the rate of an infant, your weight would be tripled one year from today. Calculate how much you would weigh."

Students should note the extremely rapid rate of growth of infants during the first year, and the comparatively slower rate of growth in the second year.

AV: The Growing Infant (30 min., Insight Media)
The First Year of Life (28 min., Films for the Humanities and Sciences)

These two films examine physical growth during infancy, including cephalocaudal and proximodistal principles, the relationship between cognitive and physical growth, and the development of vision, hearing, and perceptual abilities. *The Growing Infant* follows one child through several stages of development. *The First Year of Life* explores how newborns see, hear, and make use of skills developed even before birth to interact with their surroundings. The infant's emerging individuality is also discussed.

Sleep

Classroom Activity: The First Two Years of Sleep

Students are fascinated by sleep. Those who are parents, or who anticipate having children, will benefit from knowing developmental norms for sleep behavior during the first two years of life.

Like adults, infants cycle between rapid eye movement (REM) sleep and non-rapid eye movement (NREM) sleep. Unlike the 90-minute sleep cycle of adults, the complete sleep cycle in infants lasts about 50 to 60 minutes. As any parent knows, newborns sleep on and off, all through the day and night, averaging 15 or 16 hours out of every 24. By age 4 months, most babies sleep a 6- to 8-hour chunk at night, and by age 6 months, about 10 to 12 hours. The following table illustrates the developmental progression of nighttime and daytime sleep over the first two years of development.

Age	Nighttime Sleep (hours)	Daytime Sleep (hours)	Total Sleep (hours)
1 month	8.5 (many naps)	7.5 (many naps)	16
3 months	6–10	5–9	15
6 months	10–12	3–4.5	14.5
9 months	11	3 (2 naps)	14
12 months	11	2.5 (2 naps)	13.5
18 months	11	2.5 (1-2 naps)	13.5
2 years	11	2 (1 nap)	13

Source: University of Michigan Health System. (n.d.). *Sleep problems.* Retrieved July 10, 2007 from www.med.umich.edu/1libr/yourchild/sleep.htm.

Classroom Activity: Problem-Based Learning: Sleeping Patterns

The Introduction's Classroom Activity: Introducing Problem-Based Learning describes this relatively new pedagogical tool. Following is a sample problem that you might want to give to your students as part of your coverage of biosocial development during the first two years:

> Marysol and Belize disagree about whether their infant daughter should be allowed to sleep with them in their bed. Belize strongly feels the baby should be allowed to sleep with them because his family has done this for generations. Marysol disagrees, expressing concerns based on some information she heard on the evening news.
>
> Before you leave class today, your group must address the following questions: First, from what you have learned about co-sleeping, how prevalent is this practice and how do cultural customs affect sleeping patterns? Second, after your group agrees on an answer to the first question, determine some resulting learning issues that need to be researched to answer the question, "Where Should Babies Sleep?"
>
> Based on your group's decisions, you should devise a plan for researching the various issues. Two weeks from today's class, your group will present a recommendation for Marysol and Belize based on the issues you think are relevant.

Brain Development

AV: Birth of a Brain (33 min., CRM/McGraw-Hill)

This film shows the development of the brain from the fetal period through infancy. Two features make it particularly interesting. First, it uses moving pictures to show the development of neurons, dendrites, and axons in the brain as maturation occurs. The striking images of this process help students visualize the crucial prenatal and postnatal periods of development.

Second, it uses only one infant, from birth to about 8 months, to illustrate brain development. Beginning with her Lamaze birth—a useful review of Prenatal Development and Birth—we watch as the infant becomes more capable of coordinated motor movements and early language, and of interaction with her parents and her older sister (who is, predictably, jealous).

The interaction of biological and psychological factors is apparent throughout the film. For example, the narrator stresses the importance of avoiding toxins (both postnatally, in the form of "chemical pacifiers," as well as prenatally) and providing proper nutrition and stimulation to allow the brain to develop normally. This film includes material that can easily serve as a springboard for many of the topics in this unit as well as cognitive and psychosocial development during this period.

AV: The Development of the Human Brain (40 min., Films for the Humanities and Sciences)

This film traces the course of brain development from conception to age 8. After describing brain functions that are already present at birth, it identifies the range of motor and cognitive skills that appear as the brain matures.

AV: The Brain (50 min., BBC Films)

Using vivid graphics, animation, and three-dimensional models, this spectacular video takes students on a complete tour of the brain.

AV: Pediatric Brain Development: The Importance of a Head Start (13 min., Films for the Humanities and Sciences)

(See description in Prenatal Development and Birth.)

AV: Pediatric Neuroscience: Rage of Innocents (47 min., Films for the Humanities and Sciences)

Taking a strong sociocultural and evolutionary perspective, this film explores the impact of attentive and neglectful caregiving on the emotional and neurological development of the child. Researchers discuss studies demonstrating a biochemical link between early caregiving and the development of brain regions that regulate emotions and the individual's response to stress. It also explores parental nurturing from the perspective of evolutionary biology.

"On Your Own" Activity: BYOB: Bring Your Own Brain

To familiarize students with the overall structure of the brain—especially the cerebral cortex and other areas that develop most rapidly during the first two years—have them follow the guidelines in Handout 3 and actually prepare an edible, neuroanatomically accurate model of the brain. The model can be an appetizer, dessert, or other food item depicting the cerebral cortex, brain stem, limbic system, nerve cell, or any other part of the central nervous system.

In addition to being a fun-filled—and perhaps delicious—activity, the diversity of projects that is sure to result will expand on the text coverage of the developing brain.

Sensation and Movement

AV: The Discovery Year (52 min., Films for the Humanities and Sciences)

The late Christopher Reeve hosts this exploration of the first year of life—the discovery year—as babies learn to use their senses, crawl, explore, and finally walk. The program also examines how personality develops at this young age by focusing on how three sets of parents respond to the individual personalities of their infant daughters.

AV: Discovering the Outside World (23 min., Films for the Humanities and Sciences)

This program focuses on the extraordinary development of the individual that occurs during the first nine months. Sleep–waking cycles are described, sensory development is outlined, and the infant's expanding repertoire of communication skills is delineated.

AV: The Newborn: Development and Discovery (29 min., Magna Systems, Inc.)

This film discusses the developmental needs of the neonate, focusing on tests that determine the state of sensory, motor, cognitive, and social development. Other issues explored include bonding, breast- versus bottle-feeding, and the care of high-risk infants.

The Five Senses

AV: Seeing Infants with New Eyes (30 min., Child Development Media)

This documentary profiles infant specialist Magda Gerber and her philosophy of raising self-confident, intrinsically motivated infants.

AV: Helping Babies Learn (19 min., Child Development Media)

This brief video presents a discussion of how caregivers can create stimulating environments for infants and toddlers. It also includes developmentally appropriate learning exercises.

Observational Activity: Time Sampling of Newborn Behavior

All babies come into the world with a number of internal biological "clocks" that regulate cycles of sleeping, waking, and eating. Although all infants show the same states of sleeping and waking, the exact patterns exhibited by infants vary greatly.

Sleep is the dominant state for neonates, with newborns averaging 16 hours of sleep during each 24-hour period. Infant sleep differs from adult sleep, however, in that newborns sleep only in short stretches of 2 to 3 hours, much to the chagrin of haggard first-time parents who are used to sleeping in 7- to 8-hour stretches. Beginning at about 3 months of age, however, babies begin to sleep through the night. By 6 months of age, fully half of an infant's daily quota of sleep occurs during the night.

Newborn sleep alternates between *active sleep* and *quiet sleep*. These two stages probably represent rudimentary forms of adult REM (rapid eye movement) sleep—which is linked to dreaming—and non-REM (NREM) sleep, respectively. NREM sleep may be especially important in restoring the body's physiological resources after the day's activities. In adults, REM and NREM sleep alternate on a 90-minute cycle; in newborns, the two stages alternate in a 1-hour cycle. In the neonate, active sleep accounts for up to 80 percent of total sleep. By 6 months of age, the sleep cycle lengthens to more closely approximate the adult pattern, and active sleep is reduced to about 30 percent of total sleep. Handout 4 provides suggestions for having students observe newborns in a hospital setting. Handout 5 describes the procedure for students and provides a data sheet and follow-up questionnaire for them to complete.

Although hospital nurseries are extraordinarily busy places, most will permit a small number of students to observe the newborns (through the observation window) for half an hour or so. However, be sure to first obtain permission from the hospital administration and coordinate the scheduling of student visits with the nursing staff so that the visits will not be disruptive to the nursery.

After introducing the activity in class, distribute copies of Handout 4, which lists the five infant states identified by the questionnaire authors. Next, explain the *time sampling* method of observing behavior in order to prepare students for the observational activity. The following information should be helpful.

In the time sampling method, an observer records the frequency, or presence/absence, of an overt behavior (one that can be seen clearly and counted) during short time intervals of uniform length. As a method of observation, time sampling has several advantages: (1) it takes less time and effort than other methods, such as narrative recording; (2) it is more objective than some methods; and (3) it provides useful information on intervals and frequencies of behavior in a quantitative format that lends itself to statistical analysis. The disadvantages of time sampling are as follows: (1) it is limited to overt behaviors, (2) it takes behavior out of context and does not keep units of behavior in their original form, and (3) it does not describe the behavior, its causes, or results.

Now distribute copies of Handout 5, which includes a description of the procedure, a data sheet, and a follow-up questionnaire. After students have had a chance to review the procedure, answer any questions they might have. Have students work in teams of two, with both students in a team scoring the same infant independently. After the observation has been completed, instruct students to complete the questions on the follow-up questionnaire and hand it in, along with their data sheet.

Classroom Activity: Incorporating a Comparative Perspective Into Developmental Psychology

Psychology is usually defined as the scientific study of behavior and mental processes, yet many courses limit their focus to human behavior and cognition. When animal research findings are discussed, they are often descriptions of older research, presented in historical context (e.g., Harlow's attachment studies; early studies of learning by Pavlov and Skinner).

Suzanne Baker of James Madison University suggests that incorporating information on the behavior of nonhuman species into your class can give students a more comprehensive picture of the richness and diversity of behavior and mental processes throughout the animal kingdom. All species, including humans, face problems in their physical and social environments. These include problems related to obtaining food, shelter, safety and other resources; surviving as a member of a social group; and adapting to changing circumstances.

In this unit, you might focus on comparative differences in sensory and perceptual processes. Characteristics and limitations of the human infant's sensory capabilities are highlighted when they are compared with those of other species. A good way to start is by noting that sensory and perceptual capabilities have evolved as adaptations to the social and physical environment of the species. Animal species provide fascinating examples of specialized sensory systems. For example, bats use high-frequency sonar, outside the range of human hearing, to orient and to capture their prey in total darkness. Rats, which have poor visual acuity, communicate using ultrasound and are sensitive to light in the ultraviolet (UV) region of the spectrum. Elephants' use of infrasonic vocalizations allows them to communicate over vast distances. Almost every species of bird can see UV light, and color signals in these wavelengths often play an important role in how they select mates. Some species of fish can also see UV wavelengths.

Many teachers are reluctant to give up time to fit information on the behavior of nonhumans into an already overcrowded course curriculum. However, even the briefest diversion into the world of animal behavior can broaden students' understanding of the diversity of behavior, and deepen their appreciation of the applicability of some of developmental psychology's big principles and ideas. Additional ideas for incorporating a comparative perspective into your course can be found in other units of these resources.

Baker, S. C. *Expanding our students' horizons: Incorporating a comparative perspective into psychology courses.* Retrieved on November 8, 2010, from teachpsych.org/resources/e-books/eit2005/eit05-01.pdf.

Classroom Activity: The Development of Visual Perception

Infants come into the world with remarkably acute sensory and perceptual systems, all of which continue to develop after birth. You can expand the text discussion of the development of infant visual perception by explaining the physiological changes that cause the improvements.

Studies using Robert Fantz's preference method show that although vision is not well developed at birth, acuity improves rapidly. (In these studies the infant is shown two images; a consistent preference for one image over another indicates an ability to discriminate between the two.) The newborn's limited distance vision is due primarily to the inability of the *cornea* and *lens* of the eye to focus images on the infant's retina. At birth, the *retina* is not fully developed; although the *rods* and *cones* in the outer, peripheral region are relatively adultlike, the cones in the central region (*fovea*), which later will permit the sharpest vision, are immature. At higher levels in the visual system, including the *lateral geniculate nucleus* and the pathways to the *visual cortex*, we find a similar degree of immaturity in the neonate. Here, too, however, development is rapid; these neural pathways are nearly mature only two months after birth.

Visual focusing in the adult is largely due to the ability of the *ciliary muscles* of the eyes to contract and thereby change the shape of the lens in order to *accommodate* nearby or distant objects in the visual field. In general, the eye muscles are not well developed at birth, which limits the infant's ability to accommodate, or focus. Because these muscles also control eye movements, a baby's eyes occasionally move in different directions. Eye coordination also improves markedly during the first months after birth.

Neonates have limited color vision. One-month-old infants, for example, have difficulty distinguishing red or green stimuli from a yellow background. By the time infants reach the ripe old age of 3 months, however, they seem to possess the *trichromatic* (three-color) vision characteristic of adult color vision.

Babies seem capable of responding to visually perceived movement soon after birth. In one remarkable study, researchers presented moving cartoon faces to babies who were only 9 *minutes* old. All the babies consistently moved their heads to follow the moving cartoon figures.

Adult vision is also characterized by *perceptual constancy*, or the tendency to perceive objects as remaining the same even when their actual appearance (as represented on the retinas of the eyes) changes. Visually, adults perceive constancy of size, shape, brightness, and color. To determine whether size constancy is present in infants, researchers have relied on a technique known as the *conditioning method*. In this method, the experimenter rewards the baby for making a simple motor response, such as turning his or her head in response to an interesting visual image, perhaps by "popping up" in front of the infant in a simple game of peekaboo.

Using this conditioning method, Gordon Bower conditioned infants to turn their heads only when a particular white cube was displayed (see original cube, figure on next page). If the infants responded when the cube was not displayed, no reward was delivered.

In a later test, Bower presented the original white cube and several other test cubes, as illustrated in the figure, measuring the number of head-turning responses that each triggered in the infant subjects. Bower reasoned that the number of responses to each cube was an indication of how similar it seemed to the

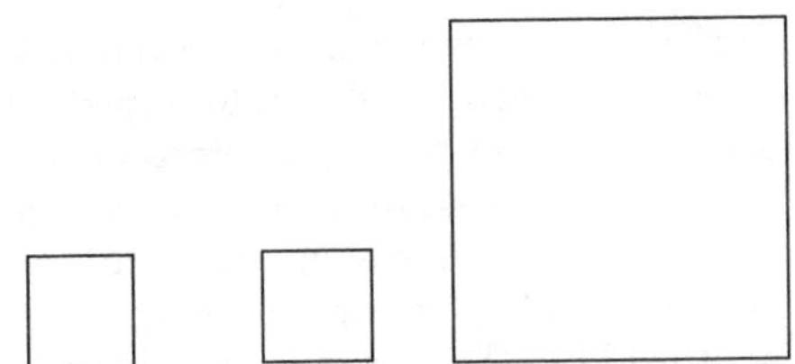

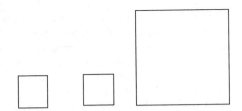

Stimulus:	Original Cube	Test Cube 1	Test Cube 2
Size:	30 cm	30 cm (same)	90 cm (larger)
Distance:	1 m	3 m	3 m

original cube. A significant number of responses to test cube 1—a cube the same size as the original cube but presented at a different distance—would indicate the presence of size constancy, or an awareness that objects remain constant in size even though their distances (and the retinal images they project) are changed. Conversely, a significant number of responses to test cube 2—a larger cube presented at a greater distance so that it projected a retinal image *the same size as the original cube*—would indicate the absence of size constancy.

Infants as young as 6 weeks of age made a total of 98 head-turns to the original stimulus, 58 head-turns to test cube 1, and only 22 head-turns to test cube 2. Bower concluded that infants do possess some size constancy.

More recent studies have failed to consistently demonstrate size constancy in such young infants. Because depth perception—which is not fully developed until about 4 months of age—may be necessary for size constancy, some researchers prefer a more conservative approach, saying that constancy is present by 6 months of age and that data from younger infants are inconclusive.

Matlin, M.W. (2005). *Cognition* (6th ed.). Hoboken, NJ: Wiley.

"On Your Own" Activity: Infants' Shape Preferences

To familiarize students with the classic preference method of assessing perceptual abilities, have them complete Handout 6, which examines infants' preferences for shape. Students are asked to construct six test stimuli consisting of cartoon faces, bull's-eyes, and blank circles. They then are asked to present the test stimuli one at a time to a 2- to 6-month-old infant while measuring the number of seconds the infant looks at each stimulus before turning away.

Students should find that infants initially prefer simple visual patterns consisting of highly contrasting elements. Researchers have also discovered that infants prefer curvilinear patterns to straight-line patterns; they prefer concentric patterns (as in the bull's-eye) to nonconcentric patterns; and they prefer shapes with multiple orientations to those with all the elements oriented in the same direction.

AV: Simple Beginnings? (24 min., Films for the Humanities and Sciences)

This short film explores child development from birth to age 5. An especially interesting feature is the description of three experiments, which test early abilities of infants to recognize faces and motion as well as their short-term memories.

Classroom Activity: Facial Expression Processing: Neurobehavioral Maturation or Cognitive Scaffolding?

From infancy through adulthood, the ability to distinguish among and interpret facial expressions plays an important part in the development and maintenance of human relationships. It is therefore not surprising that adult women, whose interactions tend to be more intimate than those of men, are more accurate at identifying nonverbal cues than are men. Although the adult female advantage in processing nonverbal cues is well documented, the process by which it develops is poorly understood.

A meta-analysis by Erin McClure of Emory University was designed to explore this issue, focusing on facial expression processing (FEP). First, here's some basic information about FEP and theories regarding its development. FEP is operationally defined in terms of performance on a variety of tasks involving facial expression discrimination, recognition, and identification. Most studies of FEP in the first months of life use visual preference or habituation techniques to evaluate discrimination among facial expressions. In preference tasks, emotional expressions are presented either in pairs or successively to an observing infant. Examiners measure the duration of the infant's gaze at differing expressions; gaze times are then compared between expressions. If infants show a preference for one expression by gazing at it longer over several trials, it is assumed that they can discriminate among the different expressions presented.

FEP habituation tasks involve repeatedly presenting a facial expression to infants until they meet a predetermined criterion, often defined as decreasing by 50 percent the time spent looking at the face before looking away. Following a short delay, a new expression is presented, and infants' duration of gaze is once again measured. If infants look longer at the novel face than they did at the last presentation of the habituated face, they are thought to perceive a difference between the two. Conversely, if they gaze at the novel expression for the same length of time as they did at the habituated expression, they are not thought to perceive any difference.

According to the *neurobehavioral maturation* model, FEP development depends on maturation of brain areas that are specialized for recognition of complex patterns such as faces. Studies have implicated a variety of brain areas, but especially several areas in the temporal cortex and the amygdala. For instance, using micro-electrodes to record single neuron activity, numerous investigators have found cells in the temporal cortex that respond more strongly to faces than to other visual stimuli. Some research indicates that these regions may develop more rapidly in females than in males. In normally developing macaques, for instance, females appear to become capable of forming visual discrimination habits—a skill thought to be mediated by the temporal cortex—earlier than do males.

From the perspective of the neurobehavioral model, sex differences in the development of FEP correspond to sex differences in the maturation of brain areas mediating this skill, particularly the amygdala and the temporal cortex. Findings from several studies suggest that areas in the temporal cortex linked to FEP mature less rapidly in male than in female primates, apparently as a consequence of hormonal surges. When human males and females reach the age of 3 to 4 years, however, their temporal cortexes appear to have reached similar developmental stages. Indeed, both girls and boys in this age range generally perform well above chance levels on tasks requiring them to identify the most common expressions as well as their meaning.

In contrast, the *social constructivist theory* of FEP development maintains that social interactions are critical to the development of nonverbal skills. Adults provide cognitive scaffolding, initially identifying facial expressions or exaggerating their own expressions for the observing child. Over repeated interactions, adults systematically reduce their involvement, leaving more and more of the task to the child. Eventually, the child becomes capable of completing the task alone. From this perspective, gender differences in FEP stem primarily from different patterns of early, scaffolded experience for boys and girls. Over time, individual differences in scaffolding history may lead to differences in boys' and girls' development of emotional understanding and FEP. Girls, who generally are exposed to a more expressive environment than are boys from infancy onward, are likely to develop FEP skills more rapidly than are boys. Later, through the greater emphasis that adults place on emotion with girls, they further encourage girls to develop their skills and guide them more carefully in doing so. This suggests a pattern in which sex differences should emerge gradually during the first year and increase through development, until they reach adult levels.

McClure's meta-analysis of 104 studies of gender differences in FEP set out to test two hypotheses: first, whether, in line with the neurobehavioral model, biological maturation could be the primary force influencing the development of gender differences. If this is the case, gender differences favoring girls should be evident in the youngest infants studied; these effects should decline gradually until children are 3 to 4 years of age. After this point, effect sizes should either remain low and constant throughout development or show an increase in adolescence, when hormonal levels rise again. Second, as suggested by the social constructivist model, gender differences in FEP should be experience-dependent and heterogeneous across age groups. In contrast to the pattern predicted from the neurobehavioral model, however, the gender differences should be nonexistent or minimal in the early months of life. They should then increase gradually over time, with girls showing an ever-increasing advantage until adult levels are reached, when they should level off and remain relatively constant.

As predicted by both the neurobehavioral and social constructivist hypotheses, both infant and child/adolescent samples of effect sizes were significantly heterogeneous. Moreover, gender differences in FEP were greatest in infancy; they then declined to lower, but still significant, levels by the preschool years. Throughout childhood and adolescence, gender differences appeared to remain relatively stable. This pattern is consistent with predictions derived from the neurobehavioral model and suggests that gender differences in FEP are linked to differences in early neurological maturation.

McClure, E. (2000). A meta-analytic review of sex differences in facial expression processing and their development in infants, children, and adolescents. *Psychological Bulletin, 126*(3), 424–453.

Motor Skills

AV: A Child Grows: The First Year (25 min., Insight Media)

This program outlines the development of motor and cognitive abilities during the first year of life. Special attention is paid to the development of eye–hand coordination and the process by which infants learn to distinguish self from non-self.

AV: Infancy: Landmarks of Development (22 min., Magna Systems, Inc.)

This film traces the major landmarks in the development of gross and fine motor skills during the first year. It also discusses influences on the timing of motor development, including nutrition, health care, opportunities for practice, and cultural patterns.

Classroom Activity: Normal Development of Motor Skills

To reinforce the idea that there is a range for the normal development of motor skills, before students read the relevant material ask them to estimate the average age at which a baby sits up without support, stands steadily without holding on, and walks a few steps without falling. The answers will show a wide range, especially if your students come from various ethnic groups. Thus, you might get:

sit up	4–8 months
stand	7–14 months
walk	9–16 months

If your students come from fewer ethnic groups, you may well get a narrower range and unusually early or late estimates. This is so simply because the sample may be less representative of the population as a whole. Thus, a class of African American students is likely to say:

sit up	4–5 months
stand	7–8 months
walk	8–11 months

After your students have made their estimates, put the norms from the Denver Developmental Screening Test on the board:

sit up	5.5 months
stand	11.5 months
walk	12.1 months

This exercise is useful for emphasizing not only the wide range of normal behavior but also the fact that norms always depend on the particular population surveyed.

This may also be a good time to point out that children who develop motor skills rapidly are not necessarily those who develop other skills quickly: The 6-year-old who can already read and write well may have been the first infant on the block to walk, or the last. Severe retardation in the development of motor skills (as in the case of an infant who is not sitting up at 9 months), however, may signal a serious problem, which helps explain why the Denver study is used by psychologists as well as physicians. Mental retardation, neurological impairment, severe malnutrition, and poor parent–infant interaction all correlate with very slow motor development.

Classroom Activity: Nature and Nurture in Motor-Skill Development

To help students understand the interaction of nature and nurture in the development of motor skills, ask any students who have at least two children to tell the class about the similarities and differences in the early motor-skill development of their children. Or you might ask a colleague to speak to the class on this subject. Among the factors that might affect the rate of development are the following:

(a) Overweight children master skills more slowly; the fact that they have more body weight than their relatively immature legs can support makes it harder for them to crawl, creep, and so forth.

(b) Infants who were born prematurely are seemingly slower than those who were full-term. However, if they are compared with children *conceived* at the same time rather than with children *born* at the same time, they are found to be developing very close to schedule.

(c) Overprotection tends to slow development; attention and encouragement tend to accelerate it. Since firstborns are often more protected than their siblings, parents frequently report that their first child was slower to develop than their later-born children.

"On Your Own" Activity: Basic Motor Skills: Learning Like an Infant

To allow students to "feel" the progressively finer motor coordination achieved by the infant, have them complete Handout 7, which asks students to re-master their motor skills as they work through the stages of development in a limited way. For instance, to master the skill of picking up objects, students are first directed to pick up a piece of paper or some other small object with the entire hand, that is, with all their fingers curled around it. Next, they are directed to hold the paper between the middle fingers and the palm of their hand.

Completion of this exercise may provide a good basis for discussing how knowledge about the acquisition of such skills can be applied in other areas, such as rehabilitation following a paralyzing stroke.

AV: See How They Move (28 min., Child Development Media)

Infants from 3 months to 2 years demonstrate the major landmarks of gross motor skill development: turning, crawling, sitting, and walking.

Observational Activity: Gross Motor Skill Development in the Infant

As noted in the text, developmentalists make a distinction between *gross motor skills*, which demand large body movements, and *fine motor skills*, which require small movements. Jumping, hopping, and clapping, for example, are gross motor skills; pouring a liquid into a glass without spilling it and turning a radio knob are fine motor skills.

In the first two years of life, the most obvious gross motor skills are those that transform the helpless newborn who cannot roll over without assistance into an active toddler who crawls, stands, walks, and finally runs. The *nonlocomotor*, or *stability*, *skills* pertain to the development of control of the head, neck, and trunk, and the eventual abilities to sit and stand. The *manipulative skills* include reaching for, grasping, and releasing objects. Finally, the *locomotor skills* include creeping, crawling, and walking.

Because motor development is such an obvious aspect of growth, it is often taken for granted. Although the development of gross motor skills occurs in a predictable cephalocaudal (head to tail) and proximodistal (near to far) sequence, and at a predictable rate closely related to maturation of the nervous system, the age at which these skills are acquired can vary considerably from infant to infant and still be considered normal. And although the rate of development of motor skills is limited by the maturity of the infant's neuromuscular system, environmental factors have a significant impact on skill attainment. A stimulating environment will encourage the child to practice movements and, therefore, promote motor development.

This observational activity is designed to increase students' understanding of how motor development is measured in young children. Have students arrange to observe a 1- or 2-year-old and his or her primary caregiver in a natural play setting for a period of approximately 30 minutes. Ideally, students will ask a relative or friend and his or her child to participate. The play setting could be in the child's home, at a local playground, in the campus child development center, or at any other mutually agreeable location. If the student does not know someone with a young child, he or she can complete this observational activity by visiting a playground or day-care center (after obtaining permission from the day-care center, of course).

During the observation period, students are to assess the child's gross motor skill development using an 11-skill checklist developed by Janice Beaty and based on the Denver norms for infant motor development (see Handout 8). The skills range in degree of difficulty from those certain to be mastered by a 1-year-old, such as standing without assistance, to skills that even some 4- and 5-year-olds will have difficulty with, such as clapping out musical rhythms and walking down steps alternating left and right feet.

If you wish, allow students to test a child anywhere between the ages of 1 and 6. This should make it easier to find children to study and allow a cross-sectional comparison of gross motor skill development over a greater span of years. If you choose this approach, the observational activity could be used again in conjunction with the discussion of biosocial development during early childhood. When students have completed the activity, collect the skill checklist data from the follow-up questionnaires (Handout 9), tabulate the percentage of children who demonstrated mastery of each skill by age in years, and put these results on the board. This information could form the basis for a general discussion of biosocial development during childhood.

Beaty, J. J. (1990). *Observing development of the young child* (3rd ed.), pp. 161–187. Copyright © 1994. Adapted by permission of Prentice Hall, Upper Saddle River, New Jersey.

Critical Thinking Activity: The Effects of Biosocial Experiences on Cognitive and Psychosocial Development

Each unit of these resources contains a critical thinking exercise designed specifically to test students' critical thinking about a topic covered in the text. Handout 10 contains a brief scenario followed by a series of questions.

Answers to this unit's critical thinking exercise are as follows:

1. In addition to biological maturation, brain development in the early years depends on normal sensory and perceptual experiences. This is most clearly demonstrated by experiments with kittens that were temporarily blindfolded for the first several weeks of life. These kittens never developed normal visual pathways. Consequently, their binocular vision and depth perception were permanently impaired.

   The fine-tuning of the visual systems of human babies is a much more gradual process than for kittens, lasting up to six years. This means that abnormal visual experiences during these years may have an irreversible effect on Samantha's neural pathways.
2. If Samantha's vision is abnormal, it is possible that the rate at which she acquires gross motor skills—such as crawling, creeping, and walking—may lag behind that of other children. This is so because her less-than-optimal depth perception may distort the perceptual feedback her brain receives as she moves about the environment.

   Samantha's fine motor skills may also suffer. For example, as a result of her faulty vision she may find it difficult to learn to coordinate the movement and trajectory of her arm and hand muscles as she reaches for toys and small objects. Her ability to "track" moving objects may also be slow to develop.
3. During the first months and years of life, there are major spurts of growth and refinement in the neural connections of the visual system and cortex. Over the course of time, neural pathways that are exercised are strengthened, while those that are not used die. These developmental processes improve the efficiency of neural communication in the brain.

   Although at birth, vision is the least developed of the senses, improvement in the perception of distance, motion, and color is rapid over the early months of life. Although scientists' understanding of the role of early experiences in cognitive development is far from complete, it is possible that abnormal visual experiences—which impair neural development in the cortex and distort learning experiences—may affect cognitive and social development. Samantha may, for example, be slower to learn about color, form, size, and other visual concepts since her vision is distorted. To the extent that her cognitive and motor skills lag behind those of other children, she may be more likely to withdraw socially from other children. If her visual, cognitive, and motor skill development does not improve, the impact on development in the social domain would probably become more severe as Samantha gets older and social play becomes more important.

Surviving in Good Health

AV: Keeping Babies Healthy and Safe (33 min., Child Development Media)

The first part of this video focuses on how caregivers keep their babies physically healthy, focusing on resistance to illness. The second part discusses the importance of parental monitoring and other ways to keep infants and toddlers safe in the home and elsewhere.

Internet Activity: Childhood Infections

Every child gets some sort of infection sooner or later. And when their children get sick, parents need answers. What are the symptoms? How can I help my child feel better? When should I call the doctor? To help students learn more about childhood infections and the Internet resources available to parents, have students search the Web to find information about the five childhood infections listed in Handout 11.

AV: Bottle Babies (26 min., University of Michigan Media)

This film exposes some of the adverse effects of marketing baby formulas in developing countries, including infant disease and malnutrition that may result from the substitution of powdered milk formulas for breast-feedings.

AV: Nutrition (15 min., Magna Systems)

This film presents a concise overview of the importance of good nutrition in each stage of childhood. The food pyramid and nutrient composition of common foods are explained.

Classroom Activity: Nutrition for Children

Nutritionists have become increasingly concerned that parents are applying their own diets to their infants, which may be hampering the infants' development. A set of dietary guidelines for children under 2 years of age published by the American Academy of Pediatrics includes the following recommendations for parents.

(a) Use your child's appetite as a feeding guide.
(b) Do not overly restrict the amount of fat and cholesterol in your infant's diet. Unless they are seriously obese, babies should be given whole or at least low-fat—not nonfat—milk until 2 years of age.
(c) High-fiber diets (often recommended for some adults) are not healthy for babies and children.
(d) A moderate amount of sodium is necessary in a child's diet to maintain the appropriate balance of minerals and water and to help the muscles and nervous system function.
(e) For children 2 and older, the amount of dietary fat should be reduced to no more than 30 percent of daily calories.

Early nutrition lays the foundation for the developing infant's future health. From a dietary standpoint, two potential problems are *obesity* and *dental disease*. Obesity is also related to increased risk of cancer, atherosclerosis (coronary artery disease), and diabetes.

Experts warn parents that infant obesity is less likely to occur when the parents encourage eating habits that will help the individual avoid obesity throughout life. This means introducing a *variety of nutritious foods*, not forcing the baby to finish the bottle or jar of food, minimizing concentrated sweets and "empty-calorie" foods, and developing a regular program of vigorous physical activity. New foods should be introduced one at a time and gradually, so that food allergies can be isolated. To prevent babies from developing a preference for sweets over vegetables, parents should introduce vegetables first and fruits later. Parents also should never use food as a reward, or teach their babies to seek food for emotional comfort, or associate punishment with food deprivation. Because babies apparently have no natural sense of "calorie counting" and because they stop eating when they feel full, they should be offered water, rather than juice or milk, when they cry from thirst.

Proper eating habits such as those just mentioned also promote healthy development of teeth. In addition, parents should avoid giving babies bottles as pacifiers. Prolonged sucking on a bottle promotes the growth of bacteria that cause tooth decay; it also pushes the jawline out of shape so that buckteeth (overbite of protruding upper and receding lower teeth) are more likely to develop.

Sizer, F., & Whitney, E. N. (2008). *Nutrition: Concepts and controversies* (11th ed.). New York: Cengage Learning.

HANDOUT 1

Developmental Fact or Myth?

T F 1. During the first year of life, most infants triple their body weight.

T F 2. By age 2, infants are already half their adult height.

T F 3. At birth, the nervous system contains only a fraction of the neurons the developing person will need.

T F 4. At birth, infants' vision is better developed than their hearing.

T F 5. At birth, newborns cannot focus well on objects at any distance.

T F 6. All healthy infants develop the same motor skills in the same sequence.

T F 7. Age norms for the development of motor skills, such as sitting up and walking, vary from group to group.

T F 8. The risks from diseases are far greater than the risks from immunizations.

T F 9. Approximately a third of the world's children are short for their age because of malnutrition.

T F 10. Chronic malnutrition during infancy may lead to permanent damage to the developing brain.

HANDOUT 2

Growth Rates During the First Two Years—On an Adult Scale

The text notes that growth in early infancy is astoundingly rapid. You can begin to appreciate just how rapid this growth is by projecting the growth patterns of the infant onto an adult, such as yourself.

1. If you were gaining weight at the rate of an infant, your weight would be tripled one year from today. Calculate how much you would weigh.

2. If you, like an infant, grew an inch a month, the change would not be as dramatic—because you are already much taller than an infant. Thus, every inch is a smaller percentage increase for you. Nevertheless, assume that you were growing at the rate of an infant during the first year, adding an inch a month. What would your height be a year from today?

3. How would you describe the growth rate of the infant?

4. The same kinds of calculations can help you make a less dramatic comparison between growth rates during the first and second years of life. During the first year, weight is tripled; thus, an infant born at a little more than 7 pounds will weigh about 22 pounds at 1 year. If growth were to continue at this rate, how much would the child weigh at 2 years?

   In fact, the average infant at 2 years weighs only 30 pounds. If a 30-inch 1-year-old continued to gain an inch a month, he or she would grow 12 inches during the second year. How tall would he or she be?

   In fact, even the fastest growing child grows only 6 inches, to reach 36 inches at age 2.

5. Compare the rates of growth during the first and second years.

HANDOUT 3

BYOB: Bring Your Own Brain

Imagine that you are a local caterer who is struggling to keep a fledgling business afloat. You've just heard that the International Association of Brain Surgeons (IABS) is holding its annual convention this year in your hometown, and you have been selected to prepare an edible, neuroanatomically accurate centerpiece for the keynote speaker's table. Your centerpiece may be an appetizer, dessert, or other food item depicting the cerebral cortex, brain stem, limbic system, nerve cell, or any other part of the central nervous system. It may represent any angle or cross section of the brain, and you will be asked to give a brief oral summary of its features and significance to the developing child's motor, emotional, and/or cognitive abilities. Grading will be based on the integration of creativity, flavor, and anatomical accuracy.

Source: Raap, D. (2002, January). *Course projects for targeted audiences.* Paper presented at the meeting of the National Institute on the Teaching of Psychology (NITOP), St. Petersburg, FL.

HANDOUT 4

Observational Activity: Time Sampling of Newborn Behavior: Infant States

Infant's State

1. Active Sleep

Eyes:	Closed, with jerky, rapid eye movements apparent beneath the eyelids
Breathing:	Shallow and irregular
Movements:	Muscles are deeply relaxed
Response to stimuli:	Sounds or changes in lighting may elicit facial reactions in the sleeping infant

2. Quiet Sleep

Eyes:	Closed, with slow, rolling movements apparent beneath the eyelids
Breathing:	Deep and regular
Movements:	Occasional generalized startle responses
Response to stimuli:	Little or no response to mild sounds and lights

3. Drowsiness

Eyes:	Open or closed
Breathing:	Irregular
Movements:	Moderately active
Response to stimuli:	Facial expressions; startle responses to stimuli

4. Awake-Quiet

Eyes:	Open
Breathing:	Inconsistent pattern in this state
Movements:	Quiet; some movement of head and limbs while examining environment
Response to stimuli:	Novel stimuli may trigger and maintain this state

5. Awake-Fussing

Eyes:	Open
Breathing:	Inconsistent pattern in this state
Movements:	Much activity characteristic of highly aroused state
Response to stimuli:	Crying, kicking, thrashing about may increase in response to feelings of physical discomfort (cold, pain, hunger, being placed in crib, etc.)

HANDOUT 5

Observational Activity: Time Sampling of Newborn Behavior: Observation Procedure

1. Each student and his or her partner will independently observe the behavior of the same infant for forty 30-second intervals.
2. Review the descriptions of infant states and make sure you are familiar with the behavioral characteristics of each state.
3. Pick an infant to observe who is *not in quiet sleep* at the start of the observation period. Doing otherwise may give you little or no variation in infant behavior during the observation period.
4. Begin timing the 30-second intervals. For each interval make a check mark on your data sheet in the column under the infant state that most accurately describes the infant's behavior (eyes, breathing, movements) during the preceding 30 seconds.
5. Following the observation period, complete the follow-up questionnaire and return your answers, along with your data sheet, to your instructor.

HANDOUT 5 *(continued)*

Time Sampling of Newborn Behavior: Data Sheet

For each 30-second interval, make a check mark in the column beneath the state that most accurately describes the newborn's behavior during the preceding 30-second period.

	Infant State				
30-Second Interval	Active Sleep	Quiet Sleep	Drowsiness	Awake-Quiet	Awake-Fussing
1					
2					
3					
4					
5					
6					
7					
8					
9					
10					
11					
12					
13					
14					
15					
16					
17					
18					
19					
20					
21					
22					
23					
24					
25					
26					
27					
28					
29					
30					
31					
32					
33					
34					
35					
36					
37					
38					
39					
40					

HANDOUT 5 *(continued)*

Time Sampling of Newborn Behavior: Follow-Up Questionnaire

1. Describe the context of your observational activity (setting, time of day, whether the nursery was busy) and the newborn you chose to observe.

2. Did you find it difficult to decide which of the five infant states your subject was displaying at any given moment? Which states were most difficult to identify?

3. Approximately what percentage of the time did you and your partner agree on the infant's state? Were there any patterns to the occasions when you and your partner disagreed?

HANDOUT 5 *(continued)*

4. Determine the percentage of the 20-minute observation period that your subject was in each of the five infant states and draw a bar graph of these percentages in the space that follows.

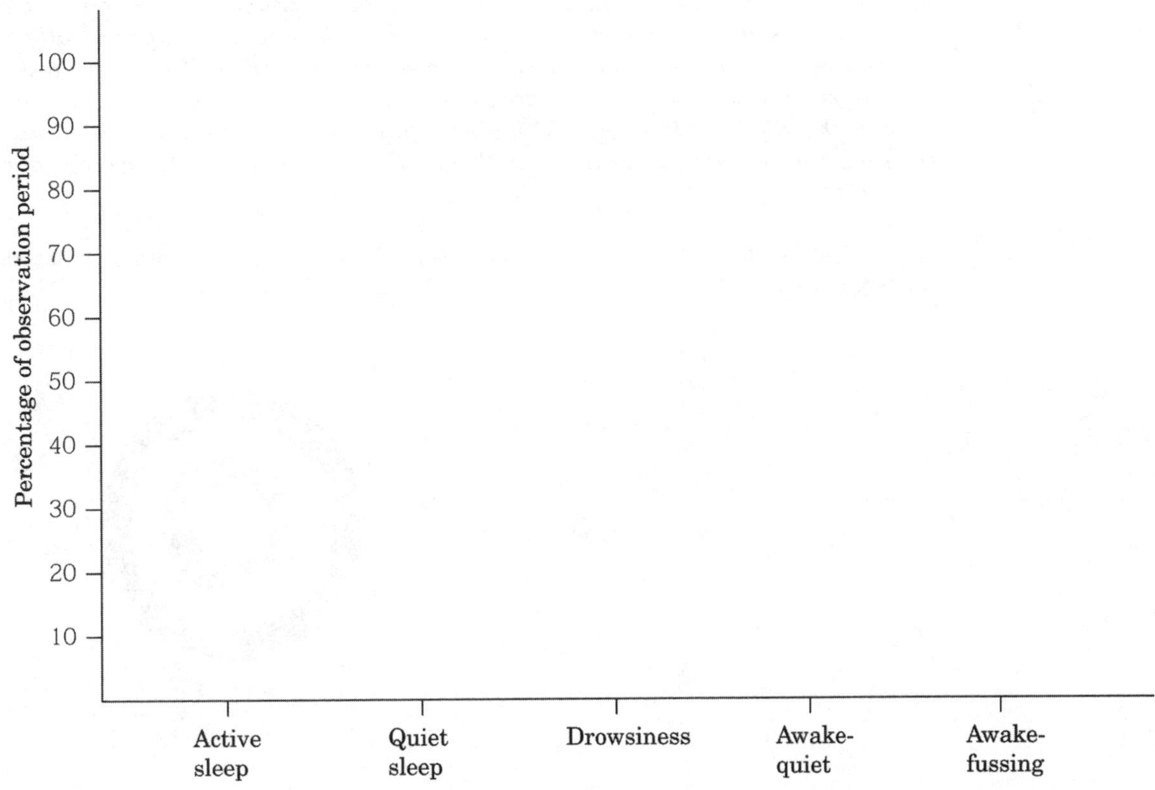

HANDOUT 6

Infants' Shape Preferences

The preference method of assessing perceptual ability is based on the idea that if infants consistently prefer to look at one image over another, they must be able to perceptually discriminate the two images.

For this demonstration you will need to make six test stimuli. Draw three circles 6 inches in diameter on a white piece of paper. Using the examples below, draw a cartoon face on one circle and a bull's-eye on another. Leave the third circle white. Cut the circles out. Cut two more circles out of brightly colored paper, ideally yellow and red, respectively. Cut the sixth circle from newsprint. Present the test stimuli one at a time to a 2- to 6-month-old infant while measuring the number of seconds the infant looks at each stimulus before turning away. Each stimulus should be presented at least twice, with gaze time computed as the average of the two tests.

Source: Matlin, M. W., & Foley, H. J. (1997). *Sensation and perception* (4th ed.). Boston: Allyn & Bacon.

1. How old was the infant you tested?

2. Describe any difficulties you encountered in conducting your test.

HANDOUT 6 *(continued)*

3. Complete the following table by entering the average number of seconds your subject gazed at each test stimulus.

Test Stimulus	Trial 1	Trial 2	Average
Cartoon Face			
Bull's-Eye			
White Circle			
Yellow Circle			
Red Circle			
Newsprint Circle			

HANDOUT 7

Basic Motor Skills: Learning Like an Infant

One way to understand the way infants master basic motor skills is by trying to re-master these skills as an adult.

You can learn to "feel" the progressively finer coordination achieved by the infant if you work through the stages of development in a limited way. A good place to start is with mastery of the motor skills involved in picking up objects.

1. Pick up a piece of paper or some other small object with your entire hand; that is, with all of your fingers curled around it.
2. Now hold the paper between your middle fingers and the palm of your hand.
3. Pick up the paper by pressing your index finger against the side of your palm.
4. Finally, use the thumb and index finger to pick up the paper. When is this grasp achieved?
5. Which of these ways of grasping a small object felt most comfortable or natural to you?

HANDOUT 8

Observational Activity: Gross Motor Skill Development in the Infant: Skill Checklist

1. *Stands Alone Without Difficulty*

   By the twelfth month of life, approximately 50 percent of all babies can stand easily without assistance; by the fourteenth month, fully 90 percent of all babies have mastered this skill.

2. *Walks Well*

   Walking separates toddler from infant and normally occurs around the end of the first year of life. One-year-olds move cautiously, walk with a wide, "waddling" stride, and often need assistance. Two-year-olds still must concentrate somewhat on their balance but typically will not need assistance, and unlike 1-year-olds, will not lose their balance as easily when forced to stop suddenly.

3. *Walks Backward*

   Walking backward requires neuromuscular coordination, balance, and perceptual skills far in excess of those required in walking forward. At 14 months, only about 50 percent of toddlers are able to walk backward with confidence; by 21 months, nearly 90 percent can do so.

4. *Walks Up (or Down) Steps Alternating Feet*

   Approximately half of all babies are, with help, able to walk up steps by 17 months of age. By 22 months, nearly 90 percent can do so. At this age, however, they will place both feet on a step before advancing upward, rather than alternating left foot, right foot, left foot, etc., as they proceed. Older 2-year-olds may be able to alternate feet going upstairs, but doing so when going down the steps will not be mastered until much later.

5. *Kicks Ball Accurately*

   The 1-year-old toddler may approach and strike a ball with his or her foot, but not until children are nearly 2 are they able to consistently muster the balance, coordination, and eye–foot control necessary for effective and accurate kicking.

6. *Is Able to Run and Control Speed and Direction*

   Although 1-year-olds often walk very rapidly in a rudimentary form of running, their feet never leave the ground. True running usually does not occur until sometime between the second and third birthday.

7. *Can Jump Over Small Obstacle and Land on Both Feet*

   Unlike hopping and leaping, which involve taking off and landing on one foot, jumping involves landing on both feet and usually is not apparent in children under 2 years of age.

8. *Hops Steadily on One Foot*

   Because hopping involves taking off and landing on the same foot, children must have a fairly well-developed sense of balance in order to demonstrate this skill. Very few children are able to hop well before the third birthday.

HANDOUT 8 *(continued)*

9. *Climbs Well*

   Climbing requires coordinated use of the upper and lower body and is considered an advanced form of *creeping*. Children begin climbing as soon as they are able to pull themselves up onto an object worthy of being climbed. By 2 years, this skill is well developed.

10. *Moves Rhythmically to Music*

    An infant's earliest movements are reflexive, involuntary responses to specific stimuli. The first voluntary movements of young children typically are elicited by sounds. These movements gradually mature into skills that include rhythmic movement to music. Following the cephalocaudal pattern of development, young children will be able to move their arms and hands and later their legs and feet to a slow rhythm tapped out on a box or drum. As rhythmic skills improve, children will learn to follow irregular beats and beats that vary in sound intensity.

11. *Claps in Rhythm*

    As discussed in the previous item, the head-to-toe sequence of development also applies to the rhythmic use of the arms and hands. Two-year-olds typically love to clap, but usually are unable to control their clapping to follow even the simplest rhythmic pattern without great difficulty.

Source: Beaty, J. J. (1990). *Observing development of the young child* (3rd ed.), pp. 161–187.

HANDOUT 9

Gross Motor Skill Development in Infants: Follow-Up Questionnaire

Before your scheduled observation period, read through the gross motor skill checklist and the questions on this handout so you will know what to look for. Observe your subject for approximately half an hour of unstructured play. After the observation period, complete the questions on the handout and return it to your instructor.

1. Describe the participant (age, sex, motor skills, etc.) and setting that you chose for this observation.

2. Describe any difficulties you encountered in completing this observational activity.

3. Complete the following skill checklist for your subject.

Skill	Demonstrated Yes	Demonstrated No	Comments
1. Stands alone			
2. Walks well			
3. Walks backward			
4. Alternates feet			
Walking up stairs			
Walking down stairs			
5. Kicks ball accurately			
6. Runs, controlling speed and direction			
7. Jumps over obstacle			
8. Hops on one foot			
9. Climbs well			
10. Moves rhythmically			
11. Claps rhythmically			

HANDOUT 9 *(continued)*

4. Assuming the normal variation in age norms for the attainment of the various motor skills you assessed, would you say that your subject was "on time," "early," or "late" in the development of gross motor skills? Give several specific examples of behaviors you observed to justify your assessment of the child's skill level.

5. Using the checklist, pick the gross motor skill at which the child was the *least accomplished*. Which skill is this, and what reasons can you suggest for the child's relatively weaker ability? Suggest at least three activities you could design for the child to promote mastery of the skill.

Source: Beaty, J. J. (1990). *Observing development of the young child* (3rd ed.), pp. 161–187.

HANDOUT 10

Critical Thinking Activity: The Effects of Biosocial Experiences on Cognitive and Psychosocial Development

Now that you have read and reviewed the material on biosocial development during the first two years, take your learning a step further by testing your critical thinking skills on this creative problem-solving exercise.

This exercise takes a creative look at how early experiences in one domain of development might also affect development in other domains. In an extensive study (Vernon-Feagens & Manlove, 1996), the researchers found that children with chronic middle ear fluid were more likely to play alone and less likely to talk with their peers than control children. Animal studies also provide evidence that early sensory experiences can have a dramatic, and sometimes irreversible, effect on developing neural connections in the brain.

In this exercise, you are asked to imagine that you are advising parents who are considering whether to have their toddler Samantha's vision disorder corrected. Samantha's disorder, which can be completely corrected only through surgery, involves an uneven curvature of the lens of each eyeball. Unless the problem is corrected, Samantha's vision will forever be slightly out of focus in both eyes, even if she wears corrective eyeglasses or contact lenses.

Samantha's parents, who are understandably concerned about the dangers of performing any operation on so young a child, have several questions. To stretch your creative imagination, see if you can answer their questions.

Vernon-Feagens, L., & Manlove, E. E. (1996). Otitis media and and the social behavior of day-care-attending children. *Child Development, 67,* 1528–1539.

The Parents' Questions

1. Is there any evidence that our child's vision problem should be corrected sooner rather than later in life? Why not wait until Samantha is older to correct the problem?
2. If we choose not to have the surgery performed now, will Samantha's physical development lag behind that of other children?
3. What about Samantha's cognitive and social development? Could her visual problem affect these areas of her life?

HANDOUT 11

Internet Activity: Childhood Infections

Every child gets some sort of infection sooner or later. And when their children get sick, parents need answers. What are the symptoms? How can I help my child feel better? When should I call the doctor? To learn more about childhood infections and the Internet resources available to help parents, search the Web to find information about the following five childhood infections. (Hint: A good starting point is www.kidshealth.org.)

Acute Otitis Media

1. What are the symptoms and causes of this condition? How does it differ from external otitis? Why are children more susceptible to this condition than are adults? What are some of the potential complications?

2. Why are breast-fed children less susceptible to otitis media than formula-fed children? State at least two reasons.

3. When should a doctor be called? What is the standard treatment for this condition? What can be done if the condition persists?

Conjunctivitis

4. What are the symptoms and causes of this condition? Why are children more susceptible to this condition than are adults? What are some of the potential complications?

HANDOUT 11 *(continued)*

5. What steps can be taken to help prevent conjunctivitis?

6. When should a doctor be called? What is the standard treatment for this condition? What can be done if the condition persists?

Reye's Syndrome

7. What is Reye's syndrome? When was it first discovered? How is it diagnosed?

8. How common is Reye's syndrome? What are some of the risk factors that are linked to this condition?

9. How serious is this syndrome? What can be done to prevent it from occurring? What is the standard treatment for this condition?

Chlamydia Trachomatis

10. What are chlamydia? What are the symptoms of chlamydia trachomatis?

HANDOUT 11 *(continued)*

11. How do children acquire this condition? What are some of its potential dangers?

12. How is the condition prevented? How is it treated?

Candidiasis

13. What are the signs and symptoms of this condition? What causes it? How common is it during infancy?

14. Is this condition contagious? How can it be prevented? How is it treated?

15. How dangerous is candidiasis to a child's overall health and well-being?

The First Two Years: Cognitive Development

Contents

Note: Worth Publishers provides online Instructor and Student Tool Kits, DVD Student Tool Kits, and Instructor and Student video resources in DevelopmentPortal for use with the text. See Part I: General Resources for general information about these materials and the text Lecture Guides for a complete list by text chapter.

Suggested Activities

Introducing The First Two Years: Cognitive Development

"On Your Own" Activity: Developmental Fact or Myth?

Before students read about cognitive development during the first two years, have them respond to the true–false statements in Handout 1.

The correct answers follow. Class discussion can focus on the origins of any developmental misconceptions that are demonstrated in the students' incorrect answers.

1. T	6. T
2. F	7. T
3. F	8. T
4. F	9. F
5. F	10. T

AV: The Journey Through the Life Span, Program 3: Infants and Toddlers

See The First Two Years: Biosocial Development for a description of Program 3 and the accompanying observation modules, which cover the entire unit on infancy and toddlerhood.

AV: Transitions Throughout the Life Span, Program 6: The Little Scientist

Program 6 is the first telecourse to focus on the domain of cognition, the mental processes involved in thinking. The program focuses on the various ways in which infant cognitive development is revealed: through perception, memory, sensorimotor intelligence, and language development. It begins by outlining Jean Piaget's theory of sensorimotor intelligence, which maintains that infants think exclusively with their senses and motor skills. Piaget's six stages of sensorimotor intelligence are examined. Psychologists Alison Gopnik, Susan Siaw, Jean Berko Gleason, and Elizabeth Bates provide expert commentary.

Next, the program turns to the most remarkable cognitive achievement of the first two years, the acquisition of language. Beginning with a description of the infant's first attempts at language, the program follows the sequence of events that leads to the child's ability to utter two-word sentences. The program concludes with an examination of language learning as teamwork involving babies and adults, who, in a sense, teach each other the unique human process of verbal communication.

AV: Growing Minds: Cognitive Development in Early Childhood (25 min., Davidson Films)

In this video, David Elkind reviews the works of Lev Vygotsky and Jean Piaget, using their ideas—and his own—to examine three aspects of cognitive development: reasoning, visual perception, and language development.

AV: Development of the Child: Infancy (20 min., HarperCollins Media/Pennsylvania State University)

Jerome Kagan and Howard Gardner show a broad range of infant behavior, from reflexes to object permanence, from attachment to familiar caregivers to fear of unfamiliar adults. Kagan's research on infant attention provides a good illustration of the cleverness of infants, as well as the creativity of the researchers who study them. Kagan's discrepancy hypothesis (that infants are most attentive to sights and sounds that are sufficiently different from the familiar to be interesting but not so different as to be unanalyzable) is demonstrated.

Classroom Activity: Design a Study

To underscore the message that developmental psychology is an empirical science, and reinforce students' understanding of quantitative and qualitative research methods, ask the class to design a research study that answers questions about development during the first two years. Divide the class into groups of three or four and display or distribute the following question.

Research Question: Many people believe that music can have a calming effect on 2-year-olds. What type of study can I conduct to find out if this is true?

Then, give the groups 15 minutes of discussion during which they

1. state a testable research hypothesis.
2. state operational definitions of independent and dependent variables.
3. choose an appropriate research design.
4. provide a detailed outline of research methods.

Afterward, a spokesperson from each group will share the group's proposed design with the rest of the class.

Teaching Tip: Personality Differences Between the Best and Worst Teachers

After serving for a dozen years on teaching award committees, Dean Keith Simonton compiled the following list of traits of the best and worst teachers. Derived from the so-called Big Five personality traits (extroversion, agreeableness, openness, conscientiousness, neuroticism), the differences are striking. How would you characterize your own personality as a teacher?

The Best Teachers Exhibit	The Worst Teachers Exhibit
High extroversion	Low extroversion
Before-class chats/enthusiasm, interactive	Arrive late/leave early/avoid eye contact/inaudible
High agreeableness	Low agreeableness
Learn names/liberal office hours	Dislike questions/minimal office hours
High conscientiousness	Low conscientiousness
Read text/complete syllabi	Unprepared/bad syllabi/dated
Low neuroticism	High neuroticism
Relaxed/easy-going/flexible	Anxious/defensive/inflexible
High openness to experience	Low openness to experience
Show connections/use cartoons, newspapers, TV shows, movies	Narrow perspective/imposes own views/ disdains application

Simonton, D. K. (2003, February). *Teaching and the Big Five.* Paper presented at the Society for Personality and Social Psychology teaching workshop, Los Angeles, CA.

Sensorimotor Intelligence

Internet Activity: Cyberspace Hunt: Jean Piaget

The Internet is an excellent resource for learning about prominent developmental theorists. For example, a Web site devoted to Piaget contains a wealth of biographical and professional information. Have students search the Internet to find answers to the questions in Handout 2.

AV: Cognitive Development (20 min., CRM/McGraw-Hill)

(See description in Theories of Development.)

"On Your Own" Activity: Ordering Exercise

To help students apply their understanding of the stages of sensorimotor intelligence, have them order the events listed in Handout 3. The answers are as follows: a. 5; b. 3; c. 1; d. 4; e. 2; f. 6.

AV: The Infant Mind (30 min., Insight Media)

This film explains and challenges Piaget's stage theory of development. Several developmentalists explain that infants possess a basic understanding of cause and effect, object permanence, and number earlier than Piaget believed.

AV: First Adaptations (30 min., RMI Media Productions)

This program explores the awesome cognitive capacities of the newborn and infant. Experts chart an infant's developing cognitive abilities as the nervous system matures. Research on the learning abilities of newborns only a few hours old is described.

AV: Tim: His Sensory-Motor Development (31 min., HarperCollins Media)

This movie follows Tim through the first two years of life, focusing on his performance on a structured set of Piagetian tasks, including tests of object permanence and goal-directed behaviors. The film helps illustrate the substages of sensorimotor development, including circular reactions. It also provides a good way to contrast methods of assessing cognitive development; although it is clear that mastery of motor skills such as sitting and walking help Tim explore his world, and thereby enhance his cognitive development, they do not in themselves lead automatically to cognitive gains.

Teaching Tip: Active Exploration for Sensorimotor Learning

To help students appreciate the degree to which the curiosity of the infant can make life difficult for the parents—especially if the parents do not understand that active exploration is a crucial aspect of sensorimotor learning—you might list, in general terms, several of a toddler's favorite activities and then give examples of amusing and exasperating instances. If your students have had experience with toddlers, they can add their own examples. Such a list might begin like this.

> Toddlers love to make things appear and disappear, so they're apt to flush toothbrushes down the toilet; turn the TV off and on and off again; drop food from the high chair to the floor; and throw toys out of the playpen.
>
> Toddlers love to put one thing into another, so they stick peas up their noses or into their ears; put bobby pins into electric sockets; stick fingers into your mouth, and unfortunately, almost anything into their own mouths (death by poisoning is more common at age 1 than at any other age).

Classroom Activity: Active Exploration

If your campus has a child development center, you might arrange a class visit there to highlight the behavior of the "little scientist." Or, you might make arrangements to bring a child between 12 and 18 months old to class and surround him or her with interesting toys and other objects. As long as the setting is not too intimidating (an observation room with a one-way mirror would be ideal; a small classroom with fewer than a dozen students should be fine), the child will probably experiment and play with many things. You will be able to point out evidence of object permanence, and so forth.

This would also provide an opportunity for students to see social learning in action. Ask the child's parent to play with a toy in a novel way that promises to capture his or her attention (for example, making a noise with it) and then give it to him or her. Usually the child will repeat the parent's actions.

Teaching Tip: Assessing Infant Cognitive Development: Three Approaches

To help students appreciate Piaget's unique approach to the study of intellectual development, contrast it with two other approaches: the *psychometric approach*, which attempts to measure cognitive development by using *standardized intelligence tests*, and the *information-processing approach*, which attempts to describe the cognitive processes used by children as they develop.

Piaget's theory of sensorimotor intelligence is primarily concerned with *qualitative* differences in the way children acquire knowledge. Conversely, psychometric tests, such as the Bayley Scales of Infant Development, represent attempts to *quantify* intelligence by comparing each child's capabilities with those shown to be normal for various age norms. The information-processing approach views intelligence not as a single entity but rather as a set of cognitive processes that includes attention, memory, and retrieval.

Further, psychometric tests of infant development tend to emphasize motor rather than verbal skills. The results of such tests generally are not very reliable, nor are they very accurate in predicting the pace or nature of a child's later cognitive development. Infants' DQ (developmental quotient) scores on the Bayley Scales, for example, do not correlate significantly with their scores on other standard IQ tests, probably because the latter tests tend to emphasize verbal, rather than motor, capabilities.

The information-processing approach attempts to measure how infants manipulate and process information by monitoring evoked brain potentials, heart rate changes, and eye movements in response to changes in the sensory environment. Many examples of the information-processing approach were provided in the text discussion of perceptual development as part of biosocial and cognitive development. These include research on attention, habituation, and shape preference.

Classroom Activity: Event-Related Potentials

Also known as an evoked potential, the event-related potential (ERP) is one of the newer tools of cognitive neuroscience. Researchers use the ERP to observe human brain activity as it reflects specific cognitive processes such as word or facial recognition. ERP is a composite measure that uses electroencephalography (EEG) to record the brain's response to a specific auditory or visual stimulus. Although the EEG is widely used, the tracings of brain waves it produces on a time scale provide only crude information regarding brain-wave frequency and amplitude. The ERP, however, averages the results of many trials together, thus providing a much clearer picture of what electrical activity is taking place in response to a specific oral or visual stimulus. Furthermore, the use of multiple electrodes allows the researcher to see not only the brain-wave activity produced, but *where* and *when* it moves over the surface of the cerebral cortex. These data are frequently used to explore how parts of the brain process individual phonemes, syllables, and words of a sentence. Worth's Instructor Media Tool Kit includes an excellent short video clip of the fun, safe manner in which ERPs are recorded from infants' brains.

Luck, S. J. (2005). *An introduction to the event-related potential technique.* Cambridge, MA: MIT Press.

Information Processing

AV: PsychNow: Interactive Experiences in Psychology (CD-ROM) (Insight Media)

(See description in the Introduction.)

AV: The Developing Child: The Crucial Early Years (26 min., Films for the Humanities and Sciences)

This interesting film deals with the importance of early experiences in fostering cognitive development in the infant. Its message is that learning begins in the cradle, as the newborn responds to sensory stimulation, and that parents can assist cognitive development by encouraging learning. The film also discusses the controversial issue of IQ testing.

AV: Mastering the Tasks of Toddlerhood (25 min., Insight Media)

Depicting toddlers in both home and day-care centers, this film probes the cognitive and emotional development that result from the child's tasks of developing autonomy and language.

AV: The Discovery Year (52 min., Films for the Humanities and Sciences)

(See description in The First Two Years: Biosocial Development.)

AV: Discovering the Outside World (30 min., Films for the Humanities and Sciences)

(See description in The First Two Years: Biosocial Development.)

Classroom Activity: Differentiating Sensation and Perception with "Puzzle Pictures" and Sounds

According to Eleanor and James Gibson, which of the many affordances children perceive in a given object depends on their developmental level, past experiences, and their sensory awareness of what that object might be used for. To dramatically differentiate the

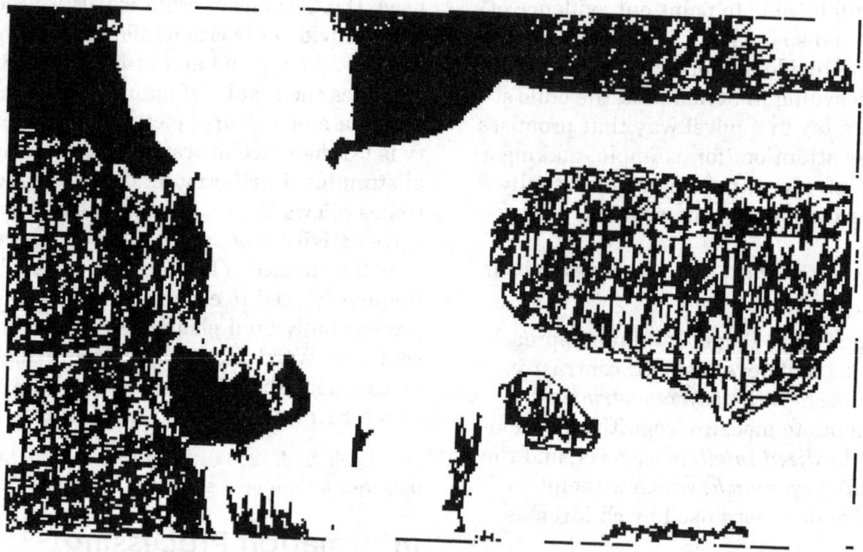

processes of sensation and perception, Douglas Bloomquist and Stanley Coren display the figure above to the class, asking students to state what they see. Many first-time observers don't immediately perceive a meaningful stimulus, seeing instead an amorphous blob—that is, a sensory stimulus without a meaningful perception. After a minute or so, begin giving the class clues, such as "it is a common animal," "you would find this animal on a farm," and so forth. At this point, someone will yell out "cow"; for those who still can't perceive the animal, sketch the drawing at the bottom of the page on the board. (Once students "get it," they will be amazed that they initially missed it.)

As a follow-up to this demonstration, you might present the classic "rat–man" demonstration. You will need three slides or overheads of the rat stimulus, the man stimulus, and the rat–man stimulus (see Bugelski & Alampay, 1961). The procedure is simple: Present the rat picture for a few seconds to half of the class (while the other students close their eyes) and then present the man picture to the other half of the class (while the first group closes its eyes). Next, have everyone open their eyes and briefly flash the rat–man picture to the entire class. Finally, by a show of hands ask the class how many saw a rat, and how many saw a man.

These two powerful demonstrations can lead to a discussion of the active nature of perception, perceptual set, and top-down processing. In the first demonstration, looking at the puzzle picture underscores the dynamic nature of perception as the person struggles to impose some organization on the meaningless image. If students think carefully, many will admit that they were, in fact, generating hypotheses about the figure and then testing them by searching for other features in the image that might confirm their hypothesis. In the rat–man demonstration, the initial

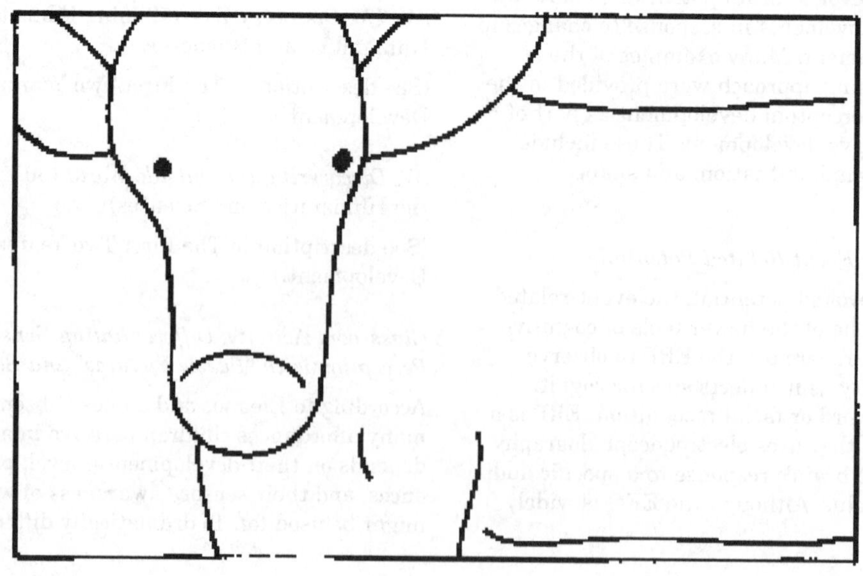

"priming" images create perceptual sets that bias later perception of what is, in fact, an ambiguous stimulus that is just as much a rat as a man.

If you want to go for a "hat trick," you might reproduce Bruce Goldstein's auditory demonstration, in which he plays a Rolling Stones recording of the song "Tumblin' Dice," first by itself and then accompanied by the actual lyrics. Seeing the words makes the initially incomprehensible lyrics immediately recognizable.

Bloomquist, D. W. (2002, January). *Introducing perception with a "puzzle picture."* Paper presented at the meeting of the National Institute on the Teaching of Psychology (NITOP), St. Petersburg, FL.

Bugelski, B. R., & Alampay, D. A. (1961). The role of frequency in developing perceptual sets. *Canadian Journal of Psychology, 15*, 205–211.

Coren, S., Ward, L. M., & Enns, J. T. (2004). *Sensation and perception* (6th ed.). New York: Wiley.

Goldstein, B. (2002, January). *Making cognitive psychology real.* Paper presented at the meeting of the National Institute on the Teaching of Psychology (NITOP), St. Petersburg, FL.

Classroom Activity: The Development of Visual Perception

If you did not use this classroom activity during your coverage of The First Two Years: Biosocial Development, you may wish to do so now. The activity explains how researchers have utilized the conditioning method to assess infants' perceptual abilities. Gordon Bower's classic study of *size constancy* in infants is also described. Because contemporary developmentalists consider perceptual development to be an important "window" through which cognitive function can be viewed, this activity could profitably be utilized while discussing cognitive development during the first two years.

AV: The First Year of Life (28 min., Films for the Humanities and Sciences)

This film, with *The Growing Infant,* examines physical growth during infancy, including cephalocaudal and proximaldistal principles, the relationship between cognitive and physical growth, and the development of vision, hearing, and perceptual abilities. It explores how newborns see, hear, and make use of skills developed even before birth to interact with their surroundings. The infant's emerging individuality is also discussed.

Classroom Activity: Gender Differences in Facial Expression Processing

If you did not use the Classroom Activity *Facial Expression Processing: Neurobehavioral Maturation or Cognitive Scaffolding?* during your coverage of biosocial development during the first two years, you may wish to do so now. The activity presents a meta-analysis designed to test two hypotheses regarding the general superiority of females in processing nonverbal cues: a neurobehavioral model and a social constructivist model. As predicted by the neurobehavioral model, gender differences in facial expression processing (FEP) (as revealed by the habituation and visual preference tasks) were greatest in infancy; they then declined to lower, but still significant, levels by the preschool years. Throughout childhood and adolescence, gender differences appeared to remain relatively stable. This pattern suggests that gender differences in FEP are linked to differences in early neurological maturation.

AV: Development of the Child: Cognition (30 min., HarperCollins Media/Pennsylvania State University)

Aspects of cognition—including perception, memory evaluation, reasoning, and hypothesis testing—are examined from a problem-solving point of view. This film also outlines Piaget's developmental stages.

Classroom Activity: Infants' Developmental Tasks

To help students better understand the developmental tasks faced by infants, you might try a classroom exercise suggested by Gregory Harper. In "lollipops and gloquex" (pronounced *glocks*), students are asked to employ the sensorimotor reflex of sucking on a lollipop to emphasize that the infant is capable of learning about his or her world only by attempting to apply new experiences to a limited repertoire of existing reflexes. You can also relate this to the Gibsons' concept of affordances.

Begin by giving each student a lollipop. As Harper indicates, the lollipop will naturally elicit sucking, the most basic of sensorimotor behaviors. As students continue to ingest their lollipops, point out that variations in sucking— for example, licking, chewing—represent elaborations of the basic reflex. Also point out that the sucking reflex can be adapted to many other objects (just as the infant discovers)—including a finger, toy, or bottle. For Piaget, such adaptations exemplify intelligent behavior.

In a second exercise, students are given the opportunity to learn about an imaginary object using the basic discovery processes of the "little scientist." Pretend to remove a large object from a cardboard box, place the object on a table or desk, and note in detail its dimensions, weight, and general appearance. As you pretend to plug it in, encourage students to ask questions in order to identify the imaginary object. Possible questions (and answers that Harper suggests) include the following.

(a) What is the object called? (gloquex)
(b) What does it do? (It counteracts bad vibrations in a room.)
(c) How does it work? (An inversely reciprocating frimfram bollixes any waves entering the aperture.)

(d) What is it made of? (hyperventilated case-hardened mollox)
(e) Why can't I see it? (You can't?)

After a few minutes, test students on their knowledge of gloquex. Beyond remembering its name and describing its appearance, students will have difficulty talking about it. They are likely to describe it with such phrases as: "It's about the same as a . . ." or "It works like a . . ." Point out the similarities between these attempts and those of a child attempting to fit a novel experience into an existing understanding or when it does not fit, causing disequilibrium, to modify the old understanding and construct a new one that fits the new experience. Using similar processes, young children are able to learn about unfamiliar objects and concepts.

Harper, G. F. (1979). Introducing Piagetian concepts through the use of familiar and novel illustrations. *Teaching of Psychology*, *6*(1), 58–59.

AV: Promoting Cognitive, Social, and Emotional Development (22 min., Films for the Humanities and Sciences)

This video discusses the caregiving of infants and young children with special needs. Among the topics explored are the importance of encouraging appropriate caregiving reactions to the child, the need for stimulation and play, and knowing how to communicate with special-needs children.

Classroom Activity: Introducing Memory with Clips from Memento

The late Martin Bolt introduced the topic of human memory in his popular psychology classes by showing clips from the 2000 feature film *Memento*. In this fascinating film, the character played by Guy Pearce attempts to avenge his wife's murder. His efforts seemingly are impossibly difficult because at the time his wife (played by Jorja Fox) was assaulted, he himself sustained a serious closed head injury that destroyed the brain mechanism by which information is transferred from short-term to long-term memory. Pearce is able to hold information only briefly, until it fades from conscious, working memory. He compensates for this form of anterograde amnesia by constantly writing Post-it Notes to himself, taking countless Polaroid snapshots, and even tattooing key facts about the crime on his body.

Two film segments are particularly useful in introducing memory. In Chapter 3 of the film, "It's Like Waking" (running from 6:25 minutes into the film until 11:05), Pearce describes his amnesia and how he is able to compensate in order to pursue his search for his wife's killer. In Chapter 6, "Memories Can Be Distorted" (running from 22:15 minutes until 28:28), a friend challenges the accuracy and reliability of Pearce's note-taking. This clip is particularly valuable for illustrating the malleable and constructive nature of human memory.

Bolt, M. (2010). Instructor's resources to accompany David G. Myers *Psychology* (9th ed.). New York: Worth. Chapter 8, p. 14.

Classroom Activity: Demonstrating the Constructive Nature of Human Memory

As noted in the text, after about 6 months, infants become capable of retaining information for longer periods of time, with less reminding. By the middle of the second year, toddlers are able to generalize their memories from particular details to the general concept. Most researchers believe there are many types of memory and that memory is a dynamic, ever-changing process, rather than a static and veridical "photocopy" of past experiences. To illustrate the constructive nature of memory and spark students' interest in your continuing discussion of information-processing theory, Doug Bernstein offers a simple, all-purpose memory demonstration that requires only that you ask the class to listen as you read aloud, at the rate of about one word per second, the following list:

bed, quilt, dark, silence, fatigue, clock, snoring, night, toss, tired, night, artichoke, turn, night, rest, dream

After you have finished reading the list, give the class about 30 seconds to write down as many of the words as they can recall. Then, ask by a show of hands how many students recalled the word "sleep." If your students are typical, a third or more of the class will remember the word but only by actively constructing it in their memory, since "sleep" was not on the list. (For an especially effective demonstration, record the list of words and play them back twice: first during the demonstration and once again after the recall period to prove to skeptics that "sleep" did not appear in the original list.)

If you wish to expand on other aspects of short- and long-term memory, you might repeat the list in order and ask for a show of hands by those who correctly recalled each word. Plotting these frequencies on the board should produce the classic, U-shaped serial position curve, with recall scores best for the beginning of the list (primacy effect) and the end of the list (recency effect), and worst in the middle of the list. Two other subtleties should also appear. Due to semantic distinctiveness, the word "artichoke" will probably have a higher recall score than its neighbors; due to the natural tendency to chunk and categorize, "night" should also have a relatively high recall score. Following the demonstration, you might discuss the development of memory span, short-term memory duration, and so on during infancy.

Bernstein, D. A. (2002, January). *Sharing ideas on the teaching of psychology.* Paper presented at the meeting of the National Institute on the Teaching of Psychology (NITOP), St. Petersburg, FL.

AV: Failures Before Kindergarten (28 min., Films for the Humanities and Sciences)

This adaptation of a Phil Donahue program explores the advantages and disadvantages of educational assessment of very young children. One panelist on the program, Madeline Duncan, describes her experiences as a teacher who held back an entire first-grade class!

Language: What Develops in the First Two Years?

AV: Development of Pre-Verbal Speech (15 min., Insight Media)

This brief video traces speech development in infants from their first cries after birth to the age of 1 year, when they can use and comprehend single words.

AV: Pre-Verbal Communication (20 min., Filmakers Library)

This film makes it clear that the language of gestures, facial expressions, and noises provides a rich communication link between mother and infant, long before the infant is able to begin speaking. In this case, a mother and an 8-month-old enjoy a conversation, even though each sees the other on a video screen rather than in person.

"On Your Own" Activity: Child-Directed Speech

This exercise asks students to make arrangements to listen to an adult having a 10- to 15-minute conversation with an infant or toddler. Afterward, students are to answer the questions in Handout 4 and return their answers to the instructor.

This exercise will help students understand and apply the text material on child-directed speech. As a follow-up, you might want to summarize the students' responses, particularly those regarding baby talk per se (questions 3 and 4). In addition, you could provide feedback regarding the accuracy of each student's assessment of the child's stage of language development (question 5).

AV: Baby Talk (60 min., Insight Media)

This video from the *Nova* series investigates the radical reappraisal of language development that stemmed from the writings of Noam Chomsky. It depicts how researchers monitor fetal response to sound and analyze patterns of crying, cooing, and babbling. Interviews with Chomsky, J. S. Bruner, and other leading psycholinguists chart the major steps in language acquisition.

AV: Beginning Language (30 min., Insight Media)

This film examines various theories of early language development, using film clips to document the development of speech. David Premack discusses his work on artificial language in chimpanzees.

AV: Child Language: Learning Without Teaching (20 min., Davidson Films)
Out of the Mouths of Babes (28 min., Filmakers Library)

Many films trace language development; these are two of the best. *Child Language* is written and narrated by Dr. Eve Clark, with emphasis on the complexities of language that the very young child learns without benefit of formal instruction. *Out of the Mouths of Babes* is an authoritative and humorous account of the course of language development over the first six years. It is written and narrated by Jill and Peter deVilliers, the language experts often cited in the text.

Critical Thinking Activity: Language Development: Nature, Nurture, or Interaction?

Each unit of these resources contains a critical thinking exercise designed specifically to test students' critical thinking about a topic covered in the text. Handout 5 briefly describes the history of language development theories followed by a series of questions. In this exercise, several examples of language use are presented; students are asked to decide whether each provides evidence of the impact of nature, nurture, or the interaction of nature and nurture in language development, and to explain their reasoning.

Answers to this unit's critical thinking exercise are as follows:

1. *Position supported:* Nurture
Explanation: The increased frequency of Juwan's utterance can be explained by the principle of reinforcement. According to learning theory, if babies are reinforced with food or attention when they utter their first babbling sounds, they will soon call "mama" and "dada" whenever they want their mother or father.

2. *Position supported:* Nature
Explanation: The fact that Melissa correctly applies this basic rule of grammar in her very first sentences—sentences that she probably never learned from her parents—suggests that she has an inborn facility for acquiring language.

3. *Position supported:* Nature
Explanation: According to Noam Chomsky, the fact that hearing and deaf children worldwide pass the various milestones of language development—such as babbling—at approximately the same age implies that the human brain is uniquely equipped with some sort of inborn language acquisition device.

4. *Position Supported:* Nature–nurture interaction
Explanation: This example demonstrates that the combination of learning experiences and biological

maturation most accurately explains how children acquire language. Hearing your native language as an infant (a learning experience) sculpts the nervous system (a biological phenomenon), which, in turn, helps shape future language development.

AV: Talking from Infancy: How to Nurture and Cultivate Early Language Development (59 min., Child Development Media)

Based on the book *Talking from Infancy,* this video provides a guide for using language interactively in play and care routines to foster early language, social, and cognitive development.

AV: Language (30 min., Insight Media)

This film looks at the interaction of nature and nurture in language development, taking the position that language in humans is biologically programmed. The question of whether animal communication qualifies as language is among the many interesting issues addressed.

AV: Language and Thinking (30 min., RMI Media Productions)

This film explores the origins of language in human development. As toddlers are observed, various experts explain the major theories about the brain's role in processing language during the play years.

Classroom Activity: Language Rhythms in Manual Babbling

For more than a century, vocal babbling sounds like "ba, ba, ba" universally uttered by infants beginning at around 7 months have attracted intense scrutiny by developmentalists. Baby babbling has been understood to mark the developmental moment when an infant begins the journey of becoming a linguistically competent individual. Laura Petitto of Dartmouth College and her colleagues have studied the hands of hearing babies born to profoundly deaf parents, discovering that they produced a class of hand activity that possessed specific rhythmic patterns found in natural language that was distinct from other uses of their hands. This form of manual "babbling" supports the idea that babies are born with sensitivity to highly specific rhythmic patterns found in natural language—a sensitivity so powerful that infants can find and produce the rhythms of language by the hand as readily as in the mouth.

Insight into the age-old question of how babies begin the remarkable process of acquiring language comes from Petitto's analysis of videotapes of babies' mouths as they make sounds. Petitto and her colleagues discovered that when babies make sounds such as "goo, goo, goo," the right side of their mouth moves more than the left side. This is intriguing because of the phenomenon of *lateralization*—brain activity in the left hemisphere (where language centers are located) controls the right side of the body, including the mouth. The researchers also discovered that the babies in their study smiled more on the left sides of their faces, presumably because the emotional centers of the brain are on the right side.

Petitto's research is concerned with uncovering the epigenetic mechanisms that determine how our species acquires language as well as how language is organized in the brain. To address these issues, she has used a number of different approaches, including PET and MRI scans of the neurological substrates in the brain underlying language representation and use; studies of language acquisition in young children acquiring spoken French and English and/or signed languages, including American Sign Language (ASL); and cross-species analyses of the extent to which chimpanzees are able to master aspects of human language. Using her findings, she has proposed an account of language acquisition based on the interaction of genetic and environmental factors. This theory is somewhat at odds with a prevailing theory, which focuses on language acquisition as the brain's struggle to gain control over the mouth, tongue, and lips. "The most prevailing view," notes Petitto, "is that first we stood up and then the jaw dropped down and then the brain got more and more control of the jaw and then later, magically, these creatures decided to invent language."

Petitto, L. A. (2005). What the hands say about the ontogeny of human language: Insights from the acquisition and cerebral organization of natural signed languages. In James McGilvray (Ed.), *The Cambridge companion to Chomsky.* Cambridge, UK: Cambridge University Press.

Petitto, L. A., Holowka, S., Sergio, L., & Ostry, D. (2001, September 6). Language rhythms in babies' hand movements. *Nature, 413*(6851), 35–36.

Petitto, L. A., & Marentette, P. (1991). Babbling in the manual mode: Evidence for the ontogeny of language. *Science, 251,* 1493–1496.

Classroom Activity: Sequence of Sensorimotor and Language Development

To help students understand the sequence and interrelationship of sensorimotor and language development, you might construct a chart of the major events, at first filling in only the age column. When completed, the chart might look like the one on the next page. If the class has already studied the material, students should be able to fill in the other two columns themselves.

Cognitive Development in Infancy

Age	Sensorimotor Stages	Language Sequence
0–1 month	1. reflexes	reflexive cries
1–4 months	2. first acquired adaptations	cooing in response to voices and faces; meaningful gestures
4–8 months	3. making interesting sights last	babbling, especially to people; games that involve turn-taking
8–12 months	4. new adaptation and anticipation	respond to "no," "hot," etc.; imitation of others' intonation; intent listening
12–18 months	5. new means through active experimentation	first words (including many words for actions and movable objects); holophrases, especially questions and commands
18–24 months	6. new means through mental combinations	underextensions; overextensions; start of two-word sentences

Alternatively, you might explain the stages yourself, filling in the columns as you lecture. Either through discussion or lecture, point out the relationship between the development of sensorimotor intelligence and language at each stage. For instance, with the emergence of anticipation, reactions to "no" and "hot" would be expected; once mental combinations are possible, two-word sentences and under- and overextensions are also possible. As will be pointed out in the discussion of cognitive development during early childhood, there is some controversy about whether thought precedes language or language development produces thought. For the moment, however, it is only necessary to point out that the two are related.

Classroom Activity: Assessing Sensorimotor and Language Development with Unedited Videotapes

As noted in the General Resources section of these resources, Debra Poole of Beloit College produces 45- to 60-minute unedited videotapes of children interacting with their parents either in the home or in a room equipped with a variety of books, toys, and games appropriate to the age of the children and the subject matter of the videotape. Poole notes that using "homemade" films without narration allows students to observe and analyze behavior themselves, without having explanations provided to them.

An observational tape on sensorimotor and language development could easily be prepared by videotaping children of various ages as they interact with their parents. The parents should be instructed to engage their children in activities that will elicit as much language use as possible. For a similar project, Poole requires her students to analyze three 10-minute segments of tape showing children who are between 18 months and 6 years of age. To analyze language development, students first prepare literal transcriptions of each segment, then analyze the speech in terms of linguistic output (number of words, mean length of utterance, etc.), phonetic constitution (vowel and consonant sounds produced, production errors such as deletion of final consonants, cluster reduction, etc.), use of grammatical rules (or, as in overextension, their absence), as well as the pragmatic usage of speech.

In assessing sensorimotor development from the videotape, students should be instructed to look for behaviors characteristic of each of the six Piagetian stages of sensorimotor intelligence—for example, reflexive sucking or grabbing, coordination of reflexive responses, and deliberate responses to people and objects. You may find it helpful to distribute copies of the table "Cognitive Development in Infancy," which outlines both language and behavioral hallmarks during the six stages.

Poole notes that her students are highly responsive to this exercise and that those who actively participate in observational activities are typically better prepared to think critically about complex developmental issues than are students who do not.

Poole, D. A. (1986). Laboratories and demonstrations in child development with unedited videotapes. *Teaching of Psychology*, *13*(4), 212–214.

Classroom Activity: Conversation with a Toddler

To expand on the text mention of baby talk, bring a tape of a dialogue between a parent and toddler to class. (You might ask students or faculty members with toddlers to make a tape for you.) Put the following questions on the board and ask students to formulate answers in relation to the taped dialogue. Then play the tape again and arrive at a consensus about what happens in the interaction between parent and child. Stop the tape whenever necessary to highlight and discuss a particular linguistic hallmark.

(a) What can you tell about the situation in which this conversation is taking place?

(b) What kinds of words does the child use most?
(c) What kinds of words does the adult use most?
(d) Is repetition of words or sounds an important part of the conversation? What function does repetition play?
(e) How well do the adult and child understand each other? How does each speaker respond to a verbalization that she or he doesn't understand?
(f) Can you give any specific examples of speech used by the child that are typical hallmarks of infant language (for example, overextensions, holophrases)?
(g) How old do you think the child is (or at what stage of language development is the child)? Explain your answer.

Classroom Activity: Evaluating Sesame Beginnings

In May 2000, the Children's Television Workshop (CTW) announced the release of *Sesame Beginnings*, a literacy program designed to increase awareness of the important role parents and caregivers play in young children's language development. Available in several languages, the program includes a 25-minute videotape, a 15-minute audiocassette, and a package of printed material. The video combines scenes shot on the *Sesame Street* set and live-action footage of parents and children. The cassette features songs that parents and children can sing along to. The printed materials include a "Parent Pages" booklet outlining the major messages and offering easy activities and a facilitator guide geared to professionals working with parents, early-childhood educators, and literacy providers.

This literacy package can be used in one of two ways in a discussion of cognitive development during the first two years. The audiovisual materials are brief enough to be presented during a one-hour class, with students instructed to write a brief one-minute reaction paper at the end of class. For a more in-depth assignment, you might assign a longer paper assessing the program's pedagogical soundness, developmental appropriateness, and so on. Either way, your students (many of whom are likely to have grown up watching Big Bird, Bert, Elmo, and Mr. Snuffleupagus) are sure to find the newest CTW materials very interesting.

Sesame Beginnings is distributed free of charge to child-care programs, family literacy programs, and public-health and community-based organizations. Additional kits are available at cost by writing to Children's Television Workshop, Health and Safety Outreach, PO Box 55742, Indianapolis, IN 46205-0742. Information will also be on its Web site: http://archive.sesameworkshop.org/sesamebeginnings/new/.

Sesame Street launches literacy program. (2000). *The Exceptional Parent, 30*(5), 20.

Classroom Activity: Classroom Debate: *"Resolved: Language Development Is the Product of Conditioning"*

To highlight the contrasting theories of language development proposed by B. F. Skinner and Noam Chomsky, follow the guidelines in the General Resources section of this manual for scheduling a classroom debate on this resolution.

The resolution is stated in favor of the behaviorist viewpoint that linguistic development is the product of imitation, shaping, reinforcement, and other basic operant conditioning processes. Although the behaviorist philosophy often provokes strong reactions from students, in the context of the acquisition of complex abilities such as language, it often is the "common sense" and model viewpoint: ("Language development innate? Nonsense. I remember how difficult it was to learn the basic rules of grammar, punctuation, spelling, and the like. Don't tell me that wasn't learning!").

Skinner's model makes a number of specific, testable predictions. For example:

(a) Language development is largely the product of learning. There should, therefore, be great individual variation in its acquisition, because no two learning environments are the same.
(b) Children imitate the early speech they hear. They should, therefore, not make grammatical mistakes, assuming that their models have not made them.
(c) Those deprived of "normal" linguistic experiences (deaf children, for example) should not develop in the same manner as those not deprived.

Encourage both teams of debaters to consider and research these predictions as they prepare their arguments. Many scholarly books and journals can provide interesting ammunition for both sides of the issue.

HANDOUT 1

Developmental Fact or Myth?

T F 1. If a 5-month-old drops a rattle out of the crib, the baby probably will not look down to search for it.

T F 2. Most developmentalists consider perception to be an automatic process that everyone experiences in the same way.

T F 3. Only infants age 9 months or older notice the difference between a solid surface and an apparent cliff.

T F 4. Infants look longer at strangers whose images and voices indicate happiness than at the familiar faces of their mothers.

T F 5. Infants' long-term memory is actually very good.

T F 6. Toward the end of the first year, infants can imitate the actions of a person they observed a day earlier.

T F 7. Children the world over follow the same sequence in early language development.

T F 8. All babies, including deaf ones, begin babbling between 6 and 9 months of age.

T F 9. When they first begin combining words, infants tend to put them in reverse order, as in "juice more."

T F 10. Most developmentalists believe that infants develop language in many ways, depending on a variety of factors.

HANDOUT 2

Internet Activity: Cyberspace Hunt: Jean Piaget

The Internet is an excellent resource for learning about prominent developmental theorists. For example, a Web site devoted to Piaget contains a wealth of biographical and professional information. Search the Web to find answers to the following questions.

1. What is the significance of the "albino sparrow" in Jean Piaget's scientific career?

2. Where did Piaget grow up? What was his childhood like?

3. What did Piaget mean by "The American question"?

4. When and where was the Jean Piaget Centennial conference held? What was the focus of the conference?

5. Piaget's theory has been criticized on many grounds. Can you find 10 common criticisms of Piaget's theory?

HANDOUT 3

Ordering Exercise

Below is a list of achievements in the life of a normal baby girl. However, these achievements are not presented in the correct order. To demonstrate your understanding of Piaget's stages of sensorimotor intelligence, number the events in the proper sequence from 1 to 6 using the blanks provided.

______ (a) The baby squeezes toothpaste out of a tube.

______ (b) The baby laughs when she is tickled and shakes her arm with pleasure when a rattle is put into her hand.

______ (c) The baby sucks the nipple and anything else that comes near her mouth.

______ (d) The baby experiments with her spoon, banging first the dish, then the high chair, and finally throwing the spoon on the floor.

______ (e) The baby refuses the pacifier and shows her displeasure by crying.

______ (f) The baby imitates a temper tantrum she has observed in an older child.

HANDOUT 4

Child-Directed Speech

To further your understanding of the nature and significance of child-directed speech, make arrangements to listen to an adult conversing with an infant or toddler for 10 to 15 minutes. You may use family members, other relatives, or friends. The conversation need not be structured in any particular way. The adult might read to the child, play with a favorite toy, or simply carry on a conversation with the child. It is important that you not *give the adult clues as to what speech patterns you are looking for. Ask the person to relax, be candid, and enjoy interacting with the child. (If you wish, you might even tape-record the conversation for a more thorough analysis later.) Then answer the following questions.*

1. Describe the participants and setting.

2. Did you encounter any difficulties in completing the exercise (for example, the adult was nervous; the child did not talk)?

3. Did the adult use child-directed speech with the child? What aspects of the adult's speech (for example, intonation, pitch, vocabulary) were different from normal conversation with another adult?

HANDOUT 4 *(continued)*

4. To which characteristics of the adult's speech (for example, repetitiveness, exaggerated intonation) was the child particularly responsive?

5. Which stage of development would you say the infant or toddler is in (for example, cooing, babbling, one-word stage)? Give examples of the child's speech to support your assessment.

HANDOUT 5

Critical Thinking Activity: Language Development: Nature, Nurture, or Interaction?

Now that you have read and reviewed the material on cognitive development during the first two years, take your learning a step further by testing your critical thinking skills on this perspective-taking exercise.

Historically, many theories of development have pitted biology, or nature, against environment, or nurture. For example, attempts to explain the ease with which babies acquire language focused either on the ways in which parents teach language to their children or on the emergence of the infant's innate language abilities. Behaviorist B. F. Skinner believed that language development could be explained entirely by principles of learning, including imitation, reinforcement, and discrimination. Arguing from the nurture position, linguist Noam Chomsky maintained that language is far too complex to be mastered so early and so easily through learning alone. Instead, Chomsky maintained that our language capacity is inborn.

More recently, developmentalists have concluded that both Skinner's and Chomsky's theories have some validity but that neither is completely correct; rather, it is the interaction of nature and nurture within a specific social context that accounts for the ease with which children acquire language.

In this exercise, review the following examples of language use and decide whether each provides evidence of the impact of nature, nurture, or the interaction of nature and nurture in language development. Explain your reasoning.

1. Whenever 8-month-old Juwan wants his mother, he calls out, "Mama," and she comes running. Consequently, Juwan utters "Mama" much more frequently now than he did at 7 months of age.

   Position Supported:

2. Even in her very first sentences, 21-month-old Melissa has obviously figured out the basics of subject–predicate word order. Seeing her mother returning from work, for example, she says, "Mommy home," rather than "home Mommy."

   Position Supported:

HANDOUT 5 *(continued)*

3. Seven-month-old Tara, who is deaf, has begun to babble manually at about the same time hearing infants begin babbling orally.

   Position Supported:

4. When Michelle was an infant, she was able to perceive differences among the spoken sounds of many languages. As she grew, her preference for hearing her native language actually influenced the development of her brain. Now a teenager, Michelle can no longer perceive certain speech sounds from languages other than her own.

   Position Supported:

The First Two Years: Psychosocial Development

Contents

Note: Worth Publishers provides online Instructor and Student Tool Kits, DVD Student Tool Kits, and Instructor and Student video resources in DevelopmentPortal for use with the text. See Part I: General Resources for information about these materials and the text Lecture Guides for a complete list by text chapter.

Classroom Activities: Child Care, Home Care, and the Quality of Infant–Caregiver Interaction, p. 24
Classroom Debate: "Resolved: Attending Day-Care Centers During the First Three Years of Life Is Psychologically Damaging to Children," p. 25
Communal Child Care, Emotional Availability, and Attachment, p. 25

Suggested Activities

Introducing the First Two Years: Psychosocial Development

"On Your Own" Activity: Developmental Fact or Myth?

Before students read about psychosocial development during the first two years, have them respond to the true–false statements in Handout 1.

The correct answers are shown below. Class discussion can focus on the origins of any developmental misconceptions that are demonstrated in the students' incorrect answers.

1. F	5. T	8. T
2. F	6. T	9. T
3. T	7. F	10. T
4. T		

"On Your Own" Activity: Revising a Textbook

The three domains of development are perhaps more closely related in infancy than in any other part of the life span. To increase your students' awareness of the interrelationship among biosocial, cognitive, and psychosocial development in infancy and toddlerhood, you might ask them to imagine that they are the editors working on a revision of one of Kathleen Berger's developmental psychology textbooks, as described in Handout 2. This exercise will help them to see that the topics treated in this unit do not fall neatly into one or another domain.

Students should come to appreciate the difficulty of treating the areas of development "piecemeal," because any important development can be covered under any of the three basic domains. Encourage students to discuss how they would revise and even rename the material when moving it from one chapter to the next. For example, the topic of "Nutrition" might become "Feeding" if presented in the context of psychosocial development. "Perception and Cognition" might become "Understanding the Environment," and so on. Your students may find that they are most often tempted to move topics out of biosocial development into the other two domains. This provides an opportunity to point out that in infancy and toddlerhood, especially, important developments tend to be expressed primarily in the biosocial domain. (For example, autonomy is expressed through the gaining of physical control over the bowels; depression would be expressed through feeding difficulties, and so on.)

AV: The Journey Through the Life Span, Program 3: Infants and Toddlers

See The First Two Years: Biosocial Development for a description of Program 3 and the accompanying observation modules, which cover the entire unit on infancy and toddlerhood.

AV: Transitions Throughout the Life Span, Program 7: Getting to Know You

Program 7 explores the emotional and social life of the developing person during the first two years. It begins with a description of the infant's emerging emotions and how they reflect increasing cognitive abilities. Newborns are innately predisposed to sociability and capable of expressing distress, sadness, contentment, and many other emotions as well as responding to the emotions of other people.

Next, the program presents Erik Erikson's theory as a tool for helping us understand how the infant's emotional and behavioral responses begin to take on the various patterns that form personality. Important research on the nature and origins of temperament, which informs virtually every characteristic of the individual's developing personality, is considered.

The final segment examines emotions from a different perspective—that of parent–infant interaction. Videotaped studies of parents and infants combined with laboratory studies have greatly expanded our understanding of psychosocial development. In the program, expert Ross Thompson explains how the intricate patterns of parent–infant interaction help infants learn to express and read emotions and promote attachment to caregivers.

Developmental psychologist Mary Ainsworth describes an experimental procedure she developed to measure the quality of attachment. The program concludes with a discussion of the impact of early day care on psychosocial development.

AV: The Child: Part III (29 min., CRM/McGraw-Hill)

A boy and girl are shown as they grow from age 1 to 2. During this period, we see their language develop from the one- to the two-word stage and their social skills emerge as they model their behavior on that of others. The stubbornness and selfishness typical of this age are well-balanced with the toddler's interest and involvement with the activities of other people. Again, because this is cinema verité, you should preview the film to know how to prepare your students.

AV: Infancy: Self and Social World (30 min., Magna Systems)

This film explores the child's expanding social world in the first year of life. It begins by examining how, in the first months of life, an infant gradually gains the awareness of being a person separate from his or her mother. A highlight of the program is the exploration of how different cultural belief systems affect the psychosocial development of the child. Infant–caregiver synchrony is also examined.

AV: The Child at Twenty-One Months (28 min., Films for the Humanities and Sciences)
The Child at Twenty-Four Months (28 min., Films for the Humanities and Sciences)
Following on *The First 365 Days in the Life of a Child*, this series follows the development of toddlers during the second year of life. The third and fourth programs in this series focus on the gradually increasing independence of children as they learn to dress themselves, handle eating utensils, distinguish objects, and use language.

Teaching Tip: Helping Students Do Well in Your Course

Within a few hours following the first exam in my course, I typically receive an e-mail or two from students who lament, "I studied so much for this exam, and yet I'm certain I did poorly! What am I doing wrong?" After years of similar experiences in her classes, Marilla Svinicki devised a simple mnemonic that she shares with students to help them study effectively. Derived from the best available evidence from research studies of learning and memory, GAMES is worth sharing with your students.

G: Goal-Oriented Study. When asked about their study goals for the day, many students report, "I'm going to study for an hour or two." While budgeting time for study is important, this type of goal doesn't match what we know about effective learning. Tallying hours of studying is not as effective a goal as understanding key concepts covered in the day's assignment. Encourage your students to set "understanding" goals for their studying. For example, the goal of understanding how developmental theory informs educational practice with children means that students should be able to explain a theory (Vygotsky, Piaget, etc.) in their own words and identify examples of the theory's application in specific educational programs. When they study, they need to keep at it until they can do these things with each theory. Like all good study goals, doing so requires that students make meaningful connections between what they already know and material they are trying to assimilate.

A: Active Study. Svinicki's students, like mine, often report spending inordinate amounts of time simply recopying notes from class and reading them over and over until they are memorized. Research on learning and memory strongly affirms the superiority of active, deep processing of material over rote repetition. Examples of active study techniques include transforming lecture notes into annotated notes that highlight main ideas and convert statements into questions. Learning to read actively includes strategies such as stopping to periodically summarize what has just been read, paraphrasing, and creating flash cards.

M: Meaningful and Memorable Study. Research demonstrates that learning occurs best when students make connections between new and existing information, major and minor points, abstractions and concrete examples, and between general and personally meaningful experiences. As Svinicki notes, "Learners create a unique, structural understanding of what they are learning in which the relationships among components and to the learners themselves are clarified." As a teacher, you can model the process of making meaningful connections as you present the course material. Students often learn the examples we give first, and then use them to recall the principles they represent. Most of all, you can encourage and even require students to create their own examples by asking for them during class and basing homework assignments on them.

E: Explaining to Someone as a Study Strategy. As a student, I was a firm believer in the old saying, "To teach is to learn twice." Before an exam, I spent many hours pacing in my dorm room as I "lectured" to an imaginary class as a test of my understanding of the material. Encourage students to find a study partner and then explain key concepts to each other. Even better, students might seek out a willing friend who is not in the class and try to explain key concepts to that person.

S: Self-Monitoring During Study. If your students are like mine, they struggle with self-evaluation and often overestimate their actual understanding of material. Accurate self-monitoring is a skill that takes many students a long time to learn. Each of the letters of the GAMES mnemonic identifies an important strategy for promoting this skill. By setting good goals, students will have a basis for evaluating their understanding. Active study strategies are a good source of feedback for monitoring understanding. As they strive to make meaningful connections between new material and what they already know, students will be testing the accuracy of their interpretation of new content. Finally, when they attempt to explain what they have learned, they will identify areas of weakness that need additional work.

Svinicki, M. D. (2006, October). Helping students do well in class: GAMES. *Association for Psychological Science Observer, 19*(10). www.psychologicalscience.org/teaching/tips.

Classroom Activity: Analysis of Videotaped Infant Development

The techniques for producing a videotape of infant development at two-month intervals during the first year and at six-month intervals during the second year are described in the General Resources section of these resources. If such a tape is available, it can be used very effectively in the classroom to demonstrate psychosocial development during the first two years. For example, emotional development (and the difficulty of measuring it) are readily apparent in the videotaped interaction between an infant and his or her primary caregiver. The emergence of certain new cognitive abilities, such as self-awareness, and the emotional advances that derive from these abilities can also be documented. During the first two months infants have no awareness of their bodies as being their own. Their hands, for example, are interesting objects that appear and disappear and are "rediscovered" each time they come into view. Even 8-month-olds have trouble knowing where their bodies end and someone else's body begins. By 1 year, however, most infants are well aware of their own bodies as distinct from those of other people. Synchrony between infant and caregiver, attachment behaviors, parent– infant interaction, and temperament styles may also be demonstrated effectively in the classroom by means of an unedited videotape of infant development.

AV: Individual Differences (18 min., CRM/McGraw-Hill)

This movie's basic theme is that a broad range of human behavior and human characteristics is considered normal: Thanks to the interaction of heredity and environment, no one of us is quite like another. Although this theme is relevant at many points in the course, the film is probably most appropriate during the infancy section. It includes descriptions of some of the tests that help professionals and parents spot infant behavior that may be so far from the norm that further investigation is needed. Among these tests is the Denver Developmental Screening Test, norms of which appear in the textbook.

Emotional Development

AV: Emotional Development of Children (18 min., Insight Media)

This short video charts the differentiation of emotions from the first weeks of life to the beginning of formal education.

AV: The Stress of Separation (20 min., Filmakers Library)

Children in a British day-care center are shown reacting to the departure of their parents, sometimes with tears, sometimes quite happily. The purpose of the movie is to show developmental changes in reaction to separation. Additional points that could be raised in class are the variations of attachment and the roles played by the day-care staff and setting. You may want to delay showing this film until you discuss the text section on attachment and day care.

Classroom Activity: Separation Anxiety, Stranger Wariness, and the Ethological Perspective

Separation anxiety and stranger wariness, which generally emerge between 6 months and 1 year, are often greeted with reactions of horror from unsuspecting parents. Although most parents have heard of these phenomena, many think it will not happen to their infants (Frankel, 2003).

According to the ethological perspective, stranger wariness and separation anxiety date back to the dawn of humankind. That is, these affective reactions are primitive survival instincts that emerged when humans were hunters and gatherers. According to Leila Beckwith, a professor of pediatrics at the University of California, Los Angeles, "The heartrending cries and screams of babies who were not being held prompted those first parents to pick them up, soothe them, and in the process, frequently protect them from hungry predators."

More commonly, this overwhelming desire of infants to be with their primary caregivers is viewed by many developmentalists as the basis of children's ability to form social relationships throughout life. Although by age 2 most children are able to cope with routine separations, their intense yearning to be with their primary caregiver is gradually transformed into "an ability and desire to forge friendships with peers, and ultimately, mature sexual relationships."

To help parents and infants survive the trauma of separation, experts offer the following recommendations (quoted from Morse, 1993):

1. Let your baby check out new faces. Studies have shown that babies are intimidated by people who approach them quickly or loudly or who try to hold them immediately. Have new caretakers (or any stranger) approach quietly, talking to you first before turning their attention to the baby.
2. Try to keep things calm at home. Avoid taking trips or having lots of new people around the baby, especially if you're returning to work.
3. Maintain a ritual when you leave. Having predictable times and routines may not make your baby smile when you leave, but knowing what's going on will give him or her a sense of control.
4. Don't prolong the agony. Instead of waiting for your baby to calm down (you could be there all day), offer a hug, a kiss, and a reminder, in a soothing voice, that you will be home later. [He or she will] be most easily distracted when you're out of sight.
5. Don't overcompensate. It's tempting to keep your baby up when you get home from work,

to squeeze in extra time together. But you're likely to end up with an overtired baby who only finds it harder to say goodbye in the morning.

6. The transition to a baby-sitter or day-care center will likely go more smoothly when your baby is either under 6 months or closer to age 2. A younger infant will get used to substitute caretakers and long separations before he or she has a chance to mind them too much, and an older toddler is better able to express his or her emotions and can form friendships that will make your absence more tolerable.
7. Keep your own reactions in check. Whether you're leaving for the grocery store or the office, any anxiety you may be feeling about going will be picked up by your baby. So keep a smile on your face.

Frankel, V. (2003, August). Separation anxieties. *Parenting, 17*(6), 93.

Morse, M. B. (1993, June). Suddenly it's cling time. *Parents*, 80–82.

Classroom Activity: The Impact of the Cultural Macrosystem on Social and Emotional Development

Educators and developmentalists have long known that child development is best understood as a holistic process. Although public awareness typically focuses primarily on intellectual and academic development, both research and practice highlight the importance of culture, social-emotional development, and individual differences in how young children learn. And play, the "work of children," is vital to children's developing imaginations, self-awareness, theory of mind, relationships with others, and developing language and problem-solving skills.

To help your students appreciate the overarching impact of the cultural macrosystem on social and emotional development, you might expand on the phenomenon of behavioral inhibition. *Behavioral inhibition* refers to biological differences in the extent to which children react with fear and wariness to unfamiliar circumstances (Fox et al., 2005). For example, wary, inhibited toddlers react to a stranger with much greater muscle tension and higher levels of cortisol (a potent stress hormone) than uninhibited toddlers do. As they grow older, inhibited children also display higher elevated resting heart rates and greater arousal of the sympathetic nervous system than uninhibited children do.

When inhibited children encounter other children for the first time, their wariness, discomfort, and social awkwardness often "mark" them for rejection by their peers. By late childhood, such children are more likely to state that they are socially incompetent, have lousy relationships with their peers, and feel lonely and depressed. Moreover, childhood behavioral inhibition has been identified as an important risk factor for social anxiety in adolescence and adulthood (West & Newman, 2007).

These negative social and emotional outcomes occur in behaviorally inhibited children in North America and Western Europe but are not seen in their counterparts in the People's Republic of China. A shy, wary reaction to an unfamiliar person or circumstance—called *hai xiu* in Mandarin—has an entirely different cultural "meaning" in Beijing or Shanghai than it does in the United States. In individualistically oriented cultures, such as those in North America and Western Europe, children tend to be socialized in a manner that endorses social assertiveness. Social reticence is considered a distinct disadvantage to individuals of all ages, including toddlers and young children. However, shyness is not regarded as maladaptive in collectivistic cultures such as China, where individualism is subordinate to the larger group. In such cultures, functioning effectively as a member of the group often requires behavioral restraint, obedience, and submission, and so it is easy to understand why these cultures value, even endorse, shy-inhibited behavior. Thus, shy, reticent Chinese children are described as well behaved and are more likely to receive praise from teachers, parents, and other adults. Moreover, restrained children are perceived as socially competent and develop positive relationships with their peers. And, unlike shy Western children, they do not report greater loneliness, depression, or feelings of social incompetence.

Fox, N. A., Henderson, H. A., Marshall, P. J., Nichols, K. E., & Ghera, M. M. (2005). Behavioral inhibition: Linking biology and behavior within a developmental framework. *Annual Review of Psychology, 56,* 235–262.

West, A. E., & Newman, D. L. (2007). Childhood behavioral inhibition and the experience of social anxiety in American Indian adolescents. *Cultural Diversity and Ethnic Minority Psychology. 13*(3), 197–206.

AV: From Here to Self-Esteem: A Roadmap for Parents of Young Children (30 min., Films for the Humanities and Sciences)

This video discusses 10 specific ways in which parents and caregivers can build self-esteem in children through everyday interactions such as responding to a baby's emotional needs, helping a child work through his or her own problems, and promoting independence.

Classroom Activity: The Dunedin Study: Childhood Temperament Predicts Adolescent and Adult Personality and Behavior Problems

Temperamental style in infancy has been linked to adjustment problems in kindergarten and later in life. Perhaps the most extensive longitudinal study was begun with a cohort of all children born between April 1, 1972, and March 31, 1973, in Dunedin, New Zealand. The sample of 1,037 children was retested with a battery of medical, psychological, and sociological measures every two years since the children were 3. (See also the Critical Thinking Activity.)

At ages 3, 5, 7, and 9, the behavior of each child was rated in terms of 22 characteristics related to temperament, including emotional stability, restlessness, impulsiveness, persistence, negativism, passivity, shyness, self-confidence, self-reliance, attentiveness, friendliness, emotional flatness, and 10 other dimensions. By age 9, each child had received four sets of ratings made independently by different examiners.

To assess behavior problems in the sample, the researchers relied on outcome data from teachers and parents who rated the children at ages 9, 11, 13, and 15 on two widely used behavior problem checklists: the Rutter Child Scales and the Revised Behavior Problem Checklist. These 26- and 31-item scales yield four subscales: Anxiety/Withdrawal, which represents feelings of inferiority, failure, and embarrassment; Attention Problems, which reflects problems in concentration; Conduct Disorder, which reflects aggressiveness and alienation; and Socialized Delinquency, which reflects norm-violating tendencies.

Factor analysis of the temperament measures yielded three dimensions at each age: *lack of control, approach, and sluggishness* (Table 1 on the next page). The lack of control factor combined elements of emotional instability, restlessness, short attention span, and negativism. Three- to 5-year-old children characterized by lack of control are unable to inhibit impulsive expressions and lack persistence in problem solving. The researchers note that this factor is similar to the cluster of traits once described as the "difficult child."

By ages 7 and 9, lack of control could be differentiated into two subcategories: *irritability* and *distractibility*. The irritability factor included extreme emotional instability and impulsive, willful, and rough behavior. The distractibility factor included ratings of withdrawal from difficult tasks, fleeting attention, and lack of persistence.

At each age, the *approach* factor included ratings of friendliness toward the experimenter, as well as self-confidence and self-reliance in adjusting to new situations. Children characterized by this factor are eager to explore novel situations and objects.

The *sluggishness* factor was based on ratings of emotional flatness, passivity, and shyness. Sluggish children react passively to changing situations and withdraw from novelty. The researchers note that this factor is similar to the trait cluster of the "slow-to-warm-up" child.

To determine whether there were predictive correlations between temperament and behavior problems, the researchers computed correlations between the examiner's ratings of children's temperament at ages 3 and 5 and teacher and parent reports of behavior problems at ages 9 and 11.

For both boys and girls, lack of control at ages 3 and 5 showed a significant positive correlation with teacher and parent reports of inattention and hyperactivity (Table 1). Lack of control was also positively correlated with reports of antisocial behavior and conduct disorder at ages 9 and 11. Interestingly, lack of control at 3 and 5 years of age was negatively correlated with parental assessment of children's competencies at 13 and 15 years. Boys and girls characterized as lacking in control in early childhood were less likely to be rated in adolescence as mature, determined, and confident.

For boys, approach ratings in early childhood were negatively correlated with anxiety and withdrawal in late childhood and adolescence. Childhood approach at age 5 was positively correlated with competence at 13 and 15 years of age. Furthermore, boys and girls described as high on approach were rated in adolescence as more caring, friendly, popular, and enthusiastic.

For girls, ratings of sluggishness in early childhood were positively correlated with internalizing anxiety and attention problems during adolescence. Boys and girls who were rated as sluggish in early childhood were rated by their parents in adolescence as immature and lacking in confidence, humor, and enthusiasm.

Caspi et al. (1995) offer two possible explanations for their intriguing results. "One possibility is that behavior disorders and temperamental characteristics are different degrees of the same phenomenon, and that, at the extreme, individual differences in childhood behavioral styles are actually early, subclinical manifestations of later behavior disorders."

Alternatively, the researchers suggest that temperamental differences may trigger "a cumulative process of person–environment interactions, culminating in psychopathological problems later in life because different individuals evoke different responses from others, react differently to similar environmental experiences, and, increasingly with age, actively select and create different environments for themselves."

The results of this extensive longitudinal study suggest that early temperament may have remarkably specific predictive validity for the development of behavior problems during adolescence and young adulthood.

Several more recent follow-up studies of the participants in the Dunedin study focused on children who had displayed signs of being emotionally undercontrolled, inhibited, or well-adjusted at an early age (Rietschel, 2008; Caspi, Harrington, Milne, & Amell, 2003). After adjusting for other childhood variables, the researchers found that being emotionally undercontrolled was associated with continuing school difficulties, problems with attention, and poor reading in adolescence. Early reading difficulties, even after adjusting for hyperactivity, predicted continuing reading problems in high school. Undercontrolled children tend to be impulsive, restless, negativistic, and unsteady in their emotional reactions. In contrast, inhibited (overcontrolled) children tend to be socially reticent, fearful, and easily upset by new experiences. Finally, well-adjusted children tend to be self-confident and not easily upset when confronting new

Table 1 Correlations Between Childhood Behavioral Styles and Behavior Problems and Competencies in Adolescence

	Behavioral Styles in Early Childhood					
	Lack of Control		Approach		Sluggishness	
	Age 3	Age 5	Age 3	Age 5	Age 3	Age 5
Girls						
Inattention						
Age 13	.23***	.28***	.01	.00	.13**	.10
Age 15	.23***	.16***	.01	–.03	.17***	.13***
Antisocial behavior						
Age 9	.11**	.17**	.05	.00	.07	.04
Age 11	.15**	.18**	.03	.02	.03	.04
Conduct disorder						
Age 13	.12	.15**	.06	.01	.08	.04
Age 15	.15**	.06	.03	–.05	.10	.04
Competence						
Number of "strengths"						
Age 13	–.20***	–.16**	.07	.13**	–.18***	–.12
Age 15	–.20***	–.14**	.03	.16**	–.15**	–.10
Boys						
Anxiety/withdrawal						
Age 13	.11	.15**	–.03	–.23**	.08	.15**
Age 15	.13**	.12**	–.01	–.20***	.06	.10
Attention problems						
Age 13	.17**	.30***	.03	–.16**	.06	.08
Age 15	.22**	.24**	.04	–.10	.08	.03
Hyperactivity						
Age 9	.26***	.38***	–.02	.00	.05	–.02
Age 11	.30***	.34***	.04	–.06	.03	–.02
Competence						
Age 13	–.10	–.14**	–.01	.14**	–.03	–.17**
Age 15	–.13**	–.13**	.03	.11	.02	–.14**

**$p \le .01$ *** $p \le .001$

Caspi, A., Henry, B., McGee, R. O., Moffitt, T. E., & Silva, P. A. (1995). Temperamental origins of child and adolescent behavior problems: From age three to age fifteen. *Child Development, 66*(1), 55–68.

situations and people. The findings of the study demonstrated that undercontrolled 3-year-olds grew up to be impulsive, unreliable, and antisocial, and had more conflict with members of their social networks and in their work. Inhibited 3-year-olds were more likely to be unassertive and depressed and had fewer sources of social support as adults. Specifically, the data showed that temperamental qualities at age 3 predicted:

- the frequency of internalizing problems (e.g., worrying, crying easily, fussing), or externalizing problems (e.g., fighting, bullying, lying, disobeying) throughout childhood.
- personality at age 18 according to the Big Five personality model.
- the quality of interpersonal relationships at age 21.
- the availability of social support in young adulthood.
- unemployment during the transition to adulthood.
- risk of psychiatric disorders in young adulthood.
- criminal behavior at age 21.

Caspi, A., Harrington, H., Milne, B., & Amell, J. W. (2003). Children's behavioral styles at age 3 are linked to their adult personality traits at age 26. *Journal of Personality, 71*(4), 495–498.

Caspi, A., Henry, B., McGee, R. O., Moffitt, T. E., & Silva, P. A. (1995). Temperamental origins of child and adolescent behavior problems: From age three to age fifteen. *Child Development, 66*(1), 55–68.

Rietschel, M. (2008). Environment is important. *Current Opinion in Psychiatry, 21*(4), 323–324.

Rimm-Kaufman, S. E., & Kagan, J. (2005). Infant predictors of kindergarten behavior: The contribution of inhibited and uninhibited temperament types. *Behavioral Disorders, 30*(4), 331-347.

Critical Thinking Activity: Early Temperament Style and Later Adjustment Problems

Each unit of these resources contains a critical thinking exercise designed specifically to test students' critical thinking about a topic covered in the text. Handout 3 contains a synopsis of the Dunedin study just described followed by a series of questions. If you have not used the Classroom Activity regarding childhood temperament as a predictor of adolescent behavior problems, you might want to assign this critical thinking exercise as an outside assignment.

Answers to this unit's critical thinking exercise are as follows:

1. Because a single sample of children is followed and retested over a period of time, this study is an example of the longitudinal research design. Because the researchers did not directly manipulate an independent variable, nor employ separate groups of children in order to control extraneous variables, the design is correlational rather than experimental. Other features of the design include naturalistic observation of the children by parents and teachers through the use of behavior checklists. Given the purpose of the study—to uncover aspects of childhood temperament that predict later behavior problems—the research design seems appropriate.
2. The researchers suggest that certain behavior problems during late childhood and adolescence may merely be more extreme manifestations of specific temperamental styles during early childhood. Based on the evidence presented, this explanation does make sense.
3. Because the evidence is correlational, not based on experimental data, we can't be sure that certain temperamental styles in young children always mature into certain behavior disorders later in life. Although the research seems valid, it makes no attempt to rule out factors other than temperament that might have influenced the results.
4. There are several other possible explanations for the results of this study. For example, early childhood behavioral styles and later behavior problems are, in fact, separate phenomena, so both may be triggered by some aspect of the child's upbringing. Alternatively, temperamental differences may have an epigenetic effect on development, triggering a process of person–environment interaction that may cause different children to evoke different responses from others, as well as react differently to similar environmental experiences. The cumulative effect of this process may be the appearance of certain behavior disorders in some individuals.

Theories of Infant Psychosocial Development

Psychoanalytic Theory

Teaching Tip: Understanding Freudian Theory

To help students understand Freud's theory of personality, you might ask them to provide everyday examples and anecdotes. (Students find Freud's ideas fascinating, but in the abstract they sometimes also find them outlandish.) You might begin, for example, by pointing out that the mouth seems to be the most important part of the infant's body: In addition to eating and sucking, biting, crying, babbling, and sticking out the tongue are among the favorite activities of children under 1 year. (You might note also that Freud is not the only theorist to emphasize the importance of oral activities in development. Piaget's theory, for example, recognizes that one of the earliest ways in which the infant explores and learns about the world is through the mouth.) By the same token, defecation is an important activity for toddlers and an obvious source of pride: When a toddler asks you to come see what he or she has done in the potty, the response the toddler expects is "How wonderful," not "Let's flush it down the toilet right away."

Go on to explain that parents who are overly concerned with cleanliness and regularity in toilet training may also be overly concerned with control and regularity in all things; it is quite possible that there is a correlation between the attitudes of the parents toward toilet training and the child's eventual personality. Then point out that, in fact, there seem to be people who fit Freud's description of an *anal personality*, which can be one of two opposing types: the *anal retentive*, who as a child was overly eager to please during toilet training and as an adult is punctual, compliant, orderly, and devoted to cleanliness; and the *anal expulsive*, who as a child was recalcitrant in affairs of the potty and as an adult is defiant, stubborn, and messy. You might want to rent a DVD of the *Odd Couple* (either the movie or the TV series) to show to your students. They should recognize in Felix Unger and Oscar Madison a classic confrontation between the two types. However, to prevent students from getting carried away with these examples, you should probably remind them that although Freudian theory on this matter is not pure fantasy, the precise link between toilet training and personality has not proved to be quite as Freud described it.

AV: Erik Erikson: A Life's Work (38 min., Insight Media)

(See description in Theories of Development.)

Behaviorism and Cognitive Theory

Classroom Activity: Social Cognitive Theory and the Self-Regulated Learner

As stated in the text, behaviorists believe that emotions and personality are shaped as parents reinforce or punish a child's spontaneous behaviors. Albert Bandura and later behaviorists expanded this idea to include the importance of social learning throughout life. Social-cognitive theory is based on the ideas that thoughts and values determine a person's perspective and that learning is the result of reciprocal interaction between a person, the environment, and already learned behaviors of the individual and group. To expand on the text discussion of cognitive theory in the context of the K-8 classroom, you might introduce the concept of the "self-regulated learner."

In the classroom, students bring to each learning situation their unique mental constructs, a "fluctuating emotional state of being," and perhaps most important of all, their own personal sense of self-efficacy, or belief in their capability. These constructs and states interact with the student's organization skills, tendency to procrastinate, and other habitual behavior patterns, as well as environmental factors such as the nature of the task, the group setting, and the modeling and reinforcement available at the moment.

As Barbara Abromitis (2010) notes, "self-regulated learners are in control of their own learning behaviors from start to finish. They plan, set goals, and strategize before taking action; they self-monitor and make adjustments as needed during an action; and after acting, they reflect and evaluate on what they have done, providing self-reinforcement for effective behaviors and planning to change those that inhibited their performance. "

As the term suggests, these processes are internalized in self-regulated learners. In addition, the skills are evident not only in school, but also in sports, musical and theatrical activities, and in the social dynamics of friendships and families. Self-regulated learning, which promotes developmental success in virtually every domain, is learned from teachers and other mentors who model and reinforce the cognitive skills and behaviors that characterize self-regulation. Good teachers scaffold their students' self-regulation by providing metacognitive feedback after each lesson. Questions such as "What strategies did you use on this task?" and "Which ones were successful?" encourage students to self-reflect and evaluate what they did well and what areas might be improved.

As a follow-up, you might ask your students to reflect on their own skills as self-regulated learners. Do they, for instance, routinely review the strategies they used in tasks such as writing term papers, studying for exams, and preparing a class presentation?

Abromitis, B. (2010). *Social cognitive theory in a K-8 classroom: Using Bandura's theory to develop elementary self-regulated learners.* Suite101.com. Retrieved December 29, 2010 from www.suite101.com/content/social-cognitive-theory-in-a-k8-classroom-a186111

"On Your Own" Activity: The Big Five Personality Trait Inventory

Students are fascinated by any discussion of the measurement of personality, and always appreciate the opportunity for self-assessment. Handout 4 provides a brief questionnaire for assessing the Big Five personality traits (extroversion, agreeableness, conscientiousness, emotional stability, and openness) designed by Oliver John and his colleagues (1991). The directions for the independent scoring of each dimension are as follows:

- Extroversion: Student should reverse their responses for items 7, 19, and 33 (1 = 5, 2 = 4, 3 = 3, 4 = 2, 5 = 1), then add all the numbers for items 1, 7, 13, 19, 33, 39, 46, 49, and 53. Scores range from 9 (weak extroversion) to 45 (strong extroversion).
- Agreeableness: Students should reverse their responses for items 2, 15, 25, and 40 (1 = 5, 2 = 4, 3 = 3, 4 = 2, 5 = 1), then add all the numbers for items 2, 8, 15, 25, 28, 34, 40, 45, and 51. Scores range from 9 to 45, with higher scores indicating greater agreeableness.
- Conscientiousness: Students should reverse their responses for items 10, 21, 29, and 52 (1 = 5, 2 = 4, 3 = 3, 4 = 2, 5 = 1), then add all the numbers in front of items 3, 10, 16, 21, 24, 29, 36, 42, and 52. Scores range from 9 to 45, with higher scores indicating greater conscientiousness.
- Emotional Stability: Students should reverse their responses for items 5, 17, 31, 37, and 47 (1 = 5, 2 = 4, 3 = 3, 4 = 2, 5 = 1), then add all the numbers in front of items 5, 11, 17, 22, 26, 31, 37, 43, and 47. Scores range from 9 to 45, with higher scores indicating greater emotional stability.
- Openness: Students should reverse their responses for items 9, 14, 32, and 54 (1 = 5, 2 = 4, 3 = 3, 4 = 2, 5 = 1), then add the numbers in front of 4, 6, 9, 12, 14, 18, 20, 23, 27, 30, 32, 35, 38, 41, 44, 48, 50, and 54. Scores range from 18 to 90, with higher scores indicating greater openness.

John, O. P., Donahue, E. M., & Kentle, R. L. (1991). *The "Big Five" Inventory—Versions 4a and 54* (Tech. Report). Berkeley, CA: Institute of Personality Assessment and Research.

Sociocultural Theory

AV: Social Development of Children (16 min., Insight Media)

This video focuses on the development of children's social skills, explaining how caregivers can nurture and scaffold skills to promote healthy social development.

The Development of Social Bonds

AV: How Relationships Are Formed (24 min., Films for the Humanities and Sciences)

Part of an excellent series on the psychological development of the child, this program discusses the infant's growing need for stimulation and love. Focusing on infants in 14 countries on 5 continents, the program demonstrates that infants around the world constantly are discovering new ways of attracting the attention of people in the world around them.

AV: And Baby Makes Three (27 min., Filmakers Library)

This is a film presentation of an important point made in the text—that the interaction between mothers, fathers, and babies, each with his or her own personality and needs, makes every family unique in its child-rearing practices. The film documents the experiences of two sets of college-educated parents, one Black and one White, and their much-loved 10-month-old children. In one case, the mother decides to quit her job; in the other, the mother decides to continue working. The real differences in these two cases are not in the demographics but in the particular style of the individuals directly involved.

AV: Welcome to Parenthood (15 min., Filmakers Library)

If you want to begin a class discussion by asking students to list the advantages and disadvantages of parenthood, this might be a good way to kick off the discussion. This film is a candid examination of parenthood, its joys and stresses, through the commentary of teenagers and young adults who have recently become parents: a new mother who wanted children but feels somewhat overwhelmed and resentful in her parental role, a father who did not want children but is now delightedly anticipating the birth of his second child, and a two-career family sharing jobs and parenthood. The film emphasizes that one of the most difficult things about being a parent is matching expectations with reality. Many new parents have to admit that they're not "naturals" at it, an admission that is often difficult to make.

AV: Babies Are People Too (27 min., Churchill Films)

This award-winning anti-child-abuse film for teenage mothers is intended to provide them with a better understanding of infant development during the first two years. The film is designed to make better mothers and better-adjusted babies.

AV: Developing the Sense of Family (21 min., Films for the Humanities and Sciences)

This brief program is part of a major series devoted to the general psychological development of the child. Filmed over a one-year period in 14 countries on 5 continents, this program focuses on the infant's developing sense of familiarity with its surroundings and caregivers.

AV: Right from the Start (55 min., Prime Time School Television)

(See description in Prenatal Development and Birth.)

AV: Mother–Infant Bonding: One More Way to Mislead Women (28 min., Films for the Humanities and Sciences)

This adaptation of a Phil Donahue program explores the controversy over whether mothers and infants must be physically close immediately after birth for their relationship to develop properly. One panelist, Diane Eyer, explains why she thinks that the theory of bonding is actually a myth—and another example of how the medical and scientific communities often mislead women.

AV: Life with Baby: How Do the Parents Feel? (27 min., Filmakers Library)

A baby is not always a joy, as shown in this film portraying three problem situations: an unwed teenage mother, an isolated young couple, and a couple who frankly admit that the baby interferes with their relationship. This film will help students see that all new parents could probably use help in adjusting to their responsibilities and that the underlying causes of child abuse or neglect are probably present to some degree in many of us.

Synchrony

AV: Benjamin (42 min., Time Life Video)

Originally produced by the BBC and aired in North America on public television as part of the *Nova* series, this film shows the development of Benjamin from birth to 6 months. It emphasizes his responsiveness to social interaction, as his seemingly random movements and noises are actually synchronized with the actions and speech of his parents. One excellent aspect of this film is that it shows the research techniques used to explore parent–infant interaction, particularly frame-by-frame analysis of videotaped behavior. The film also reveals the difference in the ways mothers and fathers play with their infants: Fathers tend to be more exciting and mothers more soothing.

Attachment

AV: First Feelings (30 min., Insight Media)

Focusing on the development of attachment during infancy, this film features interviews with Mary Ainsworth, Jerome Kagan, Alan Sroufe, and Lisa Bridges. Bowlby's evolutionary theory of attachment and the various biological factors underlying the development of temperament are also discussed.

Classroom Activity: Singing to Infants

As noted in the text, the emotional ties that bind infants and their caregivers have their roots in the communication that takes place during social interactions. Such communication can take various forms, including touching, rocking, smiling, laughing, and talking. When mothers interact with their infants, they elevate their pitch, expand its range, and speak slowly and repetitively. This type of speech appears to be universal, having been documented in numerous cultures. Although men, women, and children alter their speech in similar ways when interacting with infants, men typically engage in less vocalization, pitch range expansion, and repetition than mothers do.

Given the close connections between music and emotion, as well as the prominence of musiclike features in infant-directed speech, it is surprising that singing has received relatively little attention from developmental researchers. To fill this void, several studies have examined how parents sing to infants. In one study, researchers at the University of Toronto asked 67 families to document all instances of singing to infants on a designated day in which the families were pursuing their normal activities. They recorded in a logbook who sang what song to the infant, when singing took place, and under what situations (feeding, playing, soothing, putting the infant to bed). They also provided general information on the regularity of their singing to their offspring.

The researchers found that 74 percent of all songs were sung by mothers, 14 percent by fathers, 8 percent by siblings, and 4 percent by others. Typically, singing to infants accompanied other activities such as play, sleep preparation, feeding, traveling by car, diaper changing, and bathing. The most common songs were play songs, followed by lullabies, popular songs, and invented songs. In short, mothers were the predominant singers, play songs the predominant song type, and play the activity that typically was accompanied by singing.

In the second part of the study, 16 mothers and 15 fathers were asked to sing songs in the presence of their infants (who ranged from 4 to 18 months of age) and again when the infants were absent. Each song was electronically analyzed for its physical properties of pitch and tempo. In addition, a group of 100 adult listeners (50 women and 50 men), 18–75 years of age (M = 37.2 years), were recruited from the general community and asked to distinguish the infant-present from the infant-absent songs. The listeners also rated the degree to which the parent was emotionally engaged with the infant listener on a 9-point scale, using the following designations of emotional engagement: 1 (very low); 3 (some); 5 (intermediate); 7 (high); and 9 (total).

The results showed that adult listeners—whether men or women, musically trained or untrained, experienced or inexperienced in child care—easily distinguished between parents' singing to infants and parents singing the same songs in the absence of their infants. The researchers suggest that their findings imply that mothers and fathers intuitively adjust their singing when it is directed to an infant, just as they adjust the way they speak to infants. In other words, an infant's presence seems to be necessary for production of the full complement of infant-directed song features. A more recent study that recorded mothers speaking and singing to their infants on two occasions separated by one week or more found remarkable stability of pitch, tempo, and rhythm in maternal speech and singing (Bergeson & Trehub, 2002).

Second, the results revealed that when parents sing to their infants, they do so at a higher pitch and in a more emotionally engaging manner than is the case when they sing alone. This is consistent with other evidence that pitch is an important vocal indicator of emotion, with higher pitch associated with happiness, affection, and tenderness. Interestingly, listeners' accuracy in distinguishing infant-directed singing from simulated versions was positively correlated with ratings of emotional engagement, suggesting that the singer's emotional engagement is an important cue to the presence of an infant listener. Parents also slowed the tempo of their singing in the presence of their infants, perhaps to accommodate the infants' limited processing capacity.

A third finding was that fathers and mothers produced similar adjustments in their infant-directed singing. Despite fathers' lesser involvement in caregiving, their infant-present singing was as readily distinguished from their infant-absent singing, as was the case for mothers. Moreover, the fathers' adjustments in pitch and tempo were comparable to those of the mothers, with the result that listeners found fathers' songs to infants to be as emotionally engaging as mothers' songs.

There were, however, some differences in mothers' and fathers' singing styles. For example, mothers tended to sing simpler and more child-oriented songs such as "Twinkle, Twinkle Little Star" and "Itsy, Bitsy Spider"; fathers, on the other hand, either altered popular songs or made up complex songs especially for their child.

Bergeson, T. R., & Trehub, S. E. (2002, January). Absolute pitch and tempo in mothers' songs to infants. *Psychological Science, 13*(1), 72.

Trehub, S. E., Unyk, A. M., Kamenetsky, S. B., Hill, D. S., Trainor, L. J., Henderson, J. L., & Saraza, M. (1997). Mothers' and fathers' singing to infants. *Developmental Psychology, 33*(3), 500–507.

AV: Attachment Theory: The Baby / Caregiver Bond (24 min., Films for the Humanities and Sciences)

This classic video gives an overview of John Bowlby's attachment theory. The Strange Situation is thoroughly described, along with the impact of day care on attachment and the long-term impact of attachment patterns on individuals and society.

AV: John Bowlby: Attachment and Loss (2 programs, 60 min. each, Insight Media)

Noted attachment researcher John Bowlby discusses his theory of attachment and the research findings that led to its formulation. Using two case studies, Bowlby also describes the consequences of broken attachments. In a particularly interesting segment of Program 2, Bowlby discusses his collaboration with Sigmund Freud and Mary Ainsworth.

Classroom Activity: Temperament, Security of Attachment, and Behavioral Inhibition

In a series of studies spanning more than a decade, Nathan Fox and Susan Calkins examined the relationship between individual differences in distress reactivity during the first year and attachment status and behavioral inhibition (sociability or temperamental reactivity) during the second year.

In one early study, 52 healthy, full-term infants (25 boys and 27 girls) were tested at 2 days of age and again at 5, 14, and 24 months of age. Temperament was assessed at 2 days and 5 months of age; attachment, at 14 months; and behavioral inhibition, at 24 months. Two tests of the infants' reactivity to distress were made: a pacifier withdrawal test at 2 days and an arm restraint test at 5 months. (In the latter test, each infant's behavior was observed while his or her mother gently held the infant's hands down at the infant's side for 2 minutes [or less if the child cried].) At 14 and 24 months, infants were observed during play with their mothers, when presented with a novel animated toy, and in the classic Strange Situation test. Infant heart rate and vagal tone were recorded at each age. (Vagal tone is a measure of the variability in heart-rate pattern that occurs in relation to the frequency of breathing. Because the vagus is the primary nerve of the parasympathetic nervous system, which helps maintain the body's homeostatic state, differences in the amount of control exerted on the heart rate are believed to reflect individual differences in neural and behavioral regulation.)

The data yielded several measures for each infant: distress reactivity at 2 days of age (in response to pacifier withdrawal) and at 5 months (in response to arm restraint); maternal assessment of infant temperament at 5, 14, and 24 months of age; and attachment at 14 months (from the videotaped Strange Situation). In addition, a measure of behavioral inhibition was computed for each infant on the basis of the infant's temperament assessment at 24 months.

Some interesting findings were the following.

(a) Infants who were more likely to cry when the pacifier was withdrawn at 2 days of age were more likely to be classified as insecurely attached at 14 months. The insecure group also was quicker to cry during this test than was the secure group.

(b) Infants who exhibited greater distress during the pacifier-withdrawal test also tended to cry more frequently during the reunion episodes of the Strange Situation test at 14 months.

(c) Five-month vagal tone was correlated with both crying when the pacifier was withdrawn at 2 days of age and crying when their arms were restrained and novel toys introduced at 5 months of age. (Other research has shown that infants with high vagal tone are generally more reactive as 5-month-olds, more sociable as 14-month-olds, and more facially expressive of both positive and negative emotions.)

(d) A significant difference was found among the three attachment groups at 14 months and on the index of behavioral inhibition computed at 24 months. As Figure 1 on the next page indicates, infants who had been classified as "resistant/insecure" at 14 months were more inhibited at 24 months. Infants who scored high on this index, which has a mean equal to .00, a maximum of 2.63, and a minimum of –2.67, tended to stay very close to their mothers during free play, took the longest amount of time to approach the stranger and novel toy during these tests, and were quickest to fret or cry in response to these events.

In discussing their results, the authors note that the data suggest "a more complex process than simply a direct path between security of attachment and behavioral inhibition." One aspect of this process involves "infants who, in the first year, are highly reactive to frustrating situations or limitations on their movement. They are more active and easily aroused. Some parents may decide early on that the best way to respond to this 'independence' is to extend the bounds of autonomous activity for the child. Such a child may exhibit avoidance in the Strange Situation and, if left unchecked, might respond in an undisciplined, highly active manner to subsequent social challenges."

Following up on this study, Nathan Fox examined whether differences in infant reactivity, temperament, and attachment at 14 months predicted physiological, psychosocial, and behavioral outcomes at 4 years. The results showed that infants who scored low in behavioral inhibition had higher activity level scores and were more confident with unfamiliar peers at 4 years than infants with higher behavioral inhibition scores. In addition, infants who had an avoidant attachment with their mothers displayed significantly more externalizing problems (aggression) at 4 years than securely or ambivalently attached infants.

Burgess, K. B., Marshall, P. J., Rubin, K. H., & Fox, N. A. (2003). Infant attachment and temperament as predictors of subsequent externalizing problems and cardiac physiology. *Journal of Child Psychology and Psychiatry and Allied Disciplines, 44*(6), 819–831.

Calkins, S. D., & Fox, N. A. (1992). Mean behavioral inhibition score by attachment group (ABC). The relations

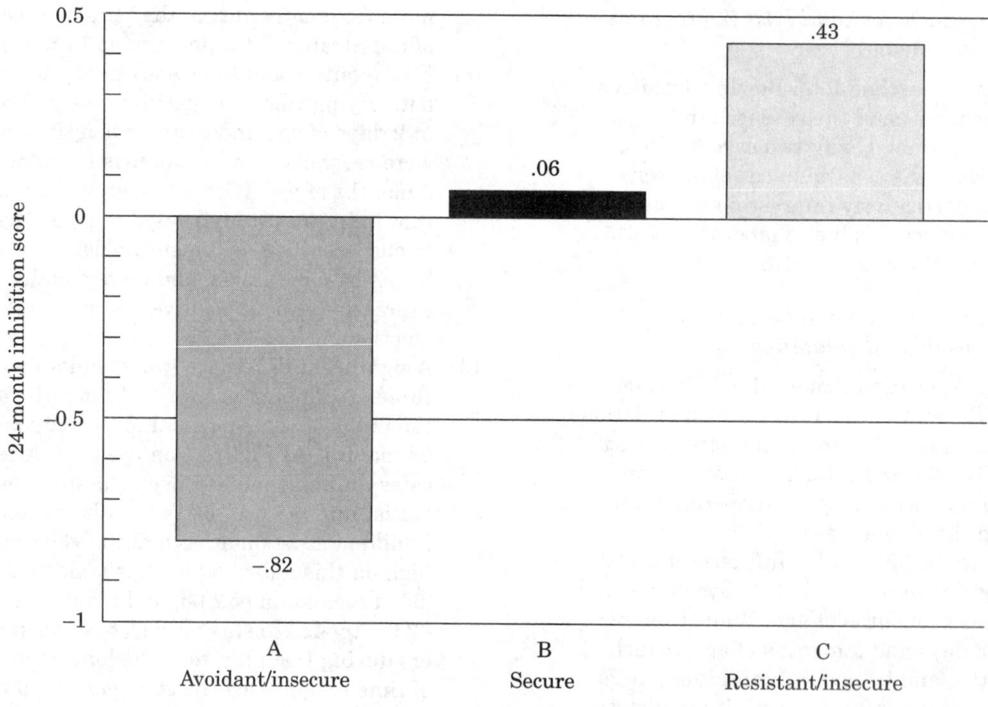

Figure 1. Mean behavioral inhibition score by attachment group (ABC). Calkins, S. D., & Fox, N. A. (1992). The relations among infant temperament, security of attachment, and behavioral inhibition at twenty-four months. *Child Development, 63,* 1456–1472. © The Society for Research in Child Development.

among infant temperament, security of attachment, and behavioral inhibition at twenty-four months. *Child Development, 63,* 1456–1472.

Fox, N. A., & Calkins, S. D. (2005). The development of self-control of emotion: Intrinsic and extrinsic influences. *Motivation and Emotion.* 27(1), 7–26.

Classroom Activity: Mary Salter Ainsworth

Mary D. Salter Ainsworth, one of the preeminent developmental psychologists of the twentieth century, died in Charlottesville, Virginia, on March 21, 1999, after a lengthy illness. She leaves behind an international family of students and friends. Her contributions to the scientific study of attachment led to groundbreaking changes in how we think about the bond between an infant and his or her caregivers. Your students might enjoy hearing some of the biographical details of her exceptional life. The following is an excerpt from her obituary, written by Inge Bretherton, Professor, Child and Family Studies, University of Wisconsin, Madison.

> Professor Ainsworth was born in Glendale, Ohio, in 1913, the daughter of Charles and Mary Salter. She spent most of her childhood in Toronto, Canada. She earned her B.A. from the University of Toronto in 1935, her M.A. in 1936, and her Ph.D. in developmental psychology in 1939. She then held a position as lecturer in the psychology department until 1942, when she was commissioned in the Canadian Women's Army Corps, attaining the rank of major. She returned to the University of Toronto as assistant professor in 1946, where she wrote an influential collaborative book with Klopfer on the Rorschach Test.
>
> In 1950, Mary Salter married Leonard Ainsworth, a WWII veteran and graduate student in psychology, and moved to London, England. There she began a lifelong collaborative partnership with John Bowlby, a child psychiatrist who was investigating the devastating effects that prolonged separation from the mother in early childhood had on young children in hospitals and institutions. From London she moved to Kampala, Uganda, where she conducted one of the first longitudinal scientific studies of mother–infant interaction in the first year of life.
>
> In 1955, Professor Ainsworth moved to Baltimore, Maryland, where she conducted clinical work and joined the faculty of the Johns Hopkins University. She was appointed Associate Professor in 1958 and full professor in 1963. In 1962, she began her renowned Baltimore study of infant–caregiver attachment. This study led to major changes in how parents, psychologists, psychiatrists, pediatricians, educators, and policymakers worldwide think about parenting infants and very young children.
>
> In 1974, Mary Ainsworth moved to the University of Virginia, first as Visiting Professor, then as Commonwealth Professor from 1975 to 1984. During this time she continued teaching developmental psychology, supervising the research of many graduate students, and publishing the results of her own research. She also played a key role in the development of the clinical psychology training program at the University of Virginia. She retired as Professor Emeritus in 1984, after which she remained professionally active until 1992.

Always active in professional organizations, she was elected president of the Society for Research in Child Development from 1977 to 1979. Among the many honors and awards she has received are Phi Beta Kappa, University of Toronto; Distinguished Contribution Award, Maryland Psychological Association (1973); Distinguished Scientific Contribution Award, Virginia Psychological Association (1983); Distinguished Scientific Contribution Award, Division 12 (Division of Clinical Psychology), American Psychological Association (APA; 1984); G. Stanley Hall Award, Division 7 (Division of Developmental Psychology), APA (1984); Salmon Lecturer, Salmon Committee on Psychiatry and Mental Hygiene, New York Academy of Medicine (1984); William T. Grant Lecturer in Behavioral Pediatrics, Society for Behavioral Pediatrics (1985); Award for Distinguished Contributions to Child Development Research, Society for Research in Child Development (1985); Award for Distinguished Professional Contribution to Knowledge, American Psychological Association (1987); C. Anderson Aldrich Award in Child Development, American Academy of Pediatrics (1987); Distinctive Achievement Award, Virginia Association for Infant Mental Health (1989); Honorary Fellowship, Royal College of Psychiatrists (1989); Distinguished Scientific Contribution Award, American Psychological Association (1989); American Academy of Arts and Sciences (1992); Distinguished Professional Contribution Award, Division 12 (Division of Clinical Psychology), American Psychological Association (1994); International Society for the Study of Personal Relationships Distinguished Career Award (1996); Mentor Award, Division 7 (Division of Developmental Psychology), American Psychological Association (1998); and the Gold Medal Award for Life Achievement in the Science of Psychology, American Psychological Foundation (1998).

Bretherton, I. (2000). Obituary for Mary D. Salter Ainsworth. *American Psychologist, 55*(10), 1148–1149.

AV: Attachment (24 min., Insight Media)

This video explores research on the development of attachment relationships, focusing on Mary Ainsworth's Strange Situation Test.

AV: First Person: Impressions of Being a Baby (30 min., Child Development Media)

Filmed over a two-and-a-half-year period, this film follows the development of several children from birth through the first few years of life. The program documents the foundations for later development provided by secure attachment, early development of social and language skills, and beginnings of the formation of self-image.

Classroom Activity: The Legacy of Childhood Attachment

To reinforce the importance that many developmentalists place on early attachment experiences, you might discuss the continuity between childhood caregiving experiences and the quality of later relationships. The next two items provide enough data to form the basis of a lecture on this topic. Before discussing specific findings, however, you may wish to elaborate a bit on the text discussion of attachment theory.

According to John Bowlby, "confidence in the availability of attachment figures, or lack of it, is built up slowly during the years of immaturity—infancy, childhood, and adolescence—and that whatever expectations are developed during those years tend to persist relatively unchanged throughout the rest of life" (Bowlby, 1973). These expectations, or "working models" of attachment relationships, incorporate expectations about how reliably and sensitively others will respond to one's needs and how worthy the individual feels of such responses. Consistent, sensitive parenting is thought to lead to secure working models: The child sees the people around him or her as dependable and supportive and feels worthy of their support. In contrast, insensitive caregiving may create insecure models: The child expects other people to be undependable or rejecting and perceives himself or herself as unworthy. Such models are thought to guide behavior throughout life, even leading individuals to re-create aspects of the very relationships that produced their attachment models.

Here are some research findings that might form the basis of your lecture.

Attachment in Preschool and Middle School: Experience in a secure relationship at home appears to facilitate a child's ability to use the preschool teacher as a secure base in the school setting (DeMulder, Denham, Schmidt, & Mitchell, 2000). The study assessed the relationships among stress at home, attachment security with the mother, attachment security with the teacher, and socialization outcomes in preschool. Children in families with lower levels of stress had more secure attachment relationships with their mothers. In addition, boys who were more securely attached to their mothers were more securely attached to their preschool teachers and were more popular with peers in preschool. Both boys and girls who were less securely attached to their mothers expressed significantly more anger and aggressive behavior in preschool.

In another study, researchers investigated associations among attachment, emotionality, teacher-reported peer competence, and style of coping with stressful experiences in fifth-grade students (Contreras, Kerns, Weimer, Gentzler, & Tomich, 2000). The results showed that children who scored higher on measures of secure attachment were rated by their teachers as more competent in their peer relationships. Secure attachment was also associated with greater use of constructive coping strategies such as instrumental problem solving and support seeking, and less reliance on avoidance, venting of emotions, or other less adaptive coping responses.

Attachment and Perfectionism in College Students: Because many of your students are likely to perceive themselves as perfectionists, they are sure to find the results of a Michigan State University study of perfectionism and attachment provocative. As background, you should note that experts have differentiated three types of perfectionism: adaptive, maladaptive, and nonperfectionism. Adaptive perfectionism involves adherence to high self-standards but not at the expense of self-esteem. Adaptive perfectionists experience positive feelings when a task is completed. In contrast, maladaptive perfectionism is distinguished by high standards that never seem to be met or achievable. Completed projects are not enjoyed, and there is considerable anxiety about even minor imperfections. Nonperfectionism, as the name indicates, refers to the absence of high self-standards.

It will probably not surprise your students to learn that maladaptive perfectionism has been correlated with several psychological problems, including depression, anxiety, and eating disorders. By comparison, adaptive perfectionism has been linked with feelings of self-efficacy and positive affect.

In one study (Rice & Mirzadeh, 2000), researchers tested the hypothesis that qualities of attachment to parents or parent figures may set the stage for the development of either adaptive or maladaptive perfectionism (data on nonperfectionism are not provided here). The researchers hypothesized that adaptive perfectionists would be more likely to report secure attachment with parents, whereas maladaptive perfectionists would indicate insecure attachments.

A total of 49 male and 129 female college students (mean age = 21.3 years) participated in the study. Ninety-four percent of the sample identified themselves as White, European American. Sixty-three percent indicated that their parents were married and living together, 14 percent reported that their parents had divorced and not remarried, and 16 percent indicated that one or both of their parents had remarried.

The researchers used the Multidimensional Perfectionism Scale (MPS) to categorize students in terms of perfectionism. The MPS consists of 35 items organized into six subscales: concern over mistakes, personal expectations for performance, parental expectations, parental criticism, doubts about competence, and the importance one places on order and organization. Attachment was assessed with the revised version of the Inventory of Parent and Peer Attachment, which measures the overall quality or security in the person's attachment bond with his or her mother and father. Other scales were used to measure students' self-reported feelings of depression, anxiety, and several other mood states.

The results were as follows:

- Students with higher "attachment to mother" scores were more likely to be adaptive perfectionists. In fact, the odds of being an adaptive perfectionist were 2.62 times greater for a student with secure attachment to mother than for a student with insecure attachment. Greater security in the attachment relationship with the father also increased the likelihood of being an adaptive perfectionist.
- Maladaptive perfectionists were less academically integrated and more depressed than adaptive perfectionists were. In fact, the average degree of depression among maladaptive perfectionists was approximately one-half a standard deviation *above* a typical cutoff for clinically significant depression.

The researchers caution that the correlational and self-report nature of their data limits the conclusions that can be drawn from their study. Nevertheless, they suggest that perfectionism may emerge from differences in the quality of parent–child interactions. Maladaptive perfectionism may develop in response to parents who set high standards for their children, yet are overly critical and unsupportive as their children attempt to meet such demands. Adverse experiences such as these may "set the stage internalizing harsh, self-defeating expectations of self and others that place the child at risk for developing later emotional as well as academic difficulties."

Fearful Attachment and the Abusive Personality: In a controversial book, Donald Dutton (2007) attempts to extend existing understandings of interpersonal violence to early developmental history—including childhood attachment. Several types of abusers are differentiated, including the overcontrolled, antisocial abuser who commits acts of violence within and outside the home, and the cyclical, or impulsive abuser, whom Dutton terms the "abusive personality." For this person, interpersonal violence is viewed as a coping response that is triggered within intimate relationships when a "cluster of difficulties co-exist." These difficulties include borderline personality organization, fearful attachment, high levels of anger, substance abuse, and the experience of violence to self or others in childhood.

Bowlby, J. (1973). *Attachment and loss: Vol. 2. Separation: Anxiety and anger.* New York: Basic Books.

Contreras, J. M., Kerns, K. A., Weimer, B. L., Gentzler, A. L., & Tomich, P. L. (2000). Emotion regulation as a mediator of associations between mother–child attachment and peer relationships in middle childhood. *Journal of Family Psychology, 14*(1), 111–124.

DeMulder, E. K., Denham, S., Schmidt, M., & Mitchell, J. (2000). Q-sort assessment of attachment security during the preschool years: Links from home to school. *Developmental Psychology, 36*(2), 274–282.

Dutton, D. (2007). *The abusive personality: Violence and control in intimate relationships* (2nd ed.). New York: Guilford Press.

Rice, K. G., & Mirzadeh, S. A. (2000). Perfectionism, attachment, and adjustment. *Journal of Counseling Psychology, 47*(2), 238–250.

Observational Activity: Attachment

About seven months after birth—when children are developing the ability to represent another person cognitively—infants develop an enduring *attachment* to their primary caregivers.

Infants express attachment by *proximity-seeking behaviors,* such as approaching, following, and clinging; and *contact-seeking behaviors*, such as crying, smiling, and calling. Parents express their attachment more by eye contact than by physical contact and by reacting to their child's vocalizations, expressions, and gestures.

As discussed in the text, on the basis of many observations, Mary Ainsworth developed a laboratory procedure in which the infant's reactions to a novel situation and the comings and goings of its mother indicate the security of the child's attachment. In this test, which is conducted in a well-equipped playroom full of toys, most infants demonstrate *secure attachment*. The presence of their mother gives them the sense of security needed to express their natural curiosity and to explore the new room. If their mother attempts to leave the room, securely attached infants will usually stop playing, protest verbally, and demonstrate contact-seeking behaviors.

Approximately one-third of the infants show insecure attachment in this test situation: They cling nervously to their mother and are unwilling to explore even if she remains in the room. Others seem aloof and engage in little or no interaction with their mother.

Have students arrange to observe a 1- or 2-year-old child and his or her caregiver in a play setting outside the child's home. During the observation period, they should measure the infant's reactions to a novel situation and the comings and goings of his or her caregiver. After the approximately 30-minute observation period, students are to complete the questions in Handout 5 and return their answers to you.

In addition to giving students firsthand experience in the developmental research method of observation, this observational activity has several purposes: (1) It assesses students' understanding and recognition of attachment behaviors in both children and parents. (2) It encourages students to think critically about the Strange Situation as a valid measure of attachment. (3) It demonstrates how research findings can be applied to everyday problems of human development (advising expectant parents and the parents of insecurely attached children).

Classroom Activity: Adult Attachment Styles, Personality, and Family Functioning

A number of developmentalists have proposed *attachment* as an organizing framework for the study of close relationships in adulthood. This proposition follows from the notion of attachment as a life-span concept that is both a prototype and a precursor of adult relationships. As John Bowlby suggested many years ago, the attachment a child forms in his or her interactions with the primary caregiver results in a prototypical internal working model that consists of basic beliefs about the self, others, and the social world in general. In addition, each individual's attachment style is believed to become an integral part of that person's overall personality.

Although this issue is not discussed in the text, your students are sure to find it fascinating as they reflect on their own memories of attachment. Most research on adult attachment has used Mary Main's Adult Attachment Interview, which measures adults' memories of their childhood relationships with parents. To expand on the discussion of child and adult attachments, you may wish to introduce your students to an alternative model proposed by Bartholomew and Horowitz (1991). This model suggests that if we look at an individual's self-image and his or her image of others as either positive or negative, then we can differentiate four prototypes of adult attachment:

- secure (positive self–positive others)
- dismissing (positive self–negative others)
- preoccupied (negative self–positive others)
- fearful attachment (negative self–negative others)

This conceptualization suggests that adult personality development proceeds along a "self" dimension, which is concerned with the establishment of a stable, positive identity; and an "other" dimension, which is concerned with establishing stable, satisfying relationships. It is therefore not surprising that researchers have found that the various attachment styles predict different patterns of interpersonal problems and different experiences of positive or negative emotions in relationships (Kapanee & Rao, 2007).

For example, researchers studied a community-based sample of 304 adults (145 men and 159 women), ranging from 20 to 87 years of age, to determine the relationship between attachment style and family context and personality variables. Demographically, the participants' annual family income ranged from less than \$10,000 to more than \$150,000 (mean = \$60,000). The majority of the participants (59.2 percent) were married, 19.4 percent were single, 12.2 percent were divorced, and 9.2 percent were widowed. Ninety-six percent of the sample were Caucasian, 1.6 percent were of Arabic descent, 1 percent were Asian American, and 1.3 percent were African American. The participants were tested in two 3-hour sessions on a battery of tests that included a questionnaire of adult attachment styles, two measures assessing past and current family climate, and several measures of personality and intellectual functioning.

A two-part relationship questionnaire was used to assess attachment style. In the first part, participants read four paragraphs describing the four adult attachment styles: secure, dismissing, preoccupied, and fearful attachment. They were asked to select the paragraph that best described their behavior in close relationships. In the second part, they were asked to reread the four paragraphs and to indicate on a 5-

point Likert scale how well each statement described their behavior in close relationships (1 = very unlike me to 5 = very like me).

The participants also completed several self-report measures regarding their views on their family of origin and their current family. These measures describe the extent to which family members support one another, are encouraged to participate in family decisions, and are allowed to express their feelings freely.

Finally, the participants also completed several inventories that measured such personality dimensions as sociability, social presence, self-acceptance, empathy, communality, well-being, tolerance, and dominance. In addition, a defense-style questionnaire was used to assess the participant's defense mechanisms (e.g., projection, denial, passive-aggression) and categorize them as one of three distinct defense styles: immature, neurotic, or mature.

The results showed that 50.7 percent of the study's participants had a secure attachment style; of the rest, 25.3 percent were classified as dismissing, 15.8 percent as fearful, and 8.2 percent as preoccupied in close relationships. Interestingly, a larger proportion of young and middle-aged adults described themselves in terms of the preoccupied or fearful attachment style. Both of these are "other-oriented" attachment styles that the authors suggest indicate that younger adults' identities are still in a formative stage apart from the influence of their family of origin.

Compared to young and middle-aged adults, a larger proportion of older adults described themselves as dismissing in close relationships. That is, they tended to downplay the importance of close relationships and to emphasize independence and self-reliance. The researchers suggest that this may be an indication of the resourcefulness of the aging self in response to age-related losses in interpersonal relationships. However, it is impossible to determine whether the disproportionate number of dismissing older adults is indicative of an age-related developmental process or whether a similar distribution of attachment styles would have emerged if the same individuals had been tested when they were younger.

Correlational analyses revealed that attachment ratings were significantly related to both family context and personality. Higher scores on the secure attachment style were associated with a more positive evaluation of the family of origin and the current family climate. Those who were securely attached scored higher on sociability, dominance, social presence, self-acceptance, empathy, communality, and lower on the immature defense style. A reversed pattern of associations was found for those participants with insecure, fearful, and preoccupied attachment styles.

Several studies have also reported continuity between caregiving experiences in childhood and marital behavior. For example, dismissing spouses tend to display fewer negative emotions than preoccupied spouses during marital interactions, analogous to the "minimizing" strategy of avoidant children. Dismissing spouses are also more likely to withdraw during conflict. Preoccupied spouses may express less positive and more negative affect than dismissing spouses, so as not to appear "soothed" and "run the risk of losing contact" with their partner. In contrast, securely attached adults are presumed to have some confidence that they will receive sensitive and supportive responses and so are be more comfortable with expressing their emotions to their romantic partners.

In a study by C. C. Paley and colleagues, the researchers explored the relationship between marital functioning and attachment in 138 couples (mean age = 28.3 years). In addition, the researchers differentiated two types of secure attachment: *continuous-secure* individuals, whose positive recollections of childhood are fairly uniform, and *earned-secure* individuals, who recount difficult childhoods but do so in a reflective manner that indicates they are not overly entangled in those experiences.

Couples were interviewed at their homes prior to the birth of their first child, and their attachments were classified according to the Adult Attachment Interview. Each spouse then completed a battery of self-report questionnaires, which included measures of marital satisfaction as well as a measure of depressive symptoms. Couples were also videotaped at home during a 15-minute problem-solving task in which they were asked to discuss and attempt to resolve a major source of disagreement in their marriage.

The results of the study revealed striking correlations between attachment stance (of both spouses) and marital behavior. However, these differences interacted with gender.

- Preoccupied wives expressed less positive affect than both continuous-secure wives and earned-secure wives.
- Dismissing wives engaged in more withdrawal than both continuous-secure wives and earned-secure wives.
- Wives whose husbands were either dismissing husbands or earned-secure expressed less positive affect and more negative affect than wives of continuous-secure husbands.
- The wives of dismissing husbands expressed less commitment to their relationship than did the wives of continuous-secure husbands.
- Wives' attachment stance was somewhat related to their marital behavior. Earned-secure wives regulated their affect during the problem-solving task as well as continuous-secure wives.
- There were no significant effects of wives' attachment stance on husbands' marital behavior or perceptions. The researchers speculate that women may be more likely than men to

carry forward the remnants of earlier attachment relationships into adult intimate relationships.

Overall, these findings suggest that attachment styles not only are important for social and personality development early in life but also are systematically related to individual differences across the life span. Adults with a secure attachment style evaluated their current family and their family of origin more positively; scored higher on personality characteristics indicative of self-confidence, psychological well-being, and ability to function in interpersonal contexts; and were less inclined to endorse immature defense styles as means to resolve conflict.

Interestingly, a number of therapists have begun to incorporate research findings such as these into a new form of *emotionally focused couple therapy* (Johnson, 2003). Findings from this type of applied case study research, along with at least one large community study of 442 women who underwent an abortion, suggest that although adult attachment styles are moderately stable over time, meaningful change can occur when new understandings of personal and interpersonal experiences are achieved (Cozzarelli, Karafa, Collins, & Tagler, 2003).

Bartholomew, K., & Horowitz L. M. (1991). Attachment styles among young adults: A test of a four-category model. *Journal of Personality and Social Psychology, 61,* 226–244.

Cozzarelli, C., Karafa, J. A., Collins, N. L., & Tagler, M. J. (2003). *Journal of Social and Clinical Psychology, 22*(3), 315–346.

Diehl, M. (1998). Adult attachment styles: Their relations to family context and personality. *Journal of Personality and Social Psychology, 74*(6), 1656–1669.

Johnson, S. M. (2003, July). The revolution in couple therapy: A practitioner-scientist perspective. *Journal of Marital and Family Therapy, 29*(3), 365–371.

Kapanee, A. R., & Rao, K. (2007). Attachment style in relation to family functioning and distress in college students. *Journal of the Indian Academy of Applied Psychology, 33*(1), 15–21.

Paley, B., Cox, M. J., Kanoy, K. W., Harter, K. S., Burchinal, M., & Margand, N. A. (2005). Adult attachment and marital interaction as predictors of whole family interactions during the transition to parenthood. *Journal of Family Psychology, 19*(3), 420–429.

Classroom Activity: Maternal Sensitivity, Infant Irritability, and the Enduring Effects of Intervention

Autonomous locomotion, symbolic representation, and linguistic advances give toddlers a wealth of new ways to explore their environments.

The child's new autonomy means that relationships between children and their primary caregivers change profoundly during toddlerhood. Developmentalists agree that how caregivers respond to the toddler's increasing autonomy can have a dramatic effect on the child's emotional development. The major challenge for caregivers is to "expand and consolidate this new autonomy without jeopardizing the feeling of security."

In one study, Dymphna van den Boom of the University of Leiden, The Netherlands, investigated whether a skill-based intervention program that promoted greater maternal sensitivity to infants would produce lasting benefits. Earlier research has demonstrated that such intervention produces favorable immediate effects in both mothers and their infants. But do these benefits endure into toddlerhood, as the child's network of relationships expands with siblings and peers?

The participants were 82 first-time mothers who were selected for the project if (1) there were no serious complications during pregnancy, (2) their newborns were assessed as "irritable" on two separate Brazelton Neonatal Assessment exams, and (3) the mother's family was of relatively low socioeconomic status.

The participants were randomly assigned to intervention and control groups. Three home intervention sessions were scheduled, once every three weeks, when the infants were between 6 and 9 months of age. The pragmatic, skill-based sessions lasted about two hours and focused on increasing maternal responsiveness to infant cues, including both positive and negative affect, requests for assistance, and so forth.

Following the brief "treatment" phase of the study, mothers and their toddlers were evaluated at home when the children were 18, 24, and 42 months of age. At 18 months, each child was observed in a 20-minute play session with toys, with the mother instructed to behave "as she normally would if mildly preoccupied—respond to the child as necessary but otherwise not to initiate interaction or direct play activities." At this age, mothers and their children were also evaluated using the Ainsworth Strange Situation.

At 24 months, three home visits were scheduled, in which the Bayley Scales of Infant Development were administered and mother–child interaction was once again observed during free play. Following the free-play period, mother–child interactions were recorded during two 40-minute sessions as they went about their everyday routine. The coded child behaviors included affect, cooperation, on-task behavior, and negativism. The coded maternal behaviors included responsiveness, teaching, monitoring, support, and uninvolvement.

At 42 months, the observations included five sets of observations, which pertained to the quality of parent–child interaction, cognitive development, security, behavior problems, and the quality of peer interaction. Each family was videotaped in their home at dinner time on two separate occasions, and four visits were made to the laboratory to collect cognitive and peer interaction data. Table 1 on the next page summarizes the procedures and measures at each age.

Was intervention effective? In terms of its effects on the quality of attachment, at 18 months only 26 percent of all untreated (comparison) irritable infants

Table 1 Procedures and Measures at 18, 24, and 42 Months

Age at Assessment	Procedures	Measures
18 months	Free play	Mother: acceptance, accessibility, cooperation, sensitivity
	Bayley Scales	Mental development index
	Strange Situation	Attachment classification
24 months	Free play	Mother: acceptance, accessibility, cooperation, sensitivity
	Bayley Scales	Mental development index
	Mother–child interaction	Child: affect, cooperation, problem solving, on-task behavior, negativism
		Mother: teaching, responsiveness, support, off-task sensitivity, monitoring, uninvolvement
42 months	Family dinner	Mother: responsiveness, assistance
		Father: responsiveness, control
		Child: reliance on mother, security, initiation of interaction
	McCarthy Scales	General cognitive index
	Attachment Q-sort	Security
	Child Behavior Checklist	Behavior problems
	Peer interaction	Peer contact, cooperation, reactive aggression, proactive aggression

were assigned the secure classification, in comparison with 72 percent of infants in the intervention group. Control group toddlers were most likely to be classified as insecure-avoidant.

At 24 months, three separate one-way MANOVAs (multivariate analyses of variance) (intervention versus comparison) were run on the 18-month play ratings, the 24-month coded child behavior, and the 24-month coded maternal behavior. In every instance, significant results emerged. Children in the intervention group had significantly higher ratings in terms of affect, cooperation, problem solving, and on-task behavior. Mothers in the intervention group were more accepting, more accessible, more cooperative, more communicative, and more sensitive than the control group mothers.

There were several sets of dependent variables at 42 months: maternal, paternal, child–mother, and child–peer behavioral components. Significant differences were obtained between intervention and comparison groups in all cases. As before, intervention mothers were more responsive and assisted their children more during peer play. In addition, fathers of children in the intervention group were also more responsive toward their children than fathers of comparison group children. Intervention children were more cooperative and secure than comparison group children. Table 2 on the next page summarizes the results for intervention and comparison groups at each age.

The results clearly support the hypothesis that the intervention improved the mother–child relationship and that this improvement was maintained long after the intervention. Somewhat surprised by the robustness of her results, van den Boom admits that "many would doubt that such a seemingly meager intervention would have effects, much less enduring ones. . . . Intervention mothers, unlike comparison group mothers, were more responsive to positive and negative child initiatives, displayed more sharing of interest in objects and activities, used verbal commands in an age-appropriate way, allowed their toddler sufficient autonomy, and issued little direct instruction. This sensitive mothering is associated in intervention children with more orienting toward their mothers, more cooperation and engaging in meaningful activities and verbal interactions, and more imitation of their mother's actions and comments compared with the control group."

A similar intervention is being conducted with adolescent mothers in Germany (Ziegenhain, 2003). The researchers note that "Adolescent mothers and their infants are a high-risk group. They are exposed to multiple stressors and experience little social support. The accumulation and the interaction of multiple risk factors have an adverse effect on both the psychological well-being of the adolescent mothers and the socio-emotional development of the children" (Ziegenhain, 2002, cited in "Relationship-based intervention," 2003). Early data from the intervention, which provides video feedback promoting sensitive parental behavior, reveal improved maternal sensitivity during the babies' first three months compared to a group of adolescent mothers who received intervention based on counseling and compared to a control group of adolescent mothers who did not receive any intervention.

Relationship-based intervention improves maternal sensitivity in young mothers. (2003, September 1). *Health & Medicine Week*, *2*.

van den Boom, D. C. (1995). Do first-year intervention effects endure? Follow-up during toddlerhood of a sample of Dutch irritable infants. *Child Development*, *66*, 1798–1816.

Ziegenhain, U. (2003). Young parenthood: Adolescent mothers and their children. *Monatsschrift Kinderheit, 151*(6), 608–612.

Table 2 Mean Factor Scores and F Ratios of Measures at 18, 24, and 42 Months

	Intervention	Control	*F*
18-month measures			
Mother free-play ratings:			
acceptance	6.86	5.95	7.04***
accessibility	6.88	5.87	7.26***
cooperation	6.70	5.18	16.92***
sensitivity	6.70	5.26	15.14
24-month measures			
Child interactive behavior:			
affect	.09	–.05	.45
cooperation	.32	–.33	9.74***
problem solving	.07	–.06	.32
on-task behavior	.02	–.06	.12
negativism	.01	.01	.00
Mother interactive behavior:			
maternal teaching	.06	–.10	.55
responsiveness	.21	–.23	4.11*
support	.11	–.13	1.21
off-task sensitivity	.22	–.22	4.09*
monitoring	.08	–.11	.69
uninvolvement	.04	–.01	.06
42-month measures:			
Mother–child interaction:			
responsiveness	.41	–.11	5.83**
assistance	.41	–.10	5.58**
Father–child interaction:			
responsiveness	.34	–.26	8.82***
control	.13	–.06	.89
Child–peer interaction:			
absence of peer contact	–.15	.15	1.82
cooperation	.17	–.27	3.90*
reactive aggression	.17	–.16	2.20
proactive aggression	.12	–.12	1.11
Child–mother interaction:			
reliance on mother	–.01	.01	.00
security	.21	–.21	4.01*

$^*p < .05$. $^{**}p < .025$. $^{***}p < .01$.

Tables 1 and 2: van den Boom, D. C. (1995). Do first-year intervention effects endure? Follow-up during toddlerhood of a sample of Dutch irritable infants. *Child Development, 66,* 1798–1816. © The Society for Research in Child Development.

Social Referencing

Classroom Activity: Infant Social Referencing, "Joint-Attention" Behaviors, and Emerging Theory of Mind

As the text notes, beginning at 9 months of age, social referencing becomes increasingly distinct and important. If you wish to elaborate on this discussion of social referencing, the following material should be helpful.

Developmentalists' understanding of social referencing has stemmed largely from research studies using the following carefully controlled, three-part paradigm: (1) the presentation of a novel event, such as a toy or a stranger; (2) an adult caregiver's emotional reaction to the event, using a standard facial expression alone or in combination with a verbalization; and (3) an assessment of the infant's reaction to the adult's emotional message.

Findings from these studies demonstrate that infants look to their mothers, fathers, and friendly strangers for affective information about ambiguous events and objects.

Warren Rosen and his colleagues elaborated on this basic paradigm to observe more fully how mothers convey emotional messages to their infants. Thirty-seven mothers and their infants (19 boys and 18 girls) participated in the study. All the infants were within two weeks of their first birthday.

On each of the 148, 90-second experimental trials, the infant was presented with a novel animated toy (a wind-up monkey or an owl robot), and the mothers were instructed to respond with an affective reaction whenever their babies glanced at them and to maintain that reaction for the duration of their babies' glance. The trials were divided into four conditions that varied two factors. The first factor was instruction: On "unconstrained trials," mothers were simply told what emotion to express; on others, they were trained to produce a specific affective reaction. The second factor was message content—either happiness or fear.

Two cameras videotaped the behaviors of the mothers and their infants during each trial. Maternal and infant behavior was then coded by separate observers. The infant coder recorded whenever the infant looked at the mother or emitted an affective display. The coder also judged the *valence* of each infant reaction (positive, negative, or ambiguous), and whether the infant's reaction was directed at the mother, the toy, or elsewhere.

Each time the infant looked toward his or her mother, the second coder judged the valence (positive or negative), clarity, and intensity of the mother's expression; in the unconstrained trials, the coder also evaluated whether the mother's expression included vocal elements, facial elements, or both.

The results provide strong evidence that 1-year-old infants actively seek and respond to their caregiver's affective appraisal of novel events. The infants looked to their mothers on 89 percent of the trials. On 45 percent of the trials, the infant reacted to the mother first. On 44 percent of the trials, the infant reacted to the toy first and then to the mother.

Infants averaged 3.7 looks to their mother per trial (SD = 2.8). When the mothers' expressions were unconstrained, the infants looked at them *more* often in the fear condition than in the happy condition (4.1 versus 3.1 gazes per trial). Conversely, when the mothers' expressions were constrained, the infants looked at them *less* often in the fear condition than in the happy condition (3.4 versus 4.0 gazes per trial).

Intensity of maternal expression was greater in the happy than in the fear conditions. During happy trials, intensity was virtually the same for both girls and boys (4.8 and 4.6 gazes per trial for girls and boys, respectively); during fear trials, the mothers' expressions were less intense for girls than for boys. Interestingly, infants who looked first to their mother before reacting to the toy received somewhat less intense reactions from her than infants who reacted first to the toy and then to their mother.

A final result is that infants referenced their mothers most frequently on trials in which the mothers' messages were judged by coders to have the lowest clarity.

The researchers noted that the results of their study support the contention that social referencing is best conceptualized as "an infant's ongoing attempt to apprehend the meaning of a novel object rather than a strategy used primarily when the infant is unable to formulate an independent appraisal. . . . Our findings suggest that infants tend to deploy social referencing persistently, flexibly, and responsively. . . . Most infants referenced their mothers repeatedly on most trials even though, given the relative position of the mother and the object, each look demanded that attention be withdrawn at least momentarily from the object."

In a more recent study, Virginia Slaughter and Danielle McConnell investigated the extent to which gaze following, social referencing, and object-directed imitation—collectively referred to as *joint-attention behaviors*—were related to each other and to vocabulary development in a sample of 60 infants between the ages of 8 and 14 months. Although earlier studies had suggested that these behaviors emerge together, this study found no evidence that infants' capacities to engage in various joint-attention behaviors were developmentally related. This is significant because it bears on the issue of when children first begin to develop a theory of mind. Earlier research indicated that a theory of mind was necessary for the development of all these behaviors. However, the results of this study suggest that a nascent theory of mind is not sufficient for the initial appearance of joint-attention behaviors at the end of the first year of life. Rather, joint-attention behaviors seem to emerge independently, as infants acquire the necessary underlying neurological mechanisms that support them. Clearly, more research is needed before this fascinating issue is resolved. [Note: This article would be very instructive as a reading assignment, along with one of the seminal joint-attention articles (see the following three references), to provoke a good discussion of how developmental theory is often built from failures to replicate, as occurred in this situation.]

Carpenter, M., Nagell, K., & Tomasello, M. (1998). Social cognition, joint attention, and communicative competence from 9 to 15 months of age. *Monographs of the Society for Research in Child Development 63*(4), Serial No. 255.

Rosen, W. D., Adamson, L. B., & Bakeman, R. (1992). An experimental investigation of infant social referencing: Mothers' messages and gender differences. *Developmental Psychology, 28*(6), 1172–1178.

Slaughter, V., & McConnell, D. (2003). Emergence of joint attention: Relationships between gaze following, social referencing, imitation, and naming in infancy. *The Journal of Genetic Psychology, 164*(1), 54–71.

Classroom Activity: Social Referencing in Chimpanzees

As noted in the text, social referencing is the seeking of information from another individual and the use of that information to evaluate an unfamiliar object or event. Thus, social referencing ability includes two defining components: referential looks alternating between another individual and the object or event and behavioral regulation stemming from the information received. Social referencing provides a context for the development of emotional communication and enables children to learn the meaning of objects and social interactions from more experienced individuals. For these reasons, social referencing has obvious adaptive value, saving individuals from the inefficient (and potentially dangerous) trial-and-error learning they would otherwise be forced to use. Given the survival value of social referencing, it is natural to ask whether this phenomenon is uniquely human or also appears in other social animals.

To find out, Connie Russell, Kim Bard, and Lauren Adamson of Georgia State University and Emory University studied 17 young chimpanzees (*Pan troglodytes*) at the Yerkes Regional Primate Research Center. Chimpanzees were chosen because they possess many competencies relevant to social referencing, including gaze modulation, the expression of emotions, and communication about objects. At the start of the study, the chimps ranged in age from 14 months to 41 months (mean = 25 months). The study used a repeated measures design with two conditions. In one condition, a caregiver expressed happy emotions about a novel object; in the other condition, the caregiver expressed fearful emotions.

To begin a trial, the caregiver took the chimpanzee into a familiar nursery room, sat in a predetermined location, and encouraged the chimp to explore. The chimps were allowed to take as much time as needed to become comfortable in the room. In a variation of the Strange Situation, when the chimpanzee left the caregiver's lap, one of four novel objects was brought into the nursery. The novel objects were brightly colored plastic figures approximately 4 inches in height attached to the top of a small remote control device that was "driven" into the room by the experimenter who remained outside. Each chimpanzee experienced four 3-minute trials, two each in the happy and fear conditions. Following a script, the caregiver expressed fear or happiness about the novel object only when the chimpanzee looked toward the caregiver. The caregivers were asked to communicate as they typically would during interactions with the chimpanzee, in order to convey that the object was dangerous for the chimpanzee to approach, or that the chimpanzee could safely and happily approach the object. Verbal expressions of feeling, along with facial expressions of fear or happiness, were encouraged. For example, the caregiver might say "It's a good toy" in an upbeat tone of voice while smiling or "That's scary!" with a low-pitched, negative tone of voice and scowling facial expression. The trials occurred at one-week intervals and were videotaped for later coding.

The chimpanzees' behavior was coded continuously into each of four coding categories: visual attention, approach to caregiver, approach to novel object, and affective displays. Visual attention was coded as (a) directed toward caregiver, (b) directed toward object, or (c) directed toward anything other than the caregiver or object. Approach to the caregiver was coded as (a) approach to the caregiver, (b) contact with the caregiver, or (c) other. Approach to the novel object was coded as (a) approach to the object, (b) contact with the object, (c) withdrawal from the object (defined as active avoidance), or (d) other. The chimpanzee's affective displays were coded as (a) positive, (b) negative, (c) neutral, and (d) unclear.

The chimpanzees' behavior showed both similarities to and differences from the behavior of human infants tested in a similar situation. All 17 of the chimps looked to the caregiver at rates similar to those found in human infants. In addition, as with human infants, social referencing in the chimps increased with age. However, in contrast to human infants, 10 to 20 percent of whom typically did not look at their caregivers, all the chimpanzees looked to the caregiver during every trial. Most important, all the chimpanzees regulated their subsequent behavior toward the novel objects according to the emotional information displayed by their caregivers. The chimpanzees withdrew from novel objects significantly more often when they received a fear message than when they received a happy message.

In a more recent study, these findings were extended to Barbary macaque monkeys (Roberts, McComb, & Ruffman, 2008). The researchers examined looking behaviors in 15 infant macaques and their mothers in the presence of a rubber snake (experimental condition) and in the absence of the snake (control condition). Older infants (aged 5 to 12 months) displayed a higher frequency of looking to their mothers than did younger infants (aged 3 to 4.5 months). Older infants also displayed more social referencing looks during the experimental condition than during the control condition. Younger infants were equally likely to look to their mothers in both conditions. These findings suggest that social referencing is at least as important for young chimpanzees as for human infants.

Roberts, S. G., McComb, K., & Ruffman, T. (2008). An experimental investigation of referential looking in free-ranging Barbary macaques (Macaca sylvanus). *Journal of Comparative Psychology, 122*(1), 94–99.

Russell, C. L., Bard, K. A., & Adamson, L. B. (1997). Social referencing by young chimpanzees *(Pan troglodytes). Journal of Comparative Psychology, 111*(2), 185–193.

AV: Fathers (24 min., Churchill Films)

Three fathers share their joys and concerns as parents. One father is grappling with the rigorous time commitments of his profession and his intense desire to spend more time with his little daughter. A second father who abandoned his wife when his child was very young is now trying to reconstruct a life with the wife he abandoned and his child plus a new baby. He struggles with the problem of being a father without being authoritarian. The film portrays his sincere attempts to change himself in order to better relate to his children. A third man mingles fathering with his professional commitments and is shown discussing issues with a colleague as he diapers his little daughter. The importance of being a good father is well articulated by all three men.

Infant Day Care

AV: Infant Development in the Kibbutz (28 min., Campus Films)

This is the best of three films produced by Joseph and Jeannette Stone and the Institute for Child Mental Health that show young children in a kibbutz. The film focuses on one 6-month-old boy, who sleeps, eats, and plays with his peers in the children's house (his mother comes daily to provide some of his care, and he also visits his family). For the most part, the film succeeds in conveying the message that the development of kibbutzim babies, cognitively and socially, is healthy and normal.

In order to use this movie profitably, you should provide some background. Kibbutzim were originally started by European Jews trying to make a homeland in the desert. In order to survive, women as well as men had to work and bear arms. The most efficient way to prepare meals, defend the kibbutz, and raise children was collectively. In addition, according to Bruno Bettelheim, many of the women felt that not every adult is necessarily good at raising children. It made more sense, they thought, for the most skilled and patient among them to be the caregivers.

When placed in context, this movie stimulates much discussion about the "ideal" way to raise children. Some students, especially those who are the parents of toddlers, will notice and appreciate the devotion and stimulation provided by the *metapalet* (the resident caregiver). New mothers are given advice and encouragement, and the setting seems clean, safe, and filled with interesting toys and language-learning opportunities. Other students will protest at the parents' separation from their children, especially at night. ("Why have them if you don't want to have them?") Finally, fathers are seen as particularly uninvolved in the infants' lives, a fact that the men in your class will probably notice and resent. The film is dated in interesting ways: An increasing number of kibbutzim now have the children stay with their parents at night, and, in general, parents are spending more time with their young children than they did before. The reason for this change is not that the children suffer from round-the-clock collective care but that the parents want more time with their children.

Classroom Activity: Child Care, Home Care, and the Quality of Infant–Caregiver Interaction

The results of a longitudinal study of 1,300 children have fanned the flames of the day-care controversy. The study reported that the more hours a child spends during the first three years of life in nonmaternal care, the less positive the child's interactions with his or her mother.

Using data from the National Institute of Child Health and Human Development (NICHD) Study of Early Child Care, the researchers investigated the relationships among the amount, quality, and stability of child care and mother–child interactions when the children were 6, 15, 24, and 36 months old. Families and their children were recruited from 10 research sites across the United States. Twenty-four percent of the recruited families were members of an ethnic minority.

According to the findings, children who regularly spend time in nonmaternal care have "somewhat less positive" interactions with their mothers than children who spend less or no time in nonmaternal care. Specifically, variation in the number of hours in child care was related to both the mother's behavior toward her children and the children's positive engagement of the mother in their interactions.

However, what is easily lost in these potentially disturbing findings is that although the setting of the care (home/center/relative's home) did not alter the results, the quality of the care did. Higher-quality child care was associated with increased maternal sensitivity. The researchers suggest two possible explanations for the quality of care/quality of interaction relationship: (1) higher-quality care settings may provide mothers with positive role models for involved, sensitive interactions with their children, and (2) greater maternal sensitivity is a function of the effect of the higher-quality child care on the child's emerging verbal skills, behavior compliance, and social competence.

The study is fertile ground for a discussion of several issues in correlational research, especially the role of sample size in tests of statistical significance and the ambiguity of nonexperimental data. For example, because of the huge size of the sample, the NICHD study data allowed researchers to detect fairly small associations between child care and mother–child interaction. As the researchers correctly point out, "The meaningfulness of these effects rests on the extent to which small degrees of difference in maternal sensitivity or the child's engagement with the mother relate to meaningful differences in children's developmental outcomes at these and later ages."

Furthermore, although the negative correlation between hours of care and mother–child interaction don't imply the existence of a causal relationship, the small *positive association* between the quality of care and the mother–child relationship offers some clues. For one, the researchers suggest that the results may be more a product of mothers who use child care than a consequence of the care itself. Specifically, they suggest that mothers who are less sensitive to their infants' needs (or who have children who are less emotionally engaging) may be inclined to use child care for more hours. Alternatively, mothers who are more sensitive may be likely to choose higher-quality care for their children than their less sensitive counterparts.

In support of this type of alternative explanation, researchers have found that family sociodemographic background (education, occupation, and income level) is the most consistent predictor of the amount of nonmaternal care infants receive. Infants who start in nonmaternal child care before the age of 3 months are more likely to come from relatively disadvantaged families (Sylva, Stein, Leach, Barnes, & Malmberg, 2007).

An earlier study produced conflicting findings regarding social interactions in the home between caregivers and infants who regularly attend day-care centers (Lieselotte, Rickert, & Lamb, 2001). The researchers recorded the home behaviors and experiences of 84 German toddlers (12 to 24 months old) who were either enrolled or not enrolled in daily child care from the time they woke up until they went to bed. They found that the total amount of daily caregiver attention the toddlers received was unrelated to whether they spent time in child care. Although the toddlers received less care from the centers, at home their mothers engaged them in more social interactions during nonworking hours than did the mothers of toddlers who were cared for only in the home.

As a follow-up to this discussion, you may wish to schedule a classroom debate on the controversial issue of day care's impact on children, as described in the Classroom Activity below.

Lieselotte, A., Rickert, H., & Lamb, M. E. (2001). Shared caregiving: Comparisons between home and child-care settings. *Developmental Psychology, 36*(3), 339–359.

Sylva, K., Stein, A., Leach, P., Barnes, J., & Malmberg, L. (2007). Family and child factors related to the use of non-maternal infant care. *Early Childhood Research Quarterly, 22*(1), 118-136.

Classroom Activity: Classroom Debate: *"Resolved: Attending Day-Care Centers During the First Three Years of Life Is Psychologically Damaging to Children"*

In recent years, no issue has been more heatedly debated than the impact of infant day care on cognitive and psychosocial development. The volatility of the issue is understandable in the United States, a country in which fully half the families with young children have both parents working.

Concern about day care became almost feverish in 1986 when prominent developmentalist Jay Belsky concluded that extended day care (more than 20 hours per week) beginning in the first year of life is a "risk factor" for the development of insecure infant attachments with parents. Although Belsky's arguments reinforced what many feared to be true about infant day care, his conclusions did not go uncriticized. Much of the criticism centered on the relatively small statistical difference in the proportion of day-care and home-reared infants who were found to be insecurely attached based on Belsky's use of the Strange Situation for measuring attachment.

One positive outcome of the day-care debate has been the increased awareness among legislators and the general public of the need for affordable, high-quality day care for infants. To broaden your students' perspectives on the day-care debate and increase their understanding of the issue's complexity, follow the guidelines in the General Resources section of these resources for scheduling a classroom debate on this resolution.

Classroom Activity: Communal Child Care, Emotional Availability, and Attachment

Developmentalists working from the sociocultural perspective have long been intrigued by the communal nature of child care among Israeli kibbutz children. For example, in the traditional kibbutz, children sleep in a collective arrangement, or *children's house*. Given the well-documented importance of early infant–caregiver relationships to development, researchers have wondered whether this type of arrangement might disrupt the formation of secure attachments.

To find out, researchers at the University of Haifa conducted a series of studies of kibbutz mother–infant dyads. Some mothers allowed their infants to sleep in the children's house at night; others had their children sleep at home. Early reports indicated that sleeping in the children's house was associated with increased rates of insecure attachments to mothers, compared with kibbutz infants who spent their nights at home with their parents. Furthermore, there was no continuity of attachment across generations for mothers of collectively sleeping infants.

More recently, Abraham Sagi-Schwartz and Ora Aviezer investigated associations among infant attachment, mothers' attachment, and emotional availability among 48 full-term, developmentally healthy infants (aged 14 to 22 months) from intact kibbutz families. Of these, 23 mothers used communal sleeping arrangements and 25 used home-based sleeping arrangements.

The infants' attachment to their mothers was observed in the well-known Strange Situation procedure, and the mothers' attachment experiences were evaluated with the Adult Attachment Inventory. In several structured play episodes, the mother–infant dyads were rated on five scales that assessed maternal sensitivity, infant responsivity, and emotional availability.

The results showed, among other things, that sleeping arrangements were unrelated to maternal sensitivity: The vast majority of mothers (93%) were sensitive when interacting with their infants, only a few showed inconsistent sensitivity, and none of the mothers were evaluated as insensitive. However, infants from the collective-sleeping arrangement showed significantly higher rates of insecure-ambivalent attachment than home-sleeping infants. None of the infants were classified as insecure-avoidant. On the other hand, secure infants, whether raised in the collective- or home-sleeping arrangements, were more responsive to and involved with their mothers.

In terms of emotional availability, the associations between infant attachment and maternal dimensions of emotional availability differed in the two child-rearing environments. Only with home-based sleeping arrangements did mothers of secure infants display higher sensitivity and structuring as compared with mothers of insecure infants. In collective sleeping, maternal sensitivity and structuring did not discriminate between dyads with secure and insecure infants.

According to the researchers, the data indicate that connections between emotional availability and attachment may be conditional on the particular "ecological context" of child care, which contributes to the risk or resiliency in the parent–child relationship. Although children who sleep in the children's house may experience sensitive maternal behavior during the day, for some children this may not have been sufficient to convey a secure sense of maternal availability. As the researchers note, "It appears that the impact of maternal inaccessibility during the night had overridden these infants' daytime interactive experiences with adequately sensitive mothers, thus obstructing the natural course of attachment formation."

Sagi-Schwartz, A., & Aviezer, O. (2005). Correlates of attachment to multiple caregivers in Kibbutz children from birth to emerging adulthood: The Haifa longitudinal study. In K. E. Grossman & K. W. Grossman (Eds.), *Attachment from Infancy to Adulthood: The Major Longitudinal Studies*. New York: Guilford Publications.

HANDOUT 1

Developmental Fact or Myth?

T F 1. Infant fear, as expressed in stranger wariness, signals abnormal development.

T F 2. Toddlers' self-awareness results more from praise than from accomplishments.

T F 3. According to Freud, an adult who eats, drinks, chews, bites, or smokes excessively may have been weaned too early.

T F 4. Like Freud, Erikson believed that problems that begin in early infancy can last a lifetime.

T F 5. Although temperament originates with the genes, its expression is modified by experience.

T F 6. Some children are more difficult to raise and harder to live with, in part because of inborn temperamental characteristics.

T F 7. Attachment patterns established in infancy almost never change.

T F 8. Social referencing—searching the expressions of others for emotional cues—becomes very important as infants reach Piaget's stage of active exploration.

T F 9. Infants use their fathers for emotional cues in uncertain situations as much as their mothers.

T F 10. High-quality day care, even during the infant's first year, does not lead to negative developmental outcomes.

HANDOUT 2

Revising a Textbook

In the text Introduction, you read that no moment of life can be fully understood without considering all three developmental domains—biosocial, cognitive, and psychosocial. Human development is conceptualized as holistic. This means that important developments, such as learning to walk, cannot be easily characterized as falling within any single domain. Although learning to walk is a physical, or motor, skill, it greatly affects cognitive development (in allowing increased exploration of the environment) and psychosocial development (in allowing and expressing greater autonomy).

The following exercise is designed to help you see how the three domains of development overlap during the first two years.

Imagine that you are an editor responsible for revising the text assigned to your course. You are attending an editorial committee meeting to plan the chapters covering the first two years.

1. The topic of locomotion, including learning to walk, is currently discussed in the chapter on biosocial development. Another editor suggests moving it to the chapter on psychosocial development. What are the advantages of this idea? Do you agree with this change? Why or why not?

2. The topic of separation anxiety appears in the chapter on psychosocial development. A reviewer suggests moving this topic to the chapter on cognitive development. What are the advantages of this idea? Do you agree with this change? Why or why not?

HANDOUT 2 *(continued)*

3. Perception and vision now appear in the chapter on biosocial development. Your assistant suggests moving these topics to the chapter on cognitive development. What are the advantages of this idea? Do you agree with this change? Why or why not?

HANDOUT 3

Critical Thinking Activity: Early Temperament Style and Later Adjustment Problems

Now that you have read and reviewed the material on psychosocial development during the first two years, take your learning a step further by testing your critical thinking skills on this scientific reasoning exercise.

A study by Caspi and others (1995) revealed that temperamental style in early childhood might be linked to adjustment problems during adolescence. The study involved a cohort of 1,037 children born between April 1, 1972, and March 31, 1973, in Dunedin, New Zealand.

At ages 3, 5, 7, and 9, the behavior of each child was rated in terms of 22 aspects of temperament, including emotional stability, restlessness, self-reliance, persistence, negativism, passivity, shyness, self-confidence, emotional flatness, and 13 other dimensions. To assess behavior problems in the sample, the researchers relied on outcome data from teachers and parents who rated the children at ages 9, 11, 13, and 15 on two widely used behavior problem checklists. These checklists included subscales measuring anxiety/withdrawal, which represents feelings of inferiority and failure; attention problems, which reflect difficulty in concentration skills; conduct disorder, which reflects aggressiveness and alienation; and socialized delinquency, which reflects norm-violating tendencies.

For both boys and girls, lack of control at ages 3 and 5 showed a significant positive correlation with teacher and parent reports of antisocial behavior and conduct disorder at ages 9 and 11. In addition, boys and girls characterized as lacking in control in early childhood were less likely to be rated in adolescence as mature and confident.

The authors suggest several possible explanations for these intriguing results. One is that certain temperamental characteristics in young children are actually early, "subclinical" manifestations of more extreme behavior disorders. Whatever the correct explanation, the results of this extensive study suggest that early temperament may have remarkably specific predictive validity for the development of behavior problems during adolescence.

1. What type of research design is used in this study (e.g., cross-sectional, longitudinal, experimental, correlational, or naturalistic observation)? Is this design appropriate?

2. What explanation do the researchers offer for their findings? Does this explanation make sense based on the evidence?

HANDOUT 3 *(continued)*

3. Given the results of this study, why can't the researchers draw a causal connection between behavior disorders and temperament?

4. Can you think of an alternative explanation for the results of this study?

Caspi, A., Henry, B., McGee, R. O., Moffitt, T. E., & Silva, P. A. (1995). Temperamental origins of child and adolescent behavior problems: From age three to age fifteen. *Child Development, 66*(1), 55–68.

HANDOUT 4

BFI–54

Here are a number of characteristics that may or may not apply to you. For example, do you agree that you are someone who *likes to spend time with others?* Please write a number next to each statement to indicate the extent to which *you agree or disagree with that statement.*

Disagree strongly	Disagree a little	Neither agree nor disagree	Agree a little	Agree strongly
1	2	3	4	5

I see myself as someone who . . .

____ 1. Is talkative
____ 2. Tends to find fault with others
____ 3. Does a thorough job
____ 4. Has a wide range of interests
____ 5. Is depressed, blue
____ 6. Is original, comes up with new ideas
____ 7. Is reserved
____ 8. Is helpful and unselfish with others
____ 9. Prefers the conventional, traditional
____ 10. Can be somewhat careless
____ 11. Is relaxed, handles stress well
____ 12. Is curious about many different things
____ 13. Is full of energy
____ 14. Prefers work that is routine and simple
____ 15. Starts quarrels with others
____ 16. Is a reliable worker
____ 17. Can be tense
____ 18. Is clever, sharp-witted
____ 19. Tends to be quiet
____ 20. Values artistic, aesthetic experiences
____ 21. Tends to be disorganized
____ 22. Is emotionally stable, not easily upset
____ 23. Has an active imagination
____ 24. Perseveres until the task is finished
____ 25. Is sometimes rude to others
____ 26. Has unwavering self-confidence
____ 27. Is inventive
____ 28. Is generally trusting
____ 29. Tends to be lazy
____ 30. Is clear-thinking, intelligent
____ 31. Worries a lot
____ 32. Wants things to be simple and clear-cut
____ 33. Is sometimes shy, inhibited
____ 34. Has a forgiving nature
____ 35. Is idealistic, can be a dreamer
____ 36. Does things efficiently
____ 37. Can be moody
____ 38. Is ingenious, a deep thinker
____ 39. Generates a lot of enthusiasm
____ 40. Can be cold and aloof
____ 41. Enjoys thinking about complicated problems
____ 42. Makes plans and follows through with them
____ 43. Remains calm in tense situations
____ 44. Likes to reflect, play with ideas
____ 45. Is considerate and kind to almost everyone
____ 46. Seeks adventure and excitement
____ 47. Gets nervous easily
____ 48. Is sophisticated in art, music, or literature
____ 49. Has an assertive personality
____ 50. Is insightful, sees different possibilities
____ 51. Likes to cooperate with others
____ 52. Is easily distracted
____ 53. Is outgoing, sociable
____ 54. Has few artistic interests

Source: John, O. P., Donahue, E. M., & Kentle, R. L. (1991). *The "Big Five" Inventory—Versions 4a and 54* (Tech. Report). Berkeley, CA: Institute of Personality Assessment and Research. Reprinted by permission.

HANDOUT 5

Observational Activity: Attachment

To better understand how attachment is measured, arrange to observe a 1- or 2-year-old and his or her primary caregiver in a play setting outside the child's home. Ideally, ask a relative or a friend and his or her child to participate. The play setting could be in your home, at a local playground, or at any other mutually agreeable location. If you do not know someone with a young child, you can complete this observational activity by visiting a playground or day-care center.

Before your scheduled observation period, read the questions on the handout so that you will know what behaviors to watch for. Observe your participants for approximately half an hour of unstructured play. If possible, during the observation period ask the caregiver to make a move as if he or she were going to leave. Observe the child's reaction. After the observation period, complete the following questions and return the response sheet to your instructor.

1. Describe the participants and setting that you chose for observing attachment.

2. Did you encounter any difficulties in completing the observational activity?

3. What signs of attachment did you observe in the child's behavior (e.g., contact-seeking, proximity-seeking)?

HANDOUT 5 *(continued)*

4. What signs of attachment did you observe in the caregiver's behavior (e.g., eye contact, responsiveness to the child's behavior)?

5. If your observation included a move by the caregiver to leave the room or area, describe the child's reactions.

6. Considering your brief observation, would you say that the child you observed was securely attached or insecurely attached, as described in the text? Give examples of the child's behavior that support your conclusion.

HANDOUT 5 *(continued)*

7. What advice would you offer to the parents of an insecurely attached child? To expectant parents hoping to foster secure attachment in their child?

8. Some critics of the Strange Situation believe that it is not a valid measure of attachment for all children. Infants who are regularly placed in day care, for example, may behave differently from home-reared infants because of their prior experiences, not because of differences in attachment. Do you feel, therefore, that this observation is a valid test of attachment? Why or why not? In what other ways could parent–child attachment be measured?

Early Childhood: Biosocial Development

Contents

Note: Worth Publishers provides online Instructor and Student Tool Kits, DVD Student Tool Kits, and Instructor and Student video resources in DevelopmentPortal for use with the text. See Part I: General Resources for information about these materials and the text Lecture Guides for a complete list by text chapter.

Classroom Activity: Using Play Therapy to Correct Balance Difficulties in Children, p. 7

Teaching Tip: The Right Age for Toilet Training, p. 8

Critical Thinking Activity: Designing a Toy, p. 8 (Handout 2, p. 18)

"On Your Own" Activity: Bubbles in the Bowl: Using Developmental Theory to Design Potty Training, p. 10 (Handout 3, p. 19)

Gross Motor Skills

Fine Motor Skills

Classroom Activity: Understanding Children's Art, p. 10

Observational Activity: Fine Motor Skills, p. 10 (Handout 4, p. 21, and Handout 5, p. 23)

Injuries and Abuse

Avoidable Injury

Audiovisual Materials: Secure Your Child's Future, p. 10
Child Care: Outdoor Safety, p. 11

Classroom Activity: Problem-Based Learning: Accident Prevention and Injury Control, p. 11

"On Your Own" Activity: Childhood Accident Record, p. 11 (Handout 6, p. 25)

Child Maltreatment

Audiovisual Materials: Child Abuse, p. 12
Childhood Physical Abuse, p. 12
No More Secrets, p. 13
Psychological Maltreatment of Children: Assault on the Psyche, p. 13
Children of Neglect, p. 13
Damage: The Effects of a Troubled Childhood, p. 13
No One Saved Dennis, p. 13
Childhood Sexual Abuse, p. 13
Toward an Understanding of Child Sexual Abuse, p. 15

Teaching Tip: Cultural Attitudes and Child Abuse, p. 12

Classroom Activities: Factors Underlying Child Abuse, p. 11
African Genital Rites and American Law: Conflict in the Cultural Macrosystem, p. 12
Interpersonal Relationships of Abused Children, p. 13

"On Your Own" Activity: Child Maltreatment in Context, p. 12 (Handout 7, p. 26)

Three Levels of Prevention, Again

Audiovisual Materials: Foster Care, p. 16

Classroom Activity: Targeting Maltreatment Interventions to Fit the Family Context, p. 15

Internet Activity: Child Maltreatment and Vulnerable-to-Crisis Families, p. 16 (Handout 8, p. 28)

Suggested Activities

Introducing Early Childhood: Biosocial Development

"On Your Own" Activity: Developmental Fact or Myth?

Before students read about biosocial development during early childhood, have them respond to the true-false statements in Handout 1.

The correct answers are shown below. Class discussion can focus on the origins of any developmental misconceptions that are demonstrated in the students' incorrect answers.

1. T 2. T 3. T 4. F 5. F 6. T 7. F 8. T 9. F 10. T

Teaching Tip: Using Humor in the Classroom

It has been said that the greatest sin in teaching is to be boring. To avoid that disastrous situation, many instructors believe that occasional, appropriate use of humor in the classroom can increase student attention, promote learning, and create a more open atmosphere that reduces academic anxiety. Classroom humor is not limited to jokes and funny stories; it can include props, anecdotes, riddles, music, video clips, and cartoons. Here are a few tips and guidelines for effectively using humor in the classroom.

Humor Should Not Be Hurtful or Offensive. Humor that furthers teaching is nonhostile. Consideration of what your students may have experienced should help you decide what subject matter lends itself to appropriate humor. Your class may include students who are struggling with eating disorders, who have been in abusive relationships, who have had a loved one unexpectedly die, or who have experienced or are experiencing other major problems. Before using humor, ask yourself, "Will this use of humor alienate or embarrass any of my students?" If the answer is "yes," try a different strategy to get the point across.

Make Humor Relevant. Humor in the classroom works best when it is connected to concepts being studied. Ted Powers offers this example, "If a class is inattentive and an instructor tells a joke like, Did you hear about the termite who walked into the saloon? The first thing he asked was, 'where's the bar tender?' that instructor may have regained the attention of the students, but no learning occurred. On the other hand, if an instructor tells that joke and follows it with a discussion of the role of top-down processing and context in communication (bar tender and bartender sound alike—how do we know when it is two words and when it is one?), then the humor facilitates learning."

Be Yourself. Eddie Murphy would probably not be funny trying to be like Robin Williams. So, too, each instructor needs to find an approach to humor that fits who he or she is. A good way is to use yourself as an example, whenever possible. If you have a funny personal experience that can help explain a concept, tell it. Don't be afraid to be funny, or to make a fool of yourself. Self-disclosure helps create an open atmosphere in the class. It can also promote class discussion from students who avoid asking questions because they fear being embarrassed.

Powers, T. (2005, December). Engaging students with humor. *Association for Psychological Science Observer, 18*(12). www.psychologicalscience.org/teaching/tips.

Teaching Tip: Keeping Students Engaged With Reading Quizzes

Because there is so much information to cover in a life-span development course, your students may actually appreciate having regularly scheduled reading quizzes throughout the term. Regular, announced quizzes are an excellent way to help ensure that student keep up with the class reading. Graded quizzes also motivate students to attend class regularly. Quizzes need not be extensive; even 5 to 10 multiple-choice questions that hit chapter high points can be effective. An easy way to generate these quizzes is by using the end-of-chapter summaries and "What Have You Learned?" questions in the textbook. Another effective strategy is to add one or more bonus questions based on something mentioned in a previous class (for example, a student's question or comment).

AV: The Journey Through the Life Span, Program 4: Early Childhood

Program 4 (24:25) introduces the developing person during early childhood. The first segment of the program, physical development (3:20), begins by outlining the changes in size, weight, and shape that accompany the loss of baby fat. The development of gross motor and fine motor skills is described, focusing on the importance of the underlying processes of brain growth and myelination that enable difficult tasks such as fastening buttons and enjoying arts and crafts.

The second segment, cognitive development (14:00), begins by describing young children's understanding of numbers and the ability to count. Unlike older children, however, young children have not developed effective strategies for remembering. The prompted scripts that adults use to stimulate memory development in young children are depicted. Charles Nelson of the University of Minnesota differentiates the explicit and implicit systems of memory, focusing on the underlying development of the brain's hippocampus and other areas that enable long-term memory. The egocentrism of the typical 4-year-old is depicted as Tom attempts to describe to Jonah, who is in another room, which tools to use to fix their space station. Piaget's conservation task is depicted. Lev Vygotsky's notion of the zone of proximal development is explained. Barbara Rogoff of the University of California, Santa Cruz, discusses the importance of learning in a cultural context by contrasting her findings in studies of guided participation and learning in Mayan children and European American children. The segment concludes by discussing the development of grammar and the fast-mapping of new vocabulary words in young children.

The discussion of language development segues into the third segment of the unit: social development (6:05). Anne Peterson of the Kellogg Foundation differentiates the authoritative, authoritarian, and laissez-faire styles of parenting. The importance of the surrounding environment in determining the appropriateness of different parenting styles is explored as Gina Morelli of Boston College contrasts these parenting styles with those of the Efe people of Africa. The conversation and play behavior of young children are used to demonstrate that, despite the efforts of some adults to de-emphasize gender differences, children still develop some gender stereotypes. The evolution and importance of mastery play, sociodramatic play, rough-and-tumble play, and parallel play are depicted, as are gender differences in the nature of play.

The observation module is divided into four segments, each focused on the importance of play. In the first segment (1:10), three young children, who range from 2 years 4 months to 3 years 2 months of age, are playing with toy trains. The second segment (5:50) illustrates the self-imposed gender segregation of young children playing with dolls, play food, and books. In the third segment (1:30), several children, between 4 and 5 years of age, are seen teasing a boy of similar age. In the fourth segment (1:35), two boys, who are 3½ to 4 years of age, can't agree on an activity.

AV: Transitions Throughout the Life Span, Program 8: Playing and Growing

Program 8 introduces the developing person between the ages of 2 and 6. The program begins by outlining the changes in size and shape that occur from ages 2 through 6. This is followed by a look at brain growth and development and its role in the development of physical and cognitive abilities. The program also addresses the important issues of injury control and accidents, the major cause of childhood death in all but the most disease-ridden or war-torn countries. A description of the acquisition of gross and fine motor skills follows, noting that mastery of such skills develops steadily during the play years along with intellectual growth. The program concludes with an in-depth exploration of child maltreatment, including its prevalence, contributing factors, consequences for future development, treatment, and prevention.

Body Changes

Growth Patterns

AV: Biological Growth: Nature's Child (60 min., Insight Media)

Focusing on the nature–nurture controversy, this program examines the relative influences of genes and environment on intelligence, temperament, and personality.

AV: Physical Development (21 min., CRM/McGraw-Hill)

This film provides an overview of physical growth from infancy to adolescence. Because it includes information about puberty, it could be shown with biosocial development in adolescence; and because it shows how body fat is measured, it is also relevant to biosocial development in middle childhood. However, it is recommended here because it highlights movement education as a way of helping normal children reduce tension and learning-disabled children improve their perceptual-motor skills. The link between movement and perceptual-motor skills may not be as direct as this film indicates, but the theme that physical growth should be accompanied by physical exercise is one almost all developmental psychologists support.

AV: Preschool Physical Development (30 min., Insight Media)

This film examines physical development between ages 3 and 6, including development of the skeletal, circulatory, and nervous systems.

Classroom Activity: The Relationship of Socioeconomic Status to Growth and Cognitive Development

Most of the children of the world live in developing nations and grow up under impoverished conditions that place them at greater risk for impaired biosocial and cognitive development. In 1975, 82 percent (1.2 billion) of all children under age 15 lived in developing countries, while only 18 percent (275 million) lived in more developed countries. These statistics are still true today; in fact, the number of children in developing countries may be even higher because of the high birth rates (World Bank, 2010). Children in developing countries are more likely to suffer malnutrition, disease, and insufficient cognitive stimulation, which detracts from optimal intellectual growth (Narayan & Petesch, 2007).

Since the early 1960s, several teams of researchers have been conducting longitudinal studies of the biosocial and cognitive development of high, low, and middle socioeconomic status (SES) children in Guatemala. Biosocial development is assessed by measuring three variables: height, weight, and skeletal age. Height reflects genetic history, as well as long-term nutrition and health care. Weight is considered a measure of more recent growth, reflecting current nutrition and health care. Skeletal age, which is measured by bone X-rays, is an index of physical maturity and is used to predict a child's potential for further growth. Cognitive development is typically assessed by comparing a child's scores on standardized tests of reading ability and general intelligence with developmental norms for the child's chronological age.

Researchers have consistently found that low-SES children have delayed biosocial growth, as compared with middle- and high-SES children. In addition, biosocial development has been found to be positively correlated with cognitive development in young children in developing countries, so that where there is delayed growth, there is slower cognitive development.

Previously, researchers had not examined whether the relationship between growth and cognitive development continues during the school years. Nor had they attempted to control for SES when comparing the cognitive status of small-for-age and normal-for-age children. These are important issues, for if the relationship between delayed growth and cognitive development persists, small-for-age children may be cognitively handicapped throughout their lives.

To address these issues, Barry Bogin and Robert MacVean studied a sample of 144 Guatemalan children: 46 of low SES, 52 of middle SES, and 46 of high SES. Height, weight, skeletal age, reading ability, and general intelligence were measured annually as the children progressed from grades 1 through 6. As in previous studies, low- and middle-SES boys and girls showed significantly delayed growth, as compared with high-SES children. However, when SES was statistically controlled, *there was no significant correlation between biosocial growth and cognitive status*.

Because large numbers of school-age children in developing nations are small for their chronological age, Bogin and MacVean's findings are highly significant. The scientists conclude that low- and middle-SES children often suffer from undernutrition that delays their biosocial development during the preschool years. Although delayed growth may persist during the years of primary schooling, the delays in cognitive development that were apparent in the preschool years may be ameliorated by education.

Bogin, B., & MacVean, R. (2003). Anthropometric variation and health: A biocultural model of human growth. *Journal of Children's Health, 1*(2), 149–172.

Narayan, D., & Petesch, P. (2007). *Moving out of poverty: Cross-disciplinary perspectives.* Washington, DC: The World Bank and Palgrave McMillan.

World Bank. (2010). *PovertyNet Home.* Retrieved December 30, 2010, from www.worldbank.org/poverty/data/trends.

Nutrition

Classroom Activity: Correcting the "Big Five" Nutritional Deficiencies in Young Children

As the text indicates, most children in developed nations are well fed. However, that doesn't mean that they are eating the right foods. In the United States, only about one-fourth of toddlers and young children eat a balanced diet, according to the U.S. Department of Agriculture. "When children stop having breast milk and jarred baby foods, their parents tend not to replace these foods with regular servings of milk, fruits, and vegetables," says Shirley Watkins, undersecretary of Food, Nutrition, and Consumer Services (cited in Vander Schaaf, 2000). One current view is that the most common nutrient deficiencies among school kids are vitamin D, calcium, fiber, and potassium (WebMD, 2011). Other sources also mention magnesium, vitamin E, and iron. Following are WebMD's recommendations:

> Vitamin D: The American Academy of Pediatrics (AAP) recommends getting at least 400 international units (IU) of vitamin D per day. The body makes vitamin D when exposed to strong sunlight, storing extra for future use. Common foods rich in vitamin D include most milk and other fortified foods, such as some brands of breakfast cereals, orange juice, and yogurt. Other foods rich in vitamin D include fattier fish, such as salmon and light tuna. Supplements are another source of vitamin D.
>
> Calcium: The IOM's daily calcium recommendations for children: ages 1-3: 500 milligrams; ages 4-8: 800 milligrams; ages 9-18: 1,300 milligrams. You get 300 milligrams of calcium from 8 ounces of any type of milk (including lactose-free) or yogurt, or from 1.5 ounces of hard cheese (such as cheddar). Orange juice with added calcium and vitamin D is a calcium-rich, but dairy-free, option. Children who don't get enough dairy or fortified choices may need a calcium supplement.
>
> Fiber: How much fiber to get depends on the child's age, according to the AAP. Figure your child's daily fiber quota in grams by adding five to his age. For example, a 5-year-old should get 10 grams of daily dietary fiber. Boost your family's fiber intake by serving a fruit or vegetable (or both) with meals and snacks. Opt for whole-grain breads and cereals, pasta, and other grains. Also, try to include legumes, including chickpeas, lentils, and white beans in salads, soups, and omelets. Coincidentally, many of these same foods provide potassium and magnesium, too.
>
> Potassium: Daily potassium recommendations for children: ages 1-3: 3,000 milligrams; ages 4-8: 3,800 milligrams; ages 9-13: 4,500 milligrams; ages 14-18: 4,700 milligrams. Besides fruits and vegetables, dairy foods, meats, and seafood are also good potassium sources. For a child to get enough potassium, at least one fruit or vegetable should be served at every meal and snack and the child should eat a balanced diet.

Vander Schaaf, R. (2000, February). The best nutrients for your child. *Parenting, 14*(1), 173.

WebMD. (2011). 4 nutrients your child may be missing. Retrieved February 17, 2011, from www.webmd.com/diet/guide/4-nutrients-your-child-may-be-missing?page=3.

Hazards of "Just Right"

Brain Development

AV: The Development of the Human Brain (40 min., Films for the Humanities and Sciences)

(See description in The First Two Years: Biosocial Development.)

AV: The Brain (23 min., Films for the Humanities and Sciences)

This program describes research on how the brain functions as the center of thinking, learning, memory, emotions, and speech. It presents a particularly effective depiction of how nerve impulses are transmitted and how chemical neurotransmitters enable communication within the brain. It concludes with an examination of the latest techniques for exploring the structure and function of the brain.

Classroom Activity: Right and Left Brain Specialization

To help students understand the specialization of the two sides of the brain and the fact that both sides participate in most tasks, you might try a simple classroom project suggested by Ernest Kemble and his colleagues. The exercise requires students to balance a wooden dowel first on the index finger of the right hand and then the left, while performing a verbal task or while remaining silent. Specialization should make balancing the dowel with the right hand (directed by the left side of the brain) more difficult when the subject is engaged in a verbal task. Conversely, balancing the dowel with the left hand (directed by the right, nonlinguistic side of the brain) should not be disrupted by the verbal activity.

In Kemble's experiment, students were first permitted a few minutes' practice with the dowel. Then they underwent eight test trials (four with each hand) in which the experimenter timed the interval between the "start" command and dropping of the dowel. Half the trials with each hand were conducted in silence, the other half while the student performed a simple verbal distraction task, such as reciting the alphabet or engaging in a "spelling bee." Mean balancing times were computed for each condition.

Kemble's results indicated that the verbal task disrupted balance in both hands, although the impairment was greater for the right hand. These results demonstrate that although the left side of the brain may be more important than the right in verbal tasks, both sides participate.

Kemble, E., Filipi, T., & Graylin, L. (1985). Some simple classroom experiments on cerebral lateralization. *Teaching of Psychology*, *12*(2), 81–83.

Classroom Activity: An Epigenetic Model of Emotional Regulation

According to Allan Schore of the UCLA School of Medicine, a major conclusion of the last few decades of infant cognitive neuroscience research is that the developing brain is epigenetically designed to be molded by the emotional environment it encounters. In other words, babies' brains develop according to a genetic timetable that must be activated by early experiences, especially interactions with caregivers.

The developing brain undergoes a growth spurt that begins in the third trimester and extends to about 124 months of age. As noted in the text, the growth spurt involves the development of the limbic system, which plays a vital role in social cognition, attachment, and emotional regulation. During the growth spurt, there is an overproduction of synaptic connections, many of which are discarded through a process of pruning that ultimately selects synaptic connections that best match incoming environmental information. Through this synaptic pruning, the structural and functional development of the brain adapts to environmental experiences.

Schore describes an extensive body of research supporting the idea that early development of the brain's right prefrontal cortex plays a critical role in attachment and the individual's lifelong pattern of emotionality. Beginning with his conceptualization of the limbic system as the brain area specialized for adapting to rapidly changing environments, Schore notes that the right prefrontal cortex has extensive connections into the limbic system and the autonomic (involuntary) nervous system. This makes it function somewhat as an executive control center for the developing person's stress response and coping behaviors.

During the first two to three years of life, Schore maintains, centers in the right prefrontal cortex respond to interactions with the primary caregiver, as he or she guides the infant's emotional development. Putting a neurobiological spin on the importance of synchronicity, Schore cites evidence that interactive mutual gazes between caregiver and infant release high levels of endogenous opiates (endorphins) in the child's brain. This synchronicity "acts as a template, as it permanently molds the individual's capacities to enter into all later emotional relationships."

In Schore's model of emotional regulation, infant mental health is viewed as the earliest expression of flexible strategies for coping with the novelty and stress inherent in everyday life. When the right prefrontal cortex is well-developed, adaptive, and flexible, it provides the person with the resilience needed for optimal development over the later stages of the life cycle.

Bradshaw, G. A., & Schore, A. N. (2007). Developmental neuroethology attachment and social context. *Ethology, 113*(5), 426–436.

Schore, A. N. (2003). *Affect regulation and the repair of the self.* New York: Norton.

Classroom Activity: Self-Regulation, the Prefrontal Cortex, and School Readiness

To supplement the text discussion of the important role that development of the prefrontal cortex plays in emotional regulation and in relation to Allan Schore's findings (discussed in the preceding classroom activity), you might describe research showing that self-regulatory skills underlie many of the behaviors and abilities that are associated with success in adjusting to school. For decades, researchers have considered intelligence to be a key predictor of success in school, but indicators of self-regulation ability may be equally powerful predictors. Children who are less distractible and who display more positive and moderate levels of emotional intensity are rated by their teachers as being more teachable and do, in fact, achieve greater academic success than do children without these self-regulatory skills.

Data from the National Center for Education Statistics survey of kindergarten teachers' ratings of characteristics considered essential or very important for kindergarten readiness indicate that teachers are deeply concerned with regulatory aspects of children's behavior (ECLS, 2008). More specifically, 84 percent of teachers stated that children need to be able to communicate wants, needs, and thoughts verbally; 76 percent felt that children need to be enthusiastic and curious; and 60 percent said that children need to be able to follow directions, not be disruptive of the class, and be sensitive to other children's feelings. In contrast, only 21 percent of teachers felt that the ability to use a pencil or paintbrush was essential; and only 10 percent and 7 percent, respectively, stated that knowing several letters of the alphabet and being able to count to 20 was essential or very important for kindergarten readiness.

Emotional reactivity and self-regulation in young children have been linked to individual variation in physiological reactivity. For example, among children characterized as inhibited (overcontrolled), novel stimuli have been associated with a high level of arousal in the limbic system, particularly in the brain's amygdala, a key structure associated with emotion. Such children have a low threshold for limbic arousal, and this arousal results in negative emotional expression, activation of the sympathetic nervous system, and ultimately withdrawal from stimulation in an attempt to self-regulate their state of arousal. High limbic arousal, social withdrawal, and sympathetic activation are all associated with a particular pattern of neural activity in the prefrontal cortex, the center of the so-called executive functions of the brain.

Early Childhood Longitudinal Study (ECLS). (2008). *Early childhood longitudinal program*. U.S. Department of Education. National Center for Education Statistics. Retrieved September 20, 2008, from http://nces.ed.gov/ecls/kindergarten.asp)

Improved Motor Skills

AV: Preschoolers: Physical and Cognitive Development (30 min., Magna Systems)

This film explores the three domains of development of the child between the ages of 3 and 6 years. The chubby toddler becomes the leaner young child whose improved motor coordination enables a variety of new activities. Perceptual development, preschool thinking, and language development are also examined.

Classroom Activity: Using Play Therapy to Correct Balance Difficulties in Children

Children maintain balance, or postural control, through a dynamic integration of internal forces and environmental feedback. They are most likely to lose their balance—and fall—when they do not maintain their center of gravity (COG) within stability limits. The child recognizes these limits through the somatosensory, vestibular, and visual senses, which provide information about current position and any adjustments needed. Once the central nervous system (CNS) receives sensory information, the information is processed, checked, and used to plan a strategy to correct for any postural imbalances.

Two key components of the CNS are involved in maintaining balance: the motor cortex and the cerebellum. The motor cortex organizes the incoming sensory information regarding balance and sends it via the peripheral nervous system to motor nerves that stimulate the proper muscles to contract, allowing the person to maintain balance. The cerebellum coordinates skeletal muscle planning. Working closely with the cerebral cortex, the cerebellum promotes muscle synergy, functioning subconsciously to make movement smooth, coordinated, and efficient.

When the cerebellum is diseased, damaged, or for other reasons malfunctioning, the person has difficulty making smooth, coordinated movements. Common characteristics and symptoms include tremors and disturbances in gait, posture, and balance. Traditional physical therapy, including balance training protocols and visual biofeedback, are often used to treat adults with cerebellar disorders. Treatment of children, however, poses special challenges.

One study investigated the effectiveness of play therapy as a treatment for young children suffering from balance problems caused by cerebellar damage. Child A participated in weekly play therapy sessions that emphasized improvement of balance, coordination, and collateral movement patterns. Among the play activities were hopscotch, marching, balance beam activities, cycling, and various isometric exercises to promote trunk stability. As a comparison, child B was recruited from the community and had no known balance, sensory, or orthopedic disorders.

During each testing session, both children were asked to perform a series of three balance tests on a force platform (a flat board with positional sensors that can measure wobble while a person is standing on it), including a two-legged stance, a left leg only stance, and a right leg only test. Force data were collected using a computer connected to the balance platform. Every five weeks (to reduce the effects of learning, which might occur in a shorter period), the children went through a testing session.

Over the course of the three sessions, child A showed a significant decrease in body sway, indicating an increased ability to maintain COG over the stability limits. This improved balance was observed with all three stance conditions. In contrast, child B exhibited no statistical differences in fore/aft sway, media/lateral sway, or total sway. The results of this study suggest that play therapy may be beneficial in the treatment of balance disorders in children. By viewing balance as a motor skill, play-based practice, experience, and feedback can be used to improve postural control in a child-oriented treatment environment that is fun.

If your students are interested in learning more about the nature of play therapy, the following information might form the basis of a mini-lecture. This form of therapy is based on two fundamental principles:

- Young children lack the cognitive maturity to benefit from talking through their problems, as takes place in most conventional forms of psychotherapy.
- Activities organized and controlled by adults do not give children the feeling of empowerment they experience in their voluntary play. In a play therapy session, children are in charge. There they create a world where they can practice social skills, overcome fears, and symbolically triumph over upsets and concerns that are threatening their sense of well-being.

A trained play therapist strives to help the child express his or her needs and discover solutions in a safe, therapeutic environment, typically a specially designed and decorated room that is furnished with the toys and equipment children need to use as tools for the dramatic scenes they direct with the therapist. Parents are important allies in the play therapy process and meet regularly with the play therapist to share important observations and support their child's therapy.

The efficacy of play therapy has become so widely accepted that many schools of education offer a graduate certificate in this specialized field. Johns Hopkins, for example, notes that "Play therapy has been applied as part of responsive services within comprehensive, developmental elementary and middle school counseling programs to facilitate self-esteem, increase self-efficacy, and decrease maladaptive behaviors to remove barriers for success in social, career, and emotional spheres." Play therapy is also used in many clinical community settings and with private practice clinicians as the preferred, developmentally appropriate treatment modality when working with young children and their families affected by parental divorce, ADHD, bereavement, trauma, and other diverse psychosocial and psychological issues that negatively affect psychosocial functioning.

Aufsesser, P. (1999, Winter). Use of play therapy in the treatment of balance disorders. *Palaestra, 15*(1), 16, 59.

Johns Hopkins University School of Education. (2008). *Play Therapy.* Retrieved September 20, 2008, from http://education.jhu.edu/counseling/counseling-certificates/playtherapy/

Topham, G. L. (2003). Innovations in play therapy: Issues, process and special populations. *Journal of Marital and Family Therapy, 29*(3), 430.

*Critical Thinking Activity: Designing a Toy**

Each unit of these resources contains a critical thinking exercise designed specifically to test students' critical thinking about a topic covered in the text. Handout 2 contains a specific task followed by a series of questions.

The answer to this unit's critical thinking activity follows:

The most significant aspect of biosocial development during early childhood is the continued maturation of the nervous system and the refinement of the visual, muscular, and cognitive skills that will be necessary for children to function in school. Appropriate toys for 2- to 6-year-old children would therefore stimulate the senses, help children to master new physical or intellectual skills, or simply provide for healthy physical exercise. Toys that encourage social play (such as some kind of ball) are also good, as long as the designer considers the limited social skills of the child.

In evaluating your toy, consider the following criteria: safety features (absence of sharp edges, appropriate size, weight, and sturdiness, no pieces small enough to choke on and nothing that might pinch, poke, or bruise the child or a playmate); sensory stimulation (visual, auditory, tactile, or olfactory properties); and developmental appropriateness (cognitive and motor skill readiness of the intended age group).

*Based on an idea from Neysmith-Roy, J. M. (1994). Constructing toys to integrate knowledge about child development. *Teaching of Psychology, 21*(2), 101–103

Teaching Tip: The Right Age for Toilet Training

A sure-fire topic for grabbing student attention in discussing children's motor control as well as their self-control is the following: What is the right age to start toilet training? Before posing this question to your students, you might summarize a large-scale study of toilet training conducted by pediatrician Bruce Taubman (1997). Taubman's study of 482 children in suburban Philadelphia is one of the first systematic investigations of toilet training since the 1960s. Among his findings:

- The average age at which parents introduced toilet training was 23 months.
- On average, boys trained somewhat later than girls.
- There was no relationship between when a child was trained and the mother's work status, the presence of siblings, or whether the child was in day care.

- About 13 percent of the children had trouble with toilet training. The vast majority of these were able to resolve their problem without special intervention.

If your class consists primarily of traditional, college-age students, chances are that parents schooled by parenting experts T. Berry Brazelton and Benjamin Spock raised most of them (cited on parenttime.com). In the last round of the toilet-training wars, these spokesmen for parents of the 1960s through the 1990s advocated a flexible toilet-training approach in the belief that parents who force toilet training can cause lasting problems in their children. "Don't rush your toddler into toilet training or let anyone else tell you it's time," said Brazelton in a television commercial for Size 6 Pampers (intended for children 35 pounds and up!). "It's got to be his choice."

As a result of this philosophy, the age at which toddlers shed their diapers has steadily increased over the past several decades. In 1957, for example, 92 percent of children were toilet trained by the age of 18 months. By 1998, that figure had dropped to less than 25 percent. Rightly so, according to experts at the University of Michigan Health System, who say that most children are ready to "begin the process between 24 to 27 months."

Another possible backlash of the permissive training policies of past decades comes from reports of pediatricians, who have noted an increase in the number of medical referrals of older children for a variety of elimination problems. Among these are withholding of urine and stool, chronic constipation, and daytime and nighttime urinary control.

Trends such as these horrify psychologist John Rosemond, syndicated columnist and author of a number of best-selling parenting books, who considers it "a slap to the intelligence of a human being that one would allow him to continue soiling and wetting himself past age 2" (cited on www.parenttime.com). Toilet training, argues Rosemond, should be no more complicated than housebreaking a new puppy.

Rosemond faults "wishy-washy" parents for delayed toilet training, and points his finger at Brazelton, who in the 1960s pioneered the "child-centered" parenting approach that lets children decide when to shed their diapers. And Rosemond believes that the problems of this philosophy may extend beyond toilet-training difficulties into disciplinary problems, when parents are slow to make the transition to "authority figure." "In a nutshell, my philosophy on toilet training is that it ought to be done between 18 and 24 months, that it's relatively easy, that we are making entirely too big a deal of it in our culture today," he says.

For his part, Brazelton attributes the increase in toilet-training problems to *escalating demands* placed on children today, rather than on fewer pressures. In his view, these pressures stem from the requirement of many day-care centers that children be toilet trained before they can be enrolled. As a result, panicky, working parents may lean too hard on their offspring. "Parents are feeling very guilty and people like Rosemond are making them feel more guilty, not less," Brazelton notes. "And the child's only recourse is to withhold urine or stool in protest."

Brazelton's advice is that parents buy a potty chair and show children what is expected of them at about age 2, but not to expect the child to become potty trained in a few days, or that every child will progress at the same rate. "If your child is afraid of the potty chair, don't put pressure on him to use it. Put toilet training aside for a month or two and give your child time to get used to the idea of the potty and to be comfortable with it," he recommends in a parenting guide on the Pampers Parenting Institute Web site. "Be patient and positive," he continues. "As with any new skill, your child will master toilet training in time."

In contrast, Rosemond's "Naked and $75" program advises parents to stay home from work with their child for a few days and allow the child to walk around naked all day long. The potty is placed where the child spends most of his or her time, and moved when necessary. Parents are urged to periodically remind the child to use the potty when needed. "Children at this age do not like urine and feces running down their legs," he notes. "When they have an accident, they stop and start to howl, and the mother comes along and says, 'Well, you forgot to use the toilet.' She puts him on the toilet, wipes him off, and speaks reassuringly to him. And within three days, or five days, he's doing it on his own." What's the $75 for, you ask? Carpet cleaning!

Taubman believes that training a child by age 2 can be done, but only with a tremendous effort. He suspects that there may be something akin to a sensitive period in development, near the age of 2 or 2½, when "kids really want their parents to get excited if they poop." If this window of opportunity is missed, training is likely to take much longer. He also believes that early toilet training was a phenomenon of another time, when children were more likely to stay at home with their mothers full time.

To check out the conflicting opinions of Brazelton and Rosemond, Google their names and you'll find a host of discussions about their views on toilet training. If you want to receive Rosemond's weekly column on paarenting, go to www.rosemond.com.

The American Academy of Pediatrics published an authoritative guide that addresses every phase of the toilet-training process (Wolraich & Tippins, 2003). Topics covered include:

- Recognizing when your child is ready
- How to choose and install a potty
- What to do when a child resists
- Positive responses to the inevitable "accidents"
- Handling constipation and other common problems

- Toilet training for children with special needs
- Special tips for boys, girls, and twins
- Coping with bed-wetting and soiling

Goode, E. (1999, January 12). Pediatricians renew battle over toilet training. *New York Times* Online. Retrieved October 23, 2008 from www.nytimes.com.

How do I know when my child is ready to start toilet training? (2008). University of Michigan Health System. Retrieved October 23, 2008 from www.med.umich.edu/1libr/yourchild/toilet.htm.

Rosemond, J. (2001). *New parent power*. Kansas City, MO: Andrews McMeel Publishing.

Rosemond, J. (2009, May 19). Parenting by John Rosemond: Keep it simple when toilet training your toddler. Retrieved February 5, 2010, from www.projo.com/lifebeat/content/lb-Parenting19_05-19-09_HTEBM68_v9.294c416.html.

Rowland, H. (1999, January 13). *Now or later? Debate over toilet training goes on.* CNN Interactive. www.CNN.com/ interactive.

Taubman, B. (1997). Toilet training and toilet refusal for stool only: Prospective study. *Pediatrics, 99*(1), 54–55.

Wolraich, M. L., & Tippins, S. (2003). *Guide to toilet training*. Washington, DC: American Academy of Pediatrics.

"On Your Own" Activity: Bubbles in the Bowl: Using Developmental Theory to Design Potty Training

To help your students apply developmental theory to practical issues in biosocial development, ask them to design a potty training plan derived from each theory of development, using Handout 3 as a guideline. A behaviorist, for instance, might note that a good way to toilet train children is to make the process entertaining and rewarding, perhaps by occasionally pouring colored shampoo into the bowl. Urinating into the bowl will be positively reinforced by the colorful bubbles that result.

Students may find it more difficult to design practical training plans based on some theories (e.g., psychoanalytic) than others. This fact by itself is worth discussing, as it will naturally lead to a consideration of what makes a good theory, the relationship of "testability" to "usefulness," and so forth. For a stimulating (and likely humorous) class discussion, ask for volunteers who are willing to share one or two of their "best" training plans.

Gross Motor Skills

Fine Motor Skills

Observational Activity: Fine Motor Skills

Fine motor skills, involving the muscles that control the extremities, are much harder for young children to master than are gross motor skills. This is because the muscles near the trunk (proximal), which control gross motor skills, mature sooner than those that control the extremities (distal). Fine motor skills also develop later because myelination of the central nervous system is incomplete during the preschool years.

Although infants and toddlers use their hands and fingers extensively, these early movements are *involuntary, reflexive responses* that are innate. Not until control of hand and finger movements shifts from lower neural centers in the brainstem to higher cortical regions does the child gain *voluntary control* over movements. Although there are wide variations in the age of neuromuscular "readiness," once voluntary control begins to emerge, practice of fine motor skills can be beneficial.

To increase students' understanding of the difficulties young children experience in mastering fine motor skills, have them make arrangements to "test" a child between 2 and 6 years old. Suggest that they assess a younger brother, sister, nephew, or niece. Alternatively, they might find a friend with a young child, or arrange to work with a child at the campus child development center. Handout 4 provides a checklist for students, and Handout 5 is a follow-up questionnaire.

Remind students that they should make the assessment a fun, playful activity for the child and that each child has his or her own developmental timetable that may be somewhat behind, or ahead of, developmental norms for that age.

Classroom Activity: Understanding Children's Art

To enhance your students' understanding of children's art, you might use samples from the local nursery school. Especially interesting would be crayon drawings by children between the ages of 3½ and 5, when the switch to representational or pictorial art occurs. Ask the nursery-school teacher to write the *exact* age of the child on the back of each sample (noting, when appropriate, if the child has any exceptional qualities, such as a disability or unusual social maturity). Show the drawings to your class. Chances are that your students will be able to tell which drawings are made by the younger children in the sample and which are by the older children. This exercise should help students see, in concrete form, the cognitive development of children, as represented in an important communication medium.

Injuries and Abuse

Avoidable Injury

AV: Secure Your Child's Future (14 min., IFB)

This straightforward film emphasizes the importance of safety seats and seatbelts for young car passengers. The class discussion could begin with the statistics. Then you could ask: Why do few states in the United States, and few parents, require their children to use seatbelts? Alternatively, why do some U.S. states, Canadian provinces, and a minority of parents require them? Ideally, a student who is a parent will volunteer the practical problems of trying to keep children safe at all times, and the class will suggest solutions. The discussion should include recognition of the role of the macro-, exo-, and microsystems, as well as the role of developmental psychology, in helping keep children safe.

AV: Child Care: Outdoor Safety (3 films, each 16–19 minutes in duration, Insight Media)

Although primarily intended as vehicles for parent and teacher training, each film illustrates numerous specific aspects of biosocial development and highlights the importance of outdoor safety in preventing accidents—the leading cause of childhood death. *Setting Up the Rules* discusses the importance of outdoor play for childhood development and identifies many common dangers presented by the outdoors. *The Playground* discusses specific dangers of common playground equipment. *Kids on the Go* explores various safety issues during field trips.

"On Your Own" Activity: Childhood Accident Record

To help your students think about childhood accidents and how they might be prevented, ask them to complete an accident record for themselves or someone in their family (see Handout 6).

Students may find it difficult to remember exactly when accidents occurred. However, the majority of accidents probably occurred in early or middle childhood. In discussing how accidents might be prevented, students should be encouraged to specify ways in which society can make the environment safer for young children.

Classroom Activity: Problem-Based Learning: Accident Prevention and Injury Control

The Introduction's Classroom Activity: Introducing Problem-Based Learning describes this relatively new pedagogical tool. Following is a sample problem that you might want to give to your students as part of your coverage of biosocial development during early childhood:

> After reading in her textbook that in developed nations more children die of violence—either accidental or deliberate—than from any other cause, Lashonda worries about her 3-year-old nephew's safety.
>
> Before you leave class today, your group must address the following questions: First, from what you have learned about accident prevention and injury control, why do public health experts prefer the latter term? Second, after your group agrees on an answer to the first question, determine some resulting learning issues that need to be researched to answer the question, "How safe is Lashonda's nephew?" Among other issues, these should focus on the three levels of prevention that apply to every childhood health and safety issue.
>
> Based on the decisions your group makes today, you should devise a plan for researching the various issues. Two weeks from today's class, your group will present an answer for Lashonda based on the issues you think are relevant.

Child Maltreatment

Classroom Activity: Factors Underlying Child Abuse

To prevent students from adopting a one-sided view of abusive or neglectful parents, you might look for ways to help them empathize with such parents. The extent to which each of us is responsible for what we do is a complicated psychological and philosophical issue—and not one you are likely to resolve in one class session. However, the tendency to blame parents, especially mothers, for everything that happens to their children is one cause of child abuse—in part because mothers feel greatly judged and very little supported where mistakes in raising children are concerned. From studies of abusive parents we know that one problem is that some parents expect perfection from themselves as well as from their children. When they don't see it, they feel guilty, harassed, and pressured, and finally they lash out. For this reason, it is probably advisable to emphasize the many social factors that underlie abuse. Unemployment, alcohol, lack of safe places for children to play, lack of good day-care facilities, lack of education, teenage pregnancy—all are correlates of abuse, and all are social problems that could be alleviated, at least to some extent, by the social network that includes each of us.

It is also a good idea to discuss actual ways in which a child might make a parent furious and to provide suggestions for coping with this behavior without harming the child. Your firsthand experiences and those of your students or colleagues who have children will most likely be more convincing than the following secondhand accounts, but here are two examples I use with my classes (both written by Kathleen Berger for an earlier edition of these resources).

> My eldest daughter, Bethany, used to cry almost every afternoon when she was about 2 months old. Feeding her, changing her, and playing with her didn't help, and I got tired of picking her up and rocking her to sleep only to have her wake up and cry as soon as I put her down. I thought of just letting her cry herself to sleep, but I felt guilty about that; I had read that "good" mothers didn't do that.
>
> A friend suggested a solution: Put her into her crib, close the door (this made the sound of her crying less annoying), and set the kitchen timer for 10 minutes. If she hadn't stopped crying when the timer rang, I should pick her up.
>
> This suggestion worked well. First, while the timer was on I could relax, because I felt I was doing something to help her: I was seeing whether she was overtired and needed some distance from me in order to go to sleep; about half the time she did go to sleep. Second, when the 10 minutes were up, I had had enough of a break to try again to comfort her.
>
> The second example involves my two oldest children when they were toddlers. One rainy Saturday afternoon, in the midst of the many little demands and quarrels

> that come naturally to a pair of toddlers, one of them asked for orange juice, which I got from the refrigerator. But the juice bottle was wet, and, naturally, it slipped from my hand and broke all over the kitchen floor. In that moment I yelled at the children so angrily that they both cried. I realized then that had I been more familiar with physical punishment, I well might have hit them—out of frustration with myself. (The solution was to hug them both, fix a bubble bath with lots of bath toys for them—at that age at any rate, they always loved to take a bath—and then, when we were finished, mop up the mess.)

AV: Child Abuse (19 min., Films for the Humanities and Sciences)

This film explores sexually and physically abused children through the experiences of a therapist and clinical social worker who deal with sex offenders and their victims. It makes the important point that the child's social interaction is often an important clue to what has happened behind closed doors.

AV: Childhood Physical Abuse (26 min., Films for the Humanities and Sciences)

This program explores a range of issues concerning the physical abuse of children, including the kinds of adults who are likely to abuse their children, the effects of abuse on children, and how abusive parents can break the cycle of their behavior.

"On Your Own" Activity: Child Maltreatment in Context

To help your students think about child maltreatment in context, ask them to respond to the questions in Handout 7.

This activity will help increase your students' awareness of the pervasive forces that contribute to child maltreatment. For a stimulating class discussion, ask for volunteers who are willing to share their answers to questions 3 and 4.

Teaching Tip: Cultural Attitudes and Child Abuse

To reinforce the idea that cultural attitudes about physical punishment affect the frequency and intensity of child abuse, you might have your students exchange their views on the subject. One way to begin the discussion is to ask for a definition of child abuse that differentiates "discipline" from "abuse." Depending on the background of your students, you might find that such questions as "Should you ever hit a child?" or "What would you do if you found your child playing with matches?" elicit considerable controversy.

Nonphysical abuse might also be explored with such questions as "Would you send a child to bed without any dessert? Without any dinner?" "Would you tell a child to go to his or her room for 10 minutes? An hour? A day?" "Would you tell a child he or she is selfish? Stupid? Stubborn? Tricky?"

Another interesting issue to explore is the father–mother relationship with regard to disciplining children. Ask your students whether both parents should play the same role and follow the same rules. Should mothers ever say, "Just wait till your father gets home"? Should fathers ever say, "Why can't you teach that child how to behave?" What do they think a parent should do if he or she feels that the other parent is too lax, too strict, or too heavy-handed in discipline?

Classroom Activity: African Genital Rites and American Law: Conflict in the Cultural Macrosystem

The text notes that definitions of child maltreatment vary with cultural norms. In some instances, these norms encourage physical rites of passage that, to other cultures, are simply sickening. To proponents, however, these rites remain sacred rituals that strengthen children's character.

One of the most vivid examples of a rite of passage that has received considerable attention in the media is "female circumcision," or genital mutilation. To stimulate critical thinking in your students about the role of the cultural macrosystem in child maltreatment, you might introduce this troubling topic with the following case study. If you wish to devote an entire lecture to this topic, you may choose to assign the article on which this case is based; your students can access it through the *New York Times* Web site (www.nytimes.com).

> Just six months after emigrating from a Somalian refugee camp to Houston, Texas, Ahmed Guled's family seems to be well on its way toward complete American acculturation. His children are enrolled in the local elementary school, enjoy Saturday morning cartoons, and dress in clothing from The Gap. Guled is proud that his children will grow up as American citizens and is already making plans for them to attend college.
>
> But despite his American aspirations, Guled still believes in an ancient tradition that is customary in parts of his ancestral African home. He believes his daughters must have their clitorises cut off and their genital lips stitched together to preserve their virginity and to follow the teachings of his Muslim faith. "It's my responsibility," he said. "If I don't do it, I will have failed my children."
>
> Guled's wife supports the practice. "We were taught that this was a way of ensuring a girl's good behavior," she said. "It prevents them from running wild. Women should be meek, simple and quiet, not aggressive and outgoing. This is something we just accept."

Although the rite is practiced in 28 African countries, its prevalence varies widely, as does its severity, ranging from removal of the clitoris to the most extreme form, infibulation, which involves sewing up the genital lips to leave only a tiny hole for passage of urine and menstrual blood.

According to the Centers for Disease Control and Prevention (CDC), each year more than 150,000 women and girls of African ancestry in the United States are at risk of having this rite performed on them. In 1996, Congress directed federal health agencies to develop a plan to educate immigrants about the harm of genital cutting. Congress also passed a law making this practice punishable by up to five years in prison.

But authorities say stopping female genital mutilation among the growing population of African immigrants will take much more. For one thing, the law is difficult to enforce. While refugees are often impoverished, those who are able to save enough money to take their daughters out of the country for cutting are probably not violating the law as it is written. For another, doctors who spot cases of genital mutilation are reluctant to report parents to authorities for fear of breaking up close-knit families and sending mothers and fathers to prison.

But the principal difficulty in preventing the practice is the secretiveness of those who believe genital cutting is an essential rite of passage. It will mean finding a way to counteract generations of cultural heritage in order to change the minds of well-meaning parents. To this end, U.S. Health Department officials have organized meetings with advocates for refugees and nonprofit groups that work closely with Africans and Asians to develop strategies for combating the practice. (Although Africa is the focus of this item, female circumcision is also practiced in parts of the Near East and Southeast Asia.) The groups may, for example, ask Muslim religious leaders to explain to immigrants that the Koran does not require the practice.

To expand students' awareness of this practice, have them research the topic on the Internet, then answer the following questions:

1. How widespread is the practice of female circumcision? Why is it practiced? Is it a form of child maltreatment? Should the answer to this question depend on whether the rite is performed by members of a certain cultural or ethnic group?
2. How might primary, secondary, and tertiary prevention be used to combat the practice of female genital cutting?

Dugger, C. W. (1996, December 28). Tug of taboos: African genital rite vs. U.S. law. *New York Times*. Retrieved from www.nytimes.com.

AV: No More Secrets (24 min., Films for the Humanities and Sciences)

Through riveting case studies of sexually abused children and adults who were abused as children, this program explores the long-term damage that results from childhood sexual abuse.

AV: Psychological Maltreatment of Children: Assault on the Psyche (19 min., Insight Media)

This brief, award-winning film dramatizes the emotional effects of verbal abuse on children. Intended primarily for teacher in-service training, experts analyze each situation portrayed and offer recommendations for intervention.

AV: Children of Neglect (30 min., Films for the Humanities and Sciences)

This film profiles the sad, yet often inspiring, stories of children who have been neglected by their parents. Because no one has ever been there for them, such children are remarkably self-sufficient.

AV: Damage: The Effects of a Troubled Childhood (55 min., Films for the Humanities and Sciences)

This film explores whether the roots of adult phobias and psychological disorders can truly be traced to childhood traumas. A variety of experts discuss the controversial notion of repressed childhood memories and the origins of adult depression.

AV: No One Saved Dennis (14 min., Films for the Humanities and Sciences)

A segment of *60 Minutes* hosted by Diane Sawyer, this brief film tells the story of Dennis, who was placed for adoption in the home of a child abuser, in a community of acquiescent family members, social workers, and health professionals who failed to intervene and prevent his death.

AV: Childhood Sexual Abuse (26 min., Films for the Humanities and Sciences)

Through interviews with psychiatrists, social workers, and law enforcement officials, this program explores the ways in which adult women learn to work out the numerous problems caused by sexually abusive fathers. It also discusses how children can be manipulated into silent acceptance of abuse, the reliability of children in giving eyewitness testimony, and various prevention skills that can be taught to children.

Classroom Activity: Interpersonal Relationships of Abused Children

Developmentalists have long believed that a family context of maltreatment can inhibit the development of normal peer relationships in abused children. For example, punishment for outgoing behaviors and gregariousness (which is frequently observed in such families) may discourage children from approaching peers and contribute to overall feelings of social wariness. Many abusive families are also characterized by threatening patterns of parent–child interactions that could promote aggression in children and impede the development of self-control.

Indeed, research has shown that abused children are both more aggressive and more withdrawn in peer interactions than nonabused children are. Abused children are also less likely than other children to approach unfamiliar children or to participate in group play and conversation. When abused children do interact with their peers, their interactions tend to be less successful, reciprocal, and positive than those of nonabused children. Not surprisingly, parents and teachers report that abused children tend to be less well-liked and more rejected by their peers.

Much of this evidence comes either from naturalistic observations of children in group settings (such as on the playground) or from reports of parents, peers, and teachers. There is, in fact, little direct evidence regarding abused children's one-on-one social interactions with children who are considered to be close friends.

In one study, Jeffrey Parker and Carla Herrera of the University of Michigan observed sixteen 9- to 14-year-old physically abused children and 32 matched nonabused children during a 1.5-hour sequence of unstructured and structured play. The children were recruited for the study through state protective services records. Selection criteria included substantiated physical abuse by a household member within the past 2.5 years; residence with biological parent(s); and absence of sexual abuse, physical or neurological impairment, or intellectual retardation.

Information on each child's friendship network was obtained from a Peer Social Network Diagram. (Your students may enjoy learning more about this research tool by drawing their own diagram in class.) In the first step of this procedure, the children listed the names of all their friends. Next, the experimenter wrote the child's name and the names of each individual in the network on small stickers and presented the child with a diagram consisting of three concentric circles. The sticker with the child's name on it was placed in the center of the diagram, and the child was asked to indicate how close he or she felt toward each listed individual by placing the sticker representing that individual in one of the three circles. The innermost circle represented "very best friends"; the next largest circle was for "good friends"; and the outermost circle was for "everyday, casual friends." Using these data, the researchers calculated for each child the overall number of friends as well as the number of friends in the innermost (very best) circle.

Each child's best friend was contacted and invited to participate in the second part of the study. The pairs of friends were observed together during a standard sequence of unstructured and structured tasks. For example, in one segment of the study the children were provided with a carton of ice cream, a bottle of chocolate syrup, a single can of soda, a serving spoon, and two bowls, cups, and spoons. The children were told that they had 20 minutes of free time for a snack. The snack segment was designed to show the children's spontaneous, casual, and unstructured conversation. In another segment, the pair of friends played a set of games that provided the opportunity for cooperation, negotiation, competition, conflict, reparation, and spontaneous generosity between the partners. Each session was videotaped and later analyzed for specific signs of intimacy, conflict, and emotional expression in each participant.

Surprisingly, the researchers found several similarities in the social network patterns of maltreated and nonmaltreated children. For example, maltreated and comparison children were similar in both the frequency of contact and the duration of their relationship with closest friends. Also, the overall size of the children's friendship networks was the same. Because other researchers have suggested that maltreated children actively avoid peer contact or antagonize peers, the unexpected similarities in the two groups highlight a common example of faulty reasoning: generalizing too quickly from broader social parameters of a group (being raised by a maltreating family) to specific characteristics of individual group members.

However, many of the behaviors of the abused children during the videotaped tasks were consistent with earlier evidence. Relative to the comparison children, the abused children interacted with other children less positively, and their interactions were characterized by greater conflict and disagreement between the partners. This is consistent with the suggestion that abusive families do not provide children with contexts conducive to the development of conflict management skills, as well as research evidence that abused children are more hostile and aggressive toward peers and lack impulse control.

Interestingly, although the abused children's interactions involved more conflict than those of control children, the conflict occurred primarily during game playing. The researchers offer several speculations as to why abused children and their friends showed higher levels of conflict in this context. First, the majority of the game-playing contexts were competitive. As several authors have argued, competitive situations in which the attainment of rewards by one individual constrains the attainment of rewards by the other may be especially challenging to best friends, who are ordinarily disposed to maintain equity in their relationship. Alternatively, the games may have affected maltreated and control children in different ways. The game contexts in this study contained several stimulating elements (e.g., time limits, buzzers, loudly ticking clocks, "exploding" game boards). Among the specific difficulties of children who are abused or who witness frequent domestic violence are problems with emotional and behavioral regulation. The arousing nature of the games may have taxed the behavioral-regulation skills of abused children to a greater extent than it did those of nonabused children, contributing to the increased conflict for these dyads in this context.

A second area in which abused children's friendships differed from the friendships of other children was that abused children exhibited fewer sustained moments of intimacy. Following an attachment theory perspective, the researchers suggest that children acquire mental representations, or internal working models, of others' emotional availability through their experiences of early care. These models are extended to future relationships, including friendships. When early care is unresponsive, insensitive, or traumatizing, children are likely to view relationships as contexts in which they are not free to reach out and share personal issues or to respond to another's emotional needs.

The researchers also found that female friends had more positive interactions and greater overall intimacy than did their male counterparts during game playing. However, abused girls displayed less positive affect than comparison girls during unstructured tasks that involved primarily conversation and discussion. These findings support previous work, suggesting that boys have more difficulty than girls in regulating their arousal under evocative conditions.

Although research on this topic has been somewhat limited, the general findings of this study have been replicated. In a more recent study, Tasha Howe and Ross Parke examined the interactional qualities of 35 severely abused children (aged 4.3 to 11.5 years) and 43 matched, nonabused children (aged 5.5 to 11.6 years). Abused children did not differ significantly from control children on several measures of friendship quality, such as resolving conflicts and helping each other. However, they were more negative in their interactions, and they reported that their friendships involved more conflicts and more betrayal and less caring.

Howe, T. R., & Parke, R. D. (2006). Friendship quality and sociometric status: Between-group differences and links to loneliness in severely abused and nonabused children. *Child Abuse and Neglect, 25*(5), 585–606.

Parker, J. G., & Herrera, C. (1996). Interpersonal processes in friendship: A comparison of abused and nonabused children's experiences. *Developmental Psychology, 32*(6), 1025–1038.

AV: Toward an Understanding of Child Sexual Abuse (4 films, each 30 min., Insight Media)

Psychosexual Development of Children describes the normal range of children's sexual development and explains the criteria for defining sexual abuse relative to these developmental norms. *Dynamics* describes the various categories of sexual abuse and presents legal definitions used in such cases. *Intervention* focuses on the roles of various legal and child protective agencies that have been established to deal with child sexual abuse. *Treatment* explores various models of treatment for sex offenders and discusses the rationale for their treatment.

Three Levels of Prevention, Again

Classroom Activity: Targeting Maltreatment Interventions to Fit the Family Context

A major challenge in preventing or stopping maltreatment is how to tailor treatment to fit the specific family context. To expand on this topic, you might summarize Patricia Crittenden's suggestion that families involved in maltreatment can be subdivided into four categories: vulnerable-to-crisis, restorable, supportable, and inadequate (Crittenden, 2006).

Vulnerable-to-crisis families are generally adequate caregiving families that are pushed over the edge by immediate stressful problems. The loss of a job or the birth of a handicapped infant, for example, can severely strain most parents' ability to cope with the normal demands and frustrations of child rearing. Especially if other relatives or friends are unresponsive, the children might become the target of their parents and be blamed for problems they never created.

About one-fourth of all substantiated maltreatment occurs in vulnerable-to-crisis families. Usually, they realize they have a problem, and this makes them receptive to services such as crisis counseling and parent training. Once the parents learn to cope with their specific problem more effectively—a process that usually takes less than a year—they are again able to provide adequate child rearing.

Restorable families make up about half of all maltreating families. The caregivers in restorable families have the potential to provide adequate care and perhaps have done so in the past, but a number of problems—caused not only by their immediate situations but also by their past histories and their temperaments—seriously impair their parenting abilities. A single mother, for example, might have untreated medical problems, inadequate housing, and poor job skills, all of which fray her quick temper and cause her to explode just as her father did when she was a disobedient child. Or a binge-drinking husband might periodically beat his children, perhaps with the tacit permission of an overly dependent, isolated wife, who herself may have come from an abusive home. Or a teenage couple might be both immature and addicted to drugs, with the result that they disregard their infant's basic needs or seriously overestimate his or her abilities.

Treatment for restorable families requires a caseworker who has the time and commitment to become a family advocate, mediating and coordinating various services (for example, making sure the local clinic provides low-cost and appropriate medical care, securing transportation and prescription medicine, or helping drug addicts not only acknowledge their dependence but also find a network of former addicts to provide support). The goal is not just child protection but family support, emotional as well as material. With such intense help, restorable families eventually become successful ones.

Supportable families make up about one-fifth of all maltreating families. They probably will never function adequately and independently, but with continual support they might meet their children's basic needs for physical, educational, and emotional care. The support might be as simple as daily home visits by a nurse or housekeeper or as involved as moving the entire family to a special residence that provides ongoing medical attention, day care, recreation, social work, and group therapy. Unfortunately, such intense support services are rarely available to the families that need them most, although some residential programs for battered women or for recovering addicts come close. Unless support is forthcoming, the children of a supportable family will need to be placed in another home.

Inadequate families constitute nearly 10 percent of maltreating families. They are so impaired by deep emotional problems or serious cognitive deficiencies that the parents or other caregivers will never be able to meet the needs of their children. For children born into these families, long-term adoption, beginning with foster care in infancy, is the best solution.

Crittenden, P. M. (2006). Why do inadequate parents do what they do? In O. Mayseless (Ed.), *Parenting representations: Theory, research, and clinical implications* (pp. 38433). New York: Cambridge University Press.

Internet Activity: Child Maltreatment and Vulnerable-to-Crisis Families

One of the biggest challenges to developmentalists in treating and preventing child maltreatment is tailoring treatment to fit a particular family's needs. One approach has been to categorize families involved in maltreatment as vulnerable-to-crisis, restorable, supportable, or inadequate, as noted in the preceding Classroom Activity. Vulnerable-to-crisis families are experiencing unusual problems such as divorce, the loss of a job, the death of a family member, or the birth of a handicapped infant. These problems strain caregivers' abilities to cope with the normal demands of child rearing. Ask students to create a fictitious vulnerable-to-crisis family, then use Internet resources to provide guidance and support. Handout 8 will guide their work.

Provide students with comments regarding their creativity, their understanding of this real-world situation, and their ability to obtain relevant information on the Internet.

AV: Foster Care (24 min., Films for the Humanities and Sciences)

Each year, 200,000 children are taken from their homes because of abuse or neglect. This heart-wrenching video profiles the foster care system, as seen through the eyes of three foster children, their parents, social workers, and the judges who must decide their fate.

HANDOUT 1

Developmental Fact or Myth?

T F 1. By age 6, the child's body is proportionately not very different from that of the adult.

T F 2. In multiethnic countries, Latinos tend to be somewhat shorter than children of African, Asian, and European descent.

T F 3. Although the right and left hemispheres of the brain have specialized functions, cognitive skill requires both sides of the brain.

T F 4. Memories of past experiences are always destructive.

T F 5. Boys are about 6 months ahead of girls in developing fine motor skills.

T F 6. Violence, either accidental or deliberate, is the leading cause of childhood death.

T F 7. All reported cases of maltreatment are substantiated.

T F 8. Child maltreatment involves not only physical abuse but also failure to meet a child's basic needs.

T F 9. Most maltreated children are friendlier than other children because they crave attention.

T F 10. Adoption is the preferred permanent option in preventing maltreatment of older children.

HANDOUT 2

Critical Thinking Activity: Designing a Toy

Now that you have read and reviewed biosocial development during early childhood, take your learning a step further by testing your critical thinking skills on this problem-solving exercise.

Developmental psychologists view play as the major means through which physical, cognitive, and social skills are mastered—especially during the preschool years. Unfortunately, many adults are so imbued with the work ethic that they tend to denigrate children's play. Some even punish their children for "horsing around," criticize preschool teachers for letting children play "too much," or schedule their children's lives so heavily with lessons and chores that there is little time for play.

Your task is to mentally design a toy suitable for a 2- to 6-year-old child, keeping in mind the physical, cognitive, and social needs of preschool children. Then answer the following questions.

1. What is the name of your toy? How does the child play with it or use it?

2. How old is the child for whom the toy is intended? What features of the toy make it developmentally appropriate?

3. What domain or domains of development is your toy designed to stimulate? How are they stimulated?

4. What are some of the specific features of the toy (e.g., size, shape, color, noise-making properties, etc.) that enhance its attractiveness and play value?

5. What considerations should be given to injury control when the toy is used?

HANDOUT 3

Bubbles in the Bowl: Using Developmental Theory to Design Potty Training

Potty training a child is an important, and sometimes stressful, milestone for both parent and child. Scores of products and training schedules have been touted as breakthroughs over the years, with some claiming that a child can be trained by the age of 1, and in only a few days.

This exercise is designed to help you bring the major developmental theories to life by considering how parents, working from each of the grand and emerging theoretical perspectives, would be advised to toilet train their child. For each theory, briefly state:

- developmental issues that might influence toilet training (e.g., muscular control, cognitive maturity)
- practical tips for promoting success (e.g., pour colored shampoo in the toilet so that urinating causes colorful bubbles to form)
- possible causes of failure (e.g., neural immaturity, cultural values)

1. Psychoanalytic theory

2. Behaviorism

3. Cognitive theory

HANDOUT 3 *(continued)*

4. Sociocultural theory

5. Universal theories (humanism and evolutionary theory)

HANDOUT 4

Observational Activity: The Development of Fine Motor Skills

Use the eight-skill checklist developed by Janice Beaty (1990) to assess the child's fine motor skill development. (Before testing, make sure all the materials, which are common items in a home with children, are available.) Then complete the questions on the accompanying handout and return your answers to your instructor.

1. **Hand Preference (lateral dominance)**

   Hand the child an easily grasped toy (such as a rattle, toy hammer, or block) several times to determine if he or she consistently prefers one hand or the other. Infants typically use both hands to grasp objects in an undifferentiated and reflexive manner. By 2½ years, about one-half of all children have established lateral dominance for their hands and feet. By age 3, this percentage has increased to about 70 percent.

   Interestingly, there are cultural differences in the development of lateral dominance. By 4½ years of age, for example, only about one-half of all Japanese children have established a dominant hand (Beaty, 1990). The earlier developmental norm in American children has been attributed to the early developmental emphasis that many parents place on handedness (particularly right-hand preference) in their children.

2. **Turns Knobs Easily**

   Turning a key in a lock, cranking an eggbeater or can opener, and twisting a lid off a jar are skills young children delight in. Most 2- and 3-year-olds can easily perform most of the above tasks, although their neuromuscular control is far from perfect and things often slip through their fingers.

3. **Pours Liquid Without Spilling**

   Renowned educator Maria Montessori made pouring exercises a regular part of her "daily living exercises" for fine motor skill development. Have the child pour liquid from a *small* pitcher into a cup or glass. Children younger than 4 may need to use both hands to prevent spilling. And even 5-year-olds, who are still perfecting their control of *grasping and releasing*, may occasionally release their grip and spill accidentally. Janice Beaty believes that too often, teachers, day-care workers, and parents do all the pouring for children, fearing that preschoolers will inevitably make a mess. "There will be accidents," she notes. "Spills are part of the price our children pay for the complicated task of growing up."

4. **Fastens and Unfastens Zippers and Buttons**

   Although most 4-year-olds can button, unbutton, and unzip with ease, they still may need assistance starting a zipper. Interestingly, preschoolers in large, single-parent, or economically disadvantaged families—who often are expected to dress themselves at an early age—tend to develop these fine motor skills at an earlier age than do only children, children within intact families, and children who are not economically disadvantaged.

HANDOUT 4 *(continued)*

5. Picks Up and Inserts Objects

Puzzles, pegboards, string beads, Lego building blocks, and Tinkertoys all require the manipulation of small parts. Virtually all preschool classrooms focus on manipulative play of this sort as an important fine motor skill. Perhaps because the play of young girls tends to focus on fine motor activities more than the play of boys, girls often have greater finger dexterity and eye–hand coordination than boys their age.

6. Controls Drawing Tools

When young children first use crayons or markers, they clumsily clamp their fists around the writing implement in what is called the *power grip*. Very young children may not use their preferred hand as they attempt to color or draw. But with practice, dexterity increases and the more delicate *precision grip*, with fingers and thumb, emerges.

7. Uses Scissors Effectively

Most 4-year-olds can make a good straight cut using scissors. Children younger than 4 show wide variations in this skill, which requires considerable practice and neuromuscular coordination. Make sure the scissors are good ones; attempting to cut paper with dull or mechanically unsound scissors is difficult, even for adults.

8. Hammers Nails with Control

Using a hammer to pound a nail held in the opposite hand is the most difficult fine motor skill on this checklist. Even many adults have difficulty hammering without hitting their thumbs, or missing the nail entirely. Young children should be tested with a plastic or very lightweight hammer, a nail with a large head (preferably plastic or wooden), and a soft material into which the nail can be pounded (such as an acoustic ceiling tile).

Beaty, J. (1990). *Observing development of the young child* (3rd ed.), pp. 191–207.

HANDOUT 5

Observational Activity: The Development of Fine Motor Skills: Follow-Up Questionnaire

1. Describe the participant (age, sex, etc.) and the setting you chose for the fine motor skill assessment.

2. Did you encounter any difficulties in completing this observational activity?

3. Fill in the following table to summarize your subject's fine motor skill performance. In the space below each checked skill, briefly describe the task on which the child demonstrated the skill in question.

Yes	No	
_____	_____	Hand preference? If yes, which hand?
_____	_____	Turns knobs easily?
_____	_____	Pours without spilling?
_____	_____	Fastens/unfastens buttons and zippers?
_____	_____	Picks up and inserts small objects?
_____	_____	Uses crayons effectively?
_____	_____	Cuts using scissors?
_____	_____	Hammers nail?

HANDOUT 5 *(continued)*

4. On the basis of your assessment of the child's fine motor skill development, pick one or two skills that need strengthening and describe at least three activities that would help the child develop each skill.

HANDOUT 6

Childhood Accident Record

Children between 2 and 6 years old are generally very susceptible to accidents because they are extremely active and unaware of potential danger. If you cannot remember accidents from your own childhood, ask a relative if he or she recalls any. Alternatively, ask a relative with children in this age group to tell you about his or her children's accidents.

1. Make a record of the accidents you sustained during early childhood. Or, if you prefer, make a record of the accidents sustained by one of your siblings or a child you know who was (or is) "accident-prone." List broken bones, cuts requiring stitches, automobile accidents, and ingestion of poisons.

Accident	Age of Occurrence

2. Review the accidents listed above. Could any of them have been prevented? If so, describe some possible preventive measures.

3. Do you know of any laws passed recently to protect children from accidents? Can you suggest any laws that might be particularly helpful?

HANDOUT 7

Child Maltreatment in Context

The following questions are designed to help you think about the significance of social context in relation to the prevalence of child abuse in the United States.

1. The most severe consequence of child abuse is obviously death. Because of the mass media's attention to these cases, members of the victims' and perpetrators' families have been offered "financial reward" for telling their stories. Does media attention contribute to or help deter child maltreatment? Explain your answer.

2. In what ways does this context of violence in the United States promote child maltreatment?

HANDOUT 7 *(continued)*

3. Have you ever encountered a situation in which you suspected a child was the victim of abuse or neglect? What did you do, and why?

4. If it were in your power to completely shape the social context in which a child grew up, what steps would you take to help ensure that he or she would be protected from maltreatment?

HANDOUT 8

Internet Activity: Child Maltreatment and Vulnerable-to-Crisis Families

In many parts of the world, any teacher, health professional, or social worker who becomes aware of a possible case of child maltreatment is legally required to report it. This policy is controversial, however, because alerting the police might backfire and actually cause the child greater harm. One solution is a policy of differential response to high-risk situations, which may require a complete investigation and the removal of the child from the family, and low-risk situations that may require only income supplementation for child care or some other form of support. This process begins by categorizing maltreating families as either vulnerable-to-crisis, restorable, supportable, or inadequate (see Classroom Activity, Targeting Maltreatment Interventions to Fit the Family Context, for descriptions of these categories). Create a fictitious family that you would categorize as vulnerable-to-crisis. Then answer the following questions.

1. List and briefly describe each of the members of this family.

2. What factors make this family "vulnerable-to-crisis"? Why isn't the family classified as "supportable," "restorable," or "inadequate"?

HANDOUT 8 *(continued)*

3. Find and describe at least one Web page that is a professional resource for clinicians, counselors, and others who provide support for families involved in child maltreatment.

4. Find and describe at least one Web page that is a resource for family members involved either as perpetrators or as victims of maltreatment.

5. On the basis of information gathered from the Internet, what specific, practical advice would you offer to your hypothetical family?

Early Childhood: Cognitive Development

Contents

Note: Worth Publishers provides online Instructor and Student Tool Kits, DVD Student Tool Kits, and Instructor and Student video resources in DevelopmentPortal for use with the text. See Part I: General Resources for information about these materials and the text Lecture Guides for a complete list by text chapter.

Children's Theories

Language

Early-Childhood Education

Suggested Activities

Introducing Early Childhood: Cognitive Development

"On Your Own" Activity: Developmental Fact or Myth?

Before students read about cognitive development during early childhood, have them respond to the true-false statements in Handout 1.

The correct answers are shown below. Class discussion can focus on the origins of any developmental misconceptions that are demonstrated in the students' incorrect answers.

1. T
2. T
3. F
4. F
5. F
6. F
7. T
8. F
9. T
10. F

AV: The Journey Through the Life Span, Program 4: Early Childhood

See Early Childhood: Biosocial Development for a description of Program 4 and the accompanying observation modules, which cover the entire unit on early childhood.

Teaching Tip: Grading

One of the most difficult tasks facing an instructor is deciding how to evaluate student work. Grading takes a lot of time and effort and in this era of "assessment overload" is sometimes viewed as a necessary evil rather than an integral part of the learning process. However, careful planning and evaluation of your grading practices can dramatically improve the reliability and validity of the marks you assign and the quality of your teaching, and promote greater student learning.

The first step in improving how you grade students is to develop a plan before putting the course syllabus together. Begin by articulating the learning goals for the course. What is most important for students to know? What should they be able to do? How should students have changed after they have completed the course? Next, you should ask yourself why you use the grading methods you currently do, and whether these methods are accomplishing what you would like them to accomplish?

If you are a relatively new instructor, it is especially important to seek input from more experienced faculty who teach similar courses. Ask them which grading practices they use, why they chose them, and how well they work. You might also consider asking your students (perhaps from a recently completed class) for their input. What did they think about your grading policies for the course? Were they fair? Did they understand the criteria you used to assign grades?

Avoid being locked in to one grading method for all course assignments. Some assignments might best be evaluated using a criterion-referenced approach. In this approach, achievement is measured against a certain standard of performance and students are graded independently of one another. Many students favor this approach over norm-referenced (curved) grading, because they are not ranked against one another and there is generally no limit to the number of high grades. Norm-referenced grading is often used to determine overall course grades because it results in a normal distribution with a small number of extremely high and low grades. A third method that may be appropriate for certain assignments is mastery grading. Using this approach, the instructor permits students to persist at learning and evaluation until they are able to demonstrate proficiency. Mastery approaches are the basis of formative assessment, as in the case of students receiving instructor feedback on rough drafts of papers before submitting their final work for a grade (summative assessment).

Martha Zlokovich offers the following additional tips to promoting grading for optimal student learning:

- As you plan for a new course or prepare the new syllabus for one you have taught many times list each course segment and assignment.
- Next to each, write one or more specific learning goals each is supposed to meet (master developmental concepts, improve critical thinking skills, etc.).
- In a third column, enter the grading procedure you will use for each assignment and exam (letter grade, points, mastery, criterion-referenced grading, etc.).
- In the last column, list the steps to mastery so that students will do well on each assignment (review class notes, complete the reading assignment, engage in active learning, submit draft of term paper for formative review).
- When you are satisfied with this table, share it with several experienced colleagues as well as with several students for their feedback.
- Finally, add a column with due dates and include it in the materials you distribute to students at the beginning of the course.

Teaching Tip: Dealing With Common Misconceptions About Child Development

Laura Levine of Central Connecticut State University suggests that a good way to create significant learning experiences in developmental psychology courses is to deal directly with student misconceptions about child development. Addressing such misconceptions is a good way to promote the "stickiness" of information after the exam, and even long after the course is over. Another benefit of this approach to teaching is to eliminate student misconceptions, which are tenacious; unless they are directly addressed, they will likely remain intact at the end of the course (Chew, 2005).

An effective way to begin a class session is to display one or more of the misconceptions listed here that are relevant to the topic you are about to address. Other misconceptions are sure to arise from your students, which you can then address in class or assign as research topics.

- Mothers care for their babies well because they have a maternal instinct.
- Babies cannot see when they are first born.
- Parents should not talk baby-talk to their children because it slows their development.
- Having kids listen to Mozart makes them smarter.
- Birth order is an important factor that determines children's intelligence and personality.
- Sugar is a major cause of hyperactive behavior.
- High self-esteem makes children perform better in school.
- Spanking is an effective way to discipline children.
- Babies 6 months and younger do not experience sadness and fear.
- Babies under 1 year are not affected by the emotions of their caregivers.

- Three-year-olds should be able to control their temper tantrums.

Levine, L. E. (2011). *Creating significant learning experiences in child development courses.* Presented at meetings of the National Institute on the Teaching of Psychology. St. Petersburg, FL.

Chew, S. L. (2005). Seldom in Doubt but Often Wrong: Addressing Tenacious Student Misconceptions. In Dunn, D. S., & Chew, S. L. (Eds.). *Best Practices in Teaching General Psychology* (pp. 211–223). Mahwah, NJ: Erlbaum.

AV: Transitions Throughout the Life Span, Program 9: Playing and Learning

Program 9 begins by comparing Piaget's and Vygotsky's views of cognitive development at this age. According to Piaget, young children's thought is prelogical: Between the ages of 2 and 6, these children are unable to perform many logical operations and are limited by irreversible, centered, and static thinking. In the program, a young mother performs the conservation experiment with her 4-year-old son, as Kathleen Berger provides expert commentary.

A discussion of the limitations of Piaget's theory leads to an overview of sociocultural theory. Lev Vygotsky, a contemporary of Piaget's, saw learning as a social activity more than as a matter of individual discovery. Vygotsky focused on the child's zone of proximal development and the relationship between language and thought. We see this zone and the benefits of guided participation in action as 4-year-old Jordan practices tennis with the helpful scaffolding provided by his father.

The program next focuses on language development during early childhood. Although young children demonstrate rapid improvement in vocabulary and grammar, they have difficulty with abstractions, metaphorical speech, and certain rules of grammar. Developmentalist Jean Berko Gleason provides expert commentary in this segment. The lesson concludes with a discussion of preschool education, including a description of quality preschool programs and an evaluation of their lifelong impact on children.

AV: The Child: Part IV (28 min., CRM/McGraw-Hill)

In a cinema-verité form, with minimal narration, the fourth film in this series shows a 2-year-old and a 3-year-old (Kathy and Ian) as they learn about their world through modeling, trial and error, discovery, and maturation. Viewing this film will help students understand the amazing learning potential of 3-year-olds, and should help focus debate on whether these children should be systematically provided with specific learning experiences or left on their own to explore their environment.

AV: Preschoolers: Physical and Cognitive Development (30 min., Magna Systems)

(See description in Early Childhood: Biosocial Development.)

AV: The Preschool Parent: Building Confidence and Curiosity (30 min., Films for the Humanities and Sciences)

This heart-warming video profiles four modern, exceptionally busy families, and their efforts to build confidence and encourage curiosity in their children.

Classroom Activity: You Want to Watch Blue's Clues *Again?*

Any parent knows that young children often ask to view and listen to storybooks and videos over and over again. Despite this fact, curriculum-based TV programs are not repeated according to any systematic schedule. This is most likely due to broadcasters' fears of losing their audience if repetitive programming causes viewers to *habituate* and change channels.

Such fears *are* valid, according to the *orienting-response theory*, which holds that young children's attention to television is primarily attracted and held by movement, scene changes, and other features that elicit orienting reactions, which generally do habituate over time. Other theorists, however, propose a *theory of invested mental effort*, according to which young children's attention to television is driven primarily by their comprehension of the content of television. Because television programs are frequently difficult for young children to understand, attention to some programs might be expected to increase with repetition until the program is fully comprehensible.

In one study, researchers at the University of Massachusetts investigated whether viewer attention and behaviors indicating program involvement necessarily diminish in young children with moderate amounts of program repetition. The 108 participants, who were recruited from three day-care centers in New York and Connecticut, included thirty-six 3-year-olds, thirty-eight 4-year-olds, and thirty-four 5-year-olds. Of these, 41 percent were African American, 36 percent were White, 21 percent were Hispanic, and 2 percent were Asian American. The program used in the study was *Blue's Clues*, a series designed to teach young children to exercise new and already acquired cognitive skills and knowledge. The program accomplishes this through Steve, the original series host, who leads the viewer through his cartoon world, solving problems left by his dog Blue, and who asks questions of the audience that can be answered verbally or through nonverbal behaviors such as pointing. (Many of your students will be familiar with this popular series. If not, you may wish to assign them the task of watching a similar program at home—*Blue's Clues* went off the air in August 2006—before you lecture on this topic. Just about any Nick or Nick Jr. program is appropriate, including *Dora the Explorer, The Backyardigans,* and *Go, Diego, Go!*

The participants were randomly assigned to one of three groups, so that all groups included an even distribution by age, gender, and ethnicity. One experimental group viewed an episode of *Blue's Clues* (called "Snacktime") only once, with a test of comprehension following immediately afterward. In this episode, Blue gives Steve and the viewers three clues to try to figure out what she wants as her snack. On the way, Steve and Blue invite viewers to help elephants paint their family (using color identification), help characters put foods of different shapes away (using shape recognition), and help chicks find their friends with matching hats (using matching skills).

A second experimental group viewed the same *Blue's Clues* episode on five consecutive days, with comprehension testing occurring immediately following the fifth exposure. The third group, the control group, watched a different program.

The results showed that repetition of the program was *not* associated with decreased attention. Moreover, verbal and nonverbal interactions, especially answers and imitations, greatly increased with episode repetition. Most important, comprehension improved, and children in the repetition experimental group showed signs of increased use of the program's problem-solving strategy during the program and afterward.

The researchers note that the results of their study are broadly consistent with the theory of invested mental effort. "Because *Blue's Clues* overtly invites viewer participation and active problem solving, we hypothesized that invested mental effort would increase as the children became familiar with the program's formats and demands. Consequences of this increased mental effort would be increased overt viewer participation, maintained visual attention, and improved comprehension, all of which were found." This comes as good news to toymaker Fisher-Price, which markets a DVD-based learning system that allows preschool children to interact and actively learn alongside SpongeBob SquarePants and other television favorites. Awarded the 2005 Australian Pre-School Toy of the Year, the educational device comes with a set of activity cards designed to make television viewing more active, rather than the passive activity it customarily is.

Crawley, A. M., Anderson, D. R., Wilder, A., Williams, M., & Santomero, A. (1999). Effects of repeated exposures to a single episode of the television program *Blue's Clues* on the viewing behaviors and comprehension of preschool children. *Journal of Educational Psychology*, *91*(4), 630–637.

Herman, M. (2005, August 2). Making TV educational. *The Press (*Christchurch, New Zealand), p. B-4.

Piaget and Vygotsky

AV: Cognitive Development (20 min., CRM/McGraw-Hill)

(See description in Theories of Development.)

AV: The Growth of Intelligence in the Preschool Years (31 min., Davidson Films)

Preschool thinking processes are in evidence when children, ages 3 to 6, are given Piagetian sorting and grouping tasks. This movie is especially useful if students are skeptical of Piaget's delineations, for it shows that overall categories, such as shape and color, are imperfectly used by young children in classification tasks.

Observational Activity: Preoperational and Concrete Operational Thinking

When they first read Piaget's description of the limits of preoperational thought, many students may have the same reaction that many psychologists did—they don't believe it. According to Piaget, preoperational and concrete operational children think about the world in very different ways. The preoperational child sees the world from his or her own perspective (egocentrism) and has not yet mastered the principle of conservation (the idea that properties such as mass, volume, and number remain the same despite changes in appearance). The concrete operational thinking of 6- to 11-year-old children, by contrast, is less egocentric and demonstrates mastery of logical thought, including conservation, where tangible objects are involved.

Make sure you have some clay, some checkers, and two different-sized glasses in the classroom. Distribute the Assignment Sheet (Handout 2) and have students read it. When they have finished, ask for two volunteers, one to be the tester, the other to play a 4-year-old. Ask the pair to demonstrate the conservation-of-liquid task. When the volunteers have finished (and the laughter has died down), begin a gentle critique of the tester's style and engage the rest of the class. Then ask for two more volunteers and have them demonstrate the conservation-of-number task. If you think it will be productive, ask for more volunteers to demonstrate the other tests of conservation.

During these trial runs, some general points about interviewing young children will probably emerge, such as working at a low table where the children are comfortable, speaking in a soft voice, introducing the activity as a game, waiting for them to respond, and so on.

You will also want to discuss the egocentric thought part of the activity, and have the class suggest other questions that tap this aspect of preschool children's cognitive development.

If time permits, you may want to touch on how the interviewer influences the outcome of the test (there will no doubt be some clear examples from the classroom "practice" interviews). Stress the importance of having a carefully prepared "presentation script," so that if a student were actually surveying many children, his or her approach with each child would be the same—and differences would be due to differences in the children.

As an outside assignment, you can ask students to actually interview young children and answer the questions in Handout 3.

Classroom Activity: In Defense of Piaget

Jean Piaget (1896–1980) was born in Neuchatel, Switzerland. When he was only 10, he published a scientific article on the albino sparrow; at age 15, he wrote several articles on mollusks. He received a PhD in biology in 1918 and only then began his study of psychology. In 1921, Piaget began to do research in child psychology at the Rousseau Institute in Geneva. He served as its co-director from 1933 to 1971 and as director of the International Bureau of Education from 1929 to 1967. Piaget was a professor of psychology at the University of Geneva from 1929 until his death.

Although most psychologists acknowledge the historical value of Piaget's developmental theory, they criticize it on several grounds, including that it is empirically false, conceptually limited, and "epistemologically untenable." Some psychologists have gone so far as to argue that the time has come to view Piaget primarily in terms of his historical impact but as largely irrelevant to our present understanding of cognitive development in children.

One of the most common criticisms of Piaget's theory is that its estimates of the competence of children, particularly 2- to 6-year-olds, are extremely conservative. As noted in the text, recent studies have found that these competencies *are* much more likely to be revealed when performance factors such as language, memory requirements, and the nature of the task are properly controlled. When testers use simplified questions, instructions, scoring indices, and the like, the true competencies of the preoperational child become apparent.

The "what to do with Piaget" controversy is a stimulating topic for discussion and/or debate throughout the course. To balance the discussion, you might introduce the arguments advanced by Orlando Lourenco of the University of Lisbon and Armando Machado of Indiana University. Lourenco and Machado maintain that while new variations on standard Piagetian tasks have "brought to light a remarkably rich, complex, and hitherto unsuspected set of cognitive competencies in the young child . . . they have provided no evidence that these competencies are equivalent to the logicomathematical and operational competencies in which Piaget was interested." Without denying that children are more competent than Piaget believed, Lourenco and Machado believe that most studies that have challenged Piaget's results on conservation, classification, and space and time representation are "generally unconvincing."

In the construction of the object concept, for example, Lourenco and Machado maintain that researchers who use the reaction of surprise instead of active search for the hidden object are misguided. In their opinion, experiments that rely on habituation–dishabituation responses indicate that the infant is aware that something has changed perceptually but provide "no conclusive evidence that a conceptual competence [i.e., object permanence] is responsible for the infant's reaction of surprise. To infer unambiguously a conceptual competence, the experimenter needs to rule out alternative, perceptual-based explanations."

As another example, Lourenco and Machado cite Piaget's transitivity task, in which children are shown that Stick A is shorter than Stick B and, *later,* that Stick B is shorter than Stick C. The crucial test, of course, is what children conclude concerning the relative lengths of Sticks A and C. In more recent studies, researchers have modified the Piagetian procedure in several ways. For example, they presented and arranged all the sticks in order of size before the test began. Then "the experimenter placed side-by-side Sticks A and B and, next, Sticks B and C, so that the child could see that A < B and B < C. Given that in these studies the stick on the right was always longer than the stick on the left, the final inference of A < C was not necessarily operational. To answer correctly, they needed to know only in which direction (right or left) the sticks increased in size, and this piece of spatial information was clearly provided by the two initial comparisons. Thus, in rigor we cannot rule out explanations of the child's correct performance based on preoperational, figurative competencies."

Critics have also maintained that Piaget was more interested in measuring children's cognitive abilities at a given age than in describing the development of these abilities. Lourenco and Machado argue that critics have simply overlooked or ignored developmental distinctions that are critical in Piagetian theory. For example, Piaget distinguished between conservation and pseudoconservation, necessity and pseudonecessity, operative and figurative thought, and deductive and transductive reasoning. "The eagerness to show how much Piaget underestimated the competence of the preoperational child has been so strong that some researchers have even questioned the very existence of preoperational thinking. . . . [H]ad Piaget tried to grasp fuzzy indicators of operational competencies, he would have been able to report them in children younger than those studied by some of his critics."

As an anonymous reviewer of a manuscript observed, assessing Piaget is somewhat like "assessing the impact of Shakespeare on English literature, or Aristotle in Philosophy—impossible." However, should you wish to elaborate on their arguments, or perhaps to assign the controversy as a topic for debate, Lourenco and Machado explore additional criticisms of Piaget's theory. Among these are that Piaget's theory characterizes development negatively, neglects the role of social factors in development, describes but does not explain, assesses thinking through language, and ignores postadolescent development.

Ferreiro, E. (2001). On the links between equilibration, causality, and "prise de conscience" in Piaget's theory. *Human Development, 44*(4), 214–219.

Lourenco, O., & Machado, A. (1996). In defense of Piaget's theory: A reply to 10 common criticisms. *Psychological Review, 103*(1), 143–164.

Weyant, R. G. (2002). Jean Piaget. *The World Book Encyclopedia*. Chicago: World Book.

Classroom Activity: Classroom Demonstration of "Preoperational" Thought . . . in Adults!

Jane Ewens Holbrook suggests a nice classroom demonstration of a conservation-like task that will give students an appreciation of preoperational thought and encourage them to examine their own thinking. The demonstration should be conducted after students are familiar with Piaget's stages and with the text material questioning the validity of standard conservation tasks (e.g., the rigidity of the test situation).

For the demonstration you will need two identical large glass jars, one filled with 200 red jelly beans and the other with 200 black jelly beans. You will also need a small scoop or measuring spoon. Set the jars of jelly beans on a table in front of the class and introduce the task as a conservation-like problem for adults. Tell the class that the scoop holds exactly 15 jelly beans and that you are going to fill it with red jelly beans and add them to the jar containing the 200 black jelly beans. (Do not actually fill the scoop.) Then say that you are going to shake the jar containing both red and black jelly beans until they are mixed. Finally, you will scoop 15 jelly beans (any 15) from the jar containing the mixed jelly beans and pour them into the jar containing the red jelly beans. (You may need to repeat the description of these steps so that students are sure of the procedure.)

After the procedure has been described, ask the class, "Will the number of red jelly beans in the jar that initially contained only black jelly beans be the same as the number of black jelly beans in the jar that originally contained only red jelly beans?"

Although some students will immediately realize that the correct answer to the question is "the same," many will answer incorrectly. (Holbrook reports that of 54 students in two classes, only 6 answered correctly after the description of the problem. After the actual pouring of jelly beans, 11 students still answered "no.") Before discussing why many students struggle with this problem, you might tell the class that 40 to 60 percent of college students typically have difficulty solving formal operations problems such as this one.

Why do adults have difficulty solving this type of problem? The answer is that adult thinking, like preoperational thinking, often is centered; students focus on one aspect of the task alone. Because they center on the mixing of the beans, students turn the task into a probability problem. Focused on the probability of scooping exactly the same number of red and black beans, they fail to realize that the actual number of each is irrelevant.

Comparing the responses of adult students on this task with the response of a typical 5-year-old on Piaget's water-pouring task, Holbrook notes that, "Like the children who are sure that the height of the water proves their point, these adults are sure that the detail they have selected is the key to the solution. In the child, the centration is perceptual; in the adult, the centration is conceptual. . . . The person worried about the mixing, the colors, and the probability of coming up with equal numbers of red and black jelly beans can also be described as being concrete, or perceptually bound. Like the child who is perceptually caught by the height of the water, the adult is trapped by the significance of the colors and particular words. . . . Only by decentering, by giving up the focus on the chosen detail, can the solution be seen."

Students who see the solution understand that it doesn't matter how many beans of each color are removed with each scoop as long as the total number in the scoop remains constant. Moving the jelly beans (and pouring the water) can be repeated endlessly without changing the answer.

Holbrook also notes that the decentering process often is gradual and may take several days. Once students understand, however, they are amazed at how they missed the obvious. More important, they are sure to gain a new appreciation for children's thinking.

Holbrook also recommends that, if time permits, the jelly bean task should be tied to a discussion of critical thinking and problem-solving techniques.

Holbrook, J. E. (1992). Bringing Piaget's preoperational thought to the minds of adults: A classroom demonstration. *Teaching of Psychology, 19*(3), 16170.

Critical Thinking Activity: Preoperational Thought in Adulthood

Each unit of these resources contains a critical thinking exercise designed specifically to test students' critical thinking about a topic covered in the chapter. Handout 4 contains several brief scenarios for which the student must identify the form of preoperational thinking illustrated.

The answers to this unit's critical thinking activity follow:

1. Though you know it's not possible, you feel as if you caused your relative's death. This is an example of *egocentrism.* Contemplating the world exclusively from your own personal perspective is an example of egocentrism.
2. Your susceptibility to deceptive packaging is an example of a failure in *conservation*—the idea that the amount of a substance is unaffected by changes in its shape or placement.
3. Because your analysis of your friend's circumstances tends to focus on one aspect of her situation to the exclusion of all others, this is an example of *centration*. You are also thinking primarily of the appearance of wealth.
4. Your thinking is static, not changing. This makes it difficult for you to reverse your earlier conclusion.

*AV: Preschool Mental Development (*30 min., Insight Media)

Focusing on cognitive development in young children, this film reviews Piaget's stage model and compares it with the behaviorist approach to cognitive development. The Head Start program is described as an example of enriching the child's learning environment.

AV: How Does the Mind Grow? (60 min., RMI Media Productions)

The program begins with an overview of the major perspectives on cognitive development that have been historically significant. Two of these, Piaget's stage theory and information-processing theory, are then explored at length, including a discussion of the strengths and weaknesses of each theory.

AV: Vygotsky's Developmental Theory: An Introduction (30 min., Davidson Films)

(See description in Theories of Development.)

Classroom Activity: Scaffolding: History and Metaphors

As noted in the text, how and when children master skills depend in part on the willingness of tutors to *scaffold*, or sensitively structure the child's participation in learning encounters. Since the 1970s, scaffolding has been formally advocated as one of the most effective instructional techniques available to classroom teachers. If you would like to elaborate on the theoretical background of scaffolding, the following information should be useful. (see also the scaffolding assignment in the General Resources section of this manual).

In *Mind in Society*, Lev Vygotsky (1978) introduced the concept of the zone of proximal development, which emerged out of his argument against the use of intelligence tests and achievement tests to form the basis of childhood education. He believed that such tests assess only those abilities that are already formed, completely overlooking the dynamic quality of human cognition. Vygotsky believed that instead of focusing on what the child had already learned, researchers should focus on what the child has the potential to learn. Vygotsky states:

> A well-known and empirically established fact is that learning should be matched in some manner with the child's developmental level. Only recently, however, has attention been directed to the fact that we cannot limit ourselves merely to determining developmental levels if we wish to discover the actual relations of the developmental process to learning capabilities. We must determine at least two developmental levels. (p. 85)

Vygotsky's two developmental levels are the actual developmental level and the level of potential development. The zone of proximal development is "the distance between the actual developmental level as determined by independent problem solving and the level of potential development as determined through problem solving under adult guidance or in collaboration with more capable peers" (p. 86).

Scaffolding is the process that allows the child to move from the actual level to fulfill his or her potential. Jerome Bruner may have been the first to use the term *scaffolding.* Just as scaffolding supports a carpenter who is working on the next floor above, cognitive scaffolding provided by adults and more capable peers supports learners as they strive to achieve new developmental levels. As the learner becomes more and more comfortable with the new concepts, the "expert" systematically begins removing the scaffolding until the learner is able to support him- or herself as the skill becomes internalized. Thus, the concepts of scaffolding and teaching a child within his or her zone of proximal development are based on a social constructivist model that assumes that all knowledge is social in nature. Working from the social constructivist perspective, Bruner describes scaffolding by stating that with the help of a more knowledgeable member of the group (i.e., the teacher), learning proceeds from the interpsychological level (between individuals) to the intrapsychological level (within an individual).

The first study to empirically test the metaphor of scaffolding may have been conducted by David Wood, Jerome Bruner, and Gail Ross (1976). Their study examined how a tutor taught thirty 3-, 4-, and 5-year-olds to build a three-dimensional structure, a task that was not yet part of the children's actual developmental level. Following this seminal study, developmental psychology has focused on six variations of scaffolding or assisting performance: modeling, contingency management, feeding back, instructing, questioning, and cognitive structuring. Many early studies focusing on the use of scaffolding were conducted in the context of parent–child scaffolding.

To further help students understand the concept of scaffolding, you might use a set of bicycle training wheels as a metaphor. As educators Michael Graves, Bonnie Graves, and Stein Braaten note, a set of training wheels is a classic example of a scaffold. "It is adjustable and temporary, providing the young rider with the support he or she needs while learning to ride a two-wheeler. Without an aid of this sort, the complex task of learning to pedal, balance, and steer all at one time would be extremely difficult, if not impossible, for many youngsters. This scaffold—training wheels—allows the learner to accomplish a goal, riding a bicycle successfully, and then to happily pedal his or her way into a wider world."

Continue the discussion of scaffolding by asking students to think of other metaphors for this concept, as well as other concrete examples of how parents and educators help learners bridge the gap between what they know and can do and an intended goal. You might also extend the discussion by asking the class to think of other examples of developmental theory and research that have found their way into the classroom environment.

Bruner, J. S. (1986). *Actual minds, possible worlds*. Cambridge, MA: Harvard University Press.

Graves, M. F., Graves, B. B., & Braaten, S. (1996, February). Scaffolded reading experiences for inclusive classes. *Educational Leadership*, 14–16.

Henderson, S. D., Many, J. E., Wellborn, H. P., & Ward, J. (2002, Summer). How scaffolding nurtures the development of young children's literacy repertoire: Insiders' and outsiders' collaborative understandings. *Reading Research and Instruction, 41*(4), 30330.

Vygotsky, L. S. (1978). *Mind in society: The development of higher psychological processes*. Cambridge, MA: Harvard University Press.

Wood, D., Bruner, J. S., & Ross, G. (1976). The role of tutoring in problem solving. *Journal of Child Psychology and Psychiatry, 17*, 8100.

Classroom Activity: Overt and Covert Verbal Problem Solving

As noted in the text, Russian psychologist Lev Vygotsky believed that a child's internal dialogue, or private speech, is essential to cognitive development. Vygotsky's theory contends that private speech increases during the preschool and early school years as children use it to rehearse what they have learned. Thereafter, private speech becomes internalized as silent thinking and gradually fades away. You may wish to expand on the text coverage of private speech with the following material.

Psychologists began studying private speech as early as the 1920s, when behaviorist John Watson wrote that private speech was simply inappropriate and a temporary verbal behavior that disappears in response to parents' and teachers' disapproval.

Jean Piaget considered private speech, which he referred to as "egocentric speech," a prime example of the prelogical, centered, and cognitively immature thought processes of the preoperational child. Such speech, he believed, served no purpose in fostering the development of language or thinking.

During the 1960s, Lawrence Kohlberg and his colleagues conducted a series of studies of children's private speech that strongly supported Vygotsky's theory. They observed nearly one hundred fifty 4- to 10-year-old children during their daily classroom activities, finding that private speech first increased and then gradually decreased as the children grew older. Most striking was the fact that although this pattern was evident in all the children, the use of private speech peaked earliest—at about age 4—in the most intelligent children, peaked between 5 and 7 years of age in children of average intelligence, and disappeared almost entirely by age 9 in all children.

Kohlberg also found that the most popular and sociable children used private speech the most, which would seem to confirm Vygotsky's belief that private speech is fostered by early social experience. Piaget's and Watson's theories, by contrast, would predict that private speech would be most typical of less socially or cognitively advanced children—due to either their egocentrism (Piaget) or their delayed responsiveness to social expectations (Watson).

Kohlberg's study indicated that the form private speech takes changes systematically over time. Very young children repeat words and sounds, often in a loud, rhythmic, and playful voice. As children get older their private speech tends to describe or guide their own activity, narrating actions as if "thinking out loud." The oldest children use a barely audible and highly abbreviated muttering so that the words cannot easily be understood by an observer.

In another study, Laura Berk and then-graduate student Ruth Garvin worked with thirty-six 5- to 10-year-old Appalachian children in the mountains of eastern Kentucky. Their studies demonstrated that the kind of egocentric private speech Piaget described accounted for less than 1 percent of a child's utterances and that children who used private speech most often also talked the most to other children. That private speech is stimulated, rather than inhibited, by social experience conflicts with Piaget's contention that children would be less likely to engage in egocentric behaviors when interacting with peers.

Berk and Garvin also found that children talked to themselves much more when they were working on difficult problems, thus supporting Vygotsky's belief that private speech facilitates thinking and problem solving. In fact, how well children performed on daily math assignments was related to the maturity of their cognitive skills and private speech. Among the most intellectually competent first-graders, for example, those who used a more mature form of private speech (soft muttering) scored higher on the tests than those who still talked aloud to themselves.

In Berk's words, the research

> shows that children need learning environments that permit them to be verbally active while solving problems and completing tasks. . . . Children who are less mature or have learning problems may . . . profit from special arrangements in their classrooms, such as study corners, where they can talk aloud more freely. Requiring such children to be quiet is likely to be counterproductive, because it suppresses forms of private speech that are crucial for learning.

The latest research supports the contention that private speech is most likely to be used when children are working on difficult problems. In fact, many researchers now prefer to refer to private speech as "covert verbal problem solving." For instance, Adam Winsler and Jack Naglieri explored age-related changes in children's use and awareness of verbal problem-solving strategies (private speech) in a large (N = 2,156) cross-sectional sample of children aged 5 to 17. The data showed that with age verbal problem solving shifted from overt to partially covert to fully covert. Similarly, children's awareness of their use of verbal problem solving was initially very low but increased with age. As for the effectiveness of the use of verbal problem solving, verbal strategies were associated with greater competence among the youngest children but were unrelated to task performance among older children.

Berk, L. E. (1986, May). Private speech: Learning out loud. *Psychology Today, 20*(5), 34–42.

Berk., L. E., & Garvin, R. A. (1999). Development of private speech among low-income Appalachian children. In P. Lloyd & C. Fernyhough (Eds.), *Lev Vygotsky: Critical assessments: Thought and language* (Vol. II, pp. 446–471). Florence, KY: Taylor & Francis/Routledge.

Winsler, A., & Naglieri, J. (2003, May/June). Overt and covert verbal problem-solving strategies: Developmental trends in use, awareness, and relations with task performance in children aged 5 to 17. *Child Development, 74*(3), 659–678.

Classroom Activity: Private Speech, Emotional Regulation, Early Literacy, and ADHD

As noted in the preceding Classroom Activity, private speech is a form of language intended for the self and is often uttered by young children as they work on cognitively challenging tasks and during creative play. It has been studied extensively as a tool for self-guidance in cognitive problem solving; children, adolescents, and adults engage in private speech to focus attention, guide and pace motor activity, make transitions, self-motivate, and offer self-feedback.

Private speech may also function as a tool for self-regulation of emotion. Natalie Broderick investigated private speech use by 24 boys and 24 girls between 4 years 9 months and 5 years 6 months of age enrolled at a Head Start center. Private speech was transcribed during three preschool activities: free play chosen by the child, an art activity, and a tabletop puzzle activity. Utterances were coded by raters blind to the study hypotheses. The results showed that both girls and boys who were characterized by their teachers as socially and emotionally well regulated used more overall private speech and less negative private speech than those characterized as poorly regulated. Well-regulated children also made greater use of "metacognitive" private speech, devoted to executive cognitive functions such as planning and decision making.

Elizabeth-Anne Benedetto-Nasho explored the relationship between private speech and performance on a math computation task in children with attention-deficit/hyperactivity disorder (ADHD). Children with ADHD demonstrated lower levels of academic efficiency, used more immature computational strategies, and exhibited increased levels of inattention and disruptive behavior during the task. Moreover, ADHD and non-ADHD children differed in their private speech patterns. Children with ADHD produced more overt on-task private speech and less internalized private speech compared with the non-ADHD comparison group. A follow-up study demonstrated that stimulant medication resulted in increased developmental maturity of private speech. Under the effects of Ritalin, ADHD children produced more internalized private speech and less overt private speech.

Developmentalists and educators have proposed that teaching early literacy skills may foster a reflective awareness of the mind's activities, particularly inner thought (Winsler, 2003). In another study examining the relationship between early literacy and awareness of inner speech (Otte, 2001), 72 kindergarten children's literacy skills were tested on a letter-naming task; the children were also rated by their teachers. Awareness of inner speech was measured by direct questioning and through the children's responses to several skits. The results showed that early literacy strongly predicted children's awareness of inner speech in others. Early literacy was also significantly related to children's ability to detect inner speech in themselves.

Benedetto-Nasho, E. (2001). Use of private speech during math computation in children with attention deficit hyperactivity disorder: Methodological challenges, task performance and effects of stimulant medication. *Dissertation Abstracts International, 62*(4-A), 1321.

Broderick, N. Y. (2001). An investigation of the relationship between private speech and emotion regulation in preschool-age children. *Dissertation Abstracts International* (Section B: The Sciences & Engineering), *61*(11-B), 6125.

Otte, L. M. (2001). The relationship between children's early literacy skills and awareness of inner speech. *Dissertation Abstracts International* (Section B: The Sciences & Engineering), *61*(9-B), 5030.

Winsler, A. (2003). Vygotskian perspectives in early childhood education. *Early Childhood Education and Development, 14*(3), 253–269.

Children's Theories

Classroom Activity: Theories of Mind Across Cultures

David Premack and Diana Woodruff introduced the term *theory of mind* to refer to a tendency to impute mental states to oneself and to others in order to understand other people's behaviors, psychological states, and traits. For example, if a friend walks by without saying "hello," one might think that she or he must be preoccupied with a problem or wishing to avoid social contact. As obvious as this example will be to most, if not all, of your students, it reflects a distinctively European American (EA) theory of mind that rules out certain beliefs and is not shared by all cultures. For example, the EA theory of mind does not normally speculate that a friend who walks by without issuing a greeting is currently occupied by a witch.

One theory of how people acquire a theory of mind is that it is inborn. By this reasoning, just as people are usually born with certain physical attributes, they are also born with certain tendencies to think about the world in certain ways. This view, which is called *nativism,* suggests that theory of mind is basically the same everywhere, because it views people as good scientists who take data in from the world and adjust their social cognition to fit those data.

However, there are many reasons to suppose that there might be important cultural variations in theory of mind. As children grow into different cultures with different practices (including different languages), it would make sense that they would form different ideas about the mind that fit those practices.

The major anthropological method for conducting research in other cultures is ethnography. In this method, an anthropologist lives among a given people, observes them, and gathers first-hand knowledge about what she or he sees. The goal is not objective observation, as in the scientific method, but rather is immersion, or deep cultural knowledge, such that the observer might actually participate in that culture.

In the EA theory of mind, although the mind is equated with the brain, and especially the "self," it is considered to be distinct from the body. The mind is believed to be the seat of all mental processes and states; thus, its primary function is to subjectively process information. And how one perceives events is more important than the events themselves. Although our minds are private, this theory holds that people can infer the contents of other people's minds.

To broaden your students' understanding that the mind is a social construction, you might prepare a brief lecture on ethnopsychology, the study of cultural variations in theory of mind, and contrast the EA model with models from one or two other cultures. For example, Angeline Lillard of the University of Virginia describes the Illongots' (a tribe in the Philippines) concept of *rinawa*, which is the closest concept in their culture to the EA concept of mind, although it is linked with the heart rather than with the brain. *Rinawa* "unites concerns for thought and feeling, inner life and social context, violent anger, and such desirable consequences as fertility and health." The importance of heart and feelings in Illongot culture has more to do with basic ideas concerning conflict and cooperation than with imputing underlying motives from a person's actions. What is important for Illongots is not what goes on in the *rinawa* but rather what happens between people. The focus is not on a world of discrete selves containing mental programs but on relationships with other people.

Rinawa also has many mystical properties: It can leave the body during sleep, it animates the body while alive, and it gradually dissipates over the life course, making it thin in older persons. Even plants have *rinawa*, but processed rice has had its *rinawa* removed. In some ways, then, *rinawa* is more like a general life force than a mediator of social cognition.

As another example of cultural variation in theory of mind, consider the EA notion of dualism, which is the separation of mind and body. In contrast, in Japanese culture there is no clear, single division between mind and body, and self is not solely identified with mind. Instead, there are several gradations in Japanese words referring to various groupings of mind, body, and spirit. *Kokoro*, translated as "heart, feeling, spirit, intention, will, mind" is usually not grouped with a rational mind concept. For EAs, minds interpret events and thereby give rise to emotions, but their primary force is in cognition. Rather than being placed with a thinking head, *kokoro* is located in the heart and has strong links to blood and genes. Even more spiritual in its nature is *hara*, "the vital center of the body-mind"; *ki*, the inner state that "circulates throughout a person's body-mind"; and *seishin*, which is even more distinctively spiritual. At the other end of the spirit–body continuum, *mi* refers to the body, but it is a body permeated with mind, combining "spirit and body, mentation and sensation, the conscious and unconscious . . . not a fixed entity but a 'relational unity' which emerges out of involvement with other persons."

Cultural variations in theories of mind are also revealed through language. Over 2,000 English words are devoted to the emotions alone. In one simple study, participants were asked to describe how advertising motivated people to buy certain products; 20 American participants mentioned more than 250 different psychological processes. The Chewong of Peninsular Malaysia contrast sharply in this regard. Over the course of 17 months living among the Chewong, one researcher attempted to map out the entire Chewong vocabulary describing psychological processes. These efforts brought to light only five such terms, translated as want, want very much, know, forget, and miss or remember. A word for thinking apparently could not be found. A paltry 23 words referred to emotions, traits, and bodily states. The researcher wrote that "whereas Western cultures encourage the doctrine 'know thyself' from which we have a rich and varied vocabulary to express our inner states, the Chewong seem to take a contrasting view, namely 'suppress thyself'."

As another example of the culture-specific concept of mind, the Baining of Papua New Guinea rarely comment on reasons for actions, even their own. For Samoans, too, the mind is unknowable and motives for actions are not important. For this reason, children in Samoa do not try to get out of trouble by saying, "I did not do it on purpose," as they do in EA culture; instead, they deny having done the deed at all. As Lillard notes, mental states undoubtedly exist in these cultures; they are simply not a topic of conversation. By making them a topic of conversation, EAs emphasize them more and prime themselves to consider these states.

The concept of mind has even differed over the course of EA history. In old English, for example, mind denoted something closer to what we might now call *soul*. The word *psyche* in ancient Greek also translates better as soul, although it is often translated as mind. The EA sense of mind has, in contrast, lost all connotation of soul. For the ancient Greeks, psyche was a life force that left the person (through the mouth, like breath) at the moment of death. This seems closer to the Illongot *rinawa* than to the EA concept of mind.

Another aspect of the EA theory of mind is the tendency to view the mind as one entity. For example, one says, "I changed my mind," not "I changed my frontal lobe." In contrast, Greeks in the time of Homer used several different words referring to different parts of the mind. For example, the *thymos* was apparently the seat of motion, whereas the *noos* caused ideas and images. Furthermore, the Greeks did not believe that the individual mind was the source of all of a person's actions. Rather, some behaviors were believed to be caused by the gods. Over time, the EA mind has become a unitary concept, has lost much of its spiritual connotation, and has come to have an especially strong rational connotation.

Callaghan, T., Rochat, P., Lillard, A., Claux, M.L., Odden, H., Itakura, S., et al. (2005). Synchrony in the onset of mental-state reasoning: Evidence from five cultures. *Psychological Science, 16*(5), 378–384.

Lillard, A. (1998). Ethnopsychologies: Cultural variations in theories of mind. *Psychological Bulletin, 123*(1), 3–32.

Language

AV: Child Language: Learning Without Teaching (20 min., Davidson Films)
Out of the Mouths of Babes (28 min., Filmakers Library)
(See descriptions in The First Two Years: Cognitive Development.)

AV: Developing Language Skills (30 min., Insight Media)

This film focuses on the ways in which language changes during early childhood. It also explores the relationship between thinking and language— looking, for example, at how the home environment, including social class, influences language learning.

AV: Language Development (32 min., Magna Systems, Inc.)

This video explores the functions of language and literacy from infancy through adolescence. The roles played by adults, society, and the child's culture in stimulating language development are also discussed.

Teaching Tip: Assessing Preoperational and Language Development with Unedited Videotapes

As noted in the General Resources section of these resources and in the Classroom Activity "Assessing Sensorimotor and Language Development with Unedited Videotapes" in The First Two Years: Cognitive Development, an observational tape on cognitive and linguistic development during childhood could easily be prepared by videotaping children of various ages as they interact with their parents.

The parents should be instructed to engage their children in activities that will elicit as much language use as possible. Have the parents discuss with their children toys, favorite activities, friends, and family. You might even give the parents some of the materials (with appropriate instructions) for administering a few standard Piagetian tests of conservation.

In assessing preoperational development on the basis of the videotape, students should look for examples of *symbolic thinking, centered thinking*, and *egocentrism* in the child's play and speech. In assessing language development, students should analyze the child's speech in terms of linguistic output (for example, number of words, extent and nature of vocabulary, sentence length, and so forth) and use of grammatical rules (or, as in overregularization, the misuse of grammar).

"On Your Own" Activity: Preschool Literature

To help your students better understand the cognitive processes and entertainment needs of young children, you might ask them to examine a well-loved children's book. Many characteristics of preoperational thought and language are reflected in such books. Guide them to choose a classic rather than a recently published book; classics are more likely to have a story or theme rather than a gimmick or didactic slant. If possible, have them read the book to a young child and then complete Handout 5.

You might list the following suggested books on the board: the *I Can Read* books by Arnold Lobel; the *Amelia Bedelia* books by Peggy Parish; the *Mr.* and *Little Miss* books by Roger Hargreaves (available in inexpensive paperbacks); books for younger children by such well-known authors as Maurice Sendak, Charlotte Zolotow, and Dr. Seuss; and fairy tales, many of which are interpreted by modern authors in picture-book format.

Most students will be able to identify several of the characteristics listed in the exercise. For example, those who choose an *Amelia Bedelia* book will find that the fun is based entirely on the main character's literal interpretation of her instructions. The Lobel *I Can Read* books (including the *Frog and Toad* books and *Owl at Home*) are full of literal and egocentric interpretations of the world (e.g., talking rocks; a moon that follows an owl home and is regretfully not invited in for dinner, and a character who, when told that spring is right around the corner, goes looking for the corner).

Other stories reflect the young child's limitations in understanding the physical world (e.g., people who change size and ice cream cones that melt to everyone's great surprise).

The *Mr.* and *Little Miss* books by Roger Hargreaves are good examples of centration used as a device in writing. For instance, when the author describes "Little Miss Helpful" or "Mr. Uppity," he is taking advantage of the young child's tendency to focus on only one characteristic at a time.

Many other children's books have a strong affiliation theme and attempt to meet children's need to believe that they will never be abandoned. Many, of course, deal with separation anxiety. If students choose fairy tales, it may be worth reviewing Bruno Bettelheim's work in some depth or to suggest other psychoanalytic interpretations.

Bettelheim, B. (1977). *The uses of enchantment: The meaning and importance of fairy tales.* New York: Vintage.

Classroom Activity: Egocentric Language in Deaf Children

Although we think most often of Piaget's studies of the development of logical, or scientific, thinking in children, Piaget also wrote on the subject of language development. Many students do, in fact, ask about Piaget's views on how children acquire language. If you would like to elaborate on this subject, the following information should prove useful.

Influenced by European psychiatrists such as Charcot, Breuer, and Freud, Piaget described language acquisition in three phases: autistic, egocentric, and social. As described in the text, the earliest signs of cognitive development appear in the prelingual (or autistic) period, through sensorimotor action. Children get to know objects by handling and acting with them; only later will they learn to refer to them symbolically, as they designate them with words. The lingual period begins when the child begins to talk, around 12 to 15 months of age. However, the *semiotic function*, which occurs when children begin to use words to substitute for actions, does not begin until about 2 years of age. Vygotsky called this phenomenon *semiotic mediation.*

Symbolic reasoning occurs during the egocentric phase. Egocentric speech (also called *private speech*—see Classroom Activity "Overt and Covert Verbal Problem Solving"), according to Piaget, is slowly replaced by social speech. Note that for Vygotsky socialization is present from the time a child is born. Inner speech replaces egocentric speech in development.

As noted in the Classroom Activity "Language Rhythms in Manual Babbling" in The First Two Years: Cognitive Development, studies of language acquisition in deaf children are increasingly being used to advance developmentalists' understanding of cognitive development in all children. For instance, researchers using Piagetian tests with deaf children have consistently found evidence of comparable levels of reasoning ability, although with some delay relative to hearing children. Deaf children, although they may have a more limited experience of life, also are able to use symbolic modes other than language to solve problems. In doing so, their thinking apparently develops through interaction with the environment, independent of the presence or absence of a symbolic language system.

In one study, Celeste Kelman (2001) explored egocentric speech in deaf children by observing variations in how the semiotic function occurs. Eight Portuguese children, ages 2 to 5 years, with profound congenital deafness were selected for the study. All the children had hearing parents and none had thus far received any formal education either in spoken or signed language. Each child participated in two play sessions, planned to last 15 minutes. Both sessions were videotaped.

An egocentric event was operationally defined as a time interval during which the child was externalizing his or her reasoning, that is, when sounds or gestures were made in an apparent effort to support planning, organizing, or deciding. Each egocentric event was classified as motor reaction activity, oral-facial mimics, body expression, silent lips articulation, murmur, or vocalization. Motor reaction activities while playing with a toy included scratching the head, chin, and ears; moving the hair with the hands; and silently moving the tongue. Oral-facial mimics included moving the jaw as if articulating, forehead wrinkling, mouth gestures, cheek and eyebrow movements, and opening and closing of the mouth. Body expressions included head movements (including "yes" and "no" movements); arm, shoulder, and trunk movements; and clapping and other hand gestures.

Like hearing children, all the deaf children displayed egocentric behaviors in each category. Body expressions were the most frequent category of egocentric behavior (34%), followed by vocalization (21%), oral-facial mimics (19%), silent articulation (12%), murmuring (9%), and motor activity reactions (6%).

Kelman, C. A. (2004). Deaf children in regular classrooms: A sociocultural approach to a Brazilian experience. *American Annals of the Deaf, 149*(3), 274–-280.

Kelman, C. A. (2001). Egocentric language in deaf children. *American Annals of the Deaf, 146*(3), 276–279.

AV: Life Is But a Dream: Parents Help Language-Delayed Kids (29 min., Filmakers Library)
Milestones: Language for the Young Deaf (14 min., Filmakers Library)

Beyond showing steps that parents can take to help hearing-impaired children learn language, both of these films provide good starting points for discussing the language-learning process in general.

*AV: The Wild Child (*85 min., black and white, United Artists)

This film, about the famous nineteenth-century French "wolf boy," is a work of art (it won first prize at the Cannes Film Festival) as well as a source for much speculation and discussion, if your class schedule allows for such a lengthy film. After the boy was found, he was exhibited in a cage until Dr. Itard persuaded the authorities to allow him to teach the boy. The teaching process is surprisingly behavioristic and meets with some success as the boy learns to talk, wear shoes, and act "civilized."

One way to use this film is to describe the idea of the critical period and then show how difficult it is to know what would have happened to this boy if he had been raised in a normal family. One difficulty is that we do not know if the child was essentially normal before he became lost or abandoned. Incidentally, Kipling's wonderful story about an infant raised by wolves is just that, a story: Children who are too young to find their own food and shelter die.

AV: Talk to the Animals (14 min., CRM/McGraw-Hill)

Originally a segment from the CBS *60 Minutes* program, this film shows chimpanzees and gorillas in experimental laboratories in Stanford, California, Oklahoma University, and the Yerkes Primate Center in Atlanta learning to communicate. The film explores possible applications of such research to children with special needs. It also raises some interesting questions about the function and structure of language, as well as about whether the creative use of language can be taught using step-by-step programmed techniques. (Most chimpanzee researchers believe that their animals use language creatively to express original ideas, but many other scientists remain skeptical.)

Early-Childhood Education

Classroom Activity: The Maria Montessori Story

A description of Maria Montessori's educational philosophy may be a useful addition to your discussion of the Montessori preschool program. Following is some basic information.

Early in her life, Montessori (1870–1952) fought doggedly for the right of women to study medicine. Not long after becoming Italy's first female physician, however, she left medicine to pursue her concern for the educational plight of poor children. Montessori developed her philosophy in the early part of the twentieth century through her work with mentally challenged and handicapped children and, later, children from impoverished families in the slums of Rome. Her views found their way to the United States as early as the 1920s, but it was not until the 1960s that they became widespread, primarily among middle-class families who started cooperative Montessori preschools. Today, Montessori preschools number around 4,000 in this country.

Central to the Montessori method are four premises: (1) children learn by using all of their senses; (2) they have an inborn love of order; (3) children prefer to choose their own activities, which they treat as serious work; and (4) during certain "sensitive periods," children are particularly ready to grasp specific intellectual concepts.

The typical Montessori curriculum reflects this philosophy. For example, in "experiences of practical life," students from an early age learn to control their sensory environment through such activities as washing tables and carrying chairs. A bit later, with the help of the sandpaper alphabet Montessori made famous, they learn to recognize the letters of the alphabet not only by sight but also by touch. Similarly, math concepts are explored through a variety of tangible materials, including rods, cylinders, bells, and blocks.

The emphasis on order in the classroom means that respect and self-sufficiency are important social goals in the Montessori program. Children learn not to disturb others, including the teacher, when they are busy with their own work.

Maria Montessori was intrigued by the ability of even the youngest children to concentrate on tasks that they themselves had chosen. Accordingly, she made many of her teaching materials "self-correcting," so that the children could grasp the relevant intellectual concepts without instruction from the teacher.

Montessori's curriculum also reveals her conviction that children are ready to master specific concepts at certain times. Children are often grouped by age, on the theory that they learn at different rates.

Some educators criticize Montessori programs as being too conformist and for disallowing the playful, spontaneous behavior that often is part of preschool development. "For a kid who is highly impulsive and disorganized, a particular Montessori school might be a perfect match," notes Sylvia Feinburg of Tufts University's Department of Child Study. "But many children already have too much control in their lives and could benefit from breaking loose a little."

This emphasis on "work" over "play" is not found to the same degree in all Montessori classrooms. Although Montessori herself was a harsh critic of teacher-initiated fantasy play, many contemporary Montessori training programs advocate classroom art, music, and drama activities.

Other critics worry about the apparent lack of structure in a typical Montessori classroom. Advocates point out that only the *materials*, rather than the specific use of children's time, are highly structured. Once a child learns how to work with the materials, he or she can choose to work with any of them for as long as desired. As one Montessori parent notes, "The teacher rarely interferes, other than to notice when a child is ready to be introduced to a new level of materials, or to make sure that the classroom's ground rules are being observed."

A number of psychologists have argued that the Montessori method is better suited to primary-grade instruction than to preschool instruction. Consistent with this argument, at least 100 public elementary schools nationwide offer some form of the Montessori program as an option. Furthermore, mixed-age grouping of children in the early years of school is now widely regarded as desirable because such groupings encourage children to learn at their own pace. Angeline Lillard and Nicole Else-Quest recently compared cognitive/academic and social/ behavioral skills among 59 students who were attending a Montessori school with those of 53 control children attending non-Montessori schools. Each group included a 5-year-old subgroup and a 12-year-old subgroup. The results revealed significant advantages for the Montessori children over the control children in both age groups.

The best advice for parents considering a Montessori program is to get a sense of the individual style of the program. Montessori schools have diverse approaches, depending on whether they're affiliated with the stricter (and more European) Association Montessori Internationale or the more liberal American Montessori Society. For more information, you might direct students to the Web sites of the Montessori Foundation (www.montessori.org).

Cushman, K. (1993, January). The Montessori story. *Parents*, 80–84.

Lillard, A., & Else-Quest, N. (2006, September). Evaluating Montessori education. *Science, 313*(5795), 1893–1894.

Shute, N. (2002, September). Madam Montessori. *Smithsonian, 33*(6), 70–74.

Classroom Activity: Preschool Testing

Parents and young children are finding that school-readiness tests and IQ tests are becoming more common as a component of the admissions process for many special and private school programs. Despite the controversy surrounding the use of such tests, including questions about their reliability and validity, nearly everyone finds the subject of intelligence testing fascinating. You may wish to elaborate on this topic with some of the following information.

Readiness tests are most often used to place children in programs appropriate to their level of ability and to differentiate children with learning disabilities. Two commonly used readiness tests are the Gesell Developmental Observation Kindergarten Assessment Test and the Metropolitan Readiness Tests. The Gesell test is a subjective test (there are no right or wrong answers) that takes about half an hour. During the test, children draw, build with blocks, and are asked to talk about things they like to do. A child's score depends as much on his or her behavior during the test as it does on the ability to perform the tasks.

The Metropolitan Readiness Tests are divided into two levels. Level 1, which is intended for beginning kindergartners, measures listening skills, letter recognition, auditory memory, and visual- and sound-matching abilities. Level 2 measures the same things as Level 1, except that it is intended for beginning first-graders and so is written at a higher level. Each level takes about 90 minutes to administer.

IQ tests are often required for admission to private schools. Although several states have banned IQ testing for use in public schools, some public-school programs continue to require them. The two most frequently used tests for measuring intelligence in early childhood are the Stanford-Binet Intelligence Scale and the Wechsler Preschool and Primary Scale of Intelligence (WPPSI). The first IQ test to be widely used in the United States, the Stanford-Binet takes 30 to 40 minutes to administer. Created to measure reasoning and memory skills, the test has children define words, trace mazes, construct with blocks, identify missing parts of pictures, and demonstrate their knowledge of numbers. The WPPSI, given to children between the ages of 3 and 7½, consists of 11 subtests that yield 3 separate scores for each child: verbal IQ, performance IQ, and a combined full-scale IQ.

A less widely used preschool IQ test is Raven's Colored Progressive Matrices. Based on nonverbal skills, the Raven measures intelligence by having children figure out visual patterns and color sequences.

A major difficulty with preschool IQ tests is that they can be inaccurate. A five-point margin of error on the Stanford-Binet and WPPSI is not uncommon. Because IQ scores are based partly on the test administrator's subjective analysis of a child's verbal responses, the same test given by two different administrators may produce scores that vary by as many as 10 points. And although WPPSI and Stanford-Binet test scores are positively correlated, a child's scores on the two tests may differ by 15 points or more.

Another problem with the tests is that scores can be influenced by many factors other than the children's cognitive abilities. One of the most important is the rapport between the child and test administrator. For example, an otherwise cooperative and socially outgoing child who doesn't hit it off with the tester may score 20 points below his or her potential. Similarly, the tests may penalize the most creative and divergent thinkers, who intentionally refuse to answer certain questions, or offer instead unusual, or quirky, responses.

Finally, many developmentalists believe that intelligence cannot be reliably tested in children before about 7 years of age, which would seem to render standardized tests for young children useless in meeting their original purpose—predicting academic performance. One reason they do not predict future performance is that the tests measure only one aspect of a child's potential, revealing nothing about personality variables, such as motivation, that might be equally important.

Cohen, R. J., & Swerdlik, M. E. (2009). *Psychological testing and assessment: An introduction to tests and measurement* (7th ed.). New York: McGraw-Hill.

Sattler, J. M. (2001). *Assessment of children: Cognitive implications* (4th ed.). La Mesa, CA: Sattler.

AV: The Preschool Experience: Four Programs (22 min., CRM/McGraw-Hill)

This film explores the functions of nursery school, day-care centers, and kindergartens, showing how children interact with one another and with teachers in various group settings. Four programs are shown: an Assistance League nursery, which provides care for 10 full hours a day; a Montessori school, which emphasizes individual curiosity and independence; the Gesell Nursery School in New Haven, Connecticut; and the Kedren Health Center in central Los Angeles, which tries to prepare children for kindergarten. Good discussion questions related to the film include the following: Are the differences among the four schools determined primarily by the formal goals of each program or by the age and background of the children? Is one type of school best for all children, or are some children better served by certain types of programs, and other children by other programs?

AV: The Impact of the Classroom Environment on Child Development (18 min., Davidson Films)

This film illustrates how three imaginative preschool teachers created an enriched learning environment for their children out of everyday materials and events. Providing a good antidote to the idea that a wealth of commercially manufactured materials is essential to preschool education, the film is particularly relevant if your class includes a large number of teachers or teachers-to-be.

AV: Men in Early Childhood Education (24 min., Davidson Films)

This film illustrates the sensitivity and value of men as preschool educators. The inescapable point of the film is that men's ideas and presence make the classroom a better place.

AV: Early Childhood Training Series: Path to Math (15 min., Magna Systems)

This series of five videos presents images of children using their senses of vision, hearing, smell, touch, and taste as they explore their environments and develop rudimentary mathematical concepts. The "path to math" consists of the following steps: (1) One-to-One Correspondence; (2) Sets and Classification (Seriation and Ordering); (3) Shape, Parts and Wholes; (4) Space and Measurement; and (5) Number and Counting.

Classroom Activity: Mandatory Pre-K Education?

Since the early 1800s, countries such as the United States have viewed education as a ticket to success. What's more, for the framers of the Constitution such as Thomas Jefferson, no democracy could function properly without literate voters. Out of this tradition grew the movement for compulsory public schooling from kindergarten to age 18.

After years of debate on the merits of pre-kindergarten (pre-K) education, researchers have found evidence that it is too late to begin schooling at age 5 or 6. Children form basic cognitive abilities in their earliest years; those who are not exposed to letters, numbers, and social skills (in preschool programs or at home) quickly fall behind those who are. Children from lower socioeconomic groups typically begin formal schooling a full year and a half behind their more affluent peers and so are late in developing language ability. Advocates of free preschool education for all children believe that providing disadvantaged kids with the chance to begin schooling earlier would make a lifelong difference. They would do better in school and as adults, when they would more likely become productive workers.

Studies show that pre-K education benefits children at all income levels, with lower socioeconomic groups reaping the most benefit. Experts point to data showing a payback of nearly $4 for every $1 invested in poor children's early education. Those figures have caught the attention of politicians such as former Vice President Al Gore, who in 2000 proposed spending $50 billion a year to offer preschool to every 3- and 4-year-old.

The Carolina Abecedarian Project followed 111 low-income North Carolina children for 21 years, starting in the 1970s. Half were enrolled in pre-K education from infancy to age 5, while a comparison group received only nutritional supplements. The program ended when the children entered kindergarten, after which those in both groups attended comparable public schools. Over the duration of the study, students who attended the pre-K program were less likely to drop out of school, repeat grades, or have unwanted pregnancies. By age 15, less than one-third had failed a grade, versus more than half of the comparison group. At age 21, they were more than twice as likely to have attended a four-year college.

On March 25, 2005, actor Rob Reiner launched an education initiative designed to ensure that all California children had access to preschool education. Under Proposition 82, the "Pre-school for All" initiative, a full year of preschool would be made available to all California 4-year-olds. Because the proposition was opposed by Governor Arnold Schwarzenegger and by 60.9 percent of those who voted in the 2006 primary election, it did not pass.

Karoly, L. A., & Bigelow, J. H. (2005). *The economics of investing in universal preschool education in California.* Santa Monica, CA: Rand Corporation Monograph Series. (www.rand.org).

Kirp, D. L. (2008). *Universal preschool's big payoff.* California State Conference. NAACP. Retrieved October 10, 2008, from http://californianaacp.org/news/preschool/200606_preschool_news/

Starr, A. (2002, August 26). Preschool education for the poor—and perhaps all children—is a must. *Business Week, 3796*, 164–165.

AV: Failures Before Kindergarten (28 min., Films for the Humanities and Sciences)

(See description in The First Two Years: Cognitive Development.)

Classroom Activity: Early Education: The Importance of Cognitive Skills

To get your students to focus on the importance of developing cognitive skills during early childhood, have them address one of the complaints that many developmental psychologists voice about most preschools: They emphasize social skills rather than cognitive skills and the development of initiative. You might want to bring advertisements and brochures from various preschools to class (or ask students to do so) to get an idea of what is available in your area.

Ask the students to form small groups and have each one plan the curriculum for a preschool, indicating how much time would be spent on reading, singing, arts and crafts, playing outside, talking, doing puzzles, and so on. Simply raising students' consciousness about such activities for children ages 3 to 5 years should be helpful.

One problem with providing good preschool training is financial, a problem not considered by most people. To get your students to address this issue, ask them how much it would cost to run their "ideal" school for a year. Be sure they include the costs of the building—rental or ownership—utilities, and insurance. Even if the teachers are paid relatively little, the cost will probably exceed $2,000 a year per child. (See also Classroom Activity "Supplemental Preschool Education" for some cost information.)

Classroom Activity: Preschool Teacher Perceptions as Predictors of Future Achievement

As each of your students can probably attest, teachers regularly make judgments about the abilities of students. Social-cognitive theorists have long been fascinated with the messages such appraisals convey to students, and especially their potential to become self-fulfilling prophecies as teachers develop expectations that alter their classroom behavior with individual students.

In a provocative longitudinal study, Jennifer Alvidrez and Rhona S. Weinstein explored relationships among preschool teachers' appraisals of intelligence, family demographics, and children's future high school performance. The study used a core sample of 128 children (64 boys and 64 girls) recruited in 1968 from two Berkeley, California, preschools when the children were 3 or 4 years of age.

The most recent report is based on data collected when the children were 4, 6, 11, and 18. These ages were chosen because both teacher ratings and Wechsler IQ scores were obtained at ages 4 and 11, assessments of the child's home environment were conducted at age 6, and high school grades, SAT Reasoning Test scores, and IQ scores were available at age 18. Teachers rated each child using the 100-item California Child Q–Set, an age-appropriate scale that contains a range of items about social, personality, and cognitive traits. When each child was 6 years old, psychologists visited their homes and completed the Environmental Q–Sort, an inventory that measures various dimensions of the home setting, including physical characteristics and social atmosphere (e.g., orderliness), the values emphasized by the family (e.g., intellectual orientation, warmth) and characteristics of behavior patterns of the mother (this test does not contain items about the father's characteristics).

Among the intriguing results of the study were the following:

- Teacher judgments of child intelligence at age 4 were frequently related to noncognitive factors as well as cognitive traits. For example, teachers tended to overestimate the intelligence of children they saw as competent, independent, and assertive and to underestimate the intelligence of children perceived as immature and insecure.
- The ability of children from higher socioeconomic status (SES) backgrounds was also judged more positively and the ability of children from lower SES backgrounds was judged more negatively than IQ scores alone would have predicted.
- IQ at age 4 accounted for the largest proportion of the variance in grade point average (GPA) at age 18 (19%). SES accounted for an additional 4 percent of the variance in GPA.
- After controlling for SES, preschool teachers' over- and underestimates of intelligence relative to IQ score significantly predicted GPA and SAT Reasoning Test scores 14 years later.
- Teacher predictions were weakest in homes rated by observers as more orderly or with mothers who were more career or community active.

However, the researchers are cautious in interpreting the results of this fascinating longitudinal study. They note, for example, that data collection for the project began almost 30 years ago. As with any longitudinal study, the findings, particularly those regarding teacher judgment and bias according to social class, may not be generalizable to school settings today.

One thing is clear: Teacher practices strongly influence student academic achievement. Research has consistently shown that, even after controlling for demographic differences in children entering school, in classrooms where teachers offer more instructional and social-emotional support, children make greater gains in math and behavioral skills, and they perceive themselves as more competent. Teachers do so by attending to students' interests and initiatives, providing scaffolded and challenging learning opportunities, and fostering a classroom environment in which positive relationships develop (Perry, Donohue, & Weinstein, 2007).

Alvidrez, J., & Weinstein, R. S. (1999). Early teacher perceptions and later student academic achievement. *Journal of Educational Psychology, 91*(4), 731–746.

Perry, K. E., Donohue, K. M., & Weinstein, R. S. (2007). Teaching practices and the promotion of achievement and adjustment in first grade. *Journal of School Psychology, 45*(3), 26292.

Classroom Activity: Supplemental Preschool Education

At a parent–teacher conference a number of years ago, Elizabeth and Antonio Trindade were informed that their son Lorenzo simply couldn't keep up with the rigorous academic curriculum of the top Manhattan public school he attended. Ms. Trindade was crushed. Her dreams of Lorenzo's future at an Ivy League university were shattered.

"Sad," you say, "but not unusual. This sort of academic screening happens all the time." What made this situation unusual was that Lorenzo was only 6 years old. He was failing kindergarten.

So distraught were Lorenzo's parents that they responded as if their child had been diagnosed with a serious illness: They sought a second (and third) opinion with a child psychologist and a pediatrician. Finally admitting Lorenzo was having trouble keeping up, they enrolled him in the Huntington Learning Center, one of the many high-powered (and expensive) tutorial and educational centers that have cropped up across the country.

For some older adults, a "preschool" child is just that: a child before school age. Since 1970, however, the number of 5-, 4-, and even 3-year-olds in organized preschool programs has skyrocketed. And for parents such as Lorenzo's, even this is not enough. Thousands of parents across the country are enrolling their children in "supplemental education" programs such as Huntington, Sylvan, and Score. This booming business caters to parents who are either dissatisfied with schools or fearful that their children need every possible advantage in an increasingly competitive world.

Learning centers are a contemporary variation of old-style tutoring. In fact, the promise of individualized attention is why many parents seek help outside their children's schools. Both Sylvan and Huntington have a ratio of one tutor per three pupils. To increase motivation, Sylvan offers an incentive plan in which students can earn points toward winning a prize, such as a pair of Rollerblades. Sylvan guarantees that a student's reading skills will jump at least one reading level after 36 hours of tutelage.

The other fast-growing component of the supplemental education industry is computer software. Such titles as "Lemonade for Sale (MathStart 3)," "Reader Rabbit," and "Where in the World Is Carmen San Diego?" already constitute something of a canon. Although the biggest sellers are aimed at children from preschool through third grade, the target group gets younger every year. Today's popular preschool offerings include "Sesame Street: Elmo's Preschool" (ages 2 to 5), "Ready to Read with Pooh" (ages 3 to 6), "Jumpstart Toddlers" (ages 1½ to 3), Disney's "The Wiggles" (ages 3+) and "Learning with Nemo" (ages 2 to 5), "Dr. Seuss Preschool" (ages 2 to 4), and the wildly popular "Jumpstart Baby" (9 to 24 months).

One concern of many developmentalists is the idea that cognitive ability can be reliably measured in young children. At some learning centers, incoming students undergo two to three hours of diagnostic testing to determine reading level, phonetic ability, reading comprehension, and overall learning strengths and weaknesses. Parents quickly buy into such testing, not realizing there are vast differences in normal cognitive development. Some children excel in early grades; others take longer to bloom. A child who achieves early academic success may simply be more mature and better organized than other children. This child may be labeled early as a high achiever, only to struggle later as the school curriculum changes.

Especially troublesome are at-home computer assessments of cognitive development. Designed to be fun, these tests are contemporary versions of the old at-home IQ tests of days past. Although experts caution parents against placing too much weight on such tests, parents find it difficult to avoid doing so.

Experts also bemoan the fact that lower-income children, many of whom would greatly benefit from extra help, are less likely to get it, causing some to fall even further behind academically. Educational software begins at around $45. In any case, most low-income families don't have home computers. One session at a learning center can cost upwards of $100 an hour, depending on the child's age and skill level, and the centers suggest three hours a week, putting the price beyond the reach of many families. A small number of public school systems, using federal grants, have contracted with Sylvan and other learning centers to provide tutoring in disadvantaged schools. These schools, however, are few and far between.

As parental demand for early learning has grown, local governments have begun stepping in. Today, 40 states offer publicly funded pre-kindergarten programs (McNeil, 2008). Although admission usually hinges on financial need, a few states are moving toward universal pre-K, so called because it provides a place for every child whose parents want one. Georgia has funded universal pre-K since 1995. And beginning in fall 1998, New York began funding 19,000 slots for pre-kindergartners, chosen mainly by lottery. As noted earlier, some states have not been as successful. California's proposal for tax-funded universal preschool was soundly defeated in June 2006.

As an informative classroom exercise, you might ask a representative from a local learning center to speak to the class. Alternatively, you might arrange for a group of students to visit a learning center and report back to the class. Still another idea is to have students evaluate popular educational Web sites touting age-appropriate activities to stimulate cognitive development in young children. One of the most widely visited sites, hosted by the "Nick Jr" television network, can be found at www.nickjr.com/kids-activities. Finally, you might have a group of students research and present to the class the current status of the universal preschool movement nationally and in their home states.

Buckleitner, W., & Orr, A. (2002, April). Mathstart: Lemonade for sale. *Instructor, 111*(7), 71.

Lohr, S. (1998, April 3). Toddlers are next hope of software industry. *New York Times.* Retrieved from www.nytimes.com.

McNeil, M. (2008, February 27). States struggle to find secure pre-K funding. *Education Week.* Retrieved February 27, 2008 from www.edweek.org/ew/index.html.

Morse, J. (1998, November 9). Preschool for everyone. *Time, 152*(19), 98.

AV: Cultural Bias in Education (28 min., Films for the Humanities and Sciences)

This program explores the various roadblocks to Latino academic advancement in the United States, including the relationship between standardized testing and cultural diversity, and the catering of early childhood education programs to majority-culture families.

Classroom Activity: Balanced Reading Instruction for ENL First Graders

Regarding children for whom English is a new language (ENL), some experts take the stance that different ethnic groups or minorities require specific kinds of instruction. For example, some argue that the usual *process* approaches are ineffective for some minority children because they do not include explicit instruction in strategies and knowledge needed to acquire "accepted" forms of reading and writing. Those who work from this perspective also argue that instruction for ENL children works best when teachers adapt their instructional methods to make them "culturally sensitive" to each child's home language and conversation style.

Other experts maintain that focusing on "what is best for one group and what is best for another group" is counterproductive and unlikely to result in the greatest success. Working from this perspective, they contend that culturally sensitive teaching promotes generic ways of teaching for specific groups, and this in itself tends to promote (and perpetuate) cultural stereotypes.

In the field of reading instruction, *balanced* teaching has recently emerged as a curriculum that distributes weight across several important features of reading and combines several major historical approaches to reading. You may wish to prepare a brief mini-lecture on this method, particularly if the class includes a number of teachers-in-training.

In a naturalistic study, Jill Fitzgerald and George Noblit examined first-grade children's emergent reading development in the context of a yearlong balanced reading instruction program. The study involved a class of 20 first-grade students at the New Hope Elementary School—a diverse school in which 43 percent of the students were White of Anglo descent, 37 percent were Black of African descent, and 18 percent were Hispanic.

At the beginning of the year, only 7 of the 20 children could write their first name correctly; only 10 could name all letters when shown in random order, and only 3 children could read any words at all. Every ethnic group was represented in the group of children with the more advanced skills, and this was the case also for the children with lower-level skills.

The balanced reading program includes four components, and the teacher in this study included at least one daily activity to represent each of those components.

- word study: learning sight words and various word-recognition strategies, including using context, phonics, and structural analysis
- responding to good literature during or after reading or listening
- writing
- guided and unguided reading "practice," which provided opportunities for students to use all the dynamic features of the reading process while reading

Throughout the school year, a graduate student/participant-observer gathered data by analyzing samples of student work, videotaping student lessons, and administering a variety of formal and informal assessments. (NOTE: As a separate topic, you may wish to elaborate on this *constant-comparison method* of gathering data in the field.)

The results attested to the effectiveness of the balanced approach to reading instruction. Specifically, several emerging themes indicated that the children were developing a balanced view of reading that paralleled their instruction.

- The development of "local" knowledge about reading. There were marked improvements in phonological awareness, sight-word vocabularies, ability to match correct letters to sounds, word recognition strategies, and knowledge of word meanings.
- The emergence of "global" knowledge about reading. Over the course of the year, the children showed increasing evidence that they were not just learning about words and word-getting strategies but rather that reading and writing were about understanding and communicating. During the fall semester, for example, when the teacher read books orally to the class, she nearly always had to erect elaborate scaffolds through questioning and guided discussion to elicit responses from her students. During the spring semester, however, the children seemed much better able to understand new books that they read independently and were developing a keener sense of how reading and writing can play a role in establishing relationships.
- The development of heightened motivation to read. The children's responsiveness and desire to read was demonstrated in a variety of ways, including the choice of "listening room" activities before school started and during play time.
- Generative moments that signaled the children's movement toward more mature reading abilities. The teacher describes one of these breakthrough moments herself:

  Today in Roberto's reading meeting, I thought I'd try to do another mini-lesson on the "compare-contrast strategy [onset-rime]," even though not many of the children seem to be getting it yet. I started writing "at," "fat," "sat," "mat" up on the dry erase board. Roberto raised his hand, and he said, "I can do them." I said, "You can *do* them?" and he nodded. He read right lickety-split through them—"at," "cat," "mat"—the whole long list. I had every "at" word that you can possibly have on there. Well, all the children in the group were just in awe. They were just staring at him, they couldn't believe it. He finished, and there was this big silence. (Teacher's journal, February 14)

Fitzgerald, J., & Noblit, G. (2000). Balance in the making: Learning to read in an ethnically diverse first-grade classroom. *Journal of Educational Psychology, 92*(1), 3–22.

Classroom Activity: Preschool and Family Support Differences in France and the United States

While Americans extol the benefits of early-childhood education, the French do far more to provide preschool to all their children. Virtually all French children attend preschool, and 8 of 10 go to free, government-supported schools. It's the same throughout much of Europe. More than 90 percent of 4-year-olds in England, Luxembourg, Germany, Denmark, Italy, and the Netherlands attend public preschool. In Greece and Spain, these percentages are nearly as high: 70 percent and 80 percent, respectively. And in virtually every industrialized country in the world, high-quality preschool is provided free-of-charge for children regardless of family income. Critics contend that the United States is the opposite, with a patchwork of preschools, many with weakly trained, poorly paid staff. John Merrow notes that, "Although 70% of American 4-year-olds and 40% of 3-year-olds are enrolled in some sort of preschool program, the quality ranges from excellent to abysmal, and the cost from $15,000 to zero. Teachers' salaries may be $38,000 a year—with benefits—or as little as $8 or $9 an hour without benefits."

Children are born into poverty in France and the United States at the same rate—25 percent in the United States and 24 percent in France. By age 6, however, child poverty in France decreases to 7 percent, while in the United States it drops only to 17 percent. The greater improvements in France are due, in large measure, to differences in government policy in the two countries. For one thing, children in France are born into a socialized system of universal health care and financial support for families. New mothers, for instance, receive 14 weeks of paid maternity leave, which many combine with the several weeks of paid summer vacation French citizens enjoy in order to stay home with their newborns much longer. When French mothers do go to work outside the home, they can place their babies in a government-subsidized child-care center—called a *crèche*—where they make co-payments based on their incomes. The directors of the crèches are public-health nurses with child-development training. And the adults who work with the children, called "young-child educators," are required to have at least two years of training.

Another difference is that French preschool teachers create lessons within a standard curriculum established by the Ministry of Education. The curriculum establishes minimum standards that all schools must meet.

Interestingly, if Congress expanded Head Start to serve all 11.2 million 3- to 5-year-olds in the United States, the cost would be an estimated $41.6 billion a year. If the French program were expanded to accommodate this many young children, the cost would be about $17.9 billion, or only about $8 billion more than the $10 billion former president Clinton asked Congress to approve just to educate underprivileged children in Head Start programs.

Jacobson, L. (2001, July 11). Looking to France. *Education Week, 20*(42), 20–21.

Merrow, J. (2002, July 17). European preschools should embarrass USA. *USA Today,* A15.

Classroom Activity: Classroom Debate: *"Resolved: A Quality Preschool Education Provides Children with Academic and IQ Gains Beyond Those of Young Children Who Remain at Home"*

A 21-year study conducted by researchers at the University of North Carolina, Chapel Hill, provides evidence that a high-quality preschool program can furnish children with academic and IQ gains that last well into their adolescent years.

The researchers followed 111 infants from low-income families from birth until age 15. Half the children were in a high-quality, five-year preschool program, beginning, on average, as a 1-year-old; the rest (the comparison group) received no preschool training. The results demonstrated a significant preschool effect. At age 3, the preschool group averaged 16.5 points higher on a standardized IQ test. At age 15, they still averaged 4.5 IQ points higher than the comparison group. On standardized reading tests (mean = 100), the preschool children scored 95; the comparison group averaged 87.5 on the test. Scores on math tests yielded similar results: 92.3 for young children, and 86 for the comparison group. Finally, during their first 10 years of school only 30 percent of the young children were held back one grade, while 56.5 percent of the comparison group were held back.

Even more dramatic are the findings from the High/Scope Educational Research Foundation's Perry Preschool study. This study followed the fortunes of low-income African American children enrolled in the program in 1962. The High/Scope researchers found that by age 27, those who had been enrolled in the program had attained higher levels of education, higher economic status, and greater social responsibility than those in a matched control group. In terms of social responsibility, as adults they stayed married longer, had fewer arrests, and owned homes and cars at a higher rate. Furthermore, those in the preschool group had spent significantly less time being dependent upon social services.

These findings come at a time when increased funding for programs such as Head Start is being debated. Those opposed to increased funding point to evidence that the effects of Head Start and other preschool programs disappear by the second or third grade and maintain that results such as those from the Perry Preschool study are simply atypical. However, the issue is far from resolved, and the debate is likely to continue for some time.

To understand the discrepancy between studies that have found long-term benefits of preschool and those that have not, education professor Steve Barnett reviewed 22 studies of preschool programs for children ages 3 and 4 that followed the children at least through the third grade (including the Head Start Synthesis study, which is often cited as evidence for the fading effects of preschool).

Barnett's analysis reveals that although preschool programs initially raise IQ scores (by some 12 IQ points in the Perry Preschool study), the effects decline after children leave the program and become insignificant by the third grade. At the same time, however, preschool often improves school outcomes, such as achievement test scores and graduation rates.

Barnett points to two reasons for the discrepancy between IQ scores and other measures of academic success. The first is that IQ is simply a poor measure of intelligence and is only one factor in school success. (The Perry Preschool study is notable for its unusually broad range of "real-life outcome measures.") The second reason is that most studies of the long-term benefits of preschool have a significant methodological flaw.

> The reason that effects on achievement appear to fade out over time in most longitudinal studies is that these studies gradually excluded from their samples children retained in grade or placed in special-education classes. . . . Thus, in most studies, grade retention and special education produce increasingly selective attrition in achievement-test scores over time that gradually equates the *tested* groups of preschool and no-preschool children on academic ability. As a result, initial differences in achievement-test scores appear to fade out over time. Long-term preschool studies show that as the differences in grade retention and special-education placements between preschool and no-preschool groups rise over time, the differences in test scores between children in the two groups remaining at grade level in regular classes decline.

Edward Zigler, the Yale professor considered the "father" of Head Start, points to another factor that may have contributed to the success of the Perry Preschool Project: the overall excellence of the program, which also had teachers visit the children's homes for an hour and a half each week. Other features of the project, as well as of any high-quality preschool program, include a developmentally appropriate curriculum that allows children to take charge of their own learning, well-trained teachers who work under knowledgeable supervision, and a ratio of students to teachers that is no higher than 10 to 1.

Quality preschool education has some long-term benefits for the public at large: monetary savings. According to the latest research, $4 to $7 is the eventual savings to the public for every dollar invested in high-quality preschool programs. In the state of Washington, for example, the Early Childhood Education and Assistance Program—which combines education, health, and social services—costs $3,000 per child. However, according to the state's Council for Educational Research and Development, "each child who does not succeed in adult life could cost the state as much as $200,000 in lost income and social dependency."

So what is to be done? First, according to Barnett, federal funding for Head Start or similar programs should be increased to the amount required to provide Perry-quality preschool programs to all poor children. Second, Barnett urges Congress to create an office of early-childhood policy research "to evaluate the results of current programs and fund experiments to investigate the long-term impacts of alternative program designs on costs and benefits so that program efficiency can be improved." Yet just as some legislators are waking up to the constructive role preschool education plays, others are moving to cut funding for the programs, offered most often to low-income families. Preschool attendance rates vary from state to state. The states with the highest preschool enrollments are New Jersey (75%), Massachusetts (72%), and Georgia (71%). The states with the lowest enrollment are Nevada (44%), Idaho (51%), and West Virginia (51%). In Mexico, where preschool is free, 81 percent of 4-year-olds were enrolled in preschool in 2005.

To increase your students' awareness of the pros and cons of preschool education, follow the guidelines in the General Resources section for scheduling a classroom debate on this resolution. This topic is an especially appropriate one for students who are parents of young children.

Barnett, W. .S. (2004). Does Head Start have lasting cognitive effects? The myth of fade-out. In E. Zigler & S. Styfco (Eds.), *The Head Start Debates.* Baltimore, MD: Brookes.

Schweinhart, L. J., Barnes, H. V., & Weikart, D. P. (Eds.). (1993) *Significant Benefits: The High / Scope Perry Preschool Study Through Age 27.* Ypsilanti, MI: High/Scope Press, 1993.

Zehr, M. A. (2007, April 12). Preschool attendance: More likely in Mexico than in the United States. *Education Week Onlihne.* http://blogs.edweek. org/edweek/learning-the-language/2007/04/preschool_attendance_more_like_1.html.

Internet Activity: Preschool Education Around the World

As efforts to expand preschool education in this country have increased, so has interest in looking to other countries to see how they are educating their youngest children. An excellent way to introduce the class to preschool education around the world is to assign small groups of students to use Internet resources to research preschool education in specific countries (see Handout 6) and then report back to the class. Alternatively, you might allow students to report on the country of their ethnic heritage. One system of early-childhood education that has captured the attention of educators and policymakers alike is that found in France (see the Classroom Activity "Preschool and Family Support Differences in France and the United States"). The French do far more to provide preschool to all their children. Virtually all French children attend preschool, and 8 of 10 go to free, government-supported schools. By contrast, 70 percent of American 4-year-olds and only 40 percent of 3-year-olds attend preschool.

In addition to their availability, French preschools are a bargain. It costs more than twice as much to enroll a child in Head Start than in a French preschool, even though French preschools are in session longer (4½ full days compared with 5 half-days for Head Start). Most important, French preschools seem to be much more uniform in their effectiveness. The French government hires highly trained teachers, who are required by the national Ministry of Education to have the equivalent of a master's degree, and pays them well. Another difference is that French preschool teachers create lessons within a standard curriculum established by the Ministry of Education. The curriculum establishes minimum standards that all schools must meet.

Ask each group to prepare a poster or brief oral presentation of their findings to the class. Provide the groups with comments regarding their presentation and their ability to obtain relevant information from the Internet.

HANDOUT 1

Developmental Fact or Myth?

T F 1. Preoperational intelligence is no longer limited to senses and motor skills.

T F 2. A 3-year-old is likely to believe that the same amount of ice cream is actually more when it is transferred from a large bowl to a small bowl.

T F 3. Research reveals that 2- to 6-year-old children are much less logical than Piaget believed.

T F 4. Older children use private speech less effectively than younger ones.

T F 5. Most 3-year-olds clearly understand that a belief can be false.

T F 6. Having an older brother or sister delays the development of a theory of mind.

T F 7. By age 6, children's vocabulary includes an average of more than 10,000 words.

T F 8. A young child who says, "You comed up and hurted me" is demonstrating a lack of understanding of English grammar.

T F 9. Research supports the idea that children who have heard two languages since birth usually master the two distinct sets of words and grammar.

T F 10. Preschool education programs, such as Head Start, have been a disappointing failure in terms of compensating for children's impoverished home environments.

HANDOUT 2

Observational Activity: Preoperational and Concrete Operational Thinking: Assignment Sheet

Piagetian concepts can be readily demonstrated if you know a 4- or 5-year-old and a 7- or 8-year-old—perhaps the children of relatives, friends, or neighbors—who are willing to participate. First, try several of the conservation tasks described in Figure 9.1 on text page 251. Choose from the tests for conservation of volume, number, matter, and length. Remember that the child should take an active part in agreeing that both quantities are equal in the first part of the experiment and that the crucial question is "Which has more—or are they both the same?" so that the child has the option of answering "The same." If the child does not understand this phrasing, the experimenter (you) can ask, "If I take this one and you take that one, who has more to drink (or whatever), or do we both have the same amount?" No matter what answer the child gives, be sure to ask the child to explain his or her reasoning in order to determine how firm the scheme is.

Then probe the ability of each child to take another person's point of view. Asked why the sun shines, the preoperational child might answer, "So that I can see." Try asking the following questions and any others that you can think of: Why does the sun shine? Why is there snow? Why does it rain?

Also, have the children shut their eyes, then ask if they think that you can still see them. Preoperational children are likely to say that you cannot. Ask how many brothers and sisters they have. Follow up by asking how many children their parents have. The preoperational child is likely to know the number of siblings but not the number of children his or her parents have.

After you have finished your tests, complete Handout 3 and return it to your instructor.

HANDOUT 3

Observational Activity: Preoperational and Concrete Operational Thinking: Follow-Up Questionnaire

1. Describe the participants (ages, sex, relationship to you) and setting that you chose for the interview.

2. Briefly describe each child's response to the conservation tests you attempted.

   (a) **Conservation of** ______________________________

   Younger child's response

   Older child's response

   (b) **Conservation of** ______________________________

   Younger child's response

   Older child's response

   (c) **Conservation of** ______________________________

   Younger child's response

   Older child's response

HANDOUT 3 *(continued)*

3. Briefly describe each child's response to the test of egocentric thought. Was egocentric thinking evident in any of the answers given? If so, give examples.

   Younger child's response

   Older child's response

4. Do the children's ages and test responses support Piaget's stage theory of cognitive development? Why or why not?

HANDOUT 4

Critical Thinking Activity: Preoperational Thought in Adulthood

Now that you have read and reviewed the material on cognitive development during early childhood, take your learning a step further by testing your critical thinking skills on this pattern recognition exercise.

When we progress to higher levels of cognitive functioning, we do not spend all our time at these higher levels. Piaget himself once observed that he spent only a fraction of each day in formal operational thought processes. This suggests that even as adults, we do not entirely leave preoperational thought behind.

To help you understand preoperational thought processes in children, see if you can recognize examples or traces of preoperational thought in everyday adult behavior in the items below. Identify the characteristic of preoperational thought that they illustrate.

1. Following an especially heated argument with an elderly relative, you shout that you would like nothing better than to have him get out of your life for good. Several days later your relative dies, leaving you feeling intensely guilty that you caused his death.

2. Your roommate complains that you are a sucker for deceptive packaging in the grocery store because you always choose taller bottles and cans over shorter, wider ones.

3. A friend from high school started an Internet business several years ago and has become one of the wealthiest, most successful entrepreneurs in the nation. Whenever you see her, you talk about her business ventures and fantasize about her material success, imagining her house, her car, her hired help. ("What must it be like to live in such luxury" is the way you put it.)

4. One day you learn that this same wealthy friend has become active in a community organization that serves the mentally challenged and their parents. You are told that her work with mentally challenged children consumes most of her weekends and a substantial part of her income and that she lives in modest circumstances. You find this hard to believe, and you suspect that somehow she is profiting from her involvement.

HANDOUT 5

Preschool Literature

You can learn much about the language and thought processes of young children by examining the literature written for them.

Visit the children's section of your local library or bookstore. Ask the librarian or salesperson to guide you to a book that is a "classic" or well-loved storybook for children from 3 to 5 years old. Examine the book carefully. If possible, read it aloud to a child or someone else. Then complete the following items.

1. Give the title, name of the author and illustrator, and date of publication of the book.

2. Summarize what the librarian or salesperson told you about the book.

3. Do you remember reading this book when you were a young child?

4. Write down examples of any of the following story elements that appear in the book:

   (a) rhyme and repetition in the story

   (b) egocentrism (e.g., animals that dress and talk like a child; misunderstandings that arise from the main character's self-centered viewpoint)

HANDOUT 5 *(continued)*

(c) centration (e.g., stories about characters who have only one prominent feature; stories about a child's focusing on one special goal, trait, or object)

(d) effects that depend on literal or figurative language (e.g., jokes that come from a character's taking things literally; misunderstandings that arise from the use of figurative language)

(e) story elements that reassure the child about the strong ties of family and friendship

(f) story elements that reflect the young child's fear of separation

5. If you read this book aloud to another person, give the age of the person and describe his or her reaction.

HANDOUT 6

Internet Activity: Preschool Education Around the World

Use the Internet to find information on preschool education in the country you selected (or that was assigned to you). Then answer the following questions.

1. If you did so, which country did you choose, and why?

2. Briefly compare this country with the United States in terms of overall affluence (e.g., percentage of children living below the poverty level) and the overall quality of its health care system.

3. What types of government support are provided for parents with young children, especially single mothers and fathers? How does this compare with the support provided in this country? (In your answer, be sure to address issues such as maternity leaves, child-care assistance, and health insurance).

HANDOUT 6 *(continued)*

4. Overall, how does the educational system of this country compare with that of the United States? (In your answer, be sure to address issues such as the length of the school year, the use of testing, and how the curriculum is set.)

5. Generally speaking, how is preschool education viewed in this country? What percentage of children attend preschool programs?

6. What is a typical preschool program like in this country? Who sets the curriculum? Are preschool teachers licensed by the government? What kind of training are preschool teachers required to complete?

7. Does the government provide financial support for parents to send their children to preschool? Are there any other incentives provided? How does this compare with the United States?

Early Childhood: Psychosocial Development

Contents

Note: Worth Publishers provides online Instructor and Student Tool Kits, DVD Student Tool Kits, and Instructor and Student video resources in DevelopmentPortal for use with the text. See Part I: General Resources for information about these materials and the text Lecture Guides for a complete list by text chapter.

Challenges for Parents

Audiovisual Materials: The History of Parenting Practices, p. 5
Families Matter, p. 5
T. Berry Brazelton: The Changing Family and Its Implications, p. 5
Families First, p. 8
Parents and Children: A Positive Approach to Child Management, p. 8
Do Parents Matter? Judith Rich Harris on the Power of Peers, p. 8
Brothers and Sisters: Love and Hate, p. 9

Teaching Tips: Authoritative or Authoritarian?, p. 6
Using Student Skits to Demonstrate Parenting Styles, p. 6

Classroom Activities: Hollywood and the Nuclear Family, p. 5
Difficulties in Being an Authoritative Parent, p. 6
You and Your Parents, p. 7
Classroom Debate: "Resolved: Parents Are Not Responsible for the Differences Among Their Children," p. 8
Parenting Behaviors in Independent and Interdependent Cultures, p. 9
Shockumentaries, p. 10

"On Your Own" Activity: Parenting Style: Do You Have a Choice?, p. 7 (Handout 2, p. 17)

Moral Development

Audiovisual Materials: The Essentials of Discipline: The Preschool Years, p. 11
Reward and Punishment, p. 11

Classroom Activities: The His and Hers of Prosocial Behavior, p. 10
Handling Spontaneous Aggression, p. 11
Punishment: Does It Work?, p. 11

Becoming Boys and Girls

Audiovisual Materials: How Boys and Girls Differ: The First Six Years, p. 13
Anything You Can Do, I Can Do Better, p. 13
The Differences Between Men and Women, p. 13
Self-Identity and Sex-Role Development, p. 14
Sex Roles: Charting the Complexity of Development, p. 14
In My Country: An International Perspective on Gender, p. 15

Classroom Activities: A Field Guide to Boys and Girls, p. 13
The Unsettled Issue of Gender Differences, p. 13
Gender Identification During Early Childhood, p. 13

"On Your Own" Activity: Gender-Role Development, p. 14 (Handout 3, p. 19, and Handout 4, p. 22)

Critical Thinking Activity: Gender Roles and Stereotypes, p. 14 (Handout 5, p. 24)

Suggested Activities

Introducing Early Childhood: Psychosocial Development

"On Your Own" Activity: Developmental Fact or Myth?

Before students read about psychosocial development during early childhood, have them respond to the true-false statements in Handout 1.

The correct answers are shown below. Class discussion can focus on the origins of any developmental misconceptions that are demonstrated in the students' incorrect answers.

1. F	6. F
2. F	7. T
3. F	8. T
4. T	9. T
5. F	10. F

Teaching Tip: Teaching Students to Distinguish Psychological Science from Pseudoscience

> *"Professor, we've spent a lot of time learning about the development of cognition and intelligence in this course. But when are we going to talk about the research that playing classical music to babies before they are born increases their I.Q. scores?"*

If your students are like mine, this question will sound familiar. Scott Lilienfeld believes the reason is that much of the "knowledge" students bring to class consists of little more than popular psychology grounded only in pseudoscience. To counter this with his students, Lilienfeld offers the following tips:

1. *"Thou shalt delineate the features that distinguish science from pseudoscience."* Although the distinction between science and pseudoscience is not always clear-cut, several warning signs will suggest you are dealing with a pseudoscience. These include an absence of the self-correcting process (*replication*) that is the hallmark of science, an emphasis on confirming existing beliefs, the tendency to place the burden of proof on skeptics rather than proponents, an excessive reliance on anecdotal rather than empirical evidence, and a lack of the scrutiny afforded by the peer review process of journal research.
2. *"Thou shalt distinguish skepticism from cynicism."* In their enthusiasm, young students of science sometimes become close-minded cynics who refuse to accept evidence that seems implausible. Skepticism, the hallmark of critical thinking and the scientific method, implies a simultaneous openness to new ideas tempered by the willingness to subject these ideas to careful scrutiny.
3. *"Thou shalt distinguish methodological skepticism from philosophical skepticism."* As students begin to grasp that scientific knowledge is tentative and subject to revision, they may mistakenly conclude that genuine knowledge is impossible. Students need to know that there is a continuum of confidence in scientific theories. Some theories, such as the theory of evolution, have acquired near-factual status while others, such as astrology, have no evidence base whatsoever. A third category of theory, such as cognitive dissonance theory, is controversial and falls in between.
4. *"Thou shalt distinguish pseudoscientific claims from claims that are merely false."* Because they are human, all scientists make mistakes. The difference between science and pseudoscience lies not so much in whether their claims are factually correct or incorrect but in their approach to evidence.
5. *"Thou shalt distinguish science from scientists."* Although the scientific method is a proven method for preventing bias in research, scientists are hardly free of biases themselves and can be just as dogmatic in their beliefs as anyone else. Good scientists acknowledge their biases and implement safeguards such as double-blind control groups to prevent them from contaminating their conclusions.
6. *"Thou shalt explain the cognitive underpinnings of pseudoscientific beliefs."* Students should recognize that human cognition is by nature faulty. We are all prone to errors in reasoning, such as false memories and the false beliefs that arise from representativeness and availability heuristics.
7. *"Thou shalt remember that pseudoscientific beliefs serve important motivational functions."* Many pseudoscientific claims appeal to proponents' heartfelt needs for hope, perceived control, and wonder. In challenging such beliefs, don't be surprised if some students become defensive, which can in turn make them even less willing to consider contrary evidence.
8. *"Thou shalt expose students to examples of good science as well as to examples of pseudoscience."* It is just as important to expose students to accurate claims as it is to debunk inaccurate ones. This makes it easier for students to give up cherished beliefs without becoming defensive. A good approach is to intersperse pseudoscientific information with information that is equally remarkable but true, such as extraordinary feats of human memory, lucid dreaming, and appropriate clinical uses of hypnosis (as opposed to the scientifically unsupported use of hypnosis for memory recovery).
9. *"Thou shalt be consistent in one's intellectual standards."* One error Lilienfeld has observed among psychology instructors is a tendency to adopt separate critical standards of evidence for theories they find plausible and for theories they find implausible. He cites the example of one psychologist who, although a proponent of psychological therapies that have been shown to be effective in controlled studies, is dismissive of electroconvulsive therapy

(ECT) for depression, despite the equally rigorous evidence for its efficacy.

10. *"Thou shalt distinguish pseudoscientific claims from purely metaphysical religious claims."* Students need to learn that metaphysical claims, unlike pseudoscientific claims, cannot be tested empirically and therefore lie outside the boundaries of the scientific method. Among these are claims regarding the existence of the soul, the afterlife, and higher beings, none of which can be confirmed or refuted by any conceivable body of scientific evidence.

Note that many of the text boxes are intended to enhance students' ability to think critically in relation to psychological science.

Lilienfeld, S. O. (2005, September). The ten commandments of helping students distinguish science from pseudoscience in psychology. *Association for Psychological Science Observer, 18*(9). www.psychologicalscience.org/observer.

AV: The Journey Through the Life Span, Program 4: Early Childhood

Early Childhood: Biosocial Development includes a description of Program 4 and the accompanying observation modules, which cover the entire unit on early childhood.

AV: Transitions Throughout the Life Span, Program 10: Playing and Socializing

Program 10 explores the ways in which young children begin to relate to others in an ever-widening social environment. The program begins with a discussion of young children's use of their new cognitive and language skills to negotiate the rules of sociodramatic and rough-and-tumble play. Gender myths, and actual differences in play, are noted.

As children play, they begin to compare themselves to others. These comparisons are almost always extremely favorable—at least in their own minds—leading to the formation of a positive self-concept and healthy self-esteem. Children's interactions are not always harmonious, of course, and learning to get along with others requires a new skill: emotional regulation. Developmentalist Nancy Eisenberg, who conducted several seminal studies of emotional regulation in children, provides expert commentary.

The program concludes by describing the increasing complexity of children's interactions with others, paying special attention to the parent–child relationship in terms of different styles of parenting and how factors such as the cultural, ethnic, and community context influence the effectiveness of parenting.

AV: The Child: Part V (30 min., CRM/McGraw-Hill)

This film shows the unfolding of personality and individuality that occurs between ages 4 and 6. Children gradually become more competent and social, just as Erikson's initiative-versus-guilt exposition would predict. The development of confidence is closely tied to the mastery of new skills, a theme throughout the text chapters on early childhood.

AV: Children in Families (30 min., Insight Media)
Preschool Personality (30 min., Insight Media)
Social Stereotyping (30 min., Insight Media)

These three titles comprise a series of films on preschool development. Designed to provide parents with practical tools for managing behavioral problems in their children, *Children in Families* examines various types of family units—nuclear, single-parent, and communal—and how they influence a child's development.

Preschool Personality explains and compares psychosocial and psychoanalytic theories of personality formation. An animated segment illustrates Erikson's crisis between initiative and guilt. Dr. Robert Liebert discusses the relationship between television viewing and childhood aggression.

Social Stereotyping takes an in-depth look at the factors that lead to the formation of social stereotypes, especially those that relate to sex roles.

Emotional Development

Classroom Activity: The Dunedin Multidisciplinary Health and Development Study

Refer back to the First Two Years: Psychosocial Development, where we introduced the Dunedin study of temperament and emotional development in children. If you did not discuss this extensive longitudinal study there, you might want to introduce it in conjunction with this material.

AV: *Emotional Intelligence: A New Vision for Educators* (40 min., Insight Media)

Daniel Goleman, author of *Emotional Intelligence: Why It Can Matter More than IQ*, explains how an understanding of EQ can help parents and teachers address such problem behaviors as violence and teen pregnancy.

AV: Emotional Intelligence: The Key to Social Skills (28 min., Films for the Humanities and Sciences)

Taken from the program *The Doctor Is In*, this video examines innovative teaching techniques designed to help children develop the social skills and emotional intelligence that will help them lead happier lives. Daniel Goleman explains his theory of emotional intelligence.

Play

Classroom Activity: How Young Children Spend Their Time

You may wish to elaborate on the text theme that how and where children spend their time has an important influence on the development of skills, relationships, attitudes, and behavior patterns. Summarizing the findings from numerous studies of how American children spend their time, Sandra Hofferth and John Sandberg (2001) note that learning activities, such as reading for pleasure, are associated with higher achievement, and family time spent at meals is linked to fewer behavior problems.

A 2005 national Harris Poll revealed that 75 percent of 355 pediatricians surveyed reported that the amount of time their young patients spend on unstructured play has decreased sharply in the past five years. Asked why, nearly all the respondents (97 percent) cited spending time in front of the television or computer as the major reason for less play. Fifty percent of the doctors also cited a lack of safe, quality play spaces within walking distance of the children's homes as another factor contributing to the decline in unstructured play. As noted in the text, most developmentalists view unstructured play as vital to a child's cognitive development. The pediatricians agreed, with the majority stating that unstructured play helps build social skills and confidence (96 percent) and improves children's problem-solving skills (82 percent).

A U.S. Census Bureau study involving a national sample of 9,925 designated parents and their 18,413 children suggests that some parents are beginning to get the message (Harvey, 2007). Sixty-seven percent of children ages 3 to 5 had limits on when and how long they could watch television, as well as which channels and specific shows could be tuned in. This figure is up from 54 percent a decade earlier.

Harvey, B. (2007, January 11). A child's day: Census report takes a look at how children spend their time. *Knight Ridder Tribune Business News*, p. 1.

Hofferth, S. L., & Sandberg, J. F. (2001). How American children spend their time. *Journal of Marriage and Family, 63*, 295–308.

Pediatricians' poll shows decrease in unstructured play, increase in overweight. (2005, August 8). *Health and Medicine Week*, 1085.

Teaching Tip: Creating Mindful Moments to Energize the Class

Amy Marin of Phoenix College encourages mindful moments in her classroom. Such moments are brief and should last only a couple of minutes, require students to actively process information, and hold students accountable for generating meaningful information at the end of the mindful moment.

Following are some examples of classroom activities Marin uses to create mindful moments in her courses.

Question of the Day. Begin class with a question (e.g., Why do children play?). Give students 3–5 minutes to write their answers, which can then be used to stimulate debate or discussion.

One Minute Biography. After learning about the work of an important researcher or theorist, give the class 3–5 minutes to write an obituary, toast, book jacket biography, or poem about that person.

Test Prep. Give the class 1–3 minutes to write a sample test question from the day's lecture. Direct students to then quiz the student next to them. Students turn in their questions at the end of class.

TwitterTalk. Give the class 1–2 minutes to summarize material (e.g., the definition of prosocial behavior) using no more than 140 characters. Call on individual students to read their "tweets."

Google It. If most students have smartphones or laptops, give them 5 minutes to find information on a specific topic. Then ask them to share with the class. This will lead to a productive discussion of the topic as well as a comparison of information sources of varying credibility.

Marin, A. J. (2011). Using active learning to energize the psychology classroom: Fifty exercises that take five minutes or less. *National Institute on the Teaching of Psychology,* St. Petersburg Beach, FL.

Challenges for Parents

AV: The History of Parenting Practices (20 min., Insight Media)

This program explores the history of parenting and the impact of historical, cultural, and governmental policy influences on how children are raised.

AV: Families Matter (60 min., Films for the Humanities and Sciences)

Journalist Bill Moyers explores why the structure of the traditional family seems to be crumbling in the United States. Taking a pragmatic approach, experts discuss the various steps needed to restore a hospitable social climate for families in this country.

AV: T. Berry Brazelton: The Changing Family and Its Implications (50 min., Films for the Humanities and Sciences)

Brazelton's books and programs on child rearing have had a tremendous impact on several generations of American parents. In this film, Dr. Brazelton focuses on the challenges faced by working parents.

Classroom Activity: Hollywood and the Nuclear Family

If you believe that Hollywood's depiction of contemporary family life is an accurate reflection of reality, you would think that the nuclear family is on the way out. In both movies and television sitcoms, the traditional family of mother, father, and 2.3 children has been replaced by an updated version consisting of single parents, divorced couples, and gay relationships. Government statistics do, in fact, support the TV trend toward the breakdown of the traditional family. In 2007, the number of children younger than 18 in the United States who were living with a single parent rose to an all-time high of 25.8 percent. The percentage of U.S. households headed by a single parent has nearly doubled since 1970.

As an informative (and fun) classroom activity, ask your students to give examples of how families are depicted in recent movies and popular television shows.

By comparison, shows of the 1950s and 1960s, such as *Father Knows Best, Ozzie and Harriet, Leave It to Beaver,* and *The Brady Bunch,* seem positively archaic. But researchers wonder whether Hollywood's depiction of the family is a healthy social force. Certainly, many more unconventional families exist today than there were in the 1950s, but are unconventional families such as those depicted by Hollywood becoming the norm?

According to one viewpoint, art is merely imitating life, and seeing unconventional relationships sensitizes people to the fact that there are other choices and that people are making them. According to another viewpoint, Hollywood's desire to create more exciting plot lines is encouraging people to model these kinds of relationships.

Pose these issues to the class and ask students for their candid opinions, based, of course, on their own upbringing, knowledge of their friends' families, and so forth.

Edwards, T. (2008, July 28). 50 million children lived with married parents in 2007. *U.S. Census Bureau News.* www.census.gov/PressRelease/www/releases/archives/marital_status_living_arrangements/012437.html.

Tank, R. (1998, May 5). So long, "Ozzie and Harriet." *CNN Interactive.* www.edition.CNN.com/interactive.

Teaching Tip: Authoritative or Authoritarian?

The Study Guide includes a Study Tip for students who have trouble distinguishing between *authoritative* and *authoritarian*. If you do not require or recommend the Study Guide, you might want to use the following tip to help your students understand the difference.

The text gives one memory trick for differentiating *authoritarian* from *authoritative*. Another involves giving a brief lecture on linguistics. Although both words have the same root noun, *authority,* which means "the power or right to give commands and enforce obedience," their suffixes have very different meanings. The suffix *-arian* denotes an occupation (as in a grammarian, antiquarian) or a person who holds rigidly to a particular social belief. An authoritarian parent is therefore one who believes in the power of authority and is in the business of enforcing obedience. The suffix *-ative* denotes a tendency toward or relationship with something. Thus, an authoritative parent is one who tends to give commands and enforce obedience, with some margin for freedom of action.

You might also encourage students to think of other uses of the word "authoritative." For example, an "authoritative biography" is one deemed reliable because it is written by a person who is properly qualified. Similarly, an "authoritative parent" is a competent authority when it comes to enforcing obedience.

Classroom Activity: Difficulties in Being an Authoritative Parent

To help students appreciate some of the difficulties involved in being the reasonable, authoritative parent that child development experts praise—and that many of the students themselves imagine they will be—you might have them try a little role-playing. Ask two students to volunteer—one to be the parent and the other to be the child. Have them begin by acting out the following situation.

A parent has just come home from the grocery store with her 5-year-old child and accidentally discovers a candy bar in the child's pocket. The child claims that someone "gave" it to him or her.

If your students are unaccustomed to role-playing, you might give them suggestions to help keep the ball rolling. For instance, the child who says the candy bar was "given" might elaborate on the story by saying that the giver was "a lady, very nice, she already paid for it, I'm not lying," and end with, "You never believe me!" Another way to help students get into role-playing is to suggest that they act like a child or a parent they know. You can also ask the class what they think the child should say next or what the parent should do. (Class participation adds to the interest and the noise level, so use this suggestion if things seem too dull and quiet.)

On the basis of this role-playing, have the class try to think of factors that correlate with permissive, authoritative, and authoritarian parenting. Students will come to realize that the parents' education and wisdom are not the only issues; the parents' patience and energy level, the child's behavior (occasional lying and stealing on the part of a 5-year-old is actually normal, but many parents have trouble being authoritative in such a situation), and the number of children in a family are also factors. It's no accident that the traditional American family, with three or four children, was more authoritarian than today's family of one or two children.

This last point may be particularly important if your students come from authoritarian families; they may need help in understanding why this parenting style made sense if there wasn't time to provide individual attention and reasoned discussion every time a child questioned a rule or quarreled with a sibling.

Teaching Tip: Using Student Skits to Demonstrate Parenting Styles

Jane Sheldon uses in-class student skits to demonstrate a variety of developmental principles, including Kohlberg's stages of moral development (preconventional, conventional, and postconventional); Freudian defense mechanisms such as regression, projection, and displacement; the operant conditioning principles of positive and negative reinforcement and punishment; categories of identity status (negative identity, foreclosure, role diffusion, and moratorium); and parenting styles (permissive, authoritative, and authoritarian). The skits take up only part of one class period, use only volunteers, and are not graded. This keeps the activity spontaneous, fun, and intrinsically motivating.

Volunteers are divided into groups of three or four. Each group randomly selects a slip of paper on which is written a particular developmental concept such as a parenting style or a Freudian defense mechanism. The groups are then given 10 to 15 minutes to create a 1- to 3-minute script and rehearse individual roles that illustrate the concept. The remainder of class time is taken up by the performances, with students in the "audience" attempting to guess and then discussing the concept or principle being depicted.

Sheldon notes that the instructor occasionally may need to provide guidelines and script editing to make the activity pedagogically sound. For example, the instructor may announce which actor is exhibiting the developmental concept to be guessed. Or the actors and class may be informed that the script is to depict children of a specific age.

Students become quite creative in the skits they write. For example, one group depicted the defense mechanism of displacement by showing a disgruntled employee taking his job-related frustration out on the family dog. Another group depicted preconventional moral reasoning by pretending to be children contemplating the consequences of shoplifting in a candy store.

While other educators have pointed out the usefulness of in-class acting, their projects typically are semester-long productions that are graded. Sheldon's method takes up very little time and doesn't create grade-related anxiety that favors extroverted students. But "even without grades at stake," notes Sheldon, "students are highly motivated to give presentations that are creative, humorous, and accurate portrayals of the concept."

Sheldon, J. P. (1996). Student-created skits: Interactive class demonstrations. *Teaching of Psychology*, *23*(2), 115–116.

"On Your Own" Activity: Parenting Style: Do You Have a Choice?

Research indicates that families with little money and many children tend to be more authoritarian. Some of your students may have difficulty understanding that social pressures, as well as parental personality and temperament, influence parenting patterns. To give them insight into the effect of the environment on parenting patterns and to increase their sensitivity to the problems of others, have students complete Handout 2.

Most students will realize that their responses to the child would not be appropriate (let alone possible) if they were very poor or under other social pressures. For example, a parent who has difficulty paying for groceries may well feel like whacking the child who spills a half-gallon of milk—to prevent the child from ever being so careless again or merely to release anger and frustration. The parent who has only one nice outfit for a child cannot calmly send the child upstairs to change clothes. Students who do not like having been manipulated into an "authoritarian" role may come up with alternatives for the economically disadvantaged parent—for example, rearranging the environment so that spillable liquids are not set on the table beforehand, or putting out only a few sheets of construction paper at a time. These are, of course, valuable responses that might be said to describe the strategies of effective parents under economic stress.

Classroom Activity: You and Your Parents

Learning is always easiest for students when they are learning about themselves. Here are several issues for classroom discussion to help your students think about their upbringing and how it has influenced their behavior.

Birth order. Firstborn and only children tend to have higher IQs and to be more conservative, more concerned about social approval, and more achievement oriented than later-born children. Although birth order interacts with other factors, such as family size and how close the children are in age, many researchers believe that later-born children are raised and socialized very differently from firstborn or only children. For example, parents are usually stricter with and encourage achievement more in their first child than in later children. Ask your students what other differences they would expect in the upbringing of only, first-, and later-born children. Ask them to think about their own birth order positions and to compare their upbringing with that of their brothers, sisters, or friends. Are there any consistent effects of birth order?

Parental style. The text identifies three classic parenting styles and discusses possible effects on the social development of children. Ask students how they would characterize their own parents and upbringing. Ask them if they can identify any particular personal traits or behaviors that may reflect this upbringing. Ask how they and their parents differ from close friends and their parents. Ask how they might be different had they been raised by other parents.

Parental malpractice. Since the early 1990s, several children have attempted to sue their parents for "parental malpractice." For example, a son sued his parents for $350,000, claiming that their neglect of him as a child was responsible for his psychological problems. Should parents be held legally accountable for the way their children turn out? If so, for what reasons and to what extent? Under what circumstances would you decide such a case in favor of the child? Although the focus here is on early childhood, you may want to extend the discussion to include parental responsibility regarding the behavior of teenagers who have "gone bad." The events at Columbine High School and other schools throughout the United States have refocused Americans on the issue of parental responsibility. One mother sued the parents of a boy who killed her daughter. Similarly, the parents of a Black, athletic student at Columbine sued the parents of the two boys who shot their son.

AV: Families First (90 min., Films for the Humanities and Sciences)

In this lengthy film, journalist Bill Moyers examines "family preservation services," an innovative intervention for troubled and vulnerable-to-crisis families that works with family members in the home. The poignant stories of families dealing with real crises, and the caseworkers who strive to keep them together, offer a provocative stimulus for class discussion.

AV: Parents and Children: A Positive Approach to Child Management (24 min., Research Press)

If your class contains many students who are parents and want practical tips for handling day-to-day problems with their children, this movie might be helpful. It is a clear presentation of behavioral principles, emphasizing appropriate use of positive reinforcement.

AV: Do Parents Matter? Judith Rich Harris on the Power of Peers (12 min., Films for the Humanities and Sciences)

In this brief video, ABC news correspondent Sylvia Chase interviews Judith Rich Harris, author of *The Nurture Assumption*. The interview focuses on Harris's controversial theory of child development through adaptation to peer groups. What makes this program particularly effective for use in the classroom is its "point–counterpoint" focus: MIT's Steven Pinker offers support for the theory and Harvard's Jerome Kagan discredits it for its lack of empirical foundation.

Classroom Activity: Classroom Debate: *"Resolved: Parents Are Not Responsible for the Differences Among Their Children"*

> Every day, tell your children that you love them. Never hit them. If they do something wrong, don't say, "You're bad!" Say, "What you did was bad." No, wait—even that might be too harsh. Say, instead, "What you did made me unhappy."

So begins an article on child rearing by Judith Rich Harris, author of the controversial books *The Nurture Assumption: Why Children Turn Out the Way They Do* and *No Two Alike: Human Nature and Human Individuality*. The thesis of both books is that parents' importance in shaping their children's development has been greatly exaggerated. According to Harris, there is a great deal of evidence that the differences in how parents rear their children are not responsible for the differences among the children.

While the media has had a frenzy over Harris, an important part of her message has largely been lost. This point is most clearly made in her analysis of Carolyn Rovee Collier's influential studies of infant memory. The major finding in these studies (which are discussed in the text under cognitive development during the first two years) was that infants retained the memory of having learned to make mobiles move by kicking their legs. In Harris's view, the standard interpretation of these results is incomplete, since they demonstrate that memories are retained "only if you haven't changed anything. If the doodads hanging from the mobile are blue instead of red, or if the liner surrounding the crib has a pattern of squares instead of circles, or if the crib is placed in a different room, they will gape at the mobile cluelessly, as if they've never seen such a thing in their lives."

This oversight is crucial to Harris. "It's not that they're stupid. Babies enter the world with a mind designed for learning and they start using it right away. But the learning device comes with a warning label: what you learn in one situation might not work in another. Babies do not assume that what they learned about the mobile with the red doodads will work for the mobile with the blue doodads. They do not assume that what worked in the bedroom will work in the den. And they do not assume that what worked with their mother will work with their father or the babysitter or their jealous big sister or the kids at the day-care center."

Thus, Harris's thesis is that children learn how to behave at home and how to behave outside the home, and parents can influence only the way they behave at home. Children behave differently in different contexts because different behaviors are required.

In response, Harris's critics—including eminent developmentalists such as Jerome Kagan, Carol Tavris, and Howard Gardner—have pointed to numerous examples of parents' pivotal role in their children's outcomes. They also have noted that Harris overstated her case by ignoring data that contradict her views and relying on measures of parental influence that were not sensitive enough to detect the subtler ways in which parents affect their children. Some studies, for example, asked parents to describe themselves and their children by asking questions such as "Are you afraid to take risks?" Their answers were then used to assess how similar the children's personality and behavior were to those of their parents. But critics note that questions such as this typically result in vague, general descriptions that do not correspond to observers' more subtle evaluations of people's behavior. They also point out that in stressing the importance of peer groups, Harris has minimized the role parents play in choosing their children's peers, moving to a particular neighborhood, or sending a child to a particular school, for instance.

To broaden your students' perspectives on the *nurture assumption* and enhance their understanding of the issue's complexity, follow the guidelines in the General Resources section for scheduling a classroom debate on this resolution.

AV: Brothers and Sisters: Love and Hate (16 min., Insight Media)

This short video explores the complex social interactions between siblings. Birth order, gender, and differences in how parents respond to siblings are also discussed.

Classroom Activity: Parenting Behaviors in Independent and Interdependent Cultures

The University of California, Davis, has prepared an information guide that focuses on cultural variations in parenting in such areas as discipline, parent–child emotional bonding, family structure and roles, gender-role development, play, and sleeping arrangements. The guide was developed to allow teachers, psychologists, and other practitioners to assess the cultural sensitivity of their programs. You may find the material helpful in preparing a unit on cultural variations in parenting.

Discipline:

- Cultures that emphasize independence in children promote parenting behaviors that provide structure while being available, involved, warm, and sensitive. Children are encouraged to think about their misbehavior and to control their impulses. Examples include using time-outs or explaining why hitting is wrong.
- Cultures that emphasize interdependence in children use strategies such as shaming to exert control over children's behavior rather than giving them choices and time to think. These strategies encourage respect for authority figures such as elder members of the family and community.
- The effectiveness of parenting strategies varies with the situation. Time-outs are most effective in middle-class environments where misbehavior is not life-threatening and time and resources are available. In dangerous environments where misbehavior can result in more serious consequences (dense traffic, unsafe environments outside the home), more controlled discipline strategies tend to be more effective and valued.

Parent–Child Emotional Bonding:

- Parents and children of all cultures share the deep, emotional connection called attachment.
- Interdependent cultures tend to use behaviors to bond with their children, while independent cultures tend to use verbal exchanges such as "I love you" and touch.
- In cultures with high infant mortality rates, bonding between parents and children is commonly delayed until that child's survival is more certain.
- In cultures with large extended families or close communities, parents often encourage children to bond with multiple people.

Family Structure and Role:

- Children in cultures that promote interdependence are viewed as part of a larger family system rather than as individuals.
- In cultures that promote interdependence in children, all members are responsible for all children in the community.
- Cultures that recognize an extended family system may increase the chances of survival for children in environments where survival rates are low. An extended network also tends to decrease children's misbehavior in the community.

Gender-Role Development:

- Cultural expectations drive the gender socialization process. In the United States, for example, girls are encouraged to express emotion more openly than boys are.
- Gender-role values vary greatly across cultures and individual families. In the United States, gender equality is valued by many. In other cultures, gender differences are highly valued.
- Immigrant families often experience conflict when their gender expectations clash with those of the majority culture and children begin to challenge traditional gender roles. These conflicts may influence children's developing sense of self and ethnic identity.

Play:

- Cultures that focus on developing independence in children encourage one-to-one play that is child-focused, such as stacking blocks and babbling with infants.
- Cultures that promote interdependence in children encourage large-group play and tend to use more observation and mimicking of normal routines.
- Games in independent cultures tend to have "winners" and "losers" more often than do games in interdependent cultures, which more often rely on cooperation.

Sleeping Arrangements:

- Sleeping arrangements for infants vary widely across cultures.
- Interdependent cultures regularly use co-sleeping in which one or both parents sleep with the infant. By some estimates, nearly two-thirds of world cultures sleep together as a family (i.e., the "family bed").

- Parents in cultures that promote independence in children believe that separate sleeping arrangements help children develop independence.

Ontai, L. L., & Mastergeorge, A. (2005). *Culture and parenting: A guide for delivering parenting curriculums to diverse families.* Davis: University of California Press.

Classroom Activity: Shockumentaries

The UCLA Television Violence Monitoring Study was a three-year project involving four broadcast networks: ABC, CBS, Fox, and NBC. The study examined every series, television movie, theatrical film shown on television, children's program, special, and advertisement aired during each of the three television seasons (over 3,000 hours of footage each year between 1995 and 2000).

The shockumentary video genre was virtually unknown until the 1995–1996 TV season, when five programs appeared, followed by 16 in the 1996–1997 season. Consider the report's synopsis of *Video Justice: Crime Caught on Tape:*

> The minute-and-a-half opening montage . . . included two shootings, 13 acts of physical violence (punching, kicking, striking with an object); eight instances of shoving, pushing or struggling; eight threats with a gun; two firings of a paintball gun and one instance of an officer being hit by a passing truck.

In another shockumentary, *Close Call: Cheating Death,*

> a member of a bomb squad leans over a chamber where a possible explosive is stored, only to have it explode in his face. The explosion itself is repeated seven different times throughout the program. Many of the repetitions are in slow motion. The camera focuses on the gore following the accident, featuring a close-up of the man's hand, which is missing three fingers as a result of the blast.

This graphic scene is followed by a later sequence in which a man, in the process of rescuing his friend from a helicopter crash, accidentally reveals the top portion of his buttocks. Remarkably, the network censors felt it necessary to digitally blur this shot, but saw no problem showing viewers a man having his face blown up seven different times!

The study reported that such sensationalistic documentaries routinely use repetition, slow motion, and other dramatic devices to heighten viewers' fears. For instance, one of the most graphic scenes in (Fox's) *When Animals Attack III* shows a bull impaling a woman with its horns and tossing her through the street like a rag doll. By the time the segment concludes, the attack has been shown no less than three times.

America's Most Wanted: America Fights Back on Fox wasn't much less restrained:

> [An] interesting instance of needlessly upping the level of violence in the program was found on Feb. 8, 1997. During a profile on a murderer, a re-enactment of him repeatedly shooting a man in a car is shown. During the re-creation, the narrator informs the audience that the man at large ruthlessly fired nine shots into his victim, killing him on the spot. However, in the re-enactment, the killer fires 14 shots into his victim.

The report also criticized some programs for putting a humorous spin on violence. One example singled out comes from the hugely popular *Buffy the Vampire Slayer,* a network show in which Buffy struggles to balance her life as a suburban teenager with her responsibilities as vampire slayer:

> A prime example of this can be found in the episode on March 31, 1997, in which Buffy fights a muscle-bound vampire at a funeral home. Just as the vampire appears to have cornered Buffy, the boy she had been on a date with earlier in the evening shows up and hits the vampire with a metal tray. Angered by the interference, the vampire slams the boy's head against a piece of metal apparently killing him. Buffy becomes infuriated, and begins beating the vampire senseless with an array of kicks and punches, all the while yelling at him, "You killed my date!"

As an effective stimulus to a good classroom discussion, assign groups of students to watch an upcoming shockumentary (some shows, such as those pertaining to police actions, are on almost weekly) or a Saturday cartoon show and report back to the class after having also reviewed the Federal Communications Commission's 2007 report on violent television programming and its impact on children.

By the way, the three UCLA Television Violence Monitoring Reports can be found on the Internet at www.media-awareness.ca/english. Alternatively, you might center the class discussion on a program such as *CSI: Crime Scene Investigation* (or any of its offshoots) with which many in the class are likely to be familiar.

Teen violence TV. (2002, May 6). *Junior Scholastic, 104*(18), 5.

Federal Communications Commission. (2007, April 6). *Violent television programming and its impact on children.* (FCC Publication No. 07-50). Washington, DC: Author.

Moral Development

Classroom Activity: The His and Hers of Prosocial Behavior

Children can feel either *empathy* for another person, which leads to *prosocial behavior,* or *antipathy,* which leads to aggression and other forms of *antisocial behavior*. By age 4 or 5, most children can be deliberately prosocial or antisocial. This occurs as a result of brain maturation, emotional regulation, advances in theory of mind, and interactions with caregivers. Prosocial behavior consists of behaviors that are beneficial to others, including comforting, sharing, helping, guiding, rescuing, and defending. Many developmentalists believe that women and men differ somewhat in their emphasis on particular classes of these behaviors. To stimulate a good class discussion of the ways in which women and men typically help others, Alice Eagly suggests starting a class by asking your students whether women or men are generally more helpful to others. She notes that ordinarily most students indicate that women are the more helpful sex. Next, ask students why they believe that women (or men for some students) are more helpful. This discussion can nicely segue into lecture material on the topics of gender differences in behavior, prosocial behavior in general, and moral development.

Eagly offers several other ideas for class exercises exploring prosocial behavior:

Organ Donation
Living organ donation is a remarkable example of prosocial behavior. Ask students under what circumstances they would consider donating a kidney. Most will likely feel ambivalent, even for close relatives. Extend the discussion by exploring reasons for their ambivalence, then by noting that women are more likely than men to become organ donors and asking students to interpret this gender difference.

Heroism
Ask students to identify heroic individuals from the community, society, the world, or in history. Then ask them to identify anyone they know personally whom they consider heroic. These questions lead naturally to a discussion of what heroism is and of gender differences, particularly if more male than female heroes are named by the class.

Prosocial Behavior in the Media
Eagly notes that Internet sites, newspapers, and other media offer many examples of prosocial behavior. Students can be directed to seek out and report on recent examples of prosocial or heroic behavior.

If your students need more specific direction for this exercise, point them to CNN, which chooses 10 heroes each year and honors one as "Hero of the Year." Another source is the Carnegie Hero Fund, established by Andrew Carnegie in 1904 (see www.carnegiehero.org). The Carnegie Fund presented 85 awards in 2010, and 9,412 since 1904. Have students analyze the criteria by which these heroes are selected.

Eagly, A. (2011). The his and hers of prosocial behavior: An examination of the social psychology of gender. Presented at meetings of the *National Institute on the Teaching of Psychology,* St. Petersburg Beach, FL.

Classroom Activity: Handling Spontaneous Aggression

To explore the problem of how to handle the spontaneous aggression of young children, you might have students air their own opinions, which are bound to differ. Some believe that children should learn to stick up for their rights and express their demands at an early age; some speak proudly of learning to fight. Others are much more concerned that children learn to control their aggressive impulses and avoid fights at almost all costs. You might ask the class, "What should parents do if their child comes crying that another child threw sand in his or her face? Or another child called him or her a baby? Or what should a parent do if his or her child bites another child? Or kicks the parent?" The answers these questions generate will increase students' awareness of our cultural assumptions about aggression.

It would also be useful to explore gender and ethnic differences. Is the same behavior expected of girls and boys? Does it make any difference whether the children who get into a fight are from different racial or religious groups, or whether the child was called a name that is an ethnic slur?

Because children begin to form attitudes about aggression during early childhood, it makes sense for adults to be clear about which values and attitudes they want to encourage.

AV: The Essentials of Discipline: The Preschool Years (3 programs, 28 min. each, Films for the Humanities and Sciences)

This three-part series explores the use of discipline during toddlerhood and early childhood (part 1), between ages 5 and 12 (part 2), and during the teenage years (part 3). Issues in the healthy use of discipline are illustrated with candid footage of real-life disciplinary situations.

AV: Reward and Punishment (14 min., CRM/McGraw-Hill)

Very clearly, albeit briefly, this film presents the merits of positive, as opposed to aversive, control procedures for dealing with children. The film is narrated by psychologist and educator James Gardner, who emphasizes affection and attention as powerful and often underutilized social reinforcers.

Classroom Activity: Punishment: Does It Work?

Punishment is one of the oldest, and most controversial, techniques for controlling behavior. But does it actually work? When a child is spanked or harshly criticized for misbehavior, will the undesirable actions be forever eliminated? Or will the child become bitter, fearful, and even more problematic in the future?

Studies of the effectiveness of punishment in humans demonstrate that punishment is most effective when it is "immediate, firm, consistent, delivered in a variety of settings, and accompanied by a clear (and fair) explanation" (Lieberman, 1999).

In one study, schoolchildren were asked to choose one of two toys and then describe it to the experimenter. One of the toys was much more attractive than the other. If a child picked the attractive toy, the experimenter punished the response by saying "No," and taking a piece of candy away from a bag of candy the child had received earlier. Some children were punished immediately; others were punished after a delay of 2, 6, or 12 seconds. This procedure was repeated for 10 pairs of toys. Surprisingly, delay of punishment appeared to have little effect on learning, because all the children avoided selecting the attractive toy after only two or three punishments. The effects of delayed punishment became apparent, however, when the children were left alone for 10 minutes with the two toys. Only half the children who had received immediate punishment played with the more attractive toys when the experimenter was absent. Nearly all of those whose punishment had been delayed *for any length of time* played with the more attractive toys when the experimenter left the room.

This experiment also tested whether an explanation for punishment made any difference in its effectiveness. Some of the children in the delayed punishment condition not only lost a candy and earned the experimenter's rather unpleasant "No," but also were told that these toys were intended only for older children. The results showed that an explanation for a punished response effectively counteracted the effects of delay. Children in this group were significantly more likely to resist the urge to play with attractive toys than were children who received delayed punishment without an explanation.

The results of such experiments indicate that under certain conditions, punishment can be an effective technique for suppressing behavior. Other researchers have suggested, however, that punishment often produces undesirable side effects. For example, an aversive stimulus that punishes a preceding response may trigger fear that becomes conditioned to the situation in which the punishment was delivered. A child who is harshly criticized by a teacher, for example, may in the future become so anxious in the classroom that little learning will take place. A vicious cycle may ensue as the child's school performance suffers even more and punishment becomes increasingly probable.

As noted in the text, punishment may also promote aggressiveness. Research involving both animals and humans demonstrates that *pain-elicited aggression* is a common side effect of physical punishment. In one experiment, college students acted as teachers by rewarding or punishing another student's efforts to learn a task. Some of the teachers completed the experiment with one hand in a painfully cold bath of water. These students were significantly more punitive toward their partners than were teachers who were not exposed to a painful stimulus.

So what can be concluded from the literature on punishment? On the one hand, there is evidence that punishment *should* be used because it is effective; on the other hand, there is evidence that punishment should be avoided because it has undesirable side effects.

Psychologists generally agree that reinforcing good behavior is preferable to punishing bad behavior. One study compared the relative effectiveness of punishment and reinforcement in encouraging first-graders to stay in their seats. After recording a six-day baseline of how often children in one classroom left their seats without permission, the teacher was asked to verbally punish seat-leaving by ordering children who got up to sit down. Surprisingly, over a 12-day period of such punishment the frequency of seat-leaving actually *increased* (see graph below). Apparently, teacher attention, even when disapproving, functioned as a reinforcer for the children. During the next phase of the experiment, the teacher discontinued punishment, instead offering frequent verbal reinforcement to children who remained in their seats. Thus, reinforcement for sitting proved much more effective in reducing seat-leaving below its baseline than did punishment for standing.

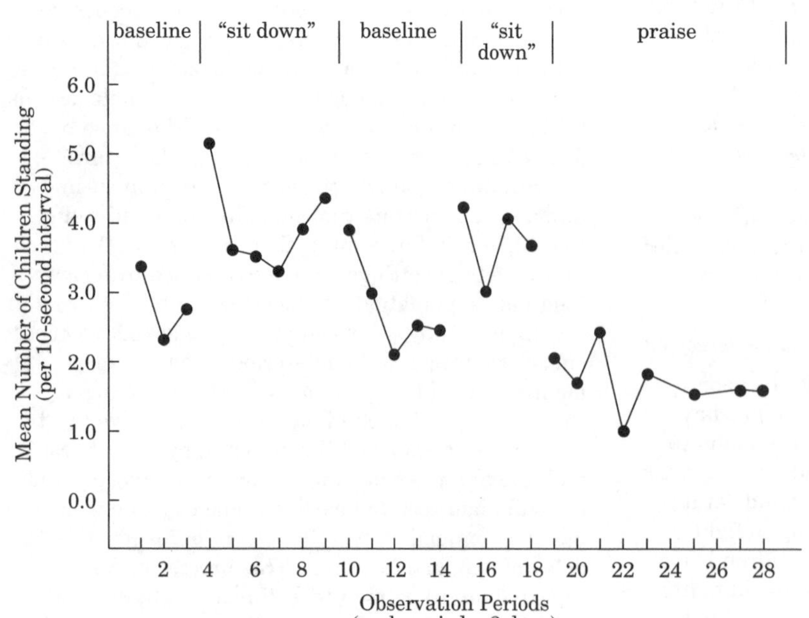

Source: Adapted from Lieberman, D. A. (1993). *Learning: Behavior and Cognition.* Pacific Grove, CA: Wadsworth.

As behaviorist David Lieberman notes:

> The use of reinforcement in this way may require considerable effort and imagination. It is far easier to yell at children when they are being bad than to think, "I wonder how I could reinforce good behavior instead?" The available evidence, however, suggests that the effort may be well worthwhile: Not only may reinforcement be more effective than punishment in eliminating the target behavior, but it also may do so at much less cost to the child's long-term social and emotional development.

Lieberman, D. A. (1999). *Learning: Behavior and cognition* (3rd ed.). Pacific Grove, CA: Brooks/Cole.

Becoming Boys and Girls

AV: How Boys and Girls Differ: The First Six Years (20 min., Insight Media)

This program examines cognitive, social, emotional, and physical differences in boys and girls, discusses the origins of these differences, and explores their meaning for parents and peers.

AV: Anything You Can Do, I Can Do Better (51 min., Films for the Humanities and Sciences)

In this captivating program, researchers debate whether male–female differences in the brain's architecture can completely explain gender differences in behavior and cognition. To illustrate the arguments being raised, children are observed at play, in the classroom, and in their families.

AV: The Differences Between Men and Women (23 min., Films for the Humanities and Sciences)

This film explores the continuing debate regarding the origins of gender differences in social and psychological traits. A particularly effective segment focuses on physiological differences in the female and male brain.

Classroom Activity: A Field Guide to Boys and Girls

In what areas do girls mature faster than boys and why? Are there gender differences in fussiness during infancy? Are boys more competitive? Are girls more emotional? Are girls better in verbal comprehension and boys better in math? How do parents treat their daughters and sons differently? These perennial questions are sure to be on the minds of your students, especially those who are parents themselves. Although many students come to the study of developmental psychology to find answers to pragmatic questions such as these, authoritative answers are often difficult to glean from the literature in peer-reviewed journals.

As an exercise in critical thinking, and to give students an opportunity to voice what's on their minds regarding their purposes in studying development, you might ask four or five volunteers to read and report on *A Field Guide to Boys and Girls*, a fascinating book written in down-to-earth language by science writer Susan Gilbert. Gilbert brings together the latest research on gender development from infancy through age 12. In her writing, she echoes an eclectic perspective that addresses several classic controversies in development, including how nature and nurture interact to make girls and boys different in some ways and similar in others.

While Gilbert acknowledges that some people feel it's politically incorrect to talk about gender differences, she believes that research findings can help parents, teachers, and other adults better understand children. At the end of each chapter, Gilbert suggests practical ways to use this information. In the health area, for example, she describes how parents who are aware of gender differences can act to change the situations that put their sons and daughters at risk.

Much of the book's advice is reassuring: "Playing with Barbie dolls will not prevent your daughter from becoming a brain surgeon or a lawyer and shooting toy guns will not bar your son from becoming a music composer or a minister." Still, parents are urged to talk to their children about the potential negative consequences (e.g., distorted body images and violence) of playing with these toys.

Gilbert, S. (2001). *A field guide to boys and girls: Differences, similarities, cutting-edge information every parent needs to know*. New York: HarperCollins.

Classroom Activity: The Unsettled Issue of Gender Differences

To make clear how unsettled the issue of gender differences is, ask each student to find one journal article that includes a report of gender differences and/or similarities among children during early childhood and have them report the basic methodology and general results to the class.

First, poll the class to see how many believe that all gender differences in personality are the result of social conditioning and how many believe that "boys will be boys," and so forth. At the end of the project, poll the class again to see whether the research has changed anyone's thinking.

Write the general conclusion of each report on the board, then ask students to summarize the research (either individually in writing, with some of the summaries being read aloud and compared, or collectively, with the final summary written on the board). Among the facts that should become apparent is that on the question of gender differences, there is no lack of conflicting findings from conflicting research. (You might also explore with students whether they ended up selecting research that confirms their original bias.)

Classroom Activity: Gender Identification During Early Childhood

To stimulate students' thinking about gender identification during early childhood, you might ask them to think of instances in which they made a mistake about the sex of a child. Were the parents sympathetic or understanding about the mistake? Were they casual about it? Or did they seem annoyed, incredulous, angry?

Most students will report reactions tending toward annoyance and surprise. For example, a mother will often say, "I don't see *how* you could think Jessica is a boy!" Sometimes the parent will pointedly direct the observer's attention to a ribbon, a pink (or blue) item of clothing, or a hairstyle, as a way of making the observer see that he or she was very much in error.

It is generally understood that boys and girls of 2 or 3 years of age look very much the same. Why, then, do parents become upset when a stranger makes a mistake? One possible explanation is that the parents see the gender of their child so clearly or they feel that they have provided the "right" clues in dressing him or her in a gender-appropriate way. Parents may also feel that their behavior toward the child makes the child's gender clear. For example, a father playing with a young daughter may feel that anyone observing them will understand that this is a father–daughter pair. Your students may have additional ideas.

AV: Self-Identity and Sex-Role Development (33 min., Magna Systems)

This video explores sex-role behavior and development as seen in the play of young children. It also presents an overview of cultural and social influences on the development of gender identity.

AV: Sex Roles: Charting the Complexity of Development (60 min., Insight Media)

Beginning with an in-depth examination of sex-role myths, this program explores various theories of sex-role development, especially in terms of the relative importance each places on biological and psychosocial factors. It also investigates the impact of gender stereotypes on child development, focusing on academic achievement and peer relationships.

"On Your Own" Activity: Gender-Role Development

This exercise explores several issues related to gender-role development, including the extent to which gender identity is a reflection of behaviors modeled by parents, historical changes in gender roles, and whether parents should encourage gender-stereotyped behaviors in their children. Have students turn in the completed quizzes (Handout 3) and follow-up questions (Handout 4) for analysis.

An appropriate follow-up to this exercise would be a summary of class answers to handout questions 2 through 6, using question 1 to classify respondents according to age group. Compare responses to question 2, which looks at gender-stereotyped behaviors (maximum score = 15), for each age group represented by the quiz respondents. Responses to question 3 could reveal changes in gender roles over time and the effect of such changes on gender-role development. Responses to questions 4 and 5 will indicate the percentage of students and others who did, and did not, feel that their parents were role models. Responses to question 6 will show the percentage of students and others who feel that parents should encourage traditional gender-role development in their children, and the percentage who feel otherwise. The exercise results could also be analyzed by groups: those whose answers did and those whose answers did not conform to traditional stereotypes. Analysis of the results will naturally lead to a lively class discussion of gender-role development.

Critical Thinking Activity: Gender Roles and Stereotypes

Each unit of these resources contains a critical thinking exercise designed specifically to test students' critical thinking about a topic covered in the text. Handout 5 contains information on gender-role theories followed by a series of questions.

The answers to this unit's critical thinking activity follow.

1. *Argument supported:* Cultural learning, because the social and cultural environment in which a child develops invariably creates stereotypes regarding "gender-appropriate" and "gender-inappropriate" occupations, and children tend to aspire to "appropriate" occupations.

   Counterargument: Biological differences in girls and boys create differences in abilities and interests, which can influence their choices of occupations. Here, boys' proven ability with spatial representation might lead to their greater choice of these three occupations.

2. *Argument supported:* Cultural learning, here perhaps mostly via observation plus reinforcement by parents and teachers of "gender-appropriate" behavior.

   Counterargument: If gender differences involving play emerge at a young age, before children have a chance to be influenced by learning, those differences may well be—at least partly—biological in nature. Researchers have also found evidence that hormones contribute to sex differences in play.

3. *Argument supported:* Biological. If gender distinctions are all learned, children would almost certainly be socialized into adopting the gender roles modeled by their parents. But this evidence says they don't adopt those roles, so some other, nonenvironmental variable is a factor in gender development.

   Counterargument: The role of the environment cannot be ruled out in this example. Gender roles are not exclusively the individual parent's choice. Such roles are strongly endorsed by the culture, and a child may mirror whatever gender distinctions the culture endorses. Children will notice, for example, that most of their teachers are women while most political leaders are men, and they will take those roles in their play.

AV: In My Country: An International Perspective on Gender (91 min., Insight Media)

This two-volume video explores cross-cultural variation in gender roles and gender-role development. It is divided into segments covering topics such as division of household labor, gender differences in discipline, care of the elderly, and attitudes toward homosexuals. It includes interviews with people from Japan, India, China, Sweden, Lebanon, Mexico, England, Zaire, and many other countries.

HANDOUT 1

Developmental Fact or Myth?

T F 1. Most young children underestimate their own abilities.

T F 2. In the United States, children are expected to play cooperatively by age 3.

T F 3. Permissive parenting is almost always the most destructive parental style.

T F 4. Most young children spend more than three hours a day using one electronic medium or another.

T F 5. To empathize means to feel sorry for someone.

T F 6. Physical aggression increases as children mature, while verbal aggression declines.

T F 7. Although physical punishment works at the moment, longitudinal research indicates that it is likely to result in children who are bullies, delinquents, and then abusive adults.

T F 8. By age 2, children can apply gender labels.

T F 9. Children tend to confuse gender and sex throughout early childhood.

T F 10. Sex roles seem more significant for females than for males.

HANDOUT 2

Parenting Style: Do You Have a Choice?

Imagine that you are the parent of a preschooler who misbehaves in perfectly normal ways. For each of the following misbehaviors, tell how you feel and what you say and do.

1. The table is set for breakfast. Your child spills a half-gallon of milk all over the table.

   How do you feel?

   What do you say or do?

2. Your little girl is dressed up to attend an important holiday function or religious service. Before you leave she falls, dirties her dress, and tears her tights.

   How do you feel?

   What do you say or do?

3. Your 3-year-old son is playing at the kitchen table while you are talking on the phone. Before you notice what he is doing, he has used up a whole package of construction paper and has made crayon marks on the plastic tablecloth.

   How do you feel?

   What do you say or do?

HANDOUT 2 *(continued)*

4. Your 5-year-old knocks over a display of glassware in the department store, breaking three glasses.

   How do you feel?

   What do you say or do?

5. After you have written your responses, reread each question, imagining now that you are a parent with three children and you have very little money. For example, suppose you have an income of no more than $500 a month after you pay your rent: Your gas and electricity, food, clothing, and any extras must come from this sum.

   Do your responses change?

   If so, how and why?

HANDOUT 3

Gender-Role Development

During early childhood, children acquire not only their gender identities but also many masculine or feminine behaviors and attitudes. These behaviors and attitudes largely reflect gender roles. A role is a set of social expectations that prescribes how those who occupy the role should act.

To what extent is your own gender identity a reflection of the behaviors modeled by your parents? This exercise asks you to reflect on the kinds of gender models your parents provided and to ask a friend or relative who is a generation older or younger than yourself to do the same.

After you and your respondent have completed the Gender-Role Quiz, answer the follow-up questions in Handout 4 and return both handouts to your instructor.

HANDOUT 3 *(continued)*

Gender-Role Quiz: Respondent #1 (Yourself)

For each question, check whether the behavior described was more typical of your mother or father as you were growing up.

	Mother	Father
1. When your family went out, who drove?		
2. Who filled out the income tax forms?		
3. Who wrote the "thank you" notes for gifts?		
4. Who was more likely to ask, "Where are my socks/stockings?"		
5. When the car needed to be repaired, who took it to the garage?		
6. Who did the laundry?		
7. Who dusted and vacuumed your house?		
8. When you had a fever, who knew where to find the thermometer?		
9. When the sink needed fixing, who knew where to find the pipe wrench?		
10. Who knew where the summer clothes were packed away?		
11. When you had guests for dinner, who made the drinks?		
12. Who watered the house plants?		
13. Who mowed the lawn?		
14. When you went on a trip, who packed the suitcases?		
15. When you went on a trip, who packed the car?		

Sources: Adapted from Doyle, J. A. (1985). *Sex and gender: The human experience.* © 1985 WCB/McGraw-Hill. Used with permission of the McGraw-Hill Companies; and Straub, R. O. (2001). *Seasons of life study guide* (4th ed.). New York: Worth Publishers.

HANDOUT 3 *(continued)*

Gender-Role Quiz: Respondent #2

For each question, check whether the behavior described was more typical of your mother or father as you were growing up.

	Mother	Father
1. When your family went out, who drove?		
2. Who filled out the income tax forms?		
3. Who wrote the "thank you" notes for gifts?		
4. Who was more likely to ask, "Where are my socks/stockings?"		
5. When the car needed to be repaired, who took it to the garage?		
6. Who did the laundry?		
7. Who dusted and vacuumed your house?		
8. When you had a fever, who knew where to find the thermometer?		
9. When the sink needed fixing, who knew where to find the pipe wrench?		
10. Who knew where the summer clothes were packed away?		
11. When you had guests for dinner, who made the drinks?		
12. Who watered the house plants?		
13. Who mowed the lawn?		
14. When you went on a trip, who packed the suitcases?		
15. When you went on a trip, who packed the car?		

Sources: Adapted from Doyle, J. A. (1985). *Sex and gender: The human experience.* © 1985 WCB/McGraw-Hill. Used with permission of the McGraw-Hill Companies; and Straub, R. O. (2001). *Seasons of life study guide* (4th ed.). New York: Worth Publishers.

HANDOUT 4

Gender-Role Development: Follow-Up Questions

1. In what age group are you and the other respondent?

2. Is there evidence of gender-stereotyped behaviors in the answers? That is, were items 1, 2, 4, 5, 9, 11, 13, and 15 checked as more typical of fathers, and items 3, 6, 7, 8, 10, 12, and 14 checked as more typical of mothers? For each respondent, indicate the total number of responses that are in agreement with the traditional gender-role breakdown just noted.

	Younger Respondent	Older Respondent
Number of items in agreement with traditional gender roles (maximum = 15)		

3. If there is a difference between your responses and those of your younger or older respondent, please explain the difference. If there is no difference, please explain this outcome.

4. To what extent do you believe your own gender identity and gender-role development were influenced by the behaviors modeled by your parents? In what ways is your own behavior modeled after that of your same-sex parent? In what ways is it different?

HANDOUT 4 *(continued)*

5. To what extent is your concept of the ideal person of the opposite sex a reflection of the behaviors modeled by your opposite-sex parent? In what ways is it different?

6. In your estimation, should parents encourage or discourage traditional gender-role development in their children? Please explain your reasoning.

HANDOUT 5

Critical Thinking Activity: Gender Roles and Stereotypes

Now that you have read and reviewed psychosocial development during early childhood, take your learning a step further by testing your critical thinking skills on this reasoning exercise.

The minor theories of development disagree about the origins of gender roles and stereotypes. Two of the theories (psychoanalytic and evolutionary) emphasize the power of genetic and biological forces on development. The remaining three theories (behaviorism, cognitive theory, and sociocultural theory) emphasize the pervasive influence of family and culture in children's learning of gender patterns.

In this exercise, you will evaluate evidence relative to the following question: *Is gender development the result of biological forces or cultural learning?* First, decide whether each of the three research findings listed below *more directly* provides evidence in support of the biological argument or the culture-learning argument, and explain your reasoning. Then, use the same research to develop a counterargument that supports the *other* side of the controversy.

1. There are more male than female engineers, physicists, and airplane pilots.

   Argument Supported:

   Counterargument:

2. Girls tend to play in small groups, with one or two friends, while boys tend to play in larger, less intimate groups.

   Argument Supported:

   Counterargument:

3. In their play, 5-year-olds aspire to sex-linked occupations, even if their parents' behavior tends to counter such stereotyping.

   Argument Supported:

   Counterargument:

Middle Childhood: Biosocial Development

Contents

Note: Worth Publishers provides online Instructor and Student Tool Kits, DVD Student Tool Kits, and Instructor and Student video resources in DevelopmentPortal for use with the text. See Part I: General Resources for information about these materials and the text Lecture Guides for a complete list by text chapter.

Measuring the Mind

Audiovisual Materials: Intelligence: A Complex Concept, p. 8
Intelligence, p. 8
A Conversation with David Wechsler, p. 8
It's Cool to Be Smart, p. 8
In a Class of His Own, p. 8
Prodigies: Great Expectations, p. 8

Classroom Activity: Test Scores and Other Criteria for Evaluating Intelligence, p. 8

"On Your Own" Activity: Developing Your Practical Intelligence, p. 9 (Handout 5, p. 21)

Children with Special Needs

Classroom Activity: What's On My Back? p. 9

"On Your Own" Activity: Physical Disabilities: Everything Is Harder, p. 9 (Handout 6, p. 23)

Audiovisual Materials: The Special Child: Maximizing Limited Potential, Dyslexia: Diagnosis and Prognosis, and Dyslexia: Disabled or Different?, p. 9

Attention-Deficit and Bipolar Disorders

Audiovisual Materials: The Diagnosis and Treatment of Attention-Deficit Disorder in Children, p. 10
ADD Children, p. 10
ADHD: What Do We Know?, p. 10
ADHD: What Can We Do?, p. 10
All About Attention-Deficit Disorder, p. 10
Coping with Attention-Deficit Disorder in Children, p. 11
Childhood Depression, p. 11

Classroom Activities: Attention-Deficit/Hyperactivity Disorder, p. 9
A Case Study of ADHD, p. 11

Learning Disabilities

Audiovisual Materials: Hidden Handicaps and Specific Learning Difficulties in the Classroom, p. 12
A Video Guide to (Dis)Ability Awareness, p. 12
Learning Disabilities, p. 12
Page Fright: Inside the World of the Learning Disabled, p. 12

Classroom Activities: Understanding and Helping Children with Learning Disabilities, p. 12
We All Learn to Compensate, p. 12

Internet Activity: Dyslexia Resources, p. 12 (Handout 7, p. 25)

Autistic Spectrum Disorders

Audiovisual Materials: Autism: A World Apart, p. 13
Autism: Diagnosis, Causes, and Treatments, p. 13
Understanding Autism, p. 13
Day by Day: Raising the Child with Autism, p. 13
A School for Robin, p. 13
Asperger's Syndrome: Autism and Obsessive Behavior, p. 15

Classroom Activity: Asperger Syndrome, p. 13

Special Education

Audiovisual Materials: LD = Learning Differences, p. 15
Learning Disabled, p. 15

Lilly: A Story About a Girl Like Me, p. 15
Mainstreaming in Action, p. 15
Who Will Teach the Water to Swim?, p. 15

Classroom Activity: *Classroom Debate:* "Resolved: Children with Learning Disabilities Should Be Mainstreamed," p. 15

Suggested Activities

Introducing Middle Childhood: Biosocial Development

"On Your Own" Activity: Developmental Fact or Myth?

Before students read about biosocial development during middle childhood, have them respond to the true-false statements in Handout 1.

The correct answers are shown below. Class discussion can focus on the origins of any developmental misconceptions that are demonstrated in the students' incorrect answers.

1.	F	6.	F
2.	F	7.	T
3.	T	8.	T
4.	F	9.	T
5.	F	10.	T

AV: The Journey Through the Life Span, Program 5: Middle Childhood

Program 5 (29:05) introduces the developing person during middle childhood. The first segment of the program, physical development (1:50), begins with a description of changes in weight and height during the school years. During these years, physical development levels off, and children have enough coordination and strength to master almost any skill. Gender differences in physical growth and skills are then described. Boys have greater muscle mass and in most cultures are encouraged to play in intricate team games. Girls have much better balance than boys and are encouraged to engage in less strenuous activities that require dexterity and poise.

The second segment, cognitive development (13:50), begins with a description of language development during the school years. Children speak with ease and have a large vocabulary and a solid understanding of grammar. The development of these skills is effectively illustrated in the joke-telling of younger and older schoolchildren and the code-switching that children use when talking with peers or adults. The development of attention, problem solving, and metacognitive skills that are important in schoolwork is depicted. In a powerful illustration of how culture shapes metacognition, Geoffrey Saxe of the University of California, Berkeley, discusses his research studies of the body-part counting system used by Oksapmin children of New Guinea. Next, Robert Siegler of Carnegie-Mellon University contrasts the problem-solving strategies of middle childhood with those of early childhood, demonstrating that the more children know, the easier it is for them to integrate new information. Ellen Winner of Boston College describes the exceptional cognitive skills of gifted children. The segment concludes with a depiction of Piaget's stage of concrete operational thought, including how 7- to 11-year-old children reason about his famous test of conservation. Patricia Greenfield, of UCLA, illustrates the newly found abilities of the concrete operational stage in the weaving of Mayan children.

The third segment of the program, social development (12:25), begins with a discussion of how schoolchildren develop moral values, emphasizing the importance of the peer group as a setting that helps children shape these values. Nicki Crick of the University of Minnesota describes gender differences in aggression, noting that while boys' aggression is more physical, girls' aggression is more relational in nature. Robert Selman of Harvard University discusses his pioneering work in developing peer therapy for aggressive and withdrawn children. On the prosocial side, Nancy Eisenberg of Arizona State University explains the development of empathy and sympathy in schoolchildren. The segment concludes with a discussion of the functions of friendships in stimulating social development and autonomy.

The observation module for the unit on middle childhood is divided into three segments. In the first (4:20), two girls talk about toys and boys, making it quite clear that they do not have boyfriends. In the second segment (3:00), a teacher leads a fifth-grade class in a lesson on sentence structure and state-of-being verbs. In the third segment (6:20), three children, ranging in age from 9 to 10 years, answer questions about themselves.

AV: Transitions Throughout the Life Span, Program 11: The Golden Years of Childhood

Program 11 introduces middle childhood, the years from 6 to 11. Changes in physical size and shape are described, and the transition to formal schooling is addressed. The discussion then turns to the increasingly common problem of obesity among children, including its various contributing factors and treatment. Next, the program takes up the continuing development of motor skills during the school years. A final segment examines the experiences of children with special needs, such as learning disabilities, and those diagnosed as having attention-deficit/hyperactivity disorder. The causes of and treatments for these problems are discussed, with emphasis placed on insights arising from the developmental psychopathology perspective. This perspective makes it clear that the manifestations of any special childhood problem will change as the child grows older and that treatment must often focus on all three domains of development.

Teaching Tip: Using Engaged Lecture

When extended lecturing can't be avoided, you might take a tip from Linda Elder and Richard Paul of The Foundation for Critical Thinking. These experts at enhancing student learning have developed an "engaged lecture" format in which they routinely stop and ask students to state in their own words their understanding of course material. Elder and Paul recommend keeping the names of the students in the class on a set of index cards, which you randomly flip through when it is time to select a student to call upon. (To keep things fair, it is a good idea to shuffle the cards frequently.) As a student's card is drawn, he or she should be asked to "state, elaborate, exemplify, or illustrate the most important points in the lecture" (see also the Teaching Tip "A One-Minute Paper").

An additional technique for breaking up an extended lecture involves randomly calling on students to summarize and make follow-up comments on those of other students. The first student can then be given the opportunity for rebuttal or to indicate if the second person accurately represented his or her comments.

Paul, R., & Elder, L. (2002). *A miniature guide for those who teach on how to improve student learning: 30 practical ideas.* Dillon Beach, CA: The Foundation for Critical Thinking.

A Healthy Time

AV: Physical Development (21 min., CRM/McGraw-Hill)

(See description in Early Childhood: Biosocial Development.)

AV: Physical Development in the Middle Years (30 min., Insight Media)

This film examines physical development between the ages of 6 and 12, emphasizing the wide range of individual differences in physical and motor-skill development. The impact of nutrition on development is also discussed.

"On Your Own" Activity: Tall and Short Classmates

To impress upon your students the extent to which schoolchildren compare themselves with classmates and focus on physical characteristics in these comparisons, you might ask them to recall students who were taller or shorter than average in their fourth- or fifth-grade classes. Or, if any of them were above or below average sizewise, ask them to recall their own feelings. Remind students that their responses to the questions in Handout 2 are for discussion only; they will not be collected.

Your students will probably be surprised at how easily they remember classmates who were significantly taller or shorter than average. Taller children, especially boys, will in most cases be recalled as having been at an advantage. Shorter or smaller children, especially boys, will be recalled as having been at a disadvantage. In many cases, the personalities of children who departed from the norm are remembered more vividly than are those of average children. This is because physical differences greatly impress the school-age child, who tends to focus on appearances and on one characteristic to the neglect of others. (For the same reason, students may remember more vividly the red-headed child, the obese child, the child with glasses, or the disabled child.) For another perspective on the importance of physical characteristics during middle childhood, you might ask how any tall or short students (who are willing to share their feelings with the class) felt about their stature when they were younger.

Health Problems in Middle Childhood

Classroom Activity: Childhood Obesity and Healthful Eating

As noted in the text, obesity is increasingly prevalent among children. The distribution of body mass index (BMI) has also shifted such that the heaviest children, who have the greatest risk of health complications, have become even heavier. The childhood obesity epidemic has affected most ethnic groups and people of every socioeconomic status. In developed countries such as the United States, obesity prevalence rates have risen more than twice as fast among ethnic minority groups, as compared with European Americans. Lower socioeconomic groups in developed countries might be especially vulnerable because of poor diet and limited opportunity for physical activity.

Nationwide, 51 million adults are dieting at any given time, according to the Calorie Control Council. But experts in pediatric nutrition caution parents who are tempted to put their obese children on calorie-cutting diets. "By restricting calories, you're putting a child at risk for growth problems," explains Terri Mandigo, coordinator of the Center for Childhood Intestinal Disorders and Nutrition at the Englewood Hospital and Medical Center in New Jersey. While an adult woman may safely reduce her calories to 1,200 a day, a 7- to 10-year-old still needs roughly 2,000 calories a day if he or she is in the 50th percentile for height and weight. Because 30 to 40 percent of children's daily calories go toward growth, weight *control* rather than weight loss should be the goal.

A better strategy is for parents to provide an environment in which balanced, low-fat meals and sensible snacks are served. "Parents have to be the gatekeepers," says William Dietz of the Tufts University School of Medicine. "They have to control what kinds of food come into the house and how they're distributed."

There is, in fact, substantial evidence that children will not automatically motivate themselves to make healthier food choices. According to one survey, the following high-fat foods were the favorites of children between the ages of 2 and 5: peanut butter, American cheese, fried potatoes, potato chips, hamburgers, eggs, and fried chicken.

Experts offer the following additional suggestions to parents of obese children.

1. Praise children for healthy eating behaviors.
2. A unified front is imperative: If one member of the family refuses to improve his or her eating habits, don't expect the child to do so.
3. Avoid making any foods off-limits: The more forbidden a food, the more desirable it becomes.
4. Provide variety in the child's diet.
5. Offer appealing substitutes for high-fat, high-calorie junk foods.
6. Start with a small goal, such as eliminating bedtime snacks.
7. Emphasize activity for activity's sake and join in with your children.
8. Encourage children to participate in meal planning, shopping, and meal preparation.
9. Set food portions on plates before they are placed on the table.
10. Encourage children to develop a positive and realistic body image.

Most recently, in response to a request from Congress, the Institute of Medicine (IOM) Committee on Prevention of Obesity in Children and Youth developed a comprehensive national strategy that recommends specific actions for families, schools, industry, communities, and government. The committee's recommendations appear in the report *Preventing Childhood Obesity: Health in the Balance,* which can be obtained through the IOM's Web site www.iom.edu/Reports/2004/Preventing-Childhood-Obesity-Health-in-the-Balance.aspx. The report presents a broad-based examination of the nature, extent, and consequences of obesity in U.S. children and youth, including the social, environmental, and dietary factors responsible for its increased prevalence. In addition, it presents an action plan that focuses on primary, secondary, and tertiary levels of prevention for obesity.

"On Your Own" Activity: Images of Obesity

To stimulate thinking about our culture's attitudes toward obese people, you might ask your students to find images of such people in the media, using Handout 3 as a guide.

Students will probably have difficulty finding a picture of an obese child, especially an attractive one. Obese adults are generally used in advertising for comic relief—for example, a middle-aged man with a big belly may be shown appreciating his mother's pasta. Heavy (not usually obese) housewives are also sometimes pictured with "tough" products, such as roach sprays, or ethnic or minority foods, such as tortillas or spaghetti sauce.

In nonadvertising contexts, obese adults are featured when they have accomplished something newsworthy. Unknown obese people tend to appear when the editor wishes to emphasize the common, ordinary, stupid, or comic aspect of an event. For example, a journalist opposed to a particular demonstration may choose to show only the overweight women in hair curlers who participated. Similarly, a journalist who wishes to make a visual comment on shady real-estate dealers, greedy politicians, and so forth, may train the camera on an obese example. Today, however, more overweight, if not obese, actors are getting star billing and "getting the girl"—for example, the star of *King of Queens.* More recently, ask students if they are familiar with the sitcom *Mike and Molly.* What is their reaction to the stars' weights?

You might ask students to share their thoughts about attitudes toward the obese, focusing especially on the psychological effects that these attitudes might have on obese people. Students from different cultural backgrounds may contribute different viewpoints, providing an interesting basis for further discussion.

Mayo Clinic (2011). *Childhood obesity: Lifestyle and home remedies.* Retrieved February 13, 2011, from www.mayoclinic.com.

Teaching Tip: A One-Minute Paper: Thinking Critically About a New Childhood Obesity Hypothesis

To improve their students' writing skills, some instructors assign frequent "one-minute" papers at the end of class. Some assignments involve summarizing the major points of the day's lecture (see also the Teaching Tip "Using Engaged Lecture"); others require responding to a particular thought question. In either case, of course, the exact amount of time allotted for writing should be determined by what you hope to get back from students. As an example of a possible thought-provoking topic for this material, you might discuss the intriguing hypothesis that prenatal and infant under- or overnutrition might increase an individual's risk of obesity throughout his or her life span, while optimal feeding (breast-feeding, in particular) serves a protective function (see figure on the next page). Among the many mechanisms proposed to account for the relationship between obesity and under- or overnutrition are the following: abnormal organ functioning that adversely affects insulin secretion, increases in the number and/or size of fat cells or alterations in adipose tissue function, and disturbances in the regulation of appetite caused by abnormalities in the central nervous system (Martorell, Stein, & Schroeder, 2003).

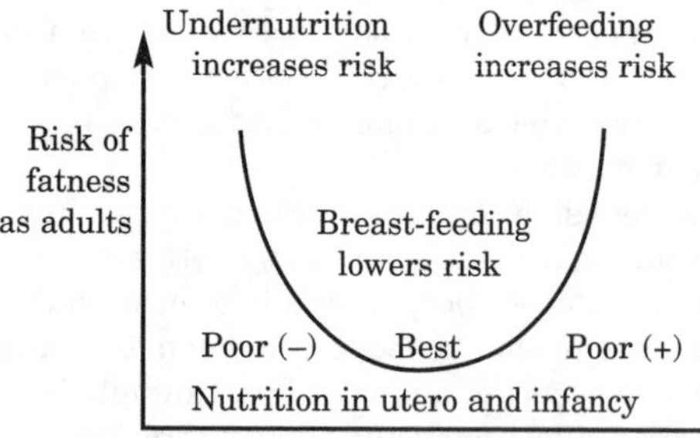

According to the developmental overnutrition hypothesis, maternal obesity increases the transfer of nutrients across the placenta, inducing permanent changes in appetite, neural and hormonal functioning, and energy metabolism. For many prenatally "overfed" children, postnatal environmental and cognitive factors add to the total risk of overweight and obesity. For instance, children who are bottle-fed seem to be more at risk of obesity later in childhood than those who are breast-fed. Several hypotheses have been advanced to explain this phenomenon, including that cow's milk, breast milk, and formula induce different permanent physiological changes that relate to lifelong risk of obesity; or that cognitive factors, such as locus of control over feeding rate (nursing baby versus parent holding a formula bottle) may create a developmental legacy of healthy or unhealthy food attitudes.

In support of the developmental overnutrition hypothesis, observational studies show strong associations among maternal obesity, a child's birthweight, and obesity later in life. In addition, animal research studies vividly demonstrate the potential long-term weight hazards of maternal obesity. For instance, the offspring of obese female rats were heavier than the offspring of rats with the same genotype but that were not obese.

However, the developmental overnutrition hypothesis is not universally accepted. In a massive study, Debbie Lawlor and her colleagues recently explored the self-reported pre-pregnancy BMIs of the parents of 4,000 children and the children's fat mass at ages 9 to 11 years using a technique called dual X-ray absorptiometry. The results showed that both maternal and paternal BMI correlated positively with the children's BMI (fatter parents had fatter children), with the effect of maternal BMI being greater than that of paternal BMI. However, there was no relationship between maternal FTO genotypes and children's BMI. Because a specific variant of the FTO gene is an accepted indicator of maternal fatness, a statistical correlation between maternal FTO genotype (the mother's genetic makeup) and the children's BMI would support the developmental overnutrition hypothesis. The researchers concluded that their results indicate that it is "unlikely that developmental overnutrition has been a major driver in the recent obesity epidemic."

The implications of this hypothesis, if ultimately confirmed, are formidable: The childhood (and adulthood) obesity epidemic could become increasingly prevalent among successive generations independent of additional genetic or environmental factors. In their one-minute papers, ask students to speculate on these implications for the individual, the family, and society. Alternatively, you might ask them to critique the hypothesis from the vantage point of the limited information they have at this point. Are there other possible explanations of these findings? What kinds of empirical evidence would be required in order to rule out possible confounding variables?

Gillman, M. W., Rifas-Shiman, S. L., Camargo, C. A., Berkey, C. S., Frazier, A. L., Rockett, H. R., Field, A. E., & Colditz, G. A. (2001). Risk of overweight among adolescents who were breastfed as infants. *Journal of the American Medical Association, 285*(19), 2461–2467.

Lawlor, D. A., Timpson, N. J., et al. (2008). Exploring the developmental overnutrition hypothesis using parental-offspring associations and FTO as an instrumental variable. *PLOS Med, 5*(3), e33.

Martorell, R., Stein, A. D., & Schroeder, D. G. (2003). Early nutrition and later adiposity. *Journal of Nutrition, 131*, 8743–8803.

von Kries, R., Koletzko, B., Sauerwald, T., von Mutius, E., Barnert, D., Grunert, V., & von Voss, H. (1999). Breast feeding and obesity: Cross sectional study. *British Medical Journal, 319*(7203), 147–150.

Whitaker, R. C., & Dietz, W. H. (1998). Role of the prenatal environment in the development of obesity. *The Journal of Pediatrics, 132*(5), 768–776.

Critical Thinking Activity: Obesity and Weight Loss

Each unit of these resources contains a critical thinking exercise designed specifically to test students' critical thinking about a topic covered in the text. Handout 4 contains a brief scenario about an overweight youngster followed by a series of questions.

Sample answers to this unit's critical thinking activity follow:

Question 1: How many hours of television does Celine watch each day?

Reason for asking: Excessive TV viewing promotes a lower level of activity and a lowered metabolic state, both of which mean that Celine is burning fewer calories than she would, say, while running and playing outdoors. In addition, Celine's television-viewing habit may also encourage her to consume more calories in the form of snack foods.

Recommendation: If Celine does spend much time watching TV, she should be encouraged to reduce her TV time and substitute some sort of physical activity.

Question: Are Celine's biological parents obese?

Reason for asking: Research on adopted children shows that heredity is at least as strong as environmental factors in most physical characteristics, including weight. Body type, height, bone structure, and individual differences in metabolic rate and activity level are all strongly influenced by heredity.

Recommendation: Knowing Celine's genetic inheritance would be of help in setting a goal for her weight-reduction program.

Question: Does Celine get much exercise? Do her adoptive parents exercise regularly?

Reason for asking: Especially during childhood, inactive people burn fewer calories and are more likely to be overweight than are active people. The best way for children to lose weight is to increase their physical activity.

Recommendation: If Celine is relatively inactive, her parents should help her to find exercises to do in which her size would not be a disadvantage, and they should exercise with her.

Question: Is the family diet low in fat, and are family attitudes toward food healthy?

Reason for asking: By equating love with food, some parents inadvertently encourage overeating, a problem that might be particularly likely if the parents are seeking to establish a loving relationship with their newly adopted child. Diets high in fat and sugar are also more likely to lead to excess weight gain than are diets that emphasize fruits, vegetables, and grains. Parents may unknowingly encourage unhealthy attitudes toward food by giving sweets to their children as rewards or by taking satisfaction when they eat unnecessarily large portions.

Recommendation: The members of Celine's family should change their eating habits, cutting down on high-fat foods, and they should examine their attitudes toward food.

Question: When did Celine's weight problem begin?

Reason for asking: It is possible that the onset of Celine's obesity may have coincided with some traumatic experience—such as being adopted or being abused at her earlier home—that created a sense of loss or diminished self-image and a corresponding need for an alternative source of gratification, such as food.

Recommendation: If so, Celine will need emotional support, along with other help, in losing weight.

Question: Is Celine's teacher aware of her self-image problem?

Reason for asking: Teachers can set the tone in a class, allowing or even endorsing teasing or, alternatively, establishing an atmosphere of mutual respect that helps each child feel appreciated.

Recommendation: Celine's parents might talk to her teacher, explaining the need for special support for Celine.

Brain Development

Coordinating Connections

AV: Growing the Mind: How the Brain Develops (50 min., Films for the Humanities and Sciences)

This program focuses on the views of renowned neuroscientist Susan Greenfield, who views learning, memory, and identity as examples of the restless brain adapting to the environment. The program charts brain development from infancy through adulthood and explores its remarkable plasticity, as revealed by its ability to reorganize after damage.

Classroom Activity: Introducing Neuroethics

Neuroethics is an emerging field that studies the ways in which developments in basic and clinical neuroscience intersect with social and ethical issues. More specifically, Michael Gazzaniga, author of *The Ethical Brain,* one of the seminal works of the young field, defines neuroethics as "the examination of how we want to deal with the social issues of disease, normality, mortality, lifestyle, and the philosophy of living informed by our understanding of underlying brain mechanisms."

Among the issues being investigated by scientists working in this field are ethical problems raised by advances in functional neuroimaging, psychopharmacology, and brain implants, as well as our growing understanding of the neural bases of behavior, personality, and consciousness. As an example, employers, marketers, and the government have a strong interest in knowing the abilities, personality, and truthfulness of people. This raises the question of whether, when, and how to ensure the privacy of our own minds at a time when brain imaging correlates of these and other traits are being investigated in the laboratory.

Another example of the scope of neuroethics is the controversial issue of brain enhancement using *psychopharmaceutical* supplements. Martha J. Farah of the University of Pennsylvania suggests posing the following example to your students (2011):

> *A middle school student is performing below his potential and finds school boring, although he does not have a learning disability or medical condition. His teacher meets with the mother to recommend trying a stimulant-like nutritional supplement, making a case that the supplement will help her son. The mother then explains the idea to her son, asks him how he feels about it, and encourages him to try the supplement.*

Several online resources are available to help you learn more about neuroethics and how to introduce the new field to your students. For example:

> The Dana Foundation's Web site offers a gateway to information about the brain and brain research: www.dana.org/neuroethics.
>
> Johns Hopkins' Berman Institute of Bioethics maintains a Brain Sciences News Roundup at www.bioethicsinstitute.org/web/page/769/sectionid/77/pagelevel/2/interior.asp.
>
> The Society for Neuroscience includes a section on neuroscience in the news: www.sfn.org.

Farah, M.J. (2011). *Resources for neuroethics teaching.* National Institute on the Teaching of Psychology. St. Petersburg Beach, Florida.

Gazzaniga, M. S. (2005). *The Ethical Brain.* New York: Dana Press.

Measuring the Mind

AV: Intelligence: A Complex Concept (20 min., CRM/McGraw-Hill)

This film uses an interesting technique to explore the question of the nature of intelligence: Random people on the street are asked to define intelligence. Their answers are diverse and sometimes surprising. The movie then presents the types of answers given by psychological theories—from the dynamic, stage-oriented, process approach of the Piagetians to the more staid, chronological, product approach of traditional intelligence testing. The difficulty of constructing a valid and reliable test is explained, and a variety of tests are shown, each with different strengths and weaknesses.

A good introduction to the film would be to have your students give their definitions of intelligence, partly to see how, if at all, their answers differ from those of the people on the street. A possible follow-up to the movie would be to ask the students (individually or in groups) to devise an intelligence test.

AV: Intelligence (30 min., Insight Media)

Focusing on the difficulty psychologists have had in defining and assessing intelligence, this short film traces the history of IQ tests, describes several failures in their development, and considers what intelligence tests really measure. Arguments as to whether IQ tests measure aptitude or achievement (as critics claim) are presented. The issue of the stability of intelligence is also considered.

AV: A Conversation with David Wechsler (55 min., Insight Media)

David Wechsler, developer of the WAIS and WISC intelligence tests, discusses his research and the development of his widely used scales.

Classroom Activity: Test Scores and Other Criteria for Evaluating Intelligence

To help students appreciate the reasons for the controversy over intelligence testing, ask them to develop a list of weighted criteria for admission to your college or university. What weight, for instance, should be given to high school grades, aptitude and achievement tests, teacher recommendations, personal interviews with the college admissions staff, and student essays on the application form? Should any consideration be given to the student's ability to pay, family background, geographical location, racial and/or ethnic background, athletic ability, unusual interests, or leadership qualities in high school? (All these factors are, in fact, taken into account by many institutions of higher learning.) Would there be anything wrong with admitting everyone who applied and simply allowing those who proved unqualified to flunk out?

From this discussion you can point out that some of the same problems and issues arise in evaluating children in elementary school. Children are passed or failed, and placed in the top or the bottom class, on the basis of many factors—which vary from school to school, teacher to teacher, and child to child.

AV: It's Cool to Be Smart (23 min., CRM/McGraw-Hill)

This film examines several programs for gifted children, all of which show children learning skills, developing talents, and exploring ideas that are unusual for children their age. Since the teacher's role is also discussed, this movie might be particularly helpful if your class contains many present or future teachers.

Before showing the film, you might ask if it is "cool" to be average, or even "dumb." The American debate about whether special programs for gifted children in fact work to the detriment of other children is still alive, although this film (produced by ABC) emphasizes only one side of the question. Indeed, one can wonder whether some gifted students, especially the dancers and musicians, are losing some of the joys of childhood as they accelerate their talents.

AV: In a Class of His Own (26 min., Films for the Humanities and Sciences)

This program covers a year in the life of Grahame, an exceptional child who startled his parents by reading from the newspaper at 2 years of age. Although his parents were determined to foster his remarkable cognitive abilities in every way, Grahame did not do well in school. The film focuses on the often frustrating problems schools, teachers, and parents face in dealing with a child who does not fit the intellectual mold.

AV: Prodigies: Great Expectations (52 min., Films for the Humanities and Sciences)

This documentary examines the advantages and disadvantages of gifted young people who, although intellectually mature, are still physically and emotionally immature.

"On Your Own" Activity: Developing Your Practical Intelligence

To help your students gain insight into their own practical intelligence (as defined by Sternberg), have them analyze the "real-world" problems in Handout 5.

The solutions follow. Students will quickly see that the problems have no right or wrong answers; each solution depends on the individual and the situation. In each case, the student may "solve" the problem in one of three ways: by adaptation—accommodating his or her behavior to the situation; by shaping—attempting to change the environment; or by selection—leaving the environment altogether. Thinking about the "solutions" of adaptation, shaping, and selection and how their personality and abilities interact with the situation should help your students to make more practical, intelligent decisions in future situations similar to those presented.

Answers to Real-World Problems:

1. a. shaping
   b. selection
   c. adaptation
2. a. adaptation
   b. shaping
   c. selection
3. a. selection
   b. adaptation
   c. shaping
4. a. adaptation
   b. shaping
   c. selection
5. a. selection
   b. shaping
   c. adaptation

Sources: Sternberg, R. J. (1986). *Intelligence applied: Understanding and increasing your intellectual skills.* New York: Harcourt Brace Jovanovich.

Sternberg, R. J. (2000). *Practical intelligence in everyday life.* New York: Cambridge University Press.

Children with Special Needs

Classroom Activity: What's On My Back

Amy Marin of Phoenix College suggests a fun classroom activity that encourages student interaction and promotes active learning. Using Post-it Notes, tape a concept that is relevant to the course unit or lecture topic on each student's back. Students then have five minutes to guess what is on their back by asking questions of other students that can only be answered by "yes" or "no." A good way to come up with the items for the notes is simply to use the key terms list at the end of the textbook chapter, as well as the names of key theorists and researchers that appear in the chapter. For the unit on children with special needs, these might include autistic spectrum disorder, bipolar disorder, dyslexia, asthma, and so forth. Examples of yes/no questions that students are permitted to ask are "Do I have impaired interpersonal skills" (autistic spectrum disorders) and "Do I have difficulty reading?" (dyslexia).

Marin, A. (2011). *Mindful Moments: 50 Micro-Activities for Energizing the College Classroom.* National Institute on the Teaching of Psychology. St. Petersburg Beach, FL.

"On Your Own" Activity: Physical Disabilities: Everything Is Harder

The developmental theory of Erik Erikson is a useful model for studying life-span changes. Erikson's theory identifies eight important psychosocial crises in life, each of which can be resolved in either a positive, growth-promoting way or in a negative manner that disrupts healthy development.

This exercise asks students to reflect on Erikson's theory and the difficulties that individuals with physical problems may have in achieving a positive resolution to each crisis. Handout 6 lists the stages and provides space for students to write their answers.

To successfully complete the exercise, students must integrate material from infancy, early childhood, and middle childhood and anticipate developmental issues that will emerge during adolescence and adulthood. You might want to check students' answers for evidence of their understanding of the eight psychosocial crises and plausible examples of how a disability might disrupt development at each stage. Students' answers could also form the basis for an effective classroom discussion of biosocial development over the life span and the interaction of the biosocial, cognitive, and psychosocial domains.

AV: The Special Child: Maximizing Limited Potential (26 min., Films for the Humanities and Sciences)
Dyslexia: Diagnosis and Prognosis (26 min., Films for the Humanities and Sciences)
Dyslexia: Disabled or Different? (26 min., Films for the Humanities and Sciences)

These films examine a variety of developmental problems. *The Special Child* covers the possible causes and forms of treatment for Down syndrome, autism, problems of neurological control, and disordered speech. Physicians, psychologists, and therapists demonstrate how a special child's developmental potential is measured and the steps taken to help him or her reach it.

The two films on dyslexia provide an overview of the symptoms, causes, diagnosis, and treatment of the various disorders falling under this heading. *Dyslexia: Disabled or Different?* focuses on learning-disabled children in the public school system and how teachers, parents, and children work together to overcome developmental barriers.

Attention-Deficit and Bipolar Disorders

Classroom Activity: Attention-Deficit/Hyperactivity Disorder

To give your students a better idea of how the clinician identifies the child with attention-deficit/hyperactivity disorder and to introduce them to the idea of "diagnostic criteria," you might read or reproduce the criteria for the disorder. The definition is derived from the *Diagnostic and Statistical Manual of Mental Disorders*, Fourth Edition, Text Revision (DSM-IV-TR). The goal of this publication is to describe each disorder in terms of its clinical features, "at the lowest order of inference necessary"—that is, focusing on the most easily identifiable behavioral signs and symptoms.

According to DSM-IV-TR, the essential features of attention-deficit/hyperactivity disorder (ADHD) are

> developmentally inappropriate degrees of inattention, impulsiveness, and hyperactivity. People with the disorder generally display some disturbance in each of these areas, but to varying degrees. Manifestations of the disorder usually appear in most situations, including at home, in school, at work, and in social situations, but to varying degrees. Some people, however, show signs of the disorder in only one setting. . . .

The diagnostic criteria for ADHD that follow are taken from DSM-IV-TR.[1]

A. A disturbance of at least six months during which at least eight of the following are present:
   (1) often fidgets with hands or feet or squirms in seat (in adolescents, may be limited to subjective feelings of restlessness)
   (2) has difficulty remaining seated when required to do so
   (3) is easily distracted by extraneous stimuli
   (4) has difficulty awaiting turn in games or group situations
   (5) often blurts out answers to questions before they have been completed
   (6) has difficulty following through on instructions from others (not due to oppositional behavior or failure of comprehension)—for example, fails to finish chores
   (7) has difficulty sustaining attention in tasks or play activities
   (8) often shifts from one uncompleted activity to another
   (9) has difficulty playing quietly
   (10) often talks excessively
   (11) often interrupts or intrudes on others (e.g., butts into other children's games)
   (12) often does not seem to listen to what is being said to him or her
   (13) often loses things necessary for tasks or activities at school or at home (e.g., toys, pencils, books, assignments)
   (14) often engages in physically dangerous activities without considering possible consequences (not for the purpose of thrill-seeking)—for example, runs into street without looking

   Note: The above items are listed in descending order of discriminating power based on data from a national field trial of the DSM-IV-TR criteria for disruptive behavior disorders.
B. Onset before the age of 7
C. Does not meet the criteria for a Pervasive Developmental Disorder

The DSM-IV-TR further specifies the following criteria for diagnosing the severity of attention-deficit/hyperactivity disorder:

> *Mild*: Few, if any, symptoms in excess of those required to make the diagnosis *and* only minimal or no impairment in school and social functioning.
>
> *Moderate*: Symptoms or functional impairment intermediate between "mild" and "severe."
>
> *Severe*: Many symptoms in excess of those required to make the diagnosis *and* significant and pervasive impairment in functioning at home and school and with peers.

AV: The Diagnosis and Treatment of Attention-Deficit Disorder in Children (27 min., Films for the Humanities and Sciences)

Taken from *The Doctor Is In* series, this program focuses on the controversial subject of how a diagnosis of attention-deficit disorder is made. The video follows several ADD children at home and school, both on and off medication and discusses the best, and worst, environments for ADD children.

AV: ADD Children (28 min., Aquarius Productions)

This short program examines the controversial issue of whether too many children are incorrectly being diagnosed with attention-deficit disorder. Focusing on who is being diagnosed and the differences between effective and ineffective treatments, the video follows several ADD children over the course of a day at home, at school, and off and on Ritalin.

AV: ADHD: What Do We Know? (35 min., Insight Media)

The etiology and prevalence of ADHD are outlined, along with the ways the disorder is manifested and its long-term outcome. A 6-year-old, an adolescent, and a man in his 20s discuss how the disorder has affected their lives.

AV: ADHD: What Can We Do? (45 min., Insight Media)

The companion to *ADHD: What Do We Know?*, this film focuses on techniques for managing the disorder in the home and classroom. The use of behavior modification techniques, such as positive and negative reinforcement, token economies, and time-out, is also discussed.

AV: All About Attention-Deficit Disorder (Part 1: 108 min.; Part II: 85 min.)

In the first installment of this highly recommended two-part film, Dr. Thomas Phelan uses clinical

[1]Consider a criterion met only if the behavior is considerably more frequent than that of most people of the same mental age. American Psychiatric Association. (1994). *Diagnostic and statistical manual of mental disorders* (4th ed., text revision). Washington, DC: Author.

examples to outline the most prominent symptoms of ADD and their effects on home, school, and social life. Part II traces the developmental course of the disorder, examines ways to diagnose its occurrence, and looks at various forms of treatment, including medication, behavioral management, and counseling.

Classroom Activity: A Case Study of ADHD

Teachers and parents often complain that children won't sit still and are unable to concentrate for very long. But does this mean that the children can be regarded as having attention-deficit/hyperactivity disorder (ADHD)? Or does it mean that the children, with their limited (and quite normal) spans of attention, won't concentrate long enough to satisfy adults? To help your students distinguish "normal" from "abnormal" conduct in children, you might want to present a case study of a child diagnosed as having ADHD. The following case was cited in David Rosenhan and Martin Seligman's abnormal psychology text.

> James was four years old when he was first admitted to the children's psychiatric ward as a day patient. Ever since infancy he had made life difficult for his elderly parents. As soon as he could crawl, he got into everything. He had no sense of danger. He slept very little at night and was difficult to pacify when upset. It was only because he was their only child and they could devote all of their time to him that his parents managed to maintain him at home.
>
> His problems were noticed by others just as soon as James began preschool at age three. He made no friends among the other children. Every interaction ended in trouble. He rushed around all day, and could not even sit still at story time. His flitting from one activity to another completely exhausted his teachers. After some eighteen months of trying, his teachers suggested that he be referred to the hospital for assessment and treatment.
>
> On examination, no gross physical damage could be found in his central nervous system. Psychological examinations revealed that James had a nearly average intelligence. In the hospital, he was just as hyperactive as he had been in school and at home. He climbed dangerously to the top of the outdoor swings. He ran from one plaything to another and showed no consideration for other children who were using them. Left to his own devices, he was constantly on the move, tearing up paper, messing with paints—all in a nonconstructive manner.
>
> James was placed in a highly structured classroom, with two teachers and five other children. There his behavior was gradually brought under control. He was given small tasks that were well within his ability, and he was carefully shown how to perform them. His successes were met with lavish praise. Moreover, patience and reward gradually increased the length of time he would spend seated at the table.
>
> Ultimately, James was placed in a small, structured, residential school. By age sixteen, he had settled down a great deal. He was no longer physically overactive, but his conversation still flitted from one subject to another. He had no friends among his peers although he could relate reasonably well to adults. He showed little initiative in matters concerning his own life, and his prospects for gaining employment were not good.

James's story highlights a number of behaviors typical of children with ADHD. Such children are overly active and impulsive and have trouble concentrating on any one task for very long. Like James, ADHD children may outgrow some of their symptoms, but the majority continue to show symptoms into adolescence and adulthood. Hyperactive children often do poorly in school; as adults, they experience more occupational difficulties than do adults without a history of ADHD. Thus, an early childhood history of ADHD casts a long shadow over an individual's life story.

Research studies also reveal that boys with ADHD differ in empathy and other emotions. In one study (Braaten & Rosen, 2000), empathy was assessed by having the participants respond to eight episodes presented in the form of short narratives. Each narrative involved a fictitious child and was illustrated by a black-and-white picture in which the character and the setting of the episode were shown. In each picture, the character's face was left blank, so that the participants would not be able to use facial cues as a way of gaining information about the characters' emotions. Following the narrative, each boy was asked three questions: (a) "How does [name of child in story] feel?" (b) "How does [name of child in story] make you feel?" and (c) "Why does he/she make you feel that way?" The results showed that boys with ADHD less frequently matched the emotion they identified in the character with the one identified in themselves and gave fewer character-centered interpretations in their descriptions of the character's emotion. Other data from the same study revealed that ADHD boys also exhibited more behavioral manifestations of sadness, anger, and guilt than did boys *without* ADHD.

Braaten, E. B., & Rosen, L. A. (2000). Self-regulation of affect in attention deficit-hyperactivity disorder (ADHD) and non-ADHD boys: Differences in empathic responding. *Journal of Consulting and Clinical Psychology. 68*(2), 313–321.

Rosenhan, D. L., & Seligman, M. E. P. (1989). *Abnormal psychology* (2nd ed., pp. 527–528). New York: Norton.

AV: Coping with Attention-Deficit Disorder in Children (24 min., Films for the Humanities and Sciences)

This film explores the causes, symptoms, diagnosis, and treatment of ADHD.

AV: Childhood Depression (19 min., Films for the Humanities and Sciences)

This brief film profiles a mother and her 3-year-old son, both of whom have depressive disorders, focusing on how genetic disorders and chemical imbalances can lead to depression.

Learning Disabilities

AV: Hidden Handicaps (23 min., CRM/McGraw-Hill)
Specific Learning Difficulties in the Classroom (23 min., Davidson Films)

With footage from actual classroom interactions, these films show the behavioral manifestations of the common learning disabilities, particularly dyslexia, found in "normal" children. Both stress the importance of early detection and patient, individualized remediation. *Hidden Handicaps* was originally produced for ABC television and hence is intended for a general audience; *Specific Learning Disabilities* is intended for educators and is more specific as well as more current. The emphasis on a historical perspective provides a good introduction to this topic.

AV: A Video Guide to (Dis)Ability Awareness (25 min., Aquarius Productions)

Former president Bill Clinton opens this realistic examination of the lives of the disabled. The award-winning video consists of a series of candid interviews with people who have a wide range of physical and developmental disabilities.

Classroom Activity: Understanding and Helping Children with Learning Disabilities

To help students understand that some of the greatest difficulties in overcoming a disability stem from others' reactions to it, you might initiate a discussion of various disabilities, asking students how they *do* react to them and then helping them to see how they *should* react. (If there are students in your class who have learning disabilities, you might ask, before class, whether they wish to talk about their experiences and then have them offer suggestions.)

People tend to expect all children to behave in certain, specified ways, and it is much easier, for example, to blame the hyperactive child for not learning to read, write, or sit still than to understand the problem. In addition, parents and teachers of learning-disabled children are apt to blame each other rather than work together to help the child—again for reasons that are understandable but destructive.

The biggest problem for blind and partially sighted children is learning to be mobile, but most people overprotect them. The result is dependent, inexperienced individuals who have little confidence in their ability to get around without help. As a consequence, many blind adults are much more restricted in their activities than necessary.

Those who are hearing-impaired have the most trouble learning language. For one thing, people avoid talking to them, or sometimes use baby talk when their language skills are far past that stage. Children and adults should be encouraged to communicate with deaf people (through writing, lipreading, and/or sign language or the manual alphabet) rather than fall back on instinctive avoidance.

Mentally challenged children are slow learners by definition, but they are not necessarily any more antisocial or emotionally disturbed than other individuals. Yet many people, including some college students, equate retardation with mental illness and avoid or tease those afflicted (the term "retard" is a favorite epithet of young children).

Development is harder for children with disabilities for many reasons. One is the additional stresses the disability places on parents and other family members. Another obstacle is the lack of good role models for disabled children. Children with disabilities may need greater self-confidence, self-esteem, and perseverance than normal children simply because most things require more effort and take longer.

AV: Learning Disabilities (19 min., Films for the Humanities and Sciences)

The point is clearly made that not every normal-looking child is a normal learner. This film focuses on a 9-year-old boy with dyslexia who was becoming emotionally disturbed because his parents, teachers, and friends did not recognize or understand his problems. Now in a special classroom, he seems to be functioning much better. This film would be a good starting point to discuss common learning disabilities and how people cope with them. Undoubtedly some of your students will recognize that they are in some way disabled. Most will acknowledge that they had to discover their own coping methods.

Internet Activity: Dyslexia Resources

Handout 7 asks students to search authoritative Internet sources to prepare answers to a series of questions regarding resources available to those with dyslexia, including treatment of the condition, public policy, testing, and local support groups.

Classroom Activity: We All Learn to Compensate

To reinforce the idea that everyone has difficulty with some skills and that most of us learn to compensate, you might invite students to talk about any specific learning disabilities they have and how they compensate for them. If you expand the list of disabilities to include such things as difficulty with spelling, doing puzzles, maintaining a sense of direction, speaking clearly, drawing, carrying a tune, and hitting a ball, most students will see that they are, in fact, disabled to a degree.

AV: Page Fright: Inside the World of the Learning Disabled (28 min., Insight Media)

Through profiles of several individuals, this video illustrates the frustration, embarrassment, and shame that the learning disabled frequently experience. It also examines alternative educational techniques that may be helpful to those with learning disabilities.

Autistic Spectrum Disorders

AV: Autism: A World Apart (29 min., Insight Media)

Recommended by numerous educational groups, this documentary uses interviews with families and experts to explore various issues related to autism, including the problems it creates for families, its possible causes and treatments, and the advantages and disadvantages of mainstreaming.

AV: Autism: Diagnosis, Causes, and Treatments (53 min., Films for the Humanities and Sciences)

Built around several case studies of children, this video differentiates high- and low-functioning autism and examines the role of genetics, neurological diseases, and immune system disorders as possible factors in autism. The last segment describes Applied Behavior Analysis, multisensory stimulation, nutrition, and other interventions in treating autism.

AV: Understanding Autism (24 min., Films for the Humanities & Sciences)

This documentary focuses on the various support services that are available for people with autism outside the home. It examines a high-functioning autistic adult and poignantly portrays the struggles of the parents of children with autism.

AV: Day by Day: Raising the Child with Autism (60 min., Insight Media)

Focusing on the coping skills and practical strategies used by parents of children with autism, this film offers a realistic look into the daily lives of a low-functioning child with no language and a difficult, overly active child with some language.

AV: A School for Robin (55 min., Filmakers Library)

This poignant, realistic film provides a longitudinal look at a preschool that attempts to bring Robin, shown from ages 3 to 7, out of his autistic shell within a mainstream context. Underlying themes are the importance of play, social interaction, and language development during early childhood. Among the several reasons you might want to show this film is that the school itself is wonderful, with a caring, well-trained interracial staff and with fine teaching materials and lots of space. At the end of three years of effort, Robin is much better—but on his way to a special class.

Classroom Activity: Asperger Syndrome

To extend the text discussion of this fascinating disorder, you might discuss the following information, much of which comes from the Online Asperger Syndrome Information and Support (OASIS@MAPP), which can be found at www.aspergersyndrome.org.

Consider the following case history:

> Adam S. was clearly a bright little boy. He began reading at age 2, and as a preschooler would lecture friendly adults—actually, any adult who would listen—about state capitals or presidents or famous painters.
>
> But something was wrong. Adam had no friends, no connection to his peers. By third grade he was adrift: isolated, troublesome and unhappy, despite his academic ability.
>
> A string of experts gave Adam a string of diagnoses: attention deficit disorder, nonverbal learning disorder, and obsessive-compulsive disorder. Then three years ago, when he was 9, doctors reached a new diagnosis—Asperger's syndrome.
>
> Adam's confusing mix of abilities and deficits and the confusion of those who tried to assess it are both typical for children with Asperger's, a condition that is generally considered a form of autism. While it remains little known, the number of diagnoses has soared since psychiatric authorities formally defined it five years ago.

Asperger syndrome (AS) is a complex neurological disorder named for a Viennese physician, Hans Asperger. In 1944, Asperger published a description of a pattern of behaviors he had observed in several young patients who had normal intelligence and language development (Asperger called his patients "little professors" who use words as their lifeline to the world), but who also exhibited autisticlike behaviors and marked deficiencies in social skills.

However, only in the past decade has AS been recognized by professionals and parents. One reason for the slow acceptance of Dr. Asperger's work is that writing in German in Vienna in 1944 (during World War II) was a poor way to spread new scientific knowledge. Asperger's work was first brought to wider attention in 1981 by a London psychiatrist, Dr. Lorna Wing, and only in 1994 was the syndrome included in the DSM-IV-TR, the latest version of the mental health profession's guidebook.

Diagnostic Criteria for 299.80 Asperger's Disorder

A. Qualitative impairment in social interaction, as manifested by at least two of the following:

   Marked impairments in the use of multiple nonverbal behaviors such as eye-to-eye gaze, facial expression, body postures, and gestures to regulate social interaction

   Failure to develop peer relationships appropriate to developmental level

   A lack of spontaneous seeking to share enjoyment, interests, or achievements with other people (e.g., by a lack of showing, bringing, or pointing out objects of interest to other people)

   Lack of social or emotional reciprocity

B. Restricted, repetitive, and stereotyped patterns of behavior, interests, and activities, as manifested by at least one of the following:

   Encompassing preoccupation with one or more stereotyped and restricted patterns of interest that is abnormal either in intensity or focus

Apparently inflexible adherence to specific, nonfunctional routines or rituals
Stereotyped and repetitive motor mannerisms (e.g., hand or finger flapping or twisting, or complex whole-body movements)
Persistent preoccupation with parts of objects

C. The disturbance causes clinically significant impairments in social, occupational, or other important areas of functioning.

D. There is no clinically significant general delay in language (e.g., single words used by age 2 years, communicative phrases used by age 3 years).

E. There is no clinically significant delay in cognitive development or in the development of age-appropriate self-help skills, adaptive behavior (other than social interaction), and curiosity about the environment in childhood.

F. Criteria are not met for another specific Pervasive Developmental Disorder or Schizophrenia.

Implicit in these criteria is the fact that persons with AS have difficulty adjusting to disruptions in their daily activities. Many develop obsessive routines that reach a point of focus in an all-consuming interest in arcane subjects. Dr. Fred Volkmar, a psychiatrist with the Yale Child Study Center who helped write the standard diagnostic definition of AS, has encountered obsessions with clocks; the Titanic; deep-fat fryers; lists of congressional members, spouses, and aides; refrigerators; and train, plane, and bus schedules.

Persons with AS also tend to have difficulty reading nonverbal body language; one manifestation of this problem is that they have trouble determining proper body space. Often hypersensitive to normal sensory stimuli, the person with AS may prefer soft clothing and certain foods and be bothered by sounds or lights that no one else seems to hear or see. Because AS victims perceive the world in a unique way, many of their behaviors that seem odd or unusual are misinterpreted as signs of intentional rudeness.

By definition, those with AS have a normal IQ, and many exhibit exceptional skill in a specific area. Young persons with AS are often viewed as eccentric and become victims of teasing and bullying. Adolescence is particularly difficult for victims of AS, in part because teachers find it hard to believe that a bright student who is disrupting class is not doing it intentionally. As a result, until recently, students with AS were grouped with other "problem students" in special classes for troublemakers. While many adults with AS manage to master enough social skills to attend college, find jobs, and even marry, others sink into isolation. Researchers report high levels of depression and suicide, and antidepressants are the most common medication given to AS patients.

Until fairly recently, researchers were unsure as to where AS fits. Some professionals felt that AS is the same as high-functioning autism; others felt that it is better described as a nonverbal learning disability. As noted in the text, scientists now refer to an autistic spectrum, with AS commonly being described as the "smart end" of the spectrum. Because AS was virtually unknown until a few years ago, many individuals either received an incorrect diagnosis or remained undiagnosed. For example, at that time it was not at all uncommon for a child who was initially diagnosed with ADD or ADHD to be rediagnosed with AS.

Many autisticlike conditions today are being referred to as "empathic disorders" in recognition of underlying social deficiencies that appear to be caused by lesions in a part of the brain that processes sensory input. In cases of classic autism, the person primarily has problems with verbal skills, which are handled by the brain's left hemisphere. In AS, the person's difficulties are largely in nonverbal skills, which are controlled by the right hemisphere, causing some experts to speculate that the syndrome may someday be known as "right-brained autism."

Two other differences in the disorders are that the genetic link appears to be stronger in Asperger syndrome than in autism and that AS often goes unnoticed for many years. Autism is usually diagnosed around age 3, but children with Asperger syndrome are not usually identified until they start school and their social inabilities begin to stand out.

Although AS can be difficult to diagnose in young children, researchers at the Yale Child Study Center recommend that parents seek help if they notice several of the following behaviors:

- A marked lack of interest in other children or a consistently inappropriate style of engaging others, such as long monologues.
- Significant difficulty in understanding other children's feelings and expressions (inability to get jokes or teasing).
- Few facial or bodily gestures; speech that is pedantic in tone or vocabulary.
- Little make-believe and much repetition in play.
- Overreaction to minor changes in routine or environment.
- Precocious verbal skills and marked self-absorption in subjects unusual for the child's age.

Treatment for AS is usually an eclectic mix of therapies, focusing on improving perceptual reactions and providing behavioral training to improve social skills. In Adam's case, this year Adam's school district has assigned him a "shadow" aide, who helps guide him away from inappropriate behavior as well as keep him working smoothly in his mainstream classes. His recent victory in his school's geography bee is the kind of positive side to his intense focus that his family and teachers can use to bolster his self-esteem. "I was very worried about his starting middle school," his mother said. "But it's turning out to be his best year."

Another way to bring autism and AS to life for the class would be read aloud portions of *The Curious Incident of the Dog in the Night-Time,* a novel by Mark

Haddon. The hero of the novel is 15-year-old Christopher John Francis Boone, who narrates the novel rather than appearing in it and who clearly has AS. Christopher is a math genius whose idiosyncrasies include "not liking being touched," "not eating food if different sorts of food are touching each other," and "not noticing that people are angry with me." Commenting on the fact that the terms "Asperger syndrome" and "autism" never appear in the book, the author notes, "The label doesn't add anything to your knowledge of anyone. In the old days you were allowed to be odd," he says. "Too many people now who would have been odd find themselves with a label and getting sucked into some kind of system."

Haddon, M. (2003). *The curious incident of the dog in the night-time.* New York: Random House.

Noonan, D. (2003, September 8). Allowed to be odd. *Newsweek, 10,* 50.

O'Neil, J. (1999, April 6). A syndrome with a mix of skills and deficits. www.nytimes.com.

AV: Asperger's Syndrome: Autism and Obsessive Behavior (29 min., Films for the Humanities and Sciences)

This BBC production takes a thorough look at Asperger syndrome. Described first in 1944, this condition makes everyday social interactions particularly difficult. The program profiles the symptoms of the syndrome and its impact on its victims and family members; it also takes an in-depth look at the role of abnormalities of the frontal cortex in the disorder.

Special Education

AV: LD = Learning Differences (60 min., Insight Media)

This program examines how specific educational handicaps affect learning and addresses the controversial question of whether learning-disabled students should be integrated into a regular school setting. It also identifies early signs of learning differences and explains how ADD and ADHD affect learning.

AV: Learning Disabled (25 min., Films for the Humanities and Sciences)

In this brief video, students and educators from Trillijum High School for the learning disabled discuss the advantages and disadvantages of special education.

AV: Lilly: A Story About a Girl Like Me (14 min., Polymorph Films)

This film was made by the mother of a 10-year-old Down syndrome child to show her daughter's daily life. Decidedly upbeat, the film demonstrates how much a special child can do and learn when aided by a favorable home environment. You should point out that not all Down syndrome children have Lilly's intellectual potential. Of course, unless home care is attempted, it is hard to know how much a particular child can learn in that milieu.

AV: Mainstreaming in Action (26 min., Insight Media)

This award-winning video takes the viewer into actual public school classrooms to watch teachers work with handicapped students in a mainstreaming environment. The teachers offer frank commentary and valuable insights into the practicality of mainstreaming and the controversial issue of socialization versus academic learning.

AV: Who Will Teach the Water to Swim? (25 min., Films for the Humanities and Sciences)

This provocative program follows two teachers who work at different schools in The Netherlands and chronicles the many problems they face in teaching children with autism.

Classroom Activity: Classroom Debate: *"Resolved: Children with Learning Disabilities Should Be Mainstreamed"*

The issue of how to best educate children with learning disabilities—either obvious problems like blindness or less apparent difficulties such as moderate mental retardation—has long been controversial. Because teachers did not feel prepared to handle them and parents wanted to protect them from loneliness and mockery, many children with special needs were kept at home, either educated by their parents or a tutor or not taught at all. Others spent their entire childhoods in schools or institutions for special children.

In the 1960s, educators and parents began to question whether separate education was always best for children with special needs. By the end of the 1960s many educators were strongly recommending the integration of special children into regular classes as much as possible and as early as possible. Such *mainstreaming* occurred gradually in the United States until federal law in 1975 mandated that all children, no matter what their limitations, receive public education in the "least restrictive" environment that is educationally sound. Moreover, in 1986, Congress passed another law extending similar provisions to children as young as 3.

Despite the many advantages it seems to offer, mainstreaming has not proven to be the simple solution that some hoped it would be. One problem is that many special children need extensive and expensive supportive services to help them learn in the regular classroom. Another is that social skills and acceptance are not necessarily furthered simply by putting children with special needs and those without such needs together in the same room. Finally, although some children with special needs can manage in a regular school, they may sometimes derive greater benefit from some form of separate education.

Although mainstreaming is not discussed in detail in the text, it remains a controversial yet widely used method for teaching disabled children. To give your class a more personal understanding of students' and families' experiences with special schools and mainstreaming, you might want to review David's experience (text Chapter 1) in light of this issue. As described by Kathleen Berger,

> David's family moved to Boston partly to be nearer the Perkins School for the Blind. As the text points out, preschool education for multihandicapped children is hard to find; it is noteworthy, and typical, that all the special schools David attended were designed for children with specific, single disabilities.
>
> David's experience with mainstreaming varied a great deal, depending on the regular teacher and the availability of special teachers. Some of the regular teachers spent extra time tutoring and helping him; others just wished he would sit quietly and do nothing. One of the latter did not mind if David did none of his work in school; she just assigned it as extra homework. This technique may have worked with a normal child, but it meant that David's family had to spend long hours getting him to sit down and do his work—a task the regular teacher found impossible.
>
> David's social skills continued to be the greatest problem, in part because he usually triggered sympathetic and patient reactions from adults and teasing or avoidance from children. As a result, it was difficult for him to learn normal social skills, such as when to join a conversation or how to play with other children.
>
> David's parents became concerned about his development during junior high school. Because the local junior high was large—with students traveling from class to class several times each day—and because junior-high students tend to be so self-absorbed and worried about their self-image, the chance of David's developing positive social skills among them seemed slim. With all of this in mind, in the fall of 1979 David's parents chose to send him to the Kentucky School for the Blind, and they were pleased with his development there. David became an active participant in the physical education program: he swam, ran around a track holding on to a guide rope, wrestled, and lifted weights. In the regular school, he had simply sat on the sidelines during gym. David's experience underscores the need for more varied activities in regular schools that want to make mainstreaming work, and shows that, at times, especially at difficult times in a child's life—such as the first years of junior high—special schools may play an important role. (See text Chapter 1 for the latest on David's progress.)

You might also point out that mainstreaming is a source of controversy and bitterness among some teachers, who note that their workloads have been increased by the addition of children with special educational needs and that help in meeting these needs is inadequate. For example, federal law requires that schools develop an individual educational plan (IEP) for each student, and in some communities, the work of developing and implementing this plan falls on the classroom teacher.

Resource rooms (rooms equipped with special learning materials) and resource teachers are not present in every school; when they are, many classroom teachers feel that they are not available to give as much help to as many students as they should. As one counselor put it: "We have children whose needs are complicated—a child in the third grade who has already been in 16 schools, children who need love and attention, and disrupt the classroom to get it. Ten percent of the students in Detroit's classrooms can't conform and can't learn. These children need a disproportionate amount of the teacher's time. It's a teacher's nightmare—she can't help them, but she never forgets them."

In addition, many regular classroom teachers are educationally and emotionally unprepared to deal with the child who is deaf, blind, retarded, palsied, or emotionally disturbed. While some school systems have provided additional coursework and counseling to help these teachers, many have not.

A more general problem is that mainstreaming may be instituted for the wrong reason—that is, as a way of cutting the education budget in times of recession. However, most professionals and parents believe that if done properly, mainstreaming is just as expensive as separate education.

To further explore the pros and cons of mainstreaming, you might want to invite a guest speaker—either a teacher who has had some experience in mainstreaming or a parent whose child has been mainstreamed—to class. Personal experiences keep this issue from becoming a purely ideological one.

Alternatively or in addition to the above, you might want to schedule a debate on this resolution. Follow the guidelines in the General Resources section for doing so.

HANDOUT 1

Developmental Fact or Myth?

T F 1. Children grow more rapidly during middle childhood than at any other time.

T F 2. Lung capacity decreases during middle childhood.

T F 3. The best way to get children to lose weight is to increase their physical activity.

T F 4. Genes alone have caused the marked increase in obesity among children.

T F 5. IQ scores are not very reliable in predicting school achievement.

T F 6. Intellectual potential does not change over the life span.

T F 7. A typical child with attention-deficit/hyperactivity disorder has great difficulty in paying attention.

T F 8. More boys than girls have attention-deficit/hyperactivity disorder.

T F 9. One of the first noticeable symptoms of autism is delayed language.

T F 10. The latest educational strategy for children in the early grades who are below average in achievement is to give them some special intervention.

HANDOUT 2

Tall and Short Classmates

Try to remember your fourth- or fifth-grade elementary school class. Without looking at class pictures, recall the personalities of the children in your class when you were between 9 and 11 years old. (Your responses will be discussed in class but not collected.)

1. Briefly describe the personality of a child whom you recall as being taller or more grown-up in appearance than most of the other children. Note his or her name, if you recall it.

2. Briefly describe the personality of a child whom you recall as being smaller or less mature in appearance than most of the other children. Note his or her name, if you recall it.

3. Describe your own size and maturity back then, relative to that of your classmates.

HANDOUT 3

Images of Obesity

Our culture's attitudes toward obese people are reflected in the media—for example, in the use (or avoidance) of obese people in print and television advertisements, as well as in nonadvertising contexts, such as news photos.

1. Find and bring to class a picture of an obese or very overweight child taken from an advertisement, news story, or magazine article. (If you cannot find an example from the print media, note an instance of an obese child appearing on television or film.) Specify the advertisement, program, or news story in which it appeared.

2. Find and bring to class at least two pictures of obese or very overweight adults taken from advertisements, news stories, or magazine articles. (If you cannot find two examples in the print media, note two instances of an obese adult appearing on television or film.) Specify the advertisement, program, or news story in which it appeared.

3. How did you react to the pictures? If possible, show the pictures to others and record their responses.

HANDOUT 4

Critical Thinking Activity: Obesity and Weight Loss

Now that you have read and reviewed Middle Childhood: Biosocial Development, take your learning a step further by testing your critical thinking skills on this practical problem-solving exercise.

Celine's parents are concerned about their daughter's weight.

Although neither of her parents is overweight, 9-year-old Celine, whom they adopted two years ago, weighs about 30 percent more than the average girl of her age and height. "We just can't understand it," they lament. "She's tried several diets and still can't lose weight! She's so upset that all she does is mope around the house all day. What can we do to help our daughter?"

To advise Celine's parents, you obviously need more information. Your task in this exercise is twofold. First, generate a list of questions you might ask to help pinpoint the cause(s) of Celine's weight problem. Each question should focus on a specific biological, social, or behavioral influence that might cause obesity. Then, for each question, explain how the answer will help you determine the cause of Celine's weight problem and what you might recommend as a result. To help you get started, one question is provided.

Question 1: How many hours of television does Celine watch each day?
Reason for asking:

Recommendation:

Question 2:
Reason for asking:

Recommendation:

Question 3:
Reason for asking:

Recommendation:

Question 4:
Reason for asking:

Recommendation:

HANDOUT 5

Developing Your Practical Intelligence

Below are five everyday situations followed by three options that represent alternative ways of handling the situation. There is no single right or wrong answer; what is "right" will depend on your assessment of the situation and on your own personality and abilities. For each situation, pick the course of action that is right for you.

1. Your 1989 Plymouth station wagon is about to give up the ghost. To avoid the inevitable breakdown, you decide to purchase a new car, a Ford Thunderbird. The local dealership, which is well stocked with the new model, has a good reputation. After describing to the salesperson just what you have in mind, you find that the price is much higher than you expected. Do you:
   a. decide to haggle and bargain for the absolute lowest price possible?
   b. resign yourself to the purchase of a different type of auto?
   c. buy the car of your dreams, knowing that you will have to get a second job to supplement your income?
2. All semester long you have been struggling to keep up with the assignments for your cognitive psychology course. Two weeks before the final, you contract a severe case of the flu. The illness robs you of a week of valuable study time, forcing you to cram for several exams in one week. Faced with the prospect of ruining your GPA, do you:
   a. pull off a superhuman series of all-nighters?
   b. ask the professor to reschedule your exam?
   c. drop one or more of the courses, as the pressure is just too great?
3. Your best friend, Jill, always cheats when the two of you play tennis. She reflexively calls any ball out that falls even remotely near a line. In the face of this inexplicable ridiculousness, do you:
   a. refuse to play tennis with her? After all, you have plenty of other tennis partners who do not cheat.
   b. decide that tennis is just a game to be enjoyed and, knowing in your heart that you are a better player, elect to tolerate her foolishness?
   c. take Jill aside, tell her with all the tact you can muster that this type of behavior is abominable, and make her promise to play squarely?
4. You arrive late for a meeting at a restaurant and are forced to sit in the smoking section (assuming that you find a restaurant that still has a smoking section). The person next to you turns out to be a heavy smoker. The area around your seat is shrouded in a cloud of blue smoke, and your allergies are stifling you. To remedy the situation, do you:
   a. go to the bathroom every time he lights up?
   b. ask him not to smoke?
   c. call for the maitre d' and demand a new table?

HANDOUT 5 *(continued)*

5. Aunt Gertrude gives you a shirt for Christmas that is not quite your style. In fact, poor Aunt Gertrude is always giving you the most hideous gifts, and this one is no exception: an ugly, red plaid, 100-percent polyester, Nehru-collared nightmare. In this delicate situation do you:
   a. exchange the shirt for a nice Oxford cloth button-down?
   b. take Aunt Gertrude aside to discuss in private the nature of the gifts that you would like to receive in the future?
   c. hang the shirt in the back of the closet and resolve to wear it at the next Halloween party you attend?

Sources: Sternberg, R. J. (1986). *Intelligence applied: Understanding and increasing your intellectual skills.* New York: Harcourt Brace Jovanovich; Sternberg, R. J. (2000). *Practical intelligence in everyday life.* New York: Cambridge University Press.

HANDOUT 6

Physical Disabilities: Everything Is Harder

When biosocial development does not proceed normally, life becomes more difficult. This exercise asks you to relate Erikson's developmental stages to the problems of people with learning disabilities resulting from impaired biosocial development. In each case, think about how a problem in biosocial development might make it more difficult to resolve one of Erikson's eight psychosocial crises in a positive way. Base your answers on material from the text, your own experiences, or the experiences of someone you know.

Note that this exercise requires you to integrate material discussed from earlier developmental periods and also to anticipate later developmental issues. You may find it helpful to review the discussion of Erikson's theory before completing this exercise.

Trust versus mistrust:

Autonomy versus shame and doubt:

Initiative versus guilt:

Industry versus inferiority:

HANDOUT 6 *(continued)*

Identity versus role confusion:

Intimacy versus isolation:

Generativity versus stagnation:

Integrity versus despair:

Source: Adapted from Straub, R. O. (2001). *Seasons of life study guide* (4th ed.). New York: Worth.

HANDOUT 7

Internet Activity: Dyslexia Resources

Use Internet resources to answer the following questions.

1. What are the addresses of three national or international Web sites that provide information regarding dyslexia?

2. What local resources, support groups, and testing facilities does your community provide for victims of dyslexia?

3. What is the "Americans with Disabilities Act"? What rights does a person with dyslexia have under this Act?

HANDOUT 7 *(continued)*

4. Are there specific educational techniques that are helpful in preventing the development of dyslexia?

5. Is there a "positive side" to dyslexia?

6. Identify a couple of well-known, accomplished personalities who were diagnosed with dyslexia as children (e.g., the TV-series creator Steven Cannell).

Middle Childhood: Cognitive Development

Contents

Note: Worth Publishers provides online Instructor and Student Tool Kits, DVD Student Tool Kits, and Instructor and Student video resources in DevelopmentPortal for use with the text. See Part I: General Resources for information about these materials and the text Lecture Guides for a complete list by text chapter.

Suggested Activities

Introducing Middle Childhood: Cognitive Development

"On Your Own" Activity: Developmental Fact or Myth?

Before students read the unit, have them respond to the true-false statements in Handout 1.

The correct answers are shown in the next column, along with the text page numbers on which the answers can be verified. Class discussion can focus on the origins of any developmental misconceptions that are demonstrated in the students' incorrect answers.

1. F
2. F
3. F
4. F
5. T
6. T
7. F
8. F
9. F
10. F

AV: The Journey Through the Life Span, Program 5: Middle Childhood

See Middle Childhood: Biosocial Development for a description of Program 5 and the accompanying observation modules, which cover the entire unit on middle childhood.

Teaching Tip: Using Student-Generated Statements to Improve Exam Performance

Many teachers believe that encouraging students to formulate questions fosters increased understanding and retention of material. Amanda O'Dell and Anthony Burrow of Loyola University, Chicago, have found that student-generated statements about lecture material may be equally effective in improving mastery of material, as well as exam performance.

Students in three relatively large developmental psychology courses (developmental psychology, $n = 51$; psychology of adolescence, $n = 47$; racial identity development, $n = 48$) were invited to write brief questions or comments about class material on note cards at the end of each class period. The instructor collected the cards at the end of every class and retained them for analysis. The cards were then coded and sorted into three mutually exclusive categories:

a. a question was asked (e.g., "Is language associated with stage 6 of the sensorimotor period?")

b. a statement was made (e.g., "I enjoyed working in groups today. The activity helped me better understand of object permanence."

c. irrelevant (e.g., "I like your shirt!")

The total number of question and statement cards was recorded for each student, and note cards deemed irrelevant to course material were excluded from further analysis. Analysis of variance showed that the number of statement-based cards predicted overall exam performance for the lecture-based course (developmental psychology, $F(2, 48) = 4.40$, $p < .05$). The effect remained after controlling for the total number of cards completed. Contrary to expectations, the number of question-based cards was unrelated to performance. For the two courses that focused less on lecture and more on class discussion (adolescence and racial identity), note card content did not predic exam performance. The researchers suggest that encouraging students to write brief statements on note cards at the end of each class can be an effective strategy for improving exam performance in courses that entail less in-class discussion.

O'Dell, A. C & Burrow, A. L (2011). Student-generated statements predict exam performance in lecture-based courses. National Institute on the Teaching of Psychology. St. Petersburg Beach, FL.

Teaching Tip: Cooperative Learning

Although many instructors believe lecturing is the only way to teach, a growing body of research supports the idea that mixing forms of pedagogy is a more effective strategy. One reason is that while lecturing fosters retention soon after a lecture, it is a poor method for fostering long-term retention. Another is that lecturing also is not as effective in promoting the ability to apply knowledge in a novel or real-world setting.

Cooperative learning (CL) involves joint intellectual efforts by students or students and instructors together. In CL, students become actively involved with the information being learned and work together to explore, apply, and think critically about new information. Unlike traditional lecture learning, CL shifts the responsibility in large measure from instructor to student. Research has demonstrated that CL increases the time and effort students put into learning, increases their motivation to succeed, provides more immediate feedback, and models learning as a dynamic process.

Many instructors who are new to CL make the mistake of simply putting students into groups and telling them to work together. As Diane Halpern notes, CL activities need to be carefully planned and structured, with clear tasks designed to achieve educational objectives. She notes that successful CL assignments share the following characteristics.

- *Each student depends on the other group members to successfully complete the task (positive interdependence).* An example is the jigsaw task, which derives its name from the puzzles in which different-shaped pieces fit together to complete a picture. Similarly, in CL, students are assigned to small groups, with each group specializing in one aspect of a problem or issue. For example, following a unit on theories of cognitive development, different groups would be formed for each major theorist. Group members would gather information on their topic and then share their information with one another.
- *Every student's learning is assessed individually (individual accountability).* Experienced CL instructors know that the most common problem in group learning is the presence of one or two group members who fail to pull their weight.
- *Groups are heterogeneous in terms of ability.* Carefully constituting groups allows stronger students to model their thinking and learning processes for others. This is easily done if you use group work frequently. By the way, this principle derives from Bandura's classic studies of self-efficacy, which found that modeling by someone who is similar to you fosters positive beliefs about your own ability and increases motivation.
- *Instructor serves as facilitator.* Your role will change dramatically when you step out from behind the podium and work with CL groups. The number of positive interactions with students is likely to increase as you monitor their progress and assist them in becoming independent learners.
- *Students need to pay attention to social skills.* Before group work begins, make sure students know that their ability to work well in groups is itself an important educational outcome, perhaps even a graded outcome. Two basic rules are (1) group members must agree to allow others to state their views without interruptions, and (2) disagreements must center on the content of the statement, not the speaker.

A simple CL activity that can be incorporated into any lecture class is to stop at some logical point in the middle of class and ask students to summarize the topic to another student who checks on his or her comprehension. Then have this student briefly summarize the topic to a third student. Another, more involved activity is to use jigsaw groups in a library assignment in which students need to find information about a complex topic, such as the treatment of adolescent substance abuse. Groups can be assigned different treatment methods and asked to find information about each. Afterward, new "mixed" groups could be formed consisting of one member from each original group. Information is synthesized in the new groups and then presented to the entire class.

Halpern, D. F. (2007). *Creating cooperative learning environments*. Association for Psychological Science. www.psychologicalscience.org/teaching/tips.

Classroom Activity: Videotaping Student Presentations

Because oral presentation skills are highly valued in both educational settings and the real world, many instructors require students to prepare and deliver short (5 minutes or so) presentations about a topic under discussion. Presentations are typically assessed using grading rubrics, peer feedback from other students, and self-assessment. However, tools such as these do not always provide students with many tangible suggestions for improving their presentations.

Merry Sleigh and Erin Sim of Winthrop University suggest videotaping classroom presentations and allowing students to watch and evaluate their own performance. In a typical class, four students make presentations that are videotaped using a camera mounted on a tripod. Afterward, all but the four presenting students are dismissed. The students review the videotapes as a group and assess one another's presentations. Each student is responsible for identifying strengths and weaknesses of each presentation, including one specific area for improvement. The students are also asked to create a strategy to address the identified weakness and employ it during a subsequent, "final" class presentation. The instructor also provides feedback to each presenter, following these same guidelines.

Students generally had very positive responses to being videotaped. Nearly all (95%) felt they "learned something about myself through this process." Most (78%) reported feeling "more confident about my speaking abilities after watching the video." Even more (84%) believed that "watching my video with my peers helped me improve my oral skills." Interestingly, students who reported being more introverted, more sensitive to criticism, and less prepared, seemed to benefit the most from having this type of feedback.

Sleigh, M. J., & Sim, E. (2011). A picture is worth a thousand words of feedback: Videotaping Student Presentations. National Institute on the Teaching of Psychology, St. Petersburg Beach, FL.

AV: Transitions Throughout the Life Span, Program 12: The Age of Reason

Program 12 examines the development of cognitive abilities in children from age 7 to 11. Following the information-processing theory, the first segment focuses on changes in the child's selective attention, sensory register, long-term memory, processing speed and capacity, and memory strategies. Next, Piaget's view of the child's cognitive development, which involves a growing ability to use logic and reasoning, is discussed. Piaget's classic tests of conservation, reversibility, and reciprocity are demonstrated with a preschool child and a 10-year-old child.

The next segment examines moral reasoning in the school years. Kohlberg's stage theory is outlined, with expert commentary provided by Kathleen Berger. The final segment focuses on language development during the school years. During this time, children develop a more analytic understanding of words and show a marked improvement in pragmatic skills, such as changing from one form of speech to another when the situation so demands. The linguistic and cognitive advantages of bilingualism are discussed, as are educational and environmental conditions that are conducive to fluency in a second language.

AV: Middle Childhood: Growth and Development (30 min., Magna Systems)

This film provides a concise overview of biosocial and cognitive development between 6 and 10 years of age. Topics explored include growth, physical coordination in sports and games, language development, characteristics of thinking, and self-concept.

AV: Middle Childhood: Sense of Industry (30 min., Magna Systems)

Following Erik Erikson's model of psychosocial development, this film analyzes middle childhood as the time when children learn the skills their society values. It also explores the impact of parents and teachers in helping children develop a sense of industry, focusing on topics such as the use of discipline, school curricula, and classroom environments.

AV: The Child's Mind (30 min., Insight Media)

This program describes the concrete operational stage of Piaget's theory, and the information-processing theory of cognitive development. Memory capacity, creativity, and metacognition are also examined. In a particularly interesting segment, developmentalist David Elkind contrasts a child's and an adult's conception of morality.

Building on Theory

Piaget and School-Age Children

AV: Cognitive Development (20 min., CRM/McGraw-Hill)

(See description in Theories of Development.)

AV: Cognitive Development (60 min., Films for the Humanities and Sciences)

This carefully crafted video takes a critical look at Piaget's theory of cognitive development. The film begins by describing Piaget's stages of cognitive development from birth to 12 years old, illustrating typical behaviors at each stage. Research findings that conflict with Piaget's ideas are then examined. The video concludes with an exploration of Jerome Bruner's views on cognitive development and a discussion of research on the topics of metacognition and theory of mind.

AV: The Elementary Mind (30 min., Insight Media)

This program focuses on Piaget's concrete operational stage of cognitive development. Featuring interviews with Robert Sternberg and Rochel Gelman, it also explores concept learning in middle childhood, childhood memory strategies, and the controversy over intelligence testing.

AV: Concrete Operations (30 min., Davidson Films)

Using structured interviews with children between 4 and 9 years of age, David Elkind illustrates Piaget's characterization of concrete operational thinking. The film also examines the development of transitive thinking, reversibility, the construction of the unit concept, and criticisms of Piaget's theory.

Teaching Tip: The Concepts of Identity, Reversibility, and Other Logical Constructs

One logical principle understood by school-age children is *identity,* the idea that certain characteristics of an object remain the same even when other characteristics are changed. Another is *reversibility,* the principle that a transformation can be restored to its original state by undoing it. To help students understand how children are tested on the concepts of identity, reversibility, and other logical constructs, bring to class copies of pages from the math programs of elementary school workbooks. On these sheets students are asked, for example, to determine whether a closely spaced group of coins remains the same number after they are spread apart or whether a ball of clay is changed in mass when it is rolled into a long, skinny snake. Then discuss the concepts illustrated, focusing on how these ideas are developed later in the study of mathematics.

Classroom Activity: Making Television Commercials to Illustrate Cognitive Development

Scott Gronlund and Stephan Lewandowsky of the University of Oklahoma suggest a clever activity that will increase your students' understanding of cognitive development during middle childhood. Working in groups of four or five, students wrote, videotaped, and orally defended a two- to three-minute television commercial based on principles covered in their cognitive psychology course.

The commercials, which advertised fictitious services and products, were screened in class and then "defended" by group members. The defense consisted of an explanation of the various cognitive principles represented in the commercial. For example, most commercials relied on cognitive chunking to make phone numbers more memorable (e.g., "1-800-CHEATIN"), spaced repetition, and the placement of important parts of the message at the beginning and end of the commercial to capitalize on the primacy and recency effects. Another group's commercial featured the concept of rehearsal by having a series of actors briefly describe recent predicaments in their lives (for example, loss of a job or an ex-spouse who refused to make child-support payments). At the conclusion of each sad story, the actor sighed and said, "We'll see." The commercial turned out to be an advertisement for a lawyer named "Will C." Gates.

The commercials were graded according to several criteria, including how well they illustrated relevant cognitive principles and the overall quality of the production. Class members conferred special recognition awards for best actor or actress, best special effects, and so forth.

Scott Gronlund and Stephan Lewandowsky offer three reasons for the resounding success of the exercise. First, active participation was ensured because the commercials were almost always humorous, making them fun to work on and watch. Second, because of everyone's familiarity with television commercials, no one felt left out or unable to contribute. Third, students almost always appreciate (and are motivated to remember) clear, practical applications of lecture and text material.

This exercise can easily be adapted to focus on developmental issues in cognition. For example, students can be instructed to produce a commercial that is targeted at a certain age group or audience. In doing so, the script should illustrate appropriate cognitive principles such as code switching and concrete operational thinking, as well as the traditional storage and retrieval skills involved in information processing.

Gronlund, S. D., & Lewandowsky, S. (1992, October). Making TV commercials as a teaching aid for cognitive psychology. *Teaching of Psychology, 19*(3), 158–160.

"On Your Own" Activity: What Do You Learn When?

To help your students understand the stages of cognitive development during childhood, have them complete the table in Handout 2 using material from the relevant text chapters. Depending on the specific abilities of your class, you may ask each student to fill out the entire table or divide it among different students.

Some of the stages are specifically discussed in the text; others will require the students to extrapolate from the material, relating what they read to what they know about the concepts that children learn.

Observational Activity: Classification and Seriation

As noted in the text, beginning at about age 7 or 8, children become true concrete operational thinkers. The hallmark of this achievement is the ability to understand certain logical operations, such as identity, reversibility, classification, and seriation. *Classification* is the concept that objects can be organized into classes, or categories. Animals, toys, and foods are some of the everyday categories familiar to children. *Seriation* refers to the arrangement of items in a series, as in shortest to longest, smallest to largest, lightest to darkest, and so forth. Classification and seriation are logical operations that underlie many of the basic ideas of elementary school science and math.

To help your students better understand classification and seriation, have them observe a 5- to 7-year-old and his or her primary caregiver in a comfortable play setting. Ideally, they should ask a relative or friend and his or her child to participate. The play setting could be the child's home or a day-care center, the campus child development center, or any other mutually agreeable location.

Remind students that they should make the assessment a fun, playful activity for the child and that each child has his or her own developmental timetable that may be somewhat behind, or ahead of, developmental norms for that age. Handout 3 is a skills checklist to guide students, and Handout 4 is a follow-up questionnaire for them to complete.

Vygotsky and School-Age Children

Classroom Activity: The Geography of Thought

Until relatively recently, Western psychologists assumed that similar fundamental processes underlie all human thought, whether in the mountains of China, the grasslands of Africa, or the streets of New York. Cultural differences might shape the *content* of thought, but the basic *strategies* people use to process information were assumed to be the same for everyone. One of these basic strategies was assumed to be logical reasoning—a need to understand situations in terms of cause and effect.

Research by Richard Nisbett at the University of Michigan, however, has called this long-held view of mental functioning into question. In a series of studies comparing European Americans to East Asians, Nisbett and his colleagues found that people who have been socialized in different cultures do not just think about different subjects; they also think in fundamentally different ways.

"We used to think that everybody uses categories in the same way, that logic plays the same kind of role for everyone in the understanding of everyday life, that memory, perception, rule application and so on are the same," Nisbett said in a 2000 *New York Times* interview. "But we're now arguing that cognitive processes themselves are just far more malleable than mainstream psychology assumed."

The research studies, which were carried out in the United States, Japan, China, and Korea, demonstrated that Easterners think more "holistically," paying much more attention to context and using experience-based knowledge rather than abstract logic. The Eastern participants also displayed more tolerance for contradiction. In contrast, Westerners were more "analytic" in their thinking and tended to detach objects from their context. They also avoided contradictions and relied more heavily on formal logic.

In one study, Nisbett and Incheol Choi of Seoul National University in Korea asked Korean and American participants to read an essay either in favor of or opposed to a nation's proposed atomic tests in a remote location in the Pacific Ocean. The participants were told that the essay writer had been given "no choice" about what to write.

As your students may remember from introductory psychology, people tend to make the fundamental attribution error and explain human behavior in terms of the traits of individual actors, even when powerful social forces seem to be at work. Told that a student was required to give a speech endorsing a particular product, for example, most people will still believe that the speaker has used and actually likes the product. Asians, according to the findings of the study, may be less susceptible to such errors. When the Korean participants first wrote an essay according to similar instructions themselves, they modified their estimates of how strongly the original essay writers believed what they wrote. The American participants, however, continued to believe that the original essay writers were sincere in their statements.

Another striking example of dissimilarities in the reasoning of East Asians and Americans concerns how the participants responded to contradiction. In a second study, Asian and American participants read a strongly worded essay supporting the funding of a research project on adoption. They were told that the essay was written by someone who had been directed to take that position. A second group was presented both with strong arguments in support of the project and weaker arguments opposing it. Both Asian and American participants in the first group expressed equivalent levels of support for the research. While Asians in the second group responded to the weaker opposing arguments by decreasing their support, the American participants *increased* their level of endorsement. Remarkably, when presented with weaker arguments that ran counter to their own, the American participants were likely to solidify their opinions, and resolve the threatened contradiction in their own minds—perhaps as an effort to reduce cognitive dissonance. Asians, however, were more likely to change their own viewpoints, acknowledging that even the weaker arguments had some merit.

As a third example of cognitive dissimilarity, the researchers reported that when logic and experiential knowledge are in conflict, Americans are more likely than Asians to adhere to the rules of formal logic. Presented with a logical sequence such as, "All animals with fur hibernate. Rabbits have fur. Therefore, rabbits hibernate," the Americans were more likely to accept the validity of the argument, separating its formal structure, that of a syllogism, from its content, which might or might not be plausible. Asians more frequently judged such syllogisms as invalid based on their implausibility—not all animals with fur do in fact hibernate.

The extent and origins of these differences in cognition are still being debated. Nisbett and his colleagues have also found that Americans tend to focus more on the self and to have a greater sense of personal agency than Asians. One thing is clear: The differences are not genetic, because Asian Americans, born in the United States, display the same style of reasoning as European Americans.

Choi, I. & Nisbett, R. E. (2000). Cultural psychology of surprise: Holistic theories and recognition of contradiction. *Journal of Personality and Social Psychology, 79*(6), 890–905.

Nisbett, R. E. (2003). *The geography of thought: How Asians and Westerners think differently . . . and why.* New York: The Free Press.

Information Processing

Classroom Activity: Autobiographical Memories

Throughout our lives, memories of personal experiences, called *autobiographical memories,* give meaning to our sense of self and place in the world. Autobiographical memories involve recurrent experiences (e.g., "Every Sunday we had a formal dinner with the extended family."); relationships (e.g., "When I was in third grade my best friend was Laney. I can see her face now, even after 20 years."); objects (e.g., "I had a wonderful music box with a dancing ballerina."), or places (e.g., "When I was afraid or mad, I used to climb a special tree in my backyard.").

Some psychologists have probed autobiographical memories (especially first memories) as a means of understanding an individual's life story. Although first memories are often a mixture of fact and fiction, they are often especially revealing glimpses into each person's identity.

Ask students to interview someone they know about his or her earliest memory. After the interview, they could report to the class, or write a short paper, in which they discuss any observed connections between the memory and the rest of the person's life story. As an alternative, end a class by asking students to think about their own first memories before the next class meeting. During the next class, ask for volunteers to discuss connections between these memories and their sense of identity.

Classroom Activity: Demonstrating the Importance of Depth of Processing in Long-Term Memory

Doug Bernstein suggests a simple classroom demonstration to help students appreciate the relationship between how deeply information is processed and the likelihood that it will be encoded and available for retrieval from long-term memory. For maximum effectiveness, the demonstration should be conducted before describing this fundamental principle of information-processing theory.

Divide the class in half before reading aloud the following list of words. Instruct half the class to count or estimate the number of vowels in the words. The other half of the class should be instructed to rate each word, on a scale from 1 (useless) to 5 (very useful), in terms of the item's value to a person stranded on a desert island. To improve separation between the groups, you might present the instructions via differing overhead transparencies to each half of the class (while the other half closes its eyes).

UMBRELLA, GASOLINE, ORCHESTRA, YACHT, HAMMER, DIAMOND, UNIVERSITY, MACARONI, EYEGLASSES, GARDEN, UNDERWEAR, NEWSPAPER, ALCOHOL, BOUQUET, MICROSCOPE, CAMOUFLAGE, POLLUTION, RESTAURANT, INSECT, ELEPHANT, SULPHUR, LEMONADE, MOSQUITO, BOTTLE

After the list has been presented, have the class spend about 30 seconds performing a distracting task, such as writing their names, addresses, phone numbers, college majors, and social security numbers on a piece of scratch paper. This task serves to displace the most recent items in the list from their short-term memories. Finally, give the students about one minute to write down as many words from the list as they can recall, and then calculate retention scores for each group (average number or percentage of words correctly recalled). Retention scores from the group that processed the words in a shallow manner (by counting or estimating vowels) should be much lower than those from the group that processed the information more deeply (by considering the usefulness of the items).

Class discussion can focus on the different stages of working and long-term memory (highlighted by asking students why you asked them to perform the distractor task) and how children's processing capacities and abilities develop during the school years.

Bernstein, D. A. (2002, January). Sharing ideas on the teaching of psychology. Paper presented at meetings of the National Institute on the Teaching of Psychology, St. Petersburg Beach, FL.

Critical Thinking Activity: Information Processing

Each unit of these resources contains a critical thinking exercise designed specifically to test students' critical thinking about a topic covered in the text. Handout 5 contains three self-activity tests and a question asking students to analyze their experience.

Information-processing theory is based on comparing the functioning of the mind with a computer. According to the theory, incoming stimuli are held for a split second in the sensory memory (also called the sensory register), after which most of it is lost or discarded. Meaningful material is transferred into working memory (also called short-term memory). This part of memory handles mental activity that is current and conscious. Long-term memory stores information for days, months, or years.

A suggested answer to this unit's critical thinking activity follows:

Test 1: In the space below, draw what is on the front of a United States penny.

Successful completion of this task presumes that the details (the information) were (1) initially processed in sensory memory; (2) encoded as meaningful material into working, or short-term, memory; (3) transferred for relatively permanent storage into long-term memory; and (4) retrieved into working memory to guide the act of reproducing the penny as a drawing.

Test 2: Give yourself 60 seconds to learn the following list of letters, then cover them up and see how many you can write down (without looking back at them!).

NAPSEFILGNIGATNEMPOLEVEDYGOLOHCYSP

As with test 1, this activity requires encoding the information from sensory memory into short-term memory, and then using the process of recall to retrieve as many letters as they can.

Test 3: Give yourself 5 seconds to learn the following letters (following the same instructions as for 2).

PSYCHOLOGY DEVELOPMENT AGING
LIFE SPAN

Test 3 presents these same 34 letters, now reorganized into four familiar words. The near impossibility of memorizing the letters as an unorganized string, in contrast to the ease of quickly storing the letters as words, illustrates the importance of meaningfulness in the processing of information.

The answer to item 4—think about the above three tasks, and explain what you experienced, using the information-processing model and terms— is included in the answers to tests 1–3.

AV: False Memories (52 min., Films for the Humanities and Sciences)

Produced by the Discovery Channel, this film explores the processes by which the brain processes, stores, and retrieves new memories and, on occasion, goes awry. Elizabeth Loftus's work on the malleability of memory is discussed, along with several case studies of induced recollections of sexual abuse in children.

Language

AV: Language Development (30 min., Magna Systems)

This film explores the functions of language (including reading and writing) from infancy through adolescence. Highlights include an examination of social and cultural factors in literacy.

Classroom Activity: The Thought Processes Behind Schoolchildren's Jokes

To help students understand the thought processes behind the jokes of school-age children, you might show them actual examples of jokes from children's magazines. Many magazines include jokes that are considered appropriate for children, or they ask children to send in jokes (in which case the child's name and age usually appear). Have students analyze popular jokes for reliance on logical operations and other examples of concrete operational thinking.

Teaching and Learning

Internet Activity: Bilingual Education on the Internet

The National Association for Bilingual Education (NABE) was created to disseminate information relating to the education of the increasingly diverse population of students in the United States. Have students use the NABE (and any other Internet resources that they discover) to answer the questions in Handout 6.

AV: Multicultural Education: Valuing Diversity (120 min., Insight Media)

In this rather lengthy but excellent lecture, Dr. James Romero of the University of Oklahoma discusses how teachers can create a classroom climate in which diversity is valued.

AV: Culture and Education of Young Children (16 min., Insight Media)

This brief film explores cultural differences in childhood development as they relate to education. Carol Phillips explains how educational programs for young children can be designed to instill respect for cultural diversity.

AV: Social-Cultural Diversity (30 min., Insight Media)

(See description in Theories of Development.)

AV: Children of the Tribe (28 min., National Film Board of Canada)

This film discusses child rearing in Japan, showing how both teachers and parents reflect the emphasis on early achievement within a nurturant setting.

AV: Success: The Marva Collins Approach (30 min., Media Five)

Marva Collins is a Black teacher in Chicago who, fed up with the attitude and bureaucracy of the public system, started her own school for ghetto children. She has been very successful, winning the loyalty of students and parents, and even former president Reagan. This film is a hymn to her success. (Note that her critics, who are not portrayed here, say that some of her claims are deceptively exaggerated.) This film can be a springboard for a discussion of what makes a "good" elementary school.

AV: Learning Without School (26 min., Films for the Humanities and Sciences)

This program profiles 11-year-old Hoppie, whose parents decided that putting their exceptional son through conventional schooling was more likely to hamper than to foster his intellectual development.

Classroom Activity: What's the Best Way to Teach Reading?

Over the last several decades, opinions about how best to teach language to children have run the gamut from the look-say and phonics approaches of the 1950s to whole-language literacy in the early 1990s and back again to phonics in more recent years. To help students understand the reasons for such varying opinions, you might prepare a lecture from the following material. Note that current views favor a combination of the different approaches, depending on the situation.

Older students in the class may remember the "great reading debate" that raged within educational circles from about 1950 on. On the one side, advocates of the *look-say* method taught children to see a word and then, focusing on the particular letters, immediately say it, connecting the visual configuration with the sound. Look-say primers repeated the same words over and over to instill this learning-by-association—a sample narrative being "Run, Spot, run. See Spot run." On the other side, devotees of the *phonics* approach insisted that children should "break the secret code" of written language by memorizing the specific sounds that various letters make: accordingly, first-graders filled page after page of workbook exercises that linked letters and sounds, circling, for example, the sound shared by "tan," "ton," and "tin," or, at a more advanced level, "nip," "not," and "dan."

According to the look-say advocates, phonics made reading seem dull and deceptively simple, ignoring complications such as "ough" in "tough," "cough," and "through." According to the leading phonics spokesperson, the look-say method destroyed equal opportunity and democracy by keeping the basic mysteries of reading (that is, phonics) from the masses, and was the "most inhuman, mean, stupid way of foisting something on a child's mind." This exaggeration arose from the conviction that look-say was based on misapplied principles of animal conditioning and that any educator who did not begin reading instruction with phonics must be elitist.

In the early 1990s, the debate quieted somewhat because a new approach, originating in New Zealand and inspired by the work of both Piaget and Vygotsky, had children discovering the principles and strategies of reading as they communicate in the classroom. This method, sometimes called *whole-language literacy*, begins with children telling stories, then drawing pictures to illustrate the stories, and then, with the teacher's encouragement, figuring out how to write, spell, and punctuate their own work, reading it to another child, and finally having it read by their teacher or a classmate. This method not only enhances the children's motivation while they are actively engaged in reading and writing but also makes the written word part of the social interaction within the classroom, encouraging the children to learn more conventional spelling, reading, and writing so that they can express themselves more clearly.

The theory behind this movement is that the skill of reading is best learned by experiencing words in context. With the whole-language approach, many experts say, students read and write earlier, and do so with much greater enthusiasm.

Whole-language advocates argue that the key to teaching reading is emphasizing what words *say* rather than decoding their symbols into sounds. Students in whole-language classrooms still learn phonics and spelling, but they do so along with reading, rather than as a prerequisite to it.

The issue of how to best teach reading remains controversial, however. Most recently, there has been a movement toward a hybrid approach, with its proponents insisting that phonics instruction is vital to learning to read. On the research front, there is an emerging consensus that fluent, accurate decoding of speech sounds is central to skilled reading.

Ask your students what they think about the age-old debate of how to teach reading. If you have older students, ask them to relate their experiences with their children.

As a fun activity, you might arrange for the class to watch an episode of the public television program *Between the Lions.* Theo and Cleo, the "librarians" who host the show, introduce classic children's literature with a menagerie of jungle animals and human celebrities. Using songs, rhymes, readings, live action, and animation, each episode is built around five important areas of reading instruction: phonemic awareness (individual sounds in spoken words), phonics (relationships between letters and sounds), fluency, vocabulary development, and text comprehension.

AV: Going to School in Japan (24 min., Insight Media)

This brief program takes an in-depth look at the actual school experience of Japanese children. Classroom size and structure, teaching styles, and competition among students are several of the topics explored.

AV: Japan's Toughest School: Nine Days of Hell (18 min., Insight Media)

This short film takes the viewer to the equivalent of an academic "boot camp" used by some Japanese parents to prepare their children (during school vacation) for the rigors and potential stresses of the Japanese school system. As the title suggests, the video questions whether this approach is truly beneficial to Japanese children.

Classroom Activity: Classroom Debate: *"Resolved: The School Year Must Be Lengthened"*

Compared with students in Asian and European countries, American students stand out—for the shortness of their school year and for their relatively poor academic performance, particularly in science and math. Another consequence of the short American school year is what many teachers call "summertime fade-out," or a decline of aptitude and knowledge that typically occurs when school is not in session. The result is that even more time is lost as teachers spend the first month or two of school reviewing last year's curriculum. Many educators and legislators use this as an argument in building the case for lengthening the number of school days in the United States from the traditional 180-day school year to a number more in line with that in European and Asian countries.

Japan's Ministry of Education, for example, prescribes a minimum of 210 calendar days of instruction, which includes half-days on Saturdays. Because local school districts have the option of adding days, the national average in Japan is a 243-day school year.

The gap in "available learning time" between Japanese and American students is even larger than the discrepancy in length of the school year would suggest. By the ninth grade, nearly half of all Japanese students spend an average of five additional hours a week attending private profit-making tutorial services. Although Japan is at the very top of a list of countries ranked by the length of their school year, the table below indicates that the United States is near the bottom.

Length of School Year (Days)

Japan	243	New Zealand	190
(West) Germany	226–240	Nigeria	190
South Korea	220	British Columbia	185
Israel	216	France	185
Luxembourg	216	Ontario	185
Soviet Union*	211	Ireland	184
Netherlands	200	New Brunswick	182
Scotland	200	Quebec	180
Thailand	200	Spain	180
Hong Kong	195	Sweden	180
England/Wales	192	**United States**	**180**
Hungary	192	French Belgium	175
Swaziland	191	Flemish Belgium	160
Finland	190		

*What is now Russia.

Source: Ansary, T. Say so long to summer: Is more school better school? Retrieved October 30, 2008, from http://encarta.msn.com/encnet/Features/Columns/?article=moreschoolmain.

Beginning in the 1960s, the International Association for the Evaluation of Educational Achievement (IEA) began to assess educational quality in countries throughout the world. For Americans, the results have been disturbing. Among the 25 nations tested in 1994–1995, for example, the United States ranked twenty-first in geometry, fifteenth in algebra, and seventeenth in arithmetic.

On the other hand, researchers have compared student achievement in Germany during two years. Shortening the school year for some students to two-thirds its normal length had no effect on the number of students attending the highest secondary school track (Pischke, 2003). This comes as good news to those who have supported the necessity to *shorten* the school year as school systems throughout the country are increasingly scrambling to make ends meet in the face of diminishing state and federal support.

To further explore this emotionally charged issue, set up a classroom debate following the guidelines in the General Resources section of this manual.

HANDOUT 1

Developmental Fact or Myth?

T F 1. During middle childhood, cognitive processes become more logical and more abstract.

T F 2. Children who get their education from selling fruits or other items on the street still score well on standard math achievement tests.

T F 3. Personal and cultural experiences are unrelated to the learning of new concepts.

T F 4. The basic cognitive processing capacity of schoolchildren does not differ greatly from that of preschoolers.

T F 5. (Thinking Critically) Whether direct instruction is more effective than discovery learning during the school years depends partly on cultures and goals.

T F 6. Children between ages 6 and 11 excel at switching between formal and informal forms of language.

T F 7. The best strategy for teaching a school-age child whose language is a nonstandard form is to conduct all instruction in standard English.

T F 8. Most developmentalists agree that there should be a standard educational system for all children.

T F 9. Both the phonic and whole-language approaches to learning have been disputed by current research.

T F 10. U.S. teachers present math at a higher level than do their German and Japanese counterparts.

HANDOUT 2

What Do You Learn When?

The learning of both abstract and concrete concepts occurs throughout childhood. Fill in the chart below by giving a brief description of children's grasp of the concept at each age. Not all topics are treated in the text. Use your knowledge to formulate a hypothesis where necessary.

Acquisition of/ Realistic Concept of	Young Childhood	Transitional	Middle Childhood
Humor			
Conservation			
Classification			
Reciprocity			
Reversibility			
Seriation			
Time and Space			
Death			
Divorce			
Gender Differences			
Religion			
Racial Differences			

HANDOUT 3

Observational Activity: Classification and Seriation: Skills Checklist

Arrange to observe a 5- to 7-year-old and his or her primary caregiver in a comfortable play setting, such as the child's home or day-care center. Before your scheduled observation period, read through this classification and seriation checklist to familiarize yourself with the activity and to gather the necessary testing materials. After the observation period, complete the questions on the handout and return the response sheet to your instructor.

1. *Recognizes Basic Geometric Shapes*

   Thinking begins in the visual, auditory, and tactile discriminations the child acquires from his or her environment. As Janice Beaty notes, children need to "distinguish between a circle, a square, a rectangle, and a triangle, not in order to do geometry, but to be able to categorize mentally. . . ."

   Show the child pictures of the four basic shapes, and see if he or she can name them. Alternatively, see if the child is able to draw the basic shapes or build large versions from blocks.

2. *Recognizes Basic Colors*

   Normally, color classification skills develop at about the same time as do shape classification skills. In addition to determining if your subject can recognize the basic colors of red, green, blue, yellow, black, and white, give your subject crayons or poker chips and see if he or she is able to sort into separate piles all of the greens, blues, reds, etc.

3. *Recognizes Differences in Musical Tones*

   Young children recognize variations in musical sounds very early in life. Sounds have several fundamental dimensions, including loudness (soft/loud), pitch (low note/high note), duration (short note/long note), and timbre (instrumental quality, as in the difference between the same note played on a flute and a xylophone). Determine how well your subject is able to categorize different sounds along these dimensions by playing in succession two sounds that differ in only one of the dimensions and asking the child to identify the louder (or higher, or shorter, etc.) of the two.

4. *Sorts Objects by Appearance*

   Piaget noted that seriation skills follow a developmental sequence that begins with the simple classification of objects and progresses through stages of increasing perceptual and cognitive complexity. By 5 years of age, most children are able to sort objects on the basis of more than one characteristic, as "all the blue trucks," for example. Give your subject several similar sorting tasks, selecting complexity on the basis of his or her age.

HANDOUT 3 *(continued)*

5. *Arranges Objects in Series According to a Rule*

   Determine if your subject can arrange objects (blocks, sticks, toy figures) in a series according to a specific rule (smallest to largest, shortest to tallest, etc.). Most children at this age will be able to see a relationship between two objects (one is bigger, for example); many will have trouble completing a series, however, finding it confusing that an object can at the same time be smaller than the next item in the series and larger than the preceding item.

Source: Beaty, J. J. *Observing development of the young child* (3rd ed.), pp. 211–232. Copyright © 1994. Adapted by permission of Prentice Hall, Upper Saddle River, New Jersey.

HANDOUT 4

Observational Activity: Classification and Seriation: Follow-Up Questionnaire

1. Describe the participant and setting that you chose for this observational activity.

2. Describe any difficulties that you encountered in completing the activity.

3. Complete the following skill checklist for your subject.

Skill	Demonstrated Yes	No	Comments
1. Recognizes basic geometric shapes			
2. Recognizes basic colors			
3. Recognizes differences in musical tones			
4. Sorts objects by appearance			
5. Arranges objects in a series			

HANDOUT 4 *(continued)*

4. Given the normal variation in age norms for the attainment of the various cognitive skills you assessed, would you say that your subject was "on time," "early," or "late" in his or her cognitive development? Specify several behaviors you observed to justify your assessment of the child's skill level.

5. Pick the skill at which your subject was the *least accomplished*. Suggest at least three games or educational activities that would promote the child's mastery of this skill.

HANDOUT 5

Critical Thinking Activity: Information Processing

Now that you have read and reviewed Middle Childhood: Cognitive Development, take your learning a step further by testing your critical thinking skills on this pattern recognition exercise.

1. In the space below, draw what is on the front of a United States penny.

2. Give yourself 60 seconds to learn the following list of letters, then cover them up and see how many you can write down (without looking back at them!).

   NAPSEFILGNIGATNEMPOLEVEDYGOLOHCYSP

3. Give yourself 5 seconds to learn the following letters (following the same instructions as for 2).

   PSYCHOLOGY DEVELOPMENT AGING LIFE SPAN

4. Think about the above three tasks, and explain what you experienced, using the information-processing model and terms.

HANDOUT 6

Internet Activity: Bilingual Education on the Internet

The National Association for Bilingual Education (NABE) disseminates information relating to the education of the increasingly diverse population of students in the United States. As part of its mission, the NABE provides information through its Internet server (www.nabe.org).

In addition, over 3,500 schools in the United States and elsewhere currently have home pages on the Web. NABE provides links to many of these sites, which share resources related to the education of culturally and linguistically diverse students.

In this Internet Activity, use the NABE (and any other Internet resources that you discover) to provide answers to the following questions.

1. What court rulings have influenced the way minority students who speak a second language are educated in the United States?

2. How has the student population with limited proficiency in English shifted in recent years?

3. What are the most common language-education groups available for students with limited proficiency in English?

HANDOUT 6 *(continued)*

4. Which school districts in the United States have the highest enrollments of students with limited proficiency in English?

5. Use the Internet to "visit" a bilingual school (perhaps one concerning a subject matter of interest to you or one devoted to a certain language or multicultural program). Then answer the following questions.

   a. What is the name of the school? Where is it located? Whom does it serve?

   b. What are some of the school's special programs?

   c. Does the Internet site offer suggestions for specific classroom activities? Describe one.

Middle Childhood: Psychosocial Development

Contents

Note: Worth Publishers provides online Instructor and Student Tool Kits, DVD Student Tool Kits, and Instructor and Student video resources in DevelopmentPortal for use with the text. See Part I: General Resources for information about these materials and the text Lecture Guides for a complete list by text chapter.

Suggested Activities

Introducing Middle Childhood: Psychosocial Development

"On Your Own" Activity: Developmental Fact or Myth?

Before students read about psychosocial development during middle childhood, have them respond to the true-false statements in Handout 1.

The correct answers are shown below. Class discussion can focus on the origins of any developmental misconceptions that are demonstrated in the students' incorrect answers.

1. T	6. F
2. T	7. T
3. F	8. T
4. T	9. T
5. F	10. F

AV: The Journey Through the Life Span, Program 5: Middle Childhood

See Middle Childhood: Biosocial Development for a description of Program 5 and the accompanying observation modules, which cover the entire unit on middle childhood.

AV: Transitions Throughout the Life Span, Program 13: A Society (Culture) of Children

Program 13 brings to a close the unit on middle childhood. We have seen that from ages 7 to 11, the child becomes stronger and more competent, mastering the biosocial and cognitive abilities that are important in his or her culture. Psychosocial accomplishments are equally impressive.

The program begins by exploring the growing social competence of children, as described by Freud, Erikson, and behaviorists as well as cognitive, sociocultural, and epigenetic theorists. The second segment focuses on the growth of social cognition and self-understanding. Next, the program explores the problems and challenges often experienced by school-age children in our society, including the experience of parental divorce and remarriage and living in single-parent and blended families. The final segments consider the various ways in which children cope with stressful situations.

AV: Middle Childhood: Social and Emotional Development (30 min., Magna Systems, Inc.)

Part of the *Developing Child* series, this module investigates a variety of issues in social and emotional development: development of the sense of self; family relationships during middle childhood; growth in social cognition; the impact of divorce and two-career families on children; the blended family; and the function of the peer group.

Teaching Tip: Text Messaging During Class Impairs Comprehension

With ever-increasing use of smart phones, tablet computers, and other electronic devices, many instructors wonder if they should adopt some sort of classroom policy regarding what is permitted in class, and what is not. Research is beginning to address some of the relevant issues. For example, one study found that cellphone ringing while students are taking notes significantly impairs their ability to correctly answer questions about the content that was disrupted (End et al., 2010).

Amanda Gingerich of Butler University conducted a demonstration over two semesters in her cognitive psychology course. Half of each class was randomly assigned to text message one another during a 10-minute lecture on a specific topic. The other half of the class did not text message during the lecture. Both groups were told that a quiz would immediately follow the lecture. Following the lecture, all students completed a short multiple-choice quiz.

Students who were permitted to send text messages during the lecture scored significantly lower on the quiz than did students who did not text ($t(42) = 2.52$, $p < .05$). In addition, students in the text condition indicated less confidence in their comprehension of the material. Earlier studies have shown that memory systems become more inflexible when we are multitasking, which can impair learning (Foerde, Knowlton, & Poldrack, 2006). Noting these findings may go a long way in encouraging your students to turn off their cell phones during lectures.

End, C. M., Worthman, S., Matthews, M., & Wetterau, K. (2010). Costly cell phones: The impact of cell phone rings on academic performance. *Teaching of Psychology, 37*(1), 55–57.

Gingerich, A.C. (2011). IDK LOL: Text messaging during class impairs comprehension of lectural material. National Institute on the Teaching of Psychology. St. Petersburg Beach, FL.

Foerde, K., Knowlton, B.J., Poldrack, R.A., & Smith, E. (2006). Modulation of competing memory systems by distraction. *PNAS Proceedings of the National Academy of Sciences of the United States of America, 103*(31), 11778–1173.

Classroom Activity: Incorporating Media Literacy Into Your Course

For many people, television, movies, video games, the Internet, and other media have been a constant, if not completely dominant, companion throughout their lives. Remarkably, the Berkeley Pop Culture Project has reported that a majority of 4- to 6-year-old children surveyed liked TV better than they liked their fathers, perhaps because TV watching is the dominant leisure activity of Americans (an average of about 70 days of nonstop viewing per year), and only about one-third of parents spend time with their children during the evening. Despite the fact that we "consume" enormous amounts of media, most of us are not very good at thinking critically about media images and content.

Media literacy has been defined as "the ability of a citizen to access, analyze, and produce information for specific outcomes" (Silverblatt, 2008). Teaching media literacy can promote broader critical thinking skills and enhanced understanding of mass communication processes; it can also increase awareness of the impact of media on individuals and society. Incorporating media literacy into your developmental psychology courses also supports many of the learning goals and outcomes published in the American Psychological Associations Assessment CyberGuide (APA, 2009). These include promoting understanding of psychological theories and concepts (Goal 1); evaluating research findings (Goal 2); increasing critical thinking skills (Goal 3); developing information and technology literacy (Goal 6); communicating effectively (Goal 7); and understanding the mechanisms surrounding privilege, power, and oppression (Goal 8).

Michael Hulsizer of Webster University offers the following suggestions for incorporating media literacy into developmental psychology courses:

Childhood perceptions: Because young children process information differently from adults, they do not fully understand adult-oriented media. Discussion topics: Examine how children might view TV shows aimed at teens or adults. Discuss the role of cognitive development in this analysis.

Children and advertising: Children are exposed to thousands of ads each year, from what cereals to eat and clothes to wear to what toys to buy. Discussion topics: How do children perceive television commercials and ads? Are they created with children in mind? Examine an advertised toy and determine whether the advertising was truthful.

Media violence. Much research suggests that violent films, TV, and video games can promote a host of undesirable outcomes among children. Discussion topics: What evidence does the class find of media violence targeted at children? Are there examples of prosocial responses by the media to published research regarding the hazards of violent programming to children?

Illusion of invulnerability: The vast majority of young adults (more than 80%) agree that the media have a strong impact on society. However, only a minority (12%) feel the media have a strong impact on them personally. Discussion topics: Is this an example of a media illusion of invulnerability? What strategies might a developmental psychologist suggest to counter this illusion among children?

Hulsizer, M. R. (2011). Incorporating media literacy into psychology courses. National Institute on the Teaching of Psychology. St. Petersburg Beach, FL.

Silverblatt, A. (2008). *Media literacy: Keys to interpreting media messages* (3rd ed.). Westport, CT: Praeger.

Classroom Activity: Busing, Charter Schools, and Government-Funded School Vouchers

To help students think about the implications of development during middle childhood, you might ask them to apply what they have learned to the issue of school busing. This issue, which originated during the 1960s, is still unresolved and is often framed in terms of racial balance and equality versus neighborhood stability. Since this ideological argument does not take into account the actual psychosocial and educational development of the school-age child, consider having your students argue for and against busing on these terms. Arguments pro and con might include the following:

Pros

(a) School-age children are able to decenter and understand another point of view; therefore, putting a school-age child in a diversified environment could help to reduce racial prejudices.
(b) A good education that offers individual attention is very important during these years. Hence, if a child is being bused from an inferior school to a better one, busing is a good thing.
(c) Social skills are as important as cognitive skills during these years. Hence, in a multiracial world, children of all races and ethnic groups should have an opportunity to learn to respect one another.
(d) Poverty and concomitant feelings of lack of control over events can be destructive to a child's ability to plan for the future. If a child is bused into a school and neighborhood in which he or she learns that one's own efforts and accomplishments can change one's future, busing would be an advantage.
(e) Modeling is important, so the child who sees and learns to like teachers of many backgrounds will learn to be more open-minded.

Cons

(a) Rejection is a common problem during middle childhood. Hence, busing a few "token" children might be destructive to their self-esteem unless the school is able to prevent rejection on racial grounds.
(b) School-age children look to adults—teachers and parents—as role models. Hence, busing children far away from their neighborhoods—especially to a school where there is mutual hostility between teachers and the parents of the bused children—is destructive.
(c) Play patterns are important. Thus, a child should be able to make friends at school, ideally friends who can come over to play at the child's home, and vice versa. If the child is bused too far from his or her neighborhood, or the neighborhoods are antagonistic, busing may not be a good idea.

Alternatively, have the class discuss the issue of geographical variation in spending per pupil, which plagues many communities today. Many cities across the United States provide very different educational opportunities for students in wealthy and poor school districts. Ask students to make a study of this issue as it pertains to your campus community. Depending on your school's location, two other "hot" local issues that could be discussed include the pros and cons of "charter schools" and the fairness of government-funded school vouchers that can be used to pay tuition of private schools, including those with religious affiliations.

In thinking about the needs and abilities of school-age children, students have an opportunity to apply their knowledge of development to an issue of social importance.

The Nature of the Child

AV: Eye of the Storm (25 min., ABC)

When Martin Luther King Jr. was assassinated in 1968, a third-grade teacher in an all-White school in Iowa decided to teach her children about prejudice. An ABC news team filmed the project. The teacher began by treating all her blue-eyed students as a privileged group; after a few days, she reversed the process, treating children with brown eyes as the privileged ones. The film reveals the children from both groups to be amazingly susceptible to the idea that they are superior to those of different eye color. They display enmity for their "inferiors" and even perform their schoolwork markedly better when they are given privileges such as being first in the lunch line. At the end, the teacher explains the purpose of the experiment, and all the children become friends again. This movie has become a classic, because it uncovers the universal wish of humans to consider themselves superior, as well as showing the courageous effort of one teacher to nip prejudice in childhood.

AV: Children, Enfants, Niños (24 min., National Film Board of Canada)

This film has some wonderful footage of children around the world, playing, eating, working, laughing. It has no narration, thus allowing the instructor to comment on the universalities in the childhood experience, as well as the cultural and geographical differences. If your college has the facilities to make it possible, you might assign your students the task of viewing and reviewing this film, and writing a narrative for it.

Classroom Activity: Poverty

If you did not discuss the U.S. Census Bureau study described in the Classroom Activity "Context, Family Structure, and Divorce Rate" in the Introduction, this material could form the basis for a supplementary lecture on the impact of poverty on development, especially in terms of the social comparisons made by school-age children.

AV: Children of Poverty (26 min., Films for the Humanities and Sciences)

This program profiles a representative sample of American children who are living in poverty—all in homes headed by single women. The program vividly illustrates the impact of poverty on children and their mothers, and focuses on the daily struggle to find safe shelter, food, and of trying to nurture self-esteem in impoverished children.

AV: Kids and Stress (28 min., Films for the Humanities and Sciences)

This highly recommended program examines the effects of stress on children. Among the more serious consequences discussed are sleep and eating disturbances, alcohol and drug abuse, depression, and suicide. The film also discusses the important psychological and social buffers that help kids help themselves avoid the negative impact of potential stressors.

AV: Dreamspeaker (75 min., Filmakers Library)

An emotionally disturbed boy runs away from society to the forests of Vancouver, where he is found by an Indian shaman. The holy man helps him work through his hostilities and slow his readiness to react violently to frustration. The film is visually and emotionally appealing and has won several awards. The interesting question, of course, is: How valid is the portrayal of the process of rehabilitation? Your students should be able to discuss this question on the basis of their newly acquired knowledge along with their long-standing opinions.

AV: Counseling Children (60 min., Insight Media)

Using vignettes, therapist Mary Bradford Ivey demonstrates an ecological intervention with troubled children, focusing on the family and community.

Teaching Tip: The Exosystem and Children's Lives

To help your students think about aspects of the exosystem that affect the lives of children, ask them to help you list recent events or problems that might be expected to have significant effects. For example, children are concerned about the possibility of a nuclear war. Children are also affected by dramatic news events—the shooting of Congresswoman Gabrielle Giffords; the crises in Egypt and other areas of the Middle East; assassinations; the events of September 11, 2001; disasters (such as airplane crashes); and more local stories (such as cyclones, hurricanes, floods, droughts, earthquakes, tornadoes, reported incidents of child abuse, and similar issues). To further explore this issue, you might ask students to interview a school-age child and share the child's concerns with the class.

If students seem unconvinced that children can be greatly affected by the political situation or other aspects of the exosystem, you might introduce them to books by Robert Coles (*The Moral Life of Children* [Boston: Houghton Mifflin, 1987] and *The Political Life of Children* [New York: Atlantic Monthly Press, 2000]). Also pertinent are the many works on the Holocaust that document profound emotional effects on children—even in cases in which the parents, rather than the children themselves, were victims.

Families and Children

AV: The History of Parenting Practices (20 min., Insight Media)

(See description in Early Childhood: Psychosocial Development.)

"On Your Own" Activity: Genograms

This exercise asks students to construct a genogram (generational map) of their family. Genograms are convenient ways of depicting how the structure of the family has changed over the years. Handout 2 provides instructions for completion.

Since the turn of the century, the typical structure of family genograms has changed in several ways. For example, families with multigenerational living members are much more common, the average size of nuclear families has declined, and there are more single-parent and stepparent households.

As a follow-up to this exercise, you might summarize the patterns in the genograms submitted. For example, how many show the step-relationships of blended families? What are the average number of intra- and intergenerational ties among relatives who are alive now? To stimulate discussion, ask your students to think about the ways in which historical changes in family structure have had an impact on their family.

"On Your Own" Activity: Children's Work at Home

To encourage students to think about the amount and kinds of responsibilities that are considered appropriate for school-age children, ask them to answer the questions in Handout 3.

In discussing students' responses, reiterate the fact that there is no consensus on the question of childhood responsibility.

Most developmental psychologists agree that children should have some responsibilities within the home and that their tasks should be discussed openly to ensure that everyone understands that a family is based on mutual respect and responsibility. At the same time, most developmental psychologists consider the child's schooling and friendships to be very important. Household responsibilities should not take so much time and energy that the child has little of either left for study and play.

In your discussion, cover such aspects as the significance of the family's size and socioeconomic status, the existence (or nonexistence) of sex differences in the students' responses, and the range of expectations reflected in responses and the reasons for it (ask students whether the tasks they assigned are similar to what they remember doing during middle childhood).

AV: The Essentials of Discipline: The Middle Years (3 programs, 28 min. each, Films for the Humanities and Sciences)

(See description in Early Childhood: Psychosocial Development.)

Classroom Activity: Cooperative (Parental) Alliance and the Binuclear Family

If your class is typical, your students' family structures while children will run the gamut of those described in the text. Although divorce is the legal end to a marriage, in ideal cases the co-parental relationship is a continuing bond that lasts for years. Even so, the social and legal systems still view divorced parents as adversaries. The language associated with divorce adds fuel to this fire: a "broken home" would seem to be one in which something needs to be fixed; "visitation rules" imply that one parent is merely a "visitor" in the home of the custodial parent who, by implication, "owns" the child.

Developmentalists agree that a parental alliance between divorced parents is generally the best situation for children. Building on this theme, legal scholars have argued that divorce attorneys should do a better job of promoting this type of alliance by preparing their clients before the divorce is finalized. You might toss this idea out for a class discussion, perhaps by asking any "experts" in the class to share their experiences, views, and tips. To get the discussion started, you might present the following information.

Following a longitudinal study of post-divorce family relationships, legal researchers coined the phrase *binuclear family* to emphasize that "sanctioning divorce means . . . developing a healthy language in which we can speak about it—words such as *binuclear* that can reflect images of a healthy divorced family, rather than words such as a *broken home*." The subtext of this idea is that language plays a significant role following divorce, and attorneys and family members need to find better ways to talk about the complex relationships that often develop when a marriage ends.

In some instances, things are relatively straightforward, as when one divorcing parent decides to relinquish his or her parental role. In such cases, parental cooperation and collaboration is a nonissue. In most instances, however, divorce necessitates a renegotiation of rules and boundaries in order to shape new co-parenting relationships.

Among the issues that need to be explored are these:

- How much time does each parent plan to spend with the children following the divorce?
- Is each parent motivated to become a collaborative co-parent, or is a "parallel parenting" arrangement preferred?
- How will the co-parents divide the child-care responsibilities?
- Do the co-parents expect the same rules to apply in each household (discipline, chores, allowances, bedtimes, curfews)?
- How will the co-parents negotiate important decisions? Are any unilateral decisions permissible?
- How will information about the children's emotional and physical states, daily routines, weekly schedules, and school issues be exchanged between the co-parents?

Legal scholars such as Mitchell Karpf and Irene Shatz note that when parents are made aware of children's basic rights during a divorce process, they often become more highly motivated to form a cooperative alliance.

The seven basic rights that children have during their parents' divorce include the right to

1. understand that the decision to divorce was their parents' decision and that the divorce was not their fault.
2. not be asked to serve as a messenger, spy, or mediator; to never be interrogated about the other parent's private life.
3. maintain independent relationships with each parent; to respect differences in parenting styles in each home.
4. be free from witnessing parental conflict and from having to side with one parent.
5. have regular access and consistent time with each parent.
6. not hear disparaging comments made by one parent about the other.
7. maintain relationships with extended family members on both sides of the family.

Karpf, M. K., & Shatz, I. M. (2005, Spring). The divorce is over—what about the kids? *American Journal of Family Law, 19*(1), 7–11.

Classroom Activity: Problem-Based Learning: Family Structure and Parenting

The Introduction's Classroom Activity: Introducing Problem-Based Learning describes this relatively new pedagogical tool. Following is a sample problem that you might want to give to your students as part of your coverage of psychosocial development during middle childhood.:

> After reading in his textbook that single-parent families are more likely than other families to change residence and family composition, and that change adds stress in middle childhood, Seth worries about his 10-year-old daughter's well-being.
>
> Before you leave class today, your group must address the following questions: First, from what you have learned about families and children, why is it generally better for children to have two parents? Second, after your group agrees on an answer to the first ques-

tion, determine some learning issues that need to be researched to answer the question, What issues should Seth be concerned about regarding his daughter's well-being in a single-parent family? Among other issues, these should focus on the various functions of a supportive family that apply to every aspect of development during middle childhood.

Based on the decisions your group makes today, you should devise a plan for researching the various issues. Two weeks from today's class, your group will present an answer for Seth based on the issues you think are relevant.

The Peer Group

The Culture of Children

AV: The Child's Personality (30 min., Insight Media)

This film discusses the increasingly important role of the peer group in personality development during middle childhood. The development of independence, the self-concept, and achievement motivation are also examined, as is the subject of child abuse.

AV: Friends and Foes: Peers in Development (60 min., RMI Media Productions)

Peer influence, both positive and negative, is the subject matter of this film. The changing nature of friendship as children grow older, the impact of conflict and negotiation, and the consequences of inadequate peer relationships are also discussed.

Teaching Tip: Peer-Group Interactions

To help your students understand the nature of peer-group interactions during middle childhood, ask them to recall the social organization of their former elementary school.

Ask students to recall the circumstances of social get-togethers—for example, birthday parties and slumber parties. Ask them about the groups that formed on their blocks, in their apartment buildings, or in their backyards; about groups that formed around other activities (for example, in day camp, in dancing school, after the school play). As students cite and describe various social occasions or institutions, they may also recall some of the feelings and problems associated with socializing during this period.

AV: All in a Summer Day (25 min., Learning Corporation of America)

This film about jealousy and forgiveness in school-age children is based on a science-fiction story by Ray Bradbury. A group of children live on a rainy planet where the sun shines only once every nine years. As they prepare for their first sunny day, one of them—once an earthling—tells of the beauty of the sun. They are envious of her and so lock her up so she can't enjoy the rare sunny day. When the day is over, she is tearful, they are penitent, and she forgives them—a happy ending not in the original story. This fable can be an interesting way to start a discussion of peer pressure, being different, and the emotional life of school-age children. An interesting question to raise: Which is harder to believe, a planet without sun or children who feel penitent and forgiving as quickly as these do?

AV: Close Harmony (30 min., Learning Corporation of America)

Winner of a 1982 Oscar as the best documentary, *Close Harmony* shows the interaction between a group of elementary school students and senior citizens who join together to perform a concert. It is easy to see why this event became significant for all involved and to admire the teacher who made it happen. A possible topic for discussion is: Are there any ways such contact can be arranged in your community? What problems would be involved?

Friendship and Social Acceptance

Teaching Tip: The Universality of Rejection

To help your students recognize the universality of rejection during middle childhood, ask if anyone remembers being teased, rejected, or called a derogatory name during the grade-school years. If there is no immediate response, you might share one of your own memories or ask whether the students remember any nicknames for children who were fat, wore braces ("tinsel teeth," "train tracks," "metal mouth"), or wore glasses ("four eyes").

This topic usually triggers lively discussion. Students realize that anyone can feel rejected at any time—even the attractive, friendly, well-adjusted students in the class may have been unpopular or lonely children. A related topic is religious, racial, or economic prejudice. You might ask your students to discuss any books or films they have read or seen that touch on this subject and may have affected them deeply.

Bullies and Victims

Observational Activity: Gender Roles and Aggression on TV

School-age children are particularly susceptible to operant conditioning, including learning by observation, or *modeling*. Children who imitate those they admire (parents, teachers, sports and entertainment figures) derive reinforcement from "being like" their heroes.

A potent source of models for the school-age child, like the younger child, is television. By watching television, for example, children learn a great deal about the various roles they may play during their lives, including gender roles, parental roles, and friendship roles. Unfortunately, many of the behaviors modeled on TV reflect undesirable stereotypes and antisocial behaviors that may cast a long shadow on the child's future social development. The good news is that prosocial behaviors, when they are modeled on television, are just as influential and apt to be imitated as are antisocial behaviors.

For this activity, ask your students to watch several hours of TV, noting the incidence of aggressive behaviors (defined as overt use of force against others) and differences in how males and females are portrayed. Have them use the guidelines in Handout 4 in conducting their study, then answer the questions in Handout 5.

Children's Moral Codes

AV: Moral Development (two programs, 28 min. each, Insight Media)

This two-part series explores the concepts of morality and moral intelligence. Part one examines the principal theories of moral development, including psychoanalytic, sociobiology, social learning, and cognitive theories. Part two explores how moral reasoning develops from early infancy through adolescence, focusing on the important roles played by parents, peers, schools, and society.

Classroom Activity: The Process of Moral Reasoning

To further explore the process of moral reasoning, you might ask your students to discuss a moral issue relevant to their lives. Although college students generally accept the notion that people should be free to express themselves sexually, they do not agree about what to do if that sexual expression leads to pregnancy. However, because 36 percent of all sexually active teenage girls become pregnant within two years of first intercourse, it is an issue worthy of their consideration.

Both the right to abortion and forced adoption are controversial subjects that would be good topics for class discussion. You may need to get the discussion going by taking one side or the other on the abortion issue or by saying that in order to secure the right to keep her infant, an unwed teenage mother should be required to prove that she can provide competent care, just as every prospective adoptive parent must.

Once students have become involved, you need only moderate the discussion, perhaps correcting errors of fact. After 5 or 10 minutes, ask the class to think about the kinds of arguments they are using. Which of Kohlberg's stages predominate? Has Kohlberg's view that values shift through the process of discussion and clarification been substantiated; that is, has anyone taken a new position on these issues? Do men and women in the class approach the problem differently?

Classroom Activity: Using Robert Cormier's Novel to Teach Moral Development

Sharon Stringer of Youngstown State University suggests assigning Robert Cormier's novel *After the First Death* to promote discussion of moral development during childhood and adolescence. Cormier's young adult protagonists face a variety of moral dilemmas that vividly illustrate the conflicts presented in the writings of Lawrence Kohlberg and Carol Gilligan. "Their stories and dilemmas," Stringer writes, "pose two tests of character. One conflict centers on the decision to conform to authority or disobey in order to preserve the rights of the individual. A second conflict is to balance a rational focus on rights and laws with an ethic of care and concern for human relationships."

To help her students make meaningful connections between the novel's characters and their own life experiences, Stringer first asks her students to discuss various ways in which their character has been tested. After reading the novel and discussing it in class, students write a paper describing the moral development of one or more of the characters in the novel. (A good strategy would be to ask students to pick the character with whom they most closely identify.)

Stringer reports that the effect of the novel on students is quite powerful. Commenting on the assignment, one student wrote, "I loved it. I'm not a big reader. I couldn't put this novel down." Another student noted that the assignment "made me draw on my own inner strength, bring out my own ideas."

Stringer, S. A. (1994). The psychological changes of adolescence: A test of character. *The Alan Review, 22*(1). Retrieved from scholar.lib.vt.edu/ejournals/ALAN/fall94/Stringer.html.

Critical Thinking Activity: Moral Reasoning Dilemma

This second critical thinking exercise is designed to test students' critical thinking about moral thinking. Handout 6 contains a brief scenario followed by a series of questions.

The answer to this critical thinking activity follows:

Preconventional Reasoning: Moral reasoning at this level is self-centered and emphasizes obtaining rewards and avoiding punishments.

Blake: "There's no way I'll be caught. I don't think the professor even knows what a Web site is."

Jennifer: "If I turn Blake in, he'll find some way to get back at me."

Sharon: "If the term papers are graded on a curve, Blake's unearned A will affect my class standing."

Conventional Reasoning: Moral reasoning at this level focuses on pleasing other people and obeying the laws set down by society.

Blake: "Who hasn't cheated at least once in school? If everyone cheats, what's the big deal?"

Jennifer: "If I turn Blake in, everyone will hate me for being a snitch."

Sharon: "Blake broke the rules; he should pay the consequences."

Postconventional Reasoning: Moral reasoning at this level emphasizes moral principles and rules of society that are established by mutual agreement, or the principles that are universal (not only in one culture).

Blake: "I'm going to be a computer programmer, not a psychologist. This type of assignment doesn't indicate anything about my likelihood of success. Besides, I've heard that the professor doesn't even read these papers."

Jennifer: "It's not my business; my only concern is whether I do a good job on the paper."

Sharon: "If people stand by while others cheat, the meaning of grades and a college education will be diminished."

HANDOUT 1

Developmental Fact or Myth?

T F 1. School-age children typically are more self-critical than they were when they were younger.

T F 2. Children's ability to cope with stress may depend on their resilience when dealing with difficult situations.

T F 3. Children in a shared home environment tend to react to family situations in a similar way.

T F 4. Extended families are more common among low-income households.

T F 5. Acceptance by their peer group is more important to school-age children than having a few close friends.

T F 6. Older children change friends more often than do younger children.

T F 7. Those in middle childhood tend to choose best friends whose backgrounds, interests, and values are similar to their own.

T F 8. Bullying during middle childhood seems to be universal.

T F 9. Bullies and their victims are usually of the same sex.

T F 10. Bullies generally are not socially perceptive.

HANDOUT 2

Genograms

As an exercise in studying trends in the constitution of families, construct a genogram of your own family. A genogram *is a map of several generations within a family, something like a family tree. By convention, in genograms males are represented by squares and females by circles. Marriage is indicated by a solid line drawn from circle to square, and divorce by a dashed line. Death is depicted by an "X" through the circle or square.*

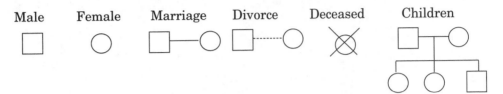

Male Female Marriage Divorce Deceased Children

The genogram is expanded horizontally to include additional individuals within a given generation, and vertically to document the family history across several generations.

It might be a good idea to make a rough draft before drawing the final version. Return your genogram to your instructor.

Straub, R. O. (2004). *Seasons of life study guide* (5th ed.). New York: Worth Publishers.

HANDOUT 3

Children's Work at Home

While middle childhood is the developmental period centered on the child's growing inclusion in the wider social world, school-age children are also able to participate more fully in the responsibilities of family life.

1. Imagine that you are the parent of a 7-year-old child. What household tasks would you assign to your 7-year-old son? to your 7-year-old daughter?

2. How might the school child's responsibilities at home affect his or her ability to cope with everyday problems in adolescence and adulthood—for better or for worse?

3. How often are these tasks performed (or how much time do they take)?

4. What tasks do you think would be appropriate for an 11-year-old son? for an 11-year-old daughter?

HANDOUT 3 *(continued)*

5. How often are these tasks performed (or how much time do they take)?

6. In your hypothetical family (indicate the number of members and their ages), how are the decisions made about the division of household responsibilities?

7. If you can remember them, describe your own responsibilities at home during the school years.

HANDOUT 4

Observational Activity: Gender Roles and Aggression on TV: Guidelines

This activity asks you to analyze a representative sampling of school-age children's TV programs, following the guidelines below. After you have finished your viewing, complete the questions on the accompanying handout and return it to your instructor.

1. Watch at least four hours of TV, spread throughout the day.
2. Select programs that provide a representative sampling of what TV has to offer. For example, pick at least one early prime-time program that is watched by schoolchildren, a Saturday morning cartoon, and an "educational" program; take note of the commercials that occur during these programs as well.
3. For each program that you watch, keep a record of the following:
   a. the number of male and female characters in "lead roles"
   b. the prosocial behaviors modeled by male and female characters, including nurturance, empathy, problem solving, and conflict resolution
   c. the antisocial behaviors modeled by male and female characters, especially the use of physical force, verbal aggression, addictive behavior, and deceit
   d. the operant outcomes of the various behaviors modeled by males and females (for example, is "action" more likely to be reinforced in males or females?)

HANDOUT 5

Observational Activity: Gender Roles and Aggression on TV: Follow-Up Questionnaire

1. In the space below, list the programs that you watched for this observational activity.

Name of Program	Time of Day	Duration

2. Was there a difference in how often males and females played lead roles in the various programs? If so, what impact do you feel this has on school-age viewers?

3. How often was aggressive behavior modeled by males and females? When aggressive behavior occurred, which sex was more likely to use physical force? nonphysical force?

HANDOUT 5 *(continued)*

4. How often were prosocial behaviors (helping, praising, sharing) modeled by females? males?

5. What were the consequences of aggression in the programs you watched? Was aggressive behavior reinforced? Was there a gender difference in the consequences of aggression?

6. What were the consequences of prosocial behaviors in the programs you watched? Was prosocial behavior reinforced? Was there a gender difference in the consequences of prosocial behavior?

HANDOUT 5 *(continued)*

7. What differences did you observe in how males and females were portrayed in the various categories of TV programs? For example, were males and females in "educational programs" portrayed differently from those in cartoons and prime-time programs?

8. Write a paragraph that summarizes how the typical female was portrayed in the programs you watched.

9. Write a paragraph that summarizes how the typical male was portrayed in the programs you watched.

10. What other values, prejudicial attitudes, or stereotypes were reinforced in the programs you watched?

HANDOUT 6

Critical Thinking Activity: Moral Reasoning Dilemma

*Now that you have read and reviewed the material on psychosocial development during middle childhood, take your learning a step further by testing your critical thinking skills on this perspective-taking exercise.**

Here is a situation that is somewhat similar to Kohlberg's dilemmas for moral reasoning. Three weeks before their developmental psychology term papers are due, Jennifer and two classmates visit the campus library to conduct online literature searches on their topics. After 30 minutes of checking sites on the Internet, Blake announces that he's found a Web site that offers inexpensive term papers on a variety of subjects, including the topic of his paper. Jennifer, who has never cheated in her academic career, says nothing and maintains her concentration on her own research. Sharon, who is appalled by Blake's intention to cheat, vows that she will report Blake to their professor.

In choosing their selected course of action, Blake, Sharon, and Jennifer each made a moral decision. Behavior alone does not indicate moral thinking, however. Your job is to write a justification that each student might use at each of Kohlberg's three levels of moral reasoning—preconventional, conventional, and postconventional. To help you get started the first one is filled in for you.

Preconventional Reasoning

Blake: "There's no way I'll be caught. I don't think the professor even knows what a Web site is."

Jennifer:

Sharon:

Conventional Reasoning

Blake:

Jennifer:

Sharon:

*Adapted from Halonen, J. (1995). *The critical thinking companion for introductory psychology.* New York: Worth Publishers, pp. 20–22.

HANDOUT 6 *(continued)*

Postconventional Reasoning

Blake:

Jennifer:

Sharon:

Adolescence: Biosocial Development

Contents

Note: Worth Publishers provides online Instructor and Student Tool Kits, DVD Student Tool Kits, and Instructor and Student video resources in DevelopmentPortal for use with the text. See Part I: General Resources for information about these materials and the text Lecture Guides for a complete list by text chapter.

Nutrition

The Transformations of Puberty

Suggested Activities

Introducing Adolescence: Biosocial Development

"On Your Own" Activity: Developmental Fact or Myth?

Before students read about biosocial development during adolescence, have them respond to the true-false statements in Handout 1.

The correct answers are shown below. Class discussion can focus on the origins of any developmental misconceptions that are demonstrated in the students' incorrect answers.

1. F	6. T
2. T	7. F
3. T	8. T
4. T	9. T
5. F	10. F

AV: The Journey Through the Life Span, Program 6: Adolescence

Program 6: Adolescence portrays the adolescent as a developing person embarking on a journey of reflection and opportunity. The program begins by outlining the physical and biological changes that accompany the growth spurt and puberty, noting the tremendous normal variation, as demonstrated by boys and girls in a school cafeteria line. The effects of nutrition, stress, and overall health on the timing of puberty are described, and Anne Peterson of the Kellogg Foundation describes the impact of early and late puberty. A highlight of the segment is a discussion of gender differences in how puberty is experienced among a group of teens gathered together from across the United States to produce a play about the Civil War draft riots.

The second segment of the program—cognitive development—centers on Jean Piaget's stage of formal operations (covered in the text discussion of cognitive development during adolescence). Adolescents' emerging skill in thinking systematically and logically about abstract and hypothetical issues is described, along with the impact of this new style of reasoning on teens' everyday lives and problem-solving ability. This description segues into the final segment of the program—social development (see the text discussion of psychosocial development during adolescence)—that explores the ways in which the cognitive advances of adolescence influence teens' thinking about justice and fairness and their relationships with peers and parents. Anne Peterson provides expert commentary on the importance of how parents listen to teenagers, and three risky adolescent behaviors: drug and alcohol use and early sexual behavior. Ellen Winner of Boston College discusses how friendships and academic challenges change during the teen years. The program concludes with an in-depth exploration of teens' emerging sexual identities.

Accompanying the narrated video segment are three un-narrated observation modules. In the first, an adolescent girl and boy talk about sexuality, including the benefits and risks of early sexual maturation and the qualities they find attractive in potential boyfriends and girlfriends. In the second module, a class of high school students discusses Tennessee Williams' play *A Streetcar Named Desire,* focusing on the morality of the character Blanche—a mature woman who has an affair with a 17-year-old male student. In the third module, two adolescent boys talk about politics, dating, and their changing relationships with parents.

AV: Transitions Throughout the Life Span, Program 14: Explosions

Between the ages of 10 and 20, young people cross the great divide between childhood and adulthood. This crossing encompasses all three domains of development—biosocial, cognitive, and psychosocial. Program 14 focuses on the dramatic changes that occur in the biosocial domain, beginning with puberty and the growth spurt. The biosocial metamorphosis of the adolescent is discussed in detail, with emphasis on sexual maturation, nutrition, and the effects of the timing of puberty, including possible problems arising from early or late maturation. Kathleen Berger provides expert commentary regarding adolescents' preoccupation with body image and the emotional impact of puberty.

Although adolescence is, in many ways, a healthy time of life, the program addresses two health hazards that too often affect adolescence: unhealthy eating and use of alcohol, tobacco, and other drugs.

AV: Adolescence (30 min., Insight Media)

This film is a very basic introduction to the key developmental issues and concepts of adolescence. Experts discuss the physical, psychological, and social changes that force the individual to make the transition from childhood to adulthood. This film could be shown before the unit on adolescence is assigned.

AV: Adolescent Development (30 min., Insight Media)

This program charts the changes in each of the three domains of development that mark the transition from childhood to adulthood.

AV: Adolescence: The Winds of Change (30 min., HarperCollins)

In this film, adolescents frankly discuss the biological and social changes they are experiencing, and developmental psychologists John Conger, David Elkind, and Jerome Kagan provide comments. A series of candid scenes highlights the importance of parental attitudes and social conditions in molding adolescent behavior, as the adolescents either follow or reject their adult models. Because political and cultural conditions make each generation of adolescents somewhat different from the others, a good discussion question to ask the class is: How typical do you think the adolescents in this movie seem, and how accurate are the experts?

Classroom Activity: Introducing Adolescents, the Risk Takers—Especially in the United States

In the early years of the new millenium, it was all too common to hear about a high school student shooting classmates and/or teachers. More recently, the tragic phenomenon of teens being used as suicide bombers for political purposes leaves many people shaking their heads and wondering, "What makes kids lash out like that? Why didn't their parents see it coming?" Other examples of destructive teen behaviors frequently in the news include cluster suicides, cutting and other forms of self-mutilation, binge drinking, and early sexual activity. As an introduction to the unit on adolescence, you might pose these questions to your class and ask for their thoughts. A good discussion is sure to follow, especially if your class includes older students and parents in addition to those who are adolescents themselves. Alternatively, you might want to delay a discussion of risk taking until you discuss psychosocial development during adolescence.

To help frame the discussion, you might present the results of a 2009 nationwide survey of students in grades 9 through 12. The survey was conducted by the Centers for Disease Control and Prevention (CDC) for their Youth Behavior Surveillance Summaries. Using an anonymous 87-question survey, the researchers asked the teens to reveal details of their private lives—especially risky behaviors. Among the notable findings of the study:

- 9.7 percent rarely or never wore a seat belt when riding in a car driven by someone else.
- During the 30 days before the survey, 28.3 percent of high school students rode in a car or other vehicle driven by someone who had been drinking alcohol, 17.5 percent had carried a weapon, 41.8 percent had drunk alcohol, and 20.8 percent had used marijuana.
- During the 12 months before the survey, 31.5 percent of high school students had been in a physical fight and 6.3 percent had attempted suicide.
- Substantial morbidity and social problems among youth also result from unintended pregnancies and STDs, including HIV infection. Among high school students nationwide, 34.2 percent were currently sexually active, 38.9 percent of currently sexually active students had not used a condom during their last sexual intercourse, and 2.1 percent of students had injected an illegal drug.
- During 2009, 19.5 percent of high school students smoked cigarettes during the 30 days before the survey.
- During the seven days before the survey, 77.7 percent of high school students had not eaten fruits and vegetables five or more times a day,

29.2 percent had drunk soda or pop at least once a day, and 81.6 percent were not physically active for at least 60 minutes per day on all seven days. One-third of high school students attended physical education classes daily, and 12.0 percent were obese.

Also as part of its Healthy Youth Project, the CDC has conducted a number of other analyses of risky behavior among teens, including violence. They have found that homicide and suicide are responsible for 25 percent of deaths among 10- to 24-year-olds in the United States. Two of the nation's health objectives, as specified in the report *Healthy People 2010,* are to reduce the prevalence of physical fighting among adolescents and the prevalence of adolescents' carrying a weapon on school property. Although there are some signs that things are improving, the picture is far from rosy. Nearly 1 in 10 high school students reported being threatened or injured with a weapon on school property during the preceding 12 months. The prevalence of weapon carrying, although down from 11.8 percent in 1993, remains a significant threat at 6.1 percent.

To add specificity to your discussion, you might ask students to dig more deeply into the CDC's Youth Risk Behavior project, perhaps by focusing on any available information for their state or local community. Among other resources, the CDC's Web site (www.cdc.gov/HealthyYouth/yrbs/index.htm) includes a copy of the full report and separate state fact sheets.

You might also present the views of Lynn Ponton, a psychiatrist at the University of California, San Francisco, who specializes in adolescence and is the author of *The Romance of Risk: Why Teenagers Do the Things They Do.* Ponton suggests that to understand tragedies such as the one that occurred at Columbine High School, we must realize that all adolescents take risks, and that even the best and brightest of teens can fall in with a destructive peer group. The key to keeping kids on the right track, she says, is parental involvement that encourages kids to take "healthy risks instead of dangerous ones." In addition, parents must be vigilant in their own risk-taking behavior, because their kids are watching closely.

Healthy risk taking, such as playing sports and travel, helps young people explore and develop identities that are distinctly their own. But when the struggle for identity leads to rebellion and anger at adults, destructive risk taking, including drinking, smoking, reckless driving, disordered eating, self-mutilation, stealing, and violence, is likely to occur. Such is the path that Eric Harris and Dylan Klebold of Littleton, Colorado, the Columbine shooters, chose, with results that the world watched in horror. More recently, Cho Seung-Hui took an even more horrific path when he shot and killed 32 students at Virginia Tech.

Ponton notes that aggression and violence directed at one's peers are often the result of scapegoating, in which young people are bullied, humiliated, or publicly ostracized by the peer group. Ponton describes working with a 17-year-old boy who had put a gun to another boy's head as revenge for being picked on. Asked how this act made him feel, the boy responded, "Strong. Powerful. I ain't never felt like that before." Sadly, this teen had never had the opportunity to feel this way in the healthier arena of academic, artistic, or athletic accomplishment.

Ponton also notes a striking gender difference in the behavior of boys and girls who take unhealthy risks during adolescence. "Boys who are unhealthy risk-takers often hurt others," she notes, whereas "girls usually turn their shame and anger on themselves, engaging in self-destructive behaviors such as cutting or extreme dieting." She describes receiving a panicky phone call from the father of an unpopular 17-year-old daughter with a history of self-mutilation, who threatened to start cutting herself again when, the day after the Colorado shooting, kids at her school mockingly asked her why she wasn't wearing her black trench coat.

After 20 years of working with adolescents, Ponton is convinced that most troubled adolescents don't give obvious signs that they are heading for trouble. Although parents should be on guard for signs of dangerous risk taking in their teens, she believes that the best strategy is for parents and other adults to encourage young people to take healthy chances and to help them grow, learn to assess danger, and cope with both failure and success.

Ponton has also applied her expertise to other risky teenage behaviors, including early sexual activity and drug use. Studies comparing American teenagers with those from other countries have consistently found that American teenagers have the highest rates of teen pregnancy and sexually transmitted diseases.

Ponton believes that one reason for these high rates is that sex education in the United States is very poor. "If you look at the other four countries," she states, "they have far better sex education in middle school and high school. We may have one hour for every 20 that they get. In addition, 49 states now accept abstinence-only money from the federal government, up from just 10 before 1998. That means that to get government funding for sex education, schools in those 49 states are under pressure to teach students that abstinence is the only way to avoid pregnancy, and 23 percent of public schools districts teach abstinence only. There's no talk about birth control or preventing sexually transmitted diseases. It's very limited. That's really a quieting of sexual education in this country. There's strong evidence that these programs don't discourage teenagers from becoming sexually active. Half of those over age 16 are sexually active."

Another factor Ponton points to is gender roles, which may be changing in the workplace but remain strongly traditional in middle schools and high schools. (Note that the following was written about Britney Spears, but clearly it is better to use another sex symbol [e.g., Miley Cyrus] to make the point of the quote.) "The media reinforces these roles. Britney Spears is an emblem: she needs to be provocative and as much of a sexual object as she can be, but she promotes herself as a virgin. Girls are encouraged to adopt a passive gender role, so they don't have the skills to deal with violence in their relationships. I see boys who are addicted to sex sites on the Internet that show sadistic behavior toward women. It affects those boys' sexual lives and also what we see with our daughters. There's also a political factor. I believe that in response to the liberal period of the 1970s and 80s, we've returned to the double standard of the 1950s."

Abma, J. C., Martinez, G. M., Mosher, W. D., & Dawson, B. S. (2004). Teenagers in the United States: sexual activity, contraceptive use, and childbearing, 2002, *Vital and Health Statistics, 2004,* Series 23, No. 24.

Centers for Disease Control and Prevention: Youth Behavior Surveillance United States, 2009. (2010, June 10). *Morbidity and Mortality Weekly Report, 59*(SS-5). Washington, DC: Department of Health and Human Services.

Gilbert, S. (2002, January 15). An expert's eye on teenage sex, risk, and abuse. *New York Times*, p. F6.

Ponton, L. E. (1998). *The romance of risk: Why teenagers do the things they do.* New York: Basic Books.

Ponton, L. E. (1999). Beyond Littleton: Their dark romance with risk. *Newsweek*, 55.

Santelli, J. S., Lindberg, L. D., Finer, L.B., & Singh, S. (2007). Explaining recent declines in adolescent pregnancy in the United States: The contribution of abstinence and improved contraceptive use. *American Journal of Public Health. 97*(1), 150–156.

Classroom Activity: Using Technology to Introduce Biosocial Development During Adolescence

Ellen Pastorino of Valencia Community College suggests discussing recent research regarding the use of cell phones, laptop computers, and other forms of technology as an effective strategy to help students make meaningful connections between their own life experiences and biosocial development. Here are a few examples to get you started.

Cell Phones, Texting, and Health: Several studies have reported increased acoustic neuromas and gliomas in heavy cell-phone users on the same side of the head typically used during calls. The risk seems to be greatest for those who began using cell phones prior to age 20, followed by 10 or more years of use (Hardell & Carlberg, 2009).

Texting while driving has been linked to increased reaction time, missed lane changes, and other hazardous changes to driving behavior (Hosking et al., 2009). A program recently developed by Robert Tower, road manager of PEER Awareness—a Michigan-based firm that promotes healthy living among young people—uses a simulation to demonstrate the dangers of texting while driving. As an example, during the simulation one teen ran over a little boy, crashed into another car, and drove on the wrong side of the road while speeding, all because she was texting on her cell phone while driving. The teens are also shown videos of interviews with families who have lost loved ones involved in crashes caused by texting while driving.

MP3 Players, Ear buds, and Hearing Loss: Contrary to what many people believe, ear buds do not effectively block out background noise. In fact, people who use ear buds in noisy environments play their iPods and other devices significantly louder (89 dB on average) than those who use conventional earphones (78 dB). (For a point of reference, hearing loss is most likely to occur in response to sounds louder than 80 dB).

Laptop Computers and Scrotal Temperature: Researchers placed thermometers on the scrotums of 29 young men who used laptops for 60 minutes under three conditions: legs closed with laptop; legs closed with lap pad under laptop; and legs apart with lap pad under laptop. After 60 minutes with legs closed and no lap pad, scrotal temperature had increased by as much as 2.5 degrees Celsius. Lower tempertures mpair sperm production and reduce fertility. (Sheynkin et al., in press)

Hardell, L., & Carlberg, M. (2009). Mobile phones, cordless phones and the risk for brain tumours. *International Journal of Oncology, 35,* 5–17.

Hosking, S. G., Young, K. L., & Regan, M. A. (2009). The effects of text messaging on young drivers. *Human Factors, 51,* 582–592.

Pastorino, E. (2011). Using the psychology of technology to connect with students. *National Institute on the Teaching of Psychology.* St. Petersburg Beach, FL.

Seltzser, A. (2011). Program exposes the dangers of texting and driving. Retrieved February 22, 2011, from www.sun-sentinel.com/news/palm-beach/fl-texting-while-driving-20110221,0,6974525.story

Sheynkin, Y., Welliver, R., Winer, A., Hajimirzaee, F., Ahn, H., & Lee, K. (in press). Protection from scrotal hyperthermia in laptop computer users. *Fertility and Sterility.*

Classroom Activity: Empathizing with Adolescents

To help your students empathize with the pubescent young person, you might ask each class member to relate some event, attitude, misconception, or worry he or she experienced in connection with the changes of puberty: having had big feet; having been the first or the last to experience menarche; having been concerned about having a small penis or being oversexed or masturbating; having had worries about acne or voice change. If the students tend to be shy, ask them to relate the experiences of their friends or of people they have empathized with in films or fiction.

Classroom Activity: Using "Radio Diaries" to Study Adolescent Development

Case studies are an excellent vehicle for teaching developmental concepts and for helping students make meaningful connections between course material and their own life experiences. Although fictional case studies from literature, television, and movies can be effective, autobiographical cases may be more engaging because they "ring true" to students.

Jane Sheldon (2004) suggests using National Public Radio's "Radio Diaries" series, available through streaming audio on the Internet (www.radiodiaries.org), to teach developmental psychology concepts. Of particular relevance to the unit on adolescence is the series "Teenage Diaries," which consists of tape recordings of the daily lives of adolescents from diverse backgrounds.

Sheldon asks students in her adolescent development class to use the major developmental theories (psychoanalytic, behaviorist, cognitive, sociocultural, and evolutionary) to analyze one of the diaries. After listening to the diary and printing out its transcript, students are instructed to interpret each segment from each theoretical perspective. In considering the different theoretical perspectives, students often apply different meanings to the same statement. Sheldon cites the example of Melissa, a teenage mother who declares that despite having a baby, she is "still going to be a party girl." As Sheldon notes, "Freud's theory suggests that Melissa's id impulses are overpowering her superego; her ego then uses the defense mechanism of denial, as shown by her thinking that her life won't change now that she has a baby. Alternatively, Erikson's theory points to the idea that Melissa is in the stage of identity versus role confusion and does not yet think of herself as a mother with adult responsibilities. According to Piaget, however, Melissa has developed a schema about what motherhood entails, and she will have to accommodate this schema to fit with the new realities of her life situation."

Although you may choose to grade students only on their analytical skills in applying the different theoretical perspectives, Sheldon suggests grading them also on their creativity and the visual appeal of the paper or poster they submit. Robert Sternberg would be pleased, since this grading strategy recognizes the different forms of intelligence (analytical, creative, and practical) that, ideally, college should stimulate.

As an alternative to asking students to listen to the diaries on their own, you might purchase an audio CD-ROM of the diariDysfuncties (available from NPR) and play segments of the diaries in class. Afterward, the class can be divided into small groups to discuss each segment.

Sheldon, J. (2004). Using "radio diaries" to teach developmental psychology concepts. *Teaching of Psychology, 31,* 47–49.

*AV: Teens: What Makes Them Tick? (*43 min., Films for the Humanities and Sciences)

In this ABC News special, correspondent John Stossel discusses the various biological and cognitive changes that occur during adolescence to make these years unique in the life span. Also discussed is the social hierarchy among teens (influencers, conformers, passives, edge kids) that leads to the development of teenage fads.

AV: Teenage Mind and Body (30 min., Insight Media)

This video charts biosocial and cognitive development during adolescence, focusing on differences between teenagers' abilities and interests and their parents' expectations. David Elkind discusses Piaget's final stage of development—formal operations—and Lawrence Kohlberg's theory of the development of moral reasoning. It works well with the discussion of biosocial development or with cognitive development during adolescence.

Classroom Activity: The "Storm and Stress" View of Adolescence

Another way to introduce the section on adolescence is to discuss G. Stanley Hall's traditional view that adolescence is inevitably a time of emotional turbulence. Hall, who coined the term *adolescence* from the Latin word for "growth," maintained that erratic physical growth coincides with erratic emotional and moral development.

Hall's views were consistent with those of most psychoanalytic theorists, who believed that the adolescent's rapid sexual maturation and powerful sex drives would inevitably conflict with the culture's traditional prohibitions against their free expression. Thus, adolescent turbulence seemed only natural to psychoanalysts such as Anna Freud, who believed that we should be more worried about the psychological health of the adolescent who does *not* seem to be emotionally upset than about the one who does. The following excerpt from Anna Freud's *The Ego and the Mechanisms of Defense* highlights "the incomprehensible and irreconcilable contradictions apparent in [adolescents'] psychic life."

> Adolescents are excessively egoistic, regarding themselves as the center of the universe and the sole object of interest, and yet at no time in later life are they capable of so much self-sacrifice and devotion. They form the most passionate love relations, only to break them off as abruptly as they began them. On the one hand, they throw themselves enthusiastically into the life of the community, and on the other, they have an overpowering longing for solitude. They oscillate between blind submission to some self-chosen leader and defiant rebellion against any and every authority. They are selfish and materially minded and at the same time full of lofty idealism. They are ascetic but will suddenly plunge into instinctual indulgence of the most primitive character. At times their behavior to other people is rough and inconsiderate, yet they themselves are extremely touchy. Their moods vary between light-hearted optimism and the blackest pessimism. Sometimes they will work with indefatigable enthusiasm and at other times they are sluggish and apathetic.

Although the "storm and stress" version of adolescence is not without some support from current research, most developmentalists today take a more balanced view. Many of your students are likely to cling to the traditional misconception, however. To initiate a lively class discussion, ask your students why earlier psychologists (and the general public) arrived at such a firm view of adolescence as a time of trouble. One reason is that they tended to concentrate on the adolescents most likely to be noticed—the disrespectful, the disturbed, and the delinquent—and to generalize from this minority to adolescents as a whole.

A second reason is that, in keeping with Hall's theories, many people believed that the problems of adolescence are directly caused by the physical changes of puberty. Since puberty is a universal biological event, it was assumed that the psychological and behavioral results of puberty must be universal as well.

Freud, A. (1967). *The ego and the mechanisms of defense.* New York: International Universities Press.

Lerner, R. M., & Steinberg, L. (2009). *Handbook of adolescent psychology* (3rd ed.). New York: Wiley.

Observational Activity: Adolescence Now and Then

One of the themes of this course is that development in each of the three domains is strongly influenced by social and cultural forces in the environment. This means that cohort effects are common and that an individual's development can be accurately understood only if it is examined in its historical context.

This activity is intended to increase students' awareness that concepts of adolescence vary as a function of historical time. Their assignment is to interview someone who is over 70 years old. They may prefer to interview a friend or a relative. Their objective is to find out what adolescence was like for the interviewee and how it differed from the typical experience of today's adolescent.

To help students unfamiliar with interview techniques, Handout 2 provides a list of questions that may serve as guidelines for structuring the interview. Students may want to copy these questions on a separate sheet of paper, leaving space for answers. By taking notes as the interviewee talks, the student will be better able to prepare a complete and accurate summary for the follow-up report (Handout 3).

Puberty Begins

AV: Adolescence: Physical Growth and Development (30 min., Child Development Media)

This video addresses the onset of puberty, focusing on reasons for timing variations among individuals and the impact of early or late maturation on males and females. It also explores the increasing openness of discussion and acceptance of sexual activity among teenagers, bringing out new dangers of sexually transmitted diseases (including the HIV virus) and pregnancies. The film also touches on the use of tobacco, alcohol, and other drugs by teens.

AV: Adolescent Physical Development (30 min., Insight Media)

This film describes the physical changes that accompany puberty and discusses their psychological impact. The psychological effects of early and late maturation, menarche, and feelings about physical appearance are also explored.

AV: Puberty (18 min., Films for the Humanities and Sciences)

This film presents a brief, but thorough overview of the physical, emotional, and sexual metamorphosis that takes place in girls and boys during puberty. In addition to outlining the neural and hormonal sequence of events that trigger puberty, and describing the development of the primary and secondary sex characteristics, this BBC documentary discusses some of the social challenges teens face in weathering this stage of the life cycle.

AV: Explosions: Biosocial Development During Adolescence (30 min., Insight Media)

This film examines how the physical changes of puberty influence an adolescent's sense of self. A particularly interesting segment focuses on how different cultural ideas about appearance can produce anxiety, stress, and negative peer pressure.

Teaching Tip: Learning to Talk About Sensitive Pubertal Topics

John Charlesworth and John Slate of Western Carolina University suggest an effective small-group exercise that can help students learn to talk about sensitive topics concerning puberty. The exercise is conducted in the classroom after students have read the text discussion of biosocial development during adolescence. The students are divided into groups of four each, with members of both sexes in each group. They then are given the following scenario:

> Each of you has two children, a boy and a girl, about to enter adolescence. At the present time, you are a long distance from your children and tomorrow you will be leaving on a long journey that will prevent you from having contact with either child for the next 10 years. Tonight is your last opportunity to inform your children of the changes they will experience during puberty, so you need to use this chance to tell your children what you consider important to help them better deal with these changes. The only form of communication available to you is the mail. Each of you is to assist your group in writing two letters, one to your daughter and one to your son. As a group you must decide what to put in your letters. The choice is yours, except in the letter to your daughter you must discuss menarche, and in the letter to your son you must discuss nocturnal emissions and spontaneous erections. You are to write these letters using a vocabulary that will be understood by these children and that will give them a positive attitude toward the changes they will experience. Each group must decide which letter it is going to write first.

When the letters have been completed (or, depending on available time, during the next class meeting), ask a representative from each group to read the group's letters. Then have class members critique the letters while you provide relevant information or clarification.

Charlesworth and Slate report that students responded very favorably to the exercise and agreed that it accomplished several objectives: (1) students' knowledge about pubertal issues (especially those pertaining to the opposite sex) increased; (2) students reported feeling more comfortable in discussing pubertal changes and issues; and (3) many students expressed increased confidence in their ability to discuss pubertal issues with their children.

Charlesworth, J. R., & Slate, J. R. (1986, December). Teaching about puberty: Learning to talk about sensitive topics. *Teaching of Psychology, 13*(4), 215–217.

Critical Thinking Activity: Early and Late Maturation

Each unit of these resources contains at least one critical thinking exercise designed specifically to test students' critical thinking about a topic covered in the text. Handout 4 contains questions to help students remember their own thoughts and feelings as they matured.

There are no answers for this exercise because the answers will be unique to each student.

Nutrition

Classroom Activity: Nutritional Value of Fast Food

Nominated for the 2005 Academy Award for Best Documentary Film, *Supersize Me* offered a two-word answer to the question "Why Are Americans So Fat?": fast food. Filmmaker Morgan Spurlock decided to find out what would happen to him if he ate nothing but fast food for an entire month. And so he did, eating only at McDonald's restaurants for 30 days. There were only three other rules: He must consume three meals a day; he must consume everything on the menu at least once; and he must supersize any meal if asked. And that he did, gaining 25 pounds in the process, which it took him 14 months to lose. A year earlier, two teenagers in New York sued the fast-food chain, claiming it had made them obese. Although a federal judge dismissed the case, the story and the documentary released shortly thereafter brought the issue of fast food into sharp public focus.

There are an estimated 300,000 (and growing daily) fast-food restaurants in the United States. Because fast food is so widely available, predictably the same wherever you are, and ready to eat within minutes, it has become part of the busy American lifestyle. Half of all Americans eat fast food at least once a week. To help your students evaluate the nutritional value of the fast foods consumed by adolescents (and, most probably, themselves), you might present some consumer information.

Consumer Reports estimates that the meal of a cheeseburger, french fries, and milk shake often ordered at a fast-food restaurant supplies 70 to 90 percent of the daily protein requirement for most people; however, people should get only a third of their protein from one meal. Extra protein just means extra calories.

Speaking of calories, the same meal would provide about 1,150 calories—about 40 percent of the calories needed to maintain the weight of a 165-pound man, or 60 percent of that needed by a 128-pound woman. The main source of all these calories is fat, which is found in the beef, cheese, and mayonnaise-type sauce used on the burgers. Chicken and fish, when fried in low-fat oils, get about half their calories from fat, as do tacos; roast beef sandwiches have a slightly lower percentage of fat. However, chicken fried in beef fat can supply twice as much fat as a regular hamburger.

Unless they have a background in nutrition, your students may find it difficult to evaluate the nutritional role of fast foods during adolescence. You might point out that while adolescents have a higher energy level and might need more calories than some adults, they are also weight-conscious and tend to see themselves as "overweight." Also, consumption of fast foods typically means a high salt (sodium) intake—a fact that may be even more important to older adults. You might point out that many fast-food restaurants now offer a salad bar, which may provide sources of vitamins, such as A and C, that are missing from the ordinary fast-food menu. Indeed, one of the problems for teenagers and others who rely heavily on fast foods is that they may not be eating a well-balanced diet that includes complex carbohydrates, vitamin- and iron-rich foods, and fiber.

Fortunately, several consumer organizations and wellness groups have rated the best and worst in fast food. Among the most nutritious choices are grilled chicken sandwiches at McDonald's and Wendy's restaurants, the barbecue chicken sandwich at KFC, Arby's Junior Roast Beef, and several items from Taco Bell's "lite" menu.

Several years ago, the Center for Science in the Public Interest (CSPI)—a top consumer watchdog organization—evaluated the nutritional value of Mexican, Italian, and Chinese cuisine. Their fundamental conclusion was that the foundations of these foods—beans, rice, fish, steamed vegetables, and pasta—can be quite healthy, at least when prepared in the traditional manner. Too often, however, American restaurants add fatty ingredients such as cheese, sour cream, and fatty cuts of meat that spoil the nutritional value.

Fortunately, there are some signs that fast-food chains are becoming more sensitive to the wishes of health-conscious consumers. Wendy's, for instance, serves an array of healthier food options, including baked potatoes (with or without toppings), chili, salads, and, at the beginning of 2002, their "Garden

Sensation" entrées. Other healthy changes include more reasonably sized servings with junior sandwiches and even encouraging consumers to customize their orders—for example, by holding the mayonnaise and adding lettuce and tomato. Wendy's also posts the complete nutrition information for every food item on its Web site (www.wendys.com) and in its nutrition guide. Similarly, in March 2005, McDonald's unveiled a new "healthy living" advertising campaign to counter the criticisms raised by the *Supersize Me* documentary. The campaign consists of TV spots in different languages around the world that feature kids snowboarding, jumping rope, and eating fruits and vegetables. To kick off the event, McDonald's restaurants offered adult Happy Meals that included bottled water, salad, and a pedometer. The company has also introduced entrée-sized salads to the menu and continues to reduce the level of trans fats in its products.

The Internet abounds with other excellent, authoritative sources of nutrition information. Among the best is the Mayo Clinic's Web site (www.mayoclinic.com), which offers almost daily nutrition updates, a library of reference articles, an "ask the dietician" column, and an interactive quiz your students can take to test their nutrition knowledge. Students can also sign up for e-mail notices of the latest research findings pertaining to nutrition. Other sites allow consumers to look up nutritional information for virtually any item on the menu at McDonald's, Burger King, Subway, and dozens of other popular fast-food chains. For an authoritative source, direct students to Wake Forest University's "Drive thru Diet" Web site at www.wfubmc.edu/Drive-Thru-Diet.htm. Another good source is the Help Guide (www.helpguide.org/life/fast_food_nutrition.htm), which compares less healthy choices with healthier choices at the popular fast-food restaurants.

Healthy fast food: Tips for making healthier fast food choices. Retrieved February 22, 2011, from www.helpguide.org/life/fast_food_nutrition.htm.

Liebman, B., & Hurley, J. (2002, September). Fast food: The best and worst. *Nutrition Action Healthletter* (Center for Science in the Public Interest), 12–15.

Read, M. (2005, March 9). McDonald's unveils healthy living campaign. Retrieved from www.theage.com.

Warshaw, H. S. (2002, October). Wendy's. *Diabetes Forecast, 55*(10), 56–58.

"On Your Own" Activity: Evaluating Dietary Macronutrients

To help your students—particularly those who are adolescents or have just completed adolescence—evaluate how well they are meeting their nutritional needs, ask them to complete Handout 5, a dietary inventory of the foods they most commonly eat.

Research studies reveal that more than two-thirds of adolescent females and more than one-third of adolescent males are trying to lose or to avoid gaining weight at any given time. Many of them do so by restricting their intake of certain types of foods. Because a variety of foods is necessary for adequate nutrition, however, restricting or eliminating certain foods may be nutritionally unwise. Completing this exercise will help students decide how well their eating habits are meeting their nutritional needs.

"On Your Own" Activity: Eating Habits: Past and Present Attitudes and Experiences

Many researchers believe that the roots of adult motivation, including attitudes toward eating, lie in early childhood experiences; it is through these experiences that the child's parents, culture, and peers exert their strongest developmental impact. The Survey of Eating Habits designed by Donn Byrne and his colleagues typically yields results that support this contention. Distribute copies of Handout 6 to your class and have students complete and score their own responses to the survey.

In the Eating Habits survey, the higher the score, the more positive is the individual's orientation to food—what Byrne refers to as *oraphilia*. Because previous studies have found sex differences in food preferences, there are separate scoring scales for males and females. When your students have completed the survey, have them compute separate totals (one point for each answer that is in agreement with the scale) for the two parts ("past attitudes and habits" and "present attitudes and habits"). Tabulate these scores on the board and have students determine (perhaps as an assignment) whether there is a significant correlation between past habits (X) and present habits (Y). The survey is a good introduction to a discussion of the many developmental influences on eating and eating disorders.

You could also determine whether there was a sex difference in food orientation. In developing the scale, the authors analyzed results for males and females separately, because prior studies of food aversion indicated significant sex differences. These separate item analyses yielded somewhat different scales for males and females.

Scoring Scales for Eating Habits Survey

Males: 2-T, 3-F, 4-T, 5-T, 7-F, 9-F, 10-T, 11-T, 12-T, 15-F, 16-F, 17-T, 18-F, 19-T, 24-T, 25-T, 26-T, 27-T, 32-T, 33-T, 34-F, 37-F, 38-T, 39-T, 42-T, 45-F, 46-F, 47-F, 51-T, 52-T, 53-T, 54-T, 58-F, 60-T, 61-T, 63-T, 64-T

Females: 1-T, 2-T, 4-T, 5-T, 6-T, 8-T, 9-F, 10-T, 11-T, 12-T, 13-F, 14-T, 15-T, 16-F, 17-T, 18-F, 19-T, 20-T, 21-T, 22-T, 23-F, 26-T, 27-T, 28-F, 29-T, 30-F, 31-F, 34-F, 35-F, 36-F, 39-T, 40-T, 41-T, 43-F, 44-T, 45-F, 48-F, 49-F, 50-T, 51-T, 52-T, 53-T, 54-T, 55-F, 56-F, 57-F, 59-T, 61-T, 62-T, 63-T, 65-T

AV: Dieting: The Danger Point (20 min., CRM/McGraw-Hill)

Dieting is viewed by this film as a potentially fatal epidemic to which American teenage girls are especially susceptible. Partly through the words of adolescent girls themselves, the egocentrism and personal fables of adolescents are shown to lead to dire consequences, including the doublethink of the girl with anorexia who, despite her emaciation, believes she is too fat.

AV: Eating Disorders: The Hunger Within (42 min., Films for the Humanities and Sciences)

An estimated 11 million people in America suffer from eating disorders. In this film, ABC News correspondent Lynn Sherr visits a Canadian counseling center that has achieved remarkable success in restoring hope and health to sufferers of anorexia and bulimia.

AV: Self-Image and Eating Disorders: A Mirror for the Heart (24 min., Films for the Humanities and Sciences)

This short film analyzes the preoccupation many women have with their body image, explaining that when this preoccupation leads to a loss of self-esteem, it often manifests itself in an obsession with food and diet. Thus, the film takes the view that eating disorders are not about food but rather are a reflection of an inner turmoil fueled by social norms for attractiveness. The program also analyzes the impact of eating disorders on the victim's family and friends and discusses various therapies for treating these disorders.

AV: Killing Us Softly—Advertising's Image of Women (30 min., Cambridge)

A powerful film that discusses how advertising reflects and perpetuates sexist cultural stereotypes of women. Jean Kilbourne provides an engaging and insightful analysis of media advertisements that at first glance appear to be harmless. In her analysis it becomes clear, however, that the media's portrayal of women is often extremely damaging.

AV: Anorexia and Bulimia (19 min., Films for the Humanities and Sciences)
Eating Disorders (26 min., Films for the Humanities and Sciences)

These two films cover the biological, social, and emotional problems of the estimated 6 million people who have eating disorders. It describes the typical personality profiles of the likeliest patients, shows how anorexia and bulimia develop, and details various possible treatments. In *Anorexia and Bulimia*, a nutritionist demonstrates the extremes to which people with these disorders commonly go and the possible effects of eating disorders on the cardiovascular and central nervous systems. *Eating Disorders* profiles the personalities of patients with eating disorders and illustrates the symptoms, development, and successful treatment of anorexia. A particularly interesting segment highlights steps that are being taken by some schools to forestall the development of such problems.

AV: An Anorexic's Tale: The Brief Life of Catherine (80 min., Films for the Humanities and Sciences)

This docudrama profiles Catherine Dunbar and her seven-year battle with anorexia nervosa. Based on the story told by her mother and her own diaries, the program traces Catherine's decline from the age of 15, when she became obsessed by her weight, became addicted to laxatives, and eventually died weighing only 40 pounds.

AV: Bulimia (12 min., CRM)

This film describes the binge–purge cycles and the motivations associated with bulimia, which is estimated to affect 30 percent of college women. Several victims of this eating disorder, including Jane Fonda, are interviewed. Treatment is also discussed.

Critical Thinking Activity: Eating Disorders on the Internet

The second critical thinking activity in this unit asks students to use the resources of the Internet to learn more about the eating disorders anorexia nervosa and bulimia nervosa. Handout 7 includes several questions to help students focus their research.

There are no "right" or "wrong" answers. Answers will vary depending on which aspects of anorexia and bulimia your students chose to research.

The Transformations of Puberty

AV: Adolescence: Current Issues (2 segments, 32 and 24 min., Child Development Media)

This two-part series offers a realistic look at the challenges facing teenagers today. Part 1 examines the challenges of pregnancy, sexually transmitted diseases, sexual abuse, and alcohol and substance abuse. Part 2, which examines the subjects of depression, suicide, delinquency, violence, runaways, and dropouts, may be more appropriate for the discussion of psychosocial development during adolescence.

AV: Teen Challenges (30 min, RMI Media Productions)

This program presents experts' and teenagers' views of teenage pregnancy, eating disorders, and other problems often faced by adolescents.

Classroom Activity: The Growth Spurt and Height Potential

At the beginning of puberty, many young people want to know whether they will be short or tall like one of their parents or closer in height to their grandparents. The answer is that their adult height will probably fall somewhere in between that of their parents. This rough estimate assumes that there is no disease or hormonal problem to hinder the individual's genetic potential. X-rays of the gaps, or *epiphyses,* between the ends of bones are often used to determine if there is a condition that would prevent further growth. As a child develops, the epiphyses shrink. Once the growth spurt is complete, the bones are fused, and no more growth takes place.

One frequently used rule of thumb is to add the heights of both parents together, divide by two, then add three inches for a boy or subtract three inches for a girl. The result is said to be correct within 2 inches about 95 percent of the time. (Your students may find it fun to call home for their parents' actual heights in inches to test the accuracy of this formula on their own stature.) Most often, however, doctors rely on normative growth charts derived from thousands of children. Because people tend to stay in the same 10 percent of all boys or girls of a given age, a doctor can estimate their eventual height based on their current percentile ranking.

Ray, C. C. (1999, February 16). Growth potential. *New York Times.* Retrieved from www.nytimes.com.

Teaching Tip: The Experience of Puberty in the Opposite Sex

To help your students understand the experience of puberty in the opposite sex, divide the class by gender and ask each group to think of two kinds of questions. The first should involve aspects of their sexual development (e.g., age of fertility, development of secondary sex characteristics) that the group thinks members of the opposite sex might not know. The second should involve aspects of sexual development in the opposite sex that they do not fully understand and would like to have clarified. After the questions have been compiled, a spokesperson for each group can present them to the other group.

AV: Teenage Pregnancy (26 min., Films for the Humanities and Sciences)

This brief, award-winning film follows several teenagers through the births of their children and early days of parenthood. It provides a sobering look at how teenage pregnancy dramatically changes lives and limits options.

AV: Male Rape (42 min., Films for the Humanities and Sciences)

Produced by the BBC, this documentary explores sex abuse against males. Members of "Survivors," a counseling support group for men who have been sexually abused, discuss how the fear of being labeled homosexual prevents many victims from disclosing their victimization.

Classroom Activity: Acquaintance Rape

In relation to the text discussion of early sexual activity, you might expand on the point that it is often unwanted, coercive, and a form of sexual abuse. You might encourage the class to discuss two topics of special concern to adolescents today: acquaintance rape (rape committed by someone known to the victim, such as a classmate or co-worker) and date rape. Perhaps because survivors may not perceive a sexual assault by someone they know as an actual rape, acquaintance rapes are more likely than stranger rapes to go unreported. Even when acquaintance rapes are reported, they are far too often dismissed as "misunderstandings" rather than being considered violent felonies. This tragedy reflects the common misconception that the typical rape involves a stranger and a woman who happens to be in the wrong place at the wrong time.

Date rape is a type of acquaintance rape. It is estimated that between 10 and 20 percent of women are forcibly raped by men they are dating. Even more remarkable is that most date rapes don't occur on blind dates but on dates with men known to the victims by nearly a year on average. One college survey found that rapes are likely to occur after a bout of heavy drinking.

Why do men rape women they know, ignoring their protests and using force to overcome their resistance? After posing this question to the class, you might discuss several of the most frequently offered explanations. Some data suggest that male sexism may partly be to blame. After reading an acquaintance rape scenario, male students who scored high on measures of sexism were more likely to blame the victim *and* showed a greater proclivity to commit acquaintance rape themselves (Abrams, Viki, Masser, & Bohner, 2003). Some date rapists wrongly believe that a woman should reciprocate with sex after a certain period of dating and being treated nicely. Others wrongly assume that women who are "picked up" at singles bars are indicating their willingness to have sex simply by being in such establishments. Still others believe that women who resist their advances are merely being coy and playing the "battle of the sexes" so as not to look "easy." They may believe that when their date says "no," she really means "maybe," and when she says "maybe," she really means "yes." Although it may seem hard to believe, men such as these actually do not see themselves as rapists. Consider Jim's story:

> I first met her at a party. She looked really hot, wearing a sexy dress that showed off her great body. We started talking right away. I knew that she liked me by the way she kept smiling and touching my arm while she was speaking. She seemed pretty relaxed so I asked her back to my place for a drink. When she said yes, I knew that I was going to be lucky! When we got to my place, we sat on the bed kissing. At first, everything was great. Then, when I started to lay her down on the bed, she started twisting and saying she didn't want to. Most women don't like to appear too easy, so I knew that she was just going through the motions. When she stopped struggling, I knew that she would have to throw in some tears before we did it. She was still very upset afterwards, and I just don't understand it! If she didn't want to have sex, why did she come back to the room with me? You could tell by the way she dressed and acted

that she was no virgin, so why did she have to put up such a big struggle? I don't know.

Ann, Jim's victim, describes the date very differently:

I first met him at a party. He was really good looking and he had a great smile. I wanted to meet him but I wasn't sure how. I didn't want to appear too forward. Then he came over and introduced himself. We talked and found we had a lot in common. I really liked him. When he asked me over to his place for a drink, I thought it would be OK. He was such a good listener, and I wanted him to ask me out again. When we got to his room, the only place to sit was on the bed. I didn't want him to get the wrong idea, but what else could I do? We talked for awhile and then he made his move. I was so startled. He started by kissing. I really liked him so the kissing was nice. But then he pushed me down on the bed. I tried to get up and I told him to stop. He was so much bigger and stronger. I got scared and I started to cry. I froze and he raped me. It took only a couple of minutes and it was terrible, he was so rough. When it was over he kept asking me what was wrong, like he didn't know. He had just forced himself on me and he thought that was OK.

As this case illustrates, many rapists appear to be perfectly ordinary people, except for their sexual violence. The ordinariness of acquaintance and date rape begs an obvious question to pose to your students: What is society doing to its sons to breed so many violent sexual predators? Many developmental psychologists and sociologists believe the answer is that young men are traditionally socialized from an early age to be aggressive and competitive. As such, some may come to see a date as a competitive event. One college student summarized his view on dating in the following manner:

A man is supposed to view a date with a woman as a premeditated scheme for getting the most sex out of her. Everything he does, he judges in terms of one criterion—"getting laid." He's supposed to constantly pressure her to see how far he can get. She is his adversary, his opponent in a battle, and he begins to view her as a prize, an object, not a person. While she's dreaming about love, he's thinking about how to conquer her.

Some experts have suggested that competitive sports may encourage violent sexual behavior. When coaches urge young football and hockey players to "do whatever it takes to win," even if it means "taking out the opposition," is there a danger that the players may generalize this philosophy from the playing field into social relationships? Statistical evidence would tend to suggest that the danger is, in fact, quite real. A disproportionate number of acquaintance rapes are committed by student athletes, including gang rapes committed by teammates.

To conclude the discussion on a constructive note, ask the class to brainstorm primary prevention strategies to socialize adolescent boys to be more respectful of girls and women. What specific strategies could be used in the home? The classroom? The locker room? How can parents, teachers, and coaches help make young men more aware of the boundaries between sexual consent and coercion? A growing body of research is demonstrating the efficacy of rape-prevention education programs with college students. In one such study, focus groups and interviews were used to explore college students' experiences during a semester-long rape prevention program at San Jose State University. Paralleling similar findings with programs for preventing bullying in schools (see Middle Childhood: Psychosocial Development), the researchers concluded that promoting greater consciousness among students was a crucial step in dismantling a campus "rape supportive culture" and in triggering healthier, violence-free cognitive, emotional, and behavior changes.

Abrams, D., Viki, G. T., Masser, B., & Bohner, G. (2003). Perceptions of stranger and acquaintance rape: The role of benevolent and hostile sexism in victim blame and rape proclivity. *Journal of Personality and Social Psychology, 84*(1), 111–125.

Freeman, M. (2002, August 25). Simply no end in sight to these transgressions. *New York Times*, p. 8.13.

Klaw, E. L., Lonsway, K. A., Berg, D. R., Waldo, C. R., Kothari, C., Mazurek, C. J., & Hegeman, K. E. (2005). Challenging rape culture: Awareness, emotion and action through campus acquaintance rape education. *Women and Therapy, 28*(2), 47–63.

HANDOUT 1

Developmental Fact or Myth?

T F 1. Although the sequence of puberty is variable, the age of onset is not.

T F 2. Adolescence is an emotional time for most teenagers.

T F 3. The level of stress in a child's family can influence the onset of puberty.

T F 4. Girls and boys who mature earlier or later than their friends have a difficult time adjusting to puberty.

T F 5. More girls than boys take steroids.

T F 6. Many adolescents do not consume enough calcium to prevent osteoporosis in adulthood.

T F 7. Physical growth in puberty proceeds from the core of the body to the extremities.

T F 8. One reason adolescents like excitement is that the brain's limbic system matures before the prefrontal cortex.

T F 9. Adolescent pregnancy correlates with birth complications.

T F 10. Sexual abuse in the United States happens most often to children 8 to 11 years old.

HANDOUT 2

Observational Activity: Adolescence Now and Then: Interview Outline

You are to interview someone who is over 70 years of age—a relative or friend—in an attempt to gain an understanding of how the concept and the experience of adolescence have changed over time.

Keep the interview friendly and informal. It should last no more than 20 minutes, depending on your subject and how much he or she is enjoying the interview. Begin the interview by identifying yourself and your purpose (a course assignment in studying historical changes in adolescence) and by assuring your subject that his or her responses will remain confidential. Here is a list of suggested questions to ask during the interview. You may add questions of your own if you wish.*

1. Did you attend high school? Did you want to? What kinds of subjects did you study? What kinds of homework did you get? Did most of the adolescents in your neighborhood go to high school?
2. How many hours per week did you work (not including school-related work)? How much did you contribute to the family income? Did you want to go to work?
3. Did you get along with your parents when you were a teenager? What kinds of restrictions or rules did your parents place on your behavior?
4. What were your clothes like? Were you concerned about fashion?
5. Did you date in high school? At what age were you allowed to date? What did you typically do on a date?
6. How did you and your friends spend your free time?
7. What was your most nagging problem as a teenager?
8. What do you see as the main difference between the teenagers of today and yourself as a teenager? What do you think of today's teenagers?

*This activity and the suggested interview questions were taken from the following article: Schwanenflugel, P. J. (1987, October). An interview method for teaching adolescent psychology. *Teaching of Psychology*, *14*(3), 167–168.

HANDOUT 3

Observational Activity: Adolescence Now and Then: Follow-Up Report

Based on the interview, prepare a written report summarizing what you learned from your subject's responses. Include your subject's sex, age (but not name), and any other pertinent demographic information. The main body of your report should focus on comparing and contrasting your subject's experiences as an adolescent with those of the "typical adolescent" today. Consider the following questions in your report: What was adolescence like then? How did it differ from adolescence today? In what ways is the "adolescent experience" the same now as it was then? Feel free to offer your own interpretation of your subject's responses, including comments on how you might have answered the questions.

Subject: age ____________ ethnic/religious background ____________

sex ____________ education level ____________

HANDOUT 4

Critical Thinking Activity: Early and Late Maturation

*Now that you have read and reviewed the material on physical development during puberty, take your learning a step further by testing your critical thinking skills on this creative problem-solving exercise.**

The physical changes of puberty have a profound effect on our self-images. Most people are able to remember at least one event, attitude, misconception, or worry they experienced in connection with the physical changes of puberty: having had big feet; having been the first or the last to experience menarche; having been concerned about having a small penis; having worried about acne or voice change. The young people who have the most difficulty are those who must adjust to these changes earlier or later than the majority of their peers. Early or late maturation may be difficult because one of the things an adolescent does not want to do is stand out from the crowd in a way that is not admirable.

To help you reason about your own adolescent body image, as well as its impact on your development, this exercise requires you to think back to your physical appearance when you were in the middle of puberty, probably age 13 or 14 and in about eighth grade.

1. What did you (or your friends and parents) consider your "best feature"? What was your "worst feature"—the aspect of your appearance that you felt required the most care or upgrading?

2. Compared to your classmates and friends, were you an average-maturing, early-maturing, or late-maturing individual? What impact do you feel the timing of your puberty had on you at the time?

3. How did the timing of your puberty affect who you are today?

HANDOUT 4 *(continued)*

4. Do the ideas you had about your physical appearance reflect your current body image? Why or why not (or to what extent)?

5. What words of advice concerning body image would you offer to your future or actual child at puberty?

*Adapted from Straub, R. O. (2004). *Seasons of life study guide* (5th ed.). New York: Worth.

HANDOUT 5

Evaluating Dietary Macronutrients

To see how well your eating habits are meeting your nutritional needs, complete the chart below for a typical 24-hour period. Also note the calories and macronutrient breakdown (grams of fat, protein, and carbohydrates) consumed in each food serving. Most packaged foods have all the nutritional information you need right on the label, in the Nutrition Facts box. For foods that don't have such labels, consult a nutritional reference guide such as *The NutriBase Nutrition Facts Desk Reference.*

When you have entered all the macronutrient data, determine the ratio of fat to protein to carbohydrates by dividing the number of calories in each macronutrient category by the total calories consumed. Fats are the densest sources of food energy: one gram provides nine calories of food energy, compared with four calories for each gram of carbohydrate or protein. For example, suppose your total of 2,500 calories breaks down as follows: 156.0 grams (624 calories) protein, 344.0 grams (1,376 calories) carbohydrates, and 56.0 grams (504 calories) fat. This results in a macronutrient ration of 20:25:55, or 20 percent fat (500/2,500), 25 percent protein (625/2,500), and 55 percent carbohydrates (1,375/2,500).

Food	Serving Size	Calories	Protein (Grams)	Carbohydrates (Grams)	Fat (Grams)

HANDOUT 6

Survey of Eating Habits

For each statement, circle "T" or "F" to indicate whether it is true or false, as applied to you.

Part I. Past Attitudes and Habits

T F 1. My family seldom argued at the dinner table.

T F 2. Many different types of meals were served at our house.

T F 3. I did not particularly care for the food served at home.

T F 4. My mother was a good cook.

T F 5. Our family seemed to be in a better disposition at and shortly after meals than before.

T F 6. My mother enjoyed cooking.

T F 7. Meals were simple but substantial in our family.

T F 8. My mother served desserts frequently.

T F 9. Discipline was usually enforced shortly before or after the evening meal.

T F 10. Mealtimes were quite unhurried; in fact, they took on the aspect of a social activity.

T F 11. My father enjoyed eating.

T F 12. I enjoyed eating.

T F 13. Younger members of the family were requested not to talk too much at meals.

T F 14. My family often celebrated something important by going to a restaurant.

T F 15. Less than an average amount of conversation occurred at mealtime in my family.

T F 16. My father tended to dampen mealtime conversation.

T F 17. Conversation at meals was more light than serious.

T F 18. Business matters were often discussed at meals (chores, etc.).

T F 19. Flowers or candles were sometimes placed on the table at evening meals.

T F 20. Sometimes my mother would give me my favorite food when I was sick or unhappy.

T F 21. My mother used to take special precautions to avoid giving us contaminated food.

T F 22. The emphasis was on nutritional meals in our family.

T F 23. My mother liked cooking least of all household chores.

T F 24. Meals were quite elaborate in our family.

T F 25. Individuals other than my immediate family, such as grandparents, usually participated in the evening meal.

T F 26. Following the main meal, I tended to linger about the table talking and so on, rather than leaving the table.

HANDOUT 6 *(continued)*

T F 27. My mother enjoyed eating.
T F 28. Sometimes I felt like leaving the table before the meal was over.
T F 29. My mother fixed my favorite foods when I was sick.
T F 30. At restaurants everything I ordered had to be eaten.
T F 31. Eating out was infrequent.
T F 32. The entire family was usually present at the evening meal.
T F 33. On my birthdays I helped plan the menu.
T F 34. My mother tended to dampen mealtime conversation.
T F 35. Discipline was often applied at mealtime.
T F 36. Family meals were more hurried than unhurried.
T F 37. My father sometimes scolded us at the evening meal.
T F 38. At breakfast, I often read what was printed on the cereal boxes.

Part II. Present Attitudes and Habits

T F 39. Mealtime is usually pleasant in my home.
T F 40. I like to smell food cooking.
T F 41. In general, I prefer a slow, leisurely meal to a quick, hurried one.
T F 42. I like many different types of food.
T F 43. I tend to be underweight.
T F 44. At a party, I tend to eat a lot of peanuts.
T F 45. I do not care much for desserts.
T F 46. I seldom like to try a new food.
T F 47. I often get indigestion or heartburn.
T F 48. If I am very busy, I may forget all about eating.
T F 49. Shopping for groceries is unpleasant.
T F 50. I like to eat foreign foods.
T F 51. A good wife must be a good cook.
T F 52. I think that going to an expensive restaurant is a good way to celebrate an important event such as an anniversary, a birthday, etc.
T F 53. I have a tendency to gain weight.
T F 54. Sometimes I have a craving for sweets.
T F 55. I tend to be quiet rather than talkative.
T F 56. If a child refuses dinner, he should be made to eat.
T F 57. I almost never eat between meals.
T F 58. I dislike many foods.
T F 59. I enjoy eating at restaurants.
T F 60. I often eat while I am watching television.
T F 61. Watching people eat makes me hungry.
T F 62. People who eat heartily in public have bad manners.
T F 63. I often buy refreshments at movies, ball games, etc.
T F 64. I sometimes reward myself by eating.
T F 65. When depressed I sometimes eat my favorite foods.

Source: Byrne, D., & Kelley, K. (1981). *An introduction to personality* (3rd ed., 135–136). Englewood Cliffs, NJ: Prentice Hall.

HANDOUT 7

Critical Thinking Activity: Eating Disorders on the Internet

Now that you have read and reviewed all the material on biosocial development during adolescence, take your learning a step further by testing your critical thinking skills on this problem-solving exercise.

In this exercise, you will examine the eating disorders anorexia nervosa and bulimia nervosa, including the symptoms, treatment options, and latest research findings that are unlocking the mysteries of these disorders. You will also be introduced to the *Internet Mental Health* Web site, one of the most authoritative sources of information on psychological disorders. The home page can be found at www.mentalhealth.com/p20-grp.html. Don't limit your exploration to this site, however; rather, use it as a starting point in your investigation to find answers to the following questions.

1. Briefly summarize the online diagnosis criteria for either anorexia nervosa or bulimia nervosa.

2. Given the many developmental contexts of anorexia nervosa and bulimia nervosa, treatment must focus on the biosocial, cognitive, and psychosocial roots of these disorders. Briefly describe the treatment options available for either anorexia or bulimia. Which have proven to be most effective?

HANDOUT 7 *(continued)*

3. Using the Research section of the Web site, find out how the recovery rates differ for anorexia nervosa and bulimia nervosa.

4. Briefly summarize one article from the Magazine Articles section of the Web site.

Adolescence: Cognitive Development

Contents

Note: Worth Publishers provides online Instructor and Student Tool Kits, DVD Student Tool Kits, and Instructor and Student video resources in DevelopmentPortal for use with the text. See Part I: General Resources for information about these materials and the text Lecture Guides for a complete list by text chapter.

Teaching and Learning

Suggested Activities

Introducing Adolescence: Cognitive Development

"On Your Own" Activity: Developmental Fact or Myth?

Before students read about cognitive development during adolescence, have them respond to the true-false statements in the handout.

The correct answers are shown below. Class discussion can focus on the origins of any developmental misconceptions that are demonstrated in the students' incorrect answers.

1. T	6. T
2. F	7. F
3. T	8. F
4. T	9. T
5. T	10. T

AV: The Journey Through the Life Span, Program 6: Adolescence

See Adolescence: Biosocial Development for a description of Program 6 and the accompanying observation modules, which cover the entire unit on adolescence.

AV: Transitions Throughout the Life Span, Program 15: What If?

Program 15 begins by describing the cognitive advances of adolescence, especially the emerging ability to think in an adult way, that is, to be logical, to think in terms of possibilities, and to reason scientifically and abstractly. Kathleen Berger provides expert commentary on the characteristics of formal operational thinking.

Not everyone attains this level of reasoning ability, however, and even those who do so spend much of their time thinking at less advanced levels. For instance, adolescents have difficulty thinking rationally about themselves and their immediate experiences, often seeing themselves as psychologically unique and more socially significant than they really are. The first segment describes this adolescent egocentrism and its manifestation in the personal fable, invincibility fable, and sensitivity toward an imaginary audience.

The next segment asks the question, "What kind of school best fosters adolescent intellectual growth?" Many adolescents enter secondary school feeling less motivated and more vulnerable to self-doubt than they did in elementary school. The rigid behavioral demands and intensified competition of most secondary schools do not, unfortunately, provide a supportive learning environment for adolescents. Schools can avoid this "volatile mismatch" by becoming more effectively organized and setting clear, attainable educational goals that are supported by the entire staff.

The final segment focuses on adolescent thinking at work: decision making regarding sexual activity and other high-risk behaviors.

Classroom Activity: Case Study of an Adolescent

John McManus of Eastern Michigan University describes an effective classroom exercise in which the case-study method is used to help students understand the problems of adolescence.

McManus divides students into groups of four to seven. Each group picks an adolescent problem—delinquency, sexual dilemmas, peer relationships, or educational difficulties, for example—then composes a hypothetical case study that illustrates the topic in a manner that is both interesting and consistent with information presented in the text and class.

When the case study has been composed, the group must generate as many potential solutions as possible for the problem described. After discussing the various solutions, they rank them from most to least favorable (an activity almost guaranteed to generate heated discussion). Each group then selects one of its members to present the case study, and its "solutions," to the class.

An optional extension of the class exercise is for each group to designate several target groups—for example, parents, friends, clergy, persons from various ethnic or socioeconomic groups—and then present the case study to a small sample from one of the targeted groups, asking them to suggest a solution. When the group reconvenes, members should discuss and integrate their findings, then present the case study to the class.

McManus reports that students responded enthusiastically to the case-study assignment. One group, for example, proposed a case in which a "14-year-old female, Cindy, lives at home with her divorced mother; her father lives in another state. She is pressured to pose nude by her mother's photographer boyfriend. He tells Cindy she will be paid well and that her mother could really use some of the extra money. Cindy's dilemma involves a serious values conflict."

The group constructed a questionnaire and administered it to a cross section of people from 13 to 65 years of age. There were clear age-related differences in the responses. Respondents under the age of 20 thought Cindy should run away from home or seek help from her friends. Twenty- to 50-year-olds recommended that Cindy seek help from community agencies such as the school or mental-health counseling centers. The oldest respondents suggested that Cindy approach her own family—a parent or a close relative—for help.

Composing case studies of this type offers several pedagogical benefits, including stimulating students' creativity and critical thinking, enhancing class discussion, and integrating and applying core concepts. And, of course, it increases student interest in the course.

McManus, J. L. (1986, April). Student-composed case study in adolescent psychology. *Teaching of Psychology*, *13*, 92–93.

AV: Adolescence: A Case Study (20 min., CRM/ McGraw-Hill)

This film shows Angie, a 17-year-old junior in a large California high school—in math and literature classes, primping in front of a mirror, and in a group of girls flirting with a group of boys. All these scenes are used to elucidate adolescent cognitive development, from the hypothetical to the most egocentric. Given adolescent self-consciousness, some of the scenes appear too staged. However, the moments when Angie is asked to explain herself ("Who am I? Well, I'm a Gemini, so I change a lot, and my moon is in Pisces so I fall in love easily") authentically reflect the poignancy of adolescence. Angie is also idealistic and aware of her roots (her parents came from Mexico), characteristics typical of many adolescents.

John Flavell and Joseph Church comment on some of the cognitive developments highlighted by the film. Church makes the radical suggestion that adolescence is perhaps the worst time for formal education as high schools and colleges now offer it. This view could be used to start a discussion of the function of school for adolescents.

AV: Teens: What Makes Them Tick? (41 min., ABC News)

(See description in Adolescence: Biosocial Development.)

AV: A Day in the Life of a Teen (25 min., Insight Media)

This interesting film is one of a series depicting the world through the eyes of a toddler, a preschooler, a child, and a teenager. Throughout the film expert commentary provides a conceptual framework for understanding cognitive development through adolescence.

AV: Pressure-Cooked Kids (28 min., Films for the Humanities and Sciences)

This highly recommended film explores the escalating pressures faced by contemporary teenagers and what can be done to teach them how to handle stress in their early years so that they can better cope when they are adults.

Teaching Tip: Revise and Resubmit

Andrew Johnson and his colleagues at Park University (2011) wondered whether certain types of student assessments more accurately predicted final grades than others. They explored this issue with two sections of students enrolled in introductory psychology, whose course assessments included a pre-post myth quiz (2% of final grade), four multiple-choice exams (48% of grade), a major position paper (23% of grade), and 16 chapter essay questions (25% of final grade). Interestingly, the answers to the chapter essay questions were scored using an artificially intelligent network-model application (SAGrader) that permitted the students to submit an unlimited number of revisions to their answers until they were satisfied with their grade on this component of the course.

The results demonstrated written essays are an important part of teaching and learning, even in large, lecture-based courses. More specifically, the written assignment that permitted students an unlimited number of revisions was the single best predictor of the final grade despite the fact that exams represented nearly twice as many points. The researchers suggest that while the opportunity for unlimited revisions creates a heavy burden for the instructor (the 56 students in the study submitted a total of 2,508 essay responses to the 16 questions!), it also introduced motivational and self-regulation components that powerfully influenced student performance. Most importantly, the opportunity to "revise and resubmit" improved students' essay scores 39.7 percent!

Johnson, A., Smyers, J., & Cowley, B. J. (2011). *Final grade predictors.* National Institute on the Teaching of Psychology,. St. Petersburg, FL.

Adolescent Thinking

Egocentrism

Classroom Activity: Adolescent Egocentrism

To broaden your students' understanding of adolescent egocentrism, you might introduce the "foundling fable," in which young people imagine that they are the offspring not of their actual parents but of much wiser and more beautiful people who were forced to give them up. This fable appeals to children and adults as well as to adolescents. Children's fairy tales and adult soap operas (as well as more serious works) often incorporate tales of people who discover their "real" parents.

You might discuss reasons behind the foundling fable's special appeal for adolescents, who (as we shall see) are wrestling with identity problems as well as with problems of physical appearance and body image (inherited physical characteristics). Why, for example, do adopted children, who have a legitimate need to discover their biological parents, become more interested in doing so upon reaching adolescence?

Formal Operational Thought

AV: Teenage Mind and Body (30 min., Insight Media)

(See description in Adolescence: Biosocial Development.)

AV: Adolescent Cognition: Thinking in a New Way (30 min., Insight Media)

Hosted by David Elkind, this video uses the theories of Piaget, Erikson, and Goffman to discuss the changes in cognition that occur during adolescence.

Classroom Activity: Adolescent Logic

To help students understand the logical thinking of adolescents, you might present the following tests for the presence of formal operational thought.

1. Construct a simple pendulum (a weight attached to a string that has been tied to a rod). Provide students with varying weights and lengths of string, and tell them that they can push the weight with varying degrees of force and begin the swing of the pendulum at varying heights. Then ask them which factors influence the number of swings the pendulum makes per minute. (Only the length of the string does, but individuals whose thinking has not yet progressed beyond the concrete operational level have a great deal of trouble figuring this out.)
2. Describe one of Piaget's reasoning tasks and ask students how they would figure it out. For example, suppose there are four bottles, each containing a colorless liquid, and a fifth bottle, also containing a liquid that is colorless. Mixing this fifth liquid with one or more of the liquids in the other bottles is supposed to produce a yellow liquid. How do they do it? (Individuals who use formal operational thought begin with a system; they do not rely on trial and error. They first determine how many single bottles they will try [4], then all the combinations of two [6], and so forth.)

Classroom Activity: Logical Versus Practical Intelligence

During adolescence, formal operational thought—reflected in scientific reasoning, logical construction of arguments, and critical thinking—first becomes possible. Not all problems encountered by adolescents and adults require formal thinking, however. And while many adolescents and adults are capable of thinking logically, they do not always do so. Indeed, older adults and experts in a field often find that a formal approach to solving problems is unsatisfactory and oversimplified.

Yale psychologist Robert Sternberg believes that a new kind of "practical intelligence" begins to emerge during late adolescence. This type of thinking is more applicable to everyday situations than formal thought is because it recognizes that many problems have no single correct answer and that "logical" answers are often impractical. Some developmentalists believe that this new way of thinking reflects the greater cognitive maturity of older adolescents in reconciling formal thought with the reality of their lives.

The following problems are designed to stimulate your students' thinking about the difference between formal thought and practical intelligence. For each problem, ask your students to think of the "logically correct" answer and a more "practical" answer. Examples of "logical" and "practical" answers are given following each problem.

1. Imagine two environmental settings for five houses of equal size. In one, representing a town, the houses are clustered in one corner of a one-acre field. In another, representing the country, the houses are scattered about the one-acre field. Would the spatial arrangement of the houses affect the amount of grass that has to be mowed? Would there be more grass to cut in the "town" or in the "country"?

   (a) What is the *logically* correct answer to this question?

   Answer: Because the spatial arrangement of the five houses does not alter the area of the field they cover, the amount of grass to mow would be the same in the town and the country.

   (b) Are there *practical* reasons that might lead one to think differently about this question? What are they?

   Answer: Mowing would be harder and take more time if the arrangement of the houses left many small spaces between them. Thus, it would require less time to mow the grass in the "country," making it seem as though there were less grass to cut than in the "town."

2. Consider the following domestic scene: "Downstairs, there are three rooms: the kitchen, the dining room, and the sitting room. The sitting room is in the front of the house, and the kitchen and dining room face onto the vegetable garden at the back of the house. The noise of the traffic is very disturbing in the front room. Mother is in the kitchen and Grandfather is reading the paper in the sitting room. The children are at school and won't be home until teatime. Who is being disturbed by the traffic noise?" (Labouvie-Vief, 1991)

   (a) What is the logical answer to this question?

   Answer: The logical relationships embedded in the passage—that the noise is most disturbing in the front room, that the sitting room is in the front, and that the grandfather is in the sitting room—suggest that the "correct" answer is the grandfather. Researchers have found that younger students almost always give this logically correct answer.

   (b) Are there practical considerations that might lead one to answer this question differently? If so, what are they?

   Answer: Older adolescents often perceive logical relationships other than those of interest to the experimenter and so answer differently. For example, some might reason that the grandfather could not possibly have been disturbed by the noise, as he would not have chosen to continue reading in a noisy room. Others may reply that the grandfather might have been hard of hearing, or that the noise was not very disruptive at that particular moment.

Labouvie-Vief, G. (1991). Intelligence and cognition. In J. E. Birren & K. W. Schaie (Eds.), *Handbook of the psychology of aging* (3rd ed.). New York: Van Nostrand Reinhold.

Straub, R. O. (2004). *Seasons of life study guide* (5th ed.). New York: Worth.

AV: Formal Thought (32 min., Davidson Films)

Adolescents are seen demonstrating logical and systematic procedures as they grapple with various tests of formal operational thought. For many classes, watching this film will bring home the fact that not all adults can master these problems as well as some of the brighter adolescents can.

"On Your Own" Activity: Formal Operational Thought: Test Yourself

To help students understand the difference between concrete operational thought and the formal operational thought that becomes possible in adolescence, you might suggest that students look closely at the kinds of intellectual tasks they are asked to perform in school. One way of doing this is to examine test questions: Some call for simple recall, others for synthesis, and others for scientific reasoning, logical conclusions, critical thinking, or the construction of an argument. Have students use Handout 2 to guide their responses.

Students who can easily distinguish between questions that require formal operational thought and those that cannot probably know how to answer the more demanding questions. The fact that not all students are comfortable with questions requiring formal operational thought supports the finding that not all adolescents (or adults) reach this level of cognitive maturity or are able to perform at this level consistently.

In responding to the last two items on the handout, some students will indicate problems with learning (remembering) details and large chunks of information; others will note problems with reasoning, criticizing, and drawing conclusions. Answers should help students to determine whether any difficulties they experience result from incomplete mastery of formal operational thought or from other problems such as poor study habits or low motivation.

If you wish to explore this subject in greater detail, you might examine graduate-level tests such as the MCAT for prospective medical students; these will provide good examples of questions requiring scientific reasoning and other thinking at the formal operational level.

AV: Adolescence: Cognitive and Moral Development (30 min., Child Development Media)

This video describes the changes in adolescent thinking and moral reasoning that accompany puberty. Among these are increasingly sophisticated logical and abstract reasoning abilities, limited by adolescent egocentrism. The video also touches on adolescents' receptivity to their culture, including the models they see at home, in school, and in the media.

Intuitive, Emotional Thought

Classroom Activity: A Virtual Reality Without Adults

In every era, teenagers have created their own private worlds in which to explore their newfound freedom, thinking skills, and emerging identities. For successive generations, this world centered around the music of rock-and-roll, heavy metal, punk, and rap. Although this rite of passage is not inevitably the "storm and stress" struggle that G. Stanley Hall believed it inevitably to be, adolescence is still full of risk. If "old-fogyism" doesn't bother you too much, a sure-fire technique for getting a good class discussion going is your personal version of the "When-I-was-a-teenager, my-parents-were-most-worried-that-I-would-fall-under-the-influence" story. Ask them whether the pop-culture influences on teenagers' minds are potentially more hazardous today, or whether this common belief is yet another example of generational forgetting.

Some experts believe the entertainment and information threats to adolescents are much more dangerous today than ever before. The new entertainment technologies threaten to make teenagers more deeply isolated from adults than ever before. MTV, the Internet, ever-more graphic video games, and no-holds-barred music are combining to create what one researcher has called "almost a virtual reality without adults." The booming computer video game business has many psychologists concerned. One of the most popular genres, known as a "first person shooter" game, or FPS, is exemplified by such games as Team Fortress, Battlefield, Call of Duty, Counter-Strike, and Doom, which was reportedly the favorite of the Columbine High School shooters. The ad for one of the games proudly promises "multiplayer gang bang death match for up to 16 thugs! Target specific body parts and actually see the damage done, including exit wounds."

Although most teenagers may not be overly influenced by the mindless violence of such games, a vulnerable minority are. And, if a teen is predisposed to violence and aggression, violent games and Internet chatrooms give them the opportunity to meet like-minded people who will validate their experience. Over time, the at-risk teen may become increasingly isolated from family and friends, as group polarization and other social dynamics work their effects on group members. Some experts argue that violent computer games and Web sites are much more harmful than movies because the viewer takes an active role. This is especially true in FPS games, in which the player becomes the aggressor. In New York, mounting concern over this issue led the state senate to approve a 2008 bill that would take steps to crack down on video game violence. These steps include establishing an Advisory Council on Interactive Media and Youth Violence, requiring that every video game sold have a clearly displayed violence rating indication, and requiring that all game consoles be equipped with parental controls.

This issue of parental perspective on content worries many experts as much as or more than the content of the information to which teens are exposed. As noted in the text, the typical teen's skills for evaluating information and thinking critically about potentially hazardous activities are still emerging, if not downright faulty. To counteract these forces, many psychologists recommend strategies that go beyond setting limits on which Web sites can be visited and which games can be played. One is to put the computer in a family room, where teens and adults have more opportunities to interact in the flow of information into the home. Another is for parents to play the video games along with their children, even if they are distasteful. Finally, parents should simply talk more to their teens about what they are watching and listening to. For example, they might say, "I don't understand this game. What is the objective?" Or "Who is this rapper Nas? What is he saying?"

Senate passes legislation to crack down on video game violence.(2008, July 7). *United States Federal News Service.* Washington, DC. Retrieved from http://0-proquest.umi.com.wizard.umd.umich.edu/pqdlink?Ver=1&Exp=10-26-2013&FMT=7&DID=1513147711&RQT=309.

Leland, J. (1999, May 10). The secret life of teens. *Newsweek*, pp. 45–50.

Teaching and Learning

AV: Education in America (three videos, 16–30 min., Insight Media)

This series of three videos discusses the evolution of education in America. Focusing on the seventeenth and eighteenth centuries, Part 1 (16 min.) takes the viewer to actual locations of dame schools, Latin grammar schools, church schools, and pauper schools. Focusing on the nineteenth century, Part 2 (16 min.) discusses the development of free public school systems. It also highlights the change to secular education, the rise of teacher education schools, and the influence of American textbooks. Focusing on developments during the first half of the twentieth century, Part 3 (30 min.) discusses the effects of the industrial revolution on education, the appearance of the junior high school, and the modern testing movement.

AV: The Middle School (30 min., Insight Media)

Using classroom visits and interviews with leading educators, this video explores why middle schools were created and the key features of successful middle school programs.

AV: American Schools: Catching Up to the Future (30 min., Insight Media)

This video probes the perennial question of what's wrong with American education. Willard Daggett discusses his belief that American schools need to be more skill-based in order to prepare students for success in today's information-based, high-tech society.

AV: Restoring Respect and Responsibility in Our Schools (44 min., Magna Films)

Profiling the work of Thomas Lickona, a leader in the Character Education Movement, this video provides a compelling argument for the role of schools in the development of student respect and responsibility. The program outlines specific classroom strategies and schoolwide curricula for creating a healthier climate in today's schools.

AV: Social-Cultural Diversity (30 min., Insight Media)

(See description in Theories of Development.)

AV: Dealing with Diversity in the Classroom (23 min., Insight Media)

This short program analyzes the diverse population of students in today's classroom. It examines how educational goals have shifted from "melting pot" assimilation to cultural pluralism and explains how teachers organize culturally diverse classrooms in order to make all students feel welcome.

AV: Going to School in Japan (24 min., Insight Media)

(See description in Middle Childhood: Cognitive Development.)

AV: Inside Britain: Education (20 min., Insight Media)

This brief film explores the history and evolution of the British educational system and provides another interesting cross-cultural contrast to education in the United States.

Classroom Activity: Problem-Based Learning: Design a Better High School

The Introduction's Classroom Activity: Introducing Problem-Based Learning describes this relatively new pedagogical tool. Following is a sample problem that you might want to give to your students as part of your coverage of cognitive development during adolescence.

> In middle school, grades usually fall because teachers mark more harshly and students become less conscientious.
>
> A good, problem-based exercise for the unit on adolescence is to have your students use the text, along with research literature and your classroom discussions, to design the ideal high school. This "perfect" high school should be one that is optimized to meet the cognitive, social, physical, and emotional needs of adolescents between the ages of 15 and 18. To promote cooperative learning, you might require that students research the topic individually, and then follow-up by dividing the class into groups of three to five students for discussion and the preparation of a final oral or collectively written report.
>
> Before sending the students off on their assignment, you might take some class time to generate critical questions the school design must address in each area of need. For example, under the category of cognitive needs questions such as these might be addressed: "How long are class periods? Is schooling year-round? Will there be high-stakes testing? Under the categories of social and emotional needs, encourage the students to add questions to this list: "Should there be a dress code? Is sex education required? Are any classes segregated by gender?"
>
> Based on the decisions your group makes today, you should devise a plan for researching the various issues. Two weeks from today's class, your group will present an answer for Seth based on the issues you think are relevant.

Classroom Activity: High-Stakes Testing: Are the SAT Reasoning Test and ACT Useful?

As an extension of the text discussion of the rigid behavioral demands and inappropriate academic standards, you might lead a discussion of high-stakes testing: the SAT Reasoning Test or ACT that students must take to gain admittance to college. College admissions officers downplay the significance of these standardized tests in the application process, teachers complain that the tests are irrelevant to the high school curriculum, and students and their parents say the entire process is too stressful. But each group continues the tradition: teachers devote class time to drills on SAT-type questions, admissions officers proudly point to their schools' increasing average scores, and parents shell out large sums of money on preparation courses. More than half of all test-takers take the SAT or ACT twice (38 percent take it three times or more), and Kaplan, Inc.—the oldest test-preparation company—estimates the business as a $250-million industry. More high school students in the class of 2010 (about 1.6 million) took the SAT than in any other graduating class in history (College Board, 2011). Another 1.57 million took the ACT (ACT News, 2011). Critics of such high-stakes tests point to the original claims that the tests measured innate intelligence. Although the College Board, which was founded in 1900 and administers both tests, no longer makes such claims, the perception that the tests are IQ tests persists. In response, the Board has changed the name of the SAT several times, from its original Scholastic Aptitude Test to Scholastic Assessment Test to the SAT to the SAT Reasoning Test, as it is called today.

Critics also charge that the tests have consistently favored affluent white students, especially males. Among the groups of students hurt the most by high-stakes testing have been African American and Latino students, who historically have been among the lowest-scoring groups and are underrepresented in colleges. Low socioeconomic status also predicts lower scores on such tests, which may be doubly discriminatory since the ACT and SAT are often used to award scholarships.

Perhaps most damaging to the tests' reputations is the fact that countless studies have questioned the tests' ability to predict freshman grade-point averages.

SAT Press Room (2011). *Course-taking patterns and academic intensity influence SAT performance*. Retrieved February 20, 2011, from http://press.collegeboard.org/sat.

ACT News (2011). *Facts about the ACT.* Retrieved February 20, 2011, from www.act.org/news/aapfacts.html.

AV: Shortchanging Girls, Shortchanging America (19 min., Insight Media)

Through interviews with educators, business executives, and developmentalists, this program explores the devastating effects of gender bias in American education. The program focuses specifically on the loss of self-esteem among girls and illustrates how they often are steered away from science and math curricular tracks.

Critical Thinking Activity: Is Tracking Effective?

Each unit of these resources contains at least one critical thinking exercise designed specifically to test students' critical thinking about a topic covered in the text. Handout 3 asks students to design an experiment to determine whether tracking is effective.

The answers to this unit's critical thinking activity follow:

1. A viable hypothesis for this experiment would be that the separation of students into tracks based on achievement scores leads to gains in academic performance.
2. The independent variable in an experiment is the factor that is manipulated by the researcher to test the hypothesis. In this case, it would be assigning students to tracks.
3. You would likely use standardized tests to track about half the volunteers and leave the other half untracked. Alternatively, you could randomly assign half of them to the proper track and the other half to a track higher or lower (again randomly) than their scores indicate.
4. The dependent variable in an experiment is always the one that, according to your hypothesis, might be affected by the independent variable. In this case, academic performance after a year or so of your special assignments seems a good choice.
5. You would test the students, assign them to classes, and then retest them.
6. Ideally, the two groups should differ only in the one independent variable—tracking, no tracking, or incorrect tracking. Any other variables that might affect the dependent variable you are measuring—here, academic performance—would need to be controlled. These include student motivation, ability (both the tracked and untracked groups should include a full range of abilities), initial achievement levels, study skills, age, and sex. The results should show whether or not one group (tracked, mistracked high, mistracked low, or not tracked) achieved more than the other.

HANDOUT 1

Developmental Fact or Myth?

T F 1. Teenagers tend to overestimate their significance to others.

T F 2. Unlike younger children, adolescents typically are *not* egocentric in their thought patterns.

T F 3. Adolescents often create an imaginary audience as they mentally picture how others will react to their behavior and physical appearance.

T F 4. Egocentrism may be a sign of cognitive maturity rather than irrational thought.

T F 5. Adolescents are able to reason about propositions that may or may not reflect reality, while younger children are still tied to concrete operational thinking.

T F 6. The brain has multiple pathways, not all used at once, for processing analytical thinking and intuitive thought.

T F 7. The organizational structure of most middle schools reflects current developmental research on the best educational system for teens.

T F 8. Engagement in school typically falls in each consecutive year of high school.

T F 9. While more U.S. schools are instituting high-stakes tests, East Asian nations are moving in the opposite direction.

T F 10. Strict punishments and installing metal detectors in high schools are likely to increase violence.

HANDOUT 2

Formal Operational Thought: Test Yourself

During adolescence, formal operational thought—including scientific reasoning, logical construction of arguments, and critical thinking—becomes possible. But not all intellectual tasks encountered by the adolescent or young adult require thinking at this level.

Consider the kinds of multiple-choice and essay questions you have been given this term. Collect questions that do not require formal operational thought and those that do. Bring them to class. If you cannot find actual examples, create your own in response to the questions below.

1. List two test questions that do not seem to require thinking at the formal operational level. (Identify by title and level the course from which they are taken.)

2. List two test questions that seem to require thinking at the formal operational level. (Identify by title and level the course from which they are taken.)

HANDOUT 2 *(continued)*

3. Describe, if you can, the kind of question that typically gives you the most trouble. Note whether or not this type of question requires thinking at the formal operational level.

4. What academic subject areas seem most difficult to you? Can you identify the main sources of difficulty?

HANDOUT 3

Critical Thinking Activity: Is Tracking Effective?

Now that you have read and reviewed the material on cognitive development during adolescence, take your learning a step further by testing your critical thinking skills on this scientific reasoning exercise.

In an effort to boost achievement, many schools employ tracking, in which students are separated into distinct groups based on standardized tests of ability and achievement. In theory, each class then contains students of about the same ability level, and teachers can direct their presentation to that level to maximize learning. Critics argue that tracking is divisive and damaging, particularly for lower-track students who often face a "dumbed-down" curriculum taught by burned-out teachers.

Your task in this exercise is to design an experiment to determine whether or not tracking is effective in boosting academic achievement in high school students of varying abilities. The principal has rounded up 100 students who have volunteered to serve as subjects. To make sure your study will be valid, she wants answers to the following questions.

1. What might be your hypothesis for this experiment?

2. What would be the independent variable?

3. How would you implement the independent variable, using the 100 volunteers?

4. What would be the dependent variable?

5. How would you perform the actual experiment?

6. What variables would you need to control in order to ensure a valid test of your hypothesis?

Adolescence: Psychosocial Development

Contents

Note: Worth Publishers provides online Instructor and Student Tool Kits, DVD Student Tool Kits, and Instructor and Student video resources in DevelopmentPortal for use with the text. See Part I: General Resources for information about these materials and the text Lecture Guides for a complete list by text chapter.

Suggested Activities

Introducing Adolescence: Psychosocial Development

Teaching Tip: The Seven Keys to Excellent Teaching

Master teacher Bill Buskist of Auburn University has extensively studied the art of teaching. Collating the musings of master teachers, and findings of studies of award-winning teachers and student evaluations, Buskist notes that excellent teachers:

- Ask the right questions about teaching. They recognize that the responsibility for improved teaching rests on their shoulders.
- Take calculated risks in teaching. Master teachers are constantly tinkering with their teaching in order to improve.
- Understand that teaching is social behavior. Master teachers recognize that high levels of rapport create positive learning environments.
- Are passionate about teaching, students, and their subject matter. Buskist puts it this way, "No passion, no inspiration. No inspiration, no powerful impact on student learning."
- Place student learning front and center. Master teachers place more emphasis on promoting thinking and analyzing than they do on content.
- Set high academic standards. Excellent teachers convey their expectations to students and work to help them achieve those expectations.
- Reflect on the quality of their teaching. Master teachers engage in frequent formative assessment.

Each of these keys is, of course, a subject worthy of extensive elaboration and discussion. However, the list is also a useful reminder for even the most experienced among us of what we all should strive for in our courses. Buskist suggests identifying specific days each week when you will pause from your busy schedule for 10–15 minutes in the solitude of your office or home to reflect on the quality of your teaching, and what you can do to improve it based on the seven keys.

Buskist, B. (2011). *7 steps to becoming an excellent teacher (or at least a better teacher)*. National Institute on the Teaching of Psychology. St. Petersburg Beach, FL.

"On Your Own" Activity: Developmental Fact or Myth?

Before students read about psychosocial development during adolescence, have them respond to the true-false statements in Handout 1. The correct answers are shown below. Class discussion can focus on the origins of any developmental misconceptions that are demonstrated in your students' incorrect answers.

1. T	6. F
2. T	7. F
3. T	8. F
4. T	9. T
5. T	10. T

AV: Journey Through the Life Span, Program 6: Adolescence

See Adolescence: Biosocial Development for a description of Program 6 and the accompanying observation modules, which cover the entire unit on adolescence.

AV: Transitions Throughout the Life Span, Program 16: Who Am I?

As young people strain to adopt adult roles, they are still in the process of discovering who they are, a process that takes place in the midst of an explosion of change—changing bodies, changing hormones, changing schools, and changing relationships. Program 16 focuses on the psychosocial development—particularly the formation of identity—required for the attainment of adult status and maturity.

The second segment discusses the influence of friends, family, community, and culture as powerful social forces that help or hinder the adolescent's transition from childhood to adulthood. Kathleen Berger provides expert commentary, and the special challenges faced by ethnic minority teens are explored.

The program concludes with the message that while no other period of life is characterized by so many changes in the three domains of development, for most young people the teenage years are happy ones. Furthermore, serious problems in adolescence do not necessarily lead to lifelong problems.

AV: Adolescence: Current Issues (2 segments, 32 and 24 min.., Child Development Media)

(See description in Adolescence: Biosocial Development.)

Classroom Activity: Using Literature to Teach Adolescent Psychosocial Development

The General Resources section includes some Classroom Activities that illustrate a broad range of developmental topics and can be used at any point during the course. One of these ("Using Literature to Teach Developmental Psychology") discusses Maya Angelou's *I Know Why the Caged Bird Sings*. The second half of Angelou's marvelous book illustrates the challenges of puberty and identity formation during adolescence, as well as the impact of the peer group, the formation of sexual identity, and the beginnings of interest in parenthood and vocations.

Following the guidelines given for this activity, instruct your students to write a term paper discussing how Angelou's adolescent experiences exemplify two or three aspects or topics of development. Alternatively, assign sections of the book to be discussed in class.

Classroom Activity: Problem-Solving Skills

To help your students appreciate some of the problems adolescents face, and to improve their problem-solving skills, you might assign groups or committees to suggest interventions in the following situations. In each case the group should provide actual names and phone numbers of organizations or agencies that would be contacted. Tell students that they can use the Internet to obtain the necessary information.

(a) You know a runaway 15-year-old girl. She is undecided about whether she wants to return home because her father, an alcoholic, is periodically abusive.
(b) A friend of your younger sister has announced her plans to drop out of high school and begin an acting/modeling career. Because she looks up to you, the younger girl asks you for guidance.
(c) You learn quite by accident that an acquaintance has made an unsuccessful suicide attempt.
(d) You are a high school English teacher. A composition written by one of your students is very confused and emotional, but it leads you to believe that the writer may be a long-term victim of sexual abuse at home.

Responses will vary depending on the resources available in your community. The goal is to provide students with experience in identifying appropriate resources for handling the specific needs of troubled adolescents.

Classroom Activity: Introducing Adolescents, the Risk Takers—Especially in the United States

This activity was introduced in the discussion of biosocial development during adolescence. If you did not use it then, you may want to use it in relation to psychosocial development in adolescence, which deals with suicide, violence, and other risky teen behaviors.

Identity

AV: The Development of Self (60 min., Insight Media)

This program explores the development of self-concept and self-esteem through research using the Perceived Competence Scale for Children, which measures self-concept in the areas of scholastic performance, athletic competence, popularity, and appearance. It also examines how self-esteem is affected by puberty and various clinical disorders associated with low self-esteem.

"On Your Own" Activity: Who Am I?

Identity formation is a primary task of adolescence. Ideally, adolescents begin to sense their own uniqueness in the larger social world of which they are a part.

To help students explore the process of their own identity formation, have them complete Handout 2, which asks them to define their identity in terms of their social roles, responsibilities, groups to which they belong, beliefs and values, personality traits and abilities, as well as their needs, feelings, and behavior patterns. They are then asked to rank each item—from 1 (most important) to 10 (least important)—according to its importance to their identity now and five years ago.

The difference between the two rankings should make it obvious that the development of identity is not confined to any one age. Older students in particular will clearly see that identity, like the life story itself, continues to unfold over the entire life span.

An interesting follow-up to this exercise would be to summarize the class's responses, noting any systematic differences in how identity is defined at younger and older ages. If you do this analysis, make sure you control for the current ages of your students. Do younger students, for example, define themselves more in terms of careers and future goals? older students in terms of family and generativity?

Note: The Instructor Media Tool Kit for this chapter contains several video clips of teenagers of varying ages responding to the question, "Who are you?" You might introduce this activity by playing several of these brief clips.

AV: Who Am I? Psychosocial Development During Adolescence (30 min., Insight Media)

Focusing on Erik Erikson's views of adolescence, this film depicts how adolescents strive to adopt adult roles and forge their identities.

AV: Adolescence: Social and Emotional Development (30 min., Child Development Media)

This video focuses on the adolescent's search for identity, noting that in the course of this search, teenagers may be in several different identity statuses at the same time. The importance of friends and the larger peer group in offering support and status is also highlighted.

AV: Adolescent Personality Development (30 min., Insight Media)

This film examines the adolescent's search for identity, the development of independence, and the exploration of sexuality during a sometimes tumultuous stage of life. The theories of personality proposed by G. Stanley Hall, Margaret Mead, Sigmund Freud, and Erik Erikson are discussed.

AV: Girls in America: Identity and Adolescence (2 parts, 57 min. each, Corporation for Public Broadcasting)

This award-winning two-part series investigates the struggle of today's teenage girls to establish identities that reflect their own hopes and perceptions rather than social stereotypes. Program One, "Run Like a Girl," probes many of the challenges of adolescence, including body image, dating, bulimia, divorce, and teen pregnancies. Centered on the world of competitive sports, the female athletes discuss their search for identity and self-esteem while resisting the social expectations of others. Program Two, "Smile Pretty," centers on the competitive world of the beauty pageant. Teenage girls from a variety of ethnic and racial backgrounds discuss the allure of pageantry, modeling, and their struggle for identity.

AV: Reviving Ophelia (38 min., Media Education Foundation)

Reviving Ophelia, by clinical psychologist Mary Pipher, was one of the most talked-about books when it was first published. In this award-winning program, the author discusses the challenges facing young persons today, especially resisting the influence of the media and popular culture in shaping their identities. She also offers concrete ideas for girls, boys, parents, and teachers to help free girls from these "toxic influences." A study guide is also available.

"On Your Own" Activity: How to Speak Gen X and Gen Y

To help students explore cohort differences in the process of identity formation, have them complete Handout 3, which explores cohort effects, stereotypes, and targeted advertising for Generation X (those born between 1965 and the late 1970s or 1980) and Generation Y (those born between the late 1970s or early 1980s and 1995). Gen Y is also known as the Millennial Generation (or Millennials), Generation Next, Net Generation, and Echo Boomers. The actual years used for each cohort is controversial; it depends on your source.

An interesting alternative to this exercise would be to have students create their own campaigns for a product (clothing, for example) and present them to the class as if they were pitching their proposal to an actual manufacturer or board of directors of an advertising agency. You might encourage them to construct posters, or use video, to bring their ideas to life in front of the class. The class could then either vote on which campaigns most accurately targeted the two cohorts or select the best individual features from various campaigns and combine them into a class campaign. To introduce this assignment, you might first present some of the information from the Classroom Activity on page 6, "The Scoop on Generation X and Generation Y."

Critical Thinking Activity: Identity Statuses: Four Cases

Each unit of these resources contains a critical thinking exercise designed specifically to test students' critical thinking about a topic covered in the text. Handout 4 contains case studies of adolescents representing each of the four identity statuses. In this case, consider distributing the handout after the text section on identity has been assigned but before the lecture on this topic, so that students will be challenged to think through the material. The cases can then be used in a lecture to elaborate upon the identity statuses.

The answers to this unit's Critical Thinking Activity follows:

1. *Rudy.* This is an example of a moratorium. In the United States, the most obvious place to engage in such a moratorium is college, which is allowing Rudy to sample a variety of academic areas before choosing a career.
2. *Melissa.* This is an example of identity achievement. Melissa is self-directed and thoughtful and has established her own career goals by abandoning some of those of her parents and society and accepting others.
3. *Lynn.* This is an example of foreclosure. You might have felt that Lynn's case falls into the identity-achievement category. However, several aspects of the description point toward foreclosure: (1) Lynn avoids exploring alternatives in her social life (she resists the influences of someone who is very different from her and her mother; she avoids men who might bring out other facets of her personality). (2) Her academic interests are "unwavering." (3) Her interests coincide with those of a much-admired parent.
4. *Daniel.* This is an example of role confusion. Daniel apparently has few goals and does not care much about finding an identity.

AV: Cultural Identity Development (64 min., Insight Media)

Although lengthy, this film presents a probing look at five levels of minority development. It also discusses how clinical psychologists and counselors incorporate an understanding of each client's cultural identity into their treatment.

Teaching Tip: "Coming of Age" in Films, TV Programs, and Music Videos

Because teenagers fit squarely in the demographic group that Hollywood strives to appeal to, there is never a shortage of recent movies that can be used to stimulate a good class discussion of key issues in adolescent psychosocial development. To broaden your students' understanding of such concepts as *identity* and *intimacy*, you might ask them to discuss recent films, television programs, and music videos that explore "coming of age." Common themes might include the loss of innocence (sexual and otherwise), the events of moratorium, rejection of parental values or eventual acceptance of them, problems of peer acceptance, and difficulties in developing intimacy. Also evident in these films are such topics as adolescent fantasies and egocentrism (see Adolescence: Cognitive Development) and adolescent decision making about sexual behavior. Ask your students what conclusions (if any) about adolescent development can be drawn from these films. You might also explore the question of why so many films, television programs, and videos focus on the adolescent experience. One reason, of course, is that so many consumers of these products are adolescents. Are there other reasons?

If your class consists mostly of traditional undergraduates, many students will already have seen the relevant films, and you need only ask for their thoughts regarding how developmental issues were addressed. Four older, but still relevant films are *Thirteen, Spider-Man* (and *Spider-Man 2* and *3*), *Finding Forrester,* and *Mean Girls*.

Thirteen is a 2003 film that depicts what many would consider a highly dysfunctional family. The family's single mother (portrayed by actress Holly Hunter) takes care of everyone except herself and her children. Her unemployed, recovering addict of a boyfriend wanders in and out of the picture, as does her former husband. But the real focus of the film is Tracy, the family's teenage daughter, who struggles to come of age in an abusive, intergenerational family, where alcohol, drugs, and sex are the main coping mechanisms. The "cutting scenes" are graphic and unsettling, as is the strongly implied abuse of Tracy and the cruelty of her best friend Evie. Be forewarned: This is an R-rated film with sexual and drug content, adult language, and mature themes.

Spider-Man was first released in 2002; *Spider-Man 2* came out in 2004, and *Spider-Man 3* appeared in 2007. The series centers on the ageless, unlikely superhero Peter Parker, an angst-ridden, geeky high schooler portrayed by Tobey Maguire. Because the comic book hero first appeared in 1962, "Spidey" has been the favorite of teenagers all over the world, who readily identify with his introspective nature and daily struggles to grow up. All the themes of adolescent psychosocial development are touched upon, including the physical and psychological changes of puberty (magnified by the superhero's daily transformation from teen to superhero), the search for identity, guilt, and unrequited love.

Finding Forrester is a 2000 film that offers a moving account of the importance of friendships and intergenerational relationships to psychosocial development. The protagonists are Jamal, a 16-year-old African American who lives with his mother in the Bronx and has a secret passion for writing, and William Forrester (played by Sean Connery), a reclusive author (and voyeur of the outside world) who eventually becomes Jamal's mentor. As their relationship develops, Jamal learns to be proud of his talents and Forrester learns how to live again and share feelings with others.

Mean Girls is a 2004 film about 16-year-old Cady Heron (played by Lindsay Lohan), who until recently was home-schooled by her zoologist parents living in African bush country. Her entry into public high school life goes well until she violates teen social rules when she falls in love with her friend's ex-boyfriend.

Teaching Tip: Vocational Identity

To help students learn more about vocational identity and career development, invite the campus career counselor to speak to the class. This will not only serve to teach students more about the process of career counseling and about issues of career development but will also expose them to someone they should get to know before they graduate.

Relationships with Adults

AV: Building on Adolescent Experience (95 min., Insight Media)

This video profiles Matthew Selekman's solution-oriented therapy approach to working with a mother and her angry adolescent daughter.

AV: Drugs and Sex (16 minutes, Magna Systems)

This short film focuses on the difficulties many parents have in discussing sex and drugs with their children. It also offers practical examples of how to do so in a manner that builds trust and resiliency.

Classroom Activity: The Scoop on Generation X and Generation Y

Gen X is generally accepted to be those 41 million people born between 1965 and the late 1970s, a shorter period than the 19 years for the baby boom (1946 through 1964). Gen Xers, who are now between the ages of 31 and 46 are caught in the middle of two much larger cohorts: baby boomers on one end (the largest population group in the history of the United

States) and Gen Y (those born since 1978) on the other. Here are some recent Gen X and Gen Y (the Millennials or Generation Next) demographic statistics:

In 2010, the estimated median age of U.S. citizens was 36.8 years (males: 35.5, females: 38.1).

Generation X:

- 31% of Gen Xers had earned a college degree.
- 81% of people in Generation X were employed full time or part time.
- 37% of Gen Xers' mothers worked outside the home when their kids were growing up.
- 16.7% of Gen Xers were Hispanic, now the largest U.S. minority group.
- 39-year-old Michael Dell, founder of Dell Computers, was the highest ranked Gen Xer on the *Forbes* list of the "World's Richest People."

Generation Y:

- 90% of Gen Yers own a computer.
- 82% own a mobile phone.
- 72% send or receive SMS (text) messages.
- Gen Yers spend more time online than they do watching television.
- In contrast to Gen Xers, who use technology when it supports a "lifestyle need," for Gen Yers, technology is embedded in everything they do. (Gen Yers have been called the first "native online population.")

The members of Gen Y in the United States number more than 57 million. Based on birth rates, the earlier Gen X has been said to represent a "baby bust" decline in births that followed the 1950s boom. Because of its larger size, Gen Y is sometimes described as an "echo boom" of rising births after 1975. At about the same time, an unprecedented bull market took hold of the economy and lasted until 2000, and baby boomers created a new, child-focused culture, which brought such innovations as no-tolerance schools and standards-based learning.

Although experts continue to debate the actual dates of the generational boundary between Gen X and Gen Y, they agree that there are major cohort differences between the groups. Among the experts who are looking most closely at these differences are marketing professionals, who determine the content of commercial advertising. A decade ago, William Strauss and Neil Howe, who prefer to refer to Gen Yers as "Millennials," predicted that by 2000, the "teen pathologies" of Generation Y, including substance abuse, crime, suicide, and adolescent pregnancy, would decline. In their most recent discussion of the Millennium generation, Strauss and Howe maintain that Millennials differ from older Gen Xers in many important ways:

- Unlike earlier generations, Gen Yers have a good relationship with their parents. According to a Gallup Poll, 90 percent of teens say they are very close to their parents; in 1974, more than 40 percent of baby boomers said they would be better off without their parents. Millennials are expected to retain these close parental bonds even after leaving home.
- Parental monitoring remains strong for this cohort, as their so-called "helicopter parents" are increasingly found on campus, guarding against threats to their offspring's development.
- Gen Y is less influenced by rebellious pop culture icons. The ability of rather ordinary-looking singers to rise to the top of their profession exemplifies their rejection of the overhyped, extreme culture of the 1990s. Consequently, marketing executives believe that the edgy brand associations that appealed to Gen X will not appeal to the more conventional Millennium generation, which seems to display a greater interest in family, religion, and community.
- Under greater pressure by their parents and society to achieve, Millennials are put off by the "slacker" archetype that was more appealing to Gen X. Advertising that belittles those who work hard and celebrates the "accidental success of airheads" doesn't impress this generation.
- In contrast to ultra-individualist Gen Xers, Millennials are more group-oriented. In addition, because of the relative success of programs such as affirmative action and Title IX, cultural and gender gaps narrowed somewhat during Gen Yers' childhood years. However, the gap between rich and poor widened. Consequently, Millennials may be less hung up on race, gender, or ethnicity than their parents, but just as, if not more, sensitive to economic class.

Central Intelligence Agency World Fact Book. Retreived February 22, 2011, from https://www.cia.gov/library/publications/the-world-factbook/geos/us.html

Crane, J. P. (2007, September 9). Boomers, Gen Yers mix it up. *The Boston Globe*. Retrieved from www.boston.com/bostonworks/news/articles/2007/09/09/boomers_gen_yers_mix_it_up?mode=PF.

Ferguson, T. (2008, July 30). Gen Y is setting the tech agenda. *Business Week*. Retrieved from www.businessweek.com/globalbiz/content/jul2008/gb20080730_562367.htm.

The scoop on Gen X. (2005, January). *Work and Family Life, 19*(1), 1.

Strauss, W., & Howe, N. (2000). *Millennials rising: The next great generation*. New York: Vintage Books.

AV: The Neglected Generation (30 min., Insight Media)

Focusing on the often-ignored subject of child neglect, this video begins by noting that half of all American teenagers suffer from a lack of parental monitoring that seriously increases their risk of developmental problems. The final segment explores the roles that families, communities, and governments can play in primary prevention of adolescent problems.

Classroom Activity: Classroom Debate: *"Resolved: Today's Parents Are Too __________."*

Parental influence on the young person's development remains strong during adolescence.

Most of your students are likely to hold very strong opinions about their own upbringing, the "best way" to raise children, and the kind of parent they either currently are or hope to become. As you discuss parenting styles in class, listen for any strongly expressed opinions, especially thoughts on "what's wrong with parents today." From these opinions, fill in the blank in the resolution above and follow the guidelines in the General Resources section of this manual for scheduling a classroom debate.

Peer Power

AV: Among Equals (57 min., Insight Media)

This program explores the crucial importance of the peer group for adolescent psychosocial development. The topics explored include identity formation, moral development, gender differences, friendship, and the emergence of intimate relationships.

AV: Teenage Relationships (30 min., RMI Media Productions)

Focusing on social and emotional development during adolescence, this engaging video features views of high school students on peer relationships, sexual activity, and other pertinent issues.

Teaching Tip: Gangs, Cliques, Crews, and "Posses"

Although most of your students will probably be only a year or two out of high school, you may find it helpful to initiate your discussion of the influence of peer groups on adolescent psychosocial development by refreshing everyone's memory of high school, where every day can be a struggle to fit in. Start the class with this brief scene in the life of one high school sophomore:

> It was one careless moment in the cafeteria that she now believes will haunt her forever, or at least until graduation, whichever comes first. Blond, smart, athletic and well off, she must have thought she could get away with sitting down with a couple of gawky skaters from the fringe of high-school society, if only to interview them about hip-hop music for the school newspaper. She should have known that in high school, appearance outweighs motive by 100 to 1. There were giggles and stares, then loss of gossip privileges and exile from her seat at the center table next to the jocks. Now, a year later, recovered from a bout of anorexia as she tried to starve her way back into favor, she has found new friends. But the formerly cool sophomore, too humiliated to bear being identified, views her years in a West Coast high school as "hell."

Although many developmentalists believe that today's teens are more tolerant of differences than they were a generation or two ago, since the invention of high school, adolescents have been forming cliques, mentally ranking them, and struggling to attain (or maintain) membership in those groups at the top of the pecking order. As an interesting discussion of a classic cohort effect, you and your students might swap stories of the various in- and out-groups from high school. Although there certainly are regional variations, the relative positions of some groups have shifted to reflect changes in society. Cheerleaders, for example, are not placed on quite so high a pedestal as they were in the past. Similarly, kids who experiment with drugs are no longer considered glamorous. In addition, today's groups are much more likely than groups a generation ago to include both boys and girls; some experts trace this development to the influence of television, which provides teens with earlier familiarity with the opposite sex.

The positions of some groups, however, have not changed. Male jocks continue to be at the top of the social dominance hierarchy in most high schools, enforcing social codes, often picking on obese, "wimpy," and "geeky" kids. Also unchanged is the tendency of groups to solidify membership with a unique uniform. As science writer Jerry Adler notes, "Chinos and button-down shirts mark kids as preppies a thousand miles from Andover; baggy jeans signify hip-hop on a Laotian kid in Iowa no less than on a homeboy straight out of Bed-Stuy." And years before the tragic shootings at Columbine High School, black trenchcoats were favored by teens at the fringe of high school society, who would rather die than conform to how other kids dressed.

As high schools have grown in size, and society has become even more stratified, the diversity of clubs, sports gangs, cliques, and "posses" has skyrocketed. At Glenbrook South, a typical high school in suburban Chicago, there are more than 70 clubs and two dozen sports teams. In addition to the athletes and members of recognized clubs, the cliques include preppies, gangsters, pot-smoking skaters, sullen punks, gays, nerds, and morbid Goths. Glenbrook has developed its own clique lexicon, which includes

- *Backstage people*, who are drama and arts students who linger in the school's auditorium to do homework, talk, and just "hang out"
- *Bandies*, or musicians who stick to themselves
- *Wall kids*, or *Abercrombies*, who favor preppy clothing and whose turf is a wall outside the school cafeteria
- *Trophy-case kids*, who oddly choose to hang out by the school's awards case, despite their favored punk clothing consisting of hooded, black sweatshirts
- *Student-council kids*, who are clean-cut and popular

The University of Michigan has also compiled a list of high school cliques, which includes jock, prep, hippie/hipster, princess/miss perfect, nerd, thespian, and bando/choir geek.

In an attempt to prevent the negative impact of cliques, stereotyping, and scapegoating on high school life, some schools have experimented with enforced, egalitarian cultures in which all students wear neutral uniforms and are required to participate on a sports team. However, the results have been mixed, at best. David Smith, the principal at Glenbrook South, notes that "there's no avoiding the fact that adolescence is a tribal society. It's just the nature of the thing." And some experts believe that efforts to completely block this high school tribalism are misguided, seeing this experience as essential practice for adult society.

Adler, J. (1999, May 10). The truth about high school. *Newsweek*, pp. 56–58.

Nieves, E. (2001, March 18). An inner-city perspective on high school violence. *New York Times*, p. 1.12.

University of Michigan. (2011). *What's your clique?* Retrieved February 23, 2011, from sitemaker.umich.edu/356.tran/true-clique.

Classroom Activity: The Role of the Peer Group

To help students understand the role of the peer group during adolescence, you might have the class talk about their own social experiences as adolescents. Did they hang out in loosely associated groups of girls and boys, gradually joining together? Did they double- or triple-date to avoid the awkwardness of being alone with someone they "liked"? Did they have a best friend of the same sex with whom they shared details of their sexual experiences in order to confirm that they were normal? Did they belong to any special groups, such as a sorority or a fraternity? Were they rejected by such a group? In either case, how did they feel?

Observational Activity: Adolescent Peer Relationships

As noted in the text, the socializing role of peers becomes especially prominent during adolescence. Teenagers help one another in many ways—by providing a sounding board of contemporaries who can function as a self-help group, by providing social support when needed, and by creating a safe arena in which the adolescent can try out various behaviors and personality characteristics.

This activity is intended to help your students explore how the concept of friendship changes during adolescence. Ask them to interview a person at least several years younger than they are, who is between the ages of 10 and 19. They may feel most comfortable interviewing a friend, a relative, or a friend's relative. They must obtain written permission from the person's parent or legal guardian before they conduct the interview.

To help students who may not be familiar with interview techniques, Handout 5 provides questions that can serve as guidelines for structuring the interview. Students may want to copy these questions onto a separate sheet of paper, leaving space for answers. By taking notes as the interviewee talks, the student will be better able to prepare a complete and accurate summary for the follow-up report (Handout 6).

Schwanenflugel, P. J. (October, 1987). An interview method for teaching adolescent psychology. *Teaching of Psychology, 14*(3), 167–168.

AV: My Bodyguard (96 min., Films Incorporated)
Breaking Away (99 min., Films Incorporated)

Two touching, amusing, insightful movies about friendship between adolescent boys. The first is about "tough guys" in Chicago, the latter about the efforts of four Indiana boys to win a bicycle race. Since they are full-length films that were successful in movie theaters, they are a splashy, expensive way to set off the discussion on adolescent psychosocial development. Depending on your students and your budget, however, they may be well worth it. For instance, *Breaking Away* is filled with examples of a father's difficulty in understanding his son's attempt to find an identity—a humorous and touching example of the differing goals and needs of the two generations and their attempts to bridge the gap. (This film is also useful for discussions of biosocial and cognitive development during adolescence.)

AV: Coping with Peer Pressure (15 min., Films for the Humanities and Sciences)

This brief film helps teen viewers learn to cope with peer pressure by realistically examining the consequences of their actions. A teenager who was nearly led astray by peers because of her low self-esteem is profiled.

"On Your Own" Activity: Survey of Sexual Knowledge

Handout 7, the Allgeiers' Survey of Sexual Knowledge, can be used to introduce adolescent sexuality and the controversy concerning sex education.

While the evidence indicates that adolescents are well informed regarding sexuality and contraception, the source of that information is generally not their parents. For example, Elizabeth and Albert Allgeier report that when students were asked to name their most useful source of information regarding sexual behavior and pregnancy, 49 percent reported their school, 20 percent books, 10 percent friends, 13 percent their mothers, 2 percent their boyfriend or girlfriend, and 0 percent their fathers.

Correct answers to the survey questions are:

1. T	13. F	25. F	37. T	49. F
2. F	14. T	26. T	38. F	50. T
3. T	15. F	27. T	39. T	51. F
4. F	16. F	28. T	40. F	52. T
5. T	17. F	29. F	41. T	53. T
6. F	18. F	30. F	42. F	54. F
7. T	19. T	31. F	43. T	55. F
8. F	20. F	32. F	44. T	56. T
9. F	21. F	33. T	45. T	57. F
10. T	22. F	34. F	46. T	58. T
11. T	23. F	35. T	47. T	59. F
12. T	24. T	36. T	48. F	60. T

AV: Woman's Talk 5: Sex Education (18 min., Corinth)

Questions from young children through adolescents are used to illustrate the parents' role in providing sex education. While the film is pretty basic, it could be a good springboard for uncovering some of the embarrassment and misinformation that most adults bring to discussions with their children about sex. As a follow-up, the class might be divided into small groups and individuals asked to tell how their parents treated the subject. Or one student might role-play a blunt, curious child, with another student playing the parent trying to cope.

AV: Good Girl (45 min., Filmakers Library)

This film examines the psychological and sociological aspects of adolescence by showing the daily activities and thoughts of a young girl growing up in America in the 1950s. Particularly interesting is her sexual development in an era when there were only two kinds of girls: good and bad.

Sadness and Anger

Depression

AV: Dealing with Teens: A Guide to Survival (52 min., Films for the Humanities and Sciences)

Taking a practical approach, this film offers suggestions for discussing a variety of issues with adolescents: dating, sexual activity, emotions, and substance abuse. Hosted by actor Howard Hesseman, the program also presents a list of warning signs for caregivers concerned about their teen's behavior.

AV: Teen Depression (16 min., Films for the Humanities and Sciences)

This brief film chronicles the lives of several teenagers diagnosed with clinical depression, analyzing how they became aware of their disorder, how it has changed their lives, and how they have been helped through therapy. Experts also explain the psychological and chemical symptoms, causes, and treatments for depression.

AV: Childhood's End: A Look at Adolescent Suicide (28 min., Filmakers Library)

A documentary look at three adolescents who tried to commit suicide. Two of them, both girls, reflect on the reasons behind their attempted suicides. The third, a boy, was "successful" and is represented by his two best friends, who wonder what they could have done to help. This film distinguishes the hype about suicide—for example, the little-known fact that suicide is much more common among the elderly—from the reality—every time an adolescent tries to kill him- or herself, it is a tragic sign that our social support system has failed.

AV: Gifted Adolescents and Suicide (26 min., Films for the Humanities and Sciences)

An adaptation of a Phil Donahue program, this video profiles two couples who lost their intellectually talented 17-year-olds to suicide. The program focuses on the need to recognize the pressure of expectations on overachievers.

AV: Everything to Live For (52 min., Films for the Humanities and Sciences)

The dramatic opening of this film points out that suicide is second only to automobile accidents as the cause of death in adolescence. This documentary profiles four adolescents: two who attempted and "failed" at suicide, and two who succeeded. Family members and the surviving "failures" talk openly about the presumed causes of the drastic measures.

AV: Suicide: The Teenager's Perspective (26 min., Films for the Humanities and Sciences)

Each year nearly half a million teenagers attempt suicide. This film deals with the tragedy of adolescent suicide and attempts to educate viewers so that they will recognize the signs of impending suicide in others. Jim Wells, a nationally recognized expert on teenage suicide, provides some unique insights.

AV: Teenage Suicide (19 min., Films for the Humanities and Sciences)

A documentary that examines the increase in teenage suicide, this film explores some of the reasons behind the increase and identifies behavior patterns that are considered to be warning signs alerting family and friends to possible problems.

AV: Teen Suicide: Sara's Diary (14 min., Magna Systems)

Based on a true story, this poignant film examines the subjects of depression, suicide, and bullying. The subject of much teasing and bullying in her school, Sara makes an unsuccessful attempt at suicide. Afterward, her main tormentor discovers her diary and learns that Sara was really no different from anyone else in the school.

Classroom Activity: Suicide Prevention

To sensitize students to the need for teen suicide prevention programs, you might ask someone from your local suicide-prevention center to report on adolescent suicide attempts in your community. What is the frequency, cause, and outcome of these attempts? How does your community compare with nationwide averages?

Alternatively, you might ask whether any of your students have had a close friend who attempted suicide. Since this is a very sensitive topic, you may want to announce the discussion in advance, so that anyone having personal experience with this issue might first talk with you about it in private. Then, you can either relate your informants' experiences to the class, or, if they wish, have them do so.

Delinquency and Disobedience

Internet Activity: Internet Resources for Troubled Adolescents

The Internet contains a wealth of information for teens and their families who are struggling with serious problems such as suicidal ideation and delinquency. For this activity, ask students to search the Web to find and explore some of these resources using information and questions from Handout 8 as a guide.

Classroom Activity: Protecting the Emotional Life of Boys

To stimulate a lively class discussion of gender differences in emotional development and the roots of adolescent lawbreaking, you might prepare a brief lecture on Dan Kindlon and Michael Thompson's thesis that boys are socialized to be emotionally illiterate. Alternatively, you might assign different groups of students to report on portions of their book *Raising Cain: Protecting the Emotional Life of Boys*, which sparked a national debate on parenting. In the biblical story of Cain and Abel, the two brothers—both eager to please God—each make an offering. The Lord expresses pleasure with Abel's offering of a prized lamb from his flock but shows little reaction to Cain's gift of the fruits of his labor. Although Cain is visibly distressed —"his countenance fell"—he is unable to express his humiliation in words. God then admonishes Cain for his self-pity and anger:

> Why are you distressed,
> And why is your face fallen?
> Surely, if you do right, there is uplift.
> But if you do not do right,
> Sin crouches at the door;
> Its urge is toward you,
> Yet you can be its master. (Genesis 4:6)

In other words, "Get over it. Sure, you're mad. But count to 10. Think about it. Do the right thing."

But Cain is either not listening or he is unable to follow the path of nonviolence. Later, out of anger and jealousy, Cain takes his brother out to the field and murders him. When the Lord confronts Cain with the question of what has become of his brother, Cain replies that he does not know. "Am I my brother's keeper?" he asks. In reply, the Lord banishes Cain to the land of Nod to become a "ceaseless wanderer on earth."

While the story of Cain and Abel has long been considered a parable of sibling rivalry, psychologists Dan Kindlon and Michael Thompson see it as a reflection of the emotional life of boys today—"a boy's desire to be loved and respected, and his propensity to respond to humiliation and shame with anger and violence rather than reflection and communication."

In the views of these theorists and clinicians, it is the legacy of Cain that surfaces in aggressive, delinquent, and violent boys. Like Cain, boys who have been disappointed, frustrated, humiliated, or disrespected often become angry and lash out. And they do so almost reflexively, without pausing to consider the consequences of their actions—to themselves or their victims. Like the shooters in the 1998 schoolyard killings in Jonesboro, Arkansas, many of these violent teenagers feel sorry afterward, but by then it is too late.

Kindlon and Thompson believe that the roots of male violence, depression, drinking, drug use, and suicidal ideation can be found in the destructive emotional training that boys receive. This emotional miseducation begins with the ways in which parents, teachers, coaches, and other influential adults respond to boys and with the ways in which they teach them to respond to others. In doing so, too often traditional gender stereotypes discourage emotional awareness in boys. Research studies of how parents interact with their male and female offspring reveal that, when girls ask questions about emotions, mothers generally give longer, more detailed explanations. Seeing a child who is crying, a young girl might ask why. In response, her mother is likely to speculate about the reasons behind the child's emotions or to validate her daughter's observation that the child is hurt or sad or has lost a toy. If a male child sees another child crying and asks why, the parent is likely to give a shorter answer that steers the child away from an emotional discussion. "I don't know, he just is. Come on, it's not polite to stare" is a typical reply.

Moreover, in these authors' view, when boys express "ordinary levels of anger or aggression, or turn surly and silent," their behavior is accepted as normal. Expressions of fear, sadness, anxiety, and other emotions that society considers "feminine" traits are treated in a way that sends the clear message that such emotions aren't acceptable in boys. For this reason, most boys—like Cain—don't know how to respond when they are frustrated with another person. Kindlon and Thompson maintain that boys' emotional miseducation biases the way that they interpret incoming emotional signals in three ways:

- In boys, the motivation for aggression is more "defensive" rather than offensive or predatory. In their view, most violent boys are not "testosterone-laden beasts"; rather, they are vulnerable, emotionally cornered individuals, who use aggression as a form of armor to protect themselves.
- Boys are primed to see the world as a threatening place and to respond to that threat with aggression. Another aspect of their emotional miseducation is that boys are caught in a trap of trying to play an impossible "macho role," in which they must, at all costs, prevent others from taking

advantage of them. This emotional illiteracy means that boys often misread emotional cues in social situations, seeing neutral situations as threatening. In addition, boys are raised in a "culture of cruelty," in which they often receive harsh discipline to "toughen them up." "Whatever else it means to be a boy in our culture," note Kindlon and Thompson, "it means that your actions are more likely to be misinterpreted as threatening or disobedient, that you are more likely than the girl next door to be punished or treated harshly."

This gender bias shows up clearly in several ways. For example, judges commit boys to residential detention centers far more often than they do girls, even for the same offenses. As another example, researchers have found that boys are much more likely than girls to receive harsh physical discipline at school and in the home. Consider: African American boys are more than three times as likely as African American girls to receive corporal punishment. For every White girl who is physically punished, six White boys are hit. Asian boys are eight times more likely than Asian girls to be hit. Should we be surprised that these experiences leave boys expecting hostility in their interactions with others?

- Boys often don't know or won't admit what it is that makes them angry. In addition to their difficulty in reading others' emotional signals, boys are often unable to pinpoint the source of their frustration and anger. As a result, they are more prone than girls to explosive outbursts or to displace their poorly understood anger toward an innocent bystander.

To protect the emotional life of boys, Kindlon and Thompson maintain that parents and educators must teach them first to attend to and understand their own emotions. How can this be accomplished? Boys must learn (a) to deal with the fact that life isn't always fair and that they can't go around hurting people every time they get angry; (b) to examine why they get angry, and then how to use words and other strategies to defuse their anger in nonviolent ways; (c) to consider how their actions affect others, to be more trusting, and not to see threats where they don't exist; (d) to communicate with others more effectively; (e) that controlling their anger doesn't make them sissies; and (f) that emotional courage and empathy are the sources of real strength in life. "If we teach our sons to honor and value their emotional lives," the authors conclude, "if we can give boys an emotional vocabulary and the encouragement to use it, they will unclench their hearts."

Kindlon, D., & Thompson, M. (1999). *Raising Cain: Protecting the emotional life of boys.* New York: Ballantine Books.

AV: Youth Terror: The View from Behind the Gun (Part I: 29 min., Part II: 19 min., CRM/McGraw-Hill)

Originally an *ABC News Close-Up!*, this film interviews young criminals, attempting to explore the reasons, attitudes, and background factors that led to their crimes. It focuses on the serious delinquent who has been arrested several times. To keep this film in perspective, you might point out that less than 1 percent of American teenagers are arrested for serious crimes; on the other hand, more than a third of all the arrests for serious crimes in the United States involve people under age 18. In fact, if a person is ever going to be arrested for committing homicide, that arrest, statistically speaking, is more likely to occur at age 15 than at any other age. You might ask your students to think about two questions as they view the film: In what ways are the young people shown here similar to other teenagers who do not become crime statistics? What can be done to prevent future generations of young people from repeating the mistakes of the young people shown here?

AV: Teens in Turmoil (26 min., Films for the Humanities and Sciences)

This program examines what it's like to be a teenager in North America today, taking the position that growing up is harder and more dangerous today than ever before. It describes a high school crisis prevention program and two distinct approaches to handling troubled adolescents: tough-love and improved parent–child communication.

AV: Breaking the Cycle of Violence (2 volumes, 30 min each, Insight Media)

The program focuses on the causes and prevention of youth violence. It features the commentary of community leaders and educators such as Archbishop Desmond Tutu, Reverend Jesse Jackson, Paul Houston, and Ed Zigler.

AV: Preventing Delinquency: The Social Developmental Approach (28 min., Filmakers Library)

Funded by the United States Department of Justice, this film explains the role parents, peers, school, and community can play in preventing delinquency. Providing the young person with legitimate sources of esteem, status, and achievement can make the delinquent path appear less attractive. Thus, prevention, rather than punishment, and a systems approach, rather than one that focuses on the "bad" boy, are highlighted.

AV: Violence Prevention: What Every Parent Should Know (28 min., Magna Systems, Inc.)

Divided into three sections, this video discusses how children today view violence and the various intervention strategies that have been applied. The first section, "Crisis Avoidance," presents basic social tools middle and high school students can use to avoid violent confrontations. The second, "Conflict Resolution," explores how students can use social skills to settle their differences nonviolently. Finally, "Problem Solving" focuses on how parents can work with their children to respond to troubling situations and ensure their safety.

Drug Use and Abuse

"On Your Own" Activity: Cohort Differences in Drug Use: A Questionnaire

Drug use among adolescents varies significantly from cohort to cohort. To demonstrate recent changes in drug-use patterns, ask students to use Handout 9 to conduct an interview with a contemporary high school student and contrast his or her responses to those of an older person (preferably one at least eight years older than the high school student).

Responses will vary. Some of the patterns mentioned in the text should emerge. For example, cocaine may be mentioned by current high school students but is less likely to be mentioned by the older person, whereas marijuana may appear to have been a bigger problem to the older interviewee. Class discussion can focus on the possible origins of cohort differences in drug use.

AV: Altered States: A History of Drug Abuse (57 min., Films for the Humanities and Sciences)

This captivating film traces the history of drug use in America from the days when the earliest immigrants developed an addiction for tobacco, through Prohibition, and up to the late twentieth century. It explores how drugs of choice have changed over time and documents the cultural, social, and political factors involved in drug use and addiction.

AV: Drugs: Uses and Abuses (8 segments, 20–34 min. each, Films for the Humanities and Sciences)

This eight-part series takes a look at the history, medicinal and illegal use, and developmental impact of sedatives (part 1), narcotics (part 2), stimulants (part 3), hallucinogens (part 4), inhalants (part 5), THC (part 6), PCP (part 7), and steroids (part 8).

AV: The Next Generation (57 min., Films for the Humanities and Sciences)

Taken from Bill Moyers' five-part series on addiction, this program looks at community and family interventions designed to prevent drug abuse. One program works by teaching parents who are heroin addicts how to repair the damage their drug abuse has caused to their families. Another targets high-risk teens with intensive counseling provided during school.

AV: The Addicted Brain (26 min., Films for the Humanities and Sciences)

This award-winning film analyzes the biochemistry of the brain, focusing on the mechanisms of "runner's high," thrill-seeking, and OCD.

AV: Obsessions: The Biological Basis of Addiction (55 min., Insight Media)

This program examines the causes and treatment of various addictions, focusing on the interaction of nature and nurture in the origins of all obsessive behaviors. Russell Sachs discusses the ways addictions to drugs, alcohol, gambling, food, work, and sex, can negatively affect the individual and his or her family.

Internet Activity: Adolescent Drug Experimentation

The National Clearinghouse for Alcohol and Drug Information (NCADI) is run by the Substance Abuse and Mental Health Services Administration (SAMHSA). SAMSHA has a Web site that includes information about the role of biopsychosocial factors in adolescent drug experimentation. Have students use the SAMSHA Web site (and any other Internet resources that they discover) to answer the questions in Handout 10.

AV: Alcohol and the Family: Breaking the Chain (25 min., Films for the Humanities and Sciences)

This video analyzes the signs of alcoholism, focusing on how family members, coworkers, and friends can intervene. It also discusses the impact of alcoholism on the children of alcoholics and provides an overview of various therapies for treating the disease.

AV: The Buzz Is Not for You: Teenage Drinking (30 min., Films for the Humanities and Sciences)

The first part of this documentary on the persistent problem of teenage drinking focuses on its disruptive effects on development. In the second part, various interventions for helping teens avoid peer pressure to drink are described. Interviews with teenagers, law enforcement officers, educators, and developmentalists explore the wide range of issues related to alcohol abuse by adolescents.

AV: The Cliffs (15 min., Films for the Humanities and Sciences)

This brief minidrama tells the story of Robbie, who, after breaking his usual pattern of getting drunk every weekend, discovers that drinking responsibly allows him to be in control and enjoy life more.

AV: Kids Under the Influence (58 min., Films for the Humanities and Sciences)

This award-winning program focuses on alcohol—the number-one drug problem among teenagers. Topics covered include physical and psychological disorders caused by alcohol abuse, the influence of peer and advertising pressure, legal issues, and various approaches to correcting this widespread social problem.

Classroom Activity: Adolescent Drunken Driving

A troubling result of adolescent drug use is revealed in age-group statistics involving traffic fatalities. The National Highway Traffic Safety Administration (NHTSA) cites three reasons that young drivers have such poor driving performance: inexperience, risk-taking behavior and immaturity, and greater risk exposure. The last two factors, of course, parallel the text discussion of possible problems during the teen years. Adolescent impulsiveness and attraction to excitement may result in poor driving judgment and participation in high-risk behaviors such as speeding, talking on cell phones or texting while driving, drinking and driving, and not using a seat belt. Peer pressure may also encourage risk-taking by young, inexperienced drivers.

NHTSA also notes that a higher proportion of teenagers than adults are responsible for their fatal crashes because of their own driving errors.

- A larger percentage of fatal crashes involving teenage drivers are single-vehicle crashes compared with those involving other drivers. In this type of fatal crash, the vehicle usually leaves the road and overturns or hits a roadside object such as a tree or a pole.
- In general, a smaller percentage of teens wear their seat belts than do other drivers.
- A larger proportion of teen fatal crashes involve going too fast for road conditions, compared with crashes of other drivers.
- More teen fatal crashes occur when passengers—usually other teenagers—are in the car than do crashes involving other drivers. Two out of three teens who die as passengers are in vehicles driven by other teenagers.

Adolescent traffic fatalities may be due in part to cognitive immaturity. However, experts are focusing on two factors that are easier to legislate: driver inexperience and alcohol use. Consider the following sober statistics:

- In 2009, about 3,000 teens in the United States aged 15–19 were killed, and more than 350,000 were treated in emergency departments for injuries suffered in motor vehicle crashes.
- Young people ages 15-24 represent only 14 percent of the U.S. population. However, they account for 30 percent ($19 billion) of the total costs of motor vehicle injuries among males and 28 percent ($7 billion) of the total costs of motor vehicle injuries among females.
- At all levels of blood alcohol concentration, the risk of involvement in a motor vehicle crash is greater for teens than for older drivers.
- Approximately 240,000 to 360,000 of the nation's 12 million current undergraduates will ultimately die from alcohol-related causes—more than the number that will get MAs and PhDs combined.

Even though the number of teen drivers continues to increase, many high schools have dropped driver education courses (only 60 percent of drivers younger than 18 get training, compared with 85 percent in the late 1970s). The National Transportation Safety Board has therefore been encouraging states to set tougher standards for young drivers. For example, 15 states have adopted a lower standard for legal drunkenness for drivers younger than 21. And because more than half of teen driver fatalities occur at night, seven states have adopted curfews for younger drivers. New York—the most stringent in this respect—prohibits all 16- and 17-year-olds who haven't taken driver's education from driving between 9 P.M. and 5 A.M. Laws such as these, along with minimum drinking age laws, have been estimated to reduce traffic fatalities involving drivers 18 to 20 years old by 13 percent. These laws have saved an estimated 18,220 lives since 1975.

Centers for Disease Control and Prevention. (2011). *Teen Drivers: Fact Sheet.* Washington, DC: National Center for Statistics and Analysis. Retrieved February 22, 2011, from www.cdc.gov/MotorVehicleSafety/Teen_Drivers/teendrivers_factsheet.html.

AV: Inhalant Abuse: Breathing Easy (24 min., Films for the Humanities and Sciences)

Inhalant abuse is a particularly troubling form of addiction because inhalants are readily available, produce a rapid drug high that quickly leads to tolerance and dependence, and can cause permanent damage to the brain in a very short time. This program analyzes adolescent drug abuse, focusing on the psychological and environmental factors that lead to abuse. Interviews of former inhalant users are particularly effective in illustrating the variables involved in addiction.

AV: Running on Empty: Teens and Methamphetamines (27 min., Films for the Humanities and Sciences)

This video probes the growing abuse of methamphetamine by teenagers. It begins by discussing the nature of the drug, and its effects on the body and central nervous system. It then traces the cycle of drug abuse, beginning with the extreme euphoria associated with initial use, and ending with the crushing lows that often lead to chronic depression.

AV: Pretty Colors: Inside America's Rave Culture (66 min., Films for the Humanities and Sciences)

This gritty film follows Sarah and Stacey, two bored teenagers who have embraced L.A.'s underground rave scene to escape their dysfunctional families. Note: Some language in this film may be objectionable.

HANDOUT 1

Developmental Fact or Myth?

T F 1. It is not unusual for young people to delay achievement by going to college.

T F 2. Generally speaking, parent–adolescent conflict is about routine, day-to-day concerns.

T F 3. During adolescence, peers have a stronger influence than parents on a young person's development.

T F 4. Socially immature adolescents generally are the first to be attracted to members of the other sex.

T F 5. Thinking about committing suicide is actually quite rare among high school students.

T F 6. Worldwide, parasuicide is higher for males but completed suicide is higher for females.

T F 7. Wealth and education decrease the incidence of suicide.

T F 8. Arrests are more likely to occur during adolescence than in any other period of life.

T F 9. Those who become career criminals show recognizable warning signs long before adulthood.

T F 10. The younger people are when they first try a drug, the more likely they are to become addicted.

HANDOUT 2

Who Am I?

Part 1. *To help you explore your own identity formation, write 10 answers to the question, "Who am I?" You may respond in terms of your social roles, responsibilities, or commitments; the groups to which you belong; your beliefs and values; your personality traits and abilities; and your needs, feelings, and behavior patterns. List only those features that are really important to you—features that, if lost, would make a real difference to your sense of who you are.*

After you have completed your list, indicate the importance of each feature to your identity today by assigning it a number from 1 (most important) to 10 (least important). Finally, rank the items according to their importance to you five years ago.

	Rank Today	Rank Five Years Ago
1. I am:	_____	_____
2. I am:	_____	_____
3. I am:	_____	_____
4. I am:	_____	_____
5. I am:	_____	_____
6. I am:	_____	_____
7. I am:	_____	_____
8. I am:	_____	_____
9. I am:	_____	_____
10. I am:	_____	_____

My current age is:_______________

HANDOUT 2 *(continued)*

Part 2. *In the space below, briefly explain any changes you observed in your rankings. What makes the item ranked 1 each time the most important?*

HANDOUT 3

How to Speak Gen X and Gen Y

Describe the cohort into which members of Generation X and Generation Y were born by answering the following questions.

1. What birth years span each generation?

   Generation X:

   Generation Y:

2. What important historical events occurred during the formative years of each generation?

   Generation X:

   Generation Y:

3. In response to the question, "What is the biggest difference between Gen X and Gen Y?" one Web site offered this tongue-in-cheek response: "Most of Gen Y actually thinks being clean and looking clean is a good idea." What are several other popular stereotypes of the members of these generations?

   Generation X stereotypes:

   Generation Y stereotypes:

HANDOUT 3 *(continued)*

4. Each generation seems to develop its own spokespersons and icons, often from the media (singers, actors and actresses, sports figures, etc.) and politics. Who are some of the icons for these two generations?

   Generation X icons:

   Generation Y icons:

5. Marketing companies develop advertising campaigns for products and events that target specific age groups. For instance, it has been suggested that Generation X advertising is edgy and focuses on the extreme pop culture of the 1990s.

   a. What are some specific examples of this type of Generation X marketing?

   b. What kinds of advertising campaigns target the members of Generation Y? What are some of the general themes in these campaigns? How do they differ from advertising that targets Generation X?

   c. If you were in charge of creating an advertising campaign for a new line of casual clothes, how would you approach it for a magazine ad or television commercial that targets each generation?

      Generation X campaign:

      Generation Y campaign:

HANDOUT 4

Critical Thinking Activity: Identity Statuses: Four Cases

Now that you have read and reviewed the material on psychosocial development during adolescence, take your learning a step further by testing your critical thinking skills on this pattern-recognition exercise.

The following brief case studies illustrate the identity statuses proposed by Erik Erikson and others. For each case, suggest the most appropriate identity status—identity achievement, foreclosure, identity diffusion, and moratorium, and describe your reasoning.

1. *Rudy.* Rudy has changed his college major so many times that it will take him six years to graduate. Since his parents have pointedly objected to paying the expenses for tuition and room and board, Rudy has cheerfully taken on a variety of jobs, ranging from bartender to shoe salesman. He likes work that allows him time to think and be alone; his few friends are very much the same way. Rudy's grades are generally high, though his record is marred by a several "incompletes." He has had one very satisfying intimate relationship and is searching rather anxiously for another. Rudy's identity status would probably be described as

   ______________________________ .

2. *Melissa.* Melissa's parents are both physicians. In college she majored in French, spending a semester in France studying art and culture. Upon graduation she surprised her parents by announcing that she had applied to medical school. A close relationship with a hospice nurse and a summer job as a hospital volunteer had helped her arrive at the decision. Melissa's identity status would probably be described as

   ______________________________ .

3. *Lynn.* Lynn's mother is a professor of women's studies who is deeply involved in feminist issues. Lynn very much admires her mother, a strong woman who, as a single parent, struggled to provide for her daughter while establishing her own career. Lynn believes that she, too, will be a strong and independent woman. She avoids people (especially men) who either don't see her in that light or try to bring out her feminine nature. She certainly steers clear of her

HANDOUT 4 *(continued)*

paternal grandmother, who (although pleasant) is a very disorganized and "artsy" person. Lynn's college grades are very high, and her course selections reflect an unwavering interest in psychology, politics, and women's studies. Lynn's identity status would probably be described as

______________________________ .

4. *Daniel.* Daniel is a freshman at a college near his old high school. He comes home nearly every weekend but does not enjoy himself once he's there. He avoids talking to his parents or old high school friends, preferring to "surf the Web" on the computer in his room. Periodically he engages in impulsive shopping; after these sprees he comes home and talks excitedly about the latest electronic gadget he's acquired. He gets angry if his parents ask what he considers to be foolish questions, and angrier still if they patronize him. Daniel is enrolled in courses he has been told are easy, and he does not have strong feelings about his studies or his grades. Daniel's identity status would probably be described as

   ______________________________ .

HANDOUT 5

Observational Activity: Adolescent Peer Relationships: Interview Questions

This activity is intended to let you explore how the concept of friendship changes during adolescence. You are to interview someone who is* at least *four years younger than you and is between the ages of 10 and 19. You may feel most comfortable interviewing a friend or relative, but no matter whom you interview, you must have written permission from your subject's parent or guardian before you begin.*

Keep the interview friendly and informal. It should last no more than 20 minutes, depending on your subject and how much he or she is enjoying the interview. Begin the interview by identifying yourself, your purpose (a course assignment on peer relationships during adolescence), and assuring your subject that his or her responses will remain confidential. Following is a list of questions you might ask during the interview. Feel free to add questions of your own if you wish.

1. I'd like you to tell me about the people in your group of friends. Which friends do you typically hang out with after school? Which friends do you typically hang out with on weekends? Which friends do you typically invite to your parties?
2. What makes a friend different from an acquaintance?
3. Do you define "friendship" differently now than you did when you were younger?
4. How many "true friends" do you have? How does the size of your current friendship group compare with its size when you were younger?
5. What happens when you and a friend have a fight? Is that person still your friend? How do you try to resolve the problem that caused the fight?
6. Who is the most popular person in your friendship group? What is that person like? Why do you think that person is popular?

---

*This activity and the suggested interview questions were taken from the following article: Schwanenflugel, P. J. (1987, October). An interview method for teaching adolescent psychology. *Teaching of Psychology*, *14*(3), 167–168.

HANDOUT 6

Observational Activity: Adolescent Peer Relationships: Follow-Up Report

After you have completed the interview, prepare a written report summarizing what you learned from your subject's responses. Include your subject's sex, age (but not name), and any other pertinent demographic information. Your report should focus on the extent to which your subject's responses confirm or refute the material on peer relationships presented in the text. Feel free to offer your own interpretation of your subject's responses, including comments on how you yourself might have answered the questions.

Subject: age ____________ ethnic/religious background ______________

sex ____________ education level ____________

HANDOUT 7

Survey of Sexual Knowledge

Please answer true or false to each of the following questions and return this sheet to your instructor. Your answers will remain completely anonymous.

T F 1. A female can become pregnant during sexual intercourse without the male having an orgasm.

T F 2. The imbalance of sexual hormones is the most frequent cause of homosexuality.

T F 3. Women can become sexually aroused when breast-feeding an infant.

T F 4. Direct contact between the penis and clitoris is necessary to produce female orgasm during sexual intercourse.

T F 5. There are no biological differences in orgasms attained through sexual intercourse, masturbation, or any other technique.

T F 6. Males are unable to have an erection until they reach puberty (adolescence).

T F 7. Women are biologically more capable of multiple orgasms than are men.

T F 8. A hysterectomy (removal of the uterus) causes the loss of sexual desire in women.

T F 9. There are two different types of biological orgasms in women: clitoral and vaginal.

T F 10. The most sensitive area of sexual stimulation in most women is the clitoris.

T F 11. Erection of the nipples is often a sign of sexual arousal in the male.

T F 12. Homosexual behavior, masturbation, and rape occur among other species of animals besides the human species.

T F 13. Rapists have an above-average sex drive.

T F 14. In this culture, some homosexual behavior is often a normal part of growing up.

T F 15. A male is not able to have an orgasm until he reaches puberty (adolescence).

T F 16. Sexual intercourse after the first six months of pregnancy is usually dangerous to the health of the mother or the fetus.

T F 17. Sex criminals use pornographic material more often in their youth than the average person in this culture.

T F 18. Most prostitutes are nymphomaniacs.

T F 19. Almost all cases of impotency are caused by psychological problems.

T F 20. The rhythm method is just as effective as the birth control pill in preventing pregnancy.

T F 21. Masturbation by a married person is almost always related to marriage problems.

HANDOUT 7 *(continued)*

T F 22. The castration of an adult male results in a loss of his sexual desire.

T F 23. Almost all homosexuals can be identified by their physical characteristics.

T F 24. Sexual satisfaction associated with the infliction of pain is called sadism.

T F 25. If a female does not have a hymen (maidenhead, "cherry"), she is not a virgin.

T F 26. Sexual stimulation often causes erection of the nipples of the female breasts.

T F 27. A majority of the sexual crimes committed against children are committed by adults who are friends or relatives of the victims.

T F 28. For a short period of time following orgasm, men usually are not able to respond to further stimulation.

T F 29. Frequent masturbation is one of the most common causes of premature ejaculation.

T F 30. During lovemaking, it usually takes the female less time to become sexually aroused and reach climax than it does the male.

T F 31. Circumcision makes it more difficult for a male to control ejaculation.

T F 32. Nocturnal emissions, or "wet dreams," often are a sign of sexual problems.

T F 33. Brain damage can be one of the results of untreated syphilis.

T F 34. Certain foods have been shown to be aphrodisiacs (sexual stimulants).

T F 35. Transvestites are individuals who receive sexual pleasure from dressing in the clothes of the opposite sex.

T F 36. Young married couples who have an active sex life are more likely to maintain regular sexual activity in their old age than less sexually active couples.

T F 37. Relatively few cases of frigidity are caused by biological problems.

T F 38. Women generally enjoy rape although they are unlikely to admit it.

T F 39. It is possible to get "crabs" without having sex with anyone.

T F 40. The condom (rubber) is the most reliable birth-control method.

T F 41. A woman can get pregnant again while she is breast-feeding her baby.

T F 42. A woman's desire for sexual activity usually shows a great decrease after the first three months of pregnancy.

T F 43. Males are capable of experiencing multiple orgasms during sexual intercourse.

T F 44. The vaginal walls secrete most of the fluid that lubricates the vagina during sexual arousal.

T F 45. There are no medical reasons why a woman cannot engage in sexual intercourse during her menstrual period.

T F 46. A female can become pregnant the first time she has sexual intercourse.

HANDOUT 7 *(continued)*

T F 47. A female does not have to experience orgasm in order to become pregnant.

T F 48. Friction along the walls of the vagina causes orgasm in the female.

T F 49. Large breasts are more sensitive to sexual stimulation than are small breasts.

T F 50. Large amounts of alcohol inhibit sexual performance.

T F 51. Sexual intercourse during pregnancy is the most frequent cause of twins.

T F 52. In studies on sexual arousal, women report being aroused by sexual material almost as frequently as men.

T F 53. Males who expose themselves in public (exhibitionists) are seldom dangerous.

T F 54. Castration of an adult male will cause his voice to change.

T F 55. The larger the penis, the more the vagina is stimulated in sexual intercourse.

T F 56. A diaphragm should remain in place for at least six hours following sexual intercourse if it is to be effective in preventing conception.

T F 57. Douching solutions sold in stores are more effective as a contraceptive than regular water.

T F 58. Once a person has been cured of syphilis, he or she can still catch the disease again.

T F 59. Most cases of gonorrhea ("clap") take several years to disappear even with medical treatment.

T F 60. A mother with syphilis can transmit the disease to her unborn child.

Source: Allgeier, Elizabeth Rice, and Albert Richard Allgeier, *Sexual interactions, First Edition.*

HANDOUT 8

Internet Activity: Internet Resources for Troubled Adolescents

The Internet contains a wealth of information for teens and their families who are struggling with serious problems such as suicidal ideation and delinquency. In this activity you are to search the Web to find and explore some of these resources. Two interesting (and, more importantly, credible) starting points are the home-pages maintained by The American Academy of Child and Adolescent Psychiatry (www.aacap.org) and the Ignitus Worldwide (www.ignitusworldwide.org). The Academy publishes dozens of fact sheets that provide concise and up-to-date material on a variety of adolescent problems. Ignitus Worldwide is a nonprofit, youth-led organization that empowers young people to take an active role in shaping the world around them.

To start your exploration, visit these Web sites (as well as others through the numerous hyperlinks) to find answers to the following questions.

1. What percentage of all crimes in the United States are committed by teenagers?

2. How many crimes occur on school campuses each year? each day?

3. How does the prevalence of suicide among gay teenagers compare with its prevalence among heterosexual teenagers?

HANDOUT 8 *(continued)*

4. What are several verbal clues that are often revealed by adolescents who are contemplating suicide?

5. Give the addresses of at least two other Web sites maintained by reputable organizations that could be consulted as resources by troubled adolescents or their family members.

HANDOUT 9

Cohort Differences in Drug Use: A Questionnaire

Drug use varies from cohort to cohort. To discover the extent of recent changes, ask a high school junior or senior questions 1 through 4. Then ask the same questions of someone who has been out of high school for at least 5 years (preferably 8 to 10 years). Use the present tense when directing questions to current high school students.

1. When you were in high school, some students probably had minor problems with drugs. Perhaps these students appeared “out of it” or seemed otherwise disturbed, but they continued to come to class. What drug do you think most of these students were using?

   a. alcohol
   b. marijuana
   c. pills
   d. cocaine
   e. heroin or “hard drugs”
   f. ecstasy
   g. other (specify)

2. When you were in high school, some students probably had serious problems with drugs—leading to withdrawal or expulsion from school or to delinquency. What drug did you know (or suspect) that a student with serious problems had been using?

3. In high school you may have tried or been tempted to try a drug. Which drug did you use (or come closest to using)? What made the drug seem somewhat appealing?

4. Parents and educators who work with high school students are often very concerned about drug use. Sometimes they institute drug education programs. When you were in high school, which drug did parents seem most concerned about? Which of the drugs listed below did they seem least concerned about?

   a. alcohol
   b. marijuana
   c. cocaine
   d. crack cocaine
   e. heroin or “hard drugs”
   f. pills (e.g., amphetamines)
   g. LSD and other potent hallucinogens
   h. PCP (“angel dust”)
   i. inhalants (“glue sniffing”)
   j. ecstasy

HANDOUT 9 *(continued)*

5. What recent changes in the pattern of drug use, if any, are suggested by the two sets of responses to your questionnaire? Can you think of any reasons for these changes?

Source: Adapted from Straub, R. (2012). *Instructor's resources and test bank for health psychology* (3rd ed.). New York: Worth.

HANDOUT 10

Internet Activity: Adolescent Drug Experimentation

To learn more about the role of biopsychosocial factors in adolescent drug experimentation, do research on the Internet to find brief answers to the following questions. Hint: One Web site you might consult is the home page of Substance Abuse and Mental Health Services Administration. Find them at http://store.samhsa.gov/home.

1. The National Parents' Resource Institute for Drug Education (PRIDE) annually conducts a survey of students in grades 6 through 12. Consult the statistical summary of their latest study to draw a bar graph depicting the percentage of students in grades 6 through 8 who reported regular use of the following substances: nicotine, beer, wine coolers, marijuana, inhalants, cocaine, uppers, downers.

2. How do the substance use data for this latest survey compare with the data reported in 1996? What trends are noticeable for various substances?

3. What aspects of the results have led some developmentalists to conclude that adolescent drug use is increasingly not merely recreational or experimental?

HANDOUT 10 *(continued)*

4. By their report, who most often discusses the hazards of early drug use with teenagers—peers, parents, or teachers? Are sixth- to eighth-graders more likely to experiment with drugs in their home, a friend's home, at school, or some other place?

5. What percent of twelfth-graders report using an illicit drug at least once each week? What percent report using an illicit drug daily?

Emerging Adulthood: Biosocial Development

Contents

Note: Worth Publishers provides online Instructor and Student Tool Kits, DVD Student Tool Kits, and Instructor and Student video resources in DevelopmentPortal for use with the text. See Part I: General Resources for information about these materials and the text Lecture Guides for a complete list by text chapter.

Good Health Habits

Suggested Activities

Introducing Emerging Adulthood: Biosocial Development

"On Your Own" Activity: Developmental Fact or Myth?

Before students read about biosocial development during emerging adulthood, have them respond to the true-false statements in Handout 1.

The correct answers are shown below. Class discussion can focus on the origins of any developmental misconceptions that are demonstrated in the students' incorrect answers.

1. T
2. T
3. T
4. F
5. F
6. F
7. T
8. T
9. T
10. F

AV: The Journey Through the Life Span, Program 7: Early Adulthood

Program 7 (21:25) introduces the developing person during emerging adulthood, a period that for most people is the healthiest of their lives. The program begins by describing the physical and biological signs of senescence—the gradual decline in physical abilities that all women and men eventually experience—focusing on changes in homeostasis and organ reserve capacity. The fertility problems experienced by about 15 percent of couples are also discussed, along with in vitro fertilization and other medical treatments. Sally Guttmacher of New York University discusses the body image problems that plague many young adult women of European ancestry. The segment concludes with an exploration of drug abuse during early adulthood.

The second segment—cognitive development—centers on the concept of postformal thinking, which is the more subjective, interpersonal, and flexible thinking that begins to dominate adult mental life. Kurt Fischer of Harvard University explains how adult thinking also is more dialectical and able to consider opposing ideas and to forge them into new beliefs. His description segues into the final segment of the program—social development—that explores changes in the settings of the social clock—the culturally set timetable that establishes when various events and endeavors in life are appropriate. Ronald Sabatelli and Paul Kindal of the University of Connecticut discuss historical changes in cohabitation, marriage, divorce, and the effects of marital conflict on children. The program concludes with an in-depth exploration of changing concepts of parenthood.

In the first of the two unnarrated observation modules for the unit on early adulthood, 24-year-old Mannes is interviewed about his work and social life following college. He reflects on why he has yet to settle into a comfortable work routine, and compares his former "experience-oriented" lifestyle as a college student with the more goal-oriented lifestyle he follows today. In the second module, 23-year-old John speaks about his recent decisions to return to college to prepare for medical school and to delay family commitments in order to focus on his career goals.

AV: Transitions Throughout the Life Span, Program 17: Early Adulthood: Biosocial Development

In Program 17, we encounter the developing person in the prime of life. Emerging adulthood is the best time for hard physical labor—because strength is at a peak—and for reproduction—because overall health is good and fertility is high. However, with the attainment of full maturity, a new aspect of physical development comes into play—that is, decline. Program 17 takes a look at how people perceive changes that occur as the body ages as well as how decisions they make regarding lifestyle affect the course of their overall development.

The first segment describes the growth, strength, and health of the individual during adulthood, as well as both visible age-related changes, such as wrinkling, and less obvious changes, such as declines in the efficiency of the body's systems. Sexual-reproductive health, a matter of great concern to young adults, is discussed in the next segment, with particular attention paid to trends in sexual responsiveness during adulthood and fertility problems that may develop. The final segment looks at three problems that are more prevalent during young adulthood than at any other period of the life span: drug abuse, compulsive eating and destructive dieting, and violence.

Growth and Strength

AV: Factors in Healthy Aging (28 min., Films for the Humanities and Sciences)

This brief film examines the ongoing study of Harvard University graduates about factors that predict health as a person ages. These include nutrition, smoking, alcohol use, personality, and heredity.

"On Your Own" Activity: Test Your Face for Symmetry

Researchers working from the evolutionary perspective have suggested that one clue to "good" genes is facial symmetry. In several studies, researchers have found that both women and men find symmetry attractive. They theorize that this is because symmetry is indicative of two copies of a gene—a sign of a healthy, fertile constitution. In this simple exercise, which requires only a mirror and a recent photograph, students can test their own faces for symmetry. Handout 2 provides instructions for students.

According to researchers who work from this perspective, symmetry is one of many "codes" used by men and women to assess a potential mate's health and fertility.

Classroom Activity: "Over the Hill": Introducing the Topic of Senescence

Classroom activities are an excellent opportunity for adolescent students to explore their personal attitudes and expectations about aging and the process of senescence. Stephen Fried of Park College describes a particularly good activity that he calls "The Aging Stereotype Game." Although the activity originally was designed to explore myths about the elderly, it can easily be modified for any age group that your students see as the threshold of being "over the hill."

Fried divides the class into groups of four to seven students. Each group is asked to develop a list of 15 to 20 negative stereotypes about older adults and a list of 15 to 20 positive stereotypes (for example, "Old people are set in their ways," and "Older people don't let little things upset them."). Each group then chooses a recorder to write down the group's list and then report it to the entire class. Once all the groups have reported, the instructor leads a discussion aimed at identifying common themes raised by the groups.

A natural extension of the class discussion would be to have students write a "one-minute paper" at the end of the class in which they examine and reflect on their own beliefs about entering adulthood.

Fried, Stephen B. (1988, October). Learning activities for understanding aging. *Teaching of Psychology, 15(3)*, 160–161.

AV: Brain Architecture and the Sexes (Films for the Humanities and Sciences)

This modularly organized series examines biological influences on male–female differences in every domain of development. Each module lasts approximately 51 minutes. Module One, "Sugar and Spice: The Facts Behind Sex Differences," discusses male–female differences in the developing prenatal brain. Module Two, "Anything You Can Do, I Can Do Better: Why the Sexes Excel Differently," explores the debate over whether differences in brain architecture account for statistical differences in performance between women and men. Module Three, "Love, Love Me, Do: How Sex Differences Affect Relationships," explores the way sex differences in the brain might influence attraction to others and parenthood.

Observational Activity: Physical Stereotyping in the Media

A number of studies have shown that males and females are usually portrayed differently by the media, leading to the perpetuation of physical and sexist stereotypes. As indicated in the text, such restrictive stereotypes can have an enormous, and negative, impact on development. Dane Archer and his colleagues evaluated 1,750 photographs of people appearing in magazine advertisements. With remarkable consistency, the photographs emphasized the faces of men and the bodies of women. The authors found that this "face-ism" effect also occurred in their own students when they were asked to draw pictures capturing the "character of a real person." Both male and female undergraduates emphasized the face of a man, drawing it about twice as large and with greater detail than they did the woman's.

To help your students appreciate the extent of sexist stereotyping in the popular media, ask each student to choose a medium and complete the assignment on Handout 3.

As students present their examples, use class time to discuss issues pertaining to physical stereotyping in the media. Good topics include the "targeting" of advertising in various periodicals to certain age, sex, and socioeconomic groups, as well as the social responsibility of advertising. Ask students whether sexist stereotyping is more prevalent in some media than in others. Encourage the class to consider the ways in which such stereotypes are self-perpetuating, and whether these traditional restrictive stereotypes are changing in contemporary society.

Archer, D., Iritani, B., Kimes, D., & Barrios, M. (1983). Face-ism: Five studies of sex differences in facial prominence. *Journal of Personality and Social Psychology, 45*, 725–735.

Psychopathology

Classroom Activity: Student-Generated Case Studies

Generally, well-being increases during emerging adulthood, but so does the rate of psychological disorders. Although the roots of such problems can be traced to earlier ages, the stresses of this period push some people over the edge. The textbook covers mood disorders, anxiety disorders, and schizophrenia, then uses the diathesis-stress model to emphasize how the social contexts of emerging adulthood tend to worsen these problems. To help bring these problems to life for students, give them 5 minutes or so to write a brief, symptom-based description of a young adult with one of these psychological disorders. When they have finished their descriptions, have students trade with one another and "diagnose" one another's case studies.

Classroom Activity: What Would Dr. Phil Say?

Before class, prepare a hypothetical case study involving an 18- to 25-year-old emerging adult who faces a personal problem. Pick one of potential problems discussed in the text, such as one involving a sexual relationship, high risk activity or other bad health habit, or even one of the several forms of psychopathology covered in the text. Read the case aloud to the class in the form of a letter to Dr. Phil, Dear Abby, or other self-help expert, and then give the class 5 to 10 minutes to write a response that is based on sound developmental science. Afterward, have students share and discuss their responses.

AV: Depression Disorders (29 min., Insight Media)

This two-part program provides a thorough overview of major depressive disorder (MDD). Part 1 explores the symptoms of MDD and examines biological theories of the disorder. Part 2 uses interviews with individuals suffering from depression to explore the role of life events and stress in MDD. Various treatments are described, including cognitive therapy, medication, and electroconvulsive shock.

AV: Exploring Psychological Disorders (CD-ROM, Insight Media)

Using video clips of actual client and patient interviews, this CD-ROM provides an overview of the criteria of the *Diagnostic and Statistical Manual of Mental Disorders (DSM-IV)* used to diagnose clinical cases. It also includes information on how biological, social, cultural, and psychological factors interact in contributing to psychological disorders.

AV: Postpartum Depression and the Yates Killings (22 min., Films for the Humanities and Sciences)

Filmed just prior to the arraignment of Andrea Yates, who was charged with drowning her five children, this *ABC News* program explores postpartum depression. A panel of experts outlines the warning signs and discusses treatment options.

"On Your Own" Activity: Zung Self-Rating Depression Scale

The Zung Self-Rating Depression Scale is a widely-used instrument for measuring depression. To score their answers to Handout 4, have students reverse their responses to items 2, 5, 6, 11, 12, 14, 16, 17, 18, and 20 (1 = 4, 2 = 3, 3 = 2, 4 = 1). They should then add together the recoded answers to obtain their total score, which can range from 20 to 80.

Scores from 50 to 59 suggest mild to moderate depression, from 60 to 69 reveal moderate to severe depression, and 70 and above may single severe depression. You might note that a version of this scale appears each year in *Parade Magazine* just before National Depression Screening Day, which was created in 1991 by Harvard psychiatrist Douglas Jacobs. Jacobs believes this effort, along with the free screening provided by mental health professionals at dozens of sites, has saved hundreds of lives.

AV: No More Shame: Understanding Schizophrenia, Depression, and Addiction (21–24 min., Films for the Humanities and Sciences)

These three programs discuss the biological, psychological, and cultural aspects of schizophrenia, major depressive disorder, and addiction. Each disorder is brought to life through the eyes of real people suffering from the disorder as a panel of experts discusses the underlying causes, prevention, and available treatments.

Critical Thinking Activity: Gender Differences in Depression

Each chapter of these resources contains a critical thinking exercise designed specifically to test students' critical thinking about a topic covered in the chapter. Handout 5 contains a synopsis of research or a brief scenario followed by a series of questions.

Answers to this chapter's critical thinking exercise are as follows:

1. Evidence indicates that brain biochemistry is a significant factor in depressive disorders. It is known, for example, that individuals with major depressive illness typically have too little or too much of certain neurotransmitters. Furthermore, significant events in women's reproductive life cycle (menstruation, pregnancy, the postpregnancy period, and menopause) may bring fluctuations in mood that for some women include depression.
2. Evidence indicates that people with certain cognitive traits (pessimistic thinking, low self-esteem, a sense of having little control over life events, and proneness to excessive worrying) are more likely to develop or have difficulty overcoming depression. Some experts have suggested that the traditional upbringing of girls might foster these traits, which may be a factor in women's higher rate of

depression. Some experts have also suggested that women are not more vulnerable to depression than men but simply express or label their symptoms differently. According to this viewpoint, women may be more likely to admit feelings of depression, brood about their feelings, or seek professional assistance. Men, on the other hand, may be socially conditioned to deny such feelings or to express them in more active ways, as reflected in the higher rates of alcoholism in men.

3. Some experts have suggested that the traditional upbringing of girls might foster the negative, self-defeating cognitive style that may be a factor in the higher rate of depression among women. Psychosocial stress also contributes to depression in persons who are vulnerable to the illness. Some experts have suggested that the higher incidence of depression in women is due to the multidimensional stresses that many women face, such as major responsibilities at home and work, single parenthood, and caring for children and aging parents. Another psychosocial factor that influences depression is the quality of a person's social relationships. For both women and men, rates of major depression are highest among the separated and divorced, and lowest among the married.
4. One way to test the hypothesis would be to create a mixed set of symptoms; some would be typical symptoms of major depression, while others would be characteristic of a disorder more commonly diagnosed in men. Randomly divide clinical psychologists into two groups: one group would be told that the patient was female; the other group would be told the patient was male. If significantly more clinicians diagnose the symptoms as signs of depression when ascribed to female patients than to male patients, this would be evidence for bias in the diagnostic process.

Good Health Habits

Teaching Tip: Forming Good Health Habits Early in Life

To emphasize the importance of forming good health habits early in life, have students prepare a list of their good and bad health habits. For each bad habit, have them explain the risks involved in persisting in the habit—for example, overeating may result in obesity, which increases the risk of heart disease. Discuss why students continue bad habits despite contraindications provided by medical research. Why do students maintain unhealthy diets, for instance? What benefits does smoking provide for them? Discuss the ways in which our culture supports and even promotes bad health habits. Then turn to the good habits, such as regular exercise. Discuss some of the ways in which these healthy patterns were developed, including the benefits of maintaining them.

"On Your Own" Activity: Eating Habits: Past and Present Attitudes and Experiences

Adolescence: Biosocial Development included this survey regarding eating habits. If you did not use the handout then, you might want to use it now (for your convenience, it's included here as Handout 6).

Also for your convenience, we repeated the somewhat different scales for males and females. When your students have completed the survey, have them compute their total score (one point for each answer that is in agreement with the scale). The higher the score, the more positive is the individual's orientation to food.

Scoring Scales for Eating Habits Survey

Males: 2-T, 3-F, 4-T, 5-T, 7-F, 9-F, 10-T, 11-T, 12-T, 15-F, 16-F, 17-T, 18-F, 19-T, 24-T, 25-T, 26-T, 27-T, 32-T, 33-T, 34-F, 37-F, 38-T, 39-T, 42-T, 45-F, 46-F, 47-F, 51-T, 52-T, 53-T, 54-T, 58-F, 60-T, 61-T, 63-T, 64-T

Females: 1-T, 2-T, 4-T, 5-T, 6-T, 8-T, 9-F, 10-T, 11-T, 12-T, 13-F, 14-T, 15-T, 16-F, 17-T, 18-F, 19-T, 20-T, 21-T, 22-T, 23-F, 26-T, 27-T, 28-F, 29-T, 30-F, 31-F, 34-F, 35-F, 36-F, 39-T, 40-T, 41-T, 43-F, 44-T, 45-F, 48-F, 49-F, 50-T, 51-T, 52-T, 53-T, 54-T, 55-F, 56-F, 57-F, 59-T, 61-T, 62-T, 63-T, 65-T

Classroom Activity: Edgework Wiki

Many young adults are drawn to edgework—recreational and career activities that entail an element of risk and even danger. You can easily get a good class discussion going on this topic by showing a video clip depicting an extreme sport such as bungee jumping, ice climbing, or any of the numerous disciplines that comprise the X Games. Then ask your students what activities they engage in, or aspire to professionally, that could be characterized as edgework. Ask why such activities are often associated with youth, and specifically, with which youth subcultures. If time permits, turn the board into an "Edgework Wiki" as you ask the class to create an entry that explains the concept of edgework to someone who knows nothing about it. Derived from "Wikipedia," the biggest free-content encyclopedia on the Internet, a "Wiki" is a collaborative Web site that can be directly edited by anyone with access to it.

AV: Altered States: A History of Drug Abuse (57 min., Films for the Humanities and Sciences)

This captivating film traces the history of drug use in America from the days when the earliest immigrants developed an addiction for tobacco, through Prohibition, and up to the present day. It explores how drugs of choice have changed over time and documents the cultural, social, and political factors involved in drug use and addiction.

AV: The Addicted Brain (26 min., Films for the Humanities and Sciences)

(See description in Adolescence: Biosocial Development.)

AV: Adult Children of Alcoholics: A Family Secret (52 min., Films for the Humanities and Sciences)

In this poignant film, adult children of alcoholic parents speak out about how their parents' disease has affected their lives, beginning with childhood nightmares and continuing into their present-day problem behaviors. The latter include marrying alcoholic spouses, abusing other drugs, gambling, and other addictive behaviors.

AV Female Alcoholism (19 min., Films for the Humanities and Sciences)

This short film offers a concise view of the changing stereotype of the female alcoholic. It also discusses the teratogenic effects of drinking alcohol during pregnancy and the psychological impact of being raised by an alcoholic mother.

Classroom Activity: Classroom Debate: *"Resolved: Alcoholism and the Abuse of Other Drugs Is Hereditary"*

The possibility that alcoholism is hereditary has been debated since the eighteenth century, when physicians believed that a "constitutional weakness" for alcohol ran in families. With more recent evidence that some people inherit a metabolic predisposition that makes alcohol more pleasurable, while others inherit a particular enzyme reaction that makes their bodies so intolerant of alcohol they are unlikely ever to abuse the drug, the debate has intensified.

A poll of your students is likely to reveal that they are divided on the issue. Some will subscribe to the disease model and see drug abuse as determined primarily by genetic factors. Others who hold the social learning view will believe that environmental factors such as cultural norms and upbringing are more important in explaining the development of alcoholism.

Several methods of addressing the heritability of drug abuse are possible, but most studies have focused on twins or adopted children. These studies suggest that the relative influence of heredity and environment in addiction is a complex problem.

To focus attention on the issue of drug abuse in early adulthood, follow the guidelines in the General Resources section of this manual and schedule a debate on the resolution. As with most debates concerning the nature–nurture issue, it is important that students not expect clear-cut, "either–or" conclusions to emerge from the literature.

"On Your Own" Activity: Cohort Differences in Drug Use: A Questionnaire

In Adolescence: Psychosocial Development, we included a questionnaire by which students could determine cohort differences in drug use, focusing on the differences between adolescents and young adults. If you did not use the handout then, you might want to use it now (for your convenience, it's included here as Handout 7). Alternatively, you might want to ask students to compare responses of people in their 20s with those of people over 30.

Responses will vary. Some of the patterns mentioned in the text should emerge. For example, students likely will find that the early 20s are the peak time for use of marijuana and other illicit drugs, heavy drinking, and chain smoking. Drug abuse tends to ease by age 30.

HANDOUT 1

Developmental Fact or Myth?

T F 1. Before middle age, women attain their full breast and hip size and men reach full shoulder and upper-arm size.

T F 2. The average young adult sees a health professional once a year.

T F 3. The older a person is, the longer it takes his or her body to adapt to, and recover from, physical stress.

T F 4. Most young adults do not condone premarital sex.

T F 5. Most people believe the primary purpose of sex is reproduction.

T F 6. The rate of serious mental illness among emerging adults is half that for adults over age 25.

T F 7. Anxiety disorders are more prevalent than depression in young adults.

T F 8. In general, men are naturally more daring than women.

T F 9. Drug abuse is more common among college students than among their peers who are not in college.

T F 10. Women actually use drugs more than men do.

HANDOUT 2

Test Your Face for Symmetry?

In order to complete this activity you will need a square or rectangular hand mirror and a recent full-face photograph of yourself (a yearbook photograph is ideal). Test your face for symmetry by holding the mirror on edge, down the middle of your photograph. A line of symmetry exists where the mirror is placed if the reflection and the reflected portion of the object together look like the whole object. Try reflecting the left side of your face, then try reflecting the right side of your face. How symmetrical is your face? Most human faces are not very symmetrical; the left and right sides of our faces are just different enough to make every face unique.

As a follow-up to this activity, see if you can test the facial symmetry of several popular actresses, actors, or other public persons who generally are considered to be very attractive. Are their faces symmetrical?

HANDOUT 3

Observational Activity: Physical Stereotyping in the Media

Choose one of the popular media and look for evidence of physical and/or sexist stereotyping. Such stereotyping may be found in the general theme or content of the article, advertisement, story, or program, and in personality characterizations. Based on your findings, answer the following questions.

1. From what medium is your sample chosen?

2. At what reference group(s) is this medium targeted?

3. How was physical and/or sexist stereotyping demonstrated in your sample?

4. For what reasons, do you believe, was stereotyping incorporated into this advertisement, story, article, or program? Was it intentional? Was it meant to boost sales?

5. Do you feel that the stereotyping serves its purpose? Why do you feel this way?

Source: Archer, D., Iritani, B., Kimes, D., & Barrios, M. (1983). Face-ism: Five studies of sex differences in facial prominence. *Journal of Personality and Social Psychology, 45*, 725–735.

HANDOUT 4

Zung Self-Rating Depression Scale

Instructions: Read each statement carefully. Use the following scale to indicate how often you have felt that way during the past two weeks. (If you are on a diet, respond to statements 5 and 7 as though you were not on a diet.)

1 = none or a little of the time
2 = some of the time
3 = good part of the time
4 = most or all of the time
5 = all the time

___ 1. I feel down-hearted, blue, and sad.
___ 2. Morning is when I feel the best.
___ 3. I have crying spells or feel like it.
___ 4. I have trouble sleeping through the night.
___ 5. I eat as much as I used to.
___ 6. I enjoy looking at, talking to, and being with attractive women/men.
___ 7. I notice that I am losing weight.
___ 8. I have trouble with constipation.
___ 9. My heart beats faster than usual.
___ 10. I get tired for no reason.
___ 11. My mind is as clear as it used to be.
___ 12. I find it easy to do the things I used to do.
___ 13. I am restless and can't keep still.
___ 14. I feel hopeful about the future.
___ 15. I am more irritable than usual.
___ 16. I find it easy to make decisions.
___ 17. I feel that I am useful and needed.
___ 18. My life is pretty full.
___ 19. I feel that others would be better off if I were dead.
___ 20. I still enjoy the things I used to do.

Source: Zung, W. K. (1965). A self-rating depression scale. *Archives of General Psychiatry, 12,* 63–70.

HANDOUT 5

Critical Thinking Activity: Gender Differences in Depression

Now that you have read and reviewed Chapter 20, take your learning a step further by testing your critical thinking skills on this perspective-taking exercise.

The symptoms of *major depressive disorder* are lethargy, loss of interest in family, friends, and activities, and feelings of worthlessness that last two weeks or longer without any notable cause. During adulthood, women are diagnosed with depression roughly twice as often as men. (Interestingly, among college-age women and men, the gender difference in depression is much smaller.)

More generally, women appear to be more vulnerable than men to *passive* (internalized) psychological disorders such as depression and anxiety. In contrast, men are generally more vulnerable to *active* (externalized) psychological disorders, including drug abuse, antisocial conduct, and poor impulse control.

This exercise asks you to examine the gender difference in the diagnosis of active and passive psychological disorders, first by thinking critically about this issue and then by reviewing ongoing research regarding its origins.

1. What factors in the biosocial domain might account for women's greater susceptibility to depression and other "passive" disorders?

2. What factors in the cognitive domain might account for women's greater susceptibility to depression?

3. What factors in the psychosocial domain might account for this gender difference?

HANDOUT 5 *(continued)*

4. Some have suggested that the gender difference may be the result of a gender bias in the diagnostic process. That is, doctors and clinicians expect women to suffer from depression more often and, consequently, are more vigilant in finding symptoms that confirm this expectation. As a researcher, how would you test this hypothesis?

(To complete this question, consult the Web sites for the *National Institute of Mental Health (NIMH)* (www.mhsource.com/hy/depwoman.html) and the *American Psychological Association (APA)* (www.apa.org/pubinfo/depress.html). Compare your answers to questions 1, 2, and 3 to the information provided by NIMH and the APA. Then briefly summarize the latest evidence regarding the biosocial, cognitive, and psychosocial factors in depression in general, and women's greater vulnerability, in particular.

HANDOUT 6

Survey of Eating Habits

For each statement, circle "T" or "F" to indicate whether it is true or false, as applied to you.

Part I. Past Attitudes and Habits

T F 1. My family seldom argued at the dinner table.

T F 2. Many different types of meals were served at our house.

T F 3. I did not particularly care for the food served at home.

T F 4. My mother was a good cook.

T F 5. Our family seemed to be in a better disposition at and shortly after meals than before.

T F 6. My mother enjoyed cooking.

T F 7. Meals were simple but substantial in our family.

T F 8. My mother served desserts frequently.

T F 9. Discipline was usually enforced shortly before or after the evening meal.

T F 10. Mealtimes were quite unhurried; in fact, they took on the aspect of a social activity.

T F 11. My father enjoyed eating.

T F 12. I enjoyed eating.

T F 13. Younger members of the family were requested not to talk too much at meals.

T F 14. My family often celebrated something important by going to a restaurant.

T F 15. Less than an average amount of conversation occurred at mealtime in my family.

T F 16. My father tended to dampen mealtime conversation.

T F 17. Conversation at meals was more light than serious.

T F 18. Business matters were often discussed at meals (chores, etc.).

T F 19. Flowers or candles were sometimes placed on the table at evening meals.

T F 20. Sometimes my mother would give me my favorite food when I was sick or unhappy.

T F 21. My mother used to take special precautions to avoid giving us contaminated food.

T F 22. The emphasis was on nutritional meals in our family.

T F 23. My mother liked cooking least of all household chores.

T F 24. Meals were quite elaborate in our family.

T F 25. Individuals other than my immediate family, such as grandparents, usually participated in the evening meal.

T F 26. Following the main meal, I tended to linger about the table talking and so on, rather than leaving the table.

HANDOUT 6 *(continued)*

T F 27. My mother enjoyed eating.
T F 28. Sometimes I felt like leaving the table before the meal was over.
T F 29. My mother fixed my favorite foods when I was sick.
T F 30. At restaurants everything I ordered had to be eaten.
T F 31. Eating out was infrequent.
T F 32. The entire family was usually present at the evening meal.
T F 33. On my birthdays I helped plan the menu.
T F 34. My mother tended to dampen mealtime conversation.
T F 35. Discipline was often applied at mealtime.
T F 36. Family meals were more hurried than unhurried.
T F 37. My father sometimes scolded us at the evening meal.
T F 38. At breakfast, I often read what was printed on the cereal boxes.

Part II. Present Attitudes and Habits

T F 39. Mealtime is usually pleasant in my home.
T F 40. I like to smell food cooking.
T F 41. In general, I prefer a slow, leisurely meal to a quick, hurried one.
T F 42. I like many different types of food.
T F 43. I tend to be underweight.
T F 44. At a party, I tend to eat a lot of peanuts.
T F 45. I do not care much for desserts.
T F 46. I seldom like to try a new food.
T F 47. I often get indigestion or heartburn.
T F 48. If I am very busy, I may forget all about eating.
T F 49. Shopping for groceries is unpleasant.
T F 50. I like to eat foreign foods.
T F 51. A good wife must be a good cook.
T F 52. I think that going to an expensive restaurant is a good way to celebrate an important event such as an anniversary, a birthday, etc.
T F 53. I have a tendency to gain weight.
T F 54. Sometimes I have a craving for sweets.
T F 55. I tend to be quiet rather than talkative.
T F 56. If a child refuses dinner, he should be made to eat.
T F 57. I almost never eat between meals.
T F 58. I dislike many foods.
T F 59. I enjoy eating at restaurants.
T F 60. I often eat while I am watching television.
T F 61. Watching people eat makes me hungry.
T F 62. People who eat heartily in public have bad manners.
T F 63. I often buy refreshments at movies, ball games, etc.
T F 64. I sometimes reward myself by eating.
T F 65. When depressed I sometimes eat my favorite foods.

Source: Byrne, D., & Kelley, K. (1981). *An introduction to personality* (3rd ed., 135–136). Englewood Cliffs, NJ: Prentice Hall.

HANDOUT 7

Cohort Differences in Drug Use: A Questionnaire

Drug use varies from cohort to cohort. To discover the extent of recent changes, ask a high school junior or senior questions 1 through 4. Then ask the same questions of someone who has been out of high school for at least five years (preferably eight to ten years). Use the present tense when directing questions to current high school students.

1. When you were in high school some students probably had minor problems with drugs. Perhaps these students appeared "out of it" or seemed otherwise disturbed, but they continued to come to class. What drug do you think most of these students were using?

   a. alcohol
   b. marijuana
   c. pills
   d. cocaine
   e. heroin or "hard drugs"
   f. other (specify)

2. When you were in high school some students probably had serious problems with drugs—leading to withdrawal or expulsion from school, or to delinquency. What drug did you know (or suspect) that a student with serious problems had been using?

3. In high school you may have tried or been tempted to try a drug. Which drug did you use (or come closest to using)? What made the drug seem somewhat appealing?

4. Parents and educators who work with high school students are often very concerned about drug use. Sometimes they institute drug education programs. When you were in high school, which drug did parents seem most concerned about? ____________________ Which of the drugs listed below did they seem least concerned about? ____________________

   a. alcohol
   b. marijuana
   c. cocaine
   d. crack cocaine
   e. heroin
   f. pills (e.g., amphetamines)
   g. LSD and other potent hallucinogens
   h. PCP ("angel dust")
   i. inhalants ("glue-sniffing")

HANDOUT 7 *(continued)*

5. **What recent changes in the pattern of drug use, if any, are suggested by the two sets of responses to your questionnaire? Can you think of any reasons for these changes?**

Source: Adapted from Straub, R. (2012). ***Instructor's resources and test bank for health psychology*** (3rd ed.). New York: Worth.

Emerging Adulthood: Cognitive Development

Contents

Note: Worth Publishers provides online Instructor and Student Tool Kits, DVD Student Tool Kits, and Instructor and Student video resources in DevelopmentPortal for use with the text. See Part I: General Resources for information about these materials and the text Lecture Guides for a complete list by text chapter.

Suggested Activities

Introducing Emerging Adulthood: Cognitive Development

"On Your Own" Activity: Developmental Fact or Myth?

Before students read about cognitive development during emerging adulthood, have them respond to the true-false statements in Handout 1.

The correct answers are shown below. Class discussion can focus on the origins of any developmental misconceptions that are demonstrated in the students' incorrect answers.

1. T 2. T 3. F 4. F 5. F 6. T 7. T 8. T 9. F 10. T

AV: The Journey Through the Life Span, Program 7: Early Adulthood

See Emerging Adulthood: Biosocial Development for a description of Program 7 and the accompanying observation modules, which cover the entire unit on emerging adulthood.

AV: Transitions Throughout the Life Span, Program 18: Early Adulthood: Cognitive Development

Program 18 closely parallels the text coverage describing the shifts in cognitive development that occur during early adulthood—for example, in the efficiency and depth of our thinking. As noted in the text, developmentalists offer three approaches to cognitive development. Like the text, this program takes a postformal approach.

The program first demonstrates the differences between adolescent and adult thinking. The thinking of young adults is more dialectical and adaptive—the kind of thinking they need to solve the problems of daily life.

Next, the program explores how the events of early adulthood can affect moral development. Of particular interest are Fowler's six stages in the development of faith.

The program also examines the effect of the college experience on cognitive growth. In general, with each year of college the individual becomes more cognitively adept. A final segment covers the effects of life events, such as parenthood, job promotion, or illness, on cognitive growth during young adulthood.

Teaching Tip: Adding a Service-Learning Project to the Course

Adding a service-learning project to a traditional lecture-based course works particularly well in a life-span development course. Students combine learning course content from the instructor with an applied outreach activity that provides opportunities for relevant experiential learning. Students then consolidate their experiences through graded assignments, such as writing an essay relating class material to outreach experiences, or drafting a mock grant proposal that describes the perceived needs of the agency or program they visited.

This unit on emerging adulthood lends itself to a variety of service-learning placements. For example, students could volunteer at a local Child or Adolescent Advocacy Center (CAC). Most nonprofit CACs depend heavily on donations and volunteer assistance to maintain operations. As students learn about development in the classroom, they can apply their knowledge to various CAC activities (e.g., the link between cognitive development during emerging adulthood and how criminal or forensic interviews are conducted; the link between social development and the benefits of support groups for various developmental problems).

Additional examples of service-learning activities include working in a Big Brother/Big Sister mentoring organization; tutoring adolescents with reading, math, or other school-based problems; or volunteering at a domestic-violence shelter. Should you decide to include a service-learning project in your course, there are many resources for finding field placements for your students. A good place to start is the National Service-Learning Clearinghouse (www.servicelearning.org/).

Postformal Thought

Classroom Activity: The Flexible Nature of Cognition

To expand on the text discussion of the nature of cognition and as a a reminder of the text earlier discussion of cognitive development during middle childhood and a prelude to the discussion of cognitive development during adulthood, you might want to cover the concept of practical intelligence. According to Sternberg, *practical intelligence* is defined as behavior that operates in real life, consisting of "the things you need to know to succeed on the job that you're never explicitly taught. . . . You have to pick this stuff up on your own. . . . Whether you get promoted, or get raises, or can move to another company or another school is going to depend in part on how well you pick it up."

Traditional IQ tests do not, of course, measure practical intelligence. In fact, by one estimate the correlation between IQ test scores and job performance is a dismal 0.2. IQ tests are poor predictors of occupational performance because they measure other skills, generally the kinds of formal operational processes discussed earlier in the text.

Sternberg believes that each individual can develop his or her practical intelligence and that practical intelligence can be taught, at least to the degree that the skills are made explicit. One of Sternberg's pet projects involves teaching his Yale graduate students the fine art of publishing journal articles—how to write for particular journals, ways of increasing one's "publishability," and the like.

Your students will probably concur with Sternberg's argument concerning the irrelevance of most intelligence tests to real-life problems and will certainly be able to cite personal examples. Handout 2 lists some of the behaviors that Sternberg and his colleagues have found to be characteristic of individuals who possess practical intelligence. Students should rate on a 1 (low) to 9 (high) scale the extent to which each of these is characteristic of their own behavior. Higher scores are associated with more adaptive behavior.

Sternberg's idea of practical intelligence (sometimes referred to as "tacit knowledge") has been applied in many different fields. As one example, military researchers have developed a method of assessing practical intelligence among military officers in order to understand why some are more effective than others (Hedlund et al., 2003). Researchers conducted interviews with Army officers at three levels of leadership in order to identify the type of practical, experience-based knowledge that is typically not part of formal training, yet is deemed crucial to leadership success. The resulting Tacit Knowledge for Military Leaders (TKML) inventory, which consists of a series of leadership scenarios, was administered to a total of 562 leaders at the platoon, company, and battalion levels. At all three levels, TKML scores were strongly correlated with ratings of leadership effectiveness as reported by peer and superior officers. After citing this study, you might challenge your students to come up with other areas of expertise that might naturally lend themselves to a good test of tacit knowledge.

Gottfredson, L. S. (2003). Dissecting practical intelligence theory: its claims and evidence. *Intelligence, 31*(4), 343–370.

Hedlund, J., Forsythe, G. B., Horvath, J. A., Williams, W. M., & Snook, S. (2003, April). Identifying and assessing tacit knowledge: understanding the practical intelligence of military leaders. *Leadership Quarterly, 14*(2), 117–124.

Sternberg, R. J. (2000). *Practical intelligence in everyday life*. New York: Cambridge University Press.

"On Your Own" Activity: Assessing Tacit Knowledge

The questionnaire in Handout 3 presents a variety of situations with which a corporate manager might be confronted. For each situation, students should rank the potential solution based on how they would most likely handle the situation. There are no right or wrong answers; what is "right" will depend on the particular individual.

After students have evaluated their responses, discussion should focus on the nature of tacit knowledge and on how each of the alternative ways of handling the test situations represents a particular style of adapting to the environment. Emphasize that tacit knowledge refers to information an individual picks up from life experiences and to his or her ability to draw upon these experiences in dealing with real-life problems. Although the tacit knowledge underlying success differs from one occupation to another (as embodied in the concept of expertise), people who are practically intelligent are better able to apply their tacit knowledge to a wide range of circumstances than those who are not.

The "answers" to the questionnaire are listed below. Note that a "+" indicates a relatively higher rating by individuals more advanced in the field relative to individuals less advanced in the field; a "–" indicates a relatively lower rating by individuals more advanced in the field. Keep in mind, then, that the +'s and –'s are relative. There are no correct answers, per se, only trends in distinguishing more from less experienced individuals.

1.	2.	3.	4.	5.
a. –	a. +	a. –	a. +	a. –
b. –	b. –	b. –	b. +	b. –
c. –	c. +	c. –	c. +	c. –
d. +	d. –	d. +	d. –	d. –
e. –	e. +	e. –	e. –	e. –

Sternberg, R. J. (1999). *Tacit knowledge in professional practice*. Mahwah, NJ: Lawrence Erlbaum.

Sternberg, R. J. (1986). *Intelligence applied: Understanding and increasing your intellectual skills.* New York: Harcourt Brace Jovanovich, pp. 321–323, 325.

Classroom Activity: Pedagogy and "Andragogy"

When adult education first became popular, experts assumed that the same methods and techniques used to teach children could be applied to adults. Although the word *pedagogy* has come to refer to the general art and science of teaching, its Greek root actually means "leading children." In the 1950s, as research began to show that adults and children do not, in fact, learn in the same ways, some European educators started using the term *andragogy,* from the Greek words "anere" for adult and "agogus," for "helping" to refer specifically to the art and science of teaching adults.

Today, andragogy has become a leading "brand" in the theory of adult education. It is based on five key assumptions, which you might wish to present to your students for discussion.

- *Motivation to learn:* Adult students need to first know why they need to learn something.
- *Learner self-concept:* As people mature, their self-concepts shift from being dependent on others toward increasing independence.
- *Role of learners' experience:* Adult learners have a variety of life experiences that represent their richest resources for learning.
- *Readiness to learn:* Adults are ready to learn those things they need to know in order to cope effectively with life situations.
- *Orientation to learning:* Adults are motivated to learn to the extent that they perceive that it will help them perform tasks they confront in their life situations. In other words, as people mature, their perspective changes from a "subject-centered" to a more "problem-centered" orientation toward learning.

Proponents draw a parallel between McGregor's Theory X and Theory Y models of management and the pedagogic and andragogic approaches to education. According to this view, Theory X managers (and teachers who follow traditional pedagogy) assume that workers (learners) are basically lazy and extrinsically motivated (by money or grades). It follows, then, that Theory X managers (and traditional teachers) direct (teach) from above (in a nonparticipatory, lecture-driven fashion). In contrast, Theory Y managers (and andragogic teachers) assume that, given challenge and responsibility, workers (students) are motivated to demonstrate competency. Theory Y managers (and andragogic teachers) are therefore most effective when they encourage participation and give employees and students more control over the work and learning environments.

Holton, E. F., Knowles, M., & Swanson, R. A. (2000). *The adult learner: The definitive classic in adult education and human resource development.* New York: Elsevier.

McGregor, D. (1960). *The human side of enterprise.* New York: Mc-Graw-Hill.

Critical Thinking Activity: Thinking in Emerging Adulthood

Each unit of these resources contains a critical thinking exercise designed specifically to test students' critical thinking about a topic covered in the text. Handout 4 contains a synopsis of research or a brief scenario followed by a series of questions. In this case, you might also ask students to share examples of the various types of thinking with the class. Discussion can focus on clarifying any misconceptions regarding the different types of thinking, as well as on the larger issue of how the commitments of adult life propel cognitive development.

Sample answers to this unit's critical thinking activity follow.

1. Formal thinking is likely to benefit college students when considering a hypothetical proposition and then deducing possible consequences: *If* this, *then* that. For example, students have to deduce the consequences of taking a particular course next semester instead of this semester. Similarly, they have to consider the outcome of a change in major. Even more obvious is any situation that requires scientific thinking or logical reasoning, such as on an exam. Analogical reasoning, for instance, requires the recognition of a higher-order relation between two lower-order relations. For example, the essence of the analogy ATOM is to MOLECULE as CELL is to ORGANISM is the recognition that molecules comprise atoms, just as organisms comprise cells. Each lower-order relation specifies a part-whole relationship.
2. Dialectical thinking involves considering both sides of an idea (thesis and antithesis) at the same time and then forging them into a synthesis. Most students, as do most people, often have to reconcile the thesis that "honesty is the best policy" with the antithesis of not hurting a friend's feelings—for example, when a student realizes that there's no need to always be brutally honest when reacting to a roommate's choice of clothing. The dialectical thinker is able to create a synthesis by deciding that honesty is a valuable goal, even when it seems hurtful at the moment.
3. Students may reflect on the impact that a particular teacher, relative, coach, or other mentor has had on their cognitive growth—as when relating "I wonder how she would handle this." Or, in describing the impact of adopting a child, they may reflect on how the event would cause a person to think and act like an adult or to put someone else's interests first.
4. Individuals at the mythic-literal stage take the myths and stories of religion literally. The sermon might therefore quote from stories in the Bible, Torah, Koran, or other respected texts that indicate that people who demonstrate commitment to the religious life of the community are rewarded. In contrast, individuals at the individual-reflective faith stage are able to articulate their own values and establish a commitment to a personal philosophy. The sermon might therefore be designed to provoke personal reflection and clarification of the congregation's values by posing pertinent questions, such as, "What are your responsibilities as a member of this religious community?"

Observational Activity: Describing the Development of a Developmental Psychologist

Kathleen Galotti of Carleton College has developed an alternative term paper assignment for her students that you may find useful (Handout 5). Each student chooses (or is assigned) a different developmental psychologist, reads as much of that person's recently published work as is feasible, and then writes a term paper describing the developmentalist's work, focusing on the question, "How has this person's work developed?"

Galotti finds that this assignment effectively addresses several objectives, including (a) to help acquaint students with the primary research literature in developmental psychology; (b) to help students understand that "entities other than infants and children (e.g., careers) also undergo development"; and (c) to provoke critical thinking about development.

Galotti notes that some of the most popular target psychologists are Diana Baumrind, Jay Belsky, Jeanne Block, Micki Chi, Carol Dweck, David Elkind, Rachel Gelman, Carol Gilligan, Susan Harter, Martin Hoffman, James Marcia, Robert Selman, and Eliot Turiel. (You may wish to limit the list to developmentalists who specialize in adulthood.) She also suggests that because of the challenging nature of the task, it is a good idea to organize voluntary discussion groups for students to share ideas in how best to tackle the project.

Galotti, K. M. (1989, February). Describing the development of a developmental psychologist: An alternative term paper assignment. *Teaching of Psychology*, *16*(1), 20.

Morals and Religion

AV: Moral Development (20 min., CRM/McGraw-Hill)

The film begins with a re-creation of Milgrim's famous experiment on obedience and then explores the relationship between level of moral reasoning (as Kohlberg defines it) and willingness to shock the victim. As one might expect, research has shown that subjects who resisted the orders to continue shocking the "learner" in the original experiment were more likely to reason at a higher stage. However, the film points out that some people at the highest stages also delivered maximum shocks, so the correlation between moral thought and behavior is by no means perfect. Then narrator David Rosenhan explains the social learning approach to moral development, again using the same experimental manipulations that Milgrim did.

AV: Socialization: Moral Development (22 min., HarperCollins)

This film explores the major theories of morality and re-creates several classic experiments addressing such questions as: What is the source of morality? Is it learned? Are ideas of good and evil universal?

Classroom Activity: Classroom Debate: *"Resolved: Males and Females Are Socialized to Approach Moral Questions in Different Ways"*

The text describes Kohlberg's stage theory of moral development in relation to psychosocial development during middle childhood. An important criticism of this theory concerns the research methodology on which the theory was based.

Kohlberg studied moral reasoning by examining the responses of children, adolescents, and adults to hypothetical stories that posed ethical dilemmas. Although only male subjects were tested, Kohlberg believed that his results applied equally to females.

As noted in the text, Carol Gilligan believes that girls and women see moral dilemmas differently from boys and men. Males tend to evaluate "right and wrong" according to abstract principles such as "justice." Females, on the other hand, tend to focus on the context of moral choices and are more concerned with the human relationships involved (a summary of her model of moral development follows). Although the latest research has not validated Gilligan's theory, debating this issue will help clarify students' understanding of moral reasoning in women and men.

Level I: Orientation of Individual Survival. The woman's thinking is based on practical and personal self-interest.

Transition I: From Selfishness to Responsibility. Recognizing her relatedness and responsibility to others, the woman begins to think of the welfare of others.

Level II: Goodness as Self-Sacrifice. Following conventional reasoning, and being overly concerned with how others view her, the woman sees goodness as the subordination of her own needs to those of others.

Transition II: From Goodness to Truth. Less concerned with what others think, the woman evaluates the morality of her behavior on the basis of its consequences and her intentions.

Level III: The Morality of Nonviolence. The woman's moral reasoning is governed by the desire to avoid hurting anyone else.

Gilligan contends that Kohlberg's theory, biased as it is toward men, interprets the male practice of reasoning from abstract principles as evidence of higher moral reasoning than the female practice of basing her moral decisions on a consideration of relationships and real-world context.

Gilligan has argued that neither pattern of moral reasoning is superior to the other and that the two perspectives simply reflect differences in how females and males are socialized. Gilligan further contends that women may be "reluctant to judge right and wrong in absolute terms because they are socialized to be nurturant, caring, and nonjudgmental."

As indicated earlier in this discussion and explained in the text, Gilligan's theory is no less controversial than Kohlberg's, however. Several extensive reviews of the literature on moral reasoning have found no evidence of systematic gender differences. When gender differences are found, they are often confounded by differences in education level and verbal fluency, which can influence scores on a test of moral reasoning.

To increase your students' understanding of the complexity of this controversy and the countless variables (gender, socialization, education, and so forth) that influence moral reasoning, follow the guidelines in the General Resources section of this manual for scheduling a classroom debate on this resolution.

How your students divide themselves into teams for this debate might itself provoke a productive classroom discussion. A natural division of teams might be males versus females. This is likely if your students focus on the issue of whether the literature on moral reasoning is biased against females. Alternatively, there may be a nature–nurture dichotomy of perspectives, reflecting student differences in the perceived importance of learning (socialization) in the moral reasoning of males and females.

Bruess, B. J., & Pearson, F. C. (2002). The debate continues: Are there gender differences in moral reasoning as defined by Kohlberg? *College Student Affairs Journal, 21*(2), 38–52.

Elm, D. R., Kennedy, E. J., & Lawton, L. (2001, September). Determinants of moral reasoning: Sex role orientation, gender, and academic factors. *Business and Society, 40*(3), 241–265.

Gilligan, C., Ward, J., & Taylor, J. (Eds.). (1988). *Mapping the moral domain.* Cambridge, MA: Harvard University Press.

Jaffee, S., & Hyde, J. S. (2000). Gender differences in moral orientation: A meta-analysis. *Psychological Bulletin, 126*(5), 703–726.

Kohlberg, L. (1981). *The philosophy of moral development.* New York: Harper & Row.

Walker, L. J., deVries, B., & Trevethan, S. D. (1987). Moral stages and moral orientations in real-life and hypothetical dilemmas. *Child Development, 58,* 842–858.

Problem-Based Learning: Cheating Teachers

The Introduction's Classroom Activity: Introducing Problem-Based Learning describes this relatively new pedagogical tool. Following is a sample problem that you might want to give to your students as part of your coverage of cognitive development during emerging adulthood.

> A few years ago, *Freakonomics* researchers Steven D. Levitt and Stephen J. Dubner broke a story about cheating schoolteachers in Chicago. Their theory was that high-stakes testing creates a strong incentive for teachers to not fail students. In support, they found that a fraction of teachers went so far as to cheat on behalf of their students. Levitt and Dubner caught on after analyzing all the individual answers of every student in the Chicago public school system. They found virtually identical patterns of answers in the same class, strongly suggesting that after students had turned in their tests, their teachers were going through and changing enough answers to boost scores.
>
> This type of cheating appears to be a global problem. In 2010, Australian teachers were caught changing students' answers on the country's National Assessment Program Literacy and Numeracy tests. In addition, some parents report that they were told to keep children with learning difficulties at home on test days. There were even reports of schools opening the tests early and preparing students accordingly.
>
> Before you leave class today, your group must address the following questions: First, from what you have learned about cognitive development during emerging adulthood, is cheating more or less likely at this age? Second, after your group agrees on an answer to the first question, determine some resulting learning issues that need to be researched to answer the question "What can be done to prevent or discourage cheating on high-stakes tests?" Among others, these issues should focus on the impact of higher education on moral development and ethical reasoning.
>
> Based on the decisions that your group makes today, you should devise a plan for researching the various issues. Two weeks from today's class, your group will present an answer based on the issues you think are relevant.

Freakonomics (2010, May 19). Cheating teachers are a global problem. the *New York Times.* http://freakonomics.blogs.nytimes.com/2010/05/19/cheating-teachers-are-a-global-problem.

Cognitive Growth and Higher Education

Teaching Tip: The Changing Nature of Higher Education

The text notes that in recent years the number of college students has increased significantly. In addition, more women, low-income, ethnic-minority, career-oriented, and part-time students make up today's student population. The number of older students attending college has also increased substantially. Although many traditional liberal-arts colleges were once resistant to the idea of older and other unconventional students, administrators today are scrambling to compensate for the enrollment decline caused by the end of the baby-boom cycle.

To amplify the text discussion of these changes, ask students to speculate on how this shift in the demographics of college student bodies might alter the impact of higher education on an individual's cognitive growth. If this trend continues, and carries over to the "typical classroom," what might be the impact on the traditional student in early adulthood? What impact might be seen by researchers studying developmental changes in cognition that occur during middle and late adulthood? If there are older students in the class who are returning to college after an absence during which their families and/or careers were established, ask them to contrast their present college experience with their earlier experience.

HANDOUT 1

Developmental Fact or Myth?

T F 1. Compared with adolescent thinking, adult thinking is more practical, flexible, and dialectical.

T F 2. Traditional models of mature thought stress abstract, impersonal logic and devalue the importance of subjective feelings and emotional experience.

T F 3. Most developmentalists believe that thinking that considers two sides of an idea or argument is an immature form of cognition.

T F 4. Dialectical thinkers tend to see situations as static.

T F 5. Studies have found that the differences between Eastern and Western thought are due to nature.

T F 6. Research indicates that the process (although not necessarily the outcome) of moral thinking improves with age.

T F 7. In matters of moral reasoning, males and females tend to be concerned with somewhat different issues.

T F 8. Emerging adults are less likely than older or younger people to attend religious services or to pray.

T F 9. Years of education per se are less strongly correlated with cognitive development than either age or socioeconomic status.

T F 10. College education leads people to become more tolerant of political, social, and religious views that differ from their own.

HANDOUT 2

Practical Intelligence

Following is a list of the attributes Robert Sternberg assigns to practical problem-solving ability. For each item, rate youself on a 1 (low) to 9 (high) scale the extent to which each is characteristic of your own behavior.

_____ 1. reasons logically and well

_____ 2. identifies connections among ideas

_____ 3. sees all aspects of a problem

_____ 4. keeps an open mind

_____ 5. responds thoughtfully to others' ideas

_____ 6. sizes up situations well

_____ 7. gets to the heart of problems

_____ 8. interprets information accurately

_____ 9. makes good decisions

_____ 10. goes to original sources for basic information

_____ 11. poses problems in an optimal way

_____ 12. is a good source of ideas

_____ 13. perceives implied assumptions and conclusions

_____ 14. listens to all sides of an argument

_____ 15. deals with problems resourcefully

HANDOUT 3

Assessing Tacit Knowledge

This questionnaire focuses on your views on matters pertaining to the work of a manager. The questions ask you to rate the importance you would assign to various items in making work-related decisions and judgments. Use a 1 to 7 rating scale—with 1 signifying "not important," 4 signifying "moderately important," and 7 signifying "extremely important."

1	2	3	4	5	6	7
not important			moderately important			extremely important

Draw upon your full knowledge of the world in order to answer these questions. Try to use the entire scale when responding, although not necessarily for each question. For example, you may decide that none of the items listed for a particular question is important or that they all are. There are, of course, no "correct" answers. You are encouraged to briefly scan the items in a given question before responding, in order to get some idea of the range of importance of all of them. Remember, you are being asked to rate the importance you personally would assign each item in making the judgment or decision noted in the question.

1. It is your second year as a mid-level manager in a company in the communications industry. You head a department of about 30 people. The evaluation of your first year on the job has been generally favorable. Performance ratings for your department are at least as good as they were before you took over, and perhaps even a little better. You have two assistants. One is quite capable, but the other just seems to go through the motions without being of much real help. You believe that although you are well liked, in the eyes of your superiors, there is little that would distinguish you from the nine other managers at a comparable level in the company. Your goal is rapid promotion to the top of the company. The following is a list of things you are considering doing in the next two months. Obviously, you cannot do them all. Rate the importance of each as a means of reaching your goal.

   ______ a. Participate in a series of panel discussions to be shown on the local public-television station.

   ______ b. Find ways to make sure your superiors are aware of your important accomplishments.

   ______ c. As a means of being noticed, propose a solution to a problem outside the scope of your immediate department that you would be willing to handle.

   ______ d. When making decisions, give a great deal of weight to the way your superior likes to have things done.

   ______ e. Accept a friend's invitation to join the exclusive country club to which many of the senior executives belong.

HANDOUT 3 *(continued)*

2. Your company has sent you to a university to recruit and interview potential trainees for management positions. You have been considering student characteristics that are important to later success in business. Rate the importance of the following characteristics according to the extent to which they lead to later success in business.

   _____ a. ability to set priorities according to the importance of the task

   _____ b. motivation

   _____ c. ability to follow through and complete tasks

   _____ d. ability to promote one's ideas and convince others of the worth of one's work

   _____ e. the need to win at everything regardless of the cost

3. A number of factors enter into the establishment of a good reputation as company manager. Consider the following factors and rate their importance.

   _____ a. critical thinking ability

   _____ b. speaking ability

   _____ c. extent of college education and the prestige of the school attended

   _____ d. no hesitancy in taking extraordinarily risky courses of action

   _____ e. a keen sense of what superiors can be sold on

4. Rate the following strategies according to how important you believe them to be as a measure of the day-to-day effectiveness of a business manager.

   _____ a. Think in terms of tasks accomplished rather than hours spent working.

   _____ b. Be in charge of all phases of every task or project with which you are involved.

   _____ c. Use a daily list of goals arranged according to your priorities.

   _____ d. Carefully consider the optimal strategy before beginning a task.

   _____ e. Reward yourself upon completion of important tasks.

5. You are looking for several new projects to tackle. You have a list of possible projects and want to pick the best two or three. Rate the importance of the following considerations when selecting projects.

   _____ a. Doing the project should prove to be fun.

   _____ b. The project should attract the attention of the local media.

   _____ c. The project is of special importance to me personally.

   _____ d. The risk of making a mistake is virtually nonexistent.

   _____ e. The project will require working directly with several senior executives.

HANDOUT 4

Critical Thinking Activity: Thinking in Emerging Adulthood

Now that you have read and reviewed the material on cognitive development during emerging adulthood, take your learning a step further by testing your critical thinking skills on this perspective-taking exercise.

This unit has explored several types of adult thinking, including formal and postformal thought, dialectical thinking, and moral reasoning. Test your understanding of these ways of thinking by writing answers to the following questions.

1. Many different kinds of problems arise in daily life. Based on your own experiences, or those of a typical college student, give an example of a problem that is likely to benefit from formal operational thinking. Then explain why a logical answer to this problem is most appropriate.

2. Dialectical thinking involves the constant integration of one's beliefs and experiences with the contradictions and inconsistencies of everyday life. Give an example of the use of dialectical thinking in your own life, or that of a typical college student.

HANDOUT 4 *(continued)*

3. One theme of this chapter is that cognitive development is often propelled by critical life experiences. Describe one life experience that strongly influenced your own cognitive development. Alternatively, explain why being a stepparent or adopting a child might lead to cognitive growth.

4. Imagine that you are a religious leader attempting to convince the members of your congregation to become more involved in their community's religious life. What kind of appeal might be most effective with members at Fowler's stage of "mythic-literal faith"? with members at the stage of "individual-reflective faith"?

HANDOUT 5

Observational Activity: Describing the Development of a Developmental Psychologist

This assignment is intended to help you explore how the thinking of developmental psychologists undergoes development over the course of their academic careers. I would like you to prepare a term paper based on the work of a recently or currently active developmental psychologist. You may select any individual from the list presented in class.

Once you have selected your target person, consult *Psychological Abstracts* and select 3 to 5 published works, *covering a range of years*, which are available in the campus library. After you have read these articles, consult the *Science Citation Index* or *Social Science Citation Index* to find two or three published works that address, or react to, some aspect of your target person's research. If you are unable to find any published reactions, find several articles written by other developmentalists working in the same area as your target person. After reading the collection of articles, prepare a 5- to 10-page (typed, double-spaced) report organized as follows:

1. *Introduction.* A paragraph that clearly and concisely describes the subject of the report, including a brief biography of the target person and a statement of the significance of his or her scholarly contributions to the field of developmental psychology.
2. *Research Section.* Two to three pages summarizing the target person's research articles, and the reaction pieces, which you consulted.
3. *Your Opinions.* A page or two of your own reactions to the articles you have read, focusing specifically on how the work and thinking of your target person have developed over the course of his or her career. You may find it helpful to consider the following questions: (a) Has the target person's research remained in one area or shifted from one topic to another? (b) In what way, if any, have scholarly reactions to the target person's early work influenced his or her subsequent research? (c) If the target person's research and writing on a particular topic span a period, how has his or her understanding of the developmental issue changed during this period?

Galotti, K. M. (1989, February). Describing the development of a developmental psychologist: An alternative term paper assignment. *Teaching of Psychology, 16*(1), 20.

Emerging Adulthood: Psychosocial Development

Contents

Note: Worth Publishers provides online Instructor and Student Tool Kits, DVD Student Tool Kits, and Instructor and Student video resources in DevelopmentPortal for use with the text. See Part I: General Resources for information about these materials and the text Lecture Guides for a complete list by text chapter.

Suggested Activities

Introducing Emerging Adulthood: Psychosocial Development

"On Your Own" Activity: Developmental Fact or Myth?

Before students read about psychosocial development during emerging adulthood, have them respond to the true-false statements in Handout 1.

The correct answers are shown below. Class discussion can focus on the origins of any developmental misconceptions that are demonstrated in the students' incorrect answers.

1. T	6. T
2. F	7. T
3. T	8. T
4. T	9. F
5. F	10. T

AV: The Journey Through the Life Span, Program 7: Early Adulthood

See Emerging Adulthood: Biosocial Development for a description of Program 7 and the accompanying observation modules, which cover the entire unit on emerging adulthood.

AV: Transitions Throughout the Life Span, Program 19: Early Adulthood: Psychosocial Development

Biologically mature and no longer bound by parental authority, the young adult typically is now free to choose a particular path of development. Today, the options are incredibly varied. Not surprisingly, then, the hallmark of psychosocial development during emerging adulthood is diversity. Nevertheless, developmentalists have identified several themes or patterns that help us understand the course of development between the ages of 20 and 40.

The program begins with a discussion of the two basic psychosocial needs of adulthood, love and work. No matter what terminology is used, these two needs are recognized by almost all developmentalists.

Next, the program addresses the need for intimacy in adulthood, focusing on the development of friendship, love, and marriage. The impact of divorce on families is also discussed.

The final segment of the program is concerned with generativity, or the motivation to achieve during adulthood, highlighting the importance of work and parenthood and addressing the special challenges facing stepparents, adoptive parents, and foster parents.

"On Your Own" Activity: When Should You . . .?

The term *social clock* is introduced in Adulthood: Psychosocial Development. However, as noted there, it applies throughout adulthood and discussion of its effects are equally relevant here. To give the class a firmer understanding of the major issues involved in adult psychosocial development, Handout 2 invites students to reflect on their own personal life experiences.

By applying theory to their own lives, students should gain a firmer grasp of the major developmental issues discussed in relation to psychosocial development during emerging adulthood. For purposes of class discussion, it might be interesting for your students to debate questions 2 and 3, and to discuss the notion of the social clock in general.

Observational Activity: The "Right Time" for Life Events

As noted in the text discussion of psychosocial development during adulthood, whatever stages of adulthood there might be are determined in large measure by a kind of social clock, a culturally set timetable that establishes when various events and behaviors in life are appropriate and called for. Each culture, subculture, socioeconomic group, and every historical period has a somewhat different social clock, with variations in the "right time" to finish school, go to work, marry, and so forth.

To help your students appreciate how the settings of the social clock vary with the above factors and to encourage them to reflect on the settings of their own social clocks, have them complete the survey in Handout 3. The survey lists nine life events or activities, with a suggested "right" age-range for each. For each event, students are to check whether they agree or disagree with the range given. (Note: To preserve confidentiality, announce that the students should not put their names on the handout.)

After the handouts have been returned, determine the percentage of students who agreed with each statement and add these percentages to those in the following table, which shows the results of the same survey presented to middle-aged, middle-class people during the late 1950s. Depending on how heterogeneous your class is, you may also choose to add additional columns to the table differentiating the percentages of women and men who agreed with each statement, as well as the percentages of those who consider themselves in the lower-, middle-, and upper-socioeconomic classes.

Once the data have been analyzed, present the table to the class and call for discussion on how the settings of the social clock vary with cohort, gender, and socioeconomic status.

Activity or Event	Appropriate Age Range	% Who Agreed (1950s survey) Men	Women
1. Best age for a man to marry	20–25	80	90
2. Best age for a woman to marry	24	85	90
3. When most people should become grandparents	45–50	84	79
4. Best age for most people to finish school and start working	20–22	86	82
5. When most people should retire	60–65	83	86
6. When a man has the most responsibilities	35–50	79	75
7. When a man accomplishes most	40–50	82	71
8. When a woman has the most responsibilities	25–40	93	91
9. When a woman accomplishes most	30–45	94	92

Adapted from Rosenfeld, A., & Stark, E. (1987). The prime of our lives. *Psychology Today, 21*(5), 62–72. Reprinted with permission from Psychology Today Magazine. Copyright © 1987 (Sussex Publishers, Inc.)

Continuity and Change

Classroom Activity: Using the Secret Identities of Superheroes to Illustrate Identity Conflict

Daniel Selvey and Tracy Griggs of Winthrop University use live-action films based on Marvel Comics and DC Comics superheroes to bring identity conflict concepts to life in their industrial/organizational psychology course. The strategy would also work well for this unit in the life-span development course. After reading and discussing concepts such as work–nonwork conflict, role integration, and self-concept differentiation, their students studied films such as *Spider-Man, Superman, The Fantastic 4, Catwoman,* and *Ironman* with an eye to analyzing the films and documenting examples of identity concepts in the protagonists.

As an example, self-concept differentiation refers to the degree to which a person's identity is variable across roles. Bruce Wayne identifies primarily as Batman and only as Bruce when he has to. In other words, "Bruce" is the mask worn by Batman. To Peter Parker, Spider-Man comes first, and the safety of New York is his top priority. He demonstrates this attitude by neglecting his work as a photographer and his girlfriend, Mary Jane. Tony Stark thrives by simultaneously occupying his two high-profile roles of Ironman and corporate mogul. Finally, Patience Phillips is unable to live a normal life alongside Catwoman, so she chooses to concentrate on the latter role.

As another example, role integration occurs when the individual cannot distinguish between home and work environments, or when and where these roles begin and end. Tony Stark of Ironman fame is a good example when he publicly declared "I am Iron Man." Clark Kent failed to integrate his roles as Superman and newspaper reporter.

Work–nonwork conflict occurs when work and nonwork roles (e.g., parenting) are incompatible in some way. Ask your students to try to identify examples of work–nonwork conflict.

Selvey and Griggs note that it is "becoming increasingly important to integrate media into college classrooms to connect with students. . . . electronic media engaged students more readily and helped them retain information better than lecture alone."

Selvey, D. L., & Griggs, T. L (2011). Teaching role dichotomy: Superheroes and their secret identities. National Institute on the Teaching of Psychology. St. Petersburg Beach, FL.

Teaching Tip: Vocational Identity

To help students learn more about vocational identity and career development, invite the campus career counselor to speak to the class. This will not only serve to teach students more about the process of career counseling and about issues of career development but will also expose them to someone they should get to know before they graduate.

Classroom Activity: The Changing Workplace

The changing workplace is a subject your students are certain to be able to connect with, so you may wish to add to the brief text discussion or you may wish to hold this discussion for the text coverage of psychosocial development during adulthood. If you have older students in your class, a particularly stimulating class discussion can be organized around cohort comparisons of how career opportunities and trajectories have changed over the decades. If not, try to arrange for some older adults to sit on a panel to discuss this issue in your class. A good resource for arranging such a panel would be your campus counseling, placement or nontraditional student outreach centers. In fact, you might consider inviting your campus career placement specialist to sit on the panel or to speak to your class.

To get the discussion started, note that for adults entering the workplace today, survival requires a very different set of skills from those needed by earlier cohorts of workers. As an example, workers who are fluent in more than one language, those who are willing to travel, and those whose work can transcend race, gender, and culture are certain to have more career opportunities than those lacking these skills and traits.

Job fields that currently are experiencing a boom include those related to business, health, education, and engineering. Fields such as computer engineering and systems analysis are flourishing because they prepare workers to do a variety of things. According to the Bureau of Labor Statistics, such fields will be among the fastest-growing occupations.

Here are some recent data on the top 10 careers to help your students' discussion.

Occupation	Employment 2008	Employment 2018	Change	Training Needed
1 Biomedical engineers	16,100	27,600	72%	Bachelor's degree
2 Network systems and data communications analysts	292,000	447,800	53%	Bachelor's degree
3 Financial examiners	27,000	38,100	41%	Bachelor's degree
4 Medical scientists, except epidemiologists	109,400	153,600	40%	Doctoral degree
5 Physician assistants	74,800	103,900	39%	Master's degree
6 Biochemists and biophysicists	23,200	31,900	37%	Doctoral degree
7 Athletic trainers	16,400	22,400	37%	Bachelor's degree
8 Computer software engineers, applications	514,800	689,900	34%	Bachelor's degree
9 Veterinarians	59,700	79,400	33%	First professional degree
10 Environmental engineers	54,300	70,900	31%	Bachelor's degree

National Data Source: Bureau of Labor Statistics, Office of Occupational Statistics and Employment Projections. Retrieved March 1, 2011, from www.acinet.org/acinet/oview1.asp?level=baplus.

AV: Careers and Babies (20 min., Polymorph Films)

Four women, two with children and two without, discuss the reasons for their respective decisions with regard to having children. The movie illustrates the pros and cons of this question and shows that childrearing has become more a matter of personal decision than the inevitable consequence of adult sexual expression.

Intimacy

AV: Gender and Relationships (30 min., RMI Media Productions)

This film explores the complexities of human emotional interactions and attachments. Based on relatively recent research findings, the film includes such subjects as the nature of love, what makes sexual behavior "normal" or "abnormal," and male–female differences in sexual attitudes and behavior.

AV: Love, Love Me, Do: How Sex Differences Affect Relationships (51 min., Films for the Humanities and Sciences)

(See description in Emerging Adulthood: Biosocial Development.)

Classroom Activity: "Seeing It" Both Ways

Dialectic is a form of reasoning based on the exchange of arguments and counterarguments, advocating propositions (theses) and counterpropositions (antitheses). The outcome of such an exchange might be the refutation of one of the relevant points of view, or a synthesis, or combination, of the opposing assertions. Amy Marin suggests a simple classroom activity that requires students to use dialectical thought as a way to actively process lecture material. At some point near the end of class, present students with a controversial statement such as "Cohabitation is wrong!" Give students a minute or two to write down as many "agree" arguments they can think of. Give them an equal amount of time to generate arguments for the "disagree" side. The responses can then be used in a number of ways, including discussion and debate.

Marin, A. (2011). Mindful moments: 50 micro-activities for energizing the college classroom. National Institute on the Teaching of Psychology. St. Petersburg Beach, FL.

Classroom Activity: An Historical Look at Marriage Age

To help students understand historical variations in development and cohort effects, introduce the concept of the *social clock*--a culturally set timetable that establishes when various events and behaviors in life are appropriate and called for. Every culture and subculture has a somewhat different social clock. Internationally, societies in developed regions tend to be quite age-stratified. A common misconception is that throughout history children, especially girls, married younger than they do today. Although some wealthy families arranged marriages for their daughters at a young age (primarily as political alliances or as an exchange for property), the average age of marriage was actually in the mid-20s. Data taken from women's birth certificates and marriage certificates reveal that the average (mean) marriage age for women in England was as follows:

1566–1619: 27.0 years

1647–1719: 29.6 years

1719–1779: 26.8 years

1770–1837: 25.1 years

Men married at a slightly older age than women did. In 1619, for instance, it was about 27 years for women, and 28 years for men. Interestingly, during the same era, the age of consent was 12 for a girl, 14 for a boy, even though for most children of that era, puberty began two to three years later than it does today. The reason for late marriage among laborers and the middle class was simple enough: It took a long time for a couple to acquire enough belongings to set up housekeeping, even in a room of their parents' home.

To foster an understanding of how the settings of the social clock have changed in the United States over the past century, display the table at the top of the next column.

	1890–1939	1940–1979	1980–1994	1995	2010
Average marriage age					
Women	22.0	21.5	19.5	25	26.1
Men	26.1	24.3	22.5	27	28.2
Average age of first-time mothers	23.7	23.1	21.1	24*	25
Average life expectancy**					
Men	53.3	60.9	65.5	72.8	75.7
Women	57.4	63.6	70.0	79.6	80.8
Average number of children	5.2	3.5	2.1	2.0	1.86**

*This takes into account the increasing number of unwed mothers.

**This is based on 2000 census data. The data for 2010 are not yet available.

The structure of families, timing of marriage, childbirth, and death have all fluctuated over the past 100 years. Currently, the average age of marriage in the United States is 26.8 years for men and 25.1 years for women. Although this represents an increase in the median age of a man's first marriage over the past several decades, it is not significantly higher than the average age of marriage a century ago. Although today's cohort of men and women in the United States marry an average of 5 years later than people did earlier, this is a misleading trend, since beginning in the 1950s young adults married younger than did any previous cohort in U.S. history. In fact, today's tendency to delay marriage is in line with the age of marriage between 1890 and 1940. Among the reasons for delaying marriage today are increased educational requirements and job training, economic insecurity, difficulties finding the "perfect mate," and the attractions of a carefree life.

The 1950s cohort of parents is a misleading benchmark for another reason: a greater proportion of the U.S. population was married (95 percent) during the 1950s than at any time before or since. Theories abound as to why the "marriage rush" of the late 1940s and 1950s occurred, but many experts believe it was a backlash that followed 15 years of severe economic depression and war. In Canada, the median age at first marriage is nearly identical to that in the United States—just over age 24 for women and nearly 27 years of age for men.

The average age at which women have their first child has also increased. On average, the first child comes along soon after marriage, followed, two-and-a-half years later, by the second child. The implications of postponing children include smaller family sizes and an increase in "only child" families, which, in turn, affect nearly every aspect of family life. For example, although delaying parenthood means that parents may be better established in their careers, it also may mean that they have less time and energy for their children. Having fewer brothers and sisters means that a child may need to look elsewhere for playmates when he or she is young, and elsewhere for family relationships at a later age. Furthermore, older parents are more likely to become frail and in need of support before their children become established in their own careers. The United States has a relatively high birth rate of 2.0 per woman for a developed country. The "total fertility rate," or average number of children a woman has, for most other industrialized countries falls well below 2.0, averaging only 1.2 in Eastern Europe. The annual fertility rate in the United States in 1900 was about 4.0 births per woman, fell to 2.2 during the Great Depression, reached a postwar peak of 3.7 in 1957, and fell again to 1.8 births in the mid-1980s. The rate has held steady at about 2.0 births per woman over the past two decades.

In discussing these trends, ask the class to consider the kind of relationship a couple in 1900 must have had, with virtually no time together free of the responsibility of children. Compare that generation with the current generation, in which a couple can expect to live together for more than 25 years without children (assuming that the children leave the nest at about age 18). How might this generational difference help to account for the rapid increase in divorce rates? What other differences between the generations might be suggested?

For students who wish to pursue historical trends in the makeup of families further, you might direct them to the United States Historical Census Data Browser at http://mapserver.lib.virginia.edu.

Birren, J. E., Schaie, K. W., Abeles, R. P., Gatz, M., & Salthouse, T. (2006). *Handbook of the psychology of aging* (6th ed). San Diego: Academic Press.

Brooke, C. N. L. (1988). *The medieval idea of marriage.* Oxford: Oxford University Press.

Dauenhauer, K. (2003, July 23). *Population: High birth rates making poor nations even poorer* (p. 1). New York: Global Information Network.

Dzado, N. (2011). 2010 average life expectancy by gender, race, and country. Retrieved March 1, 2011, from www.suite101.com/content/average-life-expectancy-in-the-united-states-and-longevity-a275686.

Edwards, E. (2002, August 26). Some fear divorce so much that they never give marriage a chance. *The Orlando Sentinel.* Knight Rider Tribune News Service. Retrieved from www.orlandosentinel.com.

Health, United States 2003, Table 27. National Center for Health Statistics. Retrieved from www.cdc.gov/nchs/fastats/lifexpec.htm.

Jayson, S. (2008, November 9). Sooner vs. later: Is there an ideal ae for first marraige? USA Today. Retrieved March 13, 2011, from www.usatoday.com/news/health/2008-11-09-delayed-marriage_N.htm.

US Census. (2010). Retrieved March 13, 2011, from www.census.gov/population/socdemo/hh-fam/tabST-F1-2000.pdf

AV: Portrait of a Family (30 min., RMI Media Productions)

This modularly organized series examines various aspects of intimacy, marriage, and families. Each module consists of three or four 30-minute programs. Modules 2 and 3 are appropriate for this chapter. Module 2, "Forming Relationships," explores various aspects of choosing partners, forming intimate relationships, sexuality, and the impact of AIDS and other sexually transmitted diseases on psychosocial development. Module 3, "The Marriage Partnership," examines a kaleidoscope of issues concerning marriage, including how the beliefs and expectations individuals bring into a marriage influence its development, communication, conflict resolution, and marital violence.

AV: Clinical Dilemmas in Marriage: The Search for Equal Partnership (44 min., Insight Media)

Family therapist Betty Carter discusses her multicontextual framework for marital assessment and intervention. Analyzing two case families, Carter discusses the importance of understanding the life cycle of each family and its particular sociocultural sphere in improving relationships.

"On Your Own" Activity: Marriages Made to Last

Jeanette and Robert Laver conducted a survey of nearly 400 couples who had been married for 15 or more years. In the survey, husbands and wives were asked to rank the reasons their marriages had lasted so long. As an introduction to this material in the text on making relationships succeed, distribute copies of Handout 4 and ask your students to list in order of frequency (1 to 15) the reasons given by husbands and wives for the longevity of their marriages.

After your students' surveys have been collected, compute an average class rank for each of the 15 items and compare these with those of the survey respondents. Class discussion could focus on several issues, including the extent of student agreement with the survey results, possible reasons for discrepancies, male–female differences in responses, and the relative importance to students of commitment, sex life, the institution of marriage, and so on. The rank-ordered frequency of responses from the Lavers' survey appears below.

Women

11 An enduring marriage is important to social stability.
8 We laugh together.
7 I want the relationship to succeed.
2 I like my spouse as a person.
6 My spouse has grown more interesting.
14 We agree about our sex life.
3 Marriage is a long-term commitment.
1 My spouse is my best friend.
15 I am proud of my spouse's achievements.
4 Marriage is sacred.
5 We agree on aims and goals.
9 We agree on a philosophy of life.
10 We agree on how and how often to show affection.
13 We discuss things calmly.
12 We have a stimulating exchange of ideas.

Men

8 An enduring marriage is important to social stability.
9 We laugh together.
7 I want the relationship to succeed.
2 I like my spouse as a person.
6 My spouse has grown more interesting.
12 We agree about our sex life.

3 Marriage is a long-term commitment.
1 My spouse is my best friend.
10 I am proud of my spouse's achievements.
4 Marriage is sacred.
5 We agree on aims and goals.
11 We agree on a philosophy of life.
13 We agree on how and how often to show affection.
14 I confide in my spouse.
15 We share outside hobbies and interests.

Laver, J., & Laver, R. (1985, June). Marriages made to last. *Psychology Today*, pp. 2–26.

Critical Thinking Activity: Explaining Changing Trends in the Age of Marriage

Each unit of these resources contains a critical thinking exercise designed specifically to test students' critical thinking about a topic covered in the text. Handout 5 contains a synopsis of research or a brief scenario followed by a series of questions.

Answers to this unit's critical thinking exercise are as follows:

1. The central thesis of sociocultural theory is that human development is the result of dynamic interaction between the developing person and his or her surrounding culture. In explaining trends in the age of marrying, a sociocultural theorist would probably point to social, economic, and cultural factors at the start of the twenty-first century. For example, the changing nature of the workplace offers most workers less security, more competition, greater educational requirements, and rapidly changing job requirements—all of which might not favor an early investment in marriage for young adults. Regarding predictions for the future, it would depend on whether the social and economic climate changes or remains the same.
2. Evolutionary theory emphasizes the interaction between genes and the environment. In emphasizing the genetic foundation, evolutionary theory stresses that we have powerful instincts that arise from our biological heritage, including, perhaps, the instinctive need to find a mate and to reproduce. However, evolutionary theory also stresses that biological predispositions are always expressed in specific environments; which may, or may not, allow for full genetic expression. Thus, an evolutionary theorist would probably argue that delaying marriage must represent an optimal strategy (in today's environment) for maximizing one's chances of establishing a long-term relationship with a mate. Regarding predictions for the future, the theorist would probably say that, biology being what it is, when environmental pressures "against" early marriage, adults will once again marry young and have children right away.
3. Answers will vary from student to student.

After your students' have completed the assignment, ask for volunteers to serve as advocates for each theoretical perspective and present their answers to the class. Discussion can then focus on filling in subtler points that follow from each theory. Finally, have students debate whether the trend toward delaying marriage and childbearing will continue into the future, focusing on the various factors in each of the developmental domains that might affect the outcome.

Internet Activity: Trends in Cohabitation, Marriage, and Divorce

The Internet contains a wealth of information for emerging adults who are struggling with questions about relationships. For this activity, ask students to search the Web to find and explore some of these resources using information and questions from Handout 6 as a guide.

HANDOUT 1

Developmental Fact or Myth?

T F 1. Unlike younger adolescents, older adolescents and emerging adults are more likely to be proud of their ethnic identity.

T F 2. Gender differences in friendship are, statistically speaking, quite small.

T F 3. Gay and lesbian couples generally follow the same relationship patterns (passion, intimacy, then commitment) as heterosexual couples.

T F 4. In some cultures, cohabitation is the norm throughout adulthood.

T F 5. Marriages that are preceded by cohabitation typically are happier and more durable.

T F 6. Most adults spend the years between ages 20 and 30 single.

T F 7. Constructive communication is key to marital satisfaction.

T F 8. Emerging adults experience more intimate partner violence than those over age 25.

T F 9. Compared with unmarried young adults in the United States, those in Italy and Japan are less likely to live with their parents.

T F 10. Parenthood begins much earlier in poor nations than in wealthy nations.

HANDOUT 2

When Should You . . . ?

1. Do the characterizations of adult development offered by Erikson and other theorists discussed in the text seem to apply to you at this particular time in your life? Why or why not?

2. At what ages do you plan to start a career, marry, have children, and retire? (If you have already done one or more of these, how old were you at the time?) What factors do you think have set or will set your social clock for these events?

3. Your sister is trying to decide between two potential marriage partners—one who is from her old neighborhood and shares her religious views, and another who is from a different city and has different religious beliefs. Which one of these persons do you believe is the better choice? Why do you feel this way?

HANDOUT 3

Observational Activity: The "Right Time" for Life Events

Each culture, subculture, socioeconomic group, and historical period has a somewhat different social clock, *the settings of which establish when various events and behaviors in life are appropriate and called for. Complete the following survey by checking "agree" or "disagree" for the age range specified for each event or activity. To ensure confidentiality, DO NOT PUT YOUR NAME ON THE RESPONSE SHEET. Return your completed survey to your instructor.*

Activity or Event	Appropriate Age Range	Agree	Disagree
1. Best age for a man to marry	20–25	______	______
2. Best age for a woman to marry	24	______	______
3. When most people should become grandparents	45–50	______	______
4. Best age for most people to finish school and start working	20–22	______	______
5. When most people should retire	60–65	______	______
6. When a man has the most responsibilities	35–50	______	______
7. When a man accomplishes most	40–50	______	______
8. When a woman has the most responsibilities	25–40	______	______
9. When a woman accomplishes most	30–45	______	______

Your gender female______ male ______

Your family's socioeconomic status lower______ middle ______ upper ______

Adapted from Rosenfeld, A., & Stark, E. (1987). The prime of our lives. *Psychology Today*, *21*(5), 62–72. Reprinted with permission from Psychology Today Magazine.

HANDOUT 4

Marriages Made to Last

List in order of frequency (from 1 to 15) the reasons women and men typically give for their marriages having lasted over the years.

Women

_____ An enduring marriage is important to social stability.
_____ We laugh together.
_____ I want the relationship to succeed.
_____ I like my spouse as a person.
_____ My spouse has grown more interesting.
_____ We agree about our sex life.
_____ Marriage is a long-term commitment.
_____ My spouse is my best friend.
_____ I am proud of my spouse's achievements.
_____ Marriage is sacred.
_____ We agree on aims and goals.
_____ We agree on a philosophy of life.
_____ We agree on how and how often to show affection.
_____ We discuss things calmly.
_____ We have a stimulating exchange of ideas.

Men

_____ An enduring marriage is important to social stability.
_____ We laugh together.
_____ I want the relationship to succeed.
_____ I like my spouse as a person.
_____ My spouse has grown more interesting.
_____ We agree about our sex life.
_____ Marriage is a long-term commitment.
_____ My spouse is my best friend.
_____ I am proud of my spouse's achievements.
_____ Marriage is sacred.
_____ We agree on aims and goals.
_____ We agree on a philosophy of life.
_____ We agree on how and how often to show affection.
_____ I confide in my spouse.
_____ We share outside hobbies and interests.

Laver, J., & Laver, R. (1985, June). Marriages made to last. *Psychology Today*, pp. 2–26. Reprinted with permission from Psychology Today Magazine.

HANDOUT 5

Critical Thinking Activity: Explaining Changing Trends in the Age of Marriage

Now that you have read and reviewed the material about psychosocial development during emerging adulthood, take your learning a step further by testing your critical thinking skills on this perspective-taking exercise.

As depicted in the figure below, both women and men, on average, are postponing marriage, reversing the trend toward younger marriages that began in the 1940s. In 1995, the median age of women in the United States at the time of their first marriage was 25 (the median age for men was 27). Today, first marriages may be later yet.

Your task in this exercise is first to use the Internet to obtain actual marriage data from 2000 to now, then make some predictions about data points for 2015 and 2020 on the graph below. In other words, what will the average age of marriage be in 2010. 2015, and 2020. You may already have formulated an opinion about where the data points will be. However, before stating this opinion, see if you can explain the trends of the past as you believe the advocates of several major theories of development would.

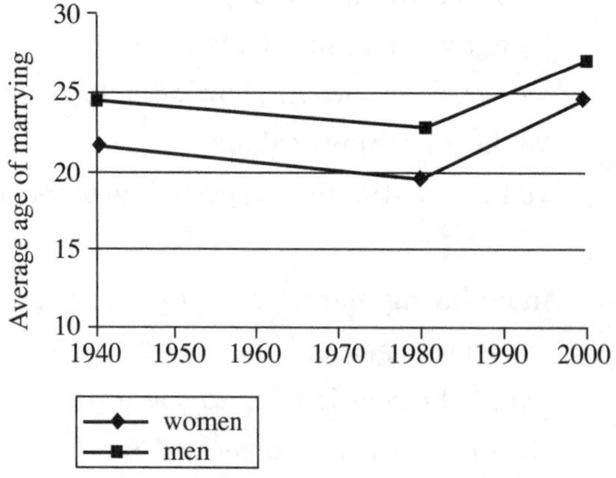

1. How might an advocate of sociocultural theory explain the trend toward postponing marriage? What might he or she predict about the average age of marrying for women and men in the future?

HANDOUT 5 *(continued)*

2. How might an advocate of evolutionary theory explain the trend toward postponing marriage. What might he or she predict about the average age of marrying for women and men in the future?

3. How do these predictions compare with your own ideas about future trends in the average age of marrying?

HANDOUT 6

Internet Activity: Trends in Cohabitation, Marriage, and Divorce

A report from the Centers for Disease Control (CDC) examines individual factors and community conditions associated with long-term marriages, as well as divorce and separation. Use this report, which can be found on the CDC's Web site (www.cdc.gov/nchs/data/series/sr_23/sr23_028.pdf), along with other resources and your own experiences, to answer the following questions.

1. How was the CDC's study conducted? Describe the demographic characteristics (age, ethnicity, socioeconomic status, etc.) of the respondents.

2. How stable are marriages in the United States today? How does this compare with the stability of marriages in your parents' and grandparents' cohorts?

3. What individual conditions are associated with longer-lasting marriages?

HANDOUT 6 *(continued)*

4. Are cohabitations more or less stable than marriages? What are some other similarities/differences between cohabitations and marriages?

5. How often do those who are divorced remarry? How do these figures compare with those for earlier cohorts?

6. Knowing a person's ethnicity, what can you predict regarding his or her marital status and likelihood of remarrying following a divorce?

7. Pick a country other than the United States—perhaps one from which your ancestors emigrated—and try to find comparable statistics on cohabitation, marriage, and divorce.

Adulthood: Biosocial Development

Contents

Note: Worth Publishers provides online Instructor and Student Tool Kits, DVD Student Tool Kits, and Instructor and Student video resources in DevelopmentPortal for use with the text. See Part I: General Resources for information about these materials and the text Lecture Guides for a complete list by text chapter.

Measuring Health

Suggested Activities

Introducing Adulthood: Biosocial Development

"On Your Own" Activity: Developmental Fact or Myth?

Before students read about biosocial development during adulthood, have them respond to the true-false statements in Handout 1.

The correct answers are shown below. Class discussion can focus on the origins of any developmental misconceptions that are demonstrated in the students' incorrect answers.

1. F	6. T
2. T	7. F
3. F	8. T
4. T	9. T
5. F	10. T

Teaching Tip: Reflecting on Your Teaching Abilities and Limitations on These Abilities

Bill Buskist of Auburn University notes the importance of continuously working at the craft of teaching. Studies indicate that award-winning teachers

- consider their teaching to be as important as any other aspect of their academic career, including their research.
- monitor both the quality of their teaching and their students' learning, and make adjustments, when necessary, to improve both.

Buskist uses the term *limiters* to refer to factors that prevent or restrict teachers from reaching their full potential. Common limiters are time constraints, other professional obligations, and stress. Buskist suggests that all teachers should take a few minutes to "identify any limiters that you believe may be preventing you from achieving your full potential as a teacher." Afterward, they should "jot down a few notes on what [they] might be able to do to reduce the impact of these limiters on [their] teaching."

Many teachers are unaware of the extensive literature on excellent teaching and master teachers. Buskist offers the following reading list as a good starting point:

Essays from E-xcellence in teaching. Available in nine volumes from http://teachpsych.org/resources/e-books/index.php.

Bain, K. (2004). What the best college teachers do. Cambridge, MA: Harvard University Press.

Buskist, B. (2011). 7 steps to becoming an excellent teacher (or at least a better teacher). National Institute on the Teaching of Psychology. St. Petersburg Beach, FL.

AV: The Journey Through the Life Span, Program 8: Middle Adulthood

Program 8 (15:25) introduces the developing person during middle adulthood. The first segment of the program—physical development—first outlines the physical and biological changes that accompany midlife, noting how nutritional needs change and ethnicity is related to overall health. Following is a discussion of gender differences in health. Richard Contrada of Rutgers University and Michelle Warren of Columbia University discuss chronic diseases that more often strike women than men. The segment ends with a discussion of menopause led by Warren and New York University's Sally Guttmacher.

The second segment—cognitive development—focuses on the cognitive flexibility that accompanies intellectual development at midlife and the role of learning and experience in stimulating cognition. Kurt Fischer of Harvard University explains plasticity and the other underlying brain processes that accompany these changes. In the final minutes of the segment, Janet Burroughs and Tommy McDonnell of the *Learning English Adult Program* discuss adult learning.

The third segment—social development—is divided into two parts. The first focuses on how personality changes, and doesn't change, during midlife. Kurt Fischer discusses gender convergence during middle adulthood, emphasizing the increasing flexibility of gender roles among people in their 40s and 50s. The second part discusses adults' relationships with their children and aging parents. Catherine Cooper of the University of California, Santa Cruz, and Anna Zimmer of Hunter College discuss the special challenges faced by adult caregivers.

In the first of the two unnarrated observation modules for the unit on middle adulthood (7:35), a 47-year-old man discusses what is important in his life. He mentions that his wife recently joined in his lifelong fishing hobby, how his relationship with his adolescent son compares with how he as a teenager related to his father, and the sense of crisis he experienced as he approached his 40s. In the second module (7:25), a 60-year-old woman speaks about being an older, single woman. She describes the difficulties she faces in finding companionship, noting that what seems to matter most to many men are youth and attractiveness.

AV: Transitions Throughout the Life Span, Program 20: Middle Adulthood: Biosocial Development

This program deals with biosocial development during the years from 35 to 64. It first describes changes in appearance and in the functioning of the sense organs and vital body systems, then discusses the potential impact of these changes for women and for men. Although declines in all the body's senses and systems occur, for most adults these changes have no significant health consequences and do not interfere with daily living. Indeed, today's cohort of middle-aged adults is healthier than in previous years.

Next, the program covers health-related behaviors of the middle-aged, focusing on smoking, drinking, eating habits, and exercise. By middle age most adults understand how lifestyle choices and health habits can affect their well-being; as a result, the number of smokers declines, and people tend toward more moderate alcohol consumption. Even so, for a number of midlife adults, risky lifestyle behaviors remain serious health hazards. The next segment deals with reasons for individual variations in health. These variations arise from a combination of many factors, including race, ethnicity, socioeconomic status, and gender.

The program concludes with a discussion of the changes in the sexual-reproductive system that occur during middle adulthood, showing why most individuals find these changes less troubling than they were led to believe.

AV: Development of the Adult (25 min., HarperCollins)

This film introduces the viewer to contemporary research on development in adulthood through interviews with Bernice Neugarten, Roger Gould, and Daniel Levinson, as well as Paul Costa and David Gutman. Among the themes explored are the influence of biological and cultural clocks and differences in male and female adult development. For instance, midlife crisis is presented as a possible rather than an inevitable event, depending in part on one's sex, career, social status, and cognitive set.

AV: Adult Development (30 min., Insight Media)

This brief film introduces the major theories of adult development and describes the major transitions of this age, including leaving home, parenthood, career selection, and retirement.

Senescence

Teaching Tip: Physical Changes with Aging

To increase students' sensitivity to the impact of physical changes that occur with age, have them select some body part or ability of which they are particularly proud, such as beautiful skin or gymnastic skill. Then ask them to imagine losing that beauty or skill with age and to think about ways to counteract the changes in self-image that may result. Students should come to see the importance of developing a well-rounded self-concept rather than overemphasizing any single characteristic.

AV: The Future of Aging (55 min., Insight Media)

This program examines research into the biological and psychological mechanisms of aging. Leading researchers discuss a variety of attempts to reverse the effects of aging, including hormone replacement therapy and genetic engineering. The program ends with a discussion of the social implications of increased longevity.

The Sexual-Reproductive System

AV: Sexuality and Aging (60 min., Insight Media)

Through interviews with elderly persons, gerontologists, and sex researchers, this film explores myths and facts about sexuality in the later years of life. Age-related physiological changes that affect sexuality are also described.

Classroom Activity: The Neuroscience of Love

Some experts believe that animal research and neuroscience are pinpointing the neural, genetic, and hormonal underpinnings of love. Larry Young of Emory University's Yerkes National Primate Research Center provides an overview of this research and discusses the implications of reducing love to a biochemical chain of events—chiefly the hormones oxytocin and vasopressin. For example, studies have shown that when a female prairie vole (a normally monogamous species) is infused with oxytocin, she becomes attached to the nearest male vole. As another example, a variant of a gene involved in regulating vasopressin seems to predict when a human male will remain unmarried, and even whether he will become involved in certain types of marital conflict. Based on such findings, Young states, "drugs that manipulate brain systems at whim to enhance or diminish our love for another may not be far away."

Martha Farah of the University of Pennsylvania suggests a good way to teach about neuroethics is to initiate an online discussion with students that can last a few days. This enables students to reflect before participating and also engages students who might be shy in class. Online discussions are a natural mode of communication for today's students and can easily be implemented in many different "blackboard"–type courses. To get the discussion started, Farah suggests posing the following questions:

Is love a sacred emotion/mental state that should not be tampered with?

Under what circumstances (if any) would the use of a love drug be unethical/ethical? For what reasons?

How about a hit of oxytocin when times get tough during a relationship?

Can/Should one maintain a long-term relationship with a short-term drug?

Could a (mandatory or voluntary) variant of the drug be used to deter ("treat") sex offenders?

Farah, M. J. (2011). Resources for neuroethics teaching. National Institute on the Teaching of Psychology. St. Petersburg Beach, FL.

Young, L. J. (2009). Love: Neuroscience reveals all. *Nature, 457,* 148.

Classroom Activity: A Healthy Sexual Relationship at All Ages

Although the text does not deal extensively with sexual relationships in adulthood, students may have questions about it, given the discussion of changes in the sexual-reproductive system. To help students recognize the factors that contribute to a healthy sexual relationship at all ages, first have them list the physical changes in sexuality experienced by adult men and women, discussed in the text—for example, lowered sex drive and orgasmic difficulties in men, and changes in reproductive capacity in women. Then ask them to assess the effects of these changes on the sexual relationship of a middle-aged couple. Next, review the three facts that sex therapists communicate to patients wishing to improve their sex life, regardless of age: (a) sex does not have to mean intercourse or orgasm; (b) partners should be able to express their personal sexual needs; and (c) almost every couple with sexual problems can be helped to achieve a better sexual relationship.

Discuss how these three ideas can enhance adult sexual relationships at any age. How might the impact of physical changes be reduced if young people knew these facts and accepted them as part of healthy sexual relationships? Why aren't these concepts understood at all ages? The role of sex-education classes in promoting these facts might be discussed, especially if the students have attended such classes in high school or college.

AV: Menopause: Passage to Paradise (24 min., Films for the Humanities and Sciences)

This film explores the experience of menopause through the eyes of a group of older women who have experienced it. Some describe their experience as a milestone without incident, while others describe it as an extremely difficult and stressful time. The husband of one woman speaks openly about how his wife's difficult menopause has affected him.

Classroom Activity: A More Realistic Picture of Menopause

To help students develop a more realistic picture of menopause, have them discuss what they have heard about menopause from their families and from the media. What do female students think menopause will be like? What do male students believe about women who are experiencing menopause? Why?

Because considerable recent evidence indicates that negative menopausal experiences are rare, ask students to suggest some reasons for the prevalence of negative images. For centuries, menopause has been viewed as the "final crash" of the female body, after a lifetime of "suffering" from the hormonal miseries of menstruation and childbearing. Why would such attitudes be popular? Who stands to gain from the idea that women ought to be miserable at this age?

The answers to these questions will be largely subjective, but they can help students grasp how cultural stereotypes hinder the development of human potential. For a broader discussion of menopause, consider a mini-lecture on cultural differences in menopausal experiences. See the next item.

Classroom Activity: Culture, Meaning, and Menopause

Dan Moerman of the University of Michigan, Dearborn, makes the provocative argument that what often appears to be an "obvious" biological matter is "richly freighted with meaning, history, tradition, or the like." Consider this definition of menopause from *The Merck Manual,* an authoritative source of medical information, which is updated periodically and is now available online (www.merckmanuals.com/professional/index.html):

> As ovaries age, response to pituitary gonadotropins (follicle-stimulating hormone [FSH] and lutenizing hormone [LH] decreases, initially resulting in shorter follicular phases, fewer ovulations, decreased progesterone production, and more irregularity in cycles. Eventually, the follicle fails to respond and does not produce estrogen. Without estrogen feedback, circulating levels of LH and FSH rise substantially . . . Hot flushes (flashes) and sweating secondary to vasomotor instability affect 75% of women.

Because every woman obviously ages, this definition would seem to imply that these biological changes would be universal. This does not appear to be the case, however. In a detailed survey of several thousand older women in Japan, Canada, and the United

States, Margaret Lock has shown that only 10 percent of Japanese women report experiencing hot flashes (compared with 31 percent and 35 percent of women in Canada and the United States, respectively). Only 4 percent of the Japanese respondents reported night sweats (compared with 20 percent and 12 percent among women in Canada and the United States).

Moerman believes that differences in what appear to be matters of biology and medicine should actually be attributed to cultural patterns.

As another example, consider the incidence of diagnosis and treatment of attention-deficit/hyperactivity disorder (ADHD). Between 1990 and 1995 in the United States, 1.5 million children between 5 and 18 years of age were receiving Ritalin. Ordinary variations in human physiology can be made into diseases as cultural conditions change. Nowhere else in the world are the behaviors and symptoms recognized as ADHD in the United States and Canada treated with the same intensity, or even recognized as disorders. Moerman's conclusion is that because of cultural differences, people in different places may experience the same biological phenomena extremely differently.

Lock, M. (1993). The politics of mid-life and menopause: Ideologies for the second sex in North America and Japan. In S. Lindenbaum & M. Lock (Eds.), *Knowledge, power and practice: The anthropology of medicine and everyday life* (pp. 330–363). Berkeley, CA: University of California Press.

Moerman, D. (2002). Meaning, medicine and the 'placebo effect.' Cambridge, UK: Cambridge University Press.

Health Habits and Age

AV: Factors in Healthy Aging (28 min., Films for the Humanities and Sciences)

Harvard University's longitudinal study of aging is the subject matter of this film. The impacts of diet, smoking, drinking, family history, and personality on aging are highlighted.

"On Your Own" Activity: Good Health Habits

To emphasize the importance of good health habits early in life, have students construct a personal chart of their good and bad health habits. Handout 2 provides a format for students to use. For each bad habit, have them explain the risks involved if the habit is continued.

Discuss why students continue bad habits despite warnings based on results of medical research. What benefits does smoking provide for smokers, for example? Why do students maintain unhealthy diets? Discuss the ways in which our culture supports and even promotes bad health habits. Then turn to the good habits. Discuss ways in which those healthy patterns were developed and the personal benefits that students experience in maintaining them.

AV: The American Alcoholic (54 min., 2 parts, CRM/McGraw-Hill)

Produced by NBC news, this film explains alcoholism and provides data about its existence in our society. It includes interviews with alcoholics who openly describe their problem. It is a useful film to show if you emphasize recognition, prevention, and treatment of adult health problems.

AV: An Easy Pill to Swallow (28 min., National Film Board of Canada)

This film describes, and critiques, our cultural tendency to rely on mood-altering prescription pills rather than self-help and psychological techniques to cure our illnesses. A fact mentioned in the film is that almost a third of all North American prescriptions are for such drugs. A fact not emphasized is that the modal recipient of such prescriptions is a middle-aged woman.

Classroom Activity: Why People Continue to Smoke

To help students understand why so many Americans continue to smoke despite decades of governmental warnings, you might discuss research indicating that the "benefits" of nicotine fall into two categories.

a. *A pleasurable life:* Nicotine is a powerful negative reinforcer that terminates the unpleasant symptoms of craving and boosts mood. Like many other psychoactive drugs, nicotine works physiologically by triggering the release of epinephrine and norepinephrine, and by stimulating increased release of the neurotransmitter dopamine in the central nervous system.
b. *Increased performance:* Nicotine maintains and increases alertness, allowing for more efficient information processing by the nervous system. Nicotine may even guard against a deficiency of the neurotransmitter dopamine, which is associated with Parkinson disease.

Researchers have found that nicotine is especially addictive for mildly depressed persons, perhaps as a result of the physiological and psychological boost the drug provides. Because it is such a powerful stimulant, nicotine also increases metabolism by about 10 percent, which accounts for the fact that many ex-smokers who don't increase their activity level gain weight after quitting. Fear of weight gain is a common reason offered by smokers for not quitting.

Social psychologist Stanley Schachter found that the body's ability to metabolize nicotine varies with its pH, becoming less efficient as pH decreases (and acidity increases). In a series of laboratory and "real-life" studies, Schachter found that as pH became more acidic, smoking behavior tended to increase. The suggestion is that smokers—like addicts of any addictive drug—attempt to maintain a constant level of nicotine in their bodies. Even more interesting was the finding that situations in which smokers report a heightened need to smoke—such as when under stress or when socializing—also tend to acidify the body's pH.

Want to kick the nicotine habit? Experts offer a variety of suggestions, including the following.

a. Throw out all cigarettes. Break several in two and place them in a jar filled with water so that you can see the sludge tobacco deposits in your lungs.
b. Clean out ashtrays and fill them with nutritious, low-calorie snacks, such as vegetable sticks, fruit, or gum.
c. Recruit friends to quit with you and offer mutual support.
d. Wear a rubber band on your wrist and snap it whenever you feel the urge to smoke. Other "urge tamers" include any activity that is incompatible with smoking, such as taking a shower or going for a long walk, and visual imagery of your greatest smoking-related fear—for example, the physical emaciation associated with lung cancer.
e. Drink plenty of water and juice to help cleanse the body of nicotine and to suppress appetite.
f. Keep track of the context in which you typically smoke (driving, sitting at a desk, etc.) and restrict your smoking (before quitting altogether) to only one place.
g. Keep trying. As Schachter's data suggest, with each attempt to quit, the odds of success increase.
h. Try a behavior-modification program. Call your local American Cancer Society office to learn about programs in your area.

The Internet also offers a number of excellent resources for people who are trying to quit smoking. One of the best is the Mayo Clinic's quit-smoking plan (www.mayoclinic.com/health/quit-smoking/MY00433).

Grunberg, N. E. (2003). The tobacco use crisis and mental health. *Psychiatry, 66*(3), 200–201.

Critical Thinking Activity: Substance-Related Disorders on the Internet

Each unit of these resources contains a critical thinking exercise designed specifically to test students' critical thinking about a topic covered in the text. This unit's critical thinking activity asks students to use the resources of the Internet to learn more about substance-related disorders. Handout 3 includes several questions to help students focus their research.

There are no "right" or "wrong" answers. Answers will vary depending on which substance-related disorder your students chose to research.

Observational Activity: How Long Will You Live?

As noted in the text, daily choices affect a person's health, not only in the short term but in the years and decades ahead as well. This is most clearly indicated by the National Academy of Sciences' Institute of Medicine's assertion that more than half the mortality from the 10 leading causes of death in the United States can be traced to people's behavior—to smoking, maladaptive coping with stress, poor nutrition, insufficient exercise, and so forth.

Based on an abridged version of Diana Woodruff-Pak's life expectancy questionnaire, Handout 4 and follow-up Handout 5 are designed to highlight several health-related issues discussed in the text. By completing the questionnaire themselves or having someone they know do so, students determine the number of years by which genetic history, personal health habits, socioeconomic status, and social and personality characteristics alter life expectancy.

AV: Women's Health (27 min., Aquarius Productions)

This video explores the male bias of medical research and how the shortage of research dedicated to women has reduced the effectiveness of treatment of various diseases. Medical experts provide an illuminating indictment of the politics of medicine.

Observational Activity: Sexism in Medicine

Historically, women have been disadvantaged in terms of health care. Beginning in middle age, women have higher morbidity rates than men. This gender difference is exacerbated by the focus of medical research on acute illnesses.

When research is conducted, women often are excluded from large clinical trials such as landmark studies on the relationship between aspirin-taking and heart disease. Although women make up 52 percent of the U.S. population, research on major diseases has been conducted primarily on men (or laboratory animals). And when women have been included in medical research, the data often are not analyzed for gender differences.

This activity has been designed to help your students better understand sexist issues in medicine and the history of the women's health care movement. Handout 6 will guide their research in recent medical journals and will help them to compare current journals to those published a generation or more ago.

Measuring Health

Internet Activity: Chronological Age Versus Real Age

The Internet contains a wealth of information for measuring a person's overall health and well-being and, in this case, "real age." For this activity, ask students to search the Web to find and explore some of these resources using information and questions from Handout 7 as a guide.

HANDOUT 1

Developmental Fact or Myth?

T F 1. Deficits in hearing conversation begin with low-frequency tones.

T F 2. Fifteen percent of all couples in the United States are infertile.

T F 3. Menopause is a time of difficulty and depression for most women.

T F 4. The average level of testosterone in men declines markedly during middle age.

T F 5. Testosterone replacement has been beneficial for both men and women.

T F 6. More women die from lung cancer than from cancers of the breast, ovaries, and uterus combined.

T F 7. Smoking rates have dropped more in European nations than in North America.

T F 8. Adults who drink alcohol in moderation may live longer than those who never drink.

T F 9. About two of every three American adults are overweight.

T F 10. Japan has the world's lowest age-adjusted mortality rate.

HANDOUT 2

Good Health Habits

As emphasized in the text, lifestyle practices show a strong relationship to variations in health and susceptibility to disease. Are you practicing a healthy lifestyle? To find out, construct a personal chart of your good and bad health habits. For each bad habit, explain the risks involved if the habit is continued—for example, obesity increases the risk of heart disease. Also indicate when and why you started the habit, along with the reasons you continue each bad habit despite evidence indicating its hazards. For each good habit, indicate how the habit was developed and the personal benefits that you derive from maintaining it.

Bad Habit	Long-Term Risks	Rationale for Habit
1.		
2.		
3.		
4.		
5.		

HANDOUT 2 *(continued)*

Good Habit	Personal Benefits	Developmental Advantages
1.		
2.		
3.		
4.		
5.		

HANDOUT 3

Critical Thinking Activity: Substance-Related Disorders on the Internet

Now that you have read and reviewed the material on drug abuse during adulthood, take your learning a step further by testing your critical thinking skills on this problem-solving exercise.

In this exercise, you will examine issues in substance-related disorders such as alcohol dependence, cannabis dependence, and hallucinogen dependence. These issues include the symptoms, treatment options, and latest research findings that are unlocking the mystery of these disorders. You will also be introduced to the Internet Mental Health Web site, one of the most authoritative sources of information on psychological disorders. The home page can be found at www.mentalhealth.com/p20-grp.html. Don't limit your exploration to this site, however; use it as a starting point in your investigation to find answers to the following questions.

1. Briefly summarize the online diagnosis criteria for one of the following substance-related disorders: alcohol dependence, amphetamine dependence, cannabis dependence, cocaine dependence, hallucinogen dependence, inhalant dependence, nicotine dependence, opiod dependence, phencyclidine dependence, sedative dependence.

2. Given the many developmental contexts of substance-related disorders, treatment must focus on the biosocial, cognitive, and psychosocial roots of these disorders. Briefly describe the treatment options available for the substance-related disorder you chose in 1. Which have proven to be most effective?

HANDOUT 3 *(continued)*

3. Using the Research section of the Web site, find out how the recovery rates differ for various substance-related disorders, including the one you chose in 1.

4. Briefly summarize one article from the Research section of the Web site for the substance-related disorder you chose in 1.

HANDOUT 4

Observational Activity: How Long Will You Live?

An individual's life span is determined by many factors, including genetic history, personal health habits, socioeconomic status, and personality. To see how these factors interact, complete the following life expectancy questionnaire for yourself (or for someone you know). The basic life expectancy for American males of all races today is 73.6 years; for females it is 79.4 years. Write this beginning number down; then, as you check through the list, add or subtract the appropriate number of years for each item.

Beginning Life Expectancy

1. Longevity of grandparents
   Add 1 year for each grandparent living beyond age 80. Add one-half year for each grandparent surviving beyond the age of 70. ________

2. Longevity of parents
   If your mother lived beyond the age of 80, add 4 years. Add 2 years if your father lived beyond 80. ________

3. Cardiovascular disease among close relatives
   If any parent, grandparent, or sibling died from cardiovascular disease before age 50, subtract 4 years for each incidence. If any died from the above before the age of 60, subtract 2 years. ________

4. Other heritable disease among close relatives
   If any parent, grandparent, or sibling died before the age of 60 from diabetes or peptic ulcer, subtract 3 years. If any died before 60 from stomach cancer, subtract 2 years. Women whose close female relatives have died before 60 from breast cancer should also subtract 2 years. Finally, if any close relatives have died before the age of 60 from any cause except accidents or homicide, subtract 1 year for each incidence. ________

5. Childbearing
   Women who cannot or do not plan to have children, and those over 40 who have never had children, should subtract one-half year. Women who have had over seven children, or plan to, should subtract 1 year. ________

6. Mother's age at your birth
   Was your mother over the age of 35 or under the age of 18 when you were born? If so, subtract 1 year. ________

7. Birth order
   Are you the first-born in your family? If so, add 1 year. ________

HANDOUT 4 *(continued)*

8. Intelligence
   If you feel that you are superior in intelligence, add 2 years. ________

9. Weight
   If you are more than 30 percent overweight, subtract 5 years. If you are more than 10 percent overweight, subtract 2 years. ________

10. Dietary habits
    If you eat a lot of vegetables and fruits, and usually stop eating before feeling full, add 1 year. If you drink five or more cups of coffee per day, subtract one-half year. ________

11. Smoking
    If you smoke two or more packs of cigarettes a day, subtract 12 years. If you smoke between one and two packs a day, subtract 7 years. If you smoke less than a pack a day, subtract 2 years. ________

12. Drinking
    If you are a moderate drinker, add 3 years. If you are a light drinker, add 1.5 years. If you are a heavy drinker, subtract 8 years. ________

13. Exercise
    If you exercise briskly at least three times a week, add 3 years. ________

14. Sleep
    If you sleep more than 10 hours or less than 5 hours a night, subtract 2 years. ________

15. Sexual activity
    If you enjoy sexual activity at least once a week, add 2 years. ________

16. Regular physical examinations
    If you have an annual physical examination by your physician, add 2 years. ________

17. Health status
    If you have a chronic illness at present, subtract 5 years. ________

18. Years of education
    If you graduated from college, add 4 years. If you attended college but did not graduate, add 2 years. If you graduated from high school but did not attend college, add 1 year. If you have less than an eighth-grade education, subtract 2 years. ________

19. Occupational level (former, if retired; spouse's, if you are not working)
    Professional, add 1.5 years; technicians, administrators, managers, and agricultural workers, add 1 year; semi-skilled workers should subtract one-half year; laborers should subtract 4 years. ________

HANDOUT 4 (continued)

20. Family income
If your family income is above average for your education and occupation, add 1 year. If it is below average for your education and occupation, subtract 1 year. ________

21. Activity on the job
If your job involves a lot of physical activity, add 2 years. If your job requires that you sit all day, subtract 2 years. ________

22. Age and work
If you are over the age of 60 and still on the job, add 2 years. If you are over the age of 65 and have not retired, add 4 years. ________

23. Rural vs. urban dwelling
If you live in an urban area and have lived in or near the city for most of your life, subtract 1 year. If you have spent most of your life in a rural area, add 1 year. ________

24. Married vs. divorced
If you are married and living with your spouse, add 1 year. Men: If you are separated or divorced and living alone, subtract 9 years (not alone: subtract 4 years). If you are widowed and living alone subtract 7 years (not alone: subtract 3 years). Women: If you are separated or divorced and living alone, subtract 4 years. If you are widowed and living alone, subtract 3 years. If you are separated, divorced, or widowed and not living alone, subtract 2 years. ________

25. Single living status
Unmarried women (living alone or with others) and unmarried men who live with family or friends should subtract 1 year for each unmarried decade past age 25. Unmarried men who live alone should subtract 2 years for each decade after 25. ________

26. Life changes
If you are always changing things in your life—jobs, residences, friends—subtract 2 years. ________

27. Friendship
If you have at least two close friends in whom you can confide almost all the details of your life, add 1 year. ________

28. Aggressive personality
If you have an aggressive and sometimes hostile personality, subtract 2 years. ________

29. Flexible personality
If you are a calm, easygoing, adaptable person, add 2 years. If you are rigid, dogmatic, and set in your ways, subtract 2 years.

HANDOUT 4 *(continued)*

30. Risk-taking personality
    If you take a lot of risks, including driving without seat belts, exceeding the speed limit, and taking any dare that is made, subtract 2 years. If you use seat belts regularly, drive infrequently, and generally avoid risks and dangerous parts of town, add 1 year. __________

31. Depressive personality
    Have you been depressed, tense, worried, or guilty for more than a period of a year or two? If so, subtract 1 to 3 years depending upon how seriously you are affected by these feelings. __________

32. Happy personality
    Are you basically happy and content, and have you had a lot of fun in life? If so, add 2 years. __________

After you have completed the longevity questionnaire, fill in the information requested on the handout and return the response sheet to your instructor.

Source: National Center for Health Statistics. 1999. *United States Department of Health and Human Services.*

HANDOUT 5

How Long Will You Live?: Follow-Up Questionnaire

1. By how many years did your predicted longevity change as a result of the factors listed below? For each factor, a negative change indicates a *decrease* in longevity; a positive change in years indicates an *increase* in predicted longevity.

   a. Genetic history. Subtract your beginning life expectancy from your total after item 8 (intelligence). ______

      Number of years by which predicted longevity changed (indicate plus or minus) ______

   b. Personal health habits. Subtract your total after item 17 (health status) from your total following item 8 (intelligence). ______

      Number of years by which predicted longevity changed ______

   c. Socioeconomic status. Subtract your total in years following item 22 (age and work) from your total following item 17 (health status). ______

      Number of years by which predicted longevity changed ______

   d. Social and personality characteristics. Subtract your total in years following item 32 (happy personality) from your total following item 22 (age and work). ______

      Number of years by which predicted longevity changed ______

2. By how many years did your predicted longevity change (increase or decrease from beginning life expectancy) as a result of factors that are under your direct control?

   Number of years by which predicted longevity changed

3. By how many years did your predicted longevity change (increase or decrease from beginning life expectancy) as a result of factors that you cannot control?

   Number of years by which predicted longevity changed

4. Did completing the questionnaire encourage you or your subject to make any changes in your personal habits or lifestyle? If so, what are those changes?

HANDOUT 5 *(continued)*

5. Which, if any, variables were you surprised to discover were related to life expectancy? Why did they surprise you?

6. a. Are there variables that did not appear in the questionnaire that you would also expect to be related to longevity? Name them.

   b. Which research methods might you use to determine whether such a relationship does, in fact, exist?

7. What are the strengths and limitations of the correlational method of research?

HANDOUT 6

Sexism in Medicine

This activity asks you to investigate gender-based issues and sexism in health care research as reflected in the range of research topics published in recent medical journals as compared with topics published a generation or more ago.

Using your library's resources, find at least five different issues of medical or health care journals published in the 1960s. Try to pick journals that have published continuously to the present day so that you can compare the 1960s issues with 2000s issues from the same journal. (Note: Although it is possible for you to complete this exercise by using the Internet, your findings will probably be more dramatic if you are able to page through the actual journals.)

As you analyze each journal, make notes on the topics discussed, the genders and demographics of subjects selected in research samples, and even the advertisements purchased by pharmaceutical companies and other health care companies.

After you have finished your observations, complete the questions that follow and return the response sheet to your instructor.

1. State the titles and volume numbers of the journals you consulted.

1960s Journals	2000s Journals
1.	1.
2.	2.
3.	3.

2. By your estimate (or actual count), what percentage of the articles dealt with conditions or diseases that affect women and men equally?

   1960s Journals:

   2000s Journals:

3. What percentage of the articles dealt with conditions or disease that primarily affect women?

   1960s Journals:

   2000s Journals:

4. What percentage of the articles dealt with conditions or disease that primarily affect men?

   1960s Journals:

   2000s Journals:

5. Describe the typical sample of subjects used in any clinical trials reported in the journals (e.g., gender, ages, ethnicity, socioeconomic status).

HANDOUT 6 *(continued)*

6. By your estimate (or actual count), what proportion of clinical trials published in the journals were conducted with women?

   1960s Journals:

   2000s Journals:

7. State your conclusions regarding this activity. Is there evidence of sexism in medicine? Has the situation changed in four decades?

HANDOUT 7

Internet Activity: Chronological Age Versus Real Age

Some scientists who study aging have argued that while your chronological age is fixed, your "real age" may be years younger or older—depending on your diet, stress control, exercise, and more than 100 other health behaviors. To explore this topic further, "surf the Net" to find brief answers to the following questions. To get started, visit www.realage.com and take the online test of biological age designed by Michael Roizen, MD.

1. What is your "real age"? How does it compare to your chronological age? If your real age is substantially different from your chronological age, what are the major health factors that account for this difference?

2. On what evidence is the concept of real age based? Is the evidence trustworthy?

3. How did proponents of the real age concept come up with the calculations by which they rated each health factor's contribution? Does this approach seem valid?

4. Assuming for the moment that the real age concept is valid, what are three minor lifestyle changes that you can make today that will lower your real age? What are three major changes that you can make that will lower your real age over the long term?

5. What are several criticisms of the real age concept that have been raised by other experts in the science of aging?

Adulthood: Cognitive Development

Contents

Note: Worth Publishers provides online Instructor and Student Tool Kits, DVD Student Tool Kits, and Instructor and Student video resources in DevelopmentPortal for use with the text. See Part I: General Resources for information about these materials and the text Lecture Guides for a complete list by text chapter.

Selective Gains and Losses

Teaching Tip: Expertise, p. 8

Suggested Activities

Introducing Adulthood: Cognitive Development

"On Your Own" Activity: Developmental Fact or Myth?

Before students read about cognitive development during adulthood, have them respond to the true-false statements in Handout 1.

The correct answers are shown below. Class discussion can focus on the origins of any developmental misconceptions that are demonstrated in the students' incorrect answers.

1. F	6. F
2. F	7. F
3. T	8. T
4. T	9. F
5. T	10. F

Classroom Activity: Problem-Based Learning: Cognitive Development During Adulthood

The Introduction's Classroom Activity: Introducing Problem-Based Learning describes this relatively new pedagogical tool. Following is a sample problem that you might want to give to your students as part of your coverage of cognitive development during adulthood.

> After reading in her textbook that some primary mental abilities decline with age while others increase, Karen worries about her grandmother's cognitive well-being. Just last week, the 75-year-old retired accountant complained that her "mind was going" because she couldn't find her car keys. She also said she found it difficult to multitask as efficiently as she once did.
>
> Before you leave class today, your group must address the following questions: First, from what you have learned about cognitive development during adulthood, should Karen be worried about her grandmother? Second, after your group agrees on an answer to the first question, determine some learning issues that need to be researched to answer the question, "What can Karen tell her grandmother about the selective gains and losses that accompany cognitive development during adulthood?"
>
> Based on the decisions that your group makes today, you should devise a plan for researching the various issues. Two weeks from today's class, your group will present an answer for Karen based on the issues that you think are relevant.

Teaching Tip: Student-Generated Lecture Summaries

Recitation—whether in front of a group, with one other person, or even alone—is a proven pedagogical technique in which a student presentation is used to demonstrate knowledge of a subject or to provide instruction to other students. You can encourage your students to use mini-recitations to assess their knowledge of course material by allotting 10 minutes at the end of a lecture for this purpose. During the first 5 minutes, instruct students to write a sentence or two summarizing the main point(s) of the lecture on a note card, which they then swap with another student. The remaining time should be used by the student pairs to comment on, and consolidate, each other's understanding of the lecture material. Alternatively, you could collect students' summaries as a means of checking how well the class is understanding your lecture material.

AV: The Journey Through the Life Span, Program 8: Middle Adulthood

See Adulthood: Biosocial Development for a description of Program 8 and the accompanying observation modules, which cover the entire unit on middle adulthood.

AV: Transitions Throughout the Life Span, Program 21: Middle Adulthood: Cognitive Development

This program deals with cognitive development during the years from 35 to 64. The way psychologists conceptualize intelligence has changed considerably in recent years. The program begins by examining the contemporary view of intelligence, which emphasizes its multidimensional nature. Most experts now believe that there are several distinct intelligences rather than a single general entity.

The program then examines the multidirectional nature of intelligence, noting that some abilities (such as short-term memory) decline with age, while others (such as vocabulary) generally increase. It also includes a discussion of the debate over whether cognitive abilities inevitably decline during adulthood, or may possibly remain stable or even increase.

The program next focuses on the fact that intelligence is characterized more by variability among people than by consistency from person to person. Each person's cognitive development occurs in a unique context influenced by variations in genes, life experiences, and cohort effects.

Next the program turns to a discussion of the cognitive expertise that often comes with experience, pointing out the ways in which expert thinking differs from that of the novice. Expert thinking is more specialized, flexible, and intuitive and is guided by more and better problem-solving strategies.

The program concludes with the message that during middle adulthood individual differences are much more critical in determining the course of cognitive development than is chronological age alone.

What Is Intelligence?

AV: Intelligence (30 min., Insight Media)
IQ Testing and the School (60 min., RMI Media Productions)

Beginning with a historical perspective on how intelligence has been defined, these films describe the origins, intended uses, varieties, and failures of traditional IQ tests. *Intelligence* also addresses the question of whether intelligence is fixed or changeable and describes the differences between intellectually gifted and cognitively disabled individuals. *IQ Testing and the School* describes three types of learning environments (competitive, individualistic, and cooperative) and their impact on student achievement.

Classroom Activity: Cohort and Intelligence

As noted in the text, cohort differences have a substantial impact on intellectual development and performance. Have students list some of the technological and educational advances of the past 10 years that will make young people (the students) today "smarter" (or in some cases "dumber") than previous generations (e.g., educational television, computer games, and the Internet). What specific skills has each affected? If time permits, develop a second list of historical events that have had an impact on the students' worldviews (e.g., assassination attempts, economic cycles, political corruption, fear of terrorist attacks or nuclear war). If several age groups are represented in class, students can compare the effects of these events on different generations. Consider how these events have resulted in today's young people being more critical or questioning in their attitudes toward authority than were older generations.

Classroom Activity: "Test-Wise" Bias

To focus on the issue of bias in testing, have students discuss the degree to which test performance is based on skills that are not related to the information the test is intended to measure. Students are likely to come up with numerous examples of the various heuristic strategies that "test-wise" students employ—such as "playing the odds" on questions phrased in certain ways—that may enhance their performance. Most students probably know at least one student who never seems to study yet manages to get higher grades than another who spends long hours cracking the books only to receive average grades.

Ask students whether they feel that this is a real problem in testing. To what extent is testing in college biased against cohort differences? What improvements in testing methodology could be made that would permit better evaluation of knowledge? Should standardized testing requirements be abolished, as some graduate schools are now doing? How can people be made more "test-wise"?

Components of Intelligence: Many and Varied

Classroom Activity: Fluid and Crystallized Intelligence

Fluid and crystallized intelligence reflect different aspects of cognitive ability. Have students develop a list of the skills and abilities used in each type of intelligence. Then have them think about the tests they have recently taken, both standardized tests (ACT, SAT, GRE) and tests given in their college courses. Which test items tapped fluid intelligence? Which tapped crystallized intelligence? If fluid intelligence does decrease with age, how do some of the timed, standardized tests discriminate against older people? In tests taken in the college classroom, which ability was tapped more? In either case, could an increase in crystallized intelligence with age be enough to make up for a decline in fluid intelligence? How might a teacher develop exams that would allow the student to use both abilities?

Classroom Activity: Sternberg's Theory of Human Intelligence

When Yale psychologist Robert J. Sternberg was a child, he did not perform well on standardized intelligence tests. Nor did many other people who later turned out to be highly successful in their own specialties. Are these people lacking in intelligence? Sternberg, who received the American Psychological Association's prestigious award for distinguished contributions to psychology, thinks not and argues that traditional IQ tests overlook certain important aspects of intelligence.

You might want to expand on the text discussion of Sternberg's theory by explaining how, in Sternberg's view, the components of intelligence are (or are not) reflected in traditional intelligence tests. Sternberg suggests that traditional psychometric tests focus only on the *analytic*, or academic, aspect of intelligence. Such tests measure how efficiently people process and analyze information. "Components," according to Sternberg, "are higher-order mental processes used in learning, and the planning, monitoring, evaluating, and executing of tasks. People with strength in this area generally do very well on standardized tests."

These intelligence tests fail, however, to measure the *creative* aspect of intelligence. This second dimension of Sternberg's theory recognizes individual differences in how insightful people are in coping with novel tasks and creatively relating new information to what they already know. The ability to automatically perform familiar verbal, mathematical, and other information-processing operations is another aspect of experience. Automatization facilitates insight by "freeing up" the mind so that it can concentrate on unfamiliar tasks.

Intelligence tests also fail to recognize a *practical* aspect of intelligence, which may be why IQ tests are only weakly correlated with job performance and "success" in life. This real-world, or "practical," intelligence develops throughout life, is probably the basis for occupational expertise, and, more generally, gives people the ability to size up situations in order to adapt to them, shape them to their liking, or quit them in the hopes of selecting others that are more comfortable.

People with practical intelligence know how to use "inside information," or *tacit knowledge*, in order to get ahead, win a promotion, or cut through bureaucratic red tape.

Your students are sure to understand the significance of Sternberg's arguments. Today, virtually no one can escape standardized intelligence testing. And all too often, students with stellar credentials (grades, letters of recommendation, professional enthusiasm, etc.) are denied admission into undergraduate, graduate, and professional programs because of marginal standardized test scores. Sternberg tells the story of a teachers' college in Mississippi that required a score of 25 on the Miller Analogy Test for admission. "A promising student was admitted to the college despite a sub-25 Miller score, and went through the program with distinction. When it came time for the student to receive a diploma, she was informed that the diploma would be withheld until she could take the test over and receive a score of at least 25. Consider the logic here: The predictor had come to surpass the criteria in importance! The test had become an end rather than a means." To help prevent absurdities such as this from happening again, Sternberg has published a popular "how to" guide for this test.

More recently, Sternberg has expanded his theory of human intelligence to include the concept of wisdom. For Sternberg, wisdom is ". . . the use of one's intelligence and experience as mediated by values toward the achievement of a common good through a balance among (1) intrapersonal, (2) interpersonal, and (3) extrapersonal interests, over the (1) short and (2) long terms, to achieve a balance among (1) adaptation to existing environments, (2) shaping of existing environments, and (3) selection of new environments."

Sternberg, R. J. (2004, January). What is wisdom and how can we develop it? *Annals of the American Academy of Political and Social Science. 591*, 164.

Sternberg, R. J. (1998). *How to prepare for the MAT-Miller analogies test.* Barron's educational series.

Sternberg, R. J. (1997). *Successful intelligence: How practical and creative intelligence determines success in life.* New York: Dutton/Plume.

AV: Intelligence, Creativity, and Thinking Styles (30 min., Films for the Humanities and Sciences)

In this interview, Robert Sternberg outlines his influential triarchic theory of intelligence and discusses how multiple intelligences and different thinking styles relate to traditional, IQ-based measures of intelligence.

AV: MI: Intelligence, Understanding, and the Mind (50 min., Into the Classroom Media)

Hosted by Harvard psychologist Howard Gardner, this program examines how outdated views of the human mind continue to dominate our views regarding intelligence. Gardner begins by discussing the cognitive revolution of the 1950s, focusing on the research of Herbert Simons, Jean Piaget, and Noam Chomsky. The major thrust of the program is Gardner's explanation of his theory of multiple intelligences.

AV: Multiple Intelligences (50 min., Into the Classroom Media)

Harvard psychologist Howard Gardner outlines his theory of multiple intelligences. As he does so, he reviews the flawed history of intelligence testing and puts forth his principal goal for education—the "attainment of genuine understanding." He explains why "understanding," which he defines as the ability to apply knowledge to new situations, is often undermined by traditional educational emphases.

Classroom Activity: Comparing Ideas About Intelligence

To further extend your discussion of the multidimensionality of intelligence, point out that although there are many studies of intelligence as measured by IQ tests, there are very few measures of intelligence as judged by people in everyday situations. To find out what average people mean when they speak of intelligence, Robert Sternberg and his colleagues interviewed or questioned by mail 475 men and women—including students, railway commuters, respondents to newspaper advertisements, and people whose names were randomly selected from the telephone book. Instead of directly asking the people to define intelligence, the researchers asked them to list what they considered to be characteristics of "intelligence," "academic intelligence," "everyday intelligence," and "unintelligence."

In a companion study, the researchers sent the questionnaire to a group of recognized authorities in the field of intelligence. After the responses of the two groups were compiled, the statistical technique of factor analysis allowed the researchers to determine the several basic dimensions underlying respondents' diverse answers. The chart that follows this item reflects the two groups' responses.

Laypersons generally conceived of intelligence as having three dimensions: practical problem-solving ability, verbal ability, and social competence. Experts separated overall problem-solving ability from practical intelligence and did not emphasize the social and cultural aspects of intelligence. In addition, the experts considered motivation to be a more important ingredient in academic intelligence than did the laypersons.

Laypersons and Experts Compare Ideas About Intelligence

Laypeople and researchers in intelligence who participated in the final phase of the author's study agreed on many characteristics of intelligent behavior but gave them somewhat different emphases. The following chart reflects the ratings. They are based on a statistical analysis of expert and lay responses to a list of characteristics mentioned by a group of laypeople in the initial phase.

Laypersons

I. Practical problem-solving ability

Reasons logically and well.
Identifies connections among ideas.
Sees all aspects of a problem.
Keeps an open mind.
Responds thoughtfully to others' ideas.
Sizes up situations well.
Gets to the heart of problems.
Interprets information accurately.
Makes good decisions.
Goes to original sources for basic information.
Poses problems in an optimal way.
Perceives implied assumptions and conclusions.
Listens to all sides of an argument.
Deals with problems resourcefully.

II. Verbal ability

Speaks clearly and articulately.
Is verbally fluent.
Converses well.
Is knowledgeable about a particular field.
Studies hard.
Reads widely.
Deals effectively with people.
Writes without difficulty.
Sets aside time for reading.
Displays a good vocabulary.
Accepts social norms.
Tries new things.

III. Social competence

Accepts others for what they are.
Admits mistakes.
Displays interest in the world at large.
Is on time for appointments.
Has social conscience.
Thinks before speaking and doing.
Displays curiosity.
Does not make snap judgments.
Makes fair judgments.
Assesses well the relevance of information to a problem at hand.
Is sensitive to other people's needs and desires.
Is frank and honest with self and others.
Displays interest in the immediate environment.

Experts

I. Verbal intelligence

Displays a good vocabulary.
Reads with high comprehension.
Displays curiosity.
Is intellectually curious.
Sees all aspects of a problem.
Learns rapidly.
Appreciates knowledge for its own sake.
Is verbally fluent.
Listens to all sides of an argument before deciding.
Displays alertness.
Thinks deeply.
Shows creativity.
Converses easily on a variety of subjects.
Reads widely.
Likes to read.
Identifies connections among ideas.

II. Problem-solving ability

Is able to apply knowledge to problems at hand.
Makes good decisions.
Poses problems in an optimal way.
Displays common sense.
Displays objectivity.
Solves problems well.
Plans ahead.
Has good intuition.
Gets to the heart of problems.
Appreciates truth.
Considers the result of actions.
Approaches problems thoughtfully.

III. Practical intelligence

Sizes up situations well.
Determines how to achieve goals.
Displays awareness to world around him or her.
Displays interest in the world at large.

Sternberg, R. J. (2000). *Practical intelligence in everyday life*. New York: Cambridge University Press.

Classroom Activity: Classroom Debate: *"Resolved: The Multidimensionality of Intelligence Makes Standardized IQ Testing Obsolete"*

The current view of intelligence as multidimensional and multidirectional has fueled the controversy over the value of IQ tests. As suggested in the text, the use of a single IQ score unfairly depicts older adults as lower in intelligence than adolescents or younger adults. To help students better understand this controversy, you might prepare a lecture on the recent history of IQ testing. Many of today's students are surprisingly unaware of how hotly these tests have been debated among psychologists and educators during the past several decades, resulting in, among other things, the publication of the answers on the SAT Reasoning Test in some states.

You might begin by explaining that tests were thought to be a fair and quick method of determining the best education for each child: By grouping children according to IQ, the gifted children would not be held back by the average students, and the slow learners would not feel hopelessly inadequate because they could not keep up. A teacher could then teach a concept to the entire class without worrying that some students would be bored and others would be lost.

However, the civil rights movement of the 1960s convinced many people that IQ tests were a way of perpetuating the status quo. The children whose parents were upper- and middle-class whites would do well on such tests because of their background rather than their innate intelligence and would therefore receive a better education; the children from poorer, non-White, or non-English-speaking families would be held back, given fewer opportunities to learn, and receive an inferior education. For them the IQ test was one more turn in a vicious circle. This later view convinced the Supreme Court of California to decide in 1978 that IQ tests, as constituted, could not be the main criterion for placing students in classes for slow learners.

Obviously, this controversy touches on deeply held values about democracy, equality of opportunity, heredity, and merit. Once the students realize these values are involved, follow the guidelines in the General Resources section of this manual and schedule a classroom debate on the resolution.

Classroom Activity: Intuition and the Intelligence of Everyday Life

As noted in the text, many contemporary developmental researchers believe that traditional measures of adult intelligence rely too heavily on little-used knowledge and skills. In contrast, newer measures of *practical intelligence* focus on conflict resolution, career decisions, and other real-life problems. Taking a similar approach to practical intelligence, Daniel Cappon and his colleagues at York University have devised the *Intuition Quotient Test*, or *IQ2*, to measure the "intelligence of everyday life."

Cappon believes that human intuition has been shaped by the evolutionary power of natural selection. "There is no way that our human ancestors could have survived without intuition," he argues. "There could not have been much conscious thinking before speech evolved, some 250,000 years ago, yet *Pithecanthropus erectus* goes back some 4.5 million years. Old Pith could not possibly have survived predators or such natural threats as the melting of the ice age without intuitive decisions—where to make a fire, when to store meat, when to move to the highlands. There was no time for thinking or laborious logic. Responses often had to be instantaneous. The sound of movement in the brush required an immediate reaction. Those who failed to respond were removed from the gene pool by voracious predators."

Despite the importance of such reasoning in our evolutionary history, intuition developed a bad reputation and, until recently, was considered by many researchers as nothing more than a "woman's gift in a man's world." Researchers in the private sector, however, have been much more willing to investigate intuition. In their endless quest for an edge in the marketplace, businesses have begun to realize that "analytical thinking arrives too late for a 24-hour global marketplace."

Cappon's studies began with an effort to test his hunch that intuition is the secret of success in most endeavors. Devising a 15-page questionnaire, he attempted to develop personality profiles of successful business leaders. His inquiries, however, were met with resistance, particularly from companies that dealt directly with people and services. Ironically, although many attributed their success at least in part to their intuitive ability, they felt the public would "lose faith in them if they were found to be running on gut feeling."

Taking another approach, Cappon interviewed and studied the writings of Nobel-laureate scientists, including Linus Pauling, Jonas Salk, and Alexander Fleming. "Of course, we have hunches," they said. "We know the answer before we work it out. Science, at its best, is the working out of things later."

After studying intuitive thinkers for several years, Cappon concludes that intuition can be operationally defined in terms of 20 specific perceptual and cognitive skills, including these:

- perceptual recognition—the ability to distinguish one thing from another—the "ability to find Waldo, for example."
- perceptual closure—the skill of knowing what something is even after minimal exposure or an obscured view.
- synthesis—the ability to put various elements together in your mind's eye to perceive a larger whole.
- foresight—the ability to anticipate, to know what will happen next.
- optimal timing—the sense of knowing when the time is ripe for something to happen. This skill has made investors and other entrepreneurs rich.
- best method—knowing how best to accomplish something. "Michelangelo wanted to paint the Sistine Chapel ceiling, but how was he going to do it? By lying on his back on a ladder for seven years."
- hindsight—the ability to use empathy and identification to put oneself so closely in a situation as to come to understand it. "Historians apply this power to explain the past."

More generally, Cappon believes that you are intuitive if you

- know what something is despite little time to see it properly.

- can identify something you haven't seen clearly.
- are good at finding Waldo.
- can distinguish elements flashed before you.
- can identify what wasn't flashed before you.
- can see the forest through the trees.
- can time three-minute eggs without a clock.
- can take in a whole scene quickly and remember details.
- are good at generating images spontaneously.
- can identify things you have never seen before.
- look at a cloud and many images come to mind.
- can anticipate what will happen next.
- always know when it's the ideal time to strike.
- are good at hunches.
- know the best way to figure something out.
- know how to apply a discovery.
- can divine the causes of things.
- are good at detective work; you know what elements fit together.
- look at a picture and know what elements don't fit.
- see the meaning of symbols.

In Cappon's one-and-one-half-hour test of intuition, subjects are presented with 320 visual images, 16 for each of the 20 specific skills. Each scene is accompanied by a simple question. To measure foresight, for example, a picture of a horse race is briefly flashed on the screen. Subjects are asked, "Which of these race horses will fall back?" (The photo was snapped a split second before one horse actually did so.) If the subject fails to answer in the brief amount of time that is allotted, the scene is repeated in slightly greater detail, until the correct answer is given. To measure hindsight, subjects are shown—in progressively greater detail—images of the devastation of a forest following the eruption of a volcano. The question asked is, "What destroyed this forest?"

Cappon believes that although everyone has some capacity for intuition, most of us fail to use it fully. And although he disagrees with Carl Jung's belief in the existence of an "intuitive personality," he admits that certain traits—such as openness, as opposed to rigidity—are positively correlated with intuitive ability. Most significantly, Cappon believes that intuitive skills can be enhanced. In fact, taking the IQ2 test seems to help many people improve their perceptual skills. People who score highest on tests of perceptual closure, for example, move their eyes differently from those who do not. Their eyes dart quickly over an image in a zigzag pattern. People who do not score as well move their eyes more slowly, in uncertain circles, until they find a point, almost at random, to focus on. "During the course of the IQ2," notes Cappon, "we could detect which people found a pathway to intuition because they changed their pattern of eye movements. Many people suspect that intuition can be trained, but the eye effect is the very first evidence that it can."

Following Cappon's lead, other researchers have begun investigating intuition. Hans Welling (2005), for example, has developed a five-phase model that explains intuition on the basis of the cognitive functions of pattern discovery and recognition. Harvard's Matthew Lieberman notes that intuition plays a prominent role in interpersonal relationships and the processes we use to understand the world around us. Lieberman believes that nonverbal decoding skills and other social cognitive heuristics that people develop with experience are examples of intuition. The literature on the development of these types of practical, intuitive skills has historically been referred to as "implicit learning," defined as ". . . the acquisition of knowledge that takes place largely independently of conscious attempts to learn and largely in the absence of explicit knowledge about what was acquired."

Most intriguing in this age of cognitive neuroscience is Lieberman's contention that implicit learning has a clear neural basis in the striatum, substantia nigra, and globus pallidus of the brain's basal ganglia. As evidence, Lieberman points to neuropsychological research on patients with Huntington disease (HD) and Parkinson disease (PD). Neuroimaging and postmortem studies demonstrate that both HD and PD are degenerative brain diseases that affect the basal ganglia, ultimately destroying the striatum.

A growing body of research demonstrates that both HD and PD patients show impaired performance on standard implicit learning tasks. One such task is the serial reaction time task (SRT), in which participants are asked, on each trial, to indicate as quickly as they can which of four quadrants on a television screen contains a target stimulus. In a typical SRT study, the target moves from quadrant to quadrant in a predictable pattern that repeats itself over an 8- to 10-trial sequence. If the participants are gaining implicit knowledge of the pattern, they should become faster in predicting the location of targets over successive trials.

Cappon, D. (1993, May). The anatomy of intuition. *Psychology Today*, *26*(3), 40–45.

Lieberman, M. D. (2000). Intuition: a social cognitive neuroscience approach. *Psychological Bulletin, 126*(1), 109–137.

Lieberman, M. D., Jarcho, J. M., & Satpute, A. B. (2004). Evidence-based and intuition-based self-knowledge: An fMRI sudy. *Journal of Personality and Social Psychology, 84*(4), 4435.

Welling, H. (2005). The intuitive process: The case of psychotherapy. *Journal of Psychotherapy Integration, 15*(1), 19–47.

"On Your Own" Activity: Measuring Creativity

Many tests of creativity have been devised. One of the most frequently used tests is the Remote Associates Test (Handout 2), devised by Sarnoff and Martha Mednick. This test is based on the idea that creativity reflects an ability to see relationships among ideas that are remote from one another. There are several ways in which you might incorporate this test into a unit on cognitive development during adulthood.

Distribute copies of the test and have students time themselves at home (about 30 minutes for completion is average). Discussion could focus on the relationship of creativity to intelligence, or you might have students compare the Remote Associates Test with the Unusual Uses Test (Handout 3), which asks respondents to generate as many uses as possible for such common objects as a paper clip, pencil, comb, or toothpick. You might also ask students to administer both tests to individuals of various ages in order to focus awareness on the relationships among age, experience, creativity, and the measurement of intelligence.

Students may have a better understanding of the multidimensional nature of intelligence after completing these exercises. Which of the two tests do they feel is a more valid measure of creativity? Based on their data, as well as on educated intuition, what relationships would they expect to find between age and performance on the two tests?

Answers to the Remote Associates Test

1. phone	11. green	21. lead
2. book	12. floor	22. top
3. fire	13. stone	23. tack
4. pin	14. bar	24. watch
5. cheese	15. fountain	25. cat
6. chair	16. ball	26. stop
7. slow	17. go	27. mail
8. foot	18. cover	28. bubble
9. party	19. type	29. black
10. hard	20. chair	30. end

Mednick, S. A., & Mednick, M. T. (1967). *Remote associates test.* Boston: Houghton Mifflin.

Critical Thinking Activity: Devising an Intelligence Test

Assign students the task of developing an "intelligence" test that is biased in favor of their own particular age cohort. As noted in Handout 4, the test could be based on knowledge and/or slang expressions that are of particular significance to members of this age cohort. It might be helpful for students to work in small groups.

By attempting to construct their own tests, students may gain a better understanding of the nature of intelligence testing and how easily tests can become biased against particular groups. Have students administer their tests to classmates who both are and are not members of the age cohort in question.

Selective Gains and Losses

Teaching Tip: Expertise

To expand on the text discussion of the cognitive expertise that often comes with experience, ask your students to think about their own areas of expertise and then complete a short, in-class writing assignment. Get their thinking started by reviewing the ways in which expert thinking differs from that of the novice. Expert thinking is more specialized, flexible, and intuitive, and is guided by more and better problem-solving strategies. In addition, many elements of expert performance are automatic and experts have more, and better, strategies for accomplishing a particular task. Finally, in developing their abilities, experts point to the importance of practice, usually 10 years or more and several hours a day before full potential is achieved.

After reviewing the features that distinguish experts from novices, give students 10–15 minutes to describe their own area(s) of expertise, specifically noting its development and how their skills have changed over the course of its development.

HANDOUT 1

Developmental Fact or Myth?

T F 1. Most developmentalists today conceive of intelligence as a single underlying ability.

T F 2. Both cross-sectional and longitudinal research indicate that intelligence declines systematically during adulthood.

T F 3. IQ scores have shown a steady upward drift over most of the last century.

T F 4. Cohort differences affect scores on intelligence tests.

T F 5. Intellectual abilities are multidirectional in that they can follow different trajectories with age.

T F 6. Cognitive abilities are not affected by number of years of formal education.

T F 7. Individual differences in intelligence are "fixed" in that they remain roughly the same over the life span.

T F 8. Declines in fluid intelligence may be masked by increases in crystallized intelligence.

T F 9. Adults believe that practical intelligence is the least useful form of intelligence during adulthood.

T F 10. Compared with novices, experts tend to rely on more formal procedures in solving problems.

HANDOUT 2

Measuring Creativity: Remote Associates Test

In this test you are presented with three words and asked to find a fourth word that is related to all three. Write this word in the space to the right.

For example, what word do you think is related to these three?

paint doll cat

The answer in this case is "house": house paint, doll house, and house cat.

1. call	pay	line	______	1
2. end	burning	blue	______	2
3. man	hot	sure	______	3
4. stick	hair	ball	______	4
5. blue	cake	cottage	______	5
6. man	wheel	high	______	6
7. motion	poke	down	______	7
8. stool	powder	ball	______	8
9. line	birthday	surprise	______	9
10. wood	liquor	luck	______	10
11. house	village	golf	______	11
12. plan	show	walker	______	12
13. key	wall	precious	______	13
14. bell	iron	tender	______	14
15. water	pen	soda	______	15
16. base	snow	dance	______	16
17. steady	cart	slow	______	17
18. up	book	charge	______	18
19. tin	writer	my	______	19
20. leg	arm	person	______	20
21. weight	pipe	pencil	______	21
22. spin	tip	shape	______	22
23. sharp	thumb	tie	______	23
24. out	band	night	______	24
25. cool	house	fat	______	25
26. back	short	light	______	26
27. man	order	air	______	27
28. bath	up	gum	______	28
29. ball	out	jack	______	29
30. up	deep	rear	______	30

Source: Gardner, R. *Exercises for general psychology*. Copyright © 1980, pp. 69–72. Adapted by permission of Prentice Hall, Upper Saddle River, New Jersey.

HANDOUT 3

Measuring Creativity: Unusual Uses Test

Name as many uses as you can for each of the following common objects.

toothpick

comb

paper clip

pencil

Styrofoam cup

door key

HANDOUT 4

Critical Thinking Activity: Devising an Intelligence Test

Now that you have read and reviewed the material on cognitive development during adulthood, take your learning a step further by testing your critical thinking skills on this creative problem-solving exercise.

As noted in the text, many standard tests of intelligence are biased against older age cohorts. Based on skills that are more pertinent to and commonly practiced by younger persons, these tests typically underestimate the capabilities of older adults.

As an exercise in studying the nature and the limitations of intelligence testing, try to design an "intelligence" test that is biased in favor of persons in your own age group. Your test may include vocabulary, expressions, and other examples of crystallized intelligence, or, if you wish, it may attempt to assess memory, speed of thinking, and other aspects of fluid intelligence that might differentiate one age group from another. Try to include 3 to 5 tasks, if your test assesses fluid intelligence, and 10 to 15 questions, if it assesses crystallized intelligence. Turn in a clear, typed copy of your test to your instructor (so that it can be reproduced for other students), along with your answers to the following questions.

1. What is the name of your test?

2. What aspect(s) of intelligence is your test designed to assess? What types of tasks or questions are included in your test?

3. Why is this test biased?

4. Who should score well on this test? Who should score poorly?

5. Have you ever taken a standardized test that you felt was unfair? Briefly describe your experience.

Adulthood: Psychosocial Development

Contents

Note: Worth Publishers provides online Instructor and Student Tool Kits, DVD Student Tool Kits, and Instructor and Student video resources in DevelopmentPortal for use with the text. See Part I: General Resources for information about these materials and the text Lecture Guides for a complete list by text chapter.

Suggested Activities

Introducing Adulthood: Psychosocial Development

"On Your Own" Activity: Developmental Fact or Myth?

Before students read about psychosocial development during adulthood, have them respond to the true-false statements in Handout 1.

The correct answers are shown below. Class discussion can focus on the origins of any developmental misconceptions that are demonstrated in the students' incorrect answers.

1. F 2. T 3. T 4. F 5. F 6. T 7. F 8. F 9. T 10. F

AV: The Journey Through the Life Span, Program 8: Middle Adulthood

See Adulthood: Biosocial Development for a description of Program 8 and the accompanying observation modules, which cover the entire unit on middle adulthood.

AV: Transitions Throughout the Life Span, Program 22: Middle Adulthood: Psychosocial Development

Program 22 is concerned with midlife, commonly believed to be a time of crisis and transition, when self-doubt, reevaluation of career goals, changes in family responsibilities, and a growing awareness of one's mortality lead to turmoil. The first segment examines the changes that occur at midlife, showing that although middle adulthood may have its share of pressures and stress, a crisis is not inevitable.

The next segment examines the question of whether there is stability of personality throughout adulthood, identifying five basic clusters of personality traits that remain fairly stable throughout adulthood. One personality trend that occurs during middle age, as gender roles become less rigid, is the tendency of both sexes to take on characteristics typically reserved for the opposite sex.

The third segment depicts the changing dynamics between middle-aged adults and their adult children and aging parents, showing why the various demands of the younger and older generations have led the middle-aged to be called the "sandwich generation." Changes in the marital relationship are also examined.

The final segment examines the evolution of work in the individual's life during middle adulthood. As many women and men begin to balance their work lives with parenthood and other concerns, many engage in a scaling back of their effort in the workplace.

Continuity and Change, Again

AV: Development of the Adult (29 min., HarperCollins)

(See description in Adulthood: Biosocial Development.)

AV: Midlife Crisis (30 min., RMI Media Productions)

Paula Hardin, author of *What Are You Doing With the Rest of Your Life?*, joins psychotherapist James Ellis in a discussion of whether there is a midlife crisis.

"On Your Own" Activity: The Social Clock and Gender Stereotypes

As noted in the text, age-graded norms once specified by the social clock are now said to be obsolete. Society, culture, cohort, family, and the individual now set multiple clocks for when to marry, have children, and so on. Although gender stereotypes may also be loosening, they continue to exert subtle pressures on our experiences. Laura Levine offers a good suggestion for stimulating class discussion about changing social norms. Ask students to think of something they don't do because of their gender (e.g., changing a tire, braiding their hair, using a snowblower, knitting) or their perceived setting of the social clock (e.g., playing an "age-inappropriate" game, sport, or other activity) and then have them learn how to do it. Ask them to be aware of resistance to this from others but also from within themselves. Class discussion, or a summary paper, can focus on how students felt once they had accomplished this task.

Levine, L. (2011). Creating significant learning experiences in child development courses. National Institute on the Teaching of Psychology. St. Petersburg Beach, FL.

Classroom Activity: Personality Testing

To help students understand the process of personality testing, you might review in class several well-known tests—for example, Rotter's Internal–External Control Scale, the Vocational Apperception Test, and the Allport-Vernon-Lindzey Study of Values. Emphasize that personality researchers do not rely on only one measure. They may use any or all of the following: interviews, standardized tests, and projective tests such as the Thematic Apperception Test (often utilized in studies of aging).

This is a good opportunity for you to outline the basic principles of test construction (standardization and sampling, for example) and the characteristics of a good test (validity, reliability, and so on).

Following this discussion, assign the "On Your Own" Activity, Designing a Personality Test, an exercise in which students are asked to construct their own personality tests; this will permit students to experience first-hand the difficulties and limitations involved in personality testing. In class, review the tests your students have devised and discuss their strengths and weaknesses. Students might also enjoy exchanging tests and comparing responses.

"On Your Own" Activity: Designing a Personality Test

To help students understand the difficulties involved in constructing an effective personality test, challenge them to devise one of their own. The test could cover any aspect of personality; students might be encouraged to focus on a dimension discussed in the text and one for which developmental data exist. This activity might be facilitated by having students work in small groups. Handout 2 will help students evaluate their own work in designing a personality test.

As the assignment is discussed in class, encourage students to describe the difficulties they encountered in designing and administering their personality tests. Students might also exchange tests with classmates and critique each other's efforts. The implications of this exercise are that the construction of an effective personality test is a difficult task. Having tried it, students should have a better understanding of the limitations of this form of testing and be more critical when evaluating conclusions based on this methodology.

"On Your Own" Activity: Measuring Your Big Five Traits

The Big Five Inventory (BFI-54) was designed by Oliver P. John and his colleagues as a quick assessment of the Big Five personality dimensions. Have your students complete the inventory in Handout 3 and calculate their scores. If your class is ethnically diverse, you might want to determine whether the Big Five applies to all groups.

Following are directions for students to measure the degree to which they exhibit each dimension:

- Extraversion: First reverse the numbers placed in front of items 7, 19, and 33 (1 = 5, 2 = 4, 3 = 3, 4 = 2, 5 = 1), then add all the numbers for items 1, 7, 13, 19, 33, 39, 46, 49, and 53. Scores can range from 9 to 45, with higher scores reflecting greater extraversion.
- Agreeableness: First reverse the numbers placed in front of items 2, 15, 25, and 40 (1 = 5, 2 = 4, 3 = 3, 4 = 2, 5 = 1), then add all the numbers for items 2, 8, 15, 25, 28, 34, 40, 45, and 51. Scores can range from 9 to 45, with higher scores reflecting greater agreeableness.
- Conscientiousness: Reverse the numbers placed in front of items 10, 21, 29, and 52 (1 = 5, 2 = 4, 3 = 3, 4 = 2, 5 = 1), then add all the numbers in front of items 3, 10, 16, 21, 24, 29, 36, 42, and 52. Total scores can range from 9 to 45, with higher scores reflecting greater conscientiousness.
- Emotional Stability: Reverse the numbers placed in front of items 5, 17, 31, 37, and 47 (1 = 5, 2 = 4, 3 = 3, 4 = 2, 5 = 1), then add all the numbers in front of items 5, 11, 17, 22, 26, 31, 37, 43, and 47. Scores can range from 9 to 45, with higher scores reflecting greater emotional stability.
- Openness: Reverse the numbers in front of items 9, 14, 32, and 54 (1 = 5, 2 = 4, 3 = 3, 4 = 2, 5 = 1), then add the numbers in front of 4, 6, 9, 12, 14, 18, 20, 23, 27, 30, 32, 35, 38, 41, 44, 48, 50, and 54. Total scores can range from 18 to 90, with higher scores reflecting greater openness.

Internet Activity: Trait Theory and Personality

The Internet contains a wealth of information about the various approaches to studying personality, including trait theory. For this activity, ask students to visit the Keirsey Temperament Web site, using questions from Handout 4 as a guide.

Classroom Activity: Classroom Debate: *"Resolved: Men and Women Are Born into Immutable Gender Roles"*

The text notes that although personality traits tend to be quite stable in adulthood, adult traits are not immutable. To focus attention on cohort effects, shifting cultural standards for the behavior of men and women, and the role of biological factors in gender personality differences, pose this question to the class: Have the concepts of the "ideal" man and the "ideal" woman changed from the previous generation to the current one?

Clinical psychologist Herbert Freudenberger has written extensively on issues facing men and women in contemporary society. In his practice, Freudenberger reports that he is seeing an increasing number of male patients who find themselves in "historically peculiar terrain" and are struggling with the problem of how to be "male" in their sexual relationships with women, in their personal identity, and in commitments to marriage, family, and career. As Freudenberger states, for men "these problems have several major sources: changes in sexual stereotypes and norms, the emphasis on material achievement, the rise of feminism and women's liberation, the lack of man-to-man intimacy, and the scarcity of acceptable mentors for men to emulate."

Freudenberger contends that today's troubled men need to learn how to open up to their feelings, to view other men and women as potential collaborators (rather than competitors) in personal relationships, and to allow themselves to feel dependent without feeling threatened. Such changes do not come easily, but when they do, Freudenberger believes that men will once again feel secure in their roles as husband, father, and friend.

Women, too, confront problems stemming from today's shifting gender-role expectations. This is particularly true when a woman is torn between traditional and nontraditional views of her role. For example, a woman who deliberately delays marriage and child rearing for education and career may also worry that she has lost status because she has not fulfilled the traditional roles of marriage partner and mother.

A spate of articles has suggested that the difficulty some men and women are having in adjusting to shifting gender role expectations is due to the biological immutability of gender differences. To explore this issue in class, follow the guidelines in the General Resources section of this manual and schedule a classroom debate on the resolution.

Intimacy

AV: The Human Animal: Family and Survival (52 min., Films for the Humanities and Sciences)

Hosted by Phil Donahue, this film begins with the sobering statistic that less than 5 percent of American households fit the profile of the traditional nuclear family. It goes on to explore the specific challenges of various family structures in contemporary America. It is also appropriate for Middle Childhood: Psychosocial Development, where different family structures are discussed.

AV: Portrait of a Family (30 min. each, RMI Media Productions)

This modularly organized series examines various aspects of intimacy, marriage, and families. Each module consists of three or four 30-minute programs. Module Four, "The Family Established," focuses on the everyday lives of married couples, discussing such issues as the social and personal impact of two-career marriages, financial difficulties, and child rearing. Module Five, "The Family in Transition," examines changing family situations, from the transition to parenthood, to midlife changes, retirement, and the loss of a spouse. Module Six, "The Family Extended," explores the special challenges of remarriage, stepfamily living, and aging relationships.

AV: Leaving Home: A Family in Transition (25 min., Direct Cinema Ltd.)

A family of four daughters is filmed as three of the daughters leave home, each to pursue a different life. The feelings of all family members are explored as the daughters go. The mother discusses "the empty nest" and her changing role, while the daughters assert their desire to be considered adults in their childhood home. They question whether one ever completely becomes an adult in the eyes of one's parents. These transitions are compared with changes the father had to face some 20 years earlier when he left his parents in Israel to come to the United States. This film provides an excellent springboard for discussion.

Classroom Activity: The Changing Family

Family members have linked lives, continuing to affect one another as they all grow older. They are less likely to live together than in earlier times and in other nations, but family members are often mutually supportive, emotionally and financially. Ask students to diagram their own families and then compare their diagrams with those of other students. How many students have traditional nuclear families? Do variations in family structure in the class match national demographics? Have students think of how their family diagrams would differ if drawn from the perspective of relatives a generation or more in the past.

Committed Partners

AV: The Broken Heart (28 min., Films for the Humanities and Sciences)

Developmentalists and health psychologists are discovering that many chronic diseases, accidents, and even auto fatalities are more common among those whose family life is disrupted or nonexistent. This specially adapted Phil Donahue program explores the link between loneliness and isolation and illness, depression, and death.

AV: Am I Wife, Mother . . . or Me? (31 min., LCA)

Excerpted from the feature movie *I Love You, Goodbye,* this film takes a critical look at the changing role of women in society. Hope Lange plays a 36-year-old wife and mother who is dissatisfied with her roles as wife and mother. Seeing herself as merely a chauffeur for her children and an audience for her egocentric husband, she leaves to begin a new life. With outstanding acting by Lange and Earl Holliman, the film is an excellent stimulus for classroom discussion.

AV: Clinical Dilemmas in Marriage: The Search for Equal Partnership (44 min., Insight Media)

(See description in Emerging Adulthood: Psychosocial Development.)

Classroom Activity: Custody and Visitation Arrangements

To help students think about the reality of custody and visitation arrangements in the recently divorced family, you might share with them the witty but sensible treatment of this subject that appears in *Miss Manners' Guide to Rearing Perfect Children* by Judith Martin.

In a section titled "The Divorced Weekend," Miss Manners begins, in some exasperation: "Why lions and tigers should have the full task of amusing the children of divorced parents on weekends Miss Manners does not know. She does know that the combined efforts of every creature in the zoo are not enough to cement a relationship between small children and a nonresident parent."

You might ask your students whether they have observed divorced fathers trying to amuse their children at zoos and other places. How does one "know" that these are divorced fathers? (Absence of a mother is one clue. Perhaps the father seems uncomfortable or full of forced cheer; perhaps the children are quieter, more well-behaved, or the reverse.)

Says Miss Manners: "Filling that time [the divorced weekend] with an occasional excursion is all very well, but only as part of sharing that parent's life and interests. First, the child must learn that he has a permanent place in that parent's life, and a realistic one, as opposed to that of a pal one goes partying with, so to speak."

Ask your students how a noncustodial parent can show a child that he or she has a "permanent place in the parent's life." Miss Manners suggests that the parent reveal his or her household routine and ask the child to share it. This includes revealing other people who are important in the parent's life (dates, new spouse, friends, or colleagues). On a practical level, Miss Manners describes what the parent should do with the child when he or she arrives on a Friday night. "The first thing," she says, "is the briefing." The parent briefs the child on what has happened in his or her life since the child was last there and in turn is briefed on what has happened in the child's life. Parent and child also brief each other on their expectations and hopes for the weekend.

Your students may be able to think of other ways in which the noncustodial parent can perform as a true parent rather than a "host." You might ask them if they agree with Miss Manners' conclusion: "Children have amazingly little emotional attachment to those who only want to entertain them."

Martin, J. (1985). *Miss Manners' guide to rearing perfect children*. New York: Viking Penguin.

Classroom Activity: Classroom Debate: *"Resolved: Divorce Laws Should Be Changed to Make Marriages More Difficult to Dissolve"*

Has the "divorce revolution" failed? This revolution—by which is meant the replacement of a culture of marriage by a culture of easy, "no-fault" divorces and single parenthood—may have been intended to foster a number of important social goals, including greater equality between marital partners. But according to groups such as the Council on Families in America (http://familyscholars.org/1995/05/01/marriage-in-america), the revolution has failed miserably and is working terrible hardships on children. A report from the group states that our culture of divorce "has generated poverty within families . . . has burdened us with insupportable social costs . . . [and has] failed to deliver on its promise of greater adult happiness and better relationships between men and women." It goes on to state that the divorce revolution has, if anything, worsened relationships among fathers, mothers, and children of divorce. "Too many women are experiencing chronic economic insecurity. Too many men are isolated and estranged from their children. Too many children are angry, sad and neglected. . . ."

Arguing the opposing position, history professor Glenda Riley states that "Divorce releases people from a lifetime of living with unsound judgments regarding their potential mates. In addition, it removes others from debilitating situations that develop after marriage." While acknowledging that some people exploit lenient divorce laws by divorcing their spouses impetuously, Riley maintains that the historical record reveals that spouses who are forced to stay in failed marriages frequently sabotage them through adultery, abuse, or desertion.

To increase your students' understanding of the complexity of this controversy and the countless variables that influence the efficacy of the home environment, follow the guidelines in the General Resources section of this manual for scheduling a classroom debate on this resolution. How your students divide themselves into teams for this debate might itself provoke a productive classroom discussion. A natural division might be students who themselves (or their parents) have gone through divorces versus those who have not.

Generativity

Teaching Tip: Life-Stage Considerations in Gender Roles

As the text notes, "Fifty years ago, kinkeepers were almost always women, usually the mother or grandmother of a large family. Now families are smaller and gender equity is more apparent, so some men and young women are kinkeepers." As developmentalist Michele Paludi notes, "The majority of students in courses on the psychology of gender roles want the opportunity to interpret and discuss the authenticity of their experiences as men and women." A common problem reported by instructors who address the issue of gender roles in their courses is the persistence of younger students' belief that many of the problems associated with gender-role stereotypes—salary inequity, discrimination in education, work, and the family, etc.—have largely been solved. This is because they have "frequently not settled certain questions that define adulthood (e.g., questions of their relationship to the existing society, of vocation, and of social roles and lifestyles)." Older, reentry students, however, understand these issues because they are more likely to have held jobs, combined family life with work roles, and had other relevant experiences.

To help her students become better informed on gender-role stereotypes, Paludi has devised a series of exercises and topics for lecture, class discussion, or term paper assignments. The topics and exercises, which are listed here, are grouped according to gender-role stereotypes; separate topics and exercises are suggested for younger undergraduates and reentry students.

Gender-Role Stereotype

a. Women succeed because of luck; men succeed because of skill.

   Topic for Younger Students: Availability of role models and mentors for career advancement

   Topics for Older Students: Type A behavior pattern, midlife crisis, women's bias against other women

   Exercise for Younger Students: Ask students to trace the history of education of the women and men in their family as far back as they can go. Have students account for the similarities and differences with respect to attitudinal barriers to the educational and occupational aspirations of women.

   Exercise for Older Students: Ask students to arrange interviews with professionals in their field of study who, like them, were reentry students. Have them ask the individuals about their educational experiences, difficulties and stresses associated with their work, and so forth.

b. Women who are unmarried and/or not mothers are unhappy and unfulfilled.

   Topics for Younger Students: Contraception, abortion, sexual double standard

   Topics for Older Students: Voluntary childlessness, remaining single throughout the life span

   Exercise for Younger Students: Have students visit Planned Parenthood and/or a feminist health center. Have them describe the services these centers provide.

   Exercise for Older Students: Have students recite a fairy tale, nursery rhyme, prayer, or song lyrics that a relative or teacher told them when they were young. Ask students to describe the gender-role stereotypes (implicit and explicit) of the relationships that appear in this tale, prayer, or song.

c. A woman's place is in the home.

   Topics for Younger Students: Dating and friendship, nonmarital cohabitation, motivations for having children

   Topics for Older Students: Depression, "empty nest," alcoholism and other drug abuse, father absence, day care, dual-work/dual-career couples

   Exercise for Younger Students: Ask students to complete a dating-rating checklist. Have them suggest some ways peer pressures or cultural influences affect their perceptions of characteristics that are essential for a date or mate.

   Exercise for Older Students: Ask students to describe their present support network. Have them investigate some support groups for life transitions (e.g., widow to widow, parents without partners, Gray Panthers).

d. Women ask to be victimized.

   Topics for Younger Students: Acquaintance (date) rape, incest

   Topics for Older Students: Wife abuse, women and psychotherapy, sexual harassment

   Exercise for Younger Students: Ask students to uncover their university's policy on sexual harassment and the steps they need to follow should they want to take formal redress.

   Exercise for Older Students: Have students inquire about the number and variety of mental health centers in their community. Ask them to pick a center and interview an individual at this center about the services provided, and so forth.

e. A woman can never be too rich, too thin, or too young.

   Topics for Younger Students: Anorexia, bulimia, early versus late puberty, premenstrual stress syndrome

   Topics for Older Students: Mastectomy, hysterectomy, menopause, teaching children about sexuality

   Exercise for Younger Students: Ask students to describe major health problems they believe women face today. Have them research women's centers or groups that deal with these problems.

   Exercise for Older Students: Have students role-play a situation in which a mother decides to discuss sex and reproduction with her daughter.

f. Men and women are born into their gender roles; these roles are immutable.

   Topic for Younger Students: Androgyny

   Topics for Older Students: On-site day care in businesses, women's liberation as men's liberation

   Exercise for Younger Students: Administer Bem's Sex-Role Inventory in class. Have students discuss the validity of their scores. (See Bem, S. L. (1974). The measurement of psychological androgyny. *Journal of Consulting and Clinical Psychology*, *42*(2), 155–162.)

Exercise for Older Students: Ask students to enumerate the expectations they see in the following roles: spouse, parent, friend, worker, lover. Have them think of the degree of power, achievement, intimacy, and competence that is related to each role. Ask students to describe a way in which they could change one of their relationships to express more of themselves.

Paludi, M. A. (1986). Teaching the psychology of gender roles: Some life-stage considerations. *Teaching of Psychology*, *13*(3), 133–137.

AV: Parenting Our Parents (26 min., Films for the Humanities and Sciences)

This film addresses an important issue for the "sandwich generation"—care of aging parents. As the size of the elderly population increases, the forecast is for a society of the old caring for the very old. Various ways of coping with the stress of caring for aging parents are also examined.

AV: The Sandwich Generation: Caring for Both Children and Parents (28 min., Films for the Humanities and Sciences)

Phil Donahue and Hugh Downs join a group of elderly Americans who don't want their adult children to be burdened with their care, and a group of adults at midlife, several of whom resent the burdens of the sandwich generation and several of whom consider it a privilege and responsibility.

Classroom Activity: The Changing Workplace

This classroom activity was described in Emerging Adulthood: Psychosocial Development. If you did not use it then, you might want to use it with the discussion of adulthood.

Conclusion for Adulthood Section

Critical Thinking Activity: The 25th High School Reunion

Each unit of these resources contains a critical thinking exercise designed specifically to test students' critical thinking about a topic covered in the text. This activity actually serves as a summary of students' understanding of the text material on adulthood. Handout 5 contains a synopsis of research or a brief scenario followed by a series of questions.

Although these answers will uniquely belong to each student, they should be checked for a general understanding of the major biosocial, cognitive, and psychosocial tasks of middle adulthood.

HANDOUT 1

Developmental Fact or Myth?

T F 1. Most middle-aged men experience a midlife crisis that provokes a radical reexamination of their lives and leads to change.

T F 2. By about age 30, several personality traits stabilize and remain so throughout adulthood.

T F 3. Friendships improve with age.

T F 4. With recent changes in the structure of the typical American family, family links have become significantly weaker.

T F 5. The relationship between parents and their children usually worsens as the parents pass through middle age.

T F 6. The longer a couple has been married, the happier they are.

T F 7. Divorce in middle adulthood is generally easier to cope with than divorce earlier or later in life.

T F 8. Remarried people generally report higher rates of happiness than people in first marriages.

T F 9. Compared with stepparents, adoptive parents often have an advantage in establishing bonds with their children.

T F 10. As people near retirement, the extrinsic rewards associated with their jobs become more important than the intrinsic rewards.

HANDOUT 2

Designing a Personality Test

After class discussion of personality throughout adulthood, select a dimension of personality, or a specific trait, that is of particular interest to you and try to construct an effective test for measuring it. (You may select any dimension of personality you like, but you may find it most interesting to choose one of those discussed in the text. Good choices would be neuroticism, openness, conscientiousness, agreeableness, or extroversion.) Then administer your test to several volunteers. It would be especially informative to give the test to men and women who represent a range of age-group cohorts. After you have constructed and administered your test, answer the questions below.

1. What type of test did you construct and why?

2. What were some of the difficulties you encountered in the construction and/or administration of your personality test?

HANDOUT 2 *(continued)*

3. How can you determine the degree to which your test is reliable and valid as a test of personality?

4. How effective is your test as a measure of personality?

HANDOUT 3

BFI-54

Here are a number of characteristics that may or may not apply to you. For example, do you agree that you are someone who likes to spend time with others? Please write a number next to each statement to indicate the extent to which you agree or disagree with that statement.

Disagree strongly	Disagree a little	Neither agree nor disagree	Agree a little	Agree strongly
1	2	3	4	5

I See Myself as Someone Who . . .

_____ 1. Is talkative
_____ 2. Tends to find fault with others
_____ 3. Does a thorough job
_____ 4. Has a wide range of interests
_____ 5. Is depressed, blue
_____ 6. Is original, comes up with new ideas
_____ 7. Is reserved
_____ 8. Is helpful and unselfish with others
_____ 9. Prefers the conventional, traditional
_____ 10. Can be somewhat careless
_____ 11. Is relaxed, handles stress well
_____ 12. Is curious about many different things
_____ 13. Is full of energy
_____ 14. Prefers work that is routine and simple
_____ 15. Starts quarrels with others
_____ 16. Is a reliable worker
_____ 17. Can be tense
_____ 18. Is clever, sharp-witted
_____ 19. Tends to be quiet
_____ 20. Values artistic, aesthetic experiences
_____ 21. Tends to be disorganized
_____ 22. Is emotionally stable, not easily upset
_____ 23. Has an active imagination
_____ 24. Perseveres until the task is finished
_____ 25. Is sometimes rude to others
_____ 26. Has unwavering self-confidence
_____ 27. Is inventive
_____ 28. Is generally trusting
_____ 29. Tends to be lazy
_____ 30. Is clear-thinking, intelligent
_____ 31. Worries a lot
_____ 32. Wants things to be simple and clear-cut
_____ 33. Is sometimes shy, inhibited
_____ 34. Has a forgiving nature
_____ 35. Is idealistic, can be a dreamer
_____ 36. Does things efficiently
_____ 37. Can be moody
_____ 38. Is ingenious, a deep thinker
_____ 39. Generates a lot of enthusiasm
_____ 40. Can be cold and aloof
_____ 41. Enjoys thinking about complicated problems
_____ 42. Makes plans and follows through with them
_____ 43. Remains calm in tense situations
_____ 44. Likes to reflect, play with ideas
_____ 45. Is considerate and kind to almost everyone
_____ 46. Seeks adventure and excitement
_____ 47. Gets nervous easily
_____ 48. Is sophisticated in art, music, or literature
_____ 49. Has an assertive personality
_____ 50. Is insightful, sees different possibilities
_____ 51. Likes to cooperate with others
_____ 52. Is easily distracted
_____ 53. Is outgoing, sociable
_____ 54. Has few artistic interests

Source: John, O. P., Donahue, E. M., & Kentle, R. L. (1991). The "big five" inventory—versions 4a and 54 (Tech. Report). Berkeley, CA: Institute of Personality Assessment and Research. Reprinted by permission.

HANDOUT 4

Internet Activity: Trait Theory and Personality

Trait theory is one of the most popular approaches to studying personality. Researchers who work from this perspective search for identifiable, enduring patterns of behavior and thought processes that seem to apply to all people. To learn more about trait theory firsthand, visit the Keirsey Temperament Web site (http://keirsey.com) and complete the Keirsey Character Sorter and the Keirsey Temperament Sorter II. Then complete the following questions:

1. How does the creator of this Web site define temperament?

2. What determines temperament?

3. How stable is temperament over the life span?

4. What are four basic temperaments? Briefly describe each type and give an example of each from the world of science, politics, or the arts.

5. Do you fit one of these patterns? Which one?

6. What role does temperament play in choosing a mate? What temperaments attract each other?

7. How valid do you believe these online scales to be as measures of personality?

HANDOUT 5

Critical Thinking Activity: The 25th High School Reunion

Now that you have read and reviewed the adulthood unit, take your learning a step further by testing your critical thinking skills on this creative problem-solving exercise.

This exercise asks you to think about your future, focusing on each of the domains of development. Your job is to imagine that you are preparing to attend your 25th high school reunion. For most undergraduates, this would mean you are projecting yourself into your future at age 43 to 58, or thereabouts. If you are an older student, simply speculate about a later reunion. Whatever your age, adjust the timeline as needed to complete the exercise.

Now, prepare two versions of "who you are" at this reunion. First, create a life story in which you experienced no major setbacks or limitations to your potential and dreams. Then write a second, more realistic version that reflects the more typical biosocial, cognitive, and psychosocial developmental patterns described in the text.

1. What issues in the biosocial domain of development will be most pressing to you at this time?

2. What issues in the cognitive domain will be most pressing to you?

3. How will your life story have been shaped by the settings of the social clock that was ticking during your adult years?

4. What career choices will you have made?

HANDOUT 5 *(continued)*

5. What relationship/family choices will you have made (for example, single, married with children, divorced)?

6. How will you have tackled the primary tasks of middle adulthood, as seen by Erik Erikson (generativity vs. stagnation)?

Source: Suggested by Halonen, J. (1995). *The critical thinking companion*. New York: Worth Publishers.

Late Adulthood: Biosocial Development

Contents

Note: Worth Publishers provides online Instructor and Student Tool Kits, DVD Student Tool Kits, and Instructor and Student video resources in DevelopmentPortal for use with the text. See Part I: General Resources for information about these materials and the text Lecture Guides for a complete list by text chapter.

Suggested Activities

Introducing Late Adulthood: Biosocial Development

"On Your Own" Activity: Developmental Fact or Myth?

Before students read about biosocial development during late adulthood, have them respond to the true-false statements in Handout 1.

The correct answers are shown below. Class discussion can focus on the origins of any developmental misconceptions that are demonstrated in the students' incorrect answers.

1. T	6. F
2. F	7. F
3. T	8. T
4. F	9. T
5. F	10. F

AV: The Journey Through the Life Span, Program 9: Late Adulthood

Program 9 (18:10) introduces late adulthood as a time when people can reap the rewards of their life's journey. Today, more than ever, elderly people are postponing the onset of chronic illness through exercise and healthy nutrition. Beyond our 65th birthdays, however, our bodies inevitably begin to show the signs of aging. The first segment of the program—physical development (2:40)—begins by outlining the physical and biological changes that accompany aging, focusing on changes in hearing, vision, and—for many, most troubling of all—loss of mobility. Anna Zimmer of the Brookdale Center on Aging of Hunter College discusses the demographics of aging, including the subclassifications of older adults as young-old, middle-old, and old-old. Robert Butler of the International Longevity Center discusses the political consequences of an aging population, noting that soon 30 to 35 percent of voters will be elderly.

The second segment of the program—cognitive development—focuses on the changes in information processing and memory that accompany aging, especially losses in the sensory register and working memory. Next, Kenneth Davis of Mount Sinai Medical Center discusses the demographics, causes, and symptoms of Alzheimer disease. Cynthia Rudder of the Nursing Home Coalition of New York State describes resident-directed, quality care in nursing homes.

The third segment of the program—social development—is divided into several parts. The first part focuses on retirement, volunteer work, and political involvement. Robert Butler counters several of the myths of aging, including that the elderly inevitably will become senile, that they are sexless, and that they are unproductive. While, for some, retirement brings a sense of loss, for many this is a time to focus on enjoying life with one's partner. Many elderly find satisfaction in being grandparents, including those who have custody of their grandchildren. Anna Zimmer discusses the impact on older adults of loss of family and friends. The segment concludes with a discussion of how older adults develop a sense of integrity at the end of their lives and strive to share their memories and wisdom.

In the first of the two unnarrated observation modules, 85-year-old Georgeanne describes her travels in Europe as a young woman, her attitudes about love and fidelity, and her feelings about death. In the second, Bill, age 99, describes his long career as a salesman, coping with hearing loss and memory problems, and life in a nursing home.

AV: Transitions Throughout the Life Span, Program 23: Late Adulthood: Biosocial Development

This program deals with biosocial development from age 65 years and on. It begins by discussing the myths and reality of this final stage of the life span. In a society such as ours, which glorifies youth, there is a tendency to exaggerate the physical decline brought on by aging. In fact, the changes that occur during the later years are largely a continuation of those that began earlier in adulthood, and the vast majority of the elderly consider themselves to be in good health.

Nonetheless, the aging process is characterized by various changes in appearance, by an increased incidence of impaired vision and hearing, and by declines in the major body systems. These are all changes to which the individual must adjust. In addition, the incidence of chronic diseases increases significantly with age.

Several theories have been advanced to explain the aging process. The most useful of these focus on cellular malfunctions, declining immune function, and our genetic makeup. However, environment and lifestyle factors also play a role, as is apparent from studies of those who live a long life.

AV: Ageless America (52 min., Films for the Humanities and Sciences)

This film addresses a number of issues in the aging of America, including care for the elderly, why women live longer than men, the "sandwich generation" of adults with responsibility for aging parents and young children, and the problems of aging itself.

AV: The Gift of Aging (30 min., Aquarius Productions)

This film examines the positive aspects of aging and the wisdom of the aged that can help people of all ages. It profiles several older adults who are aging successfully, including *Cosmopolitan* editor Helen Gurley Brown and a 77-year-old couple who embody the spirit of volunteerism.

Prejudice and Predictions

AV: Growing Old: Something to Live For (15 min., CRM/McGraw-Hill)

The basic message of this short film is that old age should and can be a wonderful time of life. One of the reasons it isn't so enjoyable for more people more of the time is the prejudice against aging that many younger people hold. Several active and alert older people, among them Margaret Mead and a leader of the Gray Panthers, express their views. The movie is an effective counter to stereotypic views of old age. However, since this is a movie with a message (it was originally written and produced by *ABC News*), the sadder facts of old age, especially for people who are ill, poor, and/or lonely, are not emphasized. You might ask your class to consider the accuracy of the overall point of view portrayed by the film, and you yourself might prepare for the discussion after the film by providing some statistics on the status of older people.

AV: Aging (25 min., Indiana University)

This film begins with the question, "What is it like to be old with life stretching out in back of you?" Although the problems of aging are honestly portrayed, the film emphasizes that aging is not all negative. Several myths or stereotypes regarding the aged are explored, among them: the aged are isolated from, and neglected by, their families; the aged are ill; retirement is bad, and the aged sicken because it brings feelings of worthlessness; the aged are rigid and reactionary. The activity theory of aging and the disengagement theory are discussed, with the conclusion that neither theory is valid by itself. A brief summary is given of the Kansas study of adult life.

Teaching Tip: Students' Fears of Growing Old

To encourage discussion of the fear of growing old, have each student compile a list of common fears and then compare these lists with actual data on the elderly. It would be helpful to have the class list steps that people might take early in life to avoid each problem later (for example, joining social groups and making friends of all ages). A speaker who works with the elderly could be called in to help outline the options available to prevent each problem.

Classroom Activity: The Aging Stereotype Game

Stephen Fried has developed a learning activity that will help your students to better understand aging. Divide the class into groups of four to seven. Ask each group to develop a list of 15 to 20 *negative* stereotypes about the elderly (for example, "All old people are senile") and as many *positive* stereotypes (for example, "All elderly people are wise"). After the groups have completed their lists, one member from each group should read the list to the entire class. You can then lead a class discussion that prompts students to identify common themes among the different lists and to examine their own beliefs.

Fried, S. B. (1988). Learning activities for understanding aging. *Teaching of Psychology*, *15*(3), 160–162.

Teaching Tip: Physical Appearance and Stereotypes

To examine how physical appearance affects stereotypes, write the word "wrinkles" on the board and have students record the first word that comes to mind. Some students will probably think of "wise" and "expressive" (like the late Ruth Gordon and Eubie Blake), while others will respond with negative images (such as the Wicked Witch). Few will have neutral associations. This should culminate in a discussion of the way in which physical characteristics influence our reactions to people (in a positive or negative way), leading us perhaps to make assumptions about their wisdom, state of mind, and so on.

"On Your Own" Activity: What Will I Be Like When I Am Seventy-Five?

This activity, designed by Stephen Reid, focuses on students' perceptions of personal aging. In Handout 2, students are asked to answer six questions regarding their probable appearance, behaviors, and traits at age 75. The "On Your Own" Activity, Role-Playing an Older Adult, in Late Adulthood: Cognitive Development also can be used to help students better understand the physical problems of the older adult.

After students have completed Handout 2, Reid recommends pairing each student with another for discussion of their answers. You might assign this activity in conjunction with a lecture on stability and change in adulthood.

Critical Thinking Activity: Ageism, the Young-Old, and the Old-Old

Each unit of these resources contains a critical thinking exercise designed specifically to test students' critical thinking about a topic covered in the text. Handout 3 contains a synopsis of research or a brief scenario followed by a series of questions.

Although these answers will uniquely belong to each student, they should be checked for a general understanding of the major biosocial, cognitive, and psychosocial tasks of late adulthood.

Observational Activity: Media Images of Aging

As noted in the text, our culture's veneration of youthfulness is so great it fosters an ageist stereotype of the elderly that makes it difficult to see them as they actually are. This stereotype is often perpetuated by the popular media of television, magazines, motion pictures, novels, and radios. To help your students better understand ageist stereotypes and the role of the media in perpetuating them, ask them to use Handout 4 to investigate attitudes about age as reflected in contemporary greeting cards and television programs, and in television programs that first aired a generation or more ago. Then, have them answer the questions in Handout 5.

Fried, S. B. (October, 1988). Learning activities for understanding aging. *Teaching of Psychology, 15*(3), 160–162.

Aging and Disease

AV: *Symptoms of Aging* (28 min., Films for the Humanities and Sciences)

Focusing on primary aging, the program examines loss of muscular strength, declining visual acuity, and coronary disease risk factors; it also discusses ways in which older adults can preserve their fitness.

AV: *Chronobiology: The Time of Our Lives* (58 min., Films for the Humanities and Sciences)

This program examines the nature and biological evolution of our bodies' biological clocks. In addition to comparing our internal timekeepers with those found in the animal kingdom, it looks at ways in which researchers are experimenting with "resetting" human biological clocks.

AV: *Factors in Healthy Aging* (28 min., Films for the Humanities and Sciences)

(See description under Adulthood: Biosocial Development.)

AV: *Aging Well* (18 min., Films for the Humanities and Sciences)

This brief program explains why the current cohort of older adults is living longer than their parents did and staying healthier. It discusses medical advances that have increased life expectancy and explores several emotional issues of aging, including the death of one's spouse, loneliness, and the need for generativity.

AV: *Never Say Die: The Pursuit of Eternal Youth* (60 min., Films for the Humanities and Sciences)

This fascinating HBO production examines the various ways Americans find to spend billions of dollars annually to beat back the ravages of time. Among the techniques examined are plastic surgery, the Pritikin diet and lifestyle, European health spas, megavitamin supplementation, and cryonic suspension. The program also explores progeria, the genetic disease that dramatically accelerates the rate of aging.

AV: *The Wit and Wisdom of Aging* (26 min., Films for the Humanities and Sciences)

Norman Cousins, himself a survivor of "terminal" cancer, discusses humor and the will to survive as potent medicines for the terminally ill. Cousins's work with other terminal patients who "refused to die" is described.

AV: *Growing Older and Better* (28 min., Films for the Humanities and Sciences)

Another in the Phil Donahue series on human development, this program asks whether the fountain of youth is just around the corner—or has it already been discovered? The show features a young-old 104-year-old; actress Estelle Getty, who started her professional career at age 60; and Dr. Stuart Berger, who describes various anti-aging strategies.

AV: *Age-Related Sensory Losses: An Empathic Approach* (15 min., University of Minnesota)

As an individual ages, the body undergoes physiological changes in eyesight and hearing that make social interactions problematic. This presentation explores the positive and not-so-positive adjustments of a family to their grandmother's aging changes. Although family interactions are portrayed, the film is also refreshingly didactic as key points are highlighted and discussed through narration.

Theories of Aging

AV: The Aging Process (19 min., Films for the Humanities and Sciences)

This brief film explores the effects of aging on the human mind and body and discusses the cellular damage and genetic clock theories of aging. The program also addresses the lifestyle habits that affect longevity, including exercise, proper diet, and moderate drinking.

AV: Aging: The Methuselah Syndrome (57 min., Michigan Media)

Taken from the *Nova* series, this film reports on research on the causes of aging and includes segments on progeria, metabolism, the immune system, the "genetic clock," the effects of antioxidants and underfeeding on aging, and the findings of the Baltimore Longitudinal Study of Aging.

AV: Man Immortal: The Human Cell and Eternal Life (53 min., Films for the Humanities and Sciences)

This program explores several paradoxes in the science of aging, including children with Hutchinson-Gilford Progeria Syndrome, who age at many times the normal rate, and cancer cells, which can survive indefinitely. From there, the program discusses the latest research on aging, life extension, and the possibility of human immortality.

Classroom Activity: Eat Less, Live Longer?

As an extension of the text discussion of biosocial development during late adulthood, you might discuss the work of gerontologist Roy Walford. He significantly extended the lives of mice and fish by reducing their caloric intake. The life span of mice, for example, has nearly been doubled—from 36 to 55 months— by cutting their daily calories 35 to 40 percent. Furthermore, by virtually every measure of health, from organ and immune system functioning to the appearance of the fur, animals on restricted diets maintain youthful vigor long after the well-fed control animals have died.

Why does eating little prolong life? Although the answer to this question is not yet known, some researchers believe that undernutrition suppresses both the metabolic rate and the activity of the immune system such that normal aging is delayed. On the basis of the findings in his animal research, Walford attempted to extend his own life by restricting his daily consumption to between 1,500 and 2,000 calories a day, compared with an average daily intake for men of about 2,500 calories (for women the figure is about 2,100). In addition, Walford limited fat consumption to 15 percent of his caloric intake, fasted two days each week, exercised regularly, and took a variety of vitamins (E, C, and pantothenic acid), minerals, and other antioxidants to detoxify the free radicals he believed promote senescence.

Unfortunately, Walford died in 2004 at the age of 79 from complications of Lou Gehrig's disease, but his work goes on. Walford had hoped to extend his own life span to 140 years. "Right now, the maximum human life span is about 110 years, and only a few people live to that age," he says. "But if what is true for other species is true for man, then with a sufficiently vigorous caloric restriction, the maximum life span could be extended to about 170. It works all the way across the animal kingdom. Calorically restricted one-celled organisms, worms, mice, rodents, rats, fish, all live a great deal longer, so it would be very surprising if it worked all across the animal kingdom and then not in humans."

Some of Walford's colleagues, however, feared their co-worker might have been overdoing it. "I wouldn't do what Roy is doing," said one. "He seems pretty healthy, but he chooses his clothes to conceal his boniness." However, many people adhere to Walford's beliefs: In North America alone, over 1,000 people are following a calorically restricted diet similar to Walford's. In fact, the Life Extension Foundation has recommended the Calorie Restriction Society's workshop to its 325,000 supporters.

You might direct students who wish to learn more about Walford's anti-aging plan to www.walford.com or www.calorierestriction.org. There they will also find summaries of the latest caloric restriction and aging research, a summary of Walford's experiences in *Biosphere 2*, and a host of other interesting, yet controversial, information about aging.

Barger, J. L., Walford, R. L., & Weindruch, R. (2003). The retardation of aging by caloric restriction: its significance in the transgenic era. *Experimental Gerontology, 38*(11-12), 1343–1351.

Calorie Restriction Society (2007). Fewer calories. More life. www.calorierestriction.org. Retrieved November 11, 2007.

Warshofsky, F. (1999). *Stealing time: The new science of aging*. New York: TV Books.

The Centenarians

AV: How to Live Longer . . . Better (25 min., Films for the Humanities and Sciences)

This program discusses lifestyle changes, with an emphasis on exercise, that are an important element in extending the life span. The need for both social involvement and good medical care is also discussed

AV: How to Live Past 100 (19 min., Films for the Humanities and Sciences)

This brief film examines the lives of several centenarians in seeking to determine the reasons for their increasing number in America today. It also looks at the most common health hazards for the elderly, the relationship between activity level and longevity, and whether intelligence declines with age.

Internet Activity: Living to 100

The Internet contains a wealth of information about health, lifestyle, and old age. For this activity, ask students to search the Web to find and explore some of these resources using information and questions from Handout 6 as a guide.

HANDOUT 1

Developmental Fact or Myth?

T F 1. By the year 2050, it is predicted that the proportion of those over 65 will double worldwide.

T F 2. Although older people are more susceptible to disease, they tend to recover faster from most illnesses.

T F 3. By late adulthood, the flu can lead to pneumonia, which can be fatal.

T F 4. The most effective treatment for insomnia is pharmacological.

T F 5. Most of the visual and auditory losses of the aged cannot be corrected.

T F 6. The most widely held theory of aging is that we wear out our bodies just by living our lives.

T F 7. Most scientists believe that aging results from the “ticking” of a genetic clock.

T F 8. Current average life expectancy for women is 5 years longer than it is for men.

T F 9. Individuals with stronger immune systems live longer than those with weaker immune systems.

T F 10. Women tend to have weaker, and less efficient, immune systems than men.

HANDOUT 2

What Will I Be Like When I Am Seventy-Five?

1. Which of your current behaviors will be similar and which ones will be different when you are 75?

2. In what ways will you look like you do now and in what ways will your appearance be different?

3. What do you think your eyesight, hearing, and physical strength will be like at age 75?

HANDOUT 2 *(continued)*

4. What might you like about being 75 years old?

5. What do you prefer about being your present age compared with being 75 years old?

6. Is it difficult to imagine yourself at 75? Why or why not?

HANDOUT 3

Critical Thinking Activity: Ageism, the Young-Old, and the Old-Old

Now that you have read and reviewed the late adulthood unit, take your learning a step further by testing your critical thinking skills on this creative problem-solving exercise.

Most people's perceptions of aging are inaccurate and reflect *ageist* stereotypes of biosocial development in late adulthood. These stereotypes stem from our preoccupation with physical decline that is more the result of disease than it is of aging per se.

Developmentalist Bernice Neugarten has drawn a distinction between the young-old—elderly persons who are, for the most part, healthy and vigorous—and the old-old—those who suffer major physical, mental, or social losses. It is an ironic fact that many professionals who work with the elderly, including those who specialize in gerontology, have inadvertently fostered ageism by focusing on the difficulties and declines of the old-old and by studying the aged residents of nursing homes, who are often frail.

In this exercise you are asked to think of two elderly adults, one who fits Neugarten's description of the young-old and one who fits her description of the old-old. They may be relatives, friends, or even public personalities. Write a paragraph or two about each person, briefly describing his or her health, personality, and lifestyle, and explain why you have classified him or her as young-old or old-old. Also indicate the extent to which each person fits, or does not fit, the usual stereotypes of the older adult. Finally, speculate as to why each person developed as he or she did. What losses, for example, might the old-old person have experienced? What gains might have helped to "age-proof" the young-old person?

Description of young-old individual:

Description of old-old individual:

Adapted from Straub, R. O. (2004). *Seasons of life study guide* (5th ed.). Worth Publishers and the Annenberg/CPB Collection.

HANDOUT 4

Observational Activity: Media Images of Aging

This activity asks you to investigate attitudes about aging as reflected in greeting cards and television programs. Arrange with the manager of a card shop to analyze at least 10 greeting cards that describe some aspect of the intended recipient of the card. As you analyze each card, make notes on the visual portrayal of the card's intended recipient and any ageist stereotypes reflected in the card's message.

For the second part of this activity, view at least five different television programs (dramas, soap operas, and situation comedies are good choices), again making notes on ageist stereotypes. If possible, try to find at least two programs that first aired in the 1960s.

After you have finished your observations, complete the questions on Handout 5 and return the response sheet to your instructor.

HANDOUT 5

Observational Activity: Media Images of Aging: Follow-Up Questionnaire

1. Describe how older adults were portrayed in the greeting cards you analyzed.

2. What common generational themes did you detect in the cards' written sentiments?

3. List the titles of the television programs you viewed, noting whether each was a current program or, if a rerun, approximately how long ago it was first broadcast.

Title of Program	First Run or Rerun?
1.	
2.	
3.	
4.	
5.	

HANDOUT 5 *(continued)*

4. Briefly describe several of the elderly characters portrayed in these programs, noting any common themes or stereotypes.

5. Compare and contrast the portrayal of older adults in the contemporary programs with their portrayal in the older program(s).

6. What role do you feel the popular media play in perpetuating ageist stereotypes? In your observations, could you detect any distinction between adults who might be described as "young-old" and those who might be described as "old-old"?

HANDOUT 6

Internet Activity: Living to 100

According to many experts on aging, the average person is born with a set of genes that would allow him or her to live to 85 years of age and maybe longer. People may add 10 or more quality years to that, or subtract a substantial number of years, by taking appropriate "age-proofing" steps or by failing to do so, respectively.

To learn more about long-lived people, and to explore your prospects for becoming a centenarian, search the Web to find answers to the following questions. (Hint: A good starting point is www.livingto100.com, a longevity Web site created by Harvard gerontologist Thomas Perls.)

1. How many centenarians are there in the United States today? Worldwide? How have these figures changed since the beginning of the twentieth century? How is this number expected to change in the future?

2. To what do aging experts attribute the change in the number of centenarians?

3. What are several traits and lifestyle habits that are common to long-lived people around the world?

4. Briefly explain the relationship of each of the following to expected longevity: education level, marital status, weight, blood pressure, stress. Then explain why, according to experts on aging.

5. What advice do centenarians offer to individuals who would like to reach 100 years of age themselves?

6. Some experts have mixed feelings about the online age-o-meters and the advice that some of them dispense. What are some of their concerns? What legal and ethical issues do online resources such as these raise?

Late Adulthood: Cognitive Development

Contents

Note: Worth Publishers provides online Instructor and Student Tool Kits, DVD Student Tool Kits, and Instructor and Student video resources in DevelopmentPortal for use with the text. See Part I: General Resources for information about these materials and the text Lecture Guides for a complete list by text chapter.

The Optimal: New Cognitive Development

Audiovisual Materials: Aging and Saging, p. 5

Classroom Activity: Problem-Based Learning: Design a More Valid Test of Cognitive Functiong for Older Adults, p. 4

Critical Thinking Activity: Personal Wisdom During Late Adulthood, p. 5 (Handout 4, p. 11, and Handout 5, p. 14)

Suggested Activities

Introducing Late Adulthood: Cognitive Development

"On Your Own" Activity: Developmental Fact or Myth?

Before students read about cognitive development during late adulthood, have them respond to the true-false statements in Handout 1.

The correct answers are shown below. Class discussion can focus on the origins of any developmental misconceptions that are demonstrated in the students' incorrect answers.

1. F	6. T
2. F	7. T
3. T	8. T
4. T	9. T
5. F	10. F

AV: The Journey Through the Life Span, Program 9: Late Adulthood

See Late Adulthood: Biosocial Development for a description of Program 9 and the accompanying observation modules, which cover the entire unit on late adulthood.

AV: Transitions Throughout the Life Span, Program 24: Late Adulthood: Cognitive Development

This program describes the changes in cognitive functioning associated with late adulthood. The program first provides evidence that suggests declines in both the information-processing and the problem-solving abilities of older adults. Next, neurological and other reasons for this decline are discussed.

Despite these cognitive declines, as the program points out, real-life conditions provide older adults with ample opportunity to compensate for the pattern of decline observed in the laboratory. It appears that, for most people, cognitive functioning in daily life remains essentially unimpaired.

The main exception to the generally positive picture of cognitive functioning during late adulthood is dementia, the subject of the fourth segment of the program. This pathological loss of intellectual ability can be caused by a variety of diseases and circumstances; risk factors, treatment, and prognosis differ accordingly.

The final segment of the program makes it clear that cognitive changes during late adulthood are by no means restricted to declines in intellectual functioning. For many individuals, late adulthood is a time of great aesthetic, creative, philosophical, and spiritual growth.

The Aging Brain

Teaching Tip: Learning Abilities in the Older Adult

To encourage students to think about learning abilities in older adults, have the class discuss the following issue: Your college is considering a program for senior citizens in which anyone over the age of 65 can take classes for free. Many schools currently offer such programs, and thousands of senior citizens are successfully earning the degrees they never had time to complete or exploring new realms of knowledge. Ask your students: How would the class differ if it included older adults? Should the teaching style be altered to accommodate the older person's needs? Do you think the course could be enriched by the older person's contributions?

If your school already has such a program, alter the discussion to include an evaluation of students' experiences with older adults in their classes. If no such program exists, students may wish to write a letter to the administration outlining suggestions for starting one.

Teaching Tip: Learning Styles for Different Ages

To enhance students' understanding of the very different learning styles of the various age groups, have them imagine that they are going to be visited by a 10-year-old and an 80-year-old who don't know each other. Ask students to design a game or activity that will accommodate the intellectual ability of both guests.

Begin by having students list the learning characteristics they expect of each individual. (You may find it necessary to refresh students' memories about the 10-year-old if it has been a while since that age group was covered.) Then have students suggest cooperative strategies that combine the skills of each—for example, a problem-solving task that can make the most of the older person's logical ability and the younger person's speed, or a game in which both long-term memory and speed are equally valuable. Intervene when students suggest such inappropriate activities as video games that require speed but few thinking skills.

The Usual: Information Processing After Age 65

"On Your Own" Activity: Role-Playing an Older Adult

To give your students an unforgettable, firsthand experience of the cognitive effects of some of the physical changes older adults must adapt to, have them put together a costume that would make them look like older adults to the casual observer. Randall Wight, who created this project for his students, also suggests they use or discard eyeglasses to reduce visual acuity, wear earplugs to impair hearing, and wrap their joints with elastic bandages to simulate stiffness.

After students have completed their sojourn as older adults, have them complete the questions on Handout 2. Class discussion can focus on any insights the students gained into the experience of aging.

Teaching Tip: Attributing Behaviors to the Aged

To demonstrate the tendency to attribute such behaviors as forgetfulness or slowness to the aged, list for students the behaviors typical of any busy person—for example, forgetting to pay an important bill, wearing socks that don't match, or spilling coffee all over the table. Ask students what they would say or do if an elderly person exhibited any of these behaviors. You may get answers such as "take over managing their finances" or "buy a more stable set of cups."

After students have suggested ways to deal with this elderly person, ask them what approach they would suggest for a younger person who behaves in the same way. This activity is especially effective if the behaviors you have listed are things you yourself have done. Have students discuss the differences in their responses to older adults and younger adults.

Teaching Tip: Cognitive Development: Specialization

To illustrate cognitive development during late adulthood, invite a professor emeritus to describe for the class the ways in which his or her field of specialization has changed over the past decade, as well as how his or her own ideas about the field have changed. Older scholars often demonstrate a "wider perspective" than younger adults in the same field, and often their own theories show creative, interesting development.

If you cannot get a speaker, you might discuss some of the ways in which well-known psychologists have experienced aging from an intellectual standpoint. Examples include Freud, Erikson, and Piaget, who continued to produce new ideas into their seventies and eighties. After retirement, the famous perceptual-development researcher J. J. Gibson moved beyond the study of "what you can see" and began to examine "what you can't see," looking at illusory effects not previously studied. In his seventies, B. F. Skinner devoted a great deal of energy to advocating world peace and demonstrating how raising children in an environment that is threatened with nuclear war can lead to social problems in the next generation (the September 1982 issue of *APA Monitor* includes a report on Skinner's presentations at the 1982 annual meetings).

Classroom Activity: Classroom Debate: *"Resolved: Research on Cognitive Decline Supports Mandatory Retirement Laws"*

Although mandatory retirement laws have been abolished in the United States, the issue remains controversial; other countries—Canada and the United Kingdom, for instance—have not necessarily followed suit. A Canadian survey shows that more Canadians are opposed to mandatory retirement today than ever before, but that number amounts to only about one-third of the population. Carrying the banner of "generational equity," many younger workers feel that opportunities for their own career advancement are more limited today than in the past because older workers are less willing to "step aside." So, mandatory retirement remains a fact of life in these countries.

A debate on this resolution can help focus students' attention on the cognitive changes of late adulthood. Both sides will find an abundance of research to support their position. In support of the resolution is evidence from studies of cognitive decline and reduced processing resources in older adults. The opposing position will find evidence from research pointing to the flawed nature of cross-sectional studies of age-related deficits, the age bias inherent in traditional research designs, and evidence that practical intelligence and problem-solving abilities remain stable or actually improve throughout adulthood.

Follow the guidelines in the General Resources section of this manual and schedule a classroom debate on the resolution.

The Impaired: Diseases That Affect the Brain

Teaching Tip: Cognitive Deficits in the Elderly

To expand on the text coverage of cognitive deficits in the elderly, invite an expert speaker to class. A representative from the local groups providing support to families of people who suffer from Alzheimer disease, a geriatric social worker or neuropsychiatrist, or a representative from the local Alcoholics Anonymous chapter who is knowledgeable about the destructive effects of alcoholism in later life could all provide interesting firsthand observations and insights.

Classroom Activity: Was Alzheimer Disease Misnamed?

The identification of a new disease rarely takes place overnight. More often, it emerges slowly from observations of countless patients' symptoms. With AIDS, for example, it took many years before the medical community recognized the symptoms as a distinct disease. Now the recovery of a long-lost hospital file has provided medical historians with the original clinical observations that led to the recognition of Alzheimer disease. Ironically, in light of newer data it now appears that this patient was misdiagnosed. More accurately, the patient should have been diagnosed with a different form of dementia.

Missing since 1910, the file is that of a 51-year-old female patient named Auguste D.—a patient of Dr. Alois Alzheimer at a German hospital. In December 1995, the hospital file was discovered in the University of Frankfurt's psychiatric archives by Konrad Maurer. Still in excellent condition, the file contains a photograph of the patient, samples of her handwriting, and Alzheimer's original clinical notes detailing her condition during the first five days of her treatment in the hospital.

"It's fantastic," notes Bengt Winblad of the Karolinska Institute in Sweden. "It will clarify the symptoms of the patient. And they are not quite the same as the textbook symptoms of Alzheimer disease. Here we've got the real thing, in Alzheimer's hand . . . ."

The file notes that Auguste D. was admitted to Frankfurt's Hospital for the Mentally Ill in 1901. She remained there until her death in 1906 from septicemia caused by bedsores. Her responses to Dr. Alzheimer's questions indicate the severity of her confusion. The record begins with Dr. Alzheimer's comment on the patient's demeanor:

("She sat on her bed with a helpless expression.")
Alzheimer: "What's your name?"
Auguste D.: "Auguste."
Alzheimer: "Last name?"
Auguste D.: "Auguste, I think."
Alzheimer: "What is your husband's name?"
Auguste D.: "Auguste, I think."

After five days of observation and testing, Alzheimer concluded that his patient suffered from "progressive cognitive impairment, speech and perception problems, hallucinations, delusions, and psychosocial incompetence," all symptoms of senile dementia, but at too early an age to be diagnosed as this disease of the aged. Over the next four-and-a-half-year period, her mental state continued to deteriorate.

At autopsy, it was discovered that Auguste D.'s brain was severely atrophied and riddled with abnormalities now referred to as neurofibrillary tangles and plaques. Although these abnormalities are characteristic of Alzheimer disease, Auguste D.'s brain also revealed significant arteriosclerosis in her cerebral blood vessels—a symptom that today is a criterion for exclusion from a diagnosis of Alzheimer disease.

Although Dr. Alzheimer reported his patient's pathology at a psychiatric conference in 1906, the naming of the disease is credited to Emil Kraepelin, director of the Royal Psychiatric Clinic in Munich, where Alzheimer transferred in 1903. Although several other psychiatrists had documented patients with symptoms similar to those of Auguste D., Kraepelin chose to mention "this Alzheimer disease" in his popular 1910 psychiatry textbook. The name stuck, even though Auguste D.'s dementia may well have been caused by reduced blood and oxygen supply to her brain.

O'Brien, C. (1996, July 5). Auguste D. and Alzheimer's disease. *Science, 273*(5271), 28.

AV: Alzheimer's: Effects on Patients and Their Families (19 min., Films for the Humanities and Sciences)
Alzheimer's Disease: The Long Nightmare (19 min., Films for the Humanities and Sciences)
Alzheimer's Disease (28 min., Films for the Humanities and Sciences)

These three films discuss exactly what contemporary researchers know, and what they do not know, about the mechanisms of Alzheimer disease. The first film also discusses the use of drugs that treat the disease by preventing the breakdown of the neurotransmitter acetylcholine and the impact of the disease on the lives of a patient's family. The second film focuses on the medical side of the disease, describing different types of patient care. The third film is a special Phil Donahue program that shows the ravages of the disease by profiling one couple, she now reduced to childlike helplessness and he to constant caregiver.

AV: New Views on Alzheimer's (28 min., Films for the Humanities and Sciences)

Hosted by Phil Donahue, this program focuses on the circumstances of four members of the Sisters of Notre Dame who are subjects in a long-term study of victims of Alzheimer disease.

Internet Activity: Alzheimer Disease

The Internet contains a wealth of information about Alzheimer disease. For this activity, ask students to search the Web to find and explore some of these resources using information and questions from Handout 3 as a guide.

AV: Understanding Depression: Through the Darkness (24 min., Films for the Humanities and Sciences)

This short program examines the symptoms and treatment of major depression. Profiling three patients, the program examines a variety of issues related to this "common cold" of mental illness, including the social stigma attached to the disorder.

The Optimal: New Cognitive Development

Classroom Activity: Problem-Based Learning: Design a More Valid Test of Cognitive Functioning for Older Adults

The Introduction's Classroom Activity: Introducing Problem-Based Learning describes this relatively new pedagogical tool. Following is a sample problem that you might want to give to your students as part of your coverage of cognitive development during adulthood.

> In daily life, most elderly people are not seriously handicapped by cognitive difficulties. The need for ecologically valid, real-life measures of cognition is increasingly apparent to developmental scientists.

Before you leave class today, your group must address the following questions: First, from what you have learned about typical tests of cognitive functioning in the elderly, are such tests valid? Second, after your group agrees on an answer to the first question, determine some learning issues that need to be researched to answer the question, "What is the best way to evaluate cognitive functioning in older adults?" Among other issues, these should focus on normal, age-related changes in sensory memory, working memory, long-term memory, and control processes.

Based on the decisions that your group makes today, you should devise a plan for researching the various issues. Two weeks from today's class, your group will present an answer based on the issues you think are relevant.

AV: Aging and Saging (24 min., Films for the Humanities and Sciences)

This film examines various cultural perspectives on aging, beginning with the message that American culture reveres youth; as a result, the elderly are expected to drop out of public life, so they will not remind the young of their own mortality. In a powerful segment, the program takes viewers to a weekend Elder Circle at the Omega Institute, a human potential center that seeks to help the elderly redefine themselves as role models of healthy and graceful aging.

Critical Thinking Activity: Personal Wisdom During Late Adulthood

Each unit of these resources contains a critical thinking exercise designed specifically to test students' critical thinking about a topic covered in the text. Handout 4 contains a questionnaire about a person's values and goals. Students should ask an older adult first to answer the questions as he or she would today, then as he or she would have answered them as a younger adult. Then ask that person to complete the questions in Handout 5. Any students over age 65 should complete the questionnaires themselves.

Although these answers will uniquely belong to each student, they should be checked for a general understanding of the major cognitive tasks of late adulthood.

HANDOUT 1

Developmental Fact or Myth?

T F 1. Neuronal loss appears to be a significant factor in cognitive slow-down.

T F 2. As long as their vision and hearing remain unimpaired, older adults are no less efficient than younger adults at inputting information.

T F 3. Older adults are less efficient than younger adults at managing control processes.

T F 4. The usual path of cognition in late adulthood is decline, at least in output.

T F 5. A majority of the elderly feel frustrated and hampered by memory loss in their daily lives.

T F 6. The general symptoms associated with dementia are essentially the same regardless of what causes the disorder.

T F 7. Alzheimer disease is in some cases inherited.

T F 8. In a TIA (mini-stroke), symptoms disappear quickly and may be so slight that no one (not even the victim) notices.

T F 9. Many older adults who are actually suffering from depression are misdiagnosed with a brain disease.

T F 10. Late adulthood is often associated with a narrowing of interests and an exclusive focus on the self.

HANDOUT 2

Role-Playing an Older Adult

To get a firsthand feeling for some of the physical changes you may have to adapt to in your later years, put together an outfit that would make you look like an elderly adult to the casual observer. To simulate physical decline, you might wear earplugs (or place cotton in your ears) to reduce hearing, use or discard glasses to reduce vision, and wrap your knees and elbows with elastic bandages to produce "stiffness" in your joints. Spend an hour or two going about your daily routine as a "senior citizen" and then complete the questions below. Return your answers to your instructor.

1. In what ways did you change your appearance and/or impair your physical abilities to simulate aging?

2. What activities did you engage in while role-playing an older adult?

3. Did you gain any insights into aging from this experience? What are they?

HANDOUT 2 *(continued)*

4. Did these physical changes alter your cognitive abilities? If so, in what ways?

5. In what ways did this activity alter your understanding of the elderly?

Source: Adapted from Hall, H. (1988, December). Trying on old age. *Psychology Today*, p. 67. Reprinted with permission from Psychology Today Magazine.

HANDOUT 3

Internet Activity: Alzheimer Disease

To learn more about Alzheimer disease (AD) and the Internet resources available to individuals affected by it, use the Internet to find brief answers to the following questions. (Hint: The Alzheimer's Disease Research Center of Washington University maintains a Web site and search engine that will help you get started [www.alzheimer.wustl.edu]. Another useful Web site is the Alzheimer Association page at www.alz.org.

1. What is AD? Is there more than one variety of this disease?

2. What are the major symptoms of AD?

3. How is AD usually diagnosed?

4. What causes AD? What areas of the brain are affected by AD?

5. What role are free radicals believed to play in AD? Briefly explain one other theory of AD.

HANDOUT 3 *(continued)*

6. Describe the typical progression of AD. What is the usual cause of death in AD victims?

7. What are the 10 warning signs of AD?

8. List 10 simple ways to help the family of a person with AD.

9. Is prenatal diagnosis of AD possible?

10. What resources are available on the Internet for AD caregivers?

HANDOUT 4

Critical Thinking Activity: Personal Wisdom During Late Adulthood

Now that you have read and reviewed the late adulthood unit, take your learning a step further by testing your critical thinking skills on this perspective-taking exercise.

Although cognitive decline may be an inevitable part of aging, it provides an incomplete picture of late adulthood, which is also characterized by positive changes. Many older adults develop new interests, new patterns of thought, and what some developmentalists refer to as *personal wisdom*. As noted in the text, many older adults become more responsive to nature, more appreciative of the arts, more philosophical, and more spiritual. To examine cognitive development in later life, ask a close older adult to complete the following Life/Values/Goals questionnaire. (If you are an older adult, complete the questionnaire for yourself.) You, or the person you ask to complete the questionnaire, should answer the questions from two life-span perspectives: as you (or your subject) felt during middle adulthood, and as you (or your subject) feel now, during late adulthood. Then complete the Critical Thinking Activity Response Sheet (Handout 5) and return it to your professor.

Sources: Bugen, L. A. (1979). *Death and dying: Theory, research, practice*. Dubuque, IA: Brown; Straub, R. O. (2004). *Seasons of life study guide* (5th ed.). New York: Worth Publishers and the Annenberg/CPB Collection.

HANDOUT 4 *(continued)*

LIFE/VALUES/GOALS

Older Adult: As you see your life now, try to answer the following.

1. What three things would your friends say about you and your life if you died today?

2. Given the likelihood that you will not die today, and have some time left to change some things in your life, what three things would you most like to have said about you and your life?

3. If someone were to witness a week of your life, what assumptions would that person make about your values, that is, what matters most to you?

4. What values do you hold that are not evident from the way you live your daily life?

5. What three goals are important to you as you plan your life?

HANDOUT 4 *(continued)*

LIFE/VALUES/GOALS

Younger Adult: Try to answer the following questions as you might have answered them when you were a younger adult.

1. What three things would your friends say about you and your life if you died today?

2. Given the likelihood that you will not die today, and have some time left to change some things in your life, what three things would you most like to have said about you and your life?

3. If someone were to witness a week of your life, what assumptions would that person make about your values, that is, what matters most to you?

4. What values do you hold that are not evident from the way you live your daily life?

5. What three goals are important to you as you plan your life?

HANDOUT 5

Critical Thinking Activity Response Sheet

Based on your responses to the Life/Values/Goals questionnaire, or those of your subject, answer the following questions.

1. Do your responses, or those of your subject, indicate a shift in life values, or goals, from early adulthood to later adulthood? What kind of shift?

2. Has the relationship between the way your subject lives life and his or her personal values changed during late adulthood? In what ways?

3. Would you say that the answers to the Life/Values/Goals questionnaire show evidence of a philosophical turn in thinking, or the emergence of a special personal wisdom, during late adulthood? Why or why not?

Late Adulthood: Psychosocial Development

Contents

Note: Worth Publishers provides online Instructor and Student Tool Kits, DVD Student Tool Kits, and Instructor and Student video resources in DevelopmentPortal for use with the text. See Part I: General Resources for information about these materials and the text Lecture Guides for a complete list by text chapter.

The Frail Elderly

Suggested Activities

Introducing Late Adulthood: Psychosocial Development

"On Your Own" Activity: Developmental Fact or Myth?

Before students read about psychosocial development during late adulthood, have them respond to the true-false statements in Handout 1.

The correct answers are shown below. Class discussion can focus on the origins of any developmental misconceptions that are demonstrated in the students' incorrect answers.

1. F	6. F
2. T	7. T
3. F	8. F
4. T	9. T
5. F	10. F

AV: The Journey Through the Life Span, Program 9: Late Adulthood

See Late Adulthood: Biosocial Development for a description of Program 9 and the accompanying observation modules, which cover the entire unit on late adulthood.

AV: Transitions Throughout the Life Span, Program 25: Late Adulthood: Psychosocial Development

"The older you are, the more important your choices are." So begins Program 25, which focuses on psychosocial development during late adulthood. Because the choices we make are so different, adults in their later years are more diverse in terms of their development than at any other time. Even so, negative stereotypes about the elderly too often distort people's perceptions of the later years. Certain changes are common during this stage of the life span—retirement, the death of a spouse, and failing health—yet people respond to these experiences in vastly different ways.

Individual experiences may help to explain the fact that theories of psychosocial aging, discussed in the first part of the program, are often contradictory. The second segment of the program focuses on the challenges to feeling fulfilled during late adulthood, such as finding new sources of achievement once derived from work. In the third segment, the importance of marriage, friends, neighbors, and family in providing social support is discussed, as are the different experiences of married and single older adults. The program concludes with a discussion of the frail elderly—the minority of older adults, often poor and/or ill, who require extensive care.

Teaching Tip: Students' Life Plans

To help students apply the information about psychosocial development during late adulthood to their own lives, have them develop life plans—including what they would like to do after retirement, where they would like to live, and how they might cope with such difficulties as being widowed, being poor, and being handicapped. Ask students to think of an elderly person they know who provides a model for good life skills. They may wish to describe this elderly person's adaptive strategies for meeting achievement and affiliation needs. If there are students who do not know any elderly people well, the class might discuss why this is so.

Theories of Late Adulthood

AV: Aging Well (18 min., Films for the Humanities and Sciences)

(See description in Late Adulthood: Biosocial Development.)

AV: To Be Old, Black, and Poor (52 min., Films for the Humanities and Sciences)

This poignant film realistically depicts the plight of the elderly African American by chronicling the difficult circumstances of Leonard and Sarah Bass over a six-month period.

AV: Close Harmony (30 min., Learning Corporation of America)

(See description in Middle Childhood: Psychosocial Development.)

Observational Activity: Recording a Life Story

Developmentalists James Birren, Jerome Bruner, and John Kotre use personal autobiographies, or life stories, as research tools for studying psychosocial development during late adulthood. These researchers have found that writing about one's life experiences is an excellent way to gain new insight into the past and give new meaning to the present.

Birren notes that the autobiographical process often triggers incredibly detailed recall of the names, events, and places of one's past. Recollection is often emotional, as when an early loss or misfortune is remembered. Frequent use of humor indicates that "the person has moved from seeing life as a series of problems to greater insight and mastery."

Bruner and his colleagues listen to an individual's life story as told in a 30-minute response to a set of simple questions. In analyzing these stories, they often find that the words and images people use to review the seemingly unconnected events in their lives bear a strong relationship to the story content. One woman, who was very family-oriented and had strong affiliation needs, used metaphors about space and environment in 37 of the first sentences she uttered. Important and complex events in one's personal history can often be clarified with just the right metaphor.

Distribute copies of Handout 2 to your students and have them collect a life story from an older adult whom they know well.

During class discussion, students will be eager to reflect on their interviews and summarize the life stories they have collected. This review of the various life stories will be a good starting point for discussing many of the themes presented in the text. Depending on the age of those interviewed, for instance, do the stories reflect preoccupation with Erikson's crisis of integrity versus despair? Does an individual's life story provide insight into his or her various psychosocial needs, such as achievement or affiliation? Is the use of metaphor frequent? humorous?

Birren, J. E. (1987, May). The best of all stories. *Psychology Today*, pp. 91–92.

Goleman, D. (1987, November 10). Reading between lines of life story. *Detroit Free Press*, pp. 3a, 3c.

Kotre, J. (1995). *White gloves: How we create ourselves through memory*. New York: The Free Press.

Activities in Late Adulthood

AV: Aging in the Future Series (5 parts, University of Michigan Media Resource Center)

Designed to point out that our traditional approach to the position of the older adult in society is changing, this series of films is hosted by Clark Tibbits of the U.S. Administration on Aging.

Part I: *Work and Retirement* (21 min.)
A fast-paced look at the historical development of retirement in the United States. In brief interviews, older adults discuss the pros and cons of retirement and the importance of continuing to work for as long as possible.

Part II: *Retirement Income Security* (14 min.)
Discusses the concerns of older adults about the economics of late adulthood, including the worry that the Social Security system may fail.

Part V: *Politics of Aging* (15 min.)
The subject of this film is the increasingly active political role many older adults are taking to protect their interests.

AV: Aging in Japan: When Traditional Mechanisms Vanish (45 min., Films for the Humanities and Sciences)

This program documents a society in flux, in which the traditional mechanisms for looking after the elderly in Japan—who once were revered as the most important members of the family—are beginning to break down. Although today's cohort of older Japanese workers created the economic miracle of modern Japan, increasingly they are finding that the happy retirement they looked forward to has been replaced by isolation. Much of this intriguing program was filmed in a Japanese public bathhouse, an ancient institution that has assumed a new role in Japan as a place where increasing numbers of displaced elderly persons congregate.

Classroom Activity: On the Street Where You Live: The Importance of Walkable Green Spaces in Naturally Occurring Retirement Communities

The text notes that older adults generally prefer to age in place, unless their family and friends have moved away. With the squaring of the demographic pyramid, urban planners are finally beginning to devote some attention to creating desirable spaces for the growing number of naturally occurring retirement communities (NORC). In one study in Tokyo, researchers investigated the association between the availability of greenery-filled public areas nearby a NORC and the longevity of senior citizens in this densely populated megacity. The researchers examined the survival rates of 3,144 people born in 1903, 1908, 1913, or 1918 over the five-year period of the study. The results were quite dramatic: The probability of survival increased in direct proportion to the availability of space for taking a walk near the residence ($p < 0.01$), the availability of nearby parks and tree-lined streets ($p < 0.05$), and the self-reported preference of the participants to continue to live in their current community ($p < 0.01$). The availability of walkable green streets and a positive attitude toward remaining in the community were the most important factors overall, and this finding was independent of age, sex, marital status, and socioeconomic status.

Takano, T., Nakamura, K., & Watanabe, M. (2002). Urban residential environments and senior citizens' longevity in megacity areas: the importance of walkable green spaces. *Journal of Epidemiology and Community Health, 56*(12), 913–918.

Friends and Relatives

Classroom Activity: Social Networking During Late Adulthood

Older people text, tweet, and stream less than younger ones. Compared with emerging adults, older adults own fewer computers, are less connected to the Internet, and avoid social networking. This is unfortunate because elders who have strong social networks and engage in cognitively stimulating activities live longer, healthier lives. Because most of your students likely use Facebook, Twitter, and other social networking sites, a surefire way to get a good discussion going is to ask them the following questions:

What are the major reasons for the digital gap between the older and younger generations?

Is the digital gap in social networking likely to increase or decrease in the future as current technologically savvy generations become "the older generation"?

Using the model of primary, secondary, and tertiary care, what steps could individuals and communities take to reduce the size of the digital gap?

Using Facebook or Twitter as a model, how would students modify popular social networking sites to be "friendlier" to older adults?

Classroom Activity: Ageism and Marital Relationships

To illustrate the role that ageist attitudes have played in the lives of older Americans, discuss how social institutions and laws have affected marital relationships among the elderly. Begin by pointing out that if two older adults receiving Social Security get married, they lose one income. As a result, they may not have enough money to live on. For this reason, many older couples literally can't afford to get married. Another problem arises when the married elderly are segregated into male and female wards or floors in nursing homes, a tragic separation for couples in which both partners are bedridden. Finally, adult children sometimes oppose the remarriage of a widowed parent because they fear the loss of an expected inheritance, or they worry that the parent will "make a mistake."

AV: Grandma Didn't Wave Back (24 min., Films for the Humanities and Sciences)

A "Young People's Special," this poignant film tells the story of the love between an aging grandmother and Debbie, her 11-year-old granddaughter. Grandma, who has lived with Debbie's family since Debbie was five, is getting old now, and the family struggles to adjust.

"On Your Own" Activity: Grandparents

A number of issues pertaining to grandparents are raised in the text. These include the changing role of grandparents due to increased life expectancy, greater financial independence, rising divorce rates, and the trend toward egalitarian relationships with grandchildren. To help students apply this information to their own life experiences, ask them to reflect on the changing role of grandparents by answering the questions on Handout 3.

As a follow-up to this exercise, you could summarize students' responses, focusing on the extent to which they concur with points made in the text regarding the changing nature of grandparenthood. For example, is there evidence of greater "noninterference" between grandparents and grandchildren today? Are grandparents today more likely to be fun-loving, indulgent playmates than the family matriarchs or patriarchs of previous generations? Are there consistent differences in the grandparenting styles of grandmothers and grandfathers? Do styles of grandparenting vary with ethnic background? If this exercise coincides with a class meeting, encouraging students to share their recollections of their grandparents should lead to an interesting class discussion.

The Frail Elderly

AV: Aging in the Future Series (5 parts, University of Michigan Media Resource Center)

Part III: *Health Maintenance and Care* (11 min.) This brief film shows older people learning about health and health care as they visit a community geriatric clinic and discuss various health care programs. Also discussed is the need for a national health care policy.

Part IV: *Living Arrangements and Services* (15 min.) This film briefly traces the historical development of specialized housing and projects future needs based on increased longevity. The problems of living arrangements for older adults—including mounting costs, loneliness, and the various needs of maintaining an independent lifestyle—are illustrated.

Teaching Tip: Housing Difficulties for the Aged

To help students understand the housing difficulties older people face, ask them to consider whether they (or their parents) could remain in their present residence if they grew frail or developed handicaps. What problems would they experience if they could no longer drive, for example? Is there a grocery store within walking distance?

Then have students consider the advantages and disadvantages of the alternative residences that now exist for the elderly, including planned retirement communities, where all residents must be over a certain age, and naturally occurring retirement communities, where more than half the residents are elderly.

A controversial option is the "guaranteed life care" retirement community. According to this plan, an individual pays a very large sum (usually a life's savings) in return for the guarantee of a residence and medical care for the rest of his or her life. Unfortunately, some developers have defaulted, leaving their elderly members penniless and homeless. Do the elderly have any recourse as victims of such fraud?

Alternatively, you could use the following problem-based learning activity to address the issue of housing for the elderly.

Classroom Activity: Problem-Based Learning: Design an Assisted-Living Residence

The Introduction's Classroom Activity: Introducing Problem-Based Learning describes this relatively new pedagogical tool. Following is a sample problem that you might want to give to your students as part of your coverage of cognitive development during adulthood.

> Sam's grandfather, who is beginning to show signs of frailty, may soon be unable to live independently. After visiting several nursing homes, assisted-living residences, and professional home care providers in the area, Sam is confused about which types of arrangement would be best for his grandfather.
>
> Before you leave class today, your group must address the following questions: First, from what you have learned about development during late adulthood, what criteria should be used to decide where Sam's grandfather should live? Second, after your group agrees on an answer to the first question, determine some learning issues that need to be researched to answer the question, "What issues should concern Sam regarding his grandfather's well-being in a new residence?" Among other issues, these issues should focus on the activities of daily life. Finally, your group should briefly describe the features, programs, and services of an optimal assisted-living residence.
>
> Based on the decisions that your group makes today, you should devise a plan for researching the various issues. Two weeks from today's class, your group will present an answer for Sam based on the issues you think are relevant.

AV: To Be Growing Older (15 min., Indiana University)

This film sympathetically and realistically presents the aging individual as a real person with very hefty problems. These include, among other things, loneliness, failing health and eyesight, and locating appropriate services. The pros and cons of nursing homes are examined, and perspectives are shared on aging by several younger people. Because of its candor, this film is provocative and even disconcerting in places.

AV: *Caring for Your Parents* (24 min., Films for the Humanities and Sciences)

This video discusses an increasingly prevalent problem for middle-aged adults: caring for elderly parents while attempting to raise one's own children and maintain a successful career. Taking a practical approach, it also discusses how to deal with a parent's advancing helplessness, problem behaviors, and role reversal.

AV: Caring for the Elderly (19 min., Films for the Humanities and Sciences)
Nursing Home Care (19 min., Films for the Humanities and Sciences)

These informative films provide an overview of the various methods of care for the aging. The first film identifies issues in elderly care through interviews with social workers, senior-citizen advocates, and nursing home administrators. The second film provides criteria for evaluating nursing homes, describes alternative care for the elderly, tours a well-run nursing home, and profiles a man of 95 who lives actively with a minimal amount of community support.

AV: Abandoning the Elderly (16 min., Films for the Humanities and Sciences)

This brief film profiles the news story involving an 80-year-old, wheelchair-bound patient who was abandoned by his family. In the program, his daughter attempts to explain the circumstances that led to this sad story. The program also reports on the increasing trend of "Granny dumping," brought on by soaring health care costs.

Teaching Tip: The Frail Elderly

To increase student understanding of the plight of the frail elderly, especially those who are suffering only from physical handicaps, a visit to a nursing home is invaluable. Try to select a home with well-designed facilities and an active roster of activities for the residents. Have students draw up a list of the physical needs of these older citizens and note how a well-designed facility meets those needs (e.g., wider doors for wheelchair access, emergency call buttons in all rooms).

Then ask students to evaluate their own living environment as a possible residence for a frail elderly person. Have them list the changes that would have to be made if an older friend, parent, or grandparent became handicapped and wanted to visit. Many older people find that the houses that have suited them perfectly for years are inaccessible or unsafe when they become frail, forcing them to make expensive changes or move. Discuss what could be done in the initial planning of homes and apartments that might prevent costly moves or changes later in life.

Critical Thinking Activity: Frailty During Late Adulthood

Each unit of these resources contains a critical thinking exercise designed specifically to test students' critical thinking about a topic covered in the text. Handout 4 contains a synopsis of research or a brief scenario followed by a series of questions.

Although the answers will uniquely belong to each student, they should be checked for a general understanding of the major themes of development during late adulthood. Some sample answers follow.

Biosocial Domain
Variable: Type of Illness
Hypothesis: Health problems that broadly restrict a person's range of activities are more likely to lead to feelings of helplessness and frailty than health problems that have a more limited impact.

Cognitive Domain
Variable: Personality Structure
Hypothesis: People who perceive a strong sense of personal control in their lives might be more resilient to frailty than people who do not have strong feelings of personal control.

Psychosocial Domain
Variable: Social Network
Hypothesis: People who have a larger network of family and friends are less likely to become frail following an injury or illness than people who are socially isolated.

HANDOUT 1

Developmental Fact or Myth?

T F 1. Developmentalists agree that in old age, the individual and society mutually withdraw from each other.

T F 2. Volunteer work attracts older people who have been strongly committed to their community.

T F 3. Nearly one in two older adults makes a long-distance move following retirement.

T F 4. Religious faith increases with age.

T F 5. Married elderly people are lower in health and happiness than are those who are divorced.

T F 6. Financial assistance and emotional support usually flow from the older generation down instead of from the younger generation up.

T F 7. Loneliness during late adulthood is greater for individuals who were never married than for any other group.

T F 8. Most older people suffer significantly from a lack of close friendships.

T F 9. Very few Asians are in nursing homes.

T F 10. Most of the frail elderly are cared for by medical personnel.

HANDOUT 2

Observational Activity: Recording a Life Story

The following questions can be used for obtaining a life story of someone you know well. Arrange to have two sessions of 30 minutes to 1 hour each. For each session you will need a tape recorder, an extension cord, several tapes, and a pen and notebook. The notebook will help you to keep an outline of the life story as it unfolds. Choose a quiet location for the interviews where your subject is comfortable and the two of you will not be disturbed.

The First Session

Begin by asking for a five-minute summary of your subject's life. This will serve as an outline for you and will help to engage the autobiographical process for the more detailed story to come.

As you record your subject's life story, encourage a narrative rather than an analytic style. For example, instead of the statement, "As a child I had a poor self-image," it would be better to evoke a specific incident, say, in which the interviewee looked in the mirror with disgust. The following questions are provided as guidelines only, and are not meant to be rigidly followed.

Family
What do you know about your family roots?
What do you remember about your grandparents?
What stories have you heard about them?
What was your mother like?
What did she tell you about her childhood?
What did she do most of her life?
What did you like to do with her?
(Same questions for father.)
Were you closer to one parent than to the other?
Which parent did you admire most?
Did you have brothers and sisters?
What was your relationship to them?
Did your parents have different ideas for boys and girls?
Do any family celebrations, rituals, or observations stand out in your mind?

Neighborhood
What was your home like?
What objects do you remember in some of the rooms?
How did you feel about your neighborhood?
Was your family different from your neighbors' in any way?
Who were your companions as a child?
What did you do with them?

School
Describe the school(s) you went to.
Were your classmates from the same background as you?
Were boys and girls treated alike?
What subjects did you like?

Work
How and when did you get your first job?
What did the work involve?
What was the best job you ever had? the worst?
If you had your choice of all the jobs in the world, looking back, what would you have chosen?

Intimacy
Did you date?

HANDOUT 2 *(continued)*

	Who was your first girlfriend (boyfriend)? What was he or she like? How did you meet your husband (wife)?
Children	How many children do you have? When were they born? What is each child like? What are your aspirations for them? Do you have grandchildren? How often do you see them?
Other	What chores or responsibilities did you have as a child? What did you daydream about becoming when you grew up? Did you have any favorite stories? What were your happiest times as a child? What were your saddest times?

After you have completed the first session, jot down your impressions of the interview. Record the sight, sound, and emotional feel of the speaker, including your subjective impressions of each of these.

If possible, allow a week between the two sessions to give your subject a chance to rummage through memorabilia and evoke deeper memories. This will also give you time to listen to the interview, make more detailed notes, and think of questions that are pertinent to the particular experiences of your subject.

The Second Session

At the beginning of the second session, ask your subject whether any additional experiences came to mind between sessions. You might also ask some of the questions generated by listening to the recording of the first session, or just continue where you left off. Near the end of your interview is the time to ask life-review questions. These questions will differ, of course, for someone in midlife and someone who is near the end of life. Sometimes going through a photograph album is a good occasion for bringing up questions of this type.

Life Review	What was the most exciting part of your life? What was the most important historical event you witnessed or were part of? Do you remember reading something, seeing a movie, or meeting someone who influenced your life dramatically? If you could relive any part of your life, what would it be? Are there any parts of your life that you regret? Are there any years you felt were wasted? Are you like the person you were 20 years ago? 10 years ago? If you had three wishes, what would they be? Looking over your entire life, when was it darkest? brightest? Is your life getting darker or brighter now? Who has been affected by your life? What are some of the things you have learned about life? Would you want your son or daughter (grandson or granddaughter) to live through your experiences? What parts would you want him or her to avoid?

Source: Kotre, J. Recording a life story. (Personal communication.)

HANDOUT 3

Grandparents

1. Describe your relationship with one of your grandparents. Was (is) it close and loving? How frequently did (do) you see him or her? To what extent did he or she participate in your upbringing?

2. In what ways was (is) your relationship to your grandparents different from that between your parents and *their* grandparents?

HANDOUT 3 *(continued)*

3. If you are a grandparent, in what ways does your role as grandparent differ from that of *your* grandparents? If you are not a grandparent, but hope to be one some day, how would you *like* your role as grandparent to differ from that of your grandparents?

4. The text notes that styles of grandparenting vary by sex, age at which one becomes a grandparent, and ethnic group. Describe how any of these factors have influenced your own relationships as a grandchild or grandparent.

HANDOUT 4

Critical Thinking Activity: Frailty During Late Adulthood

Now that you have read and reviewed the late adulthood unit, take your learning a step further by testing your critical thinking skills on this scientific problem-solving exercise.

Succumbing to a chronic illness, suffering a debilitating accident, or simply becoming "too old to function" are real fears for most elderly adults. Yet frailty is not automatically defined by illness, accident, or age. As noted in the text, the health and independence of the elderly depend not only on intrinsic impairment but also on the resources that each adult brings to the challenges of this stage of the life span. Despite suffering with health problems, many elderly persons never become frail because of four protective buffers: attitude, social network, physical setting, and financial resources.

To close out the unit on late adulthood, this exercise will help develop your skill at what some psychologists refer to as *variable-mindedness* (Halonen, 1995). Developmental psychologists are constantly striving to understand the independent variables that contribute to individual variation in developmental outcomes such as frailty. Being "variable-minded" means taking a reasoned, "educated guess" about all possible factors that might influence some developmental outcome.

Your task in this exercise is to identify several factors or variables that might influence whether an older adult becomes helpless or frail in response to a specific illness, injury, or some other health problem. For each of the three domains of development—biosocial, cognitive, and psychosocial—identify at least two independent variables that might influence an older person's vulnerability to frailty. Then translate each variable into a scientifically sound, testable research hypothesis that makes a specific prediction about the impact of that variable on the person.

For example, under the cognitive domain, one variable that might influence vulnerability to frailty is the individual's overall outlook on life. It might be expected that optimists and pessimists would respond differently to the same health problem during late adulthood. A possible hypothesis might then be "*Optimistic older adults will recover more rapidly from a given illness or injury than will pessimistic older adults.*" As another example, one variable in the biosocial domain that might influence vulnerability to frailty is the nature of the health problem.

Biosocial Domain

Variable:

1.

2.

Hypothesis:

1.

2.

HANDOUT 4 *(continued)*

Cognitive Domain
Variable:
1.

2.

Hypothesis:
1.

2.

Psychosocial Domain
Variable:
1.

2.

Hypothesis:
1.

2.

Source: Halonen, J. (1995). *The critical thinking companion*. New York: Worth, p. 25.

Death and Dying

Contents

Note: Worth Publishers provides online Instructor and Student Tool Kits, DVD Student Tool Kits, and Instructor and Student video resources in DevelopmentPortal for use with the text. See Part I: General Resources for information about these materials and the text Lecture Guides for a complete list by text chapter.

Bereavement

SUGGESTED ACTIVITIES

Introducing Death and Dying

"On Your Own" Activity: Developmental Fact or Myth?

Before students read death and dying, have them respond to the true-false statements in Handout 1.

The correct answers are shown below. Class discussion can focus on the origins of any developmental misconceptions that are demonstrated in the students' incorrect answers.

1. F	6. F
2. F	7. T
3. F	8. T
4. T	9. T
5. F	10. F

AV: Transitions Throughout the Life Span, Program 26: Death and Dying

Depending on an individual's age, experience, beliefs, and historical and cultural context, death can have many meanings. Death, like the rest of the life span, reflects the vast complexity of human development in the way people grieve and accept or deny death due to their social, religious, and cultural differences.

The program begins by exploring the dying person's emotions, noting that the reactions that death prompts vary from individual to individual. Although the concept of an unvarying sequence of stages among the dying is not universally accepted, the pioneering work of Elisabeth Kübler-Ross was instrumental in revealing the emotional gamut of terminally ill patients and the importance of honest communication.

Next, the program deals with how dying patients and their families plan for death and with the controversial issue of whether and when we should hasten the death of a loved one. This segment also discusses hospice and other forms of care designed to help the terminally ill patient to die "a good death."

The final segment explores the social context of dying, noting that perceptions of death vary markedly according to their historical and cultural context. This segment also deals with changing expressions of bereavement and how people can be aided in the process of recovery.

Death and Hope

Teaching Tip: Feelings About Death

To help students recognize and examine their own feelings about death, discuss the ideas and images they have of dying and of being dead. Ask students to list three regrets they would have if they should die immediately. Then review the discussion presented in the text and have students compare their regrets with those reported in the text (e.g., young adults are just starting to live; mothers are responsible for small children; those who are unsure about their religious beliefs are more fearful of death).

Ask students who have had a course in death education whether taking such a course has helped them and, if so, in what ways.

AV: The Biology of Death (29 min., Films for the Humanities and Sciences)

This program covers the current state of scientific knowledge regarding the causes of death and the normal aging process. It also explores cultural and legal end-of-life issues and responses.

AV: The Death Knell of Old Age: The Physical Aspects of Death (25 min., Films for the Humanities and Sciences)

This poignant program introduces the viewer to Bob, who, at the age of 87, approaches the final stage of the life cycle. Tracking the final hours of Bob's life as he quietly dies at home, the program uses 3–D computer animations of cellular damage by free radicals, optic degeneration, spinal nerve damage, and brain failure; endoscopic imaging of degeneration of the heart, blood vessels, bronchi, ears, and stomach lining; and thermal imaging of bodily heat loss illustrate the aging body's inability to mend itself.

"On Your Own" Activity: Death Anxiety Questionnaire

The Death Anxiety Questionnaire (DAQ) developed by Hope R. Conte, M. B. Weiner, and Robert Plutchik (1982) is a good way both to introduce the material on death and dying and to stimulate classroom discussion of attitudes toward death. After students have completed Handout 2, discuss their scores.

After administering the DAQ to a variety of groups—including nursing-home residents, senior citizens, and young adults—the authors found no significant differences in mean scores (mean = 8.50), despite the fact that those tested ranged in age from 30 to 80. In a separate study, however, the researchers found that adolescents often had higher DAQ scores than did older subjects. This may reflect several factors—including the emotional stresses of adolescence and cognitive maturation, which gives death a new meaning to adolescents. DAQ scores were not significantly correlated with sex, level of education, or any of a variety of other demographic characteristics tested.

The DAQ identifies four specific aspects of death anxiety: fear of the unknown (items 1, 2, 12, 14, 15), fear of suffering (items 3, 4, 5), fear of loneliness (items 6, 7), and fear of personal extinction (items 10, 11, 13). Factor analysis demonstrated that items 8 and 9 did not fit into one of these dimensions.

Conte, H. R., Weiner, M. B., & Plutchik, R. (1982). Measuring death anxiety: Conceptual, psychometric, and factor-analytic aspects. *Journal of Personality and Social Psychology, 43*, 775–785.

Teaching Tip: Cultural Denial of Death

To illustrate the ways in which Western culture "denies" death, have students list five ways in which they deny death—for example, by avoiding funerals they do not have to attend, by not talking to a bereaved person about a relative or friend who has died, by driving recklessly or taking chances, and by refusing to write a will or buy life insurance. Discuss how the outcome of each of these acts of denial might be harmful to themselves or others. What reasons do students give for their tendency to deny death? (It should, of course, be pointed out that it is likely that everyone in the class is doing some denying, so that in asking these questions no negative judgments are implied.)

If your students are a culturally diverse group, ask those whose families are from non-Western backgrounds to discuss how death and the dying are treated in their cultures.

Classroom Activity: The Day of the Dead

Many Hispanics celebrate November 2 as *El Dia de los Muertos*, or the Day of the Dead, by preparing a family altar for family members who have died. The altar is decorated with photographs, flowers, mementos, candles, and even skeleton toys. Once the altar is finished, family and friends gather to share stories and memories of the departed, give thanks for the preciousness of life, and invite the spirits of the departed to rejoin the family and enjoy a festive meal.

In Mexico, families visit cemeteries where their loved ones are buried and spend a day cleaning headstones and adorning them with photographs, flowers, and memorabilia. Afterward, altars are constructed in the home to welcome the spirits. Finally, the evening meal consists of the favorite foods of the departed.

Until fairly recently, many Mexicans who immigrated to the United States abandoned the tradition of *El Dia de los Muertos*. They did so for at least two reasons. First, their ancestors were buried in Mexico rather than in local American cemeteries. Second, most American cemeteries prohibited public gatherings like those typical of Day of the Dead celebrations.

In the 1970s, however, Hispanic artists reawakened the tradition of the Day of the Dead and the significance of the altar to the grieving process. The earliest revivals of the tradition were followed by larger community events that combined the remembrance of the dead with other traditions of Latino culture.

Roberto Vargas, a California educator and therapist, has promoted Day of the Dead ceremonies as a means of empowerment in the family and community. "The holiday brings family and friends together to share quality time, prayers, and memories. The ceremony of introducing the persons represented on the altar teaches children about their ancestors and culture and models the practice of honoring elders and respecting life. Youth and adults are re-inspired as they remind each other of the hopes of our *abuelitos*—to create a better life for their children. People who have recently lost a loved one are healed by sharing memories and tears." (For an excellent illustrative overview of how the community of Oakland, California, celebrates the Day of the Dead tradition at the Oakland Museum of California, refer to the book *El Corazón de la Muerte: Altars & Offerings for Days of the Dead*. You can find information at www.heydaybooks.com or www.museumca.org. Vargas is one of the principal founders and ceremony leaders for this annual exhibit and celebration, which has received national acclaim.)

A case in point is Rosa, a schoolteacher who remembers Day of the Dead celebrations from her childhood. As an adult she holds the tradition sacred because it provides her with affirmations of who she is today—"a Chicana with Mexican cultural roots. I remember feeling *familia*, putting photos of our relatives on the altar, holding hands together, talking to our relatives, and sharing the stories of family I grew to love."

A good source of additional material on what other cultures can teach about death and dying is the text by Colin Parkes and his colleagues referenced here. The text offers detailed examples of death rituals in various religions and societies, including Hinduism, Tibet Buddhism, Judaism, Islam, Christianity, and Native American traditions.

Parkes, C. M., Laungani, P., & Young, B. (2000). *Death and bereavement across cultures*. New York: Routledge.

Vargas, R. (1996, November). Families celebrate the day of the dead. *Hispanic, 9*(11), 72.

Vargas, R. (2011). Roberto Vargas: Leadership development & meeting facilitation to improve our world. Retrieved March 6, 2011, from http://robertovargas.com/dasdelosmuertos.

Dying and Acceptance

Classroom Activity: The High Cost of Dying

Most of your students would probably agree that every life is worth prolonging, no matter what the cost. But some may begin to question their conviction when confronted with the following statistics: In 2009, Medicare paid $55 billion just for doctor and hospital bills during the last two months of patients' lives. This amount, over 25 percent of the total Medicare budget, is more than the budget for the Department of Homeland Security or the Department of Education.

As the shape of the demographic pyramid approaches a square, the average age of Americans is increasing and the cost of care will rise proportionately. The ever-improving (and increasing) use of new technologies for diagnosing life-threatening diseases and for prolonging life adds even more to end-of-life costs. Clearly, this issue creates a moral and financial dilemma that society must face. To bluntly put the issue to the class, pose this question: Should unlimited care be spent *only* on those elderly adults who have a chance to recover?

Palliative care in a hospice setting is receiving more attention than ever, not just because many see it as more humane care but because it usually is significantly less costly than standard care; less is spent on drugs, diagnostics, tests and heroic, last-ditch treatments. At the Virginia Commonwealth University (VCU) hospital, for instance, a typical five-day stay for an end-stage cancer patient costs $5,312 in the palliative wing—57 percent less than the cost to house a similar patient elsewhere in the hospital. VCU administrators figure that the 11-bed palliative care unit, which opened in May 2000, saves the hospital at least $1 million a year.

Palliative care is slowly catching on in this country. In 2002, there were palliative-care programs in 844 community hospitals in the United States, up 18 percent from 2001. Even so, while palliative care has been recognized as a valid medical specialty in Britain since 1987, many American hospital administrators worry that palliative care could turn into a ploy for saving money off the backs of dying patients. Many doctors, patients, and their families don't like the idea of giving up until all possible avenues of treatment have been exhausted. The issue is not about to go away, however, because the aging population will fuel the demand for better end-of-life care: By 2030, the number of Americans over the age of 85 is expected to reach 8.5 million, twice the number today.

Gruen, A. (2007, September 7). Cost of dying: Planning now can save loved ones later. Retrieved from www.nj.com/starledger/stories/index.

Naik, G. (2004, March 10). Final days: unlikely ways to cut hospital costs: comfort the dying; palliative care unit offers painkillers and support, fewer tests, treatments. *Wall Street Journal,* p. A1.

60 Minutes. (2010, August 8). The cost of dying: End of life care. CBS News 60 Minutes. Retrieved March 4, 2011, from www.cbsnews.com/stories/2010/08/05/60minutes/main6747002.shtml.

Classroom Activity: The Chronosystem in Operation: Baby Boomers Avoid Talking About End-of-Life Issues

Another sign that Americans are uncomfortable talking about death comes from a study conducted by the National Hospice Foundation (NHF). The study shows that baby boomers are more likely to talk to their children about safe sex and drugs than to their terminally ill parents about choices in care as they near life's final stages. One of four Americans over the age of 45 say they would not bring up issues related to their parent's death—even if the parent had a terminal illness and less than six months to live.

The same study showed that although Americans expect their loved ones to carry out their wishes about end-of-life care, they have not made those wishes clearly known. "As difficult as it seems, we must talk with our parents, spouses and very close friends about options like hospice that provide physical and emotional support to terminally ill patients and their families," said Karen Davie, president of the NHF. "If we don't have these discussions, there is no way that thoughts can be known or respected. By sharing our wishes about end of life, we remove a heavy burden from our family and friends who will not have to wonder if they are doing the right thing."

Despite this aversion to talking about end-of-life issues, the study reported that most adults are very clear about what they want if faced with less than six months to live. In order, the Top Ten desires were as follows:

- someone to be sure that the patient's wishes are enforced
- choice among the types of services the patient could receive
- pain control tailored to the patient's wishes
- emotional support for the patient and family
- an opportunity for the patient to put his/her life in order
- spiritual support for the patient and family
- hospice care provided no matter where the patient is living
- a team of professionals, like physicians, nurses and counselors, to care for the patient
- the patient's ability to be cared for and die in his/her own home or a family member's home
- continuity with the same caregivers, no matter where the patient is staying

The study also showed that one-third of Americans admit not knowing who to contact to get the best care for a family member or close friend with a terminal illness and less than six months to live. "The entire topic of how we want to be cared for when we are dying makes us uncomfortable. It's difficult for us to even think about having that conversation, and that's a problem. We must familiarize ourselves with options now in order to make the best decisions later," notes NHF's Stuart Lazarus. "Despite the fact that hospice care has been successful in America for more than two decades, one-third of Americans do not know that only *hospice* offers what people say they want at the end of life: choice in care; control of pain; medical attention; help for the family; spiritual and emotional support; and the option to remain in their own home." A recent survey of college students' awareness of end-of-life options reported a similar level of ignorance (Newsome & Dickinson, 2000).

To help people broach end-of-life issues with their parents and loved ones, the National Hospice Foundation has developed the following guidelines:

- Choose the setting.
  Find a quiet, comfortable place free from distraction to hold a one-on-one discussion. A loved one usually wants to share his or her wishes in a private setting. And plan for the conversation—this is not a discussion to have on the spur of the moment.
- Ask permission.
  People cope with end-of-life issues in many ways. Asking permission to discuss this topic assures your loved one that you will respect his or her wishes and honor them. (Some ways of doing this could be: "I'd like to talk about how you would like to be cared for if you got really sick. Is that OK?" or "If you ever got really sick I would be afraid of not knowing the kind of care you would like. Could we talk about this now? I'd feel better if we did.")
- Talk about it.
  You have initiated this conversation because you love this person. Focus on your desire to help him or her maintain a full and happy life, even during difficult times. Use a warm and caring manner. Allow your loved one to set the pace, and use nonverbal communication to offer support. (Some ways of doing this would be to nod your head in agreement, hold your loved one's hand, or reach out to offer a hug or comforting touch.)
- Be a listener.
  This is not a debate. Sometimes just having someone to talk to is a big help. Be sure to hear what the person is saying. Listen for the wants or needs that your loved one expresses. Show empathy and respect by addressing these wants and needs in a truthful and open way.
- Do your homework.
  Before initiating the discussion, learn more about the kinds of end-of-life care options available in your community. Become familiar with what these options offer—especially so that you can determine if they will meet your loved one's end-of-life needs.

  Questions to ask your loved one about his or her end-of-life care:

  Would you like choice in care at the end of life?
  Would you like to spend your final days at home or in a homelike setting?
  Do you feel it's important to have medical attention and pain control tailored to fit your needs?
  Do you feel it's important for you—and your family—to have emotional and spiritual support?

  If your loved one responds "Yes" in answer to these questions, he or she wants the kind of end-of-life care that hospice provides.

  For more information on how to find a local hospice, guidelines on how to help a friend who is dying, and other related issues, students can be directed to the following Web sites.

  Hospice Net (www.hospicenet.org)

  American Hospice Foundation (www.americanhospice.org)

Baby boomers fear talking to parents about death (2000). *National Hospice Foundation Online* (www.nho.org).

Newsome, B. R., & Dickinson, G. E. (2000, June). Death experiences and hospice: Perceptions of college students. *Death Studies*, *24*(4), 335–341.

AV: Hospice (13 min., Indiana University)

A hospice is a place where many individuals go to die; nonetheless, this film portrays the hospice as a place of hope and peace. Individuals who have placed their loved ones in a hospice are interviewed. Hospice residents themselves also share their feelings. Although the problems and sadness connected with a hospice are not masked, viewing this film is a positive and sensitive experience.

AV: Letting Go: A Hospice Journey (90 min., Films for the Humanities and Sciences)

This excellent HBO production takes an intimate look at three hospice patients: a 9-year-old boy with an incurable brain disease, a 62-year-old man with an inoperable brain tumor, and a 46-year-old woman with lung cancer. In addition to showing how hospice care can help the terminally ill find comfort and peace in the final days of their lives, the program focuses on the decision-making processes of patients, family members, doctors, social workers, and clergy members.

Classroom Activity: Hospices and a "Good Death"

To clarify what is meant by a "good death," invite a speaker from a local hospice to address the class. Many hospice groups have a speakers' bureau and slide shows or films. Discussing the concept of a good death with someone who has helped others die comfortably should ease the students' fears as well. Also, have the class discuss whether they would want to die in a hospital, a hospice, or at home; whether they would want family and friends around them; and whether they would want to choose when to die in the event of terminal illness.

Classroom Activity: Euthanasia

The text discusses active euthanasia, in which someone takes action to bring about another person's death, and passive euthanasia, in which a person is allowed to die naturally, through the cessation of medical interventions. To help students understand the ethical issues surrounding active and passive euthanasia, ask the class whether they think life should be prolonged by artificial means. Take a vote for or against euthanasia, and then have class members explain their reasoning.

It may be helpful to present two well-publicized cases of euthanasia: the Karen Quinlan case, in which the parents of the young woman (who was in a coma and pronounced brain dead) went to court to request that life-support systems be removed; and a 1983 case, in which an elderly man (who was shot by his son) lay in a coma in a hospital. Each of these cases contains a "twist" that is likely to make the discussion more involving. In the Quinlan case, while the parents eventually won, and the life-support systems were removed, Karen lived for nine years before she finally died. In the shooting incident, the son was found guilty of attempted murder, but because a neurosurgeon testified that the bullet wound was not severe enough to have caused the father's death, the son was given a suspended 10-year sentence (over protests that others would be encouraged to commit murder if he were treated lightly). The more recent case of Terri Schiavo is discussed in the text.

If any students have had experience with a friend or relative who was kept alive by artificial means, ask them if they are willing to share their feelings about euthanasia. It should be made clear, however, that the subject may be difficult for some people, and that no one is required to speak about personal matters.

AV: "Doctor Death": Medical Ethics and Doctor-Assisted Suicide (28 min., Films for the Humanities and Sciences)

This specially adapted Phil Donahue program profiles Michigan pathologist Dr. Jack Kevorkian, who built a "suicide machine" that, at the time of this program, he had used to assist 15 patients in ending their lives. Dubbed "Dr. Death" by the popular media, Kevorkian offers his own beliefs about incurable illness and medical ethics.

Classroom Activity: Classroom Debate: *"Resolved: Euthanasia and Physician-Assisted Suicide Should Be Legalized"*

In the 1990s, the issue of assisted suicide received a great deal of attention in the media with the highly publicized assisted suicides supervised by Dr. Jack Kevorkian, the Michigan pathologist the press labeled "Dr. Death." Dr. Kevorkian devised a suicide machine that administers a lethal dose of carbon monoxide to a patient who voluntarily presses a button. In 1999, Dr. Kevorkian was sentence to 10 to 25 years in prison on a second-degree murder conviction. In June 2007, he was released on parole, on condition that he would not offer suicide advice to anyone.

Highlighting a recent or, better still, ongoing court case involving euthanasia is a particularly effective way to stimulate class discussion. For instance, in March 2004, the trial of New Zealander Lesley Martin on two charges of attempting to euthanize her mother began (euthanasia is illegal in New Zealand). Martin pleaded not guilty to both counts—one relating to administering morphine, the other to an attempt to suffocate her mother with a pillow. In her 2002 book *To Die Like A Dog,* she revealed that she killed her mother because of the pain her mother was suffering. Shortly after the book's release, Martin was arrested. She received a 15-month sentence, of which she served seven and a half months.

To further explore this controversial issue, follow the guidelines in the General Resources section of this manual and schedule a classroom debate on the resolution. You might want to direct your students to check out the Web site of Compassion and Choices, a choice-in-dying organization in North America (www.compassionandchoices.org/sslpage.aspx).

AV: Living Wills (30 min., Films for the Humanities and Sciences)
Dying Wish (52 min., Films for the Humanities and Sciences)
Medicine and Mercy (26 min., Films for the Humanities and Sciences)

These three films explore issues that pertain to dying a "good death." The first film discusses the concept of living wills and advanced directives for lifesaving care as patients, their families, and doctors present their views about this controversial issue. The second and third films look at the interplay of technology, ethics, and the quality of human life by examining the dilemmas created by advances in medical technology: Should you "pull the plug" on a ventilator that keeps a brain-dead patient alive? Should you take extraordinary measures to resuscitate a patient who will forever live in excruciating pain?

Bereavement

AV: Death: Coping with Loss (19 min., Indiana University)

Individuals of various ages discuss their feelings about death. Those people who have recently lost a loved one share their reactions toward the death of their child, sibling, or grandparent. The stages of grief and coping are outlined. Also discussed are the purposes of a funeral. Religious attitudes about an afterlife are presented briefly and without apology.

AV: Grieving: Suddenly Alone (26 min., Churchill Films)

This film is a dramatization of the course of grief that follows death as a widow experiences shock, denial, guilt, anger, depression, and, finally, acceptance.

AV: Saying Goodbye (26 min., Films for the Humanities and Sciences)

This program talks to people who have recently survived the loss of a loved one, focusing on how they dealt with their grief. A hospital chaplain and the director of a hospice also provide insights into the bereavement process.

Teaching Tip: Rituals of Death

To illustrate how our culture has ritualized death, invite a funeral director to class to discuss the typical funeral process. Who makes the arrangements? What is done to the body? What services are held? Who attends the services? Be sure to ask for the cost of a typical funeral and have the director discuss his or her role in helping the bereaved family and friends deal with their grief. If you cannot get a speaker, have students discuss their own experiences with funerals, including those they felt helped them to express their grief and those they felt denied that death had occurred.

"On Your Own" Activity: Coping with Death and Dying

To stimulate students' thinking about many of the issues discussed in the text regarding death and dying, have them complete Handout 3.

This assignment should help students integrate the text material with their own feelings. If students are willing to share their feelings with other members of the class, a stimulating and provocative discussion is certain to follow. If there is enough diversity in the ages and/or ethnic backgrounds of students, this exercise should also indicate how cohort and other demographic factors influence attitudes toward death and dying.

Critical Thinking Activity: Grief

Each unit of these resources contains a critical thinking exercise designed specifically to test students' critical thinking about a topic covered in the text. Handout 4 contains a synopsis of research or a brief scenario followed by a series of questions.

Although the answers will uniquely belong to each student, they should be checked for a general understanding of the domains and contexts of development. Some sample answers follow.

1. Biological Influences: One example is the universal (and apparently biological) capacity for experiencing grief that all humans (and some animals) seem to share. Another would be the various neural and hormonal aspects of specific emotions that accompany grieving. Cognitive Influences: Examples include age-related differences in how death is understood and how grieving varies with the perceived significance of the loss to the individual. Sociocultural: Examples include variations in the norms for grieving that are established by different cultures, religions, and age-group cohorts.
2. Microsystem: The most intimate and immediate system that shapes grieving for a child would be family traditions for mourning. Depending on the child's age, the microsystem might also include the peer group. In addition to the family, the primary microsystems that might affect an adult mourner include the particular church, temple, or mosque to which the individual belongs. Mesosystem: This context comes into play when the various microsystems interact, as when family members, friends, religious leaders, and so on coordinate their efforts to assist the mourner. Exosystem: This context of development comes into play through the influence on the bereavement process of people in the external networks, such as funeral directors and hospice workers. Macrosystem: Two examples of the macrosystem's influence are the impact of cultural values (such as whether crying is acceptable) and economic concerns (the type of burial) on mourning. Chronosystem: Finally, the chronosystem's influence is expressed in historical variation in grieving, such as the preference of recent cohorts for more private, less emotional, and less religious funerals.
3. Grief is adaptive to our species in several ways. Grief may help the mourner work through and adjust to a loss, so that he or she can eventually return to full functioning to help ensure the success of the next generation. Grieving may also cause the individual to take stock of his or her life and, in so doing, become a better person. For the group, grieving fosters empathy, strengthens social bonds, and in this collective way facilitates species' survival.
4. One implication of the absence of a formal ritual to mark the end of grieving is that grief is prolonged. This may explain why widows and widowers are less likely to remarry than those who have divorced: they simply don't know when they should stop mourning. Another implication of the myths is that "normal" grieving can't be pigeonholed: there is no single way to grieve.

HANDOUT 1

Developmental Fact or Myth?

T F 1. The dying pass through a predictable sequence of emotional stages.

T F 2. The hospice is accepted uncritically as a preferred alternative to a hospital death.

T F 3. Doctors worry about addicting the dying to painkillers.

T F 4. Modern life-prolonging medical technologies have tended to make dying a "good death" more difficult and less likely to occur.

T F 5. Today, active euthanasia is an accepted medical procedure.

T F 6. Even when there is a living will, hospitals may ignore the patient's preferences.

T F 7. Both cultures and religions design mourning to allow the expression of grief and then recovery.

T F 8. In recent times, mourning became a more private, and less emotional, affair.

T F 9. Grief is particularly difficult for those who are not allowed to mourn in public.

T F 10. The best advice to offer the bereaved is to "get on with life" as quickly as possible.

HANDOUT 2

Death Anxiety Questionnaire

For each of the following items, indicate your response according to the following scale:

0	1	2
not at all	somewhat	very much

_____ 1. Do you worry about dying?

_____ 2. Does it bother you that you may die before you have done everything you wanted to do?

_____ 3. Do you worry that you may be very ill for a long time before you die?

_____ 4. Does it upset you to think that others may see you suffering before you die?

_____ 5. Do you worry that dying may be very painful?

_____ 6. Do you worry that the persons closest to you won't be with you when you are dying?

_____ 7. Do you worry that you may be alone when you are dying?

_____ 8. Does the thought bother you that you might lose control of your mind before death?

_____ 9. Do you worry that expenses connected with your death will be a burden to other people?

_____ 10. Does it worry you that your instructions or will about your belongings may not be carried out after you die?

_____ 11. Are you afraid that you may be buried before you are really dead?

_____ 12. Does the thought of leaving loved ones behind when you die disturb you?

_____ 13. Do you worry that those you care about may not remember you after your death?

_____ 14. Does the thought worry you that with death you may be gone forever?

_____ 15. Are you worried about not knowing what to expect after death?

Conte, H. R., Weiner, M. B., & Plutchik, R. (1982). Measuring death anxiety: Conceptual, psychometric, and factor-analytic aspects. *Journal of Personality and Social Psychology*, *43*, 775–785.

HANDOUT 3

Coping with Death and Dying

1. What kind of ceremony or mourning ritual would you like to have when you die? Why would you choose this particular type of funeral?

2. What would you want to do if you had only six months to live?

3. A very close friend is in the hospital with a terminal illness. No one has told her anything about her condition, and the doctors are cheerily reassuring her that she is going to get better. Your friend asks you whether she is dying. What do you say?

HANDOUT 3 *(continued)*

4. How would you explain the death of a grandparent to a 7-year-old child?

5. Your 40-year-old friend has recently been widowed. List three things you should *not* say to her or do, and explain why.

6. Knowing that you have a terminal illness, would you prefer to be kept alive for as long as possible by artificial means or to be allowed to die peacefully in a hospice?

HANDOUT 4

Critical Thinking Activity: Grief

Now that you have read and reviewed the late adulthood unit, take your learning a step further by testing your critical thinking skills on this psychological reasoning exercise.

This exercise focuses on the various contexts and developmental domains of grief.

Grief is a multidimensional emotion, blending sadness, worry, even anger, in proportions that seem to vary from one culture to another. More obvious, how it is expressed also varies from culture to culture. For example, one study reported that mourners in 72 out of 73 sample cultures considered crying to be part of the accepted ritual (Rosenblatt, Walsh, & Jackson, 1976). Balinese mourners, however, avoid crying—not only while grieving but in other "emotional" situations as well. Rather, they tend to suppress their crying by smiling, joking, or expressing some other incompatible behavior. As a less common example, mourners in several cultures pull their hair, scratch their faces, or perform other self-injurious behaviors.

Another aspect of grieving that varies from culture to culture concerns the length of the grief period. Many cultures include formal rituals marking the end of bereavement. In the United States, however, grieving can be prolonged. Even funerals—clearly a formal ritual—are likely to mark the beginning of grieving rather than the end. As noted earlier in the text, "rites of passage" such as this generally make difficult transitions easier to bear.

Despite these cultural variations, however, people throughout the world express some form of grief when a loved one dies. This suggests that the capacity for grief is universal and presumably based, at least partly, on our shared biological makeup. Moreover, grieving also seems to occur among some animal species, including chimpanzees, who have been observed to sit in a circle around the dead body of a troop member, staring at the corpse and making wailing sounds.

Like many social behaviors, grieving is associated with a number of widely held beliefs about what is "normal." The available research evidence, however, offers little support for any of the following popular beliefs, suggesting instead that they are simply myths.

- Grieving follows a predictable time course. Although people vary in how long a period of grieving is considered acceptable, most agree that it decreases over time, typically within one year.
- Mourners must "work through" their losses through focused concentration on their emotions.
- Intense emotional distress is inevitable following the loss of a loved one, and necessary to healthy adjustment.

Use the above information, along with the text discussion of grief, to provide answers to the following questions.

1. Identify several biological, cognitive, and sociocultural influences on grief.

   Biological influences

HANDOUT 4 *(continued)*

Cognitive influences

Sociocultural influences

2. Give an example of how grieving is influenced by the various contexts of development.

   Microsystem

   Mesosystem

   Exosystem

   Macrosystem

   Chronosystem

3. Assuming that the capacity for grief is grounded in evolutionary history, how might grief be adaptive for our species?

4. What are some possible implications of the absence of a formal ritual to end grieving in a culture?

5. What are several practical implications of the myths about grieving listed earlier?